SUPERSTITION AND MAGIC
MODERN EUROPE

SUPERSTITION AND MAGIC IN EARLY MODERN EUROPE

A READER

Edited by Helen Parish

Bloomsbury Academic
An imprint of Bloomsbury Publishing Plc

B L O O M S B U R Y
LONDON · NEW DELHI · NEW YORK · SYDNEY

Bloomsbury Academic

An imprint of Bloomsbury Publishing Plc

50 Bedford Square
London
WC1B 3DP
UK

1385 Broadway
New York
NY 10018
USA

www.bloomsbury.com

BLOOMSBURY and the Diana logo are trademarks of Bloomsbury Publishing Plc

First published 2015

© Helen Parish, 2015

British Library Cataloguing-in-Publication Data
A catalogue record for this book is available from the British Library.

ISBN: HB: 978-1-4411-6876-4
PB: 978-1-4411-2222-3
ePDF: 978-1-4411-4974-9
ePub: 978-1-4411-0032-0

Library of Congress Cataloging-in-Publication Data
A catalog record for this book is available from the Library of Congress

Typeset by Integra Software Services Pvt. Ltd.
Printed and bound in India

CONTENTS

Contents

ACKNOWLEDGEMENTS

Chapter 1. K. Kamerick, 'Shaping Superstition in Late Medieval England', *Magic, Ritual and Witchcraft* 3:1 (2008), pp. 29–53. Reprinted with permission of the University of Pennsylvania Press, © 2008.

Chapter 2. E. Cameron, 'For Reasoned Faith or Embattled Creed? Religion for the People in Early Modern Europe', *Transactions of the Royal Historical Society*, 8 (1998), pp. 165–187. © The Royal Historical Society, published by Cambridge University Press, reproduced with permission.

Chapter 3. Extracts from E. Peters, 'The Medieval Church and State on Superstition, Magic and Witchcraft: From Augustine to the Sixteenth Century' in B. Ankarloo and S. Clark eds., *The Athlone History of Witchcraft and Magic, Volume 3: The Middle Ages* (2002), pp.178–186, 207–217, 223–237, 238–245. © Edward Peters 2002.

Chapter 4. H. Parish, 'Lying Histories Fayning False Miracles', *Reformation and Renaissance Review* 4:2 (2002), pp. 230–240 © Equinox Publishing Ltd 2002.

Chapter 5. L. Daston, 'Marvelous Facts and Miraculous Evidence in Early Modern Europe', *Critical Inquiry* 18:1 (1991), pp. 93–124. © 1991 by the University of Chicago. 0093-1896/91/1801-0004$01.00. All rights reserved.

Chapter 6. R. Kieckhefer 'The Specific Rationality of Medieval Magic', *American Historical Review*, 99:3 (1994), pp. 813–836. Reprinted by permission of Oxford University Press on behalf of the American Historical Association.

Chapter 7. A. Walsham, 'Sermons in the Sky: Apparitions in Early Modern Europe', *History Today* 51:4 (2001), pp. 56–63. Reprinted with permission of *History Today*.

Chapter 8. R. A. Bowyer, 'The Role of the Ghost-Story in Medieval Christianity' in H.E. Davidson and W. Russell eds., *The Folklore of* Ghosts (1981), pp. 177–192. © R. A. Bowyer 1981.

Chapter 9. W. Monter, 'Toads and Eucharists: The Male Witches of Normandy 1564–1660', *French Historical Studies* 20:4 (1997), pp. 563–595. Reprinted by permission of the publisher, Duke University Press.

Chapter 10. S. Clark, 'Witchcraft and Magic in Early Modern Culture' in B. Ankarloo ed., *The Athlone History of Witchcraft and Magic, Volume 4: The Period of the Witch Trials* (2002), pp. 97–170. © Stuart Clark 2002.

Chapter 11. E. Bever, 'Witchcraft, Female Aggression, and Power in the Early Modern Community', *Journal of Social History* 35:4 (2002), pp. 955–988. Reprinted with permission of The Journal of Social History.

Acknowledgements

Chapter 12. M.D. Bailey, 'The Disenchantment of Magic: Spells, Charms and Superstition in Early European Witchcraft Literature', *American Historical Review* 111:2 (2006), pp. 383–404. Reprinted by permission of Oxford University Press on behalf of the American Historical Association.

Chapter 13. B. Levack, 'The Decline and End of Witchcraft Prosecutions', in M. Gijswijt-Hofstra ed., *The Athlone History of Witchcraft and Magic, Volume 5: The Eighteenth and Nineteenth Centuries* (1994), pp. 1–48. © Brian P. Levack 1999.

Chapter 14. D.P. Walker, 'The Cessation of Miracles', in L. Merkel and A.G. Debus eds., *Hermeticism and the Renaissance* (1988), pp. 111–124. © Associated University Presses 1999.

GENERAL INTRODUCTION

Magic, witchcraft and superstition occupy a substantial space on the bookshelves of early modern history. The topic is certainly not the preserve of academic scholarship alone; witches, ghosts, magic and fairies make frequent appearances on our television screens, in our cinemas, and in children's – and adult – literature. Such a diversity in the representation of witchcraft and magic, and the broad chronological and methodological landscape against which these discussions take shape, reflects the popular and intellectual appeal of the topics, and the capacity for the beliefs and mentalities of the past to resonate in a modern, technologically driven world. In some respects, this is as simple as a shared vocabulary, albeit one in which words are divorced from the complexities of their original meaning. The term 'witch-hunt', for example, is readily applied to various forms of persecution and interrogation that have little, if anything, to do with 'witchcraft' as it was understood in the late medieval or early modern period. The very word 'witch' has proved to be linguistically and culturally malleable, understood in a way that is far from constant or static. But uncovering how such terms were understood in the past, and how that understanding can be revealed in the present, is part of the attraction of the topic. Witchcraft had, and has, multiple meanings. As a result, it presented a very real challenge to its opponents, for whom definition was a necessary part of the identification that justified and enabled persecution. It might be imagined that the search for legal precision in the categorization of witchcraft would provide a clear sense of what witchcraft meant, but, as Peter Maxwell-Stuart has reminded us, legal statute offers precious little clarity on this subject. For a crime to be prosecuted, there must be some definition of the offence, yet in the case of witchcraft, that definition was left (perhaps deliberately) open.[1] We can piece together a list of likely components – participation in a Sabbath, the infliction of harm by magical means (maleficia), night flight, a deliberate intent to invoke the demonic, apostasy, infanticide, cannibalism – but one of the most challenging aspects in the study of early modern witchcraft is understanding what it meant and why it mattered to those who reflected upon its impact. Multiple meanings, of course, invite multiple explanations, drawn from multiple chronological, geographical and cultural contexts and approaches, and as a result the scholarly literature is both rich and varied. Witchcraft emerged from, and embodied, a changing set of interdependent beliefs that might be pragmatic or polemical, learned or unlearned, clerical or lay, universal or the product of local or personal anger and anxiety. There is a danger in assuming that witchcraft, in any period, was understood as a rigid category of belief and action, or that witchcraft made sense – to us or to any other culture – outside more general assumptions about magic and the supernatural. The witch trials of the early modern period were without doubt one of the most sensational and controversial events of the age, but while the understanding of witchcraft that emerges from their records is a compelling caricature, it is far from complete or grounded. The trials make little sense once divorced from the wider context of beliefs in witches and witchcraft, and those beliefs are almost impossible to fathom outside an all-encompassing understanding of a universe that was governed by supernatural and magical forces at the most complex and most basic level. It is this fluidity in meaning, and the breadth of its context and impact, that shapes what follows.

The material world was neither predictable nor static; it was animated and potentially influenced by the divine, by the malign intent of demons and witches, and by the magical. We can argue that beliefs about witches need to be contextualized within a broader understanding of the magical, but 'magic' is in itself a similarly fluid term, understood in different, if not competing ways, by historians of religion and the occult, by believers and practitioners, and by its advocates and opponents. It has been described as 'more a concept than a reality', a way of organizing and categorizing a broad range of beliefs and practices held and enacted across societies and cultures.[2] Thus understood, magic might involve clergy or laity, sorcery or deception, entertainment or harm. As a label applied to the activities of others, whether by critics, sceptics or historians, the meaning of magic often lies in the eye of the beholder. This very lack of precision in meaning and definition makes the study of magic in the past a study of the evolution of ideas and categories and the conceptual thought processes that manipulated and modified that meaning. The specific rationality of magic – or a suggestion of irrationality – emerges from the process as an opposition or response to another body of knowledge and understanding, one which represented itself as religion or science and perceived in magic a challenge or an inferior world view.[3] What we witness through the study of magic is to a large extent a panorama of medieval and early modern mentalities more broadly. The study of magic is a study of an ongoing conversation among those who sought to identify, define and eradicate it and one in which magic is constantly being formed and reformed in the image and vocabulary of others. An eavesdropper on that conversation might well learn less about the practice of magic, and rather more about the cosmology and world view of its critics, but even so, magic becomes an integral part of our understanding of medieval and early modern culture. In magic, it is possible to see the convergence of science and religion; the interaction of popular and educated belief; and a meeting point of fiction, fantasy and daily life.[4]

In a similar vein, 'superstition' can be a short-hand, often derogatory, for the beliefs and practices of others – sometimes benign, sometimes more malevolent, sometimes objectively recorded and sometimes described for the purposes of proscription. Like the study of magic, any analysis of superstition is to a large extent governed by the mindset and preoccupations of its opponents, but it also serves to open up a broader discussion of more general issues and questions arising from early modern religion and belief. The cosmetic dichotomy between 'true' religion and 'superstition' belies the often ill-formed reality that lay beneath. Yet it was in the discussion and deployment of these polar opposites, whether religion/superstition, heresy/orthodoxy, that the building blocks of religious discourse were laid. Such terms reflected, conveyed and even constructed a reality in a constant process of defining and redefining boundaries and beliefs. The shifting shape of meaning need not imply that such rhetoric was ungrounded in reality but rather that superstition existed within the broader controversies outlined above. Where religion and superstition collided, this process of encounter, negotiation and redefinition reflected and remodelled beliefs about both. Euan Cameron's recent study of 'Enchanted Europe' opens with the proposition that the history of superstitious beliefs cannot be written; such practices are often idiosyncratic and disorganized, yet others can be seen to lay the foundation for a universal and plausible cosmology.[5] But despite (or perhaps even because of) this, it remains a 'profoundly instructive lesson and case study in humanity's efforts to make sense of our predicament'.

In modern parlance, the vocabulary of witchcraft, magic, and superstition all too often implies ignorance, a blind faith or a lack of rationality and understanding. Yet, as much recent scholarship has sought to demonstrate, there was often nothing irrational about such beliefs. Indeed, for many, they did indeed present a pretty plausible way in which to 'make sense of our predicament'. The representation of witchcraft in the printed pages of early modern demonological writings reflected the views and concerns of the educated and literate; these were not ill-considered ramblings but rather the fruits of a world view that was complex and made perfect sense in its context. It is possible and perhaps sensible to question the reality of early modern witchcraft and magic – the likelihood that the crimes attributed to witches actually happened and the motives of those involved. But the idea of witchcraft, and the interpretation of events and the representations of individuals in its light, was real enough. The application of 'superstition' as a pejorative term should not blind us to the reality of these beliefs or invite the conclusion that they were a passive remnant of a past age without grounding, meaning or value in the present. Whether the heart of the issue is to be found in dialectical discourse or in day-to-day activity, the study of superstition, magic and religion offers us an opportunity for real insight into the relationship between the exchange of ideas and the reality that it sought to reflect and reform.

It is this balance between the real and the imagined, the actual and the constructed, that has encouraged such an interest in these topics. In the last generation, the sheer volume of published work on religion, magic and superstition is exciting and daunting in equal measure – the rigour and vigour with which much of it engages with the source materials and the conceptual questions that they raise all the more so. An internet search for undergraduate taught courses on witchcraft and magic (although I remind my own students on a weekly basis that an internet search for anything to do with witchcraft is a perilous activity!) suggests that the subject is one of the most popular areas of interest for the current generation of scholars in early modern history. Modules – and writing – on 'Reformation Europe' have come more and more to focus not only upon the competing theologies of a confessionally divided Europe, but upon the beliefs of the faithful, broadly understood. And so we find that witches and ghosts, maleficient magic and misunderstood miracle, and superstition and sorcery are more and more deeply embedded in academic discussion. This is no bad thing. As Bob Scribner reminded us a couple of decades ago, it is incumbent upon the historian to at least attempt to discern 'the religious belief of the past in ways that might have been recognisable to the people concerned'.[6] To understand early modern beliefs about religion, nature and the supernatural, is not the same thing as to be able to explain it.[7] One consequence of recent attempts to reach a more nuanced and recognizable understanding has been a broadening of the subject matter in demographic and conceptual terms. The assertion that 'when I mean religion, I mean the Christian religion; and not only the Christian religion, but the Protestant religion; and not only the Protestant religion, but the Church of England' has long since ceased to hold water and with good reason.[8] There is much to be learned still from the doctrinal and pastoral disputes that underpinned religious and cultural change in this period, but as the focus of research turns more and more to history of belief rather than of institutions, so the range of belief that is recognized broadens and deepens. The overarching question is not that of legitimacy or veracity but, rather more practically, what religious belief and practice meant to and for those people who lived and held it. Early modern religion need not resemble (and should not be tested against) modern understandings of the Christian faith. A world view in which the natural, preternatural and supernatural had the potential to interact on a daily basis need not withstand the scrutiny of modern science, or social science. For all its strengths and immersion in the culture, for example, Evans-Pritchard's analysis of the beliefs of the Azande concluded that the thought-processes of the culture were 'unscientific', and that objective reality demonstrated that since witches, as the Azande understood them, could not exist, so their rituals might best be presented as an attempt to imagine a reality and remedy that compensated for this defect in knowledge.[9] By recognizing the capacity for (religious) beliefs to be both all-encompassing and self-reinforcing, we can perhaps better understand, though not judge or explain, their meaning and purpose in the hearts and minds of those who held them. In its complexities and ambiguities, early modern 'belief', broadly understood, offered a vocabulary – and practical guide – for dealing with the world and attached a meaning to those events and concepts that defied explanation. In a different context, Robert Parker's recent study of polytheism in the ancient world reminds us that 'gods overflowed like clothes from an over-filled drawer which no one felt obliged to tidy'.[10] Historians of belief have two options: to attempt to tidy the drawer and arrange the mental world of others into neat, colour-coded pairs or to rejoice in the apparent disorder and see in the chaos the full range of attitudes and ideas that imbued belief with meaning. In what has become an influential reference point for recent historians of medieval witchcraft and magic, Kors and Peters remind their reader of the dangers of a 'schematization of a people's entire world view upon which so many aspects of its beliefs and behaviour depend'.[11] Attitudes to magic, witchcraft and religion are best understood against the ontological backdrop of world in which demons, witches, ghosts and other manifestations of the supernatural were real. Tensions and paradoxes are, to some extent, our problem, and there is perhaps something to be learned from the assertion that 'the historian's task is to complicate, not to clarify'.[12]

It is these tensions and paradoxes that lie at the heart of what follows. Having established the sheer scale of the endeavour, it might seem perverse to attempt to present a history of the early modern belief about the supernatural in a volume of this size. But this is not a counsel of despair. The articles and essays that follow in no way purport to present a complete answer to the full range of questions that have been, and should be asked, around the general theme of magic, witchcraft and superstition in early modern Europe, but they do show us how these questions have been reflected upon and what lessons can be learned. Each makes a significant contribution to the history of magic and religion in its own right, but read together, they demonstrate the capacity for such investigations and analyses to evolve over time, to build upon methodologies and criticisms from other disciplines, and to distil general conclusions from discrete investigations (and vice versa). The approaches taken by the scholars whose work is reproduced here are varied and instructive, taken individually and together. Some engage in debate with the recent historiography, while others provide invaluable intellectual, historical and socio-political context for those readers approaching the subject for the first time. This is a book about 'early modern Europe', but it is one that sets this period against the backdrop of a broader chronology. Debates over religion, magic and superstition were not the invention of the sixteenth century; the earlier roots of these ideas and controversies, and their still contested nature by the end of our period, run as a subsidiary thread throughout.

The volume is structured around five key themes and areas of controversy. Part I tackles the vexed question of superstition as it was debated and understood in the late medieval and early modern period. Following on from this, Part II takes a more focused look at the debate over miracles and magic, and the way in which one of the most significant dichotomies established by the early Christian Church – the separation of Christian miracle from pagan magic – was contested and manipulated in an age of confessional conflict. The third part uses writing on ghosts and apparitions in various forms as an introduction to the attempts to define and redefine the supernatural, and to attach meaning to the often inexplicable intrusions made by the immaterial into the material world. Part IV examines competing and complementary explanations for the witch trials of the early modern period, with a particular focus upon the interconnections between thinking on magic and thinking on witchcraft and the much contested and debated place of gender in definitions of witchcraft. The final part invites an engagement with the question of 'disenchantment' and the gradual disintegration of the 'magical universe' in the face of scientific, religious and practical opposition. The contributions here revisit some of the key themes that underpin the collection as a whole – the decline in the persecution of witches, and perhaps belief in witchcraft; the capacity for superstition to shift shape under pressure from multiple directions; and the ongoing evolution in the relationship between religion and magic that is as evident at the end of our period as at the beginning.

Each part is prefaced by an introduction that engages with recent scholarship and debate and provides a more general overview of the historiography. These introductions are, to some extent, structured reviews of the literature; the text and footnotes provide the building blocks of a more general bibliography for readers who might wish to explore the subject in more detail. They provide a broad context for the articles that follow, alongside a brief summary of what each article contributes. Each chapter of the book might be read as a self-contained tutorial on the specific topic, but, as I hope becomes clear, this is not the point; the interconnections between each topic are sufficiently tight that the sum of the parts is rather less than the value of the whole. A 'reader' volume of this kind is a tool kit rather than a recipe book, intended to provide some of the equipment for further research as much as a simple recipe for answering a question. It is possible to dip in and out and come away with a well-focused snapshot of the issue, but there are benefits in thinking broadly, and more broadly than there is space for here, about the underlying continuities and discontinuities that make the study of magic and superstition a perennially fascinating topic.

Notes

1. Maxwell-Stuart, P. (2001), *Witchcraft in Europe and the New World, 1400–1800*. Basingstoke, Hampshire: Palgrave, p. 9.

2. Jolly, K. (2002), 'Medieval magic. Definitions, beliefs, practices', in K. Jolly, C. Raudvere and E. Peters (eds), *The Athlone History of Witchcraft and Magic in Europe Volume 3: The Middle Ages*. London: Athlone, p. 3.

3. For a fuller discussion of the 'rationality' of medieval magic see Kieckhefer, Chapter 6, below.

4. Kieckhefer, R. (2000), *Magic in the Middle Ages*. Cambridge: Cambridge University Press, pp. 1–2.

5. Cameron, E. (2010), *Enchanted Europe. Superstition, Reason, and Religion c. 1250–1750*. Oxford: Oxford University Press.

6.   Scribner, R.W. (1996), 'Introduction', in R. W. Scribner and T. Johnson (eds), *Popular Religion in Germany and Central Europe 1400–1800*. New York: St Martin's Press, p. 15.

7.   Gregory, B. (2006), 'The other confessional history: On secular bias in the study of religion', *History and Theory*, 45, p. 134.

8.   Fielding, H. (1749), *The History of Tom Jones*, Book 3. London: A. Miller.

9.   Evans-Pritchard, E.E. (1937), *Witchcraft, Oracles and Magic Among the Azande*. Oxford: Oxford University Press, p. 63.

10. Parker, R. (2005), *Polytheism and Society at Athens*. Oxford: Oxford University Press, p. 379.

11. Kors, A. and Peters, E. (2000), *Witchcraft in Europe 400–1700: A Documentary History*. Philadelphia, PA: University of Pennsylvania Press, p. 2.

12. Versnel, H. (2011), *Coping with the Gods: Wayward Readings in Greek Theology*. Leiden, The Netherlands: Brill, p. 87, 436.

PART I
SUPERSTITION

INTRODUCTION: SUPERSTITION IN LATE MEDIEVAL AND EARLY MODERN EUROPE

The exploration of the boundaries between religion, magic and superstition in early modern Europe has proved a fertile ground for historians of the Protestant and Catholic Reformations, and their impact upon popular religion, and early modern cultures. In particular, the assumption that it was the advent of the Protestant Reformations that initiated a monumental shift in attitudes to the sacred and supernatural has been modified by a range of more nuanced and reflective examinations of attitudes to magic, religion and superstition that span the increasingly fragile border between the late medieval and early modern. The agenda for the debate was established in the early twentieth century in Max Weber's *The Protestant Ethic and the Spirit of Capitalism*, in which he argued that one of the consequences of the Reformation was a process that he described as the 'disenchantment of the world', a process by which an eclectic and syncretic medieval Christianity was replaced by a more intellectual and interiorized form of religion, bereft of those magical and mysterious forces which had dominated popular understanding of the operation of the cosmos. Weber's paradigm, albeit much simplified, encouraged the modern observer to perceive the construction of a desacralized universe in the centuries after the Reformation; the advent of science and rationality and the eventual triumph of first religion and then secularism over the superstitions and distractions of medieval belief. There is, intentionally or otherwise, a sense of 'progress' here – an argument that, by definition, builds upon the supposed rationality of modern society to construct a caricature of the beliefs of the past and positions the event or process of Reformation as a turning point in the liberation of man from the shackles of ignorance and superstition. To position Weber at the start of this narrative is, perhaps, to oversimplify and exaggerate his conclusions, and there is a danger in presenting an image of more recent scholarship on the subject as the ripples formed by an ill-cast stone. Studies of the impact of Catholic and Protestant reform in the early modern period have benefited greatly from a more detailed and perceptive engagement with the history of the medieval Church and popular belief, and the extent to which the religious controversies of the sixteenth century were shaped by a rather older vocabulary and imagery surrounding religion, magic and superstition.

Reflecting upon what has informed and influenced this reinterpretation, it is hard to ignore the legacy of Keith Thomas' *Religion and the Decline of Magic*. As Jonathan Barry warns, it is not always straightforward to differentiate between Thomas' own argument and those conclusions that have been read into his work; indeed the greatest contribution that the book made was in its redefinition of the landscape in which discussions of religious change operated to include more than just matters of theology and religion narrowly understood.[1] *Religion and the Decline of Magic* has been criticized for embodying a functionalist approach, in which the purpose of beliefs and actions is at the fore rather than one that engaged with meaning in its discussions of early modern English witchcraft and for adopting a somewhat critical stance in its analysis of medieval magic which denied it an internal coherence and meaning.[2] Yet, as a study of both the differences and the interconnections between magic and religion in the late medieval and early modern period, *Religion and the Decline of Magic* continues to set the agenda for current research. The notion of the Protestant Reformation as part of an almost inexorable progress towards modern rationalism is still apparent, and still debated, albeit in a manner which is more sensitive to the structures of medieval religion and the impacts of religious change in the early modern period.[3] A substantial challenge to this model comes in the form of Michael Bailey's *Fearful Spirits, Reasoned Follies. The Boundaries of Superstition in Late Medieval Europe*, which explores the debate over the understanding of superstition and presents as both powerful and misconceived the dichotomy between the 'superstitious' Middle Ages and a more 'rational' modern Europe. A similar approach is evident in *Religion and Superstition in Reformation Europe*, in which individual essays debate the manner in which the accusations of superstition found their way into the language and debates of the Reformation and the process by which the label 'superstition' became both hotly contested and widely accepted in the vocabulary of religious controversy.[4] Drawing upon Keith Thomas' almost anthropological approach to the problem of medieval popular belief, recent historical writing has borrowed much from the theoretical models of other disciplines to inform and shape a more thoughtful approach to the problems inherent in the study of popular belief.[5] A sense of the scale of the challenge, and the value of engaging with it, is evident at the outset in Euan Cameron's *Enchanted Europe: Superstition, Reason and Religion 1250–1750*. In the opening pages, Cameron argues that history of superstition cannot be written: superstitious beliefs and practices, by their very nature, almost defy definition and compartmentalization. Some are local in their origins and meaning, others global; some derive from folklore and others from within Christianity; some appear idiosyncratic while others come close to representing an alternative cosmology. Cameron's study, unlike *Religion and the Decline of Magic*, examines not religion and superstition *per se* but rather the emergence and construction of attitudes towards superstitious beliefs and practices from the late middle ages into the early modern period. As such, it presents a rather more positive view of what superstition might mean and imbues some of these beliefs and debates with a rigour and coherence that Thomas was less inclined to see.[6] The Reformation, he argues, did not invent the concept of superstition and neither did it create the controversy over the nature of superstition which had ebbed and flowed since the first Christian centuries. Cameron's conclusion, that 'the quest to control and domesticate superstition was, in the end, a futile one [...] nevertheless it remains a profoundly instructive lesson and case study in humanity's efforts to make sense of our predicament', reflects the ongoing challenges that faced those who debated with and over superstition in this period. The most recent volume of the *Athlone History of Witchcraft and Magic in Europe* likewise reminds us of both the contemporaneity and timelessness that mark debates over magic, witchcraft and religion and the value of an examination of ideas, trends and experiences over a broad chronology.

The three essays and articles that follow engage to different degrees and in different forms with this debate over what might, or might not, be superstition, and how it might, or might not, be eradicated from the mental cosmos of the late medieval or early modern Christian. There are clearly advantages in exploring such issues and questions over a broad chronology, and the benefits of this approach are evident in Edward Peters' examination of the attitudes of the medieval Church and state to superstition, witchcraft and magic. The roots of these attitudes, he argues, are diverse, drawing upon Judaeo-Christian scripture, patristic writings, early medieval law codes, classical literature, hagiography, sermons and penitentials. Available to the historian, this range of textual materials and references was not necessarily readily accessible to those who debated magic and superstition in the millennium between the fifth and fifteenth centuries, and Peters reminds his reader that the vigour with which this debate was conducted was neither constant nor predictable. The concerns of the Church and the state were modified and formed by both context and competition, and each generation of writers, thinkers and preachers constructed their arguments upon the foundations laid by earlier contributions. Questions were clearly being asked about the relationship between religion and magic in the early Christian Church, but it was, Peters argues, in the twelfth century that the discussion of religion, magic, witchcraft and superstition occurred in its broadest range of sources. Peters' work, like that of Cameron, focuses primarily upon intellectual ideas about superstition that gave shape to legislation and attempts to control its spread, from Augustine to Isidore, in the theological and legislative priorities of the twelfth century; in attitudes to sorcery and witchcraft in the later Middle Ages; and in the debates over superstition, magic and demonology on the eve of the Reformation. It is clear that, in any age, the problem of definition was immediately apparent. 'Magic' was, from the early days of Christianity, a label that could be, and was, applied to the opponents of the nascent Church, but although the image of magic and the magician was enduring, it was also one that was modified in each generation. Magic was in this sense a palimpsest that could be wiped clean at every turn but one on which the language and priorities of any generation still showed through in the writings of the next. It is tempting to see terms such as 'magic' or 'superstition' as simple labels and terms of polemical abuse, satisfyingly broad but still potentially precise in their application to the belief system of one's opponents. But Peters suggests, influenced by Richard Kieckhefer's detailed analysis of the foundations of medieval magic, that even in its most polemical usage the term still implied a basic level of understanding as to its meaning and direction.[7] By the fourth century, it was already clear that a more precise vocabulary had shaped a more informed legal prohibition of such practices. However, it was also possible for a more generalized language to prevail; Augustine's use of the term *superstitio* to encompass what had been discrete beliefs and practices also did much to shape the debates and prohibitions that followed, not least in the connection that was beginning to be made between magic, superstition and the temptations and deceptions of the devil. Isidore of Seville's *Etymologies* were likewise influential in delineating the principles and objectives of later debates, presenting a detailed, almost exhaustive summary of magic and superstition, and attitudes towards them, collected from a broad sweep of sources. Isidore's collection was both practical and theoretical, outlining the reality of magic and superstition and the dangers that they posed and locating these dangers within the context of a changing Christian culture and its perceived opponents.[8]

The propensity of context to shape the debate was all the more apparent in twelfth-century writing on magic and superstition. Under the influence of a more confident and authoritarian ecclesiology, Gratian and Hugh of St. Victor laid out the dangers of such practices as embodied in the canon law of the Church. While earlier imagery and traditions did much to shape this representation, the language of debate certainly owed much to the pastoral, devotional and institutional concerns of the twelfth century. Thus, magic and superstition emerged a reminder of the perilous position of man, the reality of the devil and his deceptions and the hazards of a world that was filled with such temptation. Old images were pressed into the service of new preoccupations, but the debate was also enhanced by the more ready availability of new textual sources. Miracles (*miracula*) and wonders (*mira*) were contested with greater linguistic precision, and the discipline of canon law imposed more clearly defined categories of knowledge and understanding. What emerged was a model of superstition that was both recognizable and transformed, more closely linked to the agency of the devil and to the dangers of doctrinal heresy.

The increasingly determined association made between superstition and the agency of the devil had its most potent manifestation in writing on witches and witchcraft in the later Middle Ages. As Peters reminds us, particular trials, often localized in context and content, were not always well recorded, but there are individual cases where the written record survives in enough detail that it can be read alongside demonological treatises and learned discussions of witchcraft, heresy, magic and superstition. The most often studied trial of the fourteenth century is that of Alice Kyteler, whose case is notable not only for the range of accusations that were brought against the witches but also the open identification of witchcraft with heresy and the emphasis placed upon the diabolic nature of the offence. As a result of these pressures, Peters contends, the fourteenth century witnessed both a greater vigour in the prosecution of witchcraft and magic and a more focused and powerful conceptualization of the meaning of the witch. Such a discussion was informed by a sharper awareness of the natural world and the challenges that it presented to mankind; reflections upon witchcraft and superstition within a longstanding intellectual and legal tradition; and the complex affairs of the Church in the context and aftermath of the papal schism. This was also an era in which communication of ideas about such matters was more fluid and more rapid, and the interchange of news and interpretations less easy to control. Superstition remained on the agenda of academic debate, evinced in, among others, Jean Gerson's treatise *On errors concerning the magical art and the forbidden articles*, and Johann Nider's *Formicarius*. Traditional images of magic and superstition were reinterpreted in light of a polemical and pastoral imperative that was shaped by the assumption that such practices were part of a diabolic conspiracy; as such, each allegation or accusation was readily presented as part of something bigger and more hazardous. Thus, on the eve of the Reformation, demonological theory had found its way into the materials read and used by preachers and confessors. Beliefs surrounding the potential danger of magic and superstition on the eve of the reformation prepared a fertile seedbed for the reception of treatises such as the *Malleus Maleficarum* and the location of witchcraft and superstition in the context of demonic conspiracy in Ulrich Molitor's *Treatise concerning women who prophesy* and Martin of Arles' *Treatise concerning superstition and against witchcraft and sorcery which today flourish all over the world*.

Kathleen Kamerick's examination of superstition in late medieval England explores the practical consequences of such rhetoric and reflects upon the pastoral obligations that were imposed upon those charged with the eradication of superstition. In England, the position of superstition was often ambiguous; at one level it was a 'fearful portal allowing the devil's entry into human affairs', but at another level the English clergy were less inclined (or were perceived as being less inclined) to intervene to prevent such incursions than their continental counterparts. Thus, Lollard critics of the medieval English Church and Protestant reformers of the sixteenth century felt able to use 'superstition' as a powerful polemical tool in order to argue that the Catholic Church had compromised with magic. Kamerick's study of English pastoral literature of the fifteenth century reveals the many approaches taken to combat superstition and the multiplicity of meanings that were attached to the term. Those writers who were most exercised by the apparent dangers of superstition were often frustrated by a lack of precision in its definition, and the practical obstacles that impeded the erection of a clear divide between proper religious observance and superstitious distractions. The clash between religion and superstition was evident in the church courts, in printed treatises including *Dives and Pauper*, and in the *Destructionem Viciorum* that gave voice to the complaints of the Dominican preacher Alexander Carpenter. What is apparent from these sources is the sheer breadth of practices and problems that fell under the umbrella of superstition in the late Middle Ages and the manner in which this vocabulary of complaint and condemnation fed into the debates of the early reformation in England. Thus Thomas More, taking to the defence of Catholic religion in the late 1520s, not only defended popular piety from accusations of superstition but also recognized the polemical capital in turning these accusations against his evangelical opponents. This continual metamorphosis of the term 'superstition' and its meaning was not unique to the era of the Reformation; as Kamerick concludes, superstition was not, in theory or practice, a problem that was new.

This close correlation between the agenda of debate in the era of Reformation, and the content of dialogue over religion and superstition within the medieval Church, is discussed by Euan Cameron in the third article in this part. Cameron considers the representation of medieval Christianity by subsequent generations as 'folklorized', or 'enchanted', as an eclectic body of beliefs and practices that showed little attempt to differentiate between religious actions and those which might be categorized as superstitious. His responses to this schematic model invite a reconsideration of the assumption that it was not until the sixteenth century that any concerted attack was made upon magic and superstition in popular religion. As part of this reconsideration, he contends, neither the traditional narrative of a new and vigorous assault on superstition by the advocates of the Protestant Reformation nor the more recent assertion that Catholic and Protestant shared a common agenda in the reform of religion do justice to the issue. The theological controversies of the Reformation, he argues, need to be put back into any account of the early modern attack on superstition. The debate over superstition was conducted against the backdrop of debates over magic, miracles, demonology, the created world, the number and nature of the sacraments and the more conceptual issue of 'holiness'; while it would be inappropriate to divorce Protestant rhetoric from its medieval antecedents, the determination of the evangelicals to instil a radically different understanding of religion in the hearts and minds of the believer requires a closer analysis in its own right. In this age, as in any, the understanding of superstition was shaped both by continuity and by context, by conservatism and by change.

Notes

1. Barry, J. (1998), 'Introduction', in J. Barry, M. Hester and G. Roberts (eds), *Witchcraft in Early Modern Europe. Studies in Culture and Belief*. Cambridge: Cambridge University Press, pp. 1–2.

2. See, for example, the debate between Thomas and Hildred Geertz conducted in the *Journal of Interdisciplinary History* in the mid-1970s, B. Copenhaver's review of *Religion and the Decline of Magic* in *Church History* (1972), Larner, C. (1984) *Witchcraft and Religion*. Oxford: Oxford University Press, p. 145.

3. van Dülmen, R. (1999), 'The reformation and the modern age', in C. Scott Dixon (ed.), *The German Reformation: The Essential Readings*. Oxford: Oxford University Press, pp. 196–21; Nipperdey, T. (1987), 'The reformation and the modern world', in E. I. Kouri and T. Scott (eds), *Politics and Society in Reformation Europe: Essays for Sir Geoffrey Elton on His Sixty-Fifth Birthday*. Basingstoke: Macmillan, pp. 535–5; Spierenburg, P. (1991), *The Broken Spell: A Cultural and Anthropological History of Preindustrial Europe*. Basingstoke: Macmillan.

4. Bailey, M. (2013), *Fearful Spirits, Reasoned Follies. The Boundaries of Superstition in Late Medieval Europe*. Ithaca, NY: Cornell University Press; H. Parish and W. G. Naphy (2002) (eds), *Religion and Superstition in Reformation Europe*. Manchester: Manchester University Press.

5. See for example Hsu, Francis L. K. (1983), *Exorcising the Trouble Makers: Magic, Science and Culture*. Westport, CT: Greenwood Press; Merrifield, R. (1987), *The Archaeology of Ritual and Magic*. London: Batsford; Murray, A. (1992), 'Missionaries and magic in dark-age Europe', *Past and Present*, 136, 186–205; Neusner, J., Frerichs, E., and McCracken Flesher, P.V., (1989) (eds), *Religion, Science, and Magic: In Concert and in Conflict*. Oxford: Oxford University Press; Van Engen, J., (1986), 'The christian middle ages as an historiographical problem', *American Historical Review*, 91, 519–52.

6. Cameron, E. (2010), *Enchanted Europe: Superstition, Reason and Religion 1250–1750*. Oxford: Oxford University Press.

7. Kieckhefer, R. (1994), 'The specific rationality of medieval magic', *American Historical Review*, 99, 815.

8. Klingshirn, W. E. (2003), 'Isidore of seville's taxonomy of magicians and diviners', *Traditio*, 58, 59–90; Fontaine, J. (1959), *Isidore de Séville et la culture classique dans l'Espagne wisigothique*, Paris: Etudes Augustiniennes; Barney, S. A., Lewis, W. J., Beach, J. A. and Berghof, O. (trans.) (2006), *The Etymologies of Isidore of Seville*. Cambridge: Cambridge University Press; Henderson, J. (2007), *The Medieval World of Isidore of Seville: Truth from Words*. Cambridge: Cambridge University Press.

CHAPTER 1
SHAPING SUPERSTITION IN LATE MEDIEVAL ENGLAND
K. Kamerick

Superstition occupied an ambiguous place in late medieval England. While elsewhere in fifteenth-century Europe the clergy increasingly reviled superstitions in everyday practices as the fearful portal allowing the devil's entry into human affairs, this certainty faltered in England.[1] The English clergy never ignored beliefs and practices they termed 'superstitious,' describing, analyzing, and denouncing them in preachers' handbooks, confessors' manuals, and especially vernacular religious treatises intended for lay women and men. Church courts heard cases of superstition, divination, prophesying, and charm making, prohibited activities whose kinship led them to be treated as one. Still, while superstition's insidiousness and spiritual perils formed part of the laity's instruction in the Christian faith, historians have seen the English church as slow to draw the battle lines against superstition and its cohort. Keith Thomas even argued that in the interest of preserving their own status as wielders of magic, the late medieval English clergy often found it easier to overlook laypeople's superstitious beliefs than to combat them.[2]

The view of the late medieval clergy as complicit in their parishioners' superstitions contains echoes of denunciations made in the fifteenth and sixteenth centuries first by Lollards and then by evangelical reformers. Both groups reviled the English clergy not only for failing to stop superstition, but for actively promoting it. Both judged as superstitions such common devotional practices as pilgrimage, veneration of the saints, and using Gospel texts in charms; Lollards and then reformers also verbally assailed the clergy for mounting superstitious rituals, while jealously and superstitiously guarding knowledge of the scripture.

As a polemical weapon, superstition played an important rhetorical role in the attack on the traditional practices of lay Christians in the late Middle Ages in general, and on the failures of the clergy in particular. Its enduring success has obscured serious efforts made by English churchmen of the period to investigate superstition's attractions and to amputate superstitious activities from the Christian body. While the uncanonical practices and beliefs that perturbed clergymen had probably changed little over the centuries, the growing number of laypeople who read English offered a new audience for explaining the theology that undergirded licit devotions and condemned sinful superstition.[3] Religious instruction in the form of vernacular books, sermons, and church court decisions warned lay people to avoid superstition's dangers. Far from speaking with a single voice, however, these organs of lay teaching disagreed about what constituted superstition and argued too about its spiritual consequences. Their diversity arose partly from the continuing difficulty churchmen encountered in drawing the boundaries of legitimate practice: could reciting a Christian prayer, for example, become a superstitious activity if done to produce magical effects? Just as importantly, their differences reflected distinct views of lay people's religious competence. The clerics who authored these works imagined lay people in turn as simple children amenable to basic instruction, as rebellious adolescents rejecting clerical authority, and as intelligent adults capable of theologically complex thought. While some writers seemed confident in their readers' understanding, considerable anxiety yet arose about how lay women and men might read and interpret religious literature, resulting in suspicion of many texts and even efforts at censorship.[4] This article investigates superstition's transformations in this literature of religious instruction and in several other late medieval contexts, including church courts, Lollard critiques, and early reformers' debates with traditional religion's defenders. Together these sources reveal superstition's mutability, its significance and perceived dangers shifting according to each speaker's views of the laity's moral accountability or the clergy's pastoral failures.

From the clamor of conflicting notions about superstition emerge a few distinct strains of opinion. One position, which perhaps helped to inflame the church's critics, regarded superstition as a simple matter for gentle correction: ignorant laypeople who fell into such errors merely needed better teaching. This view seemed to inform decisions of the English lower ecclesiastical courts, which treated cases of superstition – which included soothsaying, charm-making, and other 'magical' activities – more lightly than heresy. One instance of this lenient stance appears in the 1499 visitation records of the Norwich diocese, when an ecclesiastical court cited a woman named Marion Clerk for using 'the art of superstition.' Marion was alleged to cure people of various diseases, to prophesy the future and inform clients of impending misfortunes, and to find hidden treasure – all the common labors of village cunning folk. Confessing her guilt, Marion told the court she received her abilities from 'God and the Blessed Mary and from *les Gracyous Fayry*' whom she described as 'little people' who gave her information whenever she needed it. Establishing their Christian credentials, Marion said *lez fayry* believed in God the Father and indeed helped her to see God and to talk with the Archangel Gabriel and Saint Stephen. The court also charged Marion's mother Agnes, who admitted she had once associated with *les Elvys*, as a practitioner of 'superstitious arts.' Agnes's husband John affirmed for the court his faith in his wife and daughter. While the judge then 'declared all arts of this kind to be superstitions and suspected of heretical depravity,' the trio were not convicted of heresy, but ordered never to take up 'superstitious arts of this kind' again.[5]

When the Clerk family renounced and abjured their former practices, the court ordered them – dressed in the penitential mode of smocks with bare feet and legs – to make public procession to and offer candles in four places: Norwich cathedral, the diocesan seat; their own parish church in Ashfield; the Bury marketplace; and the image of Saint Mary in Woolpit, a popular focus for local pilgrimages.[6] This sentence aimed to correct them and to prevent their relapse into their habitual superstitions, as the court termed them, as the multiple processions publicized the Clerks's convictions to neighbors and potential clients and also reinforced their submission to diocesan authority. In contrast, English church courts dealt with convicted heretics much more harshly, imposing such penalties as confinement, fasting, imprisonment, and wearing a badge identifying them as heretics for the rest of their lives.[7]

Other lower ecclesiastical courts around England echoed the Norwich diocese court's mild surveillance of the 'superstitious' arts, magic, and sorcery (court records use all these terms without clear differentiation). Accused and confessed necromancers, conjurers, sorcerers, spell-casters, fortune-tellers, charm purveyors, and finders of lost goods most often received light penalties.[8] Although a fuller understanding of magic and superstition's judicial treatment in England awaits a thorough investigation, a few examples sketch the courts' generally temperate posture, and their focus on correction and prevention rather that severe punishment. Those accused who confessed their guilt most often received penalties like the Clerk family's: processions to a church, candle offerings, or ritual beatings, punishments typically handed out as well to fornicators, adulterers, and other common transgressors.[9] In 1363, for example, Philip Russel admitted to a Rochester court that he practiced sorcery by using a charm with toads to prevent scabies in sheep; he was beaten through the marketplace and church.[10] In 1409 Richard Cubbul confessed to a Salisbury court that he used 'necromancy and circles on ground'; he abjured the practice on pain of six beatings.[11] Katerina Martyn, charged in 1494 with unlawful spells or enchantments (*incantacionibus illicitis*), in the Buckinghamshire (Lincoln diocese) archdeaconry court, received a ritual beating three times around the church.[12] In Wells in 1499, Kateryne Love admitted using charms, and abjured all 'manner of heresies or errors, witchcrafts and all superstitious sects'; her penance included procession to a local church and the promise to stay at least seven miles away from Wells.[13]

Accusations of sorcery and the other arts deemed superstitious could be successfully rebutted through compurgation. Judges set the number of compurgators necessary to release the accused, who would then ask honest neighbors to testify to the truth of his or her oath. Women often freed themselves from sorcery charges through this process.[14] Margaret Lindsey, defamed as a sorceress (*incantatrix*) by three men in 1435, successfully purged herself with the help of five women; her accusers were warned against making further slanders under pain of excommunication.[15] In 1446 Mariot de Belton and Isabella Brome both denied the charge that they used sorcery to help single women marry the men they wanted; each was given the chance to use compurgation to establish her innocence, although de Belton needed twelve compurgators and Brome only four.[16] In 1499 two male jurors accused Alice Fynne of using magic, a 'superstitious art' to kill one Andrew Fynne (their relationship is unknown). She successfully purged herself by bringing to court four female compurgators.[17]

Only habitual backsliding into superstitious ways or open resistance to the court's authority incurred a sentence of excommunication.[18] In 1485, for example, the Buckingham Archdeaconry court excommunicated the rector Nicholas Barton for conjuring with a psalter and keys, but Barton had previously been ordered to stop using the 'magic arts.' His excommunication followed his recidivism, and the court cited him particularly as 'a pernicious example to others,' his clerical status no doubt intensifying his crime; perhaps only incidentally his sins in magic were compounded by his adultery with the local miller's wife.[19] In another case of disobedience, Etheldreda Nyxon was cited in 1499 for using 'superstitious art, or at least the art of divination' for promising to help neighbors recover lost or stolen goods (charging a quarter of the recovered goods' value). When she denied the charge in court, the judge ordered her to appear before him again in Norwich cathedral to respond to this and other accusations. Because she refused to appear even under summons, the judge excommunicated her in writing as 'manifestly rebellious.'[20]

Late medieval England witnessed more spectacular cases of what these courts described as superstitions, involving charges of spells, image magic, and sorcery, but their notoriety and the severe punishments meted out likely stemmed from the accused persons' suspected political aims. In the 1440s, for example, Eleanor Cobham, second wife of Duke Humphrey of Gloucester, was charged with conspiring with others in using the occult arts against King Henry VI. As Henry VI's heir presumptive and a valued royal adviser, Duke Humphrey's influential voice in the king's Council had won him powerful enemies who may have pushed the case against his wife. Eleanor, it was claimed, associated with Margery Jourdemayne the so-called 'Witch of Eye,' the necromancer Roger Bolingbroke, and other magic workers, in order to discover when the king might die and if her husband would succeed him on the throne. Rumor also suggested that Eleanor used witchcraft both to induce Duke Humphrey to marry her and to shorten the king's life, so that her sorcery seemed compounded by treason and dangerous ambition. In the end, Jourdemayne and Bolingbroke were executed, while Eleanor remained in custody for the rest of her life.[21] In contrast to this infamous affair, the lower ecclesiastical courts making their rounds from one parish to another put everyday cases involving incantations and divination alongside the other ordinary wrongs committed by lay men and women. While the courts' meager documentation usually veils many things we would like to know about the charges and penalties, the accused and their accusers, this veil sometimes lifts to allow a glimpse of a court's intentions. In 1446 a Lincoln court, for instance, noted the pathetic condition of the accused as reason to hand them over for 'correction' to commissioners: the court described Isabelle Leche, accused of necromancy and sorcery, as poor and sick; Richard Fleyn, charged with necromancy, as paralytic; Isabella Baylyfson, also accused of necromancy, as decrepit.[22] Court officials seemed mostly concerned to educate and reform the practitioners of the superstitious arts. As one Richard Perkin, 'unlearned,' confessed in 1481, he had thought his charms called forth an angel, but the Archbishop of York's 'instruction and information' taught him his error, so he would henceforth shun the 'wicked spirit' he had unknowingly summoned.[23]

Neither dramatizing superstition's dangers nor dismissing them as trivial, the church courts performed the pastoral duty of correcting proven miscreants. Public processions and offerings reinforced the sinners' lessons, and broadcast a warning to the watching community. Similar views on the linked issues of superstition, magic, divination, and astrology appeared in several late medieval English treatises. In *The Repressor of Over Much Blaming of the Clergy*, for example, Bishop Reginald Pecock (c. 1395–1460) put forward as simple common sense a distinction between misbeliefs that result in heinous acts and those that are mere foolishness. Writing for a lay and clerical audience, Pecock argued that reason could persuade people to follow the right moral course. 'Some untrue opinion,' he wrote, makes people 'the worse morally, for it leads to deeds which are great moral vices.' One such error reckons there is no sin in the 'fleshly communing' of single men and women when freely consented to; another holds that a person may help himself to a neighbor's worldly goods. In contrast to these serious fallacies Pecock cited those 'untrue opinions' that do *not* pit their misguided adherents against 'notable, good, virtuous morality.' It is nonsense to believe that a man who once stole a bundle of thorns was set in the moon as punishment, or that three spirit sisters visit the cradles of infants to foretell their destinies, or that an image speaks or performs miracles. Still, no real harm arises from these notions. One could laugh at people's credulity and simplicity in their 'foolish opinions' that 'might lightly be showed to their holder for to be untrue.'[24] Instruction will correct these mistakes, which in any case, as Pecock saw it, lack gravity.

Bishop Pecock's comments on soothsaying and the man in the moon paralleled the views of the church courts (insofar as those can be discerned), but other clerical writers found superstition more threatening. Producing vernacular treatises to teach doctrinal and biblical fundamentals like the Creed, the Lord's Prayer, and the Ten Commandments to literate laypeople and lower clergy, these writers often took up superstition and magic under the rubric of idolatry, the sin against the First Commandment, 'Thou shalt not have strange gods before me' (Exodus 20:3).[25] Blinking at contemporary evidence for clerical magicians like Rector Nicholas Barton, most agreed with Bishop Pecock that superstition flourished because laypeople's ignorance made them credulous and easily seduced by its false promises. Beyond this common premise, however, disputes arose on every point. Many writers reviled all charms, spells, and divination as the devil's work that snagged simple men and women in the demonic net. As *The Pore Caitif*, a late-fourteenth-century gathering of didactic works, admonished its readers, God forbids 'belief and trust' in all 'witchcraft, dreams, charms and conjurations'; anyone who believes in them makes them 'false gods,' thereby breaking this commandment.[26] Even more harshly, the 1390s pastoral manual *Speculum Christiani* simply and resolutely censured 'all sorceries, witchcrafts, all enchantments and conjurements, with false impressions of characters' as idols that are 'utterly damned.'[27]

Yet other writers pursued superstition's origins, attractions, and permutations in more depth, perhaps prompted by the chasm between orthodox teaching and the widespread appeal of charms and divination. Lengthy treatments of these topics by two popular fifteenth-century works, the English *Dives and Pauper* and the Latin *Destructorium Viciorum*, illustrate both the zeal to combat superstition and the dilemmas the clergy faced in their efforts to erect a verbal wall separating licit devotion from superstition. An extensive commentary on the Ten Commandments likely written by a Franciscan, and printed twice before 1500 and again in the early sixteenth century, *Dives and Pauper* found a mixed lay and clerical audience. In its exhaustive evaluation of First Commandment violations, the mendicant preacher Pauper teaches the wealthy Dives about the linked sins of superstition, idolatry, magic, and witchcraft. This long section's complex discussion offered readers guidance for avoiding superstition, at the same time making plain that superstition raised dilemmas not easily resolved.[28]

Pauper calls attention to the contemporary scene by stressing then-current breaches of the First Commandment. Sun worship, for instance, was not an ancient sin found only in the Old Testament; but one that 'many fools yet do these days,' attending to the 'sun in his rising and the new moon in his first showing.'[29] Even worse, people use astronomy to prophesy the future: 'For these days,' Pauper complains, 'men take no heed of God's judgments,' but pay attention only to astronomers and the course of the planets.[30] These sky watchers go astray; like Lucifer, astronomers will fall to hell, joined there by witches who also seek to be like God and above God's laws. Attempting to foretell one's destiny through the stars distorts God's creation. The celestial bodies serve humanity; by dividing night from day and one month from another, they tell people when to work, rest, pray, eat, and fast. Acting as God's instruments, the stars order human life, but they reveal neither a person's destiny nor God's plans.[31]

Pauper's certitude and forthright denunciation soon yield, however, to a more nuanced scrutiny of astronomical practices. While Dives readily agrees to condemn astronomical prophesying, he wonders if weather forecasters might lawfully use the heavens in their art. He and Pauper concur that planets and stars can be 'tokens,' although not causes, of drought, wet, tempest, frost, wind, and thunder. Then Dives speculates whether heavenly 'wonders that occur against nature' might foreshadow future events. Unhesitatingly, Pauper responds that marvels like comets, burning castles, armed or fighting men that appear in the air, solar and lunar eclipses, and upside down rainbows reveal God's unhappiness with and intent to punish the people over whose lands these phenomena occur. Indeed a recent comet showed God's 'great offense' with the people of England who would suffer miserably unless they amend their errors of heresies, blasphemy, lechery, and idolatry.[32]

To Pauper's way of thinking, the heavens could be read for meaning, even for seeing God's wrath about to fall, but not for peering into one's fate. While early theologians, especially Augustine, had condemned astrology as incompatible with the Christian doctrine of human free will, by the thirteenth century some scholastic thinkers proposed the somewhat uneasy compromise on which Pauper based his distinction. Aquinas, for example, held that predicting celestial motions and their influences on the sublunar regions was possible, although the mutable nature of earth, air, fire, and water made these forecasts uncertain. Still, people could legitimately predict eclipses and comets, as well as the results of celestial influences like war and plague. But acts of human will belonged to the category of the contingent or accidental, known only by God. In laying out this orthodox and complex position, *Dives and Pauper*'s author displayed uncommon confidence that his lay readers would follow the subtle argument.[33]

Charms present special difficulties to Pauper, as they had to Christian thinkers for centuries. Untwining spoken or written prayers that were used as cures or accompanied medicine from illicit words summoning demonic help, was no easy matter. Saint Augustine had condemned wearing textual amulets around the neck or on other parts of the body; early medieval bishops complained of the same practice; in the thirteenth century, Thomas of Chobham prohibited it in his *Summa confessorum*. Yet Augustine also built the escape clause of intention into his critique, saying that when the reason for the 'efficacy of a thing' is unknown, then 'the intention for which it is used is important' in regards to cures.[34] Adopting this line of thought, Pauper prohibits a wide range of offenses, but asserts in several cases that the actor's intent determines or can redeem charms. Among a long list of misbegotten practices – attention to the 'dismal (unlucky) days'; leading the plow around the fire to ensure a favorable new year; divination through birds' chatter or flight – Pauper names charms used in herb gathering, and hanging on sick people and beasts scrolls 'with any scripture or figures or characters.' People guilty of these or 'any manner of witchcraft or any misbelief' forsake the faith and become God's enemies, falling in damnation without end. Still, Pauper says, one could adorn the sick person with a scroll if it held the *Pater noster, Ave*, Creed, or Gospel texts, and if one acted from devotion, not curiosity.[35] Medieval Christian moralists regarded excessive curiosity as dangerous and potentially a sin (*vitium curiositatis*), believing that the overly curious sought knowledge that belonged only to God. Since heresy, magic, and divination could all result from this sin of curiosity, Pauper cautions his readers against allowing it to seep into their practice.[36] Following Augustine and propped up by scholastic thought, Pauper insists that a pious purpose rescues the potentially suspect activity.

Biblical precedent, according to Pauper, confirms that intention should be the gauge for assessing sin in these murky areas. God and church forbid casting lots, for instance, when it is done out of vanity or to divine the future; but 'when men are in doubt what to do, and man's wit fails,' then casting lots may be done 'with reverence of God and with holy prayers before.' Pauper cites the Apostles casting lots in this way when selecting Judas's replacement (Acts 1:26). Indeed, Proverbs (16:33) says God can reveal his will through lots: 'lots are cast into the lap, but they are disposed of by the Lord.'[37] The actor's purpose and frame of mind become pivotal again when Dives asks if using 'holy words of holy writ' to charm adders, other beasts, or birds is witchcraft. If the man or woman 'takes heed,' says Pauper, 'only to the holy words and to the might of God,' this is allowed; but should their purpose waver, and they use 'any misobservance and set more trust therein than in the holy words or in God,' then they sin.[38]

Dives and Pauper sifts the elements of intention and desire, on one side, and on the other the authority of scripture and custom, before concluding whether any act deserves condemnation as superstition or witchcraft. While speaking urgently about superstition's and witchcraft's fearful dangers, *Dives and Pauper* admits the teaching of the voluminous late medieval literature on confession and pastoral care, that mortal sin must involve the consent of one's free will and deliberate intent, along with full understanding that the planned act is sinful.[39] The author's extraordinarily detailed and careful evaluations of prophecy and charms implicitly acknowledged a readership that would find inadequate the simpler proscriptions of superstitions produced in vernacular theological works like *The Pore Caitiff*.

Fuller definitions, descriptions, and commentary on 'superstitions' intended for use specifically by fifteenth-century preachers are illustrated as well in the voluminous *Destructorium viciorum* by the Dominican Alexander Carpenter (fl. c. 1429). The *Destructorium*'s utility lies not in original commentary but in its popularity, thoroughness, and its survey of authoritative opinions on superstition, especially those of the author's fellow Dominicans like Thomas Aquinas, Robert Holcot (d. 1349), and Guillaume Peyraut, author of a popular thirteenth-century work on the vices and virtues. Copies of Carpenter's work belonged to monastic libraries and individual clergymen; several late-fifteenth- and early-sixteenth-century printings indicate a continuing demand for it.[40]

After an introduction distinguishing original, mortal, and venial sin, Carpenter divided his text into seven parts corresponding to the Seven Deadly Sins. Superstition falls under Pride, as it arises, says Carpenter, from stubbornness. Drawing on Augustine, Isidore of Seville, and especially Aquinas, he defines superstition as 'the invention of empty and superfluous religion beyond what is customary' and as 'the worship of idols and demons.' Superstition branches in three directions: the first is divine worship shown to God improperly; the second, divine worship of something other than God; the third, when 'through such worship demons are consulted.'[41] From the outset, Carpenter insists on superstition's sinfulness, gravity, and ties to outcast groups. Its birth in stubbornness links it to heretics who obstinately refuse to accept the true religion; its first branch is exemplified by Jews, whom Carpenter cites as worshipping in an improper fashion (*modo indebito*) in their continued observation of Old Testament laws that figure Christ as yet to come.[42]

Superstition's second and third branches, idolatry and demon worship, raise troubling questions about apparent conflicts between scripture and custom. Carpenter describes idolatry as crediting the attributes of a living spirit to a 'dead' material object like a statue; this occurs when one swears by a statue; hopes it will grant wishes; bestows a name on the statue; or loves, worships, or makes offerings to it. As rational creatures, human beings should be ashamed to pray to a 'dead idol,' to ask for help, health, or life from this insensible material that cannot hear, walk, or see. For this reason Carpenter attacks people who seek help from the 'dead images of saints,' or who credit any help they receive to an image's 'virtue and power.' Such help likely comes from an 'illusion of the devil' because demons may inhabit images. The worship of saints' images seems 'superstitious' because scripture provides no precedent for it among the first Christians.[43]

Yet the 'custom of the church' opposes this verdict by justifying image veneration. In addition, the authoritative writings of Saint Basil, John Damascene, Gratian, Aquinas, and Holcot lead Carpenter to conclude that one may worship Christ and the saints *before* their images without worshipping the images themselves. With scripture and church custom apparently at odds over this potential superstition, Carpenter finds two ways around this impasse. First, image veneration is cleansed of superstition's taint through the devotee's inner intent, with mind and soul trained on the holy person whom the statue merely represents. Second, Carpenter adduces scripture's lacunae, since it fails to mention that the Apostles themselves introduced images into Christian worship – Saint Luke, for instance, painted portraits of Christ and the Virgin Mary.[44] Scripture, then, cannot be the final arbiter in judging superstition.

Investigating superstition's third branch, demon worship, Carpenter takes up the vexed practice of soothsaying, 'the divination of future events' done outside of divine revelation. He reiterates *Dives and Pauper*'s view, written about a decade earlier: eclipses, astronomical conjunctions, even the weather, can be known beforehand, but 'future circumstances that have contingent results cannot be foreknown.' Anyone who attempts to foretell such events looks to demons for help in seeking to usurp God's knowledge. As Augustine wrote, like all things that spring from the association of men and demons, divination is superstition.[45] Scripture also damns and prohibits all 'magical arts,' necromancy, divination by stars and planets, and by water, fire, air, animals' entrails, and the voice and flight of birds.[46] In apparent contradiction, however, scripture also shows that dream divination may be free from demonic influence. Treading paths well worn by earlier writers, Carpenter cites Old Testament cases that prove that dreams may be 'worthy of faith' and can reveal future events: the boy Joseph's dream of the sun, moon, and eleven stars worshipping him forecast his future prominence (Genesis 37:9–10); Gideon overheard a dream interpretation that foretold his eventual triumph over his enemies (Judges 7:13–15). Yet how can ordinary people judge if their dreams are prophetic? This is uncertain terrain, as dreams can arise from evil spirits as well as good ones, or they may simply result from anxiety or bodily illness. Always dangerous, dream divination leads many people to err, making those faithful people who trust in their dreams vulnerable to the seductions of evil spirits. Carpenter settles for prohibiting dream divination if done 'superstitiously and too publicly' lest one be deceived by diabolic illusions – as happens to unbelievers and 'especially to unbelieving women.'[47]

Like the vernacular *Dives and Pauper*, Carpenter's treatise for preachers condemned magic and divination as superstition, but admitted the ambiguities that allowed perilous activities like casting lots and dream divination. In reviewing these suspect practices, both works looked for guidance to scriptural example, religious authorities, and church custom, but both turned as well to the actor's intent, suggesting that superstition blossomed from the seed of a practitioner's illicit purpose. Neither author forgave evildoers, but both recognized that not all who appear to do wrong intend to do so. On this point, *Dives and Pauper* and *Destructorium viciorum* joined Bishop Pecock and the ecclesiastical courts who saw in the common folk's soothsaying and spells more foolishness and ignorance than wickedness.

Sterner views of superstition appeared in many late medieval vernacular treatises. Orthodox clerical writers targeted the laity, while Lollard authors pointed to the clergy as the guilty parties; they agreed, however, that superstition posed grave spiritual dangers that were often brushed aside. The first group insisted the laity be held responsible for their superstitions. In the early-sixteenth-century *A Werke for Housholders*, the Syon monk Richard Whytford admonishes his readers to renounce 'these superstitious witchcrafts and charms that are much used and do deceive many persons,' although he concedes 'simple people do suppose and believe they do nothing offend therein.' Whytford adds, 'For I have heard them say full often myself: Sir we mean well and we do believe well/and we think it a good and charitable deed to heal a sick person or a sick beast.' He admits the truth of this, but cautions it is 'neither good nor charitable to heal them by unlawful means.'[48] His *Werke* aimed to strip away the excuses of doctrinal illiteracy and confusion from these 'simple' folk by showing them how superstition led to sin. Yet deeply rooted custom and blind stubbornness, as such would-be educators perceived it, raised obstacles to this program. Lay people, as Whytford bemoaned, saw nothing wrong with their actions. Similarly, *The Doctrinal of Sapience* explains, 'Because many of the simple people believe and have believed and have had faith in sorceries and divinations, we shall make to you mention thereof.' Once warned, people had no pretext for waywardness. *The Doctrinal of Sapience* insists that people sin grievously unless 'they are simple people and so ignorant [from] simpleness that by ignorance they are excused. The which thing does not excuse them if they are sufficiently warned and taught.'[49]

In seeking to banish the mitigating effects of the laity's simplicity or good intentions, these religious instructional texts denounced a catalog of superstitions ranging from astronomical divination to word charms. The 'simple' and 'ignorant,' who were the chief offenders, were sometimes joined by those with secret skills, 'sorcerers of herbs, of words, and other things.'[50] Women were rarely singled out, although one Decalogue treatise indicts new mothers who 'make superstitions which are not lawful' – the example given is laying the infant in a sieve or net with bread and cheese, a practice the treatise condemns as allowing 'wicked wights' to win lifelong power over the child.[51] Many practices were derided as 'fantasies,' such as making a child gaze in a basin or crystal to see the future, or hearing in the magpie's chatter the herald of 'some strange deed,' yet people should know that demons threatened the unwary and unlearned, whose practices could be 'deadly sin.'[52]

These writers, like the author of *Dives and Pauper*, found charms a particularly vexed issue. Whytford's *Werke for Housholders* forbids abusing Christian texts by mutating prayers into charms; for example, by saying the *Pater Noster* over a piece of white bread, which is then placed in the mouth to cure an aching tooth.[53] Yet in the religious books of the late Middle Ages available to pious and educated lay women and men, this prohibition was not universal. Many Books of Hours and other prayer books included prayer charms, introduced by rubrics proclaiming their multiple benefits. Some prayers supposedly guaranteed readers remission of sins; protection from sudden death in battle or by fire, water, or deadly poison; safe travel; and freedom from childbirth's torments. While one prayer purportedly quieted storms or cured illness, another could attract love, worship, and honor from highborn persons if carried on one's body. An English rubric in one Book of Hours tells the reader to fill a cup with water, say a certain prayer over it, cast the water into the sea, and so the 'tempest shall slaked be.'[54]

To many eyes these prayer charms looked like magic, and *The Doctrinal of Sapience*, for one, condemns people who made 'writings and letters full of crosses' and who say that 'all those that bear such documents on them may not perish in fire, nor in water, nor in other perilous places.' Whether they make such things, bear them, trust in them, sell or give them, they sin 'right grievously.'[55] Neither custom, nor inscribing words taken from scripture, nor good intent, could redeem these charm users.

Some Lollard works echoed these worries about superstition, but while their authors agreed that laypeople's lack of knowledge led to superstitious actions, they lay ultimate responsibility at the clergy's feet. The thread of anticlericalism was consistently woven through the diverse views of Lollard thinkers who tended to agree in denouncing the clergy for greed, for deliberately misleading laypeople, for corruption, and for lack of pastoral care.[56] Adding to these faults, some Lollards reproached the clergy for neglecting to educate the laity in Christian basics like the Ten Commandments. Lamenting the people's lack of knowledge of these laws in saying 'I fear we are bailiffs of error for these commandments,' one writer then explains each of them. The First Commandment clearly forbids all witchcrafts, enchantments, incantations, and practices like marking 'Egyptian days,' and Augustine bade 'true priests' to warn the people that these 'crafts' could not help either sick men or beasts.[57] The priests could not teach because they themselves lacked learning, wrote another. 'Ignorant people' mistakenly believe in 'ravens greeting, pies chattering, owls calling and many such other ungrounded fantasies,' but so too 'many ignorant clerks because of the blindness of ignorance consent to this blindness of old misbelief.'[58]

An Apology for Lollard Doctrines expands on these concerns; citing Augustine, the author says 'there are a thousand species of vain superstition,' among them charms, divination through bird chattering and dreams or in any other way, necromancers, sorcerers and other snares 'of the old enemy' through whom the fiend seeks to deceive humankind. The Apology condemns the practice of using scriptural texts as charms; citing John Chrysostom, the author insists 'the gospel written is not to be worshipped.' If the gospel existed merely in words on parchment, then such leaves might reasonably be hung about the neck. But it is vain to drape one's neck with parchment pieces holding gospel words. Holy writing cannot alone drive away fiends or sickness, nor protect one from harm, as some people think who do not understand spiritual things. Miracles like this occurred in the past to benefit 'rude men,' but now 'it is vain and superstitious to the people to have such things.'[59] While God gave virtue to word, herb, and stone, only God ordains their use, so all charms and divinations are superstition and idolatry. Charms are powerless to help one; believing otherwise marks a person as easily deceived, either by fiends or one's own gullibility. God clearly forbids these charms 'that men use amiss.'[60]

The Apology goes further, however, in linking superstition's dangers to powerful leaders who deceive the people. God's mercy protects from 'the malice of charms and charmers, and conjurers, witches, sorcerers, and others' who all work for wicked ends by 'the fiends' curse or vainly without God.' These include those people who would prevent one from obeying the gospel or apostles' and prophets' teachings, as well as those who forbid people even from knowing the gospel, saying they would not understand it. These men 'hold not Christ the head' nor follow him, and even say that words of holy writ 'sound not well.' Such wicked men who lead this world in 'blindness and error and folly and malice' are the real dangers, and God keep us, prays the author, 'from the malice of their charms and from their superstitions, vanities, errors, and deceits.'[61]

Twelve Conclusions of the Lollards, a document fixed to the doors of Westminster Hall and St. Paul's in 1395, added church rituals to the demonically inspired sins against the First Commandment. Demanding church reform, the Twelve Conclusions denounced the clergy, and protested against the sacraments and traditional practices like pilgrimage. The fourth conclusion claims that the 'fained miracle of the sacrament of bread' induces men to idolatry. Then the fifth conclusion condemns 'exorcisms and blessing made in the church of wine, bread and wax, water, salt and oil and incense,' calling them the 'practice of necromancy rather than of holy theology.' Only 'false belief' as the agent of the 'devil's craft' can perceive that these rituals bestow a 'higher virtue' on these material elements of church rituals.[62]

Lollard authors, insofar as they may be grouped together, considerably broadened superstition's sphere beyond simple laypeople who sinned from ignorance, to embrace ill-educated clergy and malevolent leaders. 'Superstition' now characterized church rituals that, alongside all charms and efforts to foretell the future, worked to summon the devil. In the most extreme Lollard view, the clergy had not only abandoned their duty to instruct people against superstition, they had themselves become its purveyors.

Conflicts over superstition became even more impassioned in sixteenth-century England when early reformers, or evangelicals, reiterated Lollard views of common devotional practices as dangerous superstitions. Historians agree that heightened worries about superstition led both Catholic and Protestant clergy throughout Europe to blistering attacks on superstition, although the two groups battled over its definition.[63] Yet in England the particular medieval outlook articulated by Bishop Pecock still informed Thomas More's polemical work. During the 1520s, More confronted what he termed the 'heresies' of Martin Luther and his English followers, including William Tyndale, author of two popular works indebted to Luther. At the request of Cuthbert Tunstall, Bishop of London, More wrote *A Dialogue Concerning Heresies* (first published in 1529, followed by a second edition in 1531). Tunstall had asked More to produce English books for 'the common man' so that he might 'see through the cunning malice of heretics,' and More's *Dialogue* aimed to show this reader how to respond to 'Luther's pestilent heresies in this realm.'[64]

In More's *Dialogue* a young scholar dubbed the Messenger, who has read Tyndale and likes Luther, voices skepticism about customary devotions like venerating saints' images and relics. As the other character in the *Dialogue*, More's role is to show the Messenger his errors; jabbing at weaknesses and exposing contradictions in the Messenger's line of reasoning, More asserts the validity of pilgrimages, relics, image veneration, and a wide range of other contemporary religious practices. This serious, protracted, often repetitive discussion is enlivened at times by More's well-known 'merry tales' – mocking narratives that poke fun at the clergy and at popular beliefs.[65] The humor, however, only lightly veils their import as serious contributions to More's defense of traditional religion.

One well-known merry tale begins when the Messenger protests that harm results from the 'superstitious manner' in which people make pilgrimages and ask for 'unlawful petitions' from the saints. He emphasizes their absurdity and superstition by his story of the notorious Picardy shrine of St. Valery, where people sought a cure for 'the stone.' Most shrines received from grateful pilgrims waxen ex-votos shaped to represent a cured arm or healed leg, but at St. Valery's the offerings hung on the wall were 'none other than men's gear [genitalia] and women's gear made in wax.' Further, the shrine held two silver rings 'through which every man did put his privy member'; at an altar stood a monk blessing threads of Venice gold, which he taught male pilgrims to knit about 'their gear' while saying certain prayers to protect them from the stone. In the ludicrous finale to the Messenger's tale, a peddler at the shrine tried to sell an English pilgrim a candle the length of his gear, to burn in the chapel as guarantee against the stone. The pilgrim's earnest wife rejects this as 'witchcraft,' fearing it would 'waste up' her husband's gear.[66]

More and the Messenger enjoy a good laugh together over St. Valery's shrine, but the Messenger insists that such practices are so 'superstitious' that 'the pagan gods were worshipped with no worse.' More's response echoes Reginald Pecock from the previous century; he admits a kernel of truth in the Messenger's portrayal of saint worship, but protests his censure. Since St. Valery's shrine is in France, More puckishly suggests its defense should be left to the University of Paris, but still he claims 'there is no superstition' in asking Saint Appollonia to cure toothaches, nor in women offering oats at St. Paul's to Saint Wilgefort so she would disencumber them of their husbands. If people, and in particular women, sometimes act foolishly, it is of little concern. Pilgrimages, relic veneration, and prayers to saints are time-honored and laudable customs whose value cannot be destroyed by a few misguided people whose errors, all in all, amount to mere trivialities.[67]

In contrast to the Messenger, More finds dangerous superstition not in the credulity of simple people, but in the zealousness of reformers like the Cambridge scholar Thomas Bilney. Bilney's preaching against clerical abuses, pilgrimages, and prayers to saints led him to be charged with heresy in 1527 by More's friend Bishop Tunstall. Bilney recanted, but when he preached again on forbidden topics, even disseminating Tyndale's English New Testament, he was convicted of heresy and burned.[68] When Bilney's posthumous reputation as 'a good man and a very devout' is reported to him, More attacks Bilney's overfearful and scrupulous devotion as superstitious, alleging that Bilney bound himself so closely to follow Christ's words that he thought it a sin to 'say his service abroad' because Christ bids us to pray in our chamber. More terms this behavior more 'peevish and painful than evil and sinful,' but sees it motivated by 'superstitious fear and servile dread.' Drawing on an ancient definition of superstition as an excessively punctilious attention to rules, More declares that the devil likely cast Bilney into such superstition.[69]

Thomas More's nonchalance about the Messenger's charge of superstition in popular religious practices warned his readers to beware of quick judgments of their fellow believers, and reflected the reasoning of some medieval writers. More's indictment of Bilney, on the other hand, forecast the sixteenth century religious debates in which both Protestants and Catholics embraced 'superstition' as the defining sin of the other.[70] In his *An Answer to Sir Thomas Mores Dialogue* (1531), William Tyndale quickly denounced More's apology for devotional practices. Where More winked at the doting dames who offer oats to Saint Wilgefort, Tyndale insisted their ignorance stood at the crux of the crisis in contemporary religion. How is it possible, he asked, for people to worship images, relics, and sacraments except superstitiously, so long as prelates will not allow them to learn the true meaning of their religion? All of these devotions – carrying a piece of the cross as protection from bodily harm, saying the gospel to women in childbirth, wearing a scroll with holy words on it – are done in ignorance and sin, which good intent can neither rescue nor absolve.[71]

In the decades following More's and Tyndale's debate, Protestant reformers in England effectively linked Catholic teachings, clergy, prayers, and ritual to superstition. Sixteenth-century reform legislation expanded superstition's purview to take in not only pilgrimages; candles offered to saints; saying certain prayers with 'vain confidence' in their efficacy; and midwives' prayers to saints and their use of salt, herbs, water, wax, girdles, or relics, but also masses, belief in purgatory, all doctrine not grounded in scripture, and finally the entire era of 'papisty and superstition.'[72] Protestants denied that any material objects could contain God's power, even papers inscribed with gospel words hung around the neck, a practice still causing consternation into the seventeenth century, as a German theologian had to declare: 'it would not help against the devil if a man ate ten Bibles, and tied twenty around himself.'[73]

As a term of condemnation or reproach, 'superstition' mirrored the writer's view of the accused. While sixteenth-century Catholic and Protestant clergy might defend themselves in print, the voices of the 'unlearned' laity who found themselves so often tarred by superstition's brush are heard only through the muffling and potentially distorting court records and writings like those of Whytford, Pecock, and More. Still, they register diverse responses, from Richard Perkin's compliant gratitude for the Archbishop of York's teaching to regarding clerical intrusions as irrelevant or turning them to their own ends. Open resistance to church authority and clerical instruction occurred when people like Etheldreda Nyxon refused to show up in court to answer accusations of practicing the superstitious arts. Clerical writers bemoaned the fact that instructions on superstition were plainly rejected. As *The Doctrinal of Sapience* admits, despite admonitions and threats of excommunication, some people 'will not leave' their charms.[74] When women and men were brought into court on charges raised by their neighbors, then purged of these charges by their neighbors' oaths, the courts may have established their innocence or unwittingly acted as broadsides to advertise their skills. The laity's indictment for superstition sometimes encouraged their submission to church authority, and sometimes left them bewildered that an apparently good spirit or good deed could be the devil's handiwork, but they might also resist or defy such teachings, and presumably continued their practice of the 'superstitious arts' that seemed to serve their purposes.

Disputes over gospel words hung around the neck were almost as old as Christianity itself; their reprise in the fifteenth and sixteenth centuries reveals no new 'superstition' but points to ongoing conflicts over religious practice, as well as highlighting the word's contingent character. While the English clerical writers judged superstition a problem, they disagreed about which activities could be labeled superstitious and how the guilty should, or would, be punished. These differences arose in part from their disparate views of the laity. Along with the ecclesiastical courts, Bishop Pecock regarded superstition as an outgrowth of ignorant people's misjudgments, which could not corrode the heart of real belief and was easily corrected. Similarly, Thomas More saw more perilous superstition in Bilney's rigid correctness than in the saint-worship of foolish women. A second stance, in contrast, perceived an uneducated and stubborn laity clinging to superstitions despite warnings, teachings, and condemnations, and whose disobedience and rejection of church authority posed real spiritual dangers. The mendicant author of *Dives and Pauper* offered a third perspective: holding laypeople responsible for practices like sun-worship, soothsaying, charms, and lot-casting, he also assumed a literate audience able to follow the argumentation that insisted that good intentions might in certain cases redeem apparently superstitious behaviors. He envisioned a religious landscape in which the laity use reading and reason to participate in their own spiritual development. Finally, Lollards pictured the laity as hostages to a clerical monopoly on religious learning, which was itself a form of superstition. Along with Lollards, the reformers regarded the clergy as dealers in superstition whose product led the innocent and ignorant to spiritual harm. 'Superstition' in late medieval England thus underwent continual metamorphoses, assuming new shapes from these changing interactions of writers, their audiences, and the accused.

Notes

1. For a recent discussion see Michael D. Bailey, 'The Disenchantment of Magic: Spells, Charms, and Superstition in Early European Witchcraft Literature,' *American Historical Review* 111 (2006): 383–404; see also Françoise Bonney, 'Autour de Jean Gerson: Opinions de Théologiens sur les superstitions et la sorcellerie au début du XVe siècle,' *Le Moyen Âge* t. 26, 4th series (1971): 85–98.

2. Keith Thomas, *Religion and the Decline of Magic* (New York: Charles Scribner's Sons, 1971), 48–49.

3. Jean-Claude Schmitt discusses superstition's shifting definitions in 'Les superstitions,' in *Histoire de la France religieuse*, vol. 1, *Des dieux de la Gaule à la papauté d'Avignon (des origines au XIVe siècle)* (Paris:É ditions du Seuil, 1988), 419–21; see also his 'Les Traditions Folkloriques dans la Culture Médiévale: Quelque réflexions de méthode,' *Archives de Sciences Sociales des Religions* 52 (1981): 5–20; and Dieter Harmening, *Superstitio: Überlieferungs- und theoriegeschichtliche Untersuchungen zur kirchlich-theologischen Aberglaubensliteratur des Mittelalters* (Berlin: Erich Schmidt, 1979).

4. Kathryn Kerby-Fulton, *Books Under Suspicion: Censorship and Tolerance of Revelatory Writing in Late Medieval England* (Notre Dame, Ind.: University of Notre Dame Press, 2006), examines the plurality of views about late medieval religious writings and its readers, and argues that censorship was ineffective in a manuscript culture. Other recent studies of lay readers of religious texts include Mary C. Erler, *Women, Reading, and Piety in Late Medieval England* (Cambridge: Cambridge University Press, 2002); and several essays in *The Medieval Reader: Reception and Cultural History in the Late Medieval Manuscript*, eds. Kathryn Kerby-Fulton and Maidie Hilmo, Studies in Medieval and Renaissance History 3rd series, vol. 1 (New York: AMS Press, 2001).

5. This case is published in *The Register of John Moreton Archbishop of Canterbury 1486–1500*, volume III *Norwich Sede Vacante, 1499*, ed. Christopher Harper-Bill (Woodbridge, Suffolk: The Boydell Press for the Canterbury and York Society, 2000), 215–16. Peter Northeast also treats it in 'Superstition and Belief: A Suffolk Case of the Fifteenth Century,' *The Suffolk Review* n.s. 20 (1993): 43–46. For the activities of cunning folk in the early modern and modern eras, see Owen Davies, *Cunning Folk: Popular Magic in English History* (London and New York: Hambledon and London, 2003).

6. Diana Webb, *Pilgrimage in Medieval England* (London and New York: Hambledon and London, 2000), 99–100; C. Paine, 'The Chapel and Well of Our Lady of Woolpit,' *Proceedings of the Suffolk Institute of Archaeology and History* 38 (1993): 8–12.

7. For examples, see Norman Tanner, 'Penances imposed on Kentish Lollards by Archbishop Warham 1511–12,' in *Lollardy and the Gentry in the Later Middle Ages*, ed. Margaret Aston and Colin Richmond (New York: St. Martin's Press, 1997), 229–49.

8. Necromancy seems the most serious of these activities, as it explicitly referred to demonic magic in the late Middle Ages; see Richard Kieckhefer, *Magic in the Middle Ages* (Cambridge: Cambridge University Press, 1989), 152–53. Yet the term's meaning in these court cases is uncertain; accused people were sometimes charged with the linked crimes of necromancy, *sortilegium*, and *incantacionibus*, pointing more to general illicit trafficking with the supernatural than to summoning demons in particular. See the discussion on terminology by Karen Jones and Michael Zell, ' "The divels speciall instruments": Women and Witchcraft before the "great witch-hunt," ' *Social History* 30 (2005): 49–50, which examines church court cases from the diocese of Cambridge between 1396 and 1563.

9. On penalties given by ecclesiastical courts, see Sandra Brown, *The Medieval Courts of the York Minster Peculiar*, Borthwick Paper 66 (University of York, 1984), 25–26. Karen Jones, *Gender and Petty Crime in Late Medieval England: The Local Courts in Kent, 1460–1560* (Woodbridge: The Boydell Press, 2006), 173–79, discusses cases of witchcraft and superstition.

10. Sandra Lee Parker and L. R. Poos, 'A Consistory Court from the Diocese of Rochester, 1363–4,' *English Historical Review* 106 (1991): 657. On the use of toads in witchcraft and remedies, see Jacqueline Simpson and Steve Roud, *A Dictionary of English Folklore* (Oxford: Oxford University Press, 2000), 361–62.

11. *The Register of John Chandler Dean of Salisbury 1404–17*, ed. T. C. B. Timmins Wiltshire Record Society, vol. 39 (Devizes, 1984), 94.

12. *The Courts of the Archdeaconry of Buckingham 1483–1523*, ed. E. M. Elvey, Buckinghamshire Record Society, no. 19 (1975), 155.

13. *The Registers of Oliver King, Bishop of Bath and Wells 1496–1503 and Hadrian de Castello, Bishop of Bath and Wells 1503–1518*, ed. Henry Maxwell-Lyte, Somerset Record Society, vol. LIV (1939), 41–42.

14. R. H. Helmholz, 'The Law of Compurgation,' in Helmholz, *The Ius Commune in England: Four Studies* (Oxford and New York: Oxford University Press, 2001), 82–134.

15. *Depositions and other Ecclesiastical Proceedings from the Courts of Durham extending from 1311 to the reign of Elizabeth*, Surtees Society vol. 21 (London: J. B. Nichols and Son, 1845), 27.

16. *Depositions... from the Courts of Durham*, 29.

17. *Register of John Moreton Archbishop of Canterbury 1486–1500*, vol. III, 196. One of Alice's accusers was Thomas Fynne, who said Andrew had accused Alice on his deathbed.

18. On the church courts' use of excommunication, see Elisabeth Vodola, *Excommunication in the Middle Ages* (Berkeley: University of California Press, 1986), 28–43; and Brian L. Woodcock, *Medieval Ecclesiastical Courts in the Diocese of Canterbury* (London: Oxford University Press, 1952), 91–102.

19. *The Courts of the Archdeaconry of Buckingham 1483–1523*, 23–24. Priests convicted of adultery generally received much lighter penalties, as did laypeople convicted of sexual misdeeds. Divining with a psalter and key was likely done in the same manner as the later practice of divining with a bible and key; for the latter see *A Dictionary of Superstitions*, ed. Iona Opie and Moira Tatem (Oxford: Oxford University Press, 1989), 23–25.

20. *Register of John Moreton*, III, 217.

21. H. A. Kelly, 'English Kings and the Fear of Sorcery,' *Mediaeval Studies* 39 (1977): 219–29; for discussions of the political motivations in this case, see Ralph A. Griffiths, 'The Trial of Eleanor Cobham: An Episode in the Fall of Duke Humphrey of Gloucester,' *Bulletin of the John Rylands Library* 51 (1969): 381–99; and William R. Jones, 'Political Uses of Sorcery in Medieval Europe,' *The Historian* 34 (1972): 670–87.

22. A. Hamilton Thompson, *The English Clergy and Their Organization in the Later Middle Ages* (1947; reprint Oxford: The Clarendon Press, 1966), 220–22.

23. *The Register of Thomas Rotherham, Archbishop of York, 1480–1500*, vol. 1, ed. Eric E. Barker, Canterbury and York Society, vol. 69 (1976), 190–91.

24. Reginald Pecock, *The Repressor of Over Much Blaming of the Clergy* (London, *Rolls Series* volume 19, part I, 1860), 155–57. On the man in the moon, see *Dictionary of Superstitions*, 264; on supernatural women who visit newborns, see Stephen Wilson, *The Magical Universe: Everyday Ritual and Magic in Pre-Modern Europe* (London and New York: Hambledon and London, 2000), 197–98. On Pecock's life, thought, and heresy trial, see V. H. H. Green, *Bishop Reginald Pecock: A Study in Ecclesiastical History and Thought* (Cambridge: Cambridge University Press, 1945); and Roy Martin Haines, 'Reginald Pecock: A Tolerant Man in an Age of Intolerance,' in *Persecution and Toleration*, ed. W. J. Sheils (Oxford: Blackwell, 1984), 125–37. Kantik Ghosh discusses Pecock's audience in 'Bishop Reginald Pecock and the Idea of "Lollardy,"' in *Text and Controversy from Wyclif to Bale: Essays in Honour of Anne Hudson*, ed. Helen Barr and Ann M. Hutchinson (Turnhout, Belgium: Brepols, 2005), 251–65.

25. Biblical quotations are from the Rheims-Douay Version, rev. Richard Challoner. On the production of vernacular religious writing in late medieval England, see Judith Shaw, 'The Influence of Canonical and Episcopal Reform on Popular Books of Instruction,' in *The Popular Literature of Medieval England*, ed. Thomas J. Heffernan (Knoxville: University of Tennessee Press, 1985), 44–60; Vincent Gillespie, 'Vernacular Books of Religion,' in *Book Production and Publishing in Britain 1375–1475*, ed. Jeremy Griffiths and Derek Pearsall (Cambridge: Cambridge University Press, 1989), 317–44. On the repression of these writings, see Nicholas Watson, 'Censorship and Cultural Change in Late-Medieval England: Vernacular Theology, the Oxford Translation Debate, and Arundel's Constitutions of 1409,' *Speculum* 70 (1995): 822–64. Taking issue with Watson is

Sarah James, 'Revaluing Vernacular Theology: The Case of Reginald Pecock,' *Leeds Studies in English* n.s. 33 (2002): 135–69.

26. Mary Teresa Brady, 'The Pore Caitif, edited from MS Harley 2336 with Introduction and Notes' (Ph.D. dissertation, Fordham University, 1954), 29.

27. *Speculum Christiani: A Middle English Religious Treatise of the 14th Century*, ed. Gustaf Holmstedt, Early English Text Society, vol. 182 (1933), 16. This edition provides both the original Latin and the Middle English translation. The Latin reads 'omnia sortilegia & omnes incantaciones cum omnibus supersticionibus caracterum & huiusmodi figmentorum.' Other Middle English Decalogue commentaries that forbid superstition, magic, and witchcraft under the First Commandment include John Myrc, *Instructions for Parish Priests*, ed. Edward Peacock, Early English Text Society, vol. 31 (1868), 30; *Quattuor Sermones Printed by William Caxton*, ed. N. F. Blake (Heidelberg: Carl Winter, 1975), 26.

28. On the date and authorship of *Dives and Pauper*, see Priscilla Heath Barnum's 'Introduction' to *Dives and Pauper*, vol. I, pt. I, Early English Text Society 275 (London and New York: Oxford University Press, 1976), ix; and Francis J. Sheeran's 'Introduction' to *Dives and Pauper: A Facsimile Reproduction of the Pynson Edition of 1493* (Delmar, N.Y.: Scholars' Facsimiles & Reprints, 1973), v–x, who suggests the author was a Franciscan preacher. Anne Hudson discusses the work's authorship and orthodoxy in *The Premature Reformation: Wycliffite Texts and Lollard History* (Oxford: Clarendon Press, 1988), 417–21. For ownership, see H. G. Richardson, 'Dives and Pauper,' *The Library* 4th series, vol. 15 (June 1934): 31–37. Barnum lists manuscripts and early printed editions in *Dives and Pauper*, vol. II, Early English Text Society 323 (Oxford and New York: Oxford University Press, 2004), liv–lxxvi. Margaret Deanesly, *The Lollard Bible* (Cambridge: Cambridge University Press, 1920), 342, says copies were left as bequests in wills.

29. *Dives and Pauper*, vol. I, pt. I, 116.

30. *Dives and Pauper*, vol. I, pt. I, 144.

31. *Dives and Pauper*, vol. I, pt. I, 119–24, 136–37.

32. *Dives and Pauper*, vol. I, pt. I, 147–48.

33. See Jan R. Veenstra, 'Cataloguing Superstition: A Paradigmatic Shift in the Art of Knowing the Future,' in *Pre-Modern Encyclopaedic Texts*, ed. Peter Binkley (Leiden: Brill, 1997), 169–80. Laura Ackerman Smoller offers a concise overview of medieval discussions of astrology's conflict with Christianity and Aquinas's influential solution in *History, Prophecy, and the Stars: The Christian Astrology of Pierre D'Ailly 1350–1420* (Princeton: Princeton University Press, 1994), 25–42. Pauper's understanding of astrology agrees with Thomas Aquinas's position in *Summa Theologiae* 2.2.95.5 (New York: McGraw-Hill, 1964), vol. 40, 50–55.

34. Don. C. Skemer, *Binding Words: Textual Amulets in the Middle Ages* (University Park: The Pennsylvania State University Press, 2006), 30–33, 154, 167–68, provides the most thorough discussion of such charms. Valerie I. J. Flint, *The Rise of Magic in Early Medieval Europe* (Princeton: Princeton University Press, 1991), 301, quotes this passage from Augustine's *De Doctrina Christiana*, calling it an 'enormous loophole.'

35. *Dives and Pauper*, vol. I, pt. I, 157–8. See also Pauper's distinction between the licit and illicit use of holy candles and the *Pater noster*, vol. I, pt. I, 163. See a similar view in *Fasciculus Morum: A Fourteenth-Century Preacher's Handbook*, ed. and trans. Siegfried Wenzel (University Park: The Pennsylvania State University Press, 1989), 577. Barnum provides valuable background on this and other issues in *Dives and Pauper*, vol. II, 65–66.

36. For medieval views of curiosity, see Edward Peters, '*Libertas Inquirendi* and the *Vitium Curiositatis* in Medieval Thought,' in *La notion de liberté au Moyen Âge: Islam, Byzance, Occident* (Paris: Société d'é dition 'Les Belles Lettres,' 1985), 89–98; Richard Newhauser, 'Towards a History of Human Curiosity: A Prolegomenon to its Medieval Phase,' *Deutsche Vierteljahrsschrift für Literaturwissenschaft und Geistesge-schichte* 56 (1982): 559–75; and 'Augustinian *Vitium Curiositatis* and its Reception,' in *Saint Augustine and His Influence in the Middle Ages*, ed. Edward

King and Jacqueline Shaefer, Sewanee Medieval Studies 3 (Swanee, Tenn.: Press of the University of the South, 1988), 99–124. On curiosity's link to magic, see Edward Peters, *The Magician, the Witch and the Law* (Philadelphia: University of Pennsylvania Press, 1978), 16–17, 90.

37. *Dives and Pauper*, vol. I, pt. I, 166–67. Pauper's teaching on lots again corresponds to that of Aquinas, *Summa Theologiae*, 2.2.95.8.

38. *Dives and Pauper*, vol. I, pt. I, 169.

39. Thomas N. Tentler, *Sin and Confession on the Eve of the Reformation* (Princeton: Princeton University Press, 1977), 144–53.

40. Alexander Carpenter, *Destructorium viciorum* (Paris, 1521). A printed copy is listed in the 1558 inventory of books saved from the collection of the Benedictine priory of Monk Bretton in Yorkshire; see David N. Bell, 'Monastic Libraries: 1400– 1557,' in *The Cambridge History of the Book in Britain, volume III, 1400–1557*, ed. Lotte Hellinga and J. B. Trapp (Cambridge: Cambridge University Press, 1999), 248– 49. Copies at Syon are listed in *Syon Abbey*, ed. Vincent Gillespie, Corpus of British Medieval Library Catalogues 9 (London: The British Library in association with The British Academy, 2001), 203, 207, 209, 210, 211. Peter Heath, *The English Parish Clergy on the Eve of the Reformation* (London: Routledge & Kegan Paul, 1969), 88, identifies the work in four clerical wills in the Norwich diocese. See also G. R. Owst, *The Destructorium Viciorum of Alexander Carpenter: A Fifteenth-Century Sequel to Literature and Pulpit in Medieval England* (London: S.P.C.K., 1952); and *Oxford Dictionary of National Biography*, vol. 10 (2004), 215–16.

41. Carpenter, Part 6, chap. 43. Carpenter borrows heavily from Aquinas' arguments and examples, but his categorization of demon worship as superstition's third branch differs from Aquinas, who divides superstition into two parts: the incorrect worship of God, and worship 'due to God' that is given to another creature; see *Summa Theologiae* 2.2.92.2.

42. Carpenter, Part 6, chap. 44.

43. Carpenter, Part 6, chap. 45.

44. Carpenter, Part 6, chap. 45. On Saint Luke as the Virgin's portraitist, see Hans Belting, *Likeness and Presence: A History of the Image Before the Era of Art*, trans. Edmund Jephcott (Chicago: University of Chicago Press, 1994), 57–59.

45. Carpenter, Part 6, chap. 47. See Augustine's comments on astrology and divination in *De Doctrina Christiana*, ed. and trans. R. P. H. Green (Oxford: Clarendon Press, 1995), 93–99.

46. Carpenter Part 6, chap. 53.

47. Carpenter, Part 6, chap. 50. He cites examples from the New Testament of dreams arising from demons and from good spirits. For early medieval discussions of dream divination, see Flint, *Rise of Magic*, 194–96.

48. Richard Whytford, *A Werke for Housholders: a dayly exercyse and experyence of dethe*, ed. James Hogg, Salzburg Studies in English Literature: Elizabethan & Renaissance Studies, vol. 89 (Salzburg: Institut für Anglistik und Amerikanistik, Universität Salzburg, 1979), 21. On Whytford's work and readership, see James Hogg, 'Richard Whytford,' in *Studies in St. Birgitta and the Brigittine Order* vol. 2, *Analecta Cartusiana* 35 (1993): 254–66.

49. *The Doctrinal of Sapience, edited from Caxton's printed edition, 1489*, ed. Joseph Gallagher, Middle English Texts 26 (Heidelberg: Carl Winter, 1993), 54–55.

50. *Doctrinal of Sapience*, 55.

51. James Finch Royster, *A Middle English Treatise on the Ten Commandments: Texts, Notes and Introduction* (Chapel Hill: University of North Carolina Press, 1911), 14. Newborns were the focus of many rituals intended to protect the child and guarantee long life; see Wilson, *Magical Universe*, 165–95.

52. *Peter Idley's Instructions to His Son*, ed. Charlotte D'Evelyn (1935; reprt. Mill-wood, N.Y.: Kraus Reprint Co., 1975), 113–15.

53. Whytford, *Werke*, 22.

54. Examples of these prayer charms are in London, British Library, Harley MS 2869, fols. 95v–97v; Additional MS 37787, f. 62v.; Royal MS 6 E VI, f. 15r. See Eamon Duffy, *The Stripping of the Altars* (New Haven, Conn.: Yale University Press, 1992), 266–87, for similar rubrics and prayers which he claims belonged to the 'devotional mainstream.'

55. *Doctrinal of Sapience*, 55.

56. On disputes about the nature, importance, and even existence of Lollardy, see Andrew E. Larsen, 'Are All Lollards Lollards?' in *Lollards and Their Influence in Late Medieval England*, ed. Fiona Somerset, Jill C. Havens, and Derrick G. Pitard (Woodbridge, Suffolk: The Boydell Press, 2003), 59–72.

57. London, British Library, Harley MS 2398, f. 74 r., fols. 79v–80v. See Margaret Aston's comments on this manuscript in *Lollards and Reformers: Images and Literacy in Late Medieval Religion* (London: Hambledon Press, 1984), 153, n. 64.

58. London, British Library, MS Additional 41321, f. 84r–v, quoted at length by G. R. Owst, '*Sortilegium* in English Homilectic Literature of the Fourteenth Century,' in *Studies Presented to Sir Hilary Jenkinson*, ed. J. Conway Davies (London: Oxford University Press, 1957), 301–2.

59. *An Apology for Lollard Doctrines*, with Introduction and notes by James Henthorn Todd, Camden Society, vol. 20 (1842), 90–92. Some Lollard sermons also advocate that people not believe in the ink or skins on which the Gospel is written, 'but in the sentence that they say, which sentence is the book of life'; see *English Wycliffite Sermons* vol. II, ed. Pamela Gradon (Oxford: Clarendon Press, 1988), 227.

60. *Apology for Lollard Doctrines*, 95–97.

61. *Apology for Lollard Doctrines*, 97–99.

62. 'Twelve Conclusions of the Lollards,' in *Selections from English Wycliffite Writings*, ed. Anne Hudson (Cambridge: Cambridge University Press, 1978; reprt., Toronto: University of Toronto Press, 1997), 25–26. A recent examination of the *Twelve Conclusions*' audience is Wendy Scase, 'The Audience and Framers of the *Twelve Conclusions of the Lollards*,' in *Text and Controversy from Wyclif to Bale*, 283–301.

63. Euan Cameron, 'For Reasoned Faith or Embattled Creed? Religion for the People in Early Modern Europe,' *Transactions of the Royal Historical Society* 6th series, vol. 8 (1998): 165–87.

64. On Tyndale's works, see William A. Clebsch, *England's Earliest Protestants 1520–1535* (New Haven, Conn.: Yale University Press, 1964), 146–53. In 1523–24 More had also written against Luther in the *Responsio ad Lutheram*. Thomas More, *A Dialogue Concerning Heresies*, The Complete Works of St. Thomas More, eds. Thomas Lawler, Germain Marc'hadour, Richard C. Marius, vol. 6 (New Haven, Conn.: Yale University Press, 1981); for the *Dialogue's* history, see the Introduction, vol. 6, pt. 2, 439–54. On More's audience, see D. V. N. Bagchi, 'Tyndale, More, and the Anatomy of Heresy,' *Reformation* 2 (1997): 261–81.

65. For interpretations of the merry tales, see Anne Lake Prescott, 'The Ambivalent Heart: Thomas More's Merry Tales,' *Criticism* 45 (2003): 417–33; and Walter M. Gordon, 'The Argument of Comedy in Thomas More's *Dialogue Concerning Heresies*,' *Renaissance and Reformation* n.s. 4, no. 1 (1980), 13–32. The text's editor, Thomas Lawler, calls them 'vehicles of wisdom,' vol. 6, pt. 2, 450.

66. More, *Dialogue*, 226–29.

67. More, *Dialogue*, 229–37.

68. A.G. Dickens, *The English Reformation* 2nd ed. (London: Batsford, 1989), 102–3. On More's involvement in Bilney's execution, see Clebsch, *England's Earliest Protestants*, 279–80.

69. More, *Dialogue*, 257–59. More's use of the term seems rooted in ancient Roman understandings that linked *superstitio* to religion carried to excess (Cicero), as well as to fear and to pious actions

done by people who lack philosophical understanding (Seneca); see Dale B. Martin, *Inventing Superstition: From the Hippocratics to the Christians* (Cambridge, Mass., and London: Harvard University Press, 2004), 125–30.

70. Helen Parish and William G. Naphy, 'Introduction,' in *Religion and Superstition in Reformation Europe*, ed. Parish and Naphy (Manchester and New York: Manchester University Press, 2002), 2.

71. William Tyndale, *An Answer to Thomas Mores Dialogue*, The Independent Works of William Tyndale, eds. Anne M. O'Donnell and Jared Wicks, vol. 3 (Washington, D.C.: The Catholic University Press of America, 2000), 60.

72. *Visitation Articles and Injunctions of the Period of the Reformation*, eds. W. H. Frere and W. M. Kennedy (London: Longmans, Green & Co., 1910). For pilgrimages, candles, tapers, images, relics, beads, prayers, vol. 2: 59, 105, 108, 115, 126, 189, 200. On 'old superstitions and papistical doctrine' that lack the authority of God's word, vol. 2: 268; on transubstantiation, masses, prayers to saints, purgatory, pardons, indulgences, beads, images, vol. 2: 284; see also vol. 2: 287, 304.

73. Cited in Cameron, 'For Reasoned Faith,' 175, n. 38.

74. *Doctrinal of Sapience*, 55.

CHAPTER 2

FOR REASONED FAITH OR EMBATTLED CREED? RELIGION FOR THE PEOPLE IN EARLY MODERN EUROPE

Euan Cameron

There has long been some measure of agreement that European people in the middle ages adhered to a form of Christianity which was 'folklorised', 'enchanted', or 'magical'. Interwoven with the traditional creeds and the orthodox liturgy were numerous beliefs and practices which were intended to ensure spiritual and bodily welfare, and guard against misfortune. To the endless frustration of theologians, 'religion' and 'superstition' stubbornly refused to remain clearly separate, despite the intellectual effort expended in forcing them into different compartments.[1] 'Superstitious' rites or beliefs repeatedly intersected with the official Catholic cult. It was believed that if a talisman were placed under an altar-cloth during mass, it would acquire spiritual potency. Orthodox prayers were constantly adapted to serve the needs of popular magic. Clergy, let alone layfolk, found the line between acceptable and superstitious practice difficult to draw. For a graphic illustration of this problem, one need only look at the following recipe for curing a hailstorm caused by sorcery:

> But against hailstones and storms, besides those things said earlier about raising the sign of the cross, this remedy may be used: three little hailstones are thrown into the fire with the invocation of the most Holy Trinity; the Lord's Prayer with the Angelic Salutation is added twice or three times, and the Gospel of St John, 'In the beginning was the word', while the sign of the cross is made against the storm from all quarters, before and behind, and from every part of the earth. And then, when at the end one repeats three times, 'the Word was made flesh', and says three times after that, 'by these Gospels uttered, may that tempest flee', then suddenly, so long as the storm was caused to happen by sorcery, it will cease.

This recipe might be expected to originate in some peasant's primer; in fact it comes from none other than the notorious witch-hunting textbook, the *Malleus Maleficarum*, written by two German Dominican friars in the 1480s. It was copied, in the complete conviction of its Catholic respectability, by the papal theologian and expert on the hearing of confessions, Silvestro Mazzolini of Priero, in a work published in 1521.[2]

In the past, most historians have simply observed this phenomenon, which is copiously documented and often severely criticised in the writings of early modern commentators, especially Protestants.[3] Some who have tried to explain it have stressed the role played by surviving pagan beliefs, incompletely or even half-heartedly winnowed out by Christian missionaries in the early middle ages and after.[4] The notion of pagan survivals in Europe becomes superficially more attractive if one draws the plausible parallels between late medieval Europe and modern rural Latin America, where the Roman Catholic Church maintains its hold on the animist beliefs of indigenous villagers by a subtle, at times eclectic or syncretic, attitude to their mountain-spirit cults.[5] At the time, however, contemporary observers usually attributed 'superstitious' charms to the degradation of orthodox Christian prayers over time. Most 'charms', they said, had originally been pious prayers, which the devil had abused.[6] Such a falling-away from an imagined pristine past came more naturally to them, just as the idea of unfinished evolution offers a more plausible explanation to our world-view.

Wherever medieval 'superstitions' came from, it is widely thought that early modern Europe saw the first concentrated attempt to dissuade the people from this sort of belief-system, or at least to drive a wedge firmly and consistently between orthodox Christianity and its 'folklorised' accretions. Furthermore, it is usually argued that this campaign was waged by Protestant and Catholic reformers alike, in similar terms and with similar arguments. For all sorts of reasons, it does seem to make sense to envisage the early modern period as the one in which Europe's people were, for the first time, deliberately and systematically dissuaded from 'superstitious' patterns of thought. After the Reformation, the Protestant and Catholic confessions embarked on a massive educational enterprise, in which each sought to inculcate a uniform pattern of belief and practice among its people, from the top down.[7] The confessions backed up their educational work by strenuous, if often incomplete, efforts to institute pastoral and spiritual discipline. Such discipline produced the legions of visitation protocols found in reformed Catholicism, and the corresponding Protestant effort, which has been documented in the last generation by historians of German reformed 'confessionalism'.[8] In so far as both Protestant and Catholic educators laid claim to the mantle of Renaissance Christian humanism, both were heirs to the tradition in which Erasmus of Rotterdam had pressed for a personal, ethical piety, in place of a religion based on 'superstitious' cults and ceremonies.[9]

In different ways, the idea that 'superstitions' were first attacked in a thoroughgoing way in the early modern period also fits in with two of the most current models of early modern cultural change: the 'acculturation' model proposed by Jean Delumeau and, in his earlier works, by Robert Muchembled; and the model of a progressive separation of élite and popular cultures proposed by Peter Burke and in Muchembled's more recent writings.[10] The only issue for debate appears to be whether the enterprise of dissuading the masses from their traditional beliefs succeeded or not. If it succeeded, it was 'acculturation'; if it failed, then the outcome was a separate 'élite culture'. Most recently, Dr Stuart Clark has lent further weight to the idea that Protestant and Catholic fought on a common religious front against popular magic. His monumental study of Protestant and Catholic demonologies relegates confessional differences to the sidelines. He continually stresses the shared concepts and the similar purpose behind all demonological writers.[11]

There is considerable evidence to support that view, and this paper certainly does not propose to try to challenge all of it at once.[12] It does, however, entail certain risks, which the homogenising approach of the secular historians of culture may cause to be overlooked. Essentially, it proposes that two separate processes were at work in the religious history of early modern Europe. On the one hand there was the establishment of Protestant and Roman Catholic Christianity, and on the other the campaign to dissuade the people from their traditional sub-Christian beliefs. If there was conflict over the aims of the first enterprise, there may still (so the theory implies) have been agreement over the second. Yet I simply do not believe that the theologians of the sixteenth and early seventeenth centuries saw their task of taking true religion to the people in this fragmented, compartmentalised way. Put another way, it is not sufficient to analyse the Protestant and Roman Catholic responses to popular belief by cutting out all the theological differences between them. The writers and preachers who tried to take a reasoned, 'modern' religion to the people of Europe were also, at one and the same time, the champions of controversial, embattled, rival systems of belief. This essay seeks to put the theological controversy back into the history of the assault on 'popular superstition'. It will do so by examining some of the wide range of literature written by laity and clergy about popular religion, from both sides of the religious divide. These works include sermons, pastoral guides, pamphlets, even university theses, and survive in the European vernaculars as well as in Latin. They are important, first because they form a tradition, within which authors borrowed from each other and responded to each other's views; and secondly, because they circulated in a milieu in which future pastors and priests were trained. They bear abundant witness to the desire to inculcate a 'reasoned faith' in place of popular superstition; but their arguments show, as I shall suggest, certain important differences between one confession and another.

II

First, one important point must be conceded to the thesis that there was a common front between Protestant and Catholic reformers. Both groups of theologians started from a shared body of beliefs about the nature of the universe, and about natural causation, which they inherited from their medieval scholastic predecessors, and ultimately from Augustine and other early Fathers of the Church. Protestants concurred with the traditional belief that the universe was filled with spiritual creatures who were either good angels or fallen angels, that is, demons; they thus rejected the popular belief that there were morally neutral spirits (sprites, house-spirits and others of their kind) whose help might be invoked.[13] Demons, they agreed, were insatiably determined to injure people in body and soul. They could do this by using their great intelligence, speed, and physical power to achieve surprising, but essentially natural effects very quickly. They could also generate illusions which tricked the human senses, and convinced people that they were even more powerful and wise than they were. However, they could not perform genuine miracles; that is, they could not suspend the order of nature. They could not raise the dead, foreknow the future with certainty, see into the human heart, or change one created thing substantially into another. These things were the prerogative of God alone.[14] Philipp Melanchthon reinforced this point about the limited power of demons with a particularly graphic story in one of his lectures, which was reported by at least three other writers. At Bologna, a female musician died, but was restored to apparent life by a demonic illusion, in which she appeared to eat, drink, and play her instrument as before. Only when a sorcerer saw her, who could see through the trickery with which she had apparently been revived, was it revealed that she was just a corpse whom a demon had caused to move.[15]

Protestant and Catholic theologians then applied their shared 'demonology' to explain and condemn the two main branches of popular 'superstition' as commonly described, namely divination by unlawful means, and magical or superstitious blessing and healing. Protestants, like their medieval antecedents, firmly denied that there was any natural power inherent in words, signs, symbols, or any other inanimate thing to cause marvellous transformations in natural objects. They insisted that words and signs had meaning only to another intelligent being which could draw meaning from them.[16] Since divinations and magical healing had no natural causes, their apparently marvellous effects had to derive from the co-operation of demons, whether these were deliberately invoked in ceremonial magic, or were unconsciously invited to offer their assistance when a superstitious rite or technique was performed. This analysis led the Lutheran Johann Georg Godelmann, for example, to launch a fierce attack on the populist magical healing of Theophrastus Paracelsus (1493–1541), which encouraged the use of amulets, sympathetic magic, and the recipes of gypsies and old women to cure ailments.[17] It is striking that the Jesuit Martin Delrio, who attacked Godelmann bitterly on other issues, plagiarised the Lutheran's attack on Paracelsus more or less wholesale in Book VI of his *Magical Disquisitions*.[18]

Thus far there is broad agreement; that is, over the nature of the spiritual hierarchy, and the possible causes of supernatural events in the world. This measure of agreement is to be expected, since Protestant and Catholic churchmen were alike *theologians*. As theologians, they were reared in the same tradition of natural philosophy, neo-scholastic Aristotelianism. The natural philosophy which supported the orthodox belief in demons derived from the same roots, whether it was via the reconstructed Lutheran Aristotelianism of Philipp Melanchthon, the Calvinist scholasticism of Lambert Daneau, or the neo-Thomism of the Spanish Jesuits.[19] However, this agreement only extends as far as the broad lines of analysis and diagnosis. It does not take us very far into the realm of prescription. It does not tell us just what sort of religion was deemed acceptable for Europe's people, and conversely, how wide the net was cast to drag in those aspects of religious belief which were to be condemned as 'superstitious'. Once we look at the practical application of these general principles, we find that the religions proposed respectively by Protestants and by Catholics for Europe's people, and the things which they each denounced as 'superstitious', were significantly different.

III

The early Protestant reformers did not write a great deal about popular superstitions in the years when the reformed churches were being established. Martin Luther did offer one of the fullest discussions of such practices as conjuring weapons, love-magic, amulets, observance of unlucky days, or of omens.[20] However, the sermon-sequence expounding the Ten Commandments, where this discussion occurs, dates from June 1516 onwards. For all its critique of saint-cults, it is essentially a late medieval piece. It draws on sources such as Geiler von Kaisersberg and Johannes Nider. Its emphases were not repeated in Luther's later pastoral writings such as the *Catechisms*.[21]

One of the first Protestant pieces to address popular superstitions directly was the *Short Opinion, as to what should be thought about idolatrous blessings and conjurations,* published at Basle in 1543 by Johann Spreter of Rottweil.[22] *Segen* (which needs to be translated simultaneously as 'blessings' and 'enchantments') included all forms of words and rites used to transform something natural into something supernatural, or to give spiritual potency to any sort of cult object. *Segenspruch* was a particular preoccupation both of German and of Spanish theologians.[23] The wrongness of *Segen,* for Spreter, lay not only in their source, or whether

God or the devil was invoked, but in the very essence of what was attempted by them. God blessed all created things, and assigned to them their purposes; to try to add some additional quality to an object by one's own blessing was to try to amend God's work, and would bring a curse on the one who tried.[24] Spreter's argument was taken up in almost the same words in the *Christian Opinion and Remonstrance on Sorcery,* published under the name of Augustin Lercheimer in a manual of treatises on magic in 1586.[25] 'Segnen and *Beschweren* is to believe that one can with words, gestures, and certain shapes increase or diminish the power of creatures … or give them another power against their nature and identity, against God's will and ordinance, which in the creation gave everything its power and operation, according to which it stays …' This, it was argued, was in effect robbing God of his prerogative to assign the properties to each created thing.[26] Or, as the Tübingen academic Johann Heerbrand put it in a set of theological theses in 1570, 'Neither does the Word of God uttered in this way by the magicians confer any new properties or qualities on things, besides those which they received from God at creation.'[27]

Created things, for the Protestants, always remained just that: herbs remained herbs, water remained water. It might be inferred from this that the Protestant critique of superstition would then categorise Roman Catholic cult-objects, such as holy water, as 'superstitious' in the same way as popular charms. In fact, one does not have to rely on inference. Right from the start, Protestant critics, Lutheran and reformed alike, included Roman rituals among superstitious enchantments. Spreter said that there were two sorts of enchanters, the monks and priests who tried to make a God out of consecrated salt, water, herbs, wax, etc., and the common conjurers.[28] Jakob Heerbrand went further: 'Pontiffs and priests, satellites of the Roman Antichrist … sin much more seriously in this respect than common magicians and enchanters.'[29] Johann Georg Godelmann agreed that 'papal exorcists are to be numbered with the enchanters'.[30] These theologians and preachers attacked the entire paraphernalia of the Catholic cult as a form of sorcery, both in its purpose and in its details. Lutheran and reformed alike, it must be emphasised, denounced as magical the belief that by utterance of the words of consecration of the Eucharist, the substance of bread was instantly transformed into the body of Christ and the wine into his blood. They then went through the consecrations of the 'sacramentalia', holy salt, holy water, blessed herbs, the *agnus Dei* made of consecrated wax, the oil used in unction and baptism, and the churches, churchyards and church bells themselves.[31] All of these were enchantments, because they aspired to lock up the Holy Spirit into created things, as though they were magical instruments.

Criticism of the formulae by which Catholics blessed their holy things, their *sacramentalia,* was not confined to learned treatises or to academic debating-halls. The ultra-Lutheran Jakob Andreae preached a series of sermons at Esslingen, in which he thus denounced the rite by which the chrism was consecrated:

The chrism … is made with magical, enchanters' blessings, and when one seeks to learn the reason for these, it is no more than devil's work, that so often as the bishop consecrates the chrism, so he blows three times crosswise over the phial in which the oil is, and speaks the following words: 'I conjure you, creature of oil, by God the Father Almighty, who made heaven, earth, and sea, and all that therein is, that all power of Satan, and of all the host of the devils, all assaults and all fantasies of Satan, and their roots may be by you be torn up and driven out' … Who will not think, when he hears these words of the Bishop, that he is hearing an enchanter or conjurer of devils? that he is conjuring the poor created thing of oil, no differently than if it were possessed with a thousand devils? ... he breathes like an enchanter over the vessel in which the oil is kept; like an enchanter he makes two crosses; he conjures the devil, yea many devils, like an enchanter ... he has also just as little authority to use the name of God and the cross for this purpose, and to conjure the devil out of the oil, as any other enchanter or soothsayer, when they conjure the devil, and will tell to their neighbours where they may find their lost money or goods.[32]

When the sermons of the ultra-Lutheran Andreae and the ultra-Zwinglian Heinrich Bullinger are laid side by side, there is a remarkable measure of agreement between the arguments which they used against Roman rites. In the sixth sermon of the fifth series of his *Decades,* Bullinger devoted much care to an examination of the power of holy words, as applied to the consecrations of sacraments. He denied that in any scripture there was authority to suppose that the mere utterance of certain words could transform the natures of things, in the Eucharist or anything else. 'These imaginations', he continued, 'do rather seem more to maintain superstition than religion; as though the words, pronounced according to the form conceived, had power to call down out of heaven, to bring from one place to another, to restore health ... or to transform or change.'[33] Catholic arguments, to the effect that a 'consecration' and a 'superstition' were different things, he rebutted with some scorn. They were based on a misunderstanding of the words 'blessing' and 'sanctify'. In any case, God made things holy, not man.[34]

There is more to this Reformation assault on the 'holy things' in the Catholic rite than tendentious rhetoric. In principle, Protestants denied that the power of. God could be locked up, by the performance of certain words and ceremonies, into certain physical material objects. This entailed frontal confrontation not only with the Catholic theology of the sacraments, but also with things such as amulets, which belonged to a part of medieval popular religion which the reformed Roman Church protected and favoured. As will be discussed later, the Catholic Church still distributed the consecrated wax emblem called the *agnus Dei.* Its theologians also endorsed the wearing of texts from Scripture around the neck or in the clothing as phylacteries to guard against demonic assaults, albeit with a string of provisos and conditions. Jakob Heerbrand mocked the rhyme which claimed that the *agnus* broke the power of sin as Christ's blood did.[35] Bullinger, in his treatise *Against the Black Art,* asserted that when people crossed themselves, or used fixed forms of words to which they ascribed curative power, it was idolatry and the devil's work.[36] Godelmann said that when St John's Gospel was worn to protect against artillery, then such an amulet became a 'sacrament of the devil' which could only work by demonic pact.[37] Antonius Praetorius, in his *Basic Advice about Sorcery* of 1613, lumped popular charms and Catholic *sacramentalia* together without distinction. If the devil could be hindered by crosses, herbs, salt, bread, and words, he would have to be weaker than a person, or even a dog or a pig. Holy words hung around the neck had nothing holy in themselves, at least not used in this way. 'It would not help against the devil if a man ate ten Bibles, and tied twenty around himself'; much less would a scrap of paper with a few words hung round the neck be of any help. This was a means by which the devil deceived people and drew them into superstition through abuse of his word.[38]

There was a fundamental difference between the Protestant concept of 'holiness' and its Catholic counterpart, which has its roots in the basic teachings of the Reformation about

God's work. For Protestants, God always exercised his power directly, immediately, with absolute sovereign authority and all-encompassing providence. For Catholicism, whether medieval or reformed, God's power was often, even ordinarily, delegated: to holy Church, to holy people, into holy things. The very idea of 'Catholic' Christianity embodies the notion that divine power is authoritatively present in certain religious forms, which have been chosen and appointed by God's decree. In consequence, Protestantism was always bound to be far more hostile than Catholicism to the notion that divine power might be located reliably and consistendy in certain things and places on earth. Faith in a transcendent God, not the use of *sacramentalia,* would defend Protestants against the devil. As Andreas Althamer preached in 1532, '[St Peter] does not say, have Masses read against the devil and his delusions, or sprinkle yourself with holy water, or light a consecrated candle, or hang St John's Gospel about your neck, as the Papists teach; but "resist him strongly in the faith". Faith must do it, not the holy-water spring, but faith and trust in God through Jesus Christ ...'[39]

This difference between the two confessions is shown most glaringly in the issue which provoked the most violent disputes between them, that of ecclesiastical exorcism. Exorcism, as will be shown later, was used by militant Counter-Reformation Catholicism as a propaganda weapon against the Protestants. A successful deployment of the apostolic power of the Church to drive out evil spirits could be enormously impressive. The confirmation of Catholic truths sometimes elicited from a demon under interrogation could buttress the claims made by the Church.[40] To rebut these claims, Protestant polemical theologians such as Bullinger, Godelmann, and William Perkins all insisted that the power to exorcise had been an exceptional, miraculous gift. It was given by God directly to buttress the faith in the early days of the Church, and was not based on the use of any specific forms of words. Now that the Church had been long established, Catholic pretensions to cast out demons through such impressive-sounding formulae arose, literally, from diabolical arrogance.[41] Perkins claimed that the true power of exorcising died out after some two centuries; then, when 'Popery that mystery of iniquitie beginning to spring up, and to dilate itself in the Churches of Europe, the true gift of working miracles then ceased; and instead thereof came in delusions, and lying wonders, by the effectual working of Satan, as was foretold by the Apostle, 2. Thess. 2.9. Of which sort were and are all those miracles of the Romish Church.'[42] As Bullinger remarked, all sorts of bizarre things were done in the rites of exorcism, standing someone naked in a bath of cold water, tying a liturgical stole round his neck, sprinkling him with holy water, covering him with vestments, and so forth, which had no rational purpose.[43] Augustin Lercheimer went further: such acts actually served the devil's purposes, as they did no harm to the spiritual being, but made the victim of his possession suffer bodily.[44]

Protestant theologians linked Catholicism and superstitious magic conceptually: they argued that both these belief-systems pretended to alter the divine dispensation of the universe through words and ceremonies. However, they also linked Catholicism and magic by cruder but more memorable methods. Demonic magic, claimed Godelmann, had grown so current in the Catholic Church, that priests and clerics were not regarded as sufficiently learned unless they were magicians. A succession of popes, from Sylvester II through to Alexander VI and Paul III, were alleged to have been practising sorcerers.[45] According to Augustin Lercheimer, a canon of Halberstadt named Johannes Saxonicus used sorcery to enable him to fly, and thus celebrated three masses on the same Christmas Eve, at Halberstadt, Mainz, and Cologne.[46] Godelmann wrote about a famous practitioner of the wound-salve, called 'the Monk of

Chemnitz', who could heal injuries at a distance by anointing the sword which caused them.[47] The Danish theologian Niels Hemmingsen recalled how Catholic priests used a psalter and a key to divine who had stolen lost goods.[48] Catholicism and magic were assimilated to each other, in both directions. If clerics had practised magic, enchanters and sorcerers invariably used ecclesiastical rites and ceremonies. As John Bale said, the mass 'serveth all witches in their witchery, all sorcerers, charmers, enchanters, dreamers, soothsayers, necromancers, conjurers, cross-diggers, devil-raisers, miracle-doers, dog-leeches, and bawds; for without a mass they cannot well work their feats'.[49] Of the sign of the cross, James Calfhill argued against the Catholic Martiall, 'possible it is that, in time past, men did some good by signing them with a cross: now it is not, according to your position, "medicinable against all conjuration, enchantment, sorcery and witchcraft"; *but rather daily used in all these'*.[50]

Finally, Protestant writers asserted that Catholicism and superstition arose together, and fell together. Augustin Lercheimer claimed that since the Gospel had been preached, the black arts had declined in use, and were more widely regarded as sinful; he looked forward to these things disappearing entirely.[51] Niels Hemmingsen agreed that superstitions had declined at the time of the Reformation, but, more pessimistic, he believed that as people grew weary of the Gospel, so they resorted to their old superstitious ways.[52]

IV

For at least a generation it has been accepted wisdom that the Roman Catholic Church after the Council of Trent embarked on a campaign to suppress the traditional, popular abuses of the official cult, and to bring popular religion more strictly under the control of the now more educated, less folkloric reformed priesthood. Jean Delumeau described how the midsummer bonfires for St John Baptist's day, to which all sorts of superstitious beliefs had accrued, were domesticated. The clergy presided over the fires, prevented people from taking brands from the fire to use as talismans, ensured that the fire was thoroughly burned to ashes, and then saw to the ashes being raked into the earth.[53] This story has become a sort of emblem of the Counter-Reformation at village level. Yet the story of the Catholic response to popular belief may be a great deal more complex than the stereotype of intellectual domination of popular belief suggests. The Delumeau pattern requires, first of all, that the Catholic élites should have been absolutely clear, much clearer than their medieval forbears, as to where to draw the line between acceptable devotions and unacceptable vain observances and superstitions. Here the literature on superstitions offers a helpful guide. It is surely safe to assume that at grass-roots level Catholicism was unlikely to have been *more* rigorous and intellectual than the literature: though it may well have been less so.

Since I began earlier with a Protestant work dedicated to incantations and charms, it is appropriate to compare it with its nearest Catholic equivalent, the *First little Work on Incantations or Ensalmos*, published by the Portuguese theologian and Inquisitor Emanuele do Valle de Moura at Evora in 1620.[54] This appallingly mis-named 'little work' (*Opusculum*) of over 560 pages addressed the whole question of charms and spells with unprecedented intellectual precision, and enormous erudition. Valle de Moura himself was a rationalist, whose opinions fit closely into the Delumeau mould. His work explored the issue of enchantments in three parts. In the first part, he defined and summarised the errors of others on the subject. Secondly, he condemned the practice of uttering what he called 'constitutive *ensalmos*', meaning those charms which claimed to operate mechanically, curing or helping by the mere power of the words uttered. On the other hand, 'invocative *ensalmos*', which functioned only as prayers, might be acceptable under certain conditions. In the last part he defended the right of inquisitors to involve themselves in these issues after the reforms of Trent.[55]

The interest in Valle de Moura's work lies chiefly in his encyclopaedic treatment of the views of other writers, both theologians and medical writers, on the issue of incantations or healing charms. He cited a whole range of arguments, which claimed to justify and support some, at least, of these controversial charms. Often these arguments worked by analogy with scriptural and ecclesiastical rituals. One argument ran that God might have instilled a special sanctity in many ordinary things, both material objects and words, to help humanity, just as special power was instilled into the water used in baptism, or holy ground after it was consecrated.[56] Likewise, God might have assigned power to certain things through the intercession of saints; he cited the claims made for the *Bulla Sabbathina*, by which it was believed that the Carmelites who observed particular devotions to the Virgin would be released from Purgatory by a personal appearance of the Virgin on their behalf on the first Sunday after their death.[57] Valle de Moura also quoted the opinions of the medical writer Bravus Chamisius, who claimed that the power of words might itself have a natural curative property.[58] Some people had claimed that other natural things might have the power to drive away demons: Luther, Roman Catholics alleged, had driven away devils not only by the power of his doctoral degree but also by breaking wind.[59] Other material things were alleged to have powers against demons revealed by God, by analogy with the incense which the angel Raphael told Tobias to make with the heart and liver of a fish, which drove away a demon from his marriage-chamber.[60] Such opinions were attributed to the controversial theologian Nicolaus Serarius, as well as the medical-theological writer Francisco Valles.[61] Even Pedro Pablo Ferrer, chancellor of Evora and Valle de Moura's former teacher, was cited as taking a moderate attitude to healing spells: they were always suspect, but there might be certain healers who by a special divine grace could use *ensalmos* licitly. Other moralistic authors whose works appeared at least to show some degree of doubt included confessional writers such as Toletus and Azor.[62] Opinions, it seemed, were various and divided: Llamas and Lessius thought that some divinely communicated healing rites might be accepted, though the former thought they depended on the good morals of the person using them, the latter judged them more according to the circumstances of the action.[63]

Valle de Moura himself did not believe in any of these equivocations; he vehemently opposed any private form of words or ceremony which claimed to secure certain physical or spiritual benefits for the user or anyone else to whom it was applied. He analysed all the stories of special graces granted to saints' cults, certain prayers, or anything like. He finally concluded that any ritual, the mere performance of which was supposed to ensure benefits (for instance the certainty of not dying in mortal sin) was to be rejected.[64] However, the sheer range of controversy in this treatise illustrates two points. First, Valle de Moura thought that Catholic intellectuals, let alone the ordinary people, were often unsteady in their attitude to charms, and tended to equivocate over whether or not special powers might inhere in certain prayers or cult-objects. Secondly, 'superstitious' healing spells were often justified, or excused, by analogy with Catholic rites and practices such as exorcism. Healing powers might be genuinely delegated by God, or spuriously conferred by demonic pact: some people thought that such cures might fall into either category, and appear identical in their effects.

Especially in the Spanish-speaking world, the problem of distinguishing divine and demonic cures was made more acute by the presence of specially gifted healers or *saludadores*. These often claimed to be devotees of St Catherine or St Quiteria, and were commonly regarded as having received by some means a special personal gift to heal illnesses, and especially to close up wounds.[65] They also used particular forms of words in their healing. A most interesting discussion of this phenomenon occurs in the highly rationalistic *Six Books of Magical Disquisitions* written by the Jesuit Martin Delrio, a work mostly known for its discussion of witch-hunting (which actually occupies a very small part of the book).[66] Delrio was willing to allow that certain special people might be given the divine gift of healing, as was claimed for children born on Holy Saturday in Flanders. He noted that Vitoria, Veracruz, and Navarrus were willing to approve *saludadores* in certain circumstances, and suggested that bishops examine them. He was nevertheless worried by the claims made by some that they needed to drink plenty of wine before carrying out a cure, or that they could not cure in the presence of another, more powerful healer. Yet he did not condemn all indiscriminately as working by demonic pacts, as one might have expected.[67]

Elsewhere in the work, Delrio listed a whole range of 'vain observances': these were particular things used by ordinary people as omens or rituals to order their lives, which often drew upon the rites of the Church. Most he condemned as superstitious; only exceptionally might devotion to a saint, combined with looking to God for help, excuse them. Here he returned to the issue of *saludadores*. Spanish soldiers would apply a clean cloth to a wound. They would then utter over it a form of words, in the vernacular, which recalled the institution of the Lord's Supper, and then pray to Jesus that 'by these most holy words, and by their power, and by the merit of your most holy passion, this wound (and this evil) may be healed'. This form of words was debated at Ypres before Bishop Simon shortly before Delrio wrote, and judged superstitious. 'This condemnation,' Delrio commented, 'seemed hard to many people, but mistakenly.' The error, he thought, lay in using a healing charm without medicines; because this implied that one routinely expected a miracle from God, without natural means; it lay also in the abuse of the words of the mass.[68]

Catholic commentators experienced several problems in winnowing and purifying 'popular religion' which were not felt by their Protestant counterparts. One, obviously, was the desire to maintain continuity with the early and medieval churches. Much subtlety had sometimes to be expended in sifting claims made for the miraculous powers of holy words or gestures, or the 'certain' benefits accruing to devotees of a cult. These things could not simply be swept away as the remnants of Antichrist. A second problem concerned ecclesiastical remedies against the assaults of evil spirits. In the later middle ages several theologians had encouraged people to look for the source of their misfortunes in hostile sorcery or witchcraft, to explain illness, infertility, bad weather, or other problems.[69] Having diagnosed people's problems as the fault of demons working through sorcerers, the Church then offered an arsenal of supernatural techniques, in the shape of *sacramentalia* and exorcisms, to drive away the demons and thereby to solve the problem of ill-health, bad-weather, infertility or whatever. These *sacramentalia* and exorcisms then became, as was discussed earlier, a debating point between Catholics and Protestants. Protestants claimed that they were nothing more than another form of superstitious magic. Catholics not only rejected this claim;[70] they also alleged that the power and success of these rituals and holy things proved that theirs was the true religion. These ecclesiastical rituals and their powers became, in fact, proofs of the status and claims of Roman Catholicism itself.

From very early in the Reformation era, Catholic writers leapt to the defence of ecclesiastical 'holy things' which the Protestants attacked. Francisco de Osuna (d. c. 1540), whose *Scourge of the Devil* was translated into German in Bavaria in 1602, wrote of the effects and workings of malign sorcery in traditional late-medieval fashion. In fact he drew much of the first part of his text from the *Short Work on Witches* by the Tübingen nominalist theologian Martin Plantsch, dating from 1507.[71] In the second part, however, he departed from his source to embark on a vigorous defence of the Catholic Church's claims to exorcise, and to consecrate holy water. While he quoted Plantsch's reservations about the limits to the power of *sacramentalia*, Osuna defended the power of holy water far more fervently. 'Who is there,' he added, 'who does not know that this our holy water will remain uncorrupt for a whole year and more, while ordinary water will not remain good for more than about a month? What can be the origin of that other than the blessing?'[72]

Catholic writers learned to include, while denouncing superstitious remedies, a fervent defence of the power of holy water, holy herbs, holy wax, prayers to saints, the sign of the cross, and a range of other ministrations, including the sacraments themselves, as a far more effective defence against harmful sorcery. Just such a defence forms most of Book VI of Delrio's *Magical Disquisitions*, where he specifically replied to the charges collected by the Lutheran Godelmann from several of his own predecessors.[73] Interestingly, Delrio *disagreed* with Nicholas of Cusa's strictures against using holy water, Easter wax, or baptismal water to cure illnesses in people or animals, or sterility in fields: if these were used as a *sacramentale*, in the expectation that God would confirm faith through a marvel, that would be licit.[74] It was customary to prove the miraculous powers of Catholic rites by reference to miracle-stories, usually involving the conversion of non-Catholics. These were sometimes medieval tales from Caesarius of Heisterbach or Thomas of Chantimpré; but in Delrio's case they were often drawn from Jesuit missions, either to the Americas or to Japan, or to Protestant corners of Europe. Baptism freed a Peruvian prince called Tamaracunga from the assaults of demons; the power of the Eucharist had recently driven demons out of Netherlandish Calvinists.[75] The power of the sign of the cross was attested by a range of miracles.[76] Lopez de Gómara reported that among the American Indians the deceits and apparitions of demons amongst the Indians were best dispelled with the presence of the Eucharist, the image of the crucifix, and the sprinkling of holy water, 'and the very evil spirits have themselves confessed this to the Indians'.[77]

This calling-up of the curative and preservative powers of the Church's rites made excellent sermon fodder. Its potential was exploited to the full in a series of sermons entitled *The Panoply of the Armour of God against all the devil-worshipping of superstitions, divinations, and incantations,* preached by Friedrich Forner, suffragan bishop of Bamberg, and published at Ingolstadt in 1626. Alongside a meticulous and standard denunciation of do-it-yourself superstitious cures ran a vigorous defence of, and encouragement to use, ecclesiastical remedies. This defence occupied twenty-two of the thirty-five sermons in the cycle.[78] Like Delrio's, this work told colourful tales of successful exorcisms and cures attributed to the holy things of the Church, drawn either from Delrio himself or from Tommasso Bozio's *On the Marks of the Church*.[79]

Of all the spiritual weapons wielded by the Catholic Church in its propaganda war against the Reformation, the power to exorcise demons was the most dramatic and the most contentious. Broadly considered, exorcism might be achieved through any form of prayer or holy gesture or object; but specifically, it was performed through a series of prayers, conjurations of devils, and ritual instructions to the evil spirits to depart, which were accompanied by gestures, above all the repeated signing of the cross, and the use of cult-objects such as holy water or consecrated herbs. There is abundant evidence from recent research to show that in contested areas of Germany especially, exorcisms became celebrated and public trials of spiritual strength between Protestants and Catholics.[80] Both Delrio and Forner reported a list of instances where the devils prevailed over Protestants, only to be defeated by Catholics.[81] This, the reader was told, was how Divine providence wished to demonstrate the greater truth of Catholicism.

In the light of the persuasive role ascribed to exorcism, it is worth considering in more detail what sort of a message this rite sent to the people of Europe about the nature of the spiritual realm. There were various forms and manuals for exorcism published at this period. The multiplicity of these works proves, if nothing else, that the Roman rite established as the official means of exorcising evil spirits was far from being the only one to be used.[82] We are probably entitled, however, to assume that working exorcists would have used something akin to the works of one of the most popular authorities on the subject, the Observant Franciscan Girolamo Menghi of Viadana, whose works were published several times in Italian and Latin.[83]

Menghi's writings generally fell into two parts, a discursive part which conveyed the theology of sorcery and its remedies, and a liturgical part which contained prescriptions with which anyone might in principle perform a successful exorcism. In his *Compendium of the Exorcist's Art* (published in Italian), Menghi drew his theology of how lawfully to resist sorcery from a pre-Reformation text, Silvestro Mazzolini's *On the Marvels of witch-sorcerers* of 1521.[84] However, he specified the nature of ecclesiastical remedies rather more fully than his predecessors. Herbs, as such, had no natural power to drive away demons; yet if they were combined with ecclesiastical consecration and exorcism, one could make medicines and potions from them.[85] There was unease about amulets which contained unknown names of God; so Menghi helpfully supplied etymologies (often erroneous) for some of the most impressive ones.[86]

The exorcisms in Menghi's *Flagellum Daemonum* must have reinforced, rather than diminished, popular belief in the power of words and rituals to heal all ills. Several of these included the invocation of God in a list of impressive, powerful, and essentially incomprehensible names;[87] the demon was several times exorcised 'through the virtue of all the holy, ineffable, and most powerful names … and through the power of all those ineffable names'.[88] Earth, air, fire and water were all conjured individually, to prevent them from containing the devil; fire was conjured before it was used to burn an image of the devil, to torment the demon.[89] In the *Most Efficacious remedies for expelling malign spirits*, Menghi supplied a series of formulae for blessing holy oil. For curing ailments in the body caused by demons, he gave this recipe:

> Take white hellebore, hypericum, rose-sugar, and incense [in specified quantities], and boil them in a pound of white wine until they are reduced to half their volume; then have the boiled wine blessed and exorcised by a priest according to the form as below, and give it to the patient at a suitable time for three days; each day, notwithstanding vomiting, the sick person being duly contrite and confessed, and being in a state of grace, is to be exorcised for the space of three or four hours; because thus he will be healed, if the grace of God is favourable.[90]

Similar prescriptions were made for the preparation of holy salt, incense of blessed herbs, and for the conjuration of parchment on which amulets were to be written. One could tell whether a person was vexed by evil spirits or not by writing a list of the holy names of God on blessed parchment, and placing it on the patient when he or she was unaware of it.[91]

V

It is perfectly clear that Protestants and Roman Catiiolics both wished to dissuade their people from using do-it-yourself superstitious cures and methods of divination. The arguments by which they proved that these techniques were naturally inefficacious, and that therefore they must depend on the intervention of an obliging but deceptive demon, show close similarities. However, if one looks a little more widely, and asks what they proposed to put in place of popular superstitions, then their programmes appear to diverge rather dramatically.

Protestants taught, essentially, a different doctrine of the power of God. No earthly thing contained, or received delegated to it, one jot of the sovereign power of the Divine providence. All that one could do was to ask God, in humble petition, for one's wants and needs to be relieved, in the knowledge that providence might well have decreed otherwise. In Roman Catholicism, on the other hand, the picture was more complex. It is quite possible to find passages among Catholic authors which also stress the all-powerful nature of providence, and the way in which every religious rite depends for its working on God's will. Nevertheless, Catholics clearly believed that in ordinary circumstances, God had *chosen* to channel his holiness through the approved rites, dirough particular people, places, things, words, and ways of doing things.[92] To be in communion with these holy things on earth was to touch the expressions of the Divine. To use as many as possible of these holy things for one's spiritual and even material benefit was not disobedience, but devotion.

In practice, Protestants tried to reform the people's religion by instilling a radically different vision of God, by turning the whole form of religion into something else. For Catholics, the exercise was more one of purgation, of bringing into line, and under control, rituals and ceremonies which had grown in an uncontrolled fashion over the centuries, and had ultimately become a vulgar magic decorated with Christian names and symbols. This divergence in intent must explain why, in the succeeding centuries, parts of Europe contained no holy places or miraculous manifestations, while other parts still do demonstrate these things today. Protestants and Catholics, even as they used similar arguments and sometimes even plagiarised from each other, did not think that they were about essentially the same business in transforming people's religion. Neither should we.

Notes

1. Defining the boundaries between superstition and religion forms the main issue in St Thomas Aquinas, *Summa Theologica,* iia iiae, qq. 92–6. Several treatises on superstition were written because a 'case of conscience' had arisen over whether a particular rite or rites were superstitious or not. See e.g. Martin de Arles y Andosilla, *Tractatus de Superstitionibus*, in Nicolaus Jacquier, ed., *Flagellum Haereticorum Fascinariorum* [and other works] (Frankfurt, 1581), pp. 351ff [but first published 1517]; and Henricus de Gorihem (Henry of Gorcum), *De Superstitiosis quibusdam casibus*

(Esslingen, c. 1473). The author gratefully acknowledges the support given by the Leverhulme Trust, in awarding a Research Fellowship which made the preparation of this paper possible.

2.   Heinrich Institoris and Jakob Sprenger, *Malleus Maleficarum*, ii.2.7; and compare Silvestro Mazzolini Prierias, *De Strigimagarum Demonumque Mirandis Libri iii* (Rome, Antonius Bladis de Asula, 1521), sig. ff ii^v. For further evidence see E. Duffy, *The Stripping of the Altars: Traditional Religion in England C.1400–C.1580* (New Haven and London, 1992), 266ff.

3.   See the classic discussion in K. Thomas, *Religion and the Decline of Magic* (London, 1971), 27–57; and the appropriation of his interpretation for continental material in Stuart Clark, *Thinking with Demons: The Idea of Witchcraft in Early Modern Europe* (Oxford, 1997), 533. Further reflections on the Reformation and magical world-views are found in R. W. Scribner, 'The Impact of the Reformation on Daily Life' in *Mensch und Objekt im Mittelalter und in der frühen Neuzeit*, Österreichische Akademie der Wissenschaften, Phil.-hist. Klasse, 568 (Vienna, 1990), 315–43, and R. W. Scribner, 'The Reformation, Magic and the "Disenchantment of the World"', in *Journal of Interdisciplinary History* 23 (1993), 475–94.

4.   See the argument of V.I.J. Flint, *The Rise of Magic in Early Medieval Europe* (Oxford, 1991); for enduring paganism, note also the appropriation of evidence from Olaus Magnus, *Historia de Gentibus Septentrionalibus* (Rome, 1556), in C. Ginzburg, *Ecstasies: Deciphering the Witches' Sabbath*, trans. R. Rosenthal (London, 1992).

5.   For Mexican evidence see Jacques Lafaye, *Quetzalcoatl and Guadalupe: the Formation of Mexican National Consciousness, 1531–1813*, trans. Benjamin Keen (Chicago, 1976); N. S. Davidson, *The Counter-Reformation* (Oxford, 1987), 70ff.

6.   E.g. Johannes Nider, *Preceptorium divine legis* (Basle, c.1470), precept i, ch. 11, q. 27. [This edition has neither foliation nor quire signatures.] On the argument that the devil mocked and parodied divine ordinances, see Clark, *Demons*, ch. 6, 80–93.

7.   For catechesis, see e.g. G. Strauss, *Luther's House of Learning: Indoctrination of the Young in the German Reformation* (Baltimore, 1978); Ian Green, *The Christian's ABC: Catechisms and Catechizing in England c. 1530–1740* (Oxford, 1996); on the Roman Catholic side, the works of Peter Canisius, *Summa doctrinae christianae* (Vienna, 1555), *Catechismus minimus* (Ingolstadt, 1556), and *Catechismus minor* (Cologne, 1558), and also the Tridentine Catechism, published as *Catechismus ad parochos* (Rome, 1566).

8.   On pastoral visitations see Umberto Mazzone and Angelo Turchini, *I Visiti Pastorali: Analisi di una fonte* (Bologna, 1985); on confessional discipline see R. Po-Chia Hsia, *Social Discipline in the Reformation: Central Europe 1550–1750* (London, 1989), esp. 122–73. A recent contribution to this subject is B. Tolley, *Pastors and Parishioners in Württemberg during the Late Reformation 1581–1621* (Stanford, Calif., 1995), 64ff.

9.   For typical Erasmian satire of vulgar superstitions see *The Colloquies of Erasmus*, ed. C. R. Thompson (Chicago, 1965), esp. 'A Pilgrimage for Religion's Sake' and 'The Shipwreck'. It is noteworthy that Erasmus's works were placed on the Index in the Counter-Reformation, but extensively used as school-texts in Protestantism.

10. For acculturation, see J. Delumeau, *Catholicism between Luther and Voltaire* (London, 1977), and R. Muchembled, *Popular Culture and Elite Culture in France, 1400–1750* (Baton Rouge, 1985); also the discussion in J.K. Powis, 'Repression and Autonomy: Christians and Christianity in the Historical Work of Jean Delumeau', *Journal of Modern History* 64 (1992), 366–74; for the separation of élite and popular cultures see P. Burke, *Popular Culture in Early Modern Europe* (London, 1978) and his sources, also the more recent work of R. Muchembled, especially his *L'Invention de l'homme moderne: Sensibilités, moeurs et comportements collectifs sous l'ancien régime* (Paris, 1988).

11. Clark, *Demons*, esp. chapters 29–34.

12. This traditional view, by ascribing the attack on 'superstitions' chiefly to the early modern period, may also be unfair to late medieval pastoral theologians. That point is to be developed in a separate article.

13. For demons, see e.g. Augustin Lercheimer, *Ein Christlich Bedencken wind Erinnerung von Zauberey, woher, was, und wie vielfaeltig sie sey … in Theatrum de veneficis: Das ist: Von Teufelsgespenst, Zauberem und Giffibereitern, Schwartzkünstlern, Hexen und Unholden, vieler fürnemmen Historien und Exempel …* (Frankfurt-am-Main, Nicolaus Bassaeus, 1586), 262ff; for a Catholic example compare e.g. Pedro Ciruelo, *Reprouacion de las supersticiones y hechizerias,* translated as *Pedro Ciruelo's A Treatise Reproving all Superstitions and Forms of Witchcraft,* ed. E. A. Maio and D. W. Pearson (Madison and London, 1977), 83–8. The morally ambiguous 'house-spirits' are attested e.g. in the 'duen de casa' described by Alphonsus de Spina, *Fortalitium Fidei …* (Lyons, Guillaume Balsarin, 1487), sig. Liv, or the 'helekeppelin' described by Martin Luther in his *Decem Praecepta Wittenbergensi praedicata populo,* in *M. Luther, Werke: Kritische Gesamtausgabe,* 58 vols (Weimar, 1883–1948) [hereafter *WA*] i. 406.

14. Lercheimer, *Christlich Bedencken,* 263; *cf.* Lambert Daneau, *Dialogus de Veneficis,* in Nicolaus Jacquier, ed., *Flagellum Haereticorum Fascinariorum* [and other works] (Frankfurt, 1581), 271–4. For this 'science' of demonic activity see Clark, *Demons,* ch. 11, 161ff.

15. The story is reported by Lercheimer, *Christlich Bedencken,* fo. 281ʳ; and by Johann Georg Godelmann, *Tractatus de Magis, Veneficis et Lamiis, deque his recte cognoscendis et puniendis* (Frankfurt, 1601), 36, based on Caspar Peucer, *Commentarius, de Praecipuis Divinationum generibus, in quo a prophetiis, authoritate divine traditis, et a Physicis conjecturis, discernuntur artes et imposturae diabolicae, atque observationes natae ex superstitione, et cum hac conjunctae: Et monstrantur fontes ac causae Physicarum praedictionum: Diabolicae vero ac superstitiosae confutatae damnantur …* (Frankfurt, 1607), 14.

16. On this position see Clark, *Demons,* 281ff; and also e.g. Daneau, *Dialogus,* 265–7.

17. Godelmann, *Tractatus de Magis,* 80–3, 86–7, 92–8. Godelmann singled out Paracelsus's *De occulta Philosophic, De Caelesti Medicina, De Philosophia Magna,* and *De Philosophic ad Athenienses.* See Theophrastus Bombast von Hohenheim [Paracelsus], *Opera Omnia,* 3 vols (Geneva, 1658).

18. Maitinus Delrio S.J., *Disquisitionum Magicarum Libri Sex, in tres tomos partiti,* 3 vols. (Lyon, 1599–1600), vi, ch. 2, sect i, in vol. iii, 175ff.

19. Melanchthon's Aristotelianism is discussed in Sachiko Kusukawa, *The Transformation of Natural Philosophy: The Case of Philip Melanchthon* (Cambridge, 1995); Daneau's scholasticism in O. Fatio, *Méthode et Théobgie: Lambert Daneau et les débuts de la scholastique réformée* (Geneva, 1976); that of the Spanish Jesuits in Charles B. Schmitt, Quentin Skinner, and Eckhard Kessler (eds) *The Cambridge History of Renaissance Philosophy* (Cambridge, 1988), pp. 490–527 and refs.

20. *WA* i. 401–10.

21. *WA* i. 409 cites the story of a woman who suffered from an illusion of night-flight, from Johann Geiler von Kaisersberg, *Die Emeis* (Strasbourg, Johannes Grieninger, 1517), fo. 37ᵛ, which is in turn based on Johannes Nider's *Formicarius,* consulted as J. Nider, *De Visionibus ac revelationibus …* (Helmstedt, 1692), bk. 2 ch. 4, 200–1. On Luther see S. Brauner, *Fearless Wives and Frightened Shrews: the Construction of the Witch in Early Modern Germany* (Amherst, Mass., 1995), 53–67.

22. Johannes Spreter, *Ein Kurtzer Bericht, was von den Abgoetterischen Saegen und Beschweren zuehalten, wie der etlich volbracht, unnd das die ein Zauberey, auch greuewel vor Gott dem Herren seind* (Basle, 1543).

23. The Spanish word *ensalmo* most closely corresponds to the German *Segen.* For a sociological and theoretical approach to this issue see Irmgard Hampp, *Beschwörung, Segen, Gebet: Untersuchungen zum zauberspruch aus dem Bereich der Volksheilkunde* (Stuttgart, 1961). Tolley, *Pastors and Parishioners,* identifies the use of *Segen* as the most common form of superstitious practice *c.* 1600.

24. Spreter, *Kurtzer Bericht,* sigs. A iiʳ⁻ᵛ, A iiiʳ⁻ᵛ.

25. Lercheimer, *Christlick Bedencken,* 261–98.

26. Lercheimer, *Ckristlich Bedencken,* 289.

27. Jacobus Heerbrandus, *De Magia Disputatio ex cap. 7. Exo.,…praeside reverendo et clarissimo viro Jacobo Heerbrando, sacrae theologiae Doctore eximio, ac eiusdem in Academia Tubingensi Professore publico…Nicolaus Falco Salueldensis…respondere conabitur* (Tübingen, 1570), 12.

28. Spreter, *Kurtzer Berkht,* sig. Aiii^v.

29. Heerbrand, *De Magia Disputatio,* 13.

30. Godelmann, *Tractatus de Magis,* 55–6.

31. Heerbrand, *De Magia Disputatio,* 13–15, theses 83–92; Lercheimer, *Christlich Bedencken,* 289–90; Godelmann, *Tractatus de Magis,* 57–8.

32. Godelmann, *Tractatus de Magis,* 58–9; the original edition of Andreae's sermon has not been traced.

33. Bullinger, H., *The Decades of Henry Bullinger,* trans. 'H. I.' and ed. T. Harding, 4 vols, Parker Society (Cambridge, 1849–52), iv. 254–60.

34. *Ibid.,* 260–7.

35. Heerbrand, *De Magia Disputatio,* thesis 89, 14; also cited by Godelmann, *Tractatus de Magis,* 57.

36. Heinrich Bullinger, *Wider die Schwartzen Künst, Aberglaeubigs segnen, unwarhafftigs Warsagen, und andere dergleichen von Gott verbottne Kiinst, in Theatrum de veneficis: Das ist:Von Teufelsgespenst, Zauberem und Gifftbereitern, Schwärtzkünstlern, Hexen und Unholden, vieler fürnemmen Historien und Exempel…* (Frankfurt-am-Main, Nicolaus Bassaeus, 1586), 300.

37. Godelmann, *Tractatus de Magis,* 92.

38. Antonius Praetorius, *Gründlicher Bericht von Zauberey und Zauberem, deren Urprsung, Unterscheid, Vermögen und Handlungen, Auch wie einer Christlichen Obrigkeit, solchen schändlichen Laster zu Begegnen…* (Frankfurt, 1629), 63–5.

39. Andreas Althamer, *Eyn Predig von dan Teuffel / das er alles unglueck in der welt anrichte* (n.p., 1532), sig. B iii^v.

40. For examples of this see Clark, *Demons,* 138ff.

41. Bullinger, *Wider die Sckwartzen Kunst, in Theatrum,* 301; Godelmann, *Tractatus de Magis,* 55–6.

42. William Perkins, 'A Discourse of the Damned Art of Witchcraft', in his *Works* (Cambridge, 1618), 648.

43. Bullinger, *Wider die Sckwartzen Kunst.*

44. Lercheimer, *Christlich Bedencken,* 265.

45. Godelmann, *Tractatus de Magis,* 21f; *cf* Lercheimer, *Christlich Bedencken,* 273ff.

46. Lercheimer, *Christlich Bedencken,* fo. 279^v. [Note: leaves 277–82 of the *Theatrum* are foliated rather than paginated.]

47. Godelmann, *Tractatus de Magis,* 86.

48. Nicolaus Hemmingius [=Niels Hemmingsen], *Admonitio de superstitionibus magicis vitandis, in gratiam sincerae religionis amantium…* (Copenhagen, 1575), sigs. B viii^v -C i^r.

49. John Bale, *The Latter Examination of Mistress Anne Askewe,* in *Select Works of John Bale* (Parker Society, Cambridge, 1849), 236.

50. James Calfhill, *An Answer to John Martiall's Treatise of the Cross,* ed. Richard Gibbings (Parker Society, Cambridge, 1846), 338; italics are mine.

51. Lercheimer, *Christlich Bedencken,* 276.

52. Hemmingsen, *Admonitio,* sigs. F ii^r–iii^r.

53. J. Delumeau, *Catholicism between Luther and Voltaire* (London, 1977), 177–9.

54. Emanuele do Valle de Moura, *De Incantationibus seu Ensalmis Opusculum Primum…* (Ebora, Typis Laurentii Crasbeeck, 1620).

55. Valle de Moura, *De Incantationibus,* preface, fo. I[r] [the work is foliated to fo. I I, thereafter paginated to p. 552].

56. *Ibid.,* fos. 8[r–v].

57. *Ibid.,* fo. 9[v]–p. 12.

58. *Ibid.,* 22ff.

59. *Ibid.,* 27; in fact the power of flatulence to drive away demons was believed by others, as shown by Mazzolini, *De Strigimagarum … Mirandis,* sigs. ee ii[r–v].

60. Tobit 6:3–8:3.

61. Valle de Moura, *De Incantationibus,* 29ff; the references are to Nicolaus Serarius, *Commentarii in sacros Bibliorum libros, Josuae, Judicum, Ruth, Tobiae …* (Paris, 1611), on Tobit, ch. 8; and to Francisco Valles, *De iis quae scripta sunt physice in libris sacris, sive de sacra phibsophia liber singularis* ([Geneva], 1595), ch. 28.

62. Valle de Moura, *De Incantationibus,* 32–4, 42–3; in these passages Valle de Moura refers, amongst others, to Franciscus Toletus, *Instructio Sacerdotum* (Cologne, 1621), bk. 4 ch. 16, and to Johannes Azor, *Institutonum moralium* (3 vols in 2, Lyon, 1602–22), bk. 9 ch. 26 sect 6.

63. Valle de Moura, *De Incantationibus,* 65; in these passages Valle de Moura refers to Hieronymus Llamas, 'Methodus', [possibly =] *Summa ecclesiastica, sive instructio confessariorum et poenitentium absolutissima* (Mainz 1605); and Leonardus Lessius S.J., 'Lib. 2 de Mag.' The latter reference has not been traced. Lessius wrote many works of theology, and also the *Hygiasticon,* a treatise on preserving health.

64. Valle de Moura, *De Incantationibus,* 132.

65. On these healers, see Ciruelo, *A Treatise Reproving all Superstitions,* 255–6; for the cult of St Quiteria see also W. A. Christian, *Local Religion in Sixteenth-Century Spain* (Princeton, 1981), 108–9. Delrio, *Disquisitionum,* i. 37, compares 'saludadores' to the followers of St Catharine or of St Paul, as they were called in Italy, or the 'children of Holy Saturday' in Flanders.

66. Delrio, *Disquisitionum;* see discussion in Clark, *Demons,* e.g. 439ff.

67. Delrio, *Disquisitionum,* i. 37–42.

68. *Ibid.,* ii. 98ff, 113ff.

69. For many instances of recommended 'preservatives' against sorcery, see *Malleus Maleficarum,* pt ii, q. 2 *passim;* Geiler von Kaisersberg, *Die Emeis,* fos. 47–51; Mazzolini, *De Strigimagarum … Mirandis,* bk. ii chs. 9–12 *passim.* According to Robin Briggs, *Witches & Neighbours: The Social and Cultural Context of European Witchcraft* (London, 1996), chs. 2–4 and 9, people did not need much prompting to see the source of their problems in terms of hostile sorcery.

70. As for instance in Albertus Hungerus, *De Magia Theses Theologicae, in celebri et catholica academia Ingolstadiana An. S. N. M.D.LXXIIII, die 21 Junii per Reverendum et eruditum virum M. Hectorem Wegman Augustanum, SS. Theologiae Baccalaureum formatum, Divae Virginis apud eandem Academiam Parochum, pro impetrando Licentiae gradu, ad publicam disputationem propositae: Praeside Reverendo et Clarissimo viro ALBERTO HUNGERO, SS. Theologiae Doctore el Professore ordinario, Collegü Theologici pro tempore decano* (Ingolstadt, Weissenhorn, 1574), theses 88–95.

71. Franciscus de Osuna, *Flagelhan Diaboli, oder Dess Teufels Gaisl, darin gar lustig und artlich gehandelt wird: Von der Macht wind Gewalt dess boesen Feindts: von den effecten und Wirckungen der Zauberer/Unholdter und Hexenmaister: Warum Gott bewillige/das die Menschen von ihnen werden belaidigt am Leib und Gut: Und was fuer remedi und mittel darwider zugebrauchen. Beschliesslichen von den Teuftischm remediis, superstitionen, Aberglaubm, Agoettereyen* [sic]*/wie auch falschen Astrologia, Warsagerey/und andem dergleichen verbottenen Kuensten/die an jetzo starck im schwung gehen* (Munich, 1602); fos. 6[r]–33[v] are based on an often verbatim rendering of Martin Plantsch, *Opusculum de sagis maleficis* (Phorce, 1/1507), sigs. b iv[v]-f i[r].

72. Osuna, *Flagellum*, fo. 40^v.

73. Delrio, *Disquisitionum,* iii. 235–320.

74. *Ibid.,* iii. 191–2.

75. *Ibid.,* iii. 237ff, 253.

76. *Ibid.,* iii. 276–8 and refs, including Tommasso Bozio, *De Signis Ecclesiae libri xxiii* (Cologne, 1592) bk. 2 ch. 8, bk. 15 ch. 1; Jakob Gretser, *De Cruce Christi* (Ingolstadt, 1598), bk. 3 chs. 18–19; P. Thyraeus, *De daemoniacis* (Cologne, 1594), pt 3 ch. 44.

77. *Ibid.,* iii. 282–6.

78. Friedrich Fomer, *Panoplia armaturae Dei, adversus omnem superstitionum, divinationum, excantationum, demonolatriam, et universas magorum, veneficorum, et sagarum, et ipsiusmet Sathanae insidias, praestigias et infestationes* (Ingolstadt, 1626), 134–292.

79. Tommasso Bozio, Eugubinus, *De Signis Ecclesiae libri xxiii* (Cologne, 1592 and subsequent edns).

80. See for instance P. M. Soergel, *Wondrous in his Saints: Counter-Reformation Propaganda in Bavaria* (Berkeley, Calif, 1993), esp. 131ff.

81. Delrio, *Disquisitionum,* ii. 75ff; Forner, *Panoplia,* 98ff.

82. E.g. V. Polidoro, *Pratica exorcistarum* (Patavii, 1587); *Thesaurus exorcismorum sique coniurationum terribilium, polentissimorum, efficacissimorum cum practica probatissima: quibus spiritus maligni, daemones maleficiaque omnia de corporibus humanis obsessis, tanquam flagellis, fustibusque fugantur…* (Cologne, 1626); Maximilian van Eynatten, *Manuale exorcismorum: continens instructiones, et exorcismos ad eiiciendos e corporibus obsessis spiritus malignos…* (Antwerp, 1626); *Preces et coniurationes contra aereas tempestates…* (Campidonae, 1667); *Manuale exorcismorum et benedictionum selectorum pro exorcistarum, parochorum, at aliorum quorumvis curatorum…* (Einsiedeln, 1671).

83. Girolamo Menghi, *Compendia dell'arte essordstica, et possibilita delle mirabili, et stupende operationi delli demoni, et dei malefici. Con li rimedii opportuni alle infirmitá maleficiali* (Bologna, 1582); Girolamo Menghi, *Flagellum Daemonum, exorcismos terribiles, potentissimos, et efficaces: Remediaque probatissima, ac doctrina singularem in malignos spiritos expellendos, facturasque et maleficia fuganda de obsessis corporibus complectens; cum suis benedictionibus, et omnibus requisitis ad eorum expulsionem; Accessit postremo Pars secunda, quae Fustis daemonum inscribitur, quibus novi exorcismi, et alia nonnulla, quae prius desiderabantur, superaddita Juerunt* (Bologna, 1589); [its second part entitled] *Fustis Daemonum, adiurationes formidabiles, potentissimas, et efficaces in malignos spiritus fugandos de oppressis corporibus humanis* (Bologna, 1589); [the latter includes a separately paginated section entitled] *Remedia Efficaissima in malignos spiritus expellendos, facturasque et maleficla [sic] effuganda de obsessis corporibus; cum suis benedictionibus.*

84. Compare Menghi, *Compendia,* 528ff, 539ff, 545ff, with Mazzolini, *De Strigimagarum … Mirandis,* sigs. dd iv^r, ee ii^v, ee iv^{rff}, and bk. 2 ch. 11 passim.

85. Menghi, *Compendia,* 570–3.

86. *Ibid.,* 574–84.

87. Menghi, *Flagellum,* 112, 125, 147–8, 214, 217, 220, 225, 227.

88. *Ibid.,* 112, 133, 140ff, 201.

89. *Ibid.,* 173, 175, 179, 189.

90. *Remedia,* 25–6.

91. *Ibid.,* 36–66; for further amulets, see *ibid.,* 89–90.

92. In late scholasticism, this belief that God confined his omnipotence to working through certain normal procedures was described as God's 'ordained power', *potentia ordinata.* For discussion see E. Cameron, *The European Reformation* (Oxford, 1991), 84, n. 27 and refs.

CHAPTER 3
THE MEDIEVAL CHURCH AND STATE ON SUPERSTITION, MAGIC AND WITCHCRAFT: FROM AUGUSTINE TO THE SIXTEENTH CENTURY
Edward Peters

The roots of the attitudes of medieval ecclesiastical and secular authorities towards superstition, magic and witchcraft – as well as their definitions of these terms – may be found in a number of originally diverse sources from late antiquity that were drawn together in the thought world of the Mediterranean around the turn of the Common Era (Flint and others, in *Witchcraft and Magic in Europe* II; Markus 1974; Bernstein 1993; Russell 1977,1981,1984; Brashear 1992; Fox 1986; Pagels 1995; Beard and North 1990; Beard, North, Price 1998). Among these are the texts of Jewish scripture included in the canon of the Christian Bible (particularly Exodus 7: 8–13, 22: 18; Leviticus 20: 6, 20: 27; Numbers 22: 7, 23: 23; Deuteronomy 13: 18: 9–14; 26: 10–12; 1 Samuel 15: 23; 1 Samuel 28: 3–25; Isaiah 28: 15; Daniel 2: 1–13) and texts from Christian Scripture itself (Matthew 2: 1–12, 10: 8; Luke 8: 26–39; Acts 8: 9–24, 18: 19–20; 1 Corinthians 10: 20; 2 Thessalonians 2; 1 Timothy 4: 1; Nock, 1972a). Many of the themes of Scripture were expanded and elaborated in much of the Jewish and Christian apocryphal literature and the early Christian romances (especially the *Book of Enoch, The Clementine Recognitions* (esp. IV, 27–9; Elliott 1993: 431–8), and the later *Apostolic History of Abdias* (Elliott 1993: 525–31)).

They were further elaborated in the writings of the Church Fathers, most effectively in the writings of those Fathers whose work exerted a continuous influence through the entire period, from late antiquity to the sixteenth century, chiefly the complex thought in the voluminous works of Augustine (354–430, especially *The City of God*, books IX-X, and *On Christian Teaching (De Doctrina Christiana)* book II, 19–25) and the *Etymologies* (especially Book VIII) of Isidore of Seville (560–636; Harmening 1979: 332–9).

In terms of formal law there is also the legislation of the Roman emperors, particularly the Christian emperors of Rome from the fourth century on (especially in the *Theodosian Code*, book IX, and Justinian's legal compilations in the sixth century, both of which long influenced European learned law). There is also a variety of other texts ranging from Christian readings of Latin poets – particularly Vergil, Horace, Ovid, and Lucan on magic and sorcery, the literary reworking of classical myths, notably those of Circe and Medea (for Circe, see Yarnall 1994; Roberts 1996), the sections of the *Natural History* of Pliny the Elder that dealt with magic, especially book 30, and the interest of Roman writers like Apuleius in sorcery and shapeshifting – to historical accounts, saints' lives, sermons, collections of penitential literature and the literature of ancient magic, pagan or Christian (for pagan, Jewish, Near Eastern and Christian antiquity, see Thee 1984; Luck 1985; Neusner-Frerichs-Flesher 1989; Faraone and Obbink 1991; Gager 1992; Daxelmüller 1993; Meyer and Mirecki 1995; Graf 1997). These were supplemented after the fifth century by the law collections of the new Christian Germanic kingdoms of Europe, by the texts of early canon law and by later royal and ecclesiastical law-making from the age of Charlemagne (768–814) on, initially in the works known as penitentials and in the canons issued by Church synods and councils but later including more elaborate works of canon and secular law. These ideas guided later spiritual and temporal authorities as they encountered and became part of the still pagan peoples of late Iron-Age northern Europe and began the slow process of their conversion to a new normative Latin Christianity (Hillgarth 1986; Flint 1991; Hen 1995; Muldoon 1997; MacMullen 1997; Fletcher 1997; Milis 1998).

But not all of these ideas were readily available to all individual writers and law-makers on these subjects, nor were superstition, magic and witchcraft always matters of great concern to authorities or always clear or identified as heresy. Even in the fourteenth and fifteenth centuries when the problem of sorcery and witchcraft attracted more attention, the laws and theoretical literature concerning them remained a very small part of an immense devotional, legal and theological literature that was chiefly devoted to other aspects of the social and spiritual lives of Christian Europeans (Duffy 1992; Swanson 1995; Van Engen 1994). By focusing only on superstition, magic and witchcraft, there is a danger of overrating their importance in a much larger literature, for they are difficult to understand without their devotional and legal contexts. Definitions and the understanding of all of these terms also changed from the fourth century to the sixteenth. So did readings of Greek, Roman and biblical history. In the thirteenth, fourteenth and fifteenth centuries, many writers on magic and witchcraft read the literature of the remote past as if it spoke of contemporary concerns and meant the same things by its terminology as later thinkers did. Our concern in this chapter is with the nature of activities generally then designated as 'superstition', 'magic' and 'witchcraft' that could – or were thought to – be triable in ecclesiastical or temporal criminal courts and be subject to specific disciplinary measures such as penances or punishments. From the twelfth century on, discussions of superstition, magic and witchcraft occur in a widening variety of sources, many of which also influenced the policies of ecclesiastical and temporal justice.

This chapter will treat its subject in seven sections: (I) Superstition and Magic in the Mediterranean World from Augustine to Isidore of Seville; (II) Superstition and Magic in the Early Germanic Law Collections; (III) The Development of Early Canon Law and Carolingian Legislation to Burchard of Worms, who died in 1025; (IV) The Legal and Theological Literature of the Twelfth and Thirteenth Centuries; (V) The Outburst of Accusations of Magic and Witchcraft in High Political Circles at the Turn of the Fourteenth Century; (VI) The Sorcerer and the Witch; (VII) Superstition, Magic and Witchcraft on the Eve of the Reformation. The focus of the chapter is less upon the very wide range of practices considered to be superstitious or magical than upon the formally conceived ideas of churchmen and temporal rulers that shaped legislation and directed the operation of judicial institutions. Our focus is Latin Christian Europe rather than the Greek East (Maguire 1995, 1997), late antique or medieval and early modern Judaism (Blau 1898, 1970, 1974; Trachtenberg 1970; Goldin 1976; Schäfer 1990; Faraone and Obbink 1991; Meyer and Mirecki 1995: 111–208; and earlier works in the present series) or the Islamic world (Burnett 1996). I have cited English translations where these are available and reliable; where not, I have translated some texts myself, and I have translated all titles of literary works into English.

Although the terms *superstitio* and *magia* were regularly used throughout the period, since most of the literature was written in Latin, the term 'witchcraft' as a translation of either of these is not always appropriate before the late twelfth century, perhaps even later. There is considerable good sense in remembering that for many centuries particular terms in Greek, Latin and vernacular European vocabularies did not translate each other precisely and exactly, and that some terms – 'witch' and 'vampire' are good examples, the former better described by the Latin terms of *stria* or *striga* and the latter by *lamia* – did not appear in any language until much later than early Christianity (Burris 1936; Wagner 1939; Lecouteux 1983, 1985; Klaniczay 1990; Harmening 1990a, b; Caro Baroja 1990; Murray 1992: 189; Behringer 1998; Griffiths 1996). In fact, the Latin language maintained a particular set of terms for the subjects of this chapter that in many cases shaped the vernacular languages of Europe and imposed at least a linguistic and conceptual identity on a set of originally very diverse phenomena. Latin terms will be retained throughout this chapter where appropriate, but they will be explained at their first use. These problems are not pedantic – this chapter must take these uses and linguistic differences, and the matters that they are thought to describe, regularly into account.

Superstition and magic from Augustine to Isidore of Seville

Christian writers first encountered the Latin words *superstitio* and *magia* when Greek and Roman writers and rulers applied them to Christianity itself in their combined senses of divination, magic, secret and forbidden practices, and excessive religious fear (MacMullen 1966; Achtemeier 1976; Harmening 1979: 14–32; Fox 1986: 37; Graf 1997). Christians in turn reversed the usage: for them, superstition referred to what they considered to be the irrational and false beliefs – that is, the 'religions' – of all others besides Christians and, to a limited extent, Jews, although Christian scripture portrayed some Jews as magicians (Acts 13: 6–12; 19: 13–20; Nock 1972b: II: 308–30; Fox 1986: 143) and the poisonous image of the Jew as sorcerer survived for a long time in later European thought (Trachtenberg 1943). Christians captured for themselves the old and respected Latin word *religio* – which originally designated the bond between humans and the gods – and restricted its application to Christianity alone (Graf 1997: 254, n. 76; Beard and North 1990; Beard, North and Price 1998). To the late second-century Christian apologist Tertullian, all pagan religious practice was 'Roman superstition'. Early Christian teachers like Ignatius of Antioch also pointed out that although the Magi had used their skills as magician-astrologers to find the Christ-child, once they had found their destination, their skills ceased, since they were no longer needed after the fact of the Incarnation and Nativity (Flint 1991: 364–75; Veenstra 1998: 104). To the fourth-century Christian polemicist Lactantius the definitions were crisp and simple: 'religion is the true cult paid to God – superstition is the false' (La Roche 1957; Grodzynski 1974; Cardini 1979; Harmening 1979: 14–40; Salzman 1987; MacMullen 1997: 74–102; for a later period, Clark 1997: 472–88). In the late sixth century Martin of Braga, strongly under the influence of Augustine in his work *On the Correction of Rustics,* explained how demons had made themselves into pagan gods in order to deceive humans and receive their worship (Psalm 95 [96]: 5; Barlow 1969: 71–85). In Martin's work, Jove was described as a magician and a sexual corrupter of his wife and daughters (Hillgarth 1986: 58–60; Barlow 1969: 81–2). Shortly after Martin, Gregory of Tours in Gaul repeated the theme in his *Histories* (Hillgarth 1986: 81; de Nie 1995).

Roman religion was one thing for Christians, and although they often called it both superstition and magic, magic generally was quite another. Christians knew that Roman law had condemned magic, especially magic worked by private practitioners for their own or their clients' private and usually harmful ends, often as profoundly as Christians themselves did. Pliny the Elder had dismissed much magic in the Roman world as 'magical vanities'. The magicians' techniques included the use of incantations, inscribed amulets, images, texts, and the use of magical substances. The emperor Augustus was said to have burned the books of the diviners; the third-century emperor Septimius Severus was said to have buried all the magic books his agents could collect in the tomb of Alexander the Great; an imperial law of 297 condemned sorcerers because of the private and secret nature of their activities and their destructive powers. The Christian historian Eusebius (260–340) accused Maxentius, the opponent of the Christian-favouring imperial claimant Constantine, of using magicians to defend Rome against Constantine's legitimate invasion. Several panegyrics of Constantine and other early Christian emperors contrasted the 'divine teachings' that guided them to the 'superstitious magic' to which their pagan rivals resorted. In these instances, 'magic' seems to have meant to Christians something distinct from pagan religion in general, and the enemies of the Christian emperors were thus doubly condemned – for superstitious paganism and for the use of magic.

Richard Kieckhefer has said of these attitudes, 'While "magic" obviously served as a polemical term, even its polemical usage presupposed a shared understanding of magic as a cluster of countercultural rituals worked privately for the magicians' personal ends or those of his clients. The term "magic" was sometimes used for the rituals of insiders (even members of elites) as well as outsiders or for the rites of people who became defined as outsiders only because they used magic. To brand a Christian, a pagan, or a Jew as a magician was to use a word with a prior and independent meaning and to give it abusive, polemical application' (Kieckhefer 1994a: 815).

These attitudes and ideas were not without consequences in Roman law (MacMullen 1966; Pharr 1932). In a law of 319/320 the emperor Constantine prohibited the private consultation of diviners, but he also permitted the public practice of divination, an old and respected component of Roman religion, although he also noted that Christians could not legally be compelled to participate in public sacrifices. Constantine also prohibited any *haruspex* from entering a private house. Constantius II dealt savagely with those accused of any form of magic outside those permitted by Roman religion and custom (Barb 1963: 109). The emperor Julian, formerly a Christian, was accused by Christian critics of favouring magicians. In 371 the Christian emperor Valentinian I could still label the benevolent public divinatory practice known as the *haruspicina* as *religio*, rather than as *superstitio* or the criminal category *maleficium* (Beard and North 1990).

But Valentinian's law was issued towards the end of a period when Christian emperors were attempting to preserve some of the most cherished and otherwise respectable religious components of a Rome that was still largely pagan. With the discovery of a plot that employed sorcerers against the life of the emperor Valens in 374, the full force of Roman criminal law was brought against all magicians and those who employed them; imperial officials searched libraries for books of magic of all kinds, and the books – and sometimes whole libraries – were burned (Speyer 1992; MacMullen 1997; Bologne 1993: 18–19; Beard and North 1990). By charging the defendants with high treason, the most serious crime Roman law recognized, the emperor also automatically subjected them to torture and the most ferocious forms of public execution that the empire employed (Callu 1984; Funke 1967; Ammianus Marcellinus 1952–6: III: 215; Matthews 1989, 258–62; Cameron 1983: 163–4). Late Roman law continued to deal harshly with all those accused of magical practices. Even possession of magic books was sufficient to send a high-ranking Roman into exile and entail the loss of his property, while a lower-ranking person convicted of the same offence was to be executed. The emperors of the early fifth century, however, permitted those who owned magic books simply to purge themselves if they converted to Christianity and did not become recidivists (Barb 1963: 114). Anyone using predictive magic concerning the emperor or the future of the Roman state was to be sent to the beasts in the arena or to crucifixion, while anyone convicted of being a *magus* was to be burned alive (Pharr 1932; Lear 1965: 117). Enough cases survive from the fourth and fifth centuries to indicate that these laws were regularly used. Sorcerers were exiled from Rome in 409 (Pharr 1952: 9.16.2; MacMullen 1966: 132–4). Around the year 500, sorcerers appear to have been exiled from Rome once again, and when one of them, Basilius, returned, he was burned to death at the order of the Ostrogothic king in Italy, Theoderic (Cassiodorus 1992: 77–8).

The increasing degree of Christianization of the Roman Empire led to the ultimate prohibition of all forms of pagan religion, both public and private, by the end of the fourth century. In this context, a number of Christian thinkers reviewed the earlier ideas of superstition and magic, and a number of Christian emperors issued stiffer laws defining and condemning both. For example, several imperial laws of the fourth and early fifth centuries that were later included in the *Theodosian Code*, published in 438, prohibited all subjects of the emperors from consulting soothsayers, diviners, astrologers, augurs and seers (Pharr 1952: 9.16.1–3). The older imperial toleration for the beneficial public aspects of some of these practices had now disappeared: 'The Chaldeans and wizards, and all the rest whom the common people call *malefici*' will use their arts no more (Pharr 1952: 9.16.4; Pharr 1932; Burriss 1936; Hunt 1993). It is important to note that the terms *maleficus* and *maleficium*, which conventionally meant 'criminal' and 'criminal act', and continued to do so in law until much later, appear from this text to be now also applied 'by the common people' especially to magicians of various kinds. The term *maleficium* designated what we term some kinds of 'magic' and all kinds of 'witchcraft' down to the end of the eighteenth century (Rousseau 1979; Flint 1991: 17). The *Theodosian Code* and several abbreviated versions of it constituted what most Europeans knew of Roman law until the rediscovery of Justinian's *Digest* in the late eleventh and early twelfth century. The work of Justinian and his legal advisers in the 530s, however, preserved many of the strictures on magic and superstition in the *Theodosian Code*, especially in *Code* IX. 18 and *Digest* XLVIII.8 (Pharr 1932), so that the transition from one Roman law text to another in the twelfth century did little to change later Europeans' notions of the place of magic in Roman and later European learned law.

With the late fourth-century emperors, Church leaders, too, took a sharper and more precise position regarding superstition and magic. Assemblies of clergy in synods and councils began to lay down rules for the governance and disciplining of Christian communities. A synod at Elvira in 306 prohibited the last rites to those who had killed others by *maleficium*; a synod at Ancyra of 314 condemned to a long period of penance those who had used divination; the council of Laodicaea in the mid to late Fourth century prohibited the use of magic by the clergy, as did the fourth Council of Carthage in 398 and later councils. These rules adopted by synods and councils were collected and preserved, most importantly in the canon law collection of Dionysius Exiguus of around 500, and from Dionysius they were cited much later, since they had come to constitute a large part of the most widely known and used collection of canon law, particularly the version of Dionysius' collection augmented by Pope Hadrian I (772–95) and known as the Dionysio-Hadriana (Brundage 1995: 27–8), which was sent by Hadrian to Charlemagne (768–814) for his guidance in ecclesiastical affairs.

The work of synods and councils could also have immediate consequences. The Synod of Saragossa in 380 condemned the scholar Priscillian as a heretic, and in 385 a later relentless imperial investigation found Priscillian guilty of magical practices and sentenced him to death. The execution of Priscillian was the first one of a convicted heretic, and it is important to note both that the trial and execution were carried out by imperial officials, even against the protests of Christian bishops, and that the actual capital charges were those of magic (Chadwick 1976).

A second source in early ecclesiastical legislation for attitudes toward magic and superstition is the *indiculi superstitionum,* lists of widespread beliefs and practices that were condemned by synods, councils and individual churchmen, one of the earliest being the list drawn up by Martin of Braga mentioned above, and appended to the legislation of the Second Council of Braga in 572. Martin's list and later lists continued to be made, copied and repeated down to the beginning of the twelfth century (McNeill and Gamer 1938; Flint 1991: 41; Russell 1972: 45–62; Harmening 1979: 53–5; Dierkens 1984; Milis 1998).

Individual Christian leaders and thinkers, too, wrote vehemently against all forms of what they considered to be superstition and magic, from Tertullian and Irenaeus of Lyons in the late second and third centuries to Augustine and Jerome in the late fourth and early fifth (Thorndike 1923–58: I: 337–503), One of the most influential of Christian thinkers was Augustine, whose voluminous writings addressed subjects of all kinds that concerned Christians and exerted an enormous influence on all later Christian thought.

Augustine was a provincial from Roman north Africa whose skills as a teacher of rhetoric led him into the highest aristocratic and scholarly circles of Rome and later Milan, the effective capital of the western Roman Empire. Converted to Christianity in Milan, Augustine left the city to return home to north Africa, where he was made a priest and later bishop of Hippo Regius. He spent the rest of his life as bishop and as the most prolific and respected Christian theologian of the Latin-speaking world. One of Augustine's considerable achievements in dealing with magic was his ability to reshape the categories that included magic and to fit them into a comprehensive Christian position on all aspects of demonology, magic and superstition (Harmening 1979: 33–40; Thorndike 1923–58: I: 504–22). Magic did not figure prominently in his early thought, but as Augustine's confidence in human capacities grew less after his re-reading of the Epistles of Paul in the 390s, and his sense of human vulnerability to the temptations of the world and to demons grew greater, magic began to figure more and more prominently (Markus 1990: 47–62). It is after this period that he wrote his most important discussions of superstition and magic.

In his treatise *On Christian Doctrine* (11.20.30 Kors and Peters 2001) Augustine lists as superstition virtually all forms of pagan religion, including the making of idols and the worship of creatures. Taking up and greatly articulating the increasingly familiar Christian idea that 'the gods of the pagans are demons in disguise', Augustine then condemns the making and worship of idols, consultations and pacts made with demons, as well as soothsaying, augury, amulets, consulting books of haruspicy and augury and medical charms (Psalm 95: 5; Harmening 1979, 1989; Russell 1981; Kelly 1985). He sums up his argument in II.23, when he says:

> For it is brought about as if by a certain secret judgement of God that men who desire evil things are subjected to illusion and deception as a reward for their desire, being mocked and deceived by those fallen angels to whom, according to the most beautiful ordering of things, the lowest part of this world is subjected by Divine Providence.

The twin themes of divine permission to demons to tempt humans and the active role of demons in that process were part of Augustine's comprehensive approach to the problems of fallen human nature and the consequent vulnerability of humans to demonically inspired magic and illusion (Kelly 1968; Peters 1978; Russell 1981). To strengthen his point, Augustine draws into his discussion not only pagan practices, but several scriptural episodes, including that of King Saul and the witch of Endor (1 Kings [1 Samuel] 28: 15–19) and Paul's driving a prophetic spirit out of a woman (Acts 16: 16–18) to make his interpretation of scripture consistent with his views on pagan practices (Smelik 1977). In the first instance, Augustine states flatly that either God permitted the devil to bring back the dead prophet Samuel, or that the ghost was not Samuel at all, but a demon in Samuel's likeness, an approach that dates among Christians from the writings of Hippolytus in the early third century. Augustine prefers the latter opinion, consistent with his view of the vulnerabilty of fallen human sense perception to the illusions of demons, whose spiritual nature allowed them to operate in realms of nature that humans could not perceive. In any case his views of the episode are consistent with his views on magic generally. Augustine's views on the witch of Endor were later included in the great collection of canon law compiled by Master Gratian in the twelfth century. In the case of the prophetic woman, Paul drove out the demon that inhabited her. Here, too, illegitimate prophecy and necromancy are nothing but expressions of the power of the demons, acting with God's permission to delude and thereby test weak human nature. And for Augustine superstition is firmly linked to pacts and contracts with demons (II.22.34), an assertion that had a long and very influential history.

Augustine took up the problem of superstition and magic again in his massive work *The City of God,* a vast meditation on human history and the ultimate purpose of human existence. In book IV.30–1, Augustine condemns all of earlier Roman religion as superstition. In book VII the gods of the pagans are identified as demons. In book X.9, Augustine dismisses the pretensions of learned pagans that theirs was a purer and higher art than lowly necromancy or everyday private consultation of magicians, identifying both 'high' and 'low' magic as 'engaged in the fraudulent rites of demons'. Although Augustine acknowledged both legitimate Christian prophecy and legitimate wonder-working (which he termed 'miracle' in contrast with the Latin term *mira,* which he and other Christians understood to mean 'wonders'), he distinguished so sharply between the two categories as to separate them in most Christian minds forever (Ward 1982; Flint 1991: 31–5; Kee 1983).

In Augustine's view – and under his considerable influence – hitherto discrete magical beliefs and practices are now grouped entirely under the category of *superstitio* and condemned emphatically, their existence being blamed on the deceit of demons and the insatiable curiosity of ignorant and weak humans. In one of his later works, Augustine attributed both conditions to God's anger at human transgressions. He cited Psalm 77 [78].

'[God] has sent upon them the anger of his indignation, rage and tribulation, and possession by evil spirits' (cited in Brown 1970, 1972: 132–3). This citation effectively conveys Augustine's conviction of the power of the devil in this world and the role of superstition and magic as manifestations of that power. By reducing both pagan religion and all manifestations of magic to the category of superstition, Augustine created a Christian perspective on both past and present that had great impact in his own day and exerted an enormous influence on all later Christian thought.

Augustine was one of the most influential, but certainly not the only Church Father to deal with the themes of demonology and magic. Paul himself had identified idolatry with the worship of demons (1 Corinthians 10: 20). Justin Martyr, the second-century Christian apologist, had earlier emphasized the demons' use of magic to bind humanity to their service (Kelly 1968: 30–1). Ambrose of Milan, Augustine's older contemporary, developed the theme of the figure of Antichrist, the great apocalyptic deceiver of humanity who was to use magicians to gain power over the world (McHugh 1972). The concerns of Ambrose and Augustine were echoed by Pope Leo I in the mid-fifth century, who argued that magic was one of the many tricks of the devil through which he gains control of the greater part of humanity by means of *superstitiones*. Caesarius (469/70–542), bishop of Arles from 503 to 542, also contributed substantially to disseminating the views of Augustine, Ambrose, and other early Christian writers on the subjects of superstition and magic. Caesarius' sermons against magic and surviving pagan practices circulated widely, sometimes because of their attribution to Augustine and sometimes because they were quoted in the work of later writers, including those of the popular genre of saints' lives (Caesarius 1956; Blum 1936: 31; Harmening 1979: 49–64; Markus 1992; Klingshirn 1994; Flint 1991; 42–3; Kors and Peters 2001).

The work of Roman imperial legislators, Church synods and councils, the letters and other literary works of popes like Leo I (440–61) and Gregory I (590–604), the *indiculi superstitionum* and the writings of such figures as Augustine and others elaborated a fully developed Christian view of the role of demons and fallen human nature in the context of superstitious and magical practices. That work had depended upon the formation of an organized Christian Roman church and empire in the Mediterranean world and upon the learning and extensive means of communication available to individual thinkers. By the end of the sixth century that world slowly became subsumed in the larger and equally complex world of late Iron-Age migrating peoples who merged it into the culture of northern Europe. As the Roman world gradually folded into a sub-Roman Germanic culture in western Europe, much of the work of organized Roman law and Christian ecclesiology was preserved in summarized versions of laws, rules, and ecclesiastical legislation. Of these summaries, the most influential was that of Isidore of Seville (570–636).

Isidore's twenty books of *Etymologies* constituted a vast, but compressed, storehouse of ancient pagan and Christian learning (Flint 1991: 50–5; Kors and Peters 2001). It is important to note the context in which Isidore treats superstition and magic. Book VIII of the *Etymologies* deals with 'The Church and the Sects'. After a brief account of the Church and its difference from the Synagogue (VIII. 1–2), Isidore treats heresy and schism among Christians and Jews (VIII.3–5), pagan philosophy and poetry (VIII.6–7) and pagan prophecy in the figure of the Sibyl (VIII.8). Isidore then turns to *magi* (VIII.9), beginning with a fanciful historical account of the invention of the magical arts by the Persian king (*sic*) Zoroaster and their transmission throughout the ancient world, including to the magicians of Pharaoh whom Moses defeated, and the figure of Circe, who tempted Odysseus.

Isidore then states that *magi* are called 'by the common people' (echoing the *Theodosian Code*) *malefici* and enchanters. They disturb both the elements of nature and the minds of humans. Supported by demons, they make use of blood and sacrificial victims as well as the dead. Necromancers revive the dead and make them speak. Isidore allows for a considerably greater degree of reality in these practices rather than demonic illusion in his discussion. He then lists other types of magicians: hydromancers, geo- mancers, aeromancers, pyromancers and a long list of others, including oracles and 'mathematicians' (whose knowledge of the stars gives them their power). In the case of the latter, God permitted their skills to survive (in the Magi of the Gospels) until they predicted the birth of Jesus, after which they were forbidden. All these arts come from demons, however, 'from a pestiferous association of men and evil angels, and they are therefore to be avoided by Christians and to be repudiated and condemned savagely', because 'the demon is in all these arts' of magic and divination (VIII.9.31). But Isidore is not finished with magic in VIII.9. He goes on to conclude book VIII by discussing pagans (VIII.10) and pagan gods (VIII.11). Pagan gods were humans whom other demons persuaded later humans had been deities, thus inventing idolatry. Isidore then discusses *daemones* and their relation to fallen angels, followers of the devil, whose name and origins are also discussed, as is Antichrist and other demons in the sevice of the devil. Isidore concludes with a discussion of *lamiae* and *incubae*.

The great appeal of Isidore's work was its compact and categorical character, and hence its convenience. Not only did Isidore provide an exhaustive summary of both Roman and Christian doctrines on superstition and magic from both scripture and pagan literature, but he located those doctrines in the context of a Christian culture and the forces that challenged and disturbed it, including schism and heresy, pagan philosophy, poetry, oracles and prophecies and pagan religion, thus providing his later readers with a picture of pagan, Jewish and Christian antiquity within which superstition and magic are firmly and categorically defined and located. The legacy of Isidore proved to be as great in this respect as that of Augustine, and it shaped the transmission of much of the knowledge of the pagan and early Christian worlds to the new world of the Germanic Mediterranean and northern Europe. That knowledge became the basis, not only of the process of the Christianization of northern Europe, but of the Christian understanding of the religious practices and beliefs of the late Iron-Age northern world.

The legal and theological literature of the twelfth and thirteenth centuries

The collection of canon law of Burchard of Worms was, like most of its predecessors, individually made and hence applicable only in the diocese of Worms. But Burchard's immense industry in discovering and collecting authoritative texts made his collection a convenient repository of material that appealed to later collectors, whose work took on a distinctively scholarly character. In the case of the canon *Episcopi*, for example, Burchard's text was taken up into the more influential collections made by Ivo, Bishop of Chartres, at the beginning of the twelfth century, and from Ivo's collections it was taken up into the work that became the most important collection of classical canon law, the *Concordia Discordantium Canonum*

(*The Concord of Discordant Canons*), or *Decretum,* of Master Gratian of Bologna around 1140 (Brundage 1995; Kors and Peters 2001).

Gratian's treatment of magic and the simultaneous regularizing of the study of theology both mark a new focus in ecclesiology. But it must be noted that they were produced at a time when a great deal of literary consideration was also being given to magic, not always consistently, but reflecting nevertheless an increasing interest on the part of learned writers. Anselm of Besate in the early eleventh century and William of Malmesbury in the mid-twelfth both drew upon earlier literary tradition and local anecdote to describe in vivid terms the operations of magicians and witches who had given themselves to the devil in return for preternatural powers (Peters 1978: 21–57; Kors and Peters 2001). Not surprisingly, these subjects offered ample scope for writers to exercise their literary imaginations and rhetorical skills – much in the same way as the later visual depiction of magic and witchcraft gave similar oportunities to artists in the sixteenth and seventeenth centuries (Hoak 1985; Zika 1998). Such narratives were not intended to provoke prosecution, but rather to serve as moral reminders of the powers of the devil, the fragility of fallen human nature, and the depiction of unusual and grotesque activities as a means of morally entertaining the leisure time of nobles and rulers. In monastic circles they also served to depict the external world as temptation-filled and dangerous, hence reinforcing the monastic vocation to flee the world and its dangers.

In addition to literary adventurism, entertainment and moral exhortation, discussions of magic also occurred in considerations of the organization of knowledge in the twelfth century. The recovery of much earlier Latin literature, the absorption of Arabic learning, and the translation of Greek scientific literature at the end of the twelfth century raised serious questions about natural magic – the theory that with appropriate learning and intellectual discipline humans might acquire knowledge about the natural world that was hidden from ordinary people (occult) but was not inherently demonic in itself. But theologians also observed that demons had particular expertise in natural matters, both because of their spiritual essence and their long experience, and that even 'natural' magic could be dangerous in this regard. Peter Abelard, for example, noted that Pharaoh's priests in Exodus 7 acted against Moses because the demons gave them some of their own natural knowledge (Abelard 1971: 37). There was considerable moral, ethical and philosophical debate in the twelfth and thirteenth centuries over these questions, and it forms the background for the work of theologians and canon lawyers.

By the late twelfth century the Christian cosmology of Europe regarded human nature as innately weak, sinful and vulnerable to demonic temptation and deception (with divine permission) as a consequence of the fall of Adam and Eve, the subsequent human capacity for sin and the loss of the human ability to perceive the full spectrum of the natural world. Although human reason, to the extent that it received divine grace and was properly instructed, could distinguish right from wrong, human will might not always choose what was right. Not only could humans reason badly and misdirect their wills, but they were also unable to perceive the created world except in a limited and incomplete way. The fall of Adam and Eve also diminished the human capacity to understand fully the natural world. Those operations of nature that humans could not perceive or understand could, however, be manipulated by demons, who were believed to operate in realms of nature that were not perceptible to humans and to be able with God's permission to deceive and tempt humans. The devil could intervene in the course of 'natural causation', thereby working what seemed to humans to be 'wonders', tempt humans to pay him homage of a kind due only to God and enter agreements with humans through which humans received powers over nature and human affairs not attainable by any other means – not miracles (*miracula*), but rather *mira*, wonders. The servants of the devil could, on their own or with the devil acting through them, perform acts that harmed or illicitly influenced others in their persons, families and servants or property by occult (= 'hidden from humans', not 'supernatural') means. Pacts with the devil presumed the sins/crimes of idolatry and apostasy, because they constituted a willful rejection of Christian baptism (both a contract with God and a spiritual bond to fellow Christians) and the paying of a kind of homage to the demon that should be paid only to God or the saints. This cosmology lay beneath the development of both theology and canon law.

The work of the theologians began with the explanation of the meaning of Scripture and by the end of the twelfth century had expanded to include detailed studies of particular theological questions and from there developed the discipline of speculative theology and moral theology as a distinct field, and the arts of preaching and hearing confession. In terms of scriptural exegesis – the actual teaching explanation of the meaning of the scriptural text – the conclusions of the biblical theologians are of particular interest. In explaining the meaning of Exodus 22: 18, 'Thou shalt not suffer a witch to live', for example, the most widely accepted explanation – and the standard text used for teaching students of theology – was that

> those who perform acts by the illusions of the magical arts and the figments of the devil are to be understood as heretics, who are to be excluded from consorting with the faithful, who may truly be said to live, so that their error may die in them.

That is, sorcerers are to be excommunicated and exiled, as are other heretics, not literally killed or otherwise punished. The gloss to Leviticus 20: 6 states that

> it is a great sin to consult magicians and diviners, because this is to depart from God. There are magicians who in the name of God prophesy falsely, and there are deceitful diviners who corrupt many with poisonous words and turn them away from truth.

The comments of the exegetes were repeated by twelfth-century theologians, most notably Hugh of St Victor, who sharply denounced both the practice of magic and its entire history and exclusion from all legitimate branches of knowledge (Hugh of St Victor 1961: 154; Kors and Peters 2001):

> Magic is not accepted as a part of philosophy, but stands with a false claim outside it: the mistress of every form of iniquity and malice, lying about the truth and truly infecting men's minds, it seduces them from divine religion, prompts them to the cult of demons, fosters corruption of morals and impels the minds of its devotees to every wicked and criminal indulgence.

Although the twelfth-century theologians routinely condemned magic as sinful, they insisted that no penalty stronger than excommunication or exile was appropriate for it. But these were also considered enormous spiritual and social penalties.

Theologians had a wealth of texts to work with, but canon lawyers worked with fewer. The canon *Episcopi* passed from Regino through Burchard and Ivo of Chartres to Master

Gratian, who included it in his great and influential collection of canon law, the *Concordance of Discordant Canons,* or *Decretum,* around 1140. The text occurs in *Causa 26, quaestio 5, canon* 12 (Kors and Peters 1972: 28–31).The *Causae* were hypothetical cases, each of which was broken down into particular questions of relevant law. These in turn were answered by Gratian's assembling of apparently authoritative and sometimes apparently conflicting excerpts from older and more recent legal pronouncements, laid out and explained by Gratian's own commentary (Brundage 1995: 44–69). *Causa* 26 is located at the end of a series known as the *causae hereticorum,* 'the *causae* pertaining to heretics', and it describes the case of an unrepentant cleric who is a magician and diviner, excommunicated by his bishop, and reconciled to the Church at the point of death by another priest, without the bishop's knowledge. The various questions ask what *sortilegium* is (the answer comes from Isidore of Seville), whether it is a sin (the answer comes chiefly from Augustine), what is the nature of divination, and finally raises the question of whether magicians should be excommunicated. Gratian, following the tradition of misunderstanding Regino, attributed the canon *Episcopi* to the fourth-century Council of Ancyra and therefore allowed considerable authority to it.

Gratian also treated magic in *Causa* 33, one of a group of *causae* concerning marriage (Brundage 1987; Kors and Peters 2001). Here, Gratian was concerned with sexual impotence, and his key text is taken from Hincmar of Reims's treatise on the divorce of Lothar, which he found in the collection of Ivo of Chartres. The text, *Si per Sortiarias,* states that impotence caused by magic may indeed be an impediment to marriage and sometimes grounds for annulment.This text received greater attention from later commentators on Gratian, usually law professors, because it was a part of the rapidly developing marriage law of the Christian Church (Brundage 1987: 229–55).

Thus, like the theologians, canon lawyers by the twelfth century had a convenient location of authoritative texts and learned interpretations that identified magic as sinful, heretical (and thereby ecclesiastically criminal), and deserving of excommunication if it were not repented and penance for it performed. The actual working out of the procedures for confession and penitence took place in the work of late twelfth and early thirteenth-century theologians, canonists and writers of specialized handbooks for confessors (Peters 1978: 67–81), but these generally remained consistent with the work of Gratian and his contemporaries among the theologians.

Causa 26 and the other '*causae* of the heretics' were also central locations for Gratian's discussion of superstition as well as heresy, and the greatest influence in these sections is that of Augustine of Hippo. Augustine's bleak view of human nature and his initially reluctant insistence that the worst results of fallen human nature could legitimately be curbed by the administration of punishment in a spirit of charitable discipline were consistent with the view of the world adopted by many late eleventh and twelfth-century thinkers. In the great conflict between papacy and empire that had begun in the 1070s, as well as in the discussions of the justice of certain kinds of warfare that came out of them and were later reviewed in the context of the First Crusade of 1095–9, a new attitude toward physical coercion began to be articulated in the context of penitence and a sharpened idea of ecclesiastical sins that might be considered crimes as well. As a result, a new system of criminal law and jurisprudence emerged in both ecesiastical and secular courts around the turn of the thirteenth century. Both sets of courts were also related, since ecclesiastical courts were prohibited from shedding blood and capital punishment could only be carried out by secular courts to which convicted ecclesiastical criminals were turned over. Eventually the most important among the offences that both ecclesiastical and secular courts had to deal with was the category of heresy.

Churchmen had long known and condemned heresy, but before the twelfth century heretics were urged to repent, and the chief penalty if they did not was excommunication and exile, since these were understood to be biblically sanctioned and served to preserve the normative religious integrity of the individual community. During the eleventh and early twelfth centuries there are accounts of heretical behaviour that depict the heretics as demon-worshippers and committers of criminal acts, usually involving sexual and sacramental deviance and blasphemy (Russell 1972; Lambert 1992; Moore 1985, 1987; Peters 1980; Given 1997; Kors and Peters 2001). They were also considered to be sects – that is, anti-churches, with their own anti-equivalents of baptism, and other elements of the liturgy. By the time of Gratian, heresy loomed larger in the growing and diversifying population of western Europe and attracted public attention and concern. Increasingly, churchmen associated heretics with the service of demons, as they had earlier associated magicians, and the laws against consorting with demons had grown stiffer and carried more severe punishments. The identification of sorcery and magic with heresy and of both with diabolism increased from the mid-twelfth century on. Jeffrey Burton Russell has summarized the development by the end of the thirteenth century:

> Through its connection with heresy, witchcraft [we may add sorcery as well] in this period witnessed the addition of new elements and the further development and definition of older ones: the sex orgy, the feast, the secret meetings at night in caves, cannibalism, the murder of children, the express renunciation of God and adoration of demons, the desecration of the cross and the sacraments. All these had now become fixed elements in the composition of witchcraft. (Russell 1972: 100; *cf.* Moore 1987; Lambert 1992)

As penalties applied to unrepentant heretics became more harsh, including confiscation of property in 1184 and even stronger punishments for heretics and their supporters over the next several decades, accusations of sorcery began to resemble accusations of heresy, and they appear most prominently not at first in the work of the canon lawyers who commented on Gratian, but in the work of those theologians who composed the new genre of handbooks for confessors and preachers. In the great transformation of theology that occurred after the middle of the twelfth century a science that had once largely consisted of scriptural commentary and statements of dogma developed into speculative theology and moral theology, the latter of which guided confessors, preachers, and ecclesiastical lawyers. Confession was made mandatory for all Christians at least once a year at the Fourth Lateran Council of 1215, and the role of the confessor was one of the most important pastoral roles in the clergy. The *Summa Confessorum* (*Summa for Confessors*) of Thomas of Chobham, written around 1215, for example, emphasizes the vulnerability of humans to the temptations of demons and the central role of demons in all manifestations of magic, whether in the superstitions of the unlettered or the elaborate pretensions of learned magicians. Such views are echoed in other manuals for clergy, such as those of Bartholomew of Exeter and Robert of Flamborough (Peters 1978: 78–81). This movement toward an intensified pastoralism, of course, did not move uniformly across Europe, and it was often derailed by natural disasters and other circumstances. But it constitutes one aspect of that continuing ideal of reform that characterized Latin Christianity for centuries, and the heightened emphasis on pastoralism must always be considered when one encounters new classifications of sin and ecclesiastical crime (Harmening 1989; Paravy 1979; Duffy 1992: 53–87). Between 1320 and 1323 William of Pagula produced a very influential handbook for parish clergy called *The Pastoral Eye*. The work was often abbreviated and excerpted, and one such abbreviation, produced in 1385, succinctly stated that:

> [The parish priest] should instruct his parishoners that they should not practise the magical arts, incantations, or sorcery, since these things have no power to cure either man or beast and besides are utterly worthless and unlawful. Moreover clerics who do these things shall be degraded and lay people shall be excommunicated. (Shinners 1997: 19)

Both groups came more and more to the attention of ecclesiastical agents and officials during the thirteenth century. In the movement for pastoral reform that was marked by the Fourth Lateran Council, clergy were urged to provide better ecclesiastical care to Christians, whether in the growing cities or in the most remote rural areas. Clerics who travelled to these areas discovered some varieties of Christian belief that seemed to them to distort orthodoxy and verge on superstition (Schmitt 1983; Brooke and Brooke 1984). In other instances, the world of the growing universities produced some enthusiastic defences of non-demonic learned magic that increasingly troubled ecclesiastical authorities. On 7 March 1277, the bishop of Paris, Etienne Tempier, issued a formal condemnation of two hundred and nineteen propositions drawn from the work of Arabic, Greek and Latin thinkers. The condemnation also included a book of geomancy and

> books, scrolls, or sheets that contain details of necromancy or contain experiments of diviners, invocations of demons, or conjurations that place the soul in danger, or that in these or other similar works the orthodox faith and good morals are treated with hostility. (Peters 1980: 226; de Ridder-Symoens 1987; Kieckhefer 1997)

At the same universities and law schools at the same time, concepts of heresy, divination, magic, and sorcery were placed in consistent and clearly-defined categories of knowledge that made them easier to identify and deal with by both theologians and lawyers. In his great works of systematic theology, Thomas Aquinas (1225–74) clearly located demonic temptation and the demonic powers that humans could acquire within the context of Christian ontology and theological tradition (Kors and Peters 1972, 2001; Peters 1978: 95–8). Jurists, too, began to use other texts besides those of Gratian as new collections of canon law appeared in 1234, 1298 and 1317. The 1298 collection of canon law, the *Liber Sextus* of Pope Boniface VIII, contained a letter originally issued by Pope Alexander IV in 1258 and reissued in 1260 which stated that papally appointed inquisitors could prosecute those accused of sorcery only if their activities 'manifestly savoured of heresy':

> It is reasonable to assume that those charged with the affairs of the faith, which is the greatest of privileges, ought not thereby to intervene in other matters. The inquisitors of heretical depravity, commissioned by the apostolic see, ought not to intervene in cases of divination or sorcery unless these clearly savour of manifest heresy. Nor should they punish those who are engaged in these things, but leave them to others for punishment.

Both Alexander IV and Boniface VIII appear to have considered sorcery an offence punishable either by ordinary ecclesiastical courts or lay courts – unless it appeared that the accused had invoked demons and committed other acts that clearly constituted heretical behaviour. Boniface himself echoed Alexander IV in a statement of 1298: 'The inquisitors of heretical depratity deputed by the apostolic see should not intrude themselves into cases of divination or *sortilegium* unless these savour of manifest heresy, nor should they punish those involved in these cases, but rather turn them over to their own judges for punishment' (Trusen, 1989: 442; Kors and Peters 2001).

One example of secular law that is roughly contemporaneous with Alexander IV is the law code called *Las siete partidas* (*The Seven Parts*), designed by Alfonso X of Castile, whose text dates from the 1260s and 1270s. In the seventh *Partida*, the law states that there are two kinds of divination, one natural and connected to astronomy and hence acceptable, at least to cultivated students. The other, however, depends on the reading of omens, casting lots, making images or using forbidden means of divination – such as the head of a dead man. The latter are condemned. Necromancy, here the calling up of evil spirits and asking them for information or for power over others, is also prohibited. The condemned forms of divination and necromancy may be prosecuted by anyone in court, and those convicted shall be put to death (*Las siete partidas,* 1931; VII: 1–3). But few secular jurisdictions had such detailed laws in the late thirteenth century, and inquisitors of heretical depravity tended increasingly to take responsibility for prosecuting these offences as part of their charge against heresy generally.

By the end of the thirteenth century, of course, heresy itself had acquired sharper and more precise definitions, one of the most concise of which was that attributed to the thirteenth-century philosopher-theologian, and bishop of Lincoln, Robert Grosseteste: 'Heresy is an opinion that is contrary to sacred scripture, arrived at by human powers, openly taught and pertinaciously defended.' That is, heresy was no longer simply and vaguely any erroneous belief, but erroneous belief that was contrary to proclaimed dogma, publicly asserted (thereby giving rise to the serious offence of scandal), even after the heretic had been corrected by legitimate authorities (thereby committing the equally serious crime of contumacy, or rebellious disobedience to legitimate religious authorities). Johannes Andreae, the author of the standard teaching commentary on the *Liber Sextus,* noted that the phrase 'clearly savour' in the text of Alexander IV meant: 'as in praying at the altars of idols, to offer sacrifices, to consult demons, to elicit responses from them … or if they associate themselves publicly with heretics in order to predict the future by means of the body and blood of Christ, etc.' (Kors and Peters 1972: 79, 2001: 118; Peters 1978: 99–100). The ready identification of superstition with violation of the First Commandment against idolatry and the new learning of canon law are reflected in the questions that inquisitors are told to ask of those accused of magic and sorcery in the handbook for inquisitors written by Bernard Gui around 1323:

> Also, inquire especially into those things which smack of any possible superstition, irreverence, or insult towards the Church's sacraments, most especially towards the sacrament of the Lord's Body, and also towards divine worship and sacred places. (Hansen 1901: 47–8; Shinners 1997: 458; Rubin 1991)

Gui's handbook represents one of the earliest treatments of the crime of magic in inquisitorial literature. In the course of the fourteenth century, Gui's questions were expanded into volumes of ecclesiastical learning concerning sorcery, superstition, magic, and demonology. The legal interpretation of Johannes Andreae was echoed in a brief of legal advice for two inquisitors at the court of John XXII by the jurist Oldradus da Ponte around 1325 (Hansen 1901: 55–9) and the inquisitor Zanchino di Ugolini in 1330 (Hansen 1901: 59–63; *Bibliotheca Lamiarum* 1994: 95–6). The culmination of the inquisitorial and legal doctrine that many kinds of magic constituted the sin of idolatry was reached in the *Directorium Inquisitorum* of the inquisitor Nicolau Eymeric in 1376 (Hansen 1901: 66–71; Kors and Peters 1972: 84–92, 2001: 120–127; Cohn 1975: 177–8; Peters 1978: 196–202; *Bibliotheca Lamiarum* 1994: 98–9). Eymeric's was the most comprehensive handbook of inquisitorial procedure ever produced, and it was printed several times in the sixteenth century and remained influential into the seventeenth. The literature of canon law and inquisitorial procedure between the late thirteenth and the early fifteenth century thus laid down both a substantive and procedural groundwork for trying both heretics and sorcerers, particularly as it came to consider the latter guilty of idolatry and in violation of the First Commandment.

Three examples from the many kinds of literature that reflected some, at least, of the ideas of theologians and jurists may illuminate the distribution of some of the ideas considered above. Towards the end of the twelfth century the learned poet Walter of Châtillon produced his long epic poem, the *Alexandreis,* an account of the wars and ambitions of Alexander the Great. Almost immediately after its appearance the poem received several detailed commentaries, or glosses. It was also read and taught in the literary schools of western Europe. In one of these sets of glosses, contained in a manuscript now in Vienna and written in the second half of the thirteenth century, the commentator extended his discussion of one of Alexander's opponents in the poem, a magician-king named Zoroas of Memphis. In his discussion the commentator offered a systematic survey of the magical arts, one far more relevant to his own time than to the age of Alexander (Colker 1978: 394–5; Townsend 1996: 193–4). Magic, the commentator says, includes the five categories of prophecy, conjuring, mathematics, witchcraft (*maleficium*) and fortune-telling. Prophecy contains five categories: pyromancy, aeromancy, hydromancy, geomancy and necromancy. Conjuring includes making oneself invisible and shapeshifting. Mathematics contains haruspicy, horospicy and auspicy – that is, with foretelling the future and divination. *Maleficium* entails finding out the future by the aid of demons. Fortune-telling is the discovery of the future by casting lots. The key element here is that while many of these forms may be forbidden, it is specifically *maleficium* that requires the assistance of demons, and hence would bring the *maleficus/a* under the jurisdiction of the inquisitors of heretical depravity. King Zoroas of Memphis illustrates an important feature of thirteenth-century thought, the rediscovery (or discovery) of learned magic; that is, of magic performed without the aid of demons by skilfully exploiting occult (hidden) natural and spiritual powers. Such learned magic spread quickly throughout Europe from the late twelfth and thirteenth centuries to the sixteenth, and intermittently played an important role in general discussions of magic of all kinds (Thorndike 1923–58; Cohn 1975: 164–79; Peters 1978; Kieckhefer 1990: 116–50; Fanger 1998), often, especially after the fifteenth century, running the risk of being condemned as diabolical magic regardless of its practitioners' claims to innocence and spiritual purity. The material for the stories of Alexander the Great circulated widely through the sixteenth century, and they often emphasized their authors' interest in sorcery. In the Alexander romance written by Johannes Hartlieb in Bavaria between 1451 and 1454, the story found an author who was also widely known for his studies and books on various aspects of magic and sorcery, particularly the work known as 'The Book of All Forbidden Arts' (Fürbeth 1992; Lea 1957: 275; Hansen 1901: 130–3; Behringer 1998; Kors and Peters 2001: 170).

Another example, one that bridges learned and unlearned cultures, is the vast collection of materials concerning saints' lives and the ecclesiastical calendar compiled around 1260 by the Dominican friar Jacobus de Voragine (Jacobus deVoragine 1993). Here the preacher or confessor could find material on the Magi (Jacobus deVoragine 1993:I: 78–84), the identification of sorcery with demons (Voragine, 1993, I: 108–13, 129, 1512–13, 318–21, 340–50, II: 3–10, 106–8, 192–5, 260–5) and a late thirteenth-century perspective on the entire length of Church history and the festivals of the eccesiastical calendar that familiarized a wider public with the concerns of the early Church and tended to treat all of the lives and events that they considered as if they were contemporary with thirteenth and fourteenth-century western Europeans (Boureau 1984; Duffy 1992: 155–205; Swanson 1995: 142–71; Sticca 1996;Vauchez 1997; Kors and Peters 2001). Early Christian legends of sorcerers like the convert Cyprian and the magician Hermogenes and his contest with St James the Greater thus returned to wider familiarity in an age that understood them very differently from that in which they were first written. The *Golden Legend* and its adaptations were the main sources for hagiographical knowledge in the fourteenth, fifteenth and sixteenth centuries, and they were used as material for preachers and in the celebration of individual saints' cults, as well as for general edification. The stories of ancient and more recent conflicts between saints and demons and sorcerers had long been part of a Christian moral literature, and their periodical retellings kept them part of the narrative stock of preachers and moralists. Nearly a century before Jacobus de Voragine, the reformer and critic Gerald of Wales had included several of them in his work the *Gemma Ecclesiastica* of around 1190, including the story of St James and the magician Hermogenes as well as that of the sorcerer Cyprian (Gerald of Wales 1979: 51–4, 74–6). The career of Cyprian can thus be readily traced through Gerald ofWales, the encyclopedist Vincent of Beauvais, through Jacobus da Voragine into the demonological tract of Nicholas Jaquier in 1458 (see below).

Dante, whose great poem, the *Comedy,* was written in the second decade of the fourteenth century, treated heretics and diviners in two separate places in the *Inferno,* but his heretics in canto 10 were specifically only those who denied the immortality of the soul. In canto 20, however, his diviners ranged from classical seers and prophets to learned and well-known figures of the thirteenth century – his representative figure is Michael Scot, a scholar and ritual magician in the service of the emperor Frederick II, who had produced a large book on ritual magic for the emperor – to poor women who abandoned their families to make a living by telling fortunes. Although Dante was aware of the elaborate portraits of witches in classical literature – notably Lucan's portrayal of Erictho in the *Pharsalia* – and called the Siren an *antica strega,* 'an ancient witch,' in the *Purgatorio,* he did not elaborate further on the theme of contemporary sorcery. Dante, a lay theologian with an extensive knowledge of both Roman and canon law, and greatly concerned with human sinfulness, may thus be considered as representing some of the most important currents of twelfth and thirteenth-century thought on the nature of sorcery and divination in both their theological and legal contexts (Brucker 1963; Peters 1978; Harmening 1979: 217–58; Larner 1980: 16–18, 169–70). It is also worth noting that Dante himself, in a papal charge of magic against another figure, was suspected, because of his legendary learning and his reputation as a living man who had walked through hell, of having been solicited to perform magical injury against Pope John XXII (Kieckhefer 1997: 19).

Sorcerer and witch

The political cases of sorcery were generally widely known, because they were extensively discussed and recorded. The many local trials that took place in the thirteenth and fourteenth centuries were neither well known nor often recorded, and it is pointless to try counting local cases until the fifteenth century, when the inquisitorial criminal procedure had come into more widespread use, written records were both made and preserved, and information concerning trials and convictions circulated more and more widely throughout western Europe (Hansen 1901: 445–613; Russell 1972: 209–18; Kieckhefer 1976: 106–47).

One of these early fourteenth-century cases, however, is both well documented and well worth consideration. In 1324 the bishop of Ossory in Ireland, Richard Ledrede, accused Alice Kyteler, a wealthy and prominent woman in Kilkenny, and several others, charging them with being a group of heretics and witches who held nocturnal meetings at which they made sacrifices to the devil and performed forbidden magical acts in order to injure others. Alice herself was also accused of having a familiar demon (Russell 1972: 189–93; Cohn 1975: 198–204; Davidson and Ward 1993). As its most recent historians have noted,

> the Kyteler witch trial is of great historical interest because it is the first witchcraft trial in European history to treat the accused as members of an organized sect of heretics, and the first to accuse a woman of having acquired the power of sorcery through sexual intercourse with a demon. It is also the first occasion on which a woman was burnt for heresy on charges deriving from witchcraft and occult practices rather than from the familiar sectarian heresies. (Davidson and Ward 1993: 1)

Richard Ledrede had been trained on the Continent and resided at the papal court at Avignon and had probably learned his views about witchcraft in the world of John XXII and brought them with him when he was appointed to the Irish diocese (Cohn 1975: 202–3; Davidson and Ward 1993: 2). If this is true, it supports the argument that the later fully developed concepts and prosecutions of sorcerers and witches were more the product of learned theology and jurisprudence, particularly of the conflicts between different kinds of laws, than the result of the discovery of popular, folkloric practices (Ginzburg 1991). But there is more to the problem than this stark contrast.

Ledrede ran afoul, not only of Alice Kyteler's local supporters, but also of the resistance of English judges. The society of Kilkenny abounded with local alliances and resentments, many of the latter directed against Alice Kyteler, both for her several marriages and for the considerable wealth she had acquired from them. Alice's good fortune sems to have excited her local enemies, including her stepchildren, to charge her before the new bishop and the new bishop himself to understand the charges in terms of his own background and the confession he wrung from the torture and burning in 1324 of Petronilla of Meath, one of Alice's servants. One of Alice's strongest supporters was Arnold le Poer, seneschal of Kilkenny and Carlow, whom Ledrede eventually imprisoned until le Poer died. But Ledrede never managed to obtain custody of Alice Kyteler, and he was later discredited in a number of political conflicts with local Irish and English rivals.

The trial of Alice Kyteler is an important early case, particularly well documented, that illustrates not only the conflict of canon and secular law in early fourteenth-century Ireland (and, by implication, elsewhere), but the battery of charges that it was thought possible to bring in a local conflict of this kind and the prominence of what appears to be a new kind of diabolical witchcraft among them. The case, however, is virtually unique, and it started no general hunt for sorcerers or witches in either Ireland or England. Continentally inspired, the concept of sorcery and witchcraft used in the Kyteler case developed more strongly and regularly on the Continent from the later fourteenth century.

At first glance, the fourteenth century seems to offer many explanations for the growth in the conceptualization and prosecution of magic and witchcraft, but the considerable number and varying degrees of scale in these explanations are of different orders of magnitude and cannot be cited simply in a direct causal way to explain the changes in conceptualization and prosecution that took place, after all, in very different regions at different times – and in many regions not at all (Briggs 1996: 287–316; Nirenberg 1996; Behringer 1998). It is necessary to consider the macro-conditions of the late fourteenth and fifteenth centuries at some length, because they have sometimes been used indiscriminately to 'explain' the new ideas about sorcery, magic and witchcraft that emerged at the time.

A vast series of large-scale natural disasters struck western Europe from 1315 until well into the fifteenth century, but their connection with ideas of sorcery and witchcraft has not been established. We must first consider the macro-scale. In 1315–17 a great famine occurred throughout most of western Europe (Jordan 1996). From 1348 on, the Black Death, a pandemic of bubonic, septicaemic and pneumonic plague followed (Ziegler 1969; Piatt 1996). Throughout the century warfare devastated many areas, and it was waged on a larger scale of destruction and injury to both combatants and non-combatants and with a high degree of mobilization of state resources unheard of earlier. Finally a wave of financial collapse struck both the great and small banking firms of northern Italy, causing economic ruin and confusion throughout Europe. Certainly these disasters must have affected Europeans' confidence in both material and spiritual protectors, but in no case can a direct causal connection with ideas of magic and witchcraft be established.

There is also the intellectual and legal tradition that had developed especially since the eleventh century, shaped by a growing body of criminal law theory and a sharper and more precise concept of the offence and punishment of heresy. The new and comprehensive legal doctrines were not exclusively those of the schools or of judicial theory generally, nor of canon law exclusively, but they had begun to be applied in both ecclesiastical and secular courts from the late twelfth century on. They were part of what has been called the *ius commune* of Continental Europe, a legal system with an increasingly developed concept of both crime and criminal law and the distinctive Romano-canonical legal procedure (Bellomo 1995; Fraher 1989). From its origins in the schools of northern Italy and southern France, the new *ius commune* moved out irregularly across most of western Europe, introducing both new rules of evidence and the Romano-canonical inquisitorial judicial procedure and giving to new and centralizing court systems and the magistrates who operated them a learned law that could – and did – successfully challenge local and traditional legal systems. Romano-canonical procedure also used the inquisitorial method – the control of a case by a single magistrate simultaneously as investigator, prosecutor, and judge – and the use of torture as a legal incident; in the presence of what is now called extensive circumstantial evidence, the absence of the identical testimony of two eyewitnesses, or of a confession by the accused, torture was permitted in order to obtain a confession when significant other evidence indicated the probable guilt of the accused (Peters 1996b; Pennington 1993: 132–64).

The best way to approach these elements on the macro-scale and use them as evidence in particular instances – if they can be used as evidence at all – is to look at specific regions in which new kinds of accusations and trials appear to have taken place and to ask whether famine, plague, war or social and economc disorder is particularly marked in them and what role these might have played in conjunction with any other factors that may be relevant. As a number of historians have pointed out, the particular mix of the 'factor-bundle' will largely determine the resulting understanding and explanation. Arno Borst has said, 'We have … to attend to the dirty details of the first witchcraft trials and put them into the historical context of their specific locations, instead of spending time on religious and social history at large' (Borst 1992: 104). Among the mid-level factors, for example, is the redesign of local economies or local legal structures: that is, changing the forms of rural livelihood in ways that made many regions less self-reliant and brought them into more contact with larger markets and made them more vulnerable to their influence and fluctuations, hence losing some sense of economic autonomy (and sensing more anxiously the relative prosperity or economic misfortune that such changes entailed); or the intrusion of new legal systems in the place of old, thereby making certain practices criminal that had earlier not been thought to be criminal. There are also, finally, the particular circumstances and experience of individual jurisdictions in which the earliest trials were held. These 'middle-scale' changes might then be considered in relation to particular outbreaks of larger-scale troubles (Briggs 1996).

Finally, the fourteenth century also witnessed the long residence of the papacy outside Rome, at Avignon, from 1305 to 1378, the return to Rome, a bitterly contested papal election in 1378 that was followed by the Great Schism, that is, by a period between 1378 and 1409 when two men claimed to be the legitimate pope, and from the Council of Pisa in 1409 to 1415, when three men did so. Although the Schism was healed at the Council of Constance in 1415–18, the Council of Basel in 1439 elected Amadeus VIII, Duke of Savoy, pope as Felix V (1439–51) in place of the living Eugenius IV (and thus 'Felix V' is conventionally recorded as an antipope). Such disorder at the very top of the hierarchy of Latin Christendom did little to calm the anxieties of Christians throughout Europe, although as František Graus has shown, 'the most shattering crisis for the people of the period was not the duplication of the papacy and the college of cardinals, but the doubtful validity of the communion, the concern about the earthly and eternal salvation of every Christian, and the loss of the community of living and dead in heaven and on earth' (Borst 1992: 121). One might add that such a sense of loss and uncertainty complemented a heightened sense that the assaults of Satan were growing more powerful, that defences against them were weaker, and that this awareness was linked to ideas about the end of the world, especially those aspects of it that dealt with the growth in strength of the assaults by Satan and the coming of the Antichrist. Against these fears, the intensity of devotion increased; the rise of all forms of devotionalism, as Richard Kieckhefer has said, was 'perhaps the most significant development in late medieval Christianity' (Kieckhefer 1987: 75).

In the wake of the Avignon papacy and the Great Schism, there were many calls for reform, not only of the papacy, but of Christian life on all levels, and one of the results was a series of Church councils that dealt with a wide range of matters and the emergence of a number of religious reform movements within particular dioceses and ecclesiastical provinces. These brought to the attention of both learned scholars and political and legal authorities an entire panorama of local beliefs and practices that came to be reassessed in the light of the entire experience of fourteenth and fifteenth-century Europe and many of them condemned as superstitions. Some of these began in certain places to be condemned as sorcery and witchcraft, others as manifestations of regrettable superstition. Such ideas circulated effectively in fifteenth-century Europe among the mutual contacts on the part of university scholars, in treatises and handbooks, and among certain classes of officials, notably the Dominican and Franciscan inquisitors of heretical depravity and energetic lay magistrates, as well as groups of reform-minded prelates. Church councils also provided occasions for churchmen and laymen from all corners of Europe to meet and exchange ideas. Important councils were held at Pisa in 1409, at Constance in 1414–18, at Pavia-Siena in 1423–4, and at Basel in 1431–9. The Council of Basel in particular was one of the most important and influential occasions for such contacts and exchanges of ideas. At the council a number of new ideas concerning the diabolical character of sorcery, superstition and witchcraft circulated and spread outside the orbit of Basel itself as members of the Council and their companions and servants returned to their homes elsewhere, carrying ideas with them, and a number of treatises were written and discussed at the Council, one of them dealing with some of the earliest cases of prosecution for sorcery (see below).

Basel is an important example of the new role of communications in fifteenth-century Europe. As Margaret Aston has said of the Councils of Constance and Basel: 'They might in fact be regarded as a combined form of summit conference, trade fair and ecumenical council, with membership drawn from all parts of Europe, including both secular and ecclesiastical rulers, accompanied and provided for by all the enormous following of retainers, craftsmen, and traders who were deemed necessary for the wants of such numbers. Never before had people met together from so many parts on such a scale' (Aston 1968: 79). At these new-style assemblies, ideas, books, stories, and gossip moved easily and quickly. The assemblies became an entirely new source of information as well as an extremely efficient circulation system. Nor were Church councils the only such large-scale meetings in fifteenth-century Europe; the Congress of Arras in 1435, assembled to settle diplomatic differences among France, England and Burgundy, numbered around five thousand people (Dickinson 1955).

Of course other means of more rapid and extensive communications also appeared, print being perhaps the best known, but there were others as well. Messenger services among great and lesser powers, the regularizing of the post messengers carrying both public and private written communications, the internal communications systems of diplomatic missions, commercial corporations, religious orders, and the attendant sharing of information and ideas, including conversations and gossip that these systems inevitably permitted suggest the speed and extent of the circulation of ideas and information across Europe after the late fourteenth century, even independently of the spread of printed matter (Aston 1968: 49–116).

In this milieu, news – and texts – travelled rapidly and widely. And when the news of new kinds of sorcery and superstition began to circulate in the late fourteenth and early fifteenth centuries, it circulated far more widely and more rapidly than had news of earlier cases, for example, that of Alice Kyteler. At the Council of Basel the theologian Johann Nider first learned of the trial and execution of Joan of Arc several years earlier, in 1431 (see below). These circumstances provide the context for the spread of ideas about sorcery and witchcraft that circulated from the early fifteenth century on.

The conciliarist movement was accompanied by a number of efforts to reform the beliefs and behaviour of ordinary Christians. The 1398 condemnation of sorcery by the faculty of theology of the University of Paris was one of the earliest, but larger and more ambitious projects soon followed (Veenstra, 1998: 343–55). Jean Gerson (1363–1429), chancellor of the University of Paris, preached a number of sermons and wrote several tracts against what he considered the superstitious religious practices of his own day, including one 'On errors concerning the magical art and the forbidden articles' (Thorndike 1923–58: IV: 114–31; Bonney 1971: 88–9; Hansen 1901: 86–7; Brown 1988: 159–60; Veenstra 1998: 142–3). Gerson's criticisms focused on the interpretation of particular events – the croaking of a crow above the roof, for example – as signs of impending disaster or bad luck, the fear of 'unlucky days', that is, days that were unpropitious, as well as on the use of incantations, images and certain herbs, and the misuse of astrology, a discipline that straddled both the world of learning and that of 'superstition.' Gerson also insisted that while it was permissible to have recourse to good angels when faced with illness or temptations, it was absolutely forbidden to have recourse to demons. Gerson also insisted that the moment one even considers entering into a pact with demons, he has already made such a pact. Shortly after Gerson's tract, in 1412, John of Frankfurt, professor of theology at the University of Heidelberg and an inquisitor at Wurzburg, condemned such beliefs as the supernatural powers of infants born with a caul (Hansen 1901: 71–82; Veenstra 1998: 147; Lorenz 1994a: 87), and tracts by Nicholas Jauer in 1405, the anonymous treatise *Tractatus de Daemonibus* (*Treatise Concerning Demons*) of 1415, and a treatise on superstitions by Henry of Gorkum in 1425 all regarded these and other superstitious practices as bringing humans closer to the power of demons (Thorndike 1923–58: IV: 274–307, 683–7; Bonney 1971; Hansen 1901: 82–6, 87–8; Paton 1992; Veenstra 1998: 138–53; Cameron 1998). In one case, that of Werner of Freiburg, an Augustinian friar tried at Speyer and Heidelberg in 1405 for maintaining superstitious beliefs, Nicholas Jauer perceived a link between superstitious beliefs and the performance of magic (Lerner 1991; Veenstra 1998: 151). During the late fourteenth and early fifteenth centuries a number of other sermons and treatises in Italy, England, France and the German lands both echoed and expanded the criticisms of Gerson, particularly the remarkable collection of sermons delivered at Siena in 1427 by Bernardino of Siena, a reader of Passavanti and one of the earliest theoreticians of the relations among superstition, sorcery, and witchcraft (Owst 1957; Bonney 1971; Paton 1992: 264–306; Swanson 1995: 182–99, 235–56, 267–310; Duffy 1992: 266–98; Bossy 1985; Veenstra 1998: 137–201; Kors and Peters 2001: 133–137; on Bernardino, Mormando 1998). As Duffy has said, what the reformers found when they looked at what they called 'superstitions' was 'not paganism, but lay Christianity' (Duffy 1992: 187; Segl 1990; Monter 1983: 6–22; Clark 1997: 473–88, and 821, s.v. superstition).

During the mid-fifteenth century Cardinal Nicholas of Cusa (1401–64) made a reforming journey throughout much of western Europe, and his agenda was remarkably similar to those of Gerson and his successors earlier in the century (Sullivan 1974). At the point at which the general criticism of superstitious practices blended into the specific topic of sorcery, the sermon by Bernardino of Siena of 1427 is a good example from Italy (Kieckhefer 1990: 194–5; Paton 1992; Shinners 1997: 242–5; Mormando 1998), and on the local level both handbooks for confessors and sermons, particularly sermons on the First Commandment, reinforced the connection between superstitious practices and sorcery by linking both to the sin of idolatry. A fifteenth-century English manual for confessors requires the confessor to ask the penitent, regarding the First Commandment, 'Have you had any belief, trust, and faith in witchcraft or sorcery, "necromancy" or in dreams, or in any conjurations, for theft or in any "other" writings or charms for sickness or for peril of bodily enemies, or for any other thing, "disease", for all of this is against the faith?' (Harmening 1988, 1989, 1990a, 1990b; Maggioni 1993: 54). John Bossy has persuasively argued that one of the major transformations in the characterization of sin in the later Middle Ages and especially in the sixteenth century was the shift in penitential emphasis from the seven deadly sins to the Ten Commandments (Bossy 1988; Harmening in Blauert 1990: 68–90; Clark 1997: 493–508, 562–3). In this shift, the sin of idolatry (now emphatically including magic and witchcraft) was committed against the First Commandment and thus became the greatest of all sins.

The power of demons to tempt humans with God's permission, said Gerson, had four causes: to achieve the damnation of the obstinate, the punishment of sinners, a testing of the faithful and to manifest God's glory. Such occasions of temptation were the constant material of sermons and confessional manuals, and they were often thought to employ rituals and materials analogous to normative Christian devotional practices and objects, always for personal benefit or the benefit of clients to the exclusion of the charitable and fraternal concern for the spiritual and material welfare of the entire local community.

Certain rites and certain objects were believed to possess innate power. Not only liturgical books, and bibles and the texts they contained, but books of magic or necromancy themselves were thought to possess such powers (Kieckhefer 1997). So did prayers. So did the consecrated host. So did the class of objects known as sacramentals: the water used in baptism, holy oil and blessed candles and palms. So might the bodies of the dead. These were material exchanges between the sacred liturgical order of reality and the desires of individuals to appropriate such power for themselves, sometimes in a socially harmless way – as protections against illness or other harm or – at somewhat greater risk – to find lost or stolen objects, but at other times in asocial ways – to curse rather than bless, to cause illness instead of curing it or to use them as techniques of sorcery exclusively for private, rather than socially beneficial purposes. Once such objects left the control of the clergy who administered them and normally regulated their proper use – and hosts, water, oil, candles, blessed palms, and the texts of prayers routinely did so – they became potentially dangerous in the hands of private individuals who hoped to use their innate or acquired power for personal gain, even when those who misused them might themselves be hermits, monks or other members of what Richard Kieckhefer has termed 'the clerical underworld' and Peters, following Peter Brown, the 'demimonde' (Peters 1978: 110–37; Carey 1992). The same problem existed in the case of prayers and liturgical rituals (Franz 1909; Harmening 1988: 191), particularly those rituals concerning exorcisms and blessings.

As the idea of heresy came to define the offence not only as a violation of the bonds between the individual and God but also between individuals in the Christian community, the image of heretical groups as anti-churches also developed. These counter-societies were then accused of possessing their own rites, perversions of the normative rites of the Christian liturgy: baptism was perverted by blasphemous initiation rites; benedictions and blessings were perverted into curses; worship due only to God was paid to the devil; sacramentals were perverted for blasphemous misuse, as were such rites as exorcism. The ideal of Christian chastity was perverted by accusations of indiscriminate sexual orgies, and the sanctity of the consecrated host was perverted in obscene sexual contact with demons and unholy banquets and collective, grotesque festivities. Some of these ideas had long been understood as signs indicating the increasing and despairing fury of Satan as the end of the world – and his own final defeat – drew near, doubling his onslaught against the people of God. Such eschatological ideas were widespread in the fifteenth century (Cohn 1975; Clark 1997: 321–74, with extensive references). Such anti-churches came to be considered the norm of heretical individual and social existence several centuries before the fifteenth. But with the larger changes in devotional and material life after the late fourteenth century, all of these features came to be brought to bear, no longer exclusively on heretical groups, but upon all enemies of God and man, however these may have been thought to be constituted.

Beginning in the early fifteenth century many of the different kinds of offences that had earlier constituted the separate offences of magic, sorcery, divination, necromancy and even learned natural magic began to be considered in some places by some theologians and magistrates, both ecclesiastical and civil, as a single type of crime whose essence was defined as a conspiratorial alliance with the devil whose purpose was to ruin human society. At its most comprehensive (and not all demonologists included all of the features that collectively came to distinguish it) individuals were believed to have made a pact with the devil, signed it with their blood, rendered homage and entered into sexual relations with him, travelled by flight to assemblies at which they participated in blasphemous rites and carried with them, usually on their bodies, a mark or sign of their membership in the diabolical conspiracy of witches and were sometimes accompanied by a familiar demon, often in the shape of an animal.

The novelty of this definition lay in the application to formerly individually accused magicians and others of the idea of conspiracy, that is, of collective enmity toward the human race, and of collective action that was undertaken to accomplish its destruction. The earlier separate categories and the distinctions reflected in the canon *Episcopi* between fantasy and actuality gave way to a new and inclusive understanding of both. As Paravy notes: 'It is this fundamental distinction [that of the canon *Episcopi* between fantasy and reality] that disappears. The diverse worlds of throwers and raisers of *sortes,* of men and women who cure illnesses, are uniformly included without mercy in a single condemnation, to the extent that every kind of magic, when investigated, reveals a member of the devil's sect .... None of these elements is new, and all of them are attested in a complex intellectual and psychological heritage that unified pagan Mediterranean and [northern] Germanic traditions. What was new was the rigorous tie that bound and combined these elements to and with each other, coordinating them in a system that was at the same time fantastic and coherent' (Paravy 1981: 121, 124; Trusen 1989; Harmening 1988: 187). These elements may be seen in the 1405 *Treatise Concerning Superstitions* of Nicholas Jauer (Lorenz 1994a: 86; Veenstra 1998: 149–50).

Such a transformation of thought also permitted earlier accounts of magic and sorcery from many different periods and contexts to be reinterpreted according to the new theories. When monastic writers, for example, had depicted the world outside the monastery as filled with demonic temptation and power and weak human beings who regularly succumbed to these, such depictions reinforced the monk's original decision to leave the troubled world for the cloister and perhaps to transfer onto that world his own fears – what some psychologists now call cognitive dissonance. But when these texts were read in the late fourteenth and fifteenth centuries by a non-monastic audience outside the original cloister context, they confirmed the new beliefs about the alarming vulnerability of the world and its inhabitants to the powers of Satan and were added to the new literature of demonology, sorcery and witchcraft. As early as 1409 Pope Alexander V spoke of a 'new heresy', and by 1450 the Dominican inquisitor of Carcassone, Jean Vineti, in his *Tractatus contra Demonum Invocatores, Treatise against Those Who Invoke Demons,* argued that diabolical sorcery – witchcraft in its later classical meaning – was a new heresy (Lea 1957: 272–3; Hansen 1901: 124–30; *Bibliotheca Lamiarum* 1994: 100–1).

What was also new was the legal argument that the immediacy and imminent danger of this crime, its inherently monstrous character, made it one of those 'excepted crimes' for which there was to be no possible expiation short of death, since there was no way by which an accused person could adequately repent, and hence no justification for mercy in sentencing. Every individual manifestation of 'magic' became simply one of many tips of a gigantic iceberg – the 'new' conspiracy directed by Satan to destroy the human race (Larner 1984: 35–67). The spread of learned law gave great moral, as well as legal authority to the secular magistrate, and these, too, were expected to engage vigorously in prosecuting the enemies of the human race.

A heightened consciousness of the unified and irreparably grave character of the crime of witchcraft and news of actual instances of magic, sorcery and witchcraft seen as new crimes had to have a basis in both theory and practice. There needed to be actual prosecutions of the new crime, and accounts of these prosecutions had to circulate in order to attract the attention of devotional reformers and magistrates in other regions and thus constitute news that needed to be known by them. Although a number of isolated trials had been held in Italy in the last several decades of the fourteenth century (Bonomo 1959; Paton 1992; Brucker 1963), the key geographical areas in which such trials and reports of them first appear to have occurred are in the region from the lower Rhone valley east and northeast in the area of the Dauphiné, the Pays de Vaud, Piedmont, Savoy and the valley of Aosta, and in what is now western Switzerland – Lucerne, Fribourg, Bern and the dioceses of Geneva, Lausanne, Neuchâtel and Sion. From these areas the new ideas and legal procedures concerning sorcery and witchcraft spread along familiar and heavily used communications routes into northern and northeastern Italy – Lombardy, including the region around Como, and into eastern Switzerland, the Tirol, Swabia, Bavaria and the upper and lower Rhineland. These are the earliest sites of what became the first significant movements of witchcraft prosecution in western Europe. But these were not remote mountain backwaters of residual folk paganism, as some historians once claimed. They were lively and fluid areas of contact between different linguistic regions and cultures and exchange points for the transmission of ideas, governed by ambitious state-building rulers and cities, and strategically placed in the view of the Council of Basel. In the light of the complexity of the late fourteenth and fifteenth centuries, it is certainly necessary to look initially at the earliest particular local instances of a new conception of sorcery and witchcraft before invoking the large-scale disasters and other macro-conditions as explanatory devices.

The key years appear to be 1430–40 (Blauert 1989: 26; Ostorero et al. 1999). Neither the records of episcopal visitations in the diocese of Geneva from 1412 to 1414, nor the five books of the *Decreta sen Statuta Sabaudiae* (*The Decrees or Statutes of Savoy*), a general law code for the duchy of Savoy issued by Amadeus VIII in 1430, reveal any concern for a new kind of sorcery. A single tract, the *Errores Gazariorum* (*The Errors of the Gazars [Cathars]*), written in the francophone section of western Switzerland and recently redated to the early 1430s, however, spoke for the first time since the Alice Kyteler trial of a sect, or 'synagogue', whose members paid homage to and entered a pact with the devil, bestowed the *osculum infame,* feasted on the dead bodies of infants, held sexual orgies and received ointments and powders to kill their enemies and destroy harvests. Although they pretended to be good Catholic Christians, they represented the most dangerous of all enemies of the human race and the Christian Church (Lea 1957: 273–5; Hansen 1901: 118–22; Lorenz 1994a: 85; Ostorero et al. 1999; Kors and Peters 2001: 159–162). The *Errores Gazariorum* also identified the heresies of

Catharism and Waldensianism with one another and attributed to their members many of the features that later applied to sorcerers and witches.

Two narrative sources, both written in the same general area around 1437, attribute the appearance of a new kind of sorcery to the years beginning in the 1390s. At the Council of Basel between 1435 and 1437, the Dominican theologian and prior of the Dominican convent at Basel, Johann Nider, wrote his large, reform-minded theological work, the *Formicarius* (*The Antheap; printed in 1479*). In book V, Nider recounted conversations that he had had with a judge in the service of the city of Bern, Peter von Greyerz, concerning von Greyerz's cases tried in the Simme Valley under the jurisdiction of the city of Bern between 1392 and 1406, when von Greyerz retired. Nider's account of von Greyerz's cases depicted them as dealing both with traditional individual acts of sorcery, and also with an association of sorcerers who adored the devil, caused damage to the property and persons of others and enriched themselves (Borst, 1992; Kors and Peters 2001: 155–159). The most recent student of these cases, Andreas Blauert, has argued that the cases that von Greyerz tried had been indeed conventional cases of individual sorcery, but that in Nider's understanding and retelling they became something different – the account of a new phenomenon, diabolical, collaborative sorcery (Blauert 1989: 56–9; *Bibliotheca Lamiarum* 1994: 100–1; Bailey 1998). The cases tried by Peter von Greyerz and retold by Nider at Basel and in the *Formicarius* were those of damage to persons (including infanticide) and possessions, including crops and animals, by individuals from the middling levels of communities, who, in a period of economic and social transformation, had achieved some measure of economic success, but had also behaved in an ambitious, self-dependent and unneighbourly way and were accused by jealous or at least suspicious neighbours. They seem also to have been people who were rising in social status by these methods, earning the resentment of a traditional set of elites.

A second source, also written around 1437, the chronicle of the Lucerne scribe Hans Fründ, told of earlier cases in which sworn testimony indicated that the devil approached people who were depressed and melancholic, promising them riches and revenge on their enemies, organizing them into a group dedicated to his service, demanding sacrifices from them, and teaching them flight and shape-shifting. Fründ, like Nider, also appears to have read back into these earlier localized instances ideas of diabolical temptation, the existence of sects and homage to the demon that had recently become current in his own day.

The most persuasive piece of evidence, however, is the remarkable treatise *Ut Magorum et Maleficorum Errores* (*In order that the Errors of Sorcerers and Witches*), written by the judge Claude Tholosan, who served for several years in the district of Briançon in the Dauphine. Pierette Paravy, who edited the treatise, has dated it to 1437 (Paravy 1979; Ostorero *et al.* 1999; Kors and Peters 2001: 162–166). The Tholosan document is important for several reasons. First, it is the work of a lay judge, and second, it reveals that judge drawing upon all the learning available to him, including consultations with learned jurists at Aix-en-Provence, Avignon and elsewhere, in order to characterize a sect of diabolical sorcerers, identify and justify the punishment they deserve, assemble the juristic rationale for the crime and justify the legitimate power of the prince who had commissioned his magistrates to carry out the law. Tholosan used canon and Roman law extensively, as well as the opinions of Zanchino de Ugolini and other jurists from the early fourteenth century. The treatise is important, not only for its use and reinterpretation of substantial theological and legal learning and for its timing, but because the author was a working lay magistrate, not a hunter after superstitions like Jauer, an inquisitor like Eymeric, a theologian like Nider or a chronicler like Fründ and others. In these cases, the theologians, the chronicler and the magistrate alike could point to direct contact with actual prosecutions – which two of them understood to have been for conspiratorial and diabolical sorcery and during which the magistrate had actually tried, convicted and executed people for these offences – that had taken place within recent human memory and in readily identifiable nearby places.

All of these sources, as well as others written just after them, agreed that the origins of the 'new sect' of sorcerers and witches lay in the last half, and particularly in the last quarter of the fourteenth century. In these cases social memory recognized that the offences of sorcery and witchcraft that were being commited in the first quarter of the fifteenth century were relatively recent, but all sources located their origin at around the same time a generation or two before the present at the end of the first quarter of the fifteenth century.

The geography of these instances lies just to the west of the great mountain passes of Mont Cenis, Lesser St Bernard, Greater St Bernard and the Simplon. From Lucerne and Bern, the territory in which these cases and theoretical works took place extends southwest to Fribourg, Lausanne, Geneva and Chambéry, and from there southeast to Briançon. That is, these instances occurred in the territory of two newly formed and ambitious states: part of the Swiss Confederation, particularly the city of Bern, and in the territories of the ambitious, state-building dukes of Savoy, especially Amadeus VIII. Savoy was the principal overland route into Italy for French travellers and into France for Italians, and since the twelfth century its dukes had added a number of contiguous territories to the original duchy and exerted their influence over several more.

Nider wrote his book and circulated his narrative at the Council of Basel, at the time virtually the crossroads of Christian Europe and the point at which diverse regional ideas about sorcery – and other topics – could conveniently encounter and influence each other. It was at Basel, after all, where Nider himself heard for the first time of the prosecution and burning of Joan of Arc, informed by a fellow Dominican from the Sorbonne, another case which Nider understood as one of diabolical sorcery (Kay 1988: 304–5). The Council of Basel also had business with the duke of Savoy, Amadeus VIII (1391–1451). Amadeus VIII and his immediate predecessors had greatly increased the territory ruled or dominated by the dukes of Savoy, and their court patronized French artists, resembling in this aspect the contemporary lavish courts and patronage of the dukes of Burgundy in Burgundy and the Low Countries, especially Flanders. Disillusioned with Pope Eugenius IV (1431–47), the members of the Council of Basel declared him deposed, and they elected the widowed duke Amadeus VIII of Savoy as pope in his place. Taking the papal name Felix V (1439–51), Amadeus/Felix proceeded to attempt to increase the number of areas that recognized him as pope and to hasten the reform of Christian society, especially in his own ducal territories.

No pope ever took deposition lightly, and one of the responses on the part of Eugenius IV against Amadeus/Felix V was the charge that both heresy and diabolical sorcery flourished widely in the lands of the duke of Savoy. Eugenius IV had written other letters in the same vein (Hansen 1901: 17–19; Kors and Peters 1972: 98–101; 2001: 153–155), revealing himself to be an austere and devout prelate with a strong fear of diabolical magic. One of Eugenius' correspondents on the matter of diabolical sorcery was the inquisitor Pontus Fougeyron, whose work in the early fifteenth century contributed substantially to the demonization of heretics (Blauert 1989: 27). The response of Amadeus/Felix V was to intensify the search for diabolical sorcerers and witches in his territories. It is in these circumstances that the work of Claude Tholosan and a number of contemporary inquisitors in the area exerted a strong influence.

But magistrates, inquisitors, theologians and chroniclers did not produce the only sources that make this period a key one. The canon of Lausanne and secretary of Amadeus/Felix at the Council of Basel, Martin le Franc, wrote a long and illustrated poem around 1440 called *Le champion des dames (The Defender of Ladies)*, which was generally a poem in praise of womanhood, except for its section concerning women sorcerers. Here, le Franc described a group of old women going to the 'synagogue' – that is, the sabbat – and paying homage to the devil in the form of a goat. Le Franc's information appears to have come from the same region near Briançon as the cases of Claude Tholosan. Amadeus/Felix V later made le Franc provost of the cathedral chapter in Lausanne (Veenstra 1998: 152; Kors and Peters 2001: 166–169). Not only did le Franc's poem echo the concerns of both his own master and Eugenius IV, but in its illustrated margins the manuscript depicted for the first time witches riding on broomsticks to the sabbat. By 1440 all of the elements of the later theories of witchcraft had assembled in place and had even begun to acquire a distinctive visual imagery.

From 1440 on, a number of local trials and works on demonology – with a new insistence on the diabolical character of sorcery – took place and were produced in this region, although not on a large scale and not everywhere. But the occurrence of trials and convictions gave a new immediacy to the works of demonology, and the works of demonology framed the investigations and trials for diabolical sorcery. The results were conveyed in the words of preachers and chroniclers. From the core areas in which they began, both doctrines and trials influenced areas both adjacent and further away. These new trials and works of demonology became the province of both ecclesiastical (including ordinary episcopal jurisdiction and inquisitorial jurisdiction) and lay magistrates. It is also possible to correlate periods and places of prosecutions of diabolical sorcery in the mid to late fifteenth century with periods of severe social and economic crisis: 1447–56, 1457–66, the exceptional decade 1477–86 and the nearly as exceptional decade 1487–96 (Blauert 1989: 18; Behringer 1998). Rather than see the social and economic crises as causing the persecutions, however, it may be more advisable to consider diabolical sorcery as a crime particularly suited – because of its alleged rejection of God and its conspiratorial hostility and destructiveness to neighbours – to be invoked in periods of such crisis, at least from the fifteenth century on.

Superstition, magic and witchcraft on the eve of the reformation

During the half-century after 1440 numerous trials, usually of individuals or relatively small groups were held in the Valais (Strobino 1996), and at Lausanne, Vevey (Ostorero 1995), Neuclâtel, Bern, Fribourg and Basel (Blauert 1989: 37–60). From these origins both works of demonology and trials spread east into Austria, south into Italy, and north into the Rhineland. At the same time, the number of treatises dealing with diabolical sorcery also increased. From being particular subjects treated in longer works – as in Nider's *Formicarius* or le Franc's *Champion des dames* – the new offence continued to be treated in this way, but it also soon became the subject of separate works of demonology in its own right. Among the former were the commentary on the Bible by Alfonso Tostado around 1440, which treated the problem of demonic transportation of human beings from one place to another (Lea 1957: 189–91;

Hansen 1901: 105–9; *Bibliotheca Lamiarum* 1994: 101), and the *Fortalicium Fidei* (*The Fortification of Faith*) of Alfonso de Spina just after mid-century (Lea 1957: 285–92; Hansen 1901: 145–8; *Bibliotheca Lamiarum* 1994: 105–6; Clark 1997: 81). These works incorporated current demonological theory into the kind of literature read by preachers, confessors and academics – thus bringing these views into the awareness of clerics who normally might not have been aware of individual demonological treatises. Among the latter, however, such works as Jean Vineti's *Tractatus contra Daemonum Invocatores* of 1450 (Lea 1957: 272–3; Hansen 1901: 124–30), and Nicholas Jacquier's *Flagellum Haereticorum Fascinariorum* (*The Lash of Heretics who Fascinate [Enchant]*) of 1458 (Lea 1957: 276–80; Hansen 1901: 133–45; *Bibliotheca Lamiarum* 1994: 104–5; Ostorero *et al.* 1999; Kors and Peters 2001: 169–172), indicate the increasing importance of demonology and diabolical sorcery as subjects of separate and detailed investigation and analysis.

The most important and influential example of the latter, however, was the result of an inquisitorial career that differed from those of other inquisitors. Heinrich Kramer (Latinized: *Institoris*), a Dominican, worked during the 1470s in the area of Constance, concentrating chiefly on the heresy of diabolical sorcery (Segl 1988: 103–26, esp. 109, n. 35; Schnyder 1991, 1993). In 1485 Institoris received permission from Georg Golser, the bishop of Brixen, to investigate heresy in the bishop's domains, and he undertook his investigations in the city of Innsbruck. Institoris, a furious misogynist, questioned particularly the women who came before him in great detail concerning their sexual lives, dismaying his fellow inquisitors, incurring judicial irregularity, and bringing the inquisitorial investigation in Innsbruck to a halt. The bishop of Brixen said of him that 'because of his advanced age, Institoris had become senile (*propter senium gantz chindisch*)' – although Institoris was only fifty-nine at the time.

Aged, misogynist and senile Institoris may have been in 1485, but he had lost neither his zealous determination to combat diabolical sorcerers – particularly women – nor his literary energy (on the problem of witchcraft accusations and gender history, see Edith Ennen in Segl 1988: 7–21; Burghartz 1988: 57–74; Dienst 1990; review of the question and the scholarly literature in Purkiss 1996; extensive discussions in Briggs 1996: 257–86; Sharpe 1997: 169–99; Clark 1997: 106–33). In 1487 he published the most important of all demonological treatises, the *Hammer of Witches* (*Malleus Maleficarum,* literally *The Hammer of Women Who Commit Maleficia:* on the metaphor of the hammer, see Arbesmann 1945; later editions, which included other works of demonology along with the *Malleus,* were called the *Malleus Maleficorum,* expanding the gender definition by shifting to the masculine). The work appeared with what appeared to be a letter of approbation, *Summis desiderantes affectibus,* issued by Pope Innocent VIII in 1484, an endorsement from the faculty of theology at the University of Cologne, and with Jacob Sprenger, a Dominican inquisitor from Cologne with whom Institoris had often worked, identified as co-author, although Sprenger's role in the project is now generally doubted (Anglo 1977a; Segl 1988; *Bibliotheca Lamiarum* 1994: 107–10). But both the papal letter and the Cologne endorsement are problematic. The letter of Innocent VIII is not an approval of the book to which it was appended, but rather a charge to inquisitors to investigate diabolical sorcery and a warning to those who might impede them in this duty, that is, a papal letter in the by then conventional tradition established by John XXII and other popes through Eugenius IV and Nicholas V (1447–55). The approval of the theological faculty of Cologne was arranged through a complicated series of academic negotiations – it, too, does not address the remarkable qualities of the work itself. It is doubtful whether either Innocent VIII or the theological faculty of Cologne ever read the work. The work was essentially a defence of prosecutions for witchcraft written in the face of considerable scepticism – its arguments, especially in part III, are clearly aimed at reluctant lay magistrates.

The treatise itself is in three parts (Hansen 1901: 360–407; summary in Lea 1957: 306–36; English translation in Summers 1971; excerpts in Kors and Peters 1972: 105–89, 2001: 176–229; see also Schnyder in Segl 1988: 127–49; Clark 1997) in the form of scholastic questions. Part I insists on the reality of diabolical *maleficium*, part II deals with the kinds of witches and the nature of their activities, and part III consists of describing the legal procedures by which both ecclesiastical and civil magistrates should proceed against them. The scholastic question format allowed Institoris to draw upon the work of earlier inquisitors and demonologists such as Eymeric, Nider, Jacquier and Spina, as well as virtually all other sources that touched, however remotely, on the subject. The purpose of the treatise was thus to demonstrate the nature and ubiquity of the offence of witchcraft, to refute those who expressed even the slightest scepticism about its reality, to prove that witches were more often women than men, and to educate magistrates on the procedures that could find them out and convict them. The first two parts of the treatise prepare for the third – the urging of more widespread and intense prosecutions, chiefly by lay magistrates, in spite of any theological or legal scepticism or opposition they might encounter – by arming them with apparendy irrefutable arguments against such opposition. The *Malleus* strengthened its arguments from theology and law by providing copious detail about recent, actual cases and insisting upon the consistency of its arguments with daily life (Segl in Tanz 1993: 127–54).

The *Malleus* was not, however, all-inclusive of the features of witchcraft as these emerged in the sixteenth century. It makes 'no mention of familiar spirits, of the obscene kiss, or even of the feasting and orgies of the sabbat. Nor is there any reference to the witches' or Devil's mark. The *Malleus* defined witchcraft as the most abominable of all heresies, its four essential characteristics being the renunciation of the Christian faith, the sacrifice of unbaptized infants to Satan, the devotion of body and soul to evil, and sexual relationships with incubi' (Russell 1972: 232; there is a pictorial representation of the devil as a he-goat and the obscene kiss in a mid-fifteenth-century (about 1460) manuscript of Johannes Tinctoris' tract, *Contra Sectam Valdensium* (*Against the Sect of Waldensians*) reproduced in Cohn 1975: Plate 1, and below). Even with these features, the *Malleus* had a durable publication history. Thirteen editions appeared between 1487 and 1520 and sixteen more between 1574 and 1669. Although these editions did not necessarily have large print-runs (and the phenomenon of print played a considerable role in circulating these ideas), they were printed in various cities in Gemany, France and Italy, and they suggest the appeal and durability of the work until more elaborate and specific demonological treatises began to appear after 1580. Copies of the *Malleus* were in the libraries of the early sixteenth-century magician Johannes Trithemius as early as 1492 and slightly later in that of Gianfrancesco Pico della Mirandola. Moreover, some of the omissions in the *Malleus* were compensated for in other works of demonology, so that by 1500 a reading of the *Malleus* and a few other works provided a virtual encyclopedia for the investigation of diabolical sorcery and witchcraft. One such work was the 1524 treatise *Tractatus de Haereticis et Sortilegis* by Paulus Grillandus, which contributed substantially to the image of the witches' sabbat (Lea 1957: 395–412; Hansen 1901: 337–41; *Bibliotheca Lamiarum* 1994: 133–5; on the sabbat, see Bonomo 1959; Cohn 1975: 206–24; Ginzburg 1991; Jacques-Chaquin and Préaud

1993). Later editions of the *Malleus* often included editions of Grillandus's and other related and by then supplementary works.

Nor was the *Malleus* immediately regarded as a definitive work. Its appearance triggered no prosecutions in areas where there had been none earlier, and in some cases its claims encountered substantial scepticism (for Italy, Paton 1992: 264–306). In 1538 the Spanish Inquisition cautioned its members not to believe everything the *Malleus* said, even when it presented apparently firm evidence. Long before then, however, the *Malleus* was the subject of considerable debate among both clerics and lay thinkers (Caro Baroja 1990: 19–43). Indeed, the chief function of the work was to serve as a centrepiece in demonological theory whose arguments might be expanded and added to by such works as that of Grillandus, as well as a focus for arguments and debates concerning particular points it made, some of the latter reflecting traditional rivalry between religious orders and ecclesiastical schools of theology. For example, an attack on some of the central arguments of the *Malleus* was made by the Franciscan Samuel de Cassini in 1505 and answered in favour of the *Malleus* by the Dominican Vincente Dodo in 1507 (Max 1993: 55–62; Lea 1957: 366–8; Hansen 1901; 262–84; *Bibliotheca Lamiarum* 1994: 114–15; Clark 1997: 486–7, 538). A similar criticism by Gianfrancesco Ponzinibio of Florence in 1520 was countered by the support of the *Malleus* position by the Dominican Bartolommeo de Spina in 1523 (Caro Baroja 1990: 32; Max 1993: 55–62; Lea 1957: 385–95; Hansen 1901: 326–7; *Bibliotheca Lamiarum* 1994: 120–2). The cautionary advice of the Spanish Inquisition in 1538 was merely another instance of the kinds of interest, and objections, that the *Malleus* raised.

Ulrich Molitor, doctor of laws and advocate of Archduke Sigismund of Austria, published his treatise *Tractatus de Pythonicis Mulieribus* (*Treatise Concerning Women Who Prophesy*) in 1489. The treatise is important in several respects. The territories of the archduke were contiguous with those in which the trials for diabolical sorcery and witchcraft had begun in the mid-fifteenth century and included lands in which Institoris had worked as an inquisitor. The archduke of Austria had every reason to discover whether the crime occurred in his territories and evidently – like many others – had considerable doubts about the details depicted in the *Malleus*. Molitor's treatise was intended to dispel those archducal doubts. It is cast as a discussion among Molitor himself, the archduke and Conrad Schatz, the chief magistrate of the ducal city of Constance. In the dialogue, the archduke raises sceptical questions which Molitor and Schatz answer (Lea 1955: 542–3; Lea 1957: 348–53; Hansen 1901: 243–6; *Bibliotheca Lamiarum* 1994: 110–11). Another feature of Molitor's work is the series of woodcut illustrations that it included, depicting various forms of witchcraft and diabolical sorcery. Illustrations of witchcraft had occurred as early as the few in Martin le Franc's poem, in the work of Johannes Tinctoris, and in a 1487 treatise on the vices and virtues by Johannes Vintler. From Molitor on, however, the visual depiction of the witch became virtually a genre subject, inviting such artists as Baldung Grien, Cranach, Dürer, Bruegel and others, and adding an important and still perplexing art-historical dimension to the study of the subject (Jacques-Chaquin and Préaud 1993: 397–438; Muchembled 1994: 322; Kors and Peters 1972, 2001: 30–40; Clark 1997: 11–30; Hoak 1985; Davidson 1987; Levack 1992; Lorenz 1994a: 209–19; *Bibliotheca Lamiarum* 1994; Zika 1998).

Shortly after the middle of the fifteenth century similar accusations were made in trials at Evreux in Normandy and at Arras (Hansen 1901: 149–83; Cohn 1975: 230–2; Kieckhefer 1994b: 35–8). In the first, in 1453, Guillaume Adeline, a doctor of theology, was convicted of having made a pact with Satan, of being forced by that pact to preach against the reality of the sabbat, and to have attended sabbats himself. In the second, in 1459–60, known as the 'Vauderie of Arras', the trial of a hermit who was later executed as a witch elicited the names of several other people, who were arrested, named still others, and were themselves executed. In all, thirty-four people were arrested as witches and twelve were executed by burning. As the round of accusations and convictions grew wider still, the duke of Burgundy, Philip the Good, began an investigation that ultimately slowed the accusations and arrests, until the furore died down and the Parlement of Paris finally delivered its verdict on an appeal in 1491, which rehabilitated the memory of all those who had been executed. In his treatise on the Arras trials of 1460 the theologian Johannes Tinctoris provided an illustration of the performance of homage to the devil in the form of a goat (Cohn 1975, Plate l; Veenstra 1998: 152). By the second half of the fifteenth century similar prosecutions had reached as far down the Rhine as Cologne, where two women were burned for witchcraft in 1456 – by then the Rhine valley and its vicinity had also come to serve as a conduit for the new conception of diabolical sorcery and witchcraft, as did southwestern Germany (Lorenz 1994a,b). With several trials in Dommartin in 1498 and Kriens in 1500, the initial outbreak of trials for the new crime of witchcraft and diabolical sorcery slowed dramatically, not to be resumed extensively until the Reformation was well under way, after the middle of the sixteenth century (Blauert 1989: 87–109), although individual trials were held in some parts of western Europe in the early sixteenth century, as was the trial at Orleans reported sharply in one of the letters ot Erasmus in 1501 (Allen 1906: 334–41; Kors and Peters 2001: 231–236).

Throughout the fifteenth century a temporarily distinctive set of material and psychological circumstances in a particular geographical and jurisdictional area had drawn together a number of perennial concerns of Latin Christianity into a single concept of collaborative, conspiratorial, diabolical sorcery, which became 'witchcraft' as the term was used during the later great wave of persecutions after the middle of the sixteenth century and as it is still generally understood. Those circumstances generated a profound mistrust in both certain kinds of neighbours, their attitudes, and their reputations, and in the ability of traditional devotional practices to protect ordinary people from the assaults of those neighbours and their master, the devil. Even the developing arguments on behalf of learned, 'natural' magic – a beneficent and benevolent practice that claimed to help humans by using the occult powers of the stars and celestial spirits as a high and pure learned art – came to be regarded by both theologians and inquisitors potentially at least as a learned variant of diabolical sorcery, even though its most eminent practitioners and defenders passionately attempted to distinguish it from the traditionally despised and feared necromancy, now incorporated into diabolical sorcery (Peters 1978, 1996b; Vickers 1984; Kieckhefer 1990, 1994b, 1997; Clark 1997: 214–32, 236–40).

After the beginning of the sixteenth century, trials for witchcraft declined in number quickly, even in those regions in which the trials had most quickly developed. In Lucerne, Lausanne, Fribourg, Bern and Neuchâtel, for example, where the number of trials had reached more than thirty in the decade between 1477 and 1486, and nearly twenty in the following decade, there were only ten trials in the decade 1497–1506, and none during the decade 1507–16 (Blauert 1989: 18). The cases cited in Dommartin in 1498 and Kriens in 1500 were among a very few until after the middle of the sixteenth century. Although the new doctrines – and the new crime – remained in place and were further considered in a substantial literature during these years, the particular circumstances that had led to the accusations, trials and executions between 1430 and 1500 no longer seem to have existed after the turn of the century. And western Europe had new and pressing devotional and ecclesiological concerns after 1519 that may have pushed sorcery and witchcraft temporarily into the background (Clark 1997: 488–545; Cameron 1998).

But they left a substantial legacy, not only in the literature of demonology and witchcraft produced in the last three-quarters of the fifteenth century, but in a series of new laws and legal and theological/pastoral works produced in the first decade of the sixteenth century. In 1507, for example, the bishop of Bamberg issued a new set of laws concerning capital offences, in which the crime of magic figured prominently and justified the use of torture and execution by burning and which were invoked later in the century during large-scale witchcraft persecutions in Bamberg and elsewhere (Hansen 1901: 278–9). In 1508 the Dominican Bernard of Como published his *Tractatus de Strigiis* (*Treatise concerning Witches*), an extensive discussion of witchcraft that was often reprinted during the next two centuries (Hansen 1901: 279–84; Lea 1957: 370–3; *Bibliotheca Lamiarum* 1994: 119–20; Clark 1997: 522). The popular sermons of the theologian Johann Geiler von Kaisersberg, preached in Strassburg in 1508, condemned not magic (*Zauberei*), but witches (*Von den Unholden oder von den Hexen*) (Hansen 1901: 284–91; Lea 1957: 358–9; *Bibliotheca Lamiarum* 1994: 115–19; Behringer 1998: 56–8, 79–80; Kors and Peters 2001: 236–239). The 1510 *Mirror for Layfolk* (*Layenspiegel*) by Ulrich Tengler identified witchcraft firmly with heresy, fortune-telling, the black art, and magic and included a woodcut depicting various kinds of these being performed (Hansen 1901: 296–306; Lea 1957: 374; Clark 1997: 588). In 1515 the fifteenth-century work of the Spanish theologian Martin of Aries was first printed as *Tractatus de Superstitionibus contra Maleficia seu Sortilegia, quam Hodie Vigent in Orbe Terrarum* (*A Treatise Concerning Superstitions and against Witchcraft and Sorcery which Today Flourish All over the World*) (Hansen 1901: 308–9; Lea 1957: 296–8; Clark 1997: 480, 486–7; *Bibliotheca Lamiarum* 1994: 104; Cameron 1998: 165).

Martin of Aries's title thus drew together the key terms with whose historical development in western Europe this chapter has been concerned – superstition, magic and witchcraft, the latter two now designated *sortilegium* and *maleficium*. These were certainly not synonymous with the kinds of concerns with 'magic' expressed in Greek and Latin antiquity and in early Christianity with which this chapter opened, and Martin of Arles's work appears to have been written primarily because of a problem of determining whether or not a particular religious practice was superstitious. But those who held ideas like those of Martin of Arles and others in the early sixteenth century could now read their contemporary concepts of diabolical sorcery and witchcraft back into the texts of antiquity, and earlier Latin Christianity and see their own concerns mirrored in them, as they could also read Jewish and Christian scripture. The earliest printed and illustrated editions of Ovid and Apuleius, for example, clearly indicate sixteenth-century interpretations of the magic described in them, and that magic is now diabolical sorcery and witchcraft as sixteenth-century thinkers understood it. Even the distant past now appeared to have had the same concerns and fears that plagued the sixteenth-century present. The trials had temporarily slowed and grown fewer; the literature continued to be produced and even increased as the sixteenth century wore on. The pictures kept appearing, now in the hands of gifted artists, now in those of hacks. The crimes, as defined, remained on the books and appeared in new ones. It only remained for the new concerns to continue, the pictures to be produced in greater numbers, and the books to be opened during the political and religious crises later in the sixteenth century.

Bibliography

Abelard, Peter (1971) *Peter Abelard's Ethics*, ed. D. E. Luscombe (Oxford).

Achtemeier, P. J. (1976) 'Jesus and the disciples as miracle workers in the Apocryphal New Testament', in Schüssler-Fiorenza (1976): 49–86.

Affeldt, W., ed. (1990) *Frauen in Spdtantike und Friihmittelalter: Lebensbedingungen – Lebensnormen – Lebensformen* (Sigmaringen).

Allen, P. S. (1906) *Opus Epistolarum Des, Erasmi Roterodami,* I (Oxford).

Ammianus Marcellinus (1952–6) *Res Gestae*, ed. J. C. Rolfe (Cambridge, MA).

Anglo, S. (1977a) 'Evident authority and authoritative evidence: the *Malleus Maleftcarum*', in Anglo (1977b): 1–31.

———— ed. (1977b) *The Damned Art: Essays in the Literature of Witchcraft* (London and Boston).

Ankarloo, B., and Henningsen, G., eds. (1990) *Early Modem European Witchcraft: Centres and Peripheries (Oxford).*

Arbesmann, R. (1945) 'The "Malleus" metaphor in medieval civilization', *Traditio*, 3: 389–91.

Aston, M. (1968) *The Fifteenth Century: The Prospect of Europe (London and New York).*

Bailey, M. (1998) 'Heresy, Witchcraft, and Reform: Johannes Nider and the Religious World of the Late Middle Ages', Ph.D. dissertation (Northwestern University).

Barb, A. A. (1963) 'The survival of the magic arts', in Momigliano (1963): 100–25.

Barlow, C., ed. and trans. (1969) *The Iberian Fathers,* I (Washington, DC).

Behringer, W. (1998) *Witchcraft Persecutions in Bavaria: Popular Magic, Religious Zealotry and Reason of State in Early Modern Europe*, trans. J. C. Grayson and D. Lederer (Cambridge).

Bellomo, M. (1995) *The Common Legal Past of Europe 1000–1800* (Washington, DC).

Bernstein, A. E. (1993) *The Formation of Hell: Death and Retribution in the Ancient and Early Christian Worlds* (Ithaca and London).

Bibliotheca Lamiarum: documenti e immagini della stregoneria dal medioevo all'età moderna (1994) (Pisa).

Blau, L. (1898, repr. 1970, 1974) *Das altjüdische Zauberwesen* (Budapest, Westmead and Graz).

Blauert, A. (1989) *Frühe Hexenvefolgung. Ketzer-, Zauberei- und Hexenprozessen des 15. Jahrhunderts (Hamburg).*

———— ed. (1990) *Ketzer, Zauberer, Hexen. Die Anfänge der europäischen Hexenverfolgung* (Frankfurt).

Blum, E. (1936) *Das staatliche und kirchliche Recht des Frankenreichs in seiner Stellung zu Dämonen-, Zauber- und Hexenwesen (Paderborn).*

Bologne, J. C. (1993) *Du flambeau au bûcher: magie et superstition au Moyen Age (Paris).*

Bonney, F. (1971) 'Autour de Jean Gerson. Opinions de théologiens sur les superstitions et la sorcellerie au début du Xve siècle', *Le Moyen Age*, 77: 85–98.

Bonomo, G. (1959, repr. 1986) *Caccia alle streghe: la credenza nelle streghe dal sec. XIII al XIX connparticolare referimento all'Italia* (Palermo).

Borst, A. (1992) 'The Origins of the Witch-craze in the Alps', in Borst, *Medieval Worlds: Barbarians, Heretics, and Artists* (Chicago): 101–22; original German version in Blauert (1990): 43–67.

Bossy, J. (1985) *Christianity in the West 1400–1700* (Oxford and New York).

———— (1988) 'Moral arithmetic: Seven Sins into Ten Commandments', in Leites (1988): 214–34.

Boureau, A. (1984) *La légende dorée. Le système narratif de Jacques de Voragine* (Paris).

Bozóky, E. (1994) 'From matter of devotion to amulets', *Medieval Folklore*, 3: 91–107.

Brady, T., Oberman, H., and Tracy, J., eds. (1994) *Handbook of European History 1400–1600. Late Middle Ages, Renaissance, Reformation*, I (Leiden, New York and Cologne).

Brashear, W (1992) 'Magical papyri: magic in bookform', in Ganz (1992): 25–58.

Braune, W., and Ebbinghaus, E. A. (1969) *Althochdeutsches Lesebuch*, 15th edn (Tübingen).

Briggs, R. (1996) *Witches and Neighbours: The Social and Cultural Context of European Witchcraft* (London).

Brooke, R., and Brooke, C. (1984) *Popular Religion in the Middle Ages: Western Europe 1000–1300* (London).

Brown, D. C. (1988) *Pastor and Laity in the Theology of Jean Gerson* (Cambridge).

Brown, P. (1970) 'Sorcery, demons and the rise of Christianity: from Late Antiquity to the Middle *Ages*', in *Witchcraft Confessions and Accusations,* Association of Social Anthropologists Monographs, 9: 17–45, repr. in Brown (1972): 119–46.

——— (1972) *Religion and Society in the Age of Saint Augustine* (London and New York).

Brucker, G. A. (1963) 'Sorcery in early Renaissance Florence', *Studies in the Renaissance*, 10: 7–24.

Brundage, J. A. (1987) *Law, Sex, and Christian Society in Medieval Europe* (Chicago and London).

Brundage, J. A. (1995) *Medieval Canon Law* (London and New York).

Burghartz, S. (1988) 'The equation of women and witches: a case study of witchcraft trials in Lucerne and Lausanne in the fifteenth and sixteenth centuries', in Evans (1988): 57–74.

Burnett, C. (1996) *Magic and Divination in the Middle Ages:Texts and Techniques in the Islamic and Christian Worlds* (Aldershot).

Burriss, E. E. (1936) 'The terminology of witchcraft', *Classical Philology*, 31: 137–45.

Caesarius of Aries (1956) *Saint Caesarius of Aries: Sermons*, I, ed. M. M. Mueller (Washington, DC).

Callu, J.-P. (1984) 'Le jardin des supplices au Bas-Empire', in *Du châtiment dans la cité*, 313–57.

Cameron, A. (1983) *The Later Roman Empire* (Cambridge, MA).

Cameron, E. (1998) 'For reasoned faith or embattled creed? Religion for the people in early modern Europe', *Transactions of the Royal Historical Society*, Sixth Series, VIII: 165–87.

Cardini, F. (1979) *Magia, stregoneria, superstizioni nell'occidente medievale (Florence).*

Carey, H. M. (1992) *Courting Disaster: Astrology at the English Court and University in the Later Middle Ages* (London).

Caro Baroja, J. (1990) 'Witchcraft and Catholic theology', in Ankarloo and Henningsen (1990): 19–43.

Cassiodorus (1992) *Variae*, trans. S.J. B. Barnish (Liverpool and Philadelphia).

Chadwick, H. (1976) *Priscillian of Avila* (Oxford).

Clark, S. (1997) *Thinking with Demons: The Idea of Witchcraft in Early Modern Europe* (Oxford).

Cohn, N. (1975) *Europe's Inner Demons: An Enquiry Inspired by the Great Witch-Hunt* (London and New York).

Colker, M. (1978): see under Walter of Châtillon.

Davidson, J. P. (1987) *The Witch in Northern European Art, 1470–1750* (Freven).

Davidson, L. S., and Ward, J. O. (1993) *The Sorcery Trial of Alice Kyteler* (Binghamton).

Daxelmüller, C. (1993) *Zauberpraktiken: eine Ideengeschichte der Magie* (Zurich).

Dickinson, J. G. (1955, repr. 1972) *The Congress of Arras 1435: A Study in Medieval Diplomacy* (Oxford, New York).

Dienst, H. (1990) 'Zur Rolle von Frauen im magischen Vorstellungen und Praktiken – nachausgewählten mittelalterlichen Quellen', in Affeldt (1990): 173–94.

Dierkens, A. (1984) 'Superstitions, christianisme et paganisme à la fin de l'époque mérovingienne: à propos de l'Indiculus superstitionum et paganiarum', in Hasquin (1984): 9–26.

Dinzelbacher, P., with Bauer, D. R., eds. (1990) *Volksreligion im hohen und spciten Mittelalter* (Paderborn and Munich).

Duffy, E. (1992) *The Stripping of the Altars: Traditional Religion in England c. 1400 – c. 1580* (New Haven).

Edel, D. (1995) *Cultural Identity and Cultural Integration: Ireland and Europe in the Early Middle Ages* (Dublin).

Eichberger, D., and Zika, C., eds. (1998) *Durer and His Culture* (Cambridge).

Elliott, J. K. (1993) *The Apocryphal New Testament* (Oxford).

Fanger, C., ed. (1998) *Conjuring Spirits: Texts and Traditions of Late Medieval Ritual Magic* (University Park, PA).

Faraone, C. A., Obbink, D., eds. (1991) *Magika Hiera: Ancient Greek Magic and Religion* (NewYork).

Ferreiro, A., ed. (1998) *The Devil, Heresy and Witchcraft in the Middle Ages: Essays in Honor of Jeffrey B. Russell* (Leiden).

Fletcher, R. (1997) *The Barbarian Conversion from Paganism to Christianity* (Berkeley and Los Angeles).

Flint, V. I. J. (1991) *The Rise of Magic in Early Medieval Europe* (Princeton).

Fox, R. L. (1986) *Pagans and Christians* (Cambridge and New York).

Fraher, R. M. (1989) 'Conviction according to conscience: the medieval jurists' debate concerning judicial discretion and the law of proof', *Law and History Review*, 7: 23–88.

Franz, A. (1909) *Die kirchlichen Benediktionen im deutschen Mittelalter,* 2 vols. (Freiburg im Breisgau, Graz).

Funke, H. (1967) 'Majestäts- und Magieprozesse bei Ammianus Marcellinus', *Jahrbuch für Antike und Christentum,* 10:145–75.

Fürbeth, F. (1992) *Johannes Hartlieb. Leben und Werk* (Tübingen).

Gager, J. (1992) *Curse Tablets and Binding Spells in the Ancient World* (New York).

Ganz, P., ed. (1992) *Das Buch als magisches und als Reprdsentationsobjekt* (Wiesbaden).

Gerald of Wales (1979) *The Jewel of the Church: A Translation of' Gemma Ecclesiastica' by Giraldus Cambrensis,* trans.J.J. Hagen (Leiden).

Ginzburg, C. (1991) *Ecstasies: Deciphering the Witches' Sabbath,* trans. R. Rosenthal (New York).

Given, J. B. (1997) *Inquisition and Medieval Society: Power, Discipline, and Resistance in Languedoc* (Ithaca and London).

Goldin, J. (1976) 'The magic of magic and superstition', in Schüssler-Fiorenza (1976): 115–47.

Gottfried von Strassburg (1960, rev. 1967) *Tristan,* trans. A.T. Hatto (New York).

Graf, F. (1997) *Magic in the Ancient World* (Cambridge, MA).

Griffiths, B. (1996) *Aspects of Anglo-Saxon Magic* (Hockwold-cum-Wilton).

Grodzynski, D. (1974) 'Superstitio', *Revue des études anciennes,* 76:36–60.

Hansen, J. (1901) *Quellen und Untersuchungen zur Geschichte des Hexenwahns und der grossen Hexenverfolgung im Mittelalter* (Bonn).

Harmening, D. (1979) *Superstitio. Überlieferungs- und theoriegeschichtliche Untersuchungen zur kirchlich-theologischen Aberglaubensliteratur des Mittelalters* (Berlin).

—— (1988) 'Hexenbilder des späten Mittelalters – Kombinatorische Topik und ethnographischer Befund', in Segl (1988): 177–94.

—— (1989) 'Magiciennes et sorcières: la mutation du concept de magie à la fin du moyen âge', *Heresis,* 13–14: 421–45.

—— (1990a) 'Spätmittelalterliche Aberglaubenskritik in Dekalog- und Beichtliteratur. Perspektiven ihrer Erforschung', in Dinzelbacher and Bauer (1990): 243–52.

—— (1990b) 'Zauberinnen und Hexen.Vom Wandel des Zaubereibegriffs im späten Mittelalter', in Blauert (1990): 68–90.

Hasquin, H., ed. (1984) *Magie, sorcellerie, parapsychologie* (Brussels).

Hen, Y. (1995) *Culture and Religion in Merovingian Gaul, A.D. 481–751* (Leiden and New York).

Hillgarth, J. N. (1986) *Christianity and Paganism, 350–750: The Conversion of Western Europe* (Philadelphia).

Hoak, D. (1985) 'Art, culture, and mentality in Renaissance society: the meaning of Hans Baldung Grien's *Bewitchced Groom* (1544)', *Renaissance Quarterly,* 38: 488–510.

Hugh of St Victor (1961) *The 'Didascalicon' of Hugh of St. Victor: A Medieval Guide to the Arts* trans. J.Taylor (New York).

Hunt, D. (1993) 'Christianising the Roman Empire: the Evidence of the Code', in *The Theodosian Code,* 143–58.

Jacobus de Voragine (1993) *The Golden Legend: Readings on the Saints,* 2 vols., trans. W. G. Ryan (Princeton).

Jacques-Chaquin, N., and Préaud, M., eds. (1993) *Le sabbat des sorciers en Europe (XVe–XVIIe siècles),* Colloque international E. N. S. Fontenay–Saint–Cloud (4–7 novembre, 1992) (Grenoble).

Jonge, M. de (1985) *Outside the Old Testament* (Cambridge).

Jordan, W. C. (1996) *The Great Famine: Northern Europe in the Early Fourteenth Century* (Princeton).

Kay, R. (1988) *The Broadview Book of Medieval Anecdotes* (Lewiston, NY).

Kee, H. C. (1983) *Miracle in the Early Christian World* (New Haven).

Kelly, H. A. (1968, repr. 1974) *The Devil, Demonology, and Witchcraft* (New York).

—— (1985) *The Devil at Baptism: Ritual, Theology, and Drama* (Ithaca and London).

Kieckhefer, R. (1976) *European Witch Trials: Their Foundations in Popular and Learned Culture* (London).

—— (1987) 'Main Currents in Late Medieval Devotion', in Raitt (1987): 75–108.

—— (1990) *Magic in the Middle Ages* (Cambridge).

———— (1994a) 'The holy and the unholy: sainthood, witchcraft, and magic in late medieval Europe', *Journal of Medieval and Renaissance Studies*, 24: 355–85.

———— (1994b) 'The specific rationality of medieval magic', *American Historical Review*, 99: 813–36.

———— (1997) *Forbidden Rites: A Necromancer's Manual of the Fifteenth Century* (Sutton Press, and University Park, PA).

Klaniczay, G. (1990) *The Uses of Supernatural Power: The Transformation of Popular Religion in Medieval and Early Modern Europe*, trans. S. Singerman, ed. K. Margolis (Princeton).

Klingshirn, W. E. (1994) *Caesarius of Arles: The Making of a Christian Community in Late Antique Gaul* (Cambridge).

Kors, A. C., and Peters, E. (1972) *Witchcraft in Europe, 1100-1700: A Documentary History* (Philadelphia).

———— (2001) *Witchcraft in Europe, 400-1700: A Documentary History*, rev. Edward Peters, (Philadelphia).

Kramer, Heinrich (1991) *Malleus Maleficarum von Heinrich Institoris (alias Kramer) unter Mithilfe Jakob Sprengers. Aufgrund der damonologischen Tradition zusammengestellt. Wiedergabe des Erstdrucks von 1487 (Haiti 9238)*, ed. A. Schnyder (Göppingen).

———— (1971) *The Malleus Maleficarum of Heinrich Kramer and James Sprenger*, trans. M. Summers (New York).

La Roche, R. (1957) *La divination* (Washington, DC).

Lambert, M. (1992) *Medieval Heresy: Popular Movements from the Gregorian Reform to the Reformation* (Oxford and Cambridge, MA).

Larner, C. (1984) *Witchcraft and Religion: The Politics of Popular Belief* (Oxford and New York).

Larner, J. (1980) *Italy in the Age of Dante and Petrarch 1216–1380* (London and New York).

Las siete partidas (1931), trans, and annotated by S. P. Scott (New York).

Lea, H. C. (1955) *A History of the Inquisition of the Middle Ages*, III: 379–549 (New York).

———— (1957) *Materials toward a History of Witchcraft*, I (New York).

Lear, F. S. (1965) *Treason in Roman and Germanic Law* (Austin).

Lecouteux, C. (1983) 'Hagazussa – Striga – Hexe.The Origins of these Terms and Concepts', *Études germaniques*, 38: 161–78.

———— (1985) 'Hagazussa – Striga – Hexe', *Hessische Blätter für Volks- und Kulturforschung*, n.f. 18: 57–70.

Leites, E., ed. (1988) *Conscience and Casuistry in Early Modern Europe* (Cambridge and Paris).

Lerner, R. E. (1991) 'Werner di Friedberg intrappolato dalla lege', in Maire Vigueur (1991): 268–81.

Levack, B. P. ed. (1992) *Articles on Witchcraft, Magic and Demonology: A Twelve Volume Anthology of Scholarly Articles*, 12 vols. (New York and London).

Lorenz, S., ed.. (1994a) *Hexen und Hexenverfolgung in deutschen Südwesten*, I: *Katalogband* (Karlsruhe).

————, ed. (1994b) *Hexen und Hexenverfolgung in deutschen Südwesten*, II, *Aufsatzband* (Karlsruhe).

Luck, G. (1985) *Arcana Mundi: Magic and the Occult in the Greek and Roman Worlds* (Baltimore).

MacMullen, R. (1966) *Enemies of the Roman Order: Treason, Unrest, and Alienation* (Cambridge, MA).

———— (1997) *Christianity and Paganism in the Fourth to Eighth Centuries* (New Haven).

Maggioni, M. L. (1993) *Un manuale per confessori del quattrocento inglese* (Ms. St. John's College, Cambridge S. 35) (Milan).

Maguire, H., ed. (1995) *Byzantine Magic* (Cambridge, MA).

———— (1997) 'Magic and money in the early Middle Ages', *Speculum*, 72:1037–54.

Maire Vigueur, J.-C., ed. (1991) *La parola all' accusato* (Palermo).

Markus, R.A. (1974) *Christianity in the Roman World* (London).

———— (1990) *The End of Ancient Christianity* (Cambridge).

———— (1992) 'From Caesarius to Boniface: Christianity and paganism in Gaul', in Fontaine and Hillgarth (1992): 154–72.

Matthews, J. (1989) *The Roman Empire of Ammianus Marcellinus* (London).

Max, F. (1993) 'Les premières controverses sur la réalité du sabbat dans l'Italie du XVIe siècle', in Jacques-Chaquin and Préaud (1993): 55–62.

McHugh, M. (1972) 'Satan in St. Ambrose', *Classical Folia*, 26: 94–103.

McNeill, J. T., and Gamer, H. M. (1938, repr. 1965,1990) *Medieval Handbooks of Penance* (New York).

Meyer, M., and Mirecki, P. (1995) *Ancient Magic and Ritual Powers* (NewYork).

Milis, L., ed. (1998) *The Pagan Middle Ages* (Woodbridge).

Momigliano, A. (1963) *The Conflict Between Paganism and Christianity in the Fourth Century* (Oxford).

Moore, R. I. (1985) *The Origins of European Dissent* (Oxford and New York).

—— (1987) *The Formation of a Persecuting Society: Power and Deviance in Western Europe, 950–1250* (Oxford and New York).

Mormando, F. (1998) *The Preacher's Demons: Bernardino of Siena and the Social Underworld of Early Renaissance Italy* (Chicago).

Muchembled, R., ed. (1994) *Magie et sorcellerie en Europe du Moyen Age à nos jours* (Paris).

Muldoon, J., ed. (1997) *Varieties of Religious Conversion in the Middle Ages* (Gainesville).

Murray, A. (1992) 'Missionaries and magic in Dark-Age Europe', *Past and Present*, 136: 186–205.

Neusner, J., Frerichs, E. S., and Flesher, P., eds. (1989) *Religion, Science, and Magic: In Concert and in Conflict* (Oxford and New York).

Nie, G. de (1995) 'Caesarius of Aries and Gregory of Tours: two sixth-century bishops and 'Christian magic'', in Edel (1995): 170–96.

Nirenberg, D. (1996) *Communities of Violence: Persecution of Minorities in the Middle Ages* (Princeton).

Nock, A. D. (1972a) 'Paul and the Magus', in Nock (1972b), II: 308–30.

—— (1972b) *Essays on Religion and Magic in the Ancient World*, 2 vols. (Cambridge, MA).

Ostorero, M. (1995) *Folâtrer avec les démons': sabbat et chasse aux sorciers à Vevey, 1448* (Lausanne).

——, Paravicini Bagliani, A., and Utz Tremp, K., eds. (1999) *L'imaginaire du sabbat: édition critique des textes les plus anciens (1430c. – 1440c.)*, Cahiers lausannois d'histoire medievale (Lausanne).

Owst, G. R. (1957) '*Sortilegium* in English homiletic literature of the fourteenth century', in Davies (1957): 272–303.

Pagels, E. (1995) *The Origin of Satan* (New York).

Paravy, P. (1979) 'À propos de la genèse médiévale des chasses aux sorcières: le traité de Claude Tholosan, juge Dauphinois (vers 1436)', in *Mélanges de l'École française de Rome. Moyen Age–Temps Modernes* 91: 373–9; German trans, in Blauert (1990): 118–59.

—— (1981) 'Faire croire. Quelques hypothèses de recherche basées sur l'étude des procès de sorcellerie du Dauphiné au XVe siècle', *Faire Croire*, 119–30.

Paton, B. (1992) *Preaching Friars and the Civic Ethos: Siena, 1380–1480* (London).

Pennington, K. (1993) *The Prince and the Law 1200–1600: Sovereignty and Rights in* the Western Legal Tradition (Berkeley and Los Angeles).

Peters, E. (1978) *The Magician, the Witch, and the Law* (Philadelphia).

—— (1980) *Heresy and Authority in Medieval Europe* (Philadelphia).

—— (1996b) '*Rex curiosus*: a preface to Prospero', *Majestas* 4: 61–84.

Pharr, C. (1932) 'The interdiction of magic in Roman law', *Transactions of the American Philological Association*, 63:269–95.

—— (1952): see under *The Theodosian Code*.

Platt, C. (1996) *King Death: The Black Death and Its Aftermath in Late-Medieval England* (Toronto).

Purkiss, D. (1996) *The Witch in History: Early Modern and Twentieth-Century Representations* (London and New York).

Raitt, J., ed. (1987) *Christian Spirituality: High Middle Ages and Reformation* (New York).

Ridder-Symoens, H. de (1987) 'The intellectual and political backgrounds of the witch-craze in Europe', in Dupont-Bouchat (1987): 37–64.

Roberts, G. (1996) 'The descendants of Circe: witches and Renaissance fictions', in Barry, Hester and Roberts (1996): 183–206.

Rousseau, P. (1979) 'The death of Boethius: the charge of *Maleficium*', *Studi Medievali*, ser. Ill, 20: 871–89.

Rubin, M. (1991) *Corpus Christi: The Eucharist in Late Medieval Culture* (Cambridge).

Russell, J. B. (1972) *Witchcraft in the Middle Ages* (Ithaca, NY).

—— (1977) *The Devil: Perceptions of Evil from Antiquity to Primitive Christianity* (Ithaca and London).

—— (1981) *Satan:The Early Christian Tradition* (Ithaca and London).

—— (1984) *Lucifer: The Devil in the Middle Ages* (Ithaca and London).

Salzman, M. R. (1987) '*Superstitio* in the Codex Theodosianus and the persecution of pagans', *Vigiliae Christianae*, 41: 172–88.

Schäfer, P. (1990) 'Jewish magic literature in late Antiquity and early Middle Ages', *Journal of Jewish Studies*, 41: 75–91.

Schmitt, J.-C. (1983) *The Holy Greyhound: Guinefort, Healer of Children since the Thirteenth Century* (Cambridge and Paris).

Schnyder, A. (1991): see under Kramer.

—— (1993) *Malleus Maleficarum. Kommentar zur Wiedergabe des Erstdrucks von 1487 (Hain 9238)* (Göppingen).

Segl, P., ed. (1988) *Der Hexenhammer. Entstehung und Umfeld des Malleus Maleficarum von 1487* (Cologne andVienna).

—— (1990) 'Spätmittelalterliche Volksfrömmigkeit im Spiegel von Antiketzertraktaten und Inquisitionsakten des 13. und 14. Jahrhunderts', in Dinzelbacher and Bauer (1990): 163–76.

—— (1993) 'Der Hexenhammer – eine Quelle der Altags- und Mentalitätsgeschichte', in Tanz (1993): 127–54.

Sharpe, J. (1997) *Instruments of Darkness: Witchcraft in Early Modern England* (Philadelphia).

Shinners J. (1997) *Medieval Popular Religion, 1000-1500: A Reader* (Peterborough, Ontario).

Smelik, K. A. D. (1977) 'The witch of Endor: 1 Samuel 28 in Rabbinic and Christian exegesis till 800 A.D.', *Vigiliae Christianae*, 33:160–79.

Speyer, W (1992) 'Das Buch als magisch-religioser Kraftträger im griechischen und römischen Altertum', in Ganz (1992): 59–86.

Sticca, S. (1996) *Saints: Studies in Hagiography* (Binghamton).

Strobino, S. (1996) *Francoise sauvée des flammes? Une Valaisienne accusée de sorcellerie au XVsiècle* (Lausanne).

Sullivan, D. (1974) 'Nicholas of Cusa as a reformer: the papal legation to the Germanies, 1451–1452', *Medieval Studies*, 36: 382–428.

Summers, M. (1971): see under Kramer.

Swanson, R. N. (1995) *Religion and Devotion in Europe c. 1215 – c. 1515* (Cambridge).

Tanz, S., ed. (1993) *Mentalitat und Gesellschaft im Mittelalter. Gedenkschrift für Ernst Werner,* (Frankfurt, Berlin and New York).

The Theodosian Code (1952), ed. and trans. C. Pharr (Princeton).

Thee, F. C. R. (1984) *Julius Africanus and the Early Christian View of Magic* (Tübingen).

Thomas, K. (1971) *Religion and the Decline of Magic* (New York).

Thorndike, L. (1923–58, repr. 1964) *A History of Magic and Experimental Science*, 8 vols. (New York and London).

Townsend, D. (1996): see under Walter of Châtillon.

Trachtenberg, J. (1939, repr. 1970) *Jewish Magic and Superstition* (NewYork).

—— (1943) *The Devil and the Jew* (New Haven).

Trusen, W. (1989) 'Vom Inquisitionsverfahren zum Ketzer- und Hexenprozess. Fragen der Abgrenzung und Beeinflussung', in *Staat, Kirche, Wissenschaft*, 435–50.

Van Engen, J. (1994) 'The Church in the fifteenth century', in Brady, Oberman and Tracy (1994): 305–30.

Vauchez, A. (1997) *Sainthood in the Later Middle Ages*, trans. J. Birrell (Cambridge).

Veenstra, J. R. (1998) *Magic and Divination at the Courts of Burgundy and France:Text and Context of Laurens Pignon's 'Contre les devineurs' (1411)* (Leiden, New York, Cologne).

Vickers, B., ed. (1984) *Occult and Scientific Mentalities in the Renaissance* (Cambridge and New York).

Wagner, R.-L. (1939) *'Sorcier'et 'Magicien'* (Paris).

Walter of Châtillon (1978) *Alexandreis: Galteri de Castellione Alexandras,* ed. M. Colker (Padua); *The Alexandreis of Walter of Châtillon: A Twelfth-Century Epic*, trans. D.Townsend (Philadelphia, 1996).

Ward, B. (1982) *Miracles and the Medieval Mind: Theory, Record and Event 1000–1215* (Philadelphia).

Yarnall, J. (1994) *The Transformations of Circe* (Urbana).

Ziegler, P. (1969) *The Black Death* (New York).

Zika, C., ed. (1998) 'Dürer's witch, riding women, and moral order', in Eichberger and Zika (1998): 118–40.

PART II
MIRACLES AND MAGIC

INTRODUCTION: MAGIC AND MIRACLE: CONTESTED CATEGORIES

And he was casting out a devil, and it was dumb. And it came to pass, when the devil was gone out, the dumb spake; and the people wondered. But some of them said, He casteth out devils through Beelzebub the chief of the devils. [Luke 11:14–15]

The debate over the boundary between the Christian miraculous and the realm of magic has its origins in these first responses to the ministry of Christ. The miracles recorded in the Christian Gospels, in the eyes of the faithful, presented evidence of God's approval of the actions of his Son; to opponents of the new faith, such wonders were just that: wonders, marvels and magic. As the Christian Church sought to draw a clear and rigid boundary between magic and miracle, it became clear that any such border would be permeable and contested in the eyes of critics and under pressure from controversy and debate. Simon Magus witnessed the miracles of the apostles and hoped that he could purchase such magical powers, 'so that everyone on whom I lay my hands may receive the Holy Spirit' (Acts 8:18–24). Simon was rebuked for assuming that the ability to work miracles could be learned or purchased, but this tension between miracle and magic was still apparent in early patristic writings in which the representation of Jesus as a magician was debated. Thus Origen was obliged to rebut Celsus' allegation that Jesus was nothing more than a magician, and Justin Martyr's *First Apology* and *Dialogue with Trypho* both engaged with this highly charged controversy.[1] As Christianity expanded and encountered alternative forms and structures of belief, the nascent Christian Church was forced to engage at a practical and philosophical level with the problem of defining magic and religion and of imposing that definition upon rituals and practices that were deeply embedded in societies and cultures. The challenges that motivated and resulted from this encounter have been widely discussed and debated. The foundations of the modern debate were laid by Valerie Flint's *The Rise of Magic in the Early Middle Ages*, now perhaps best read in light of Alexander Murray's recent critique and re-evaluation of her conclusions.[2] In Flint's analysis, the encounter between Christian and non-Christian in early medieval Europe was not simply a narrative of the way in which orthodox Christianity confronted a resilient paganism and addressed its persistence. Rather, Flint argued that even the most energetic defenders of Christian orthodoxy saw a benefit in non-Christian ritual and practice, and attempted to appropriate that which they thought valuable. This was not mere survivalism but rather a conscious attempt to build and construct, with magic 'rescued in the service of human aspiration', and certainly in defiance of certain aspects of reason and regulation'. In this model, precision in the separation of miracle and magic mattered rather less. Covering the later Middle Ages, Catherine Rider's *Magic and Religion in Medieval England* presents a detailed examination of the occult practices and rituals that existed alongside or even within orthodox Christianity. Rider explores both the attempts made to prohibit and arrest such practices and the entanglement of the clergy in the rituals themselves, as well as their suppression. In the three centuries between the Fourth Lateran Council and the Reformation, she argues, the Catholic clergy were exposed more directly to the full panoply of popular religion and were, increasingly, motivated to define the boundary between religion and magic more rigidly and to enforce this distinction.[3]

The medieval Church had presented consistently, at the most basic level, two conceptual categories which shaped discussions of the visible and the invisible. The first, the miraculous, was the preserve of the Church; the second, the demonic, was constructed as its antithesis and rival. The precise boundary between the two, even in the works of the churchmen charged with its delineation, was often no more than speculative and was certainly malleable in the face of conflict and debate within the Christian Church and under pressure from outside. The eighth-century *Indiculus superstitionum et paganiarum*, for example, probably composed within the circle of Boniface, provided a basic reference tool for religious practices which are to be condemned. Many might fall under the loose definition of paganism, but others appeared more closely related to the misunderstanding or misappropriation of the Christian message particularly in relation to devotion to the saints and sacrilege. In this context, superstition (*superstitio*) was defined clearly as something that was uncanonical, not part of true Christianity.[4] However, the Augustinian legacy still loomed large over the medieval debate over true religion and false, miracles and magic. God's intervention in the world, Augustine argued, was manifest both in miracles, extraordinary events and in nature in its ordinary course. The greatest miracle was the miracle of creation, in which all others were located, and the distinction in this respect between miracle and wonder was the intellectual endeavour of man rather than a divinely established truth. The wonders of God exceeded explanation by the mind of men.[5] Thus, the drive to search for the meaning in miracles soon surpassed any attempt to identify causation. Chronicles, lives and legends of the saints recorded miracles and expounded upon them as signs with a meaning to impart, a lesson to be learned. What brought those miracles or wonders to be was scarcely debated.[6] For the twelfth century writer Oderic Vitalis, the duty of the chronicler was to record the events of history as the record of God's interventions in His world and to imbue these with meaning. The 'calamities' that befell Oderic's world in 1134 were handled in this fashion, with 'some men punished by them, as their sins deserved, while others looked on at strange and terrible happenings, and grew pale with fear'.[7]

The area of uncertainty that lay between miracle and magic provided a battle ground for opponents of the medieval Church and for the confessional polemics of the Reformation era. While few would argue against the existence of potential incursions of the divine into the realm of the material, the precise form of these interventions was vigorously contested. Questions of causation, as well as interpretations of meaning, became a crucial part of the debate over the miraculous and the magical, as both acted as indiscriminate terms of abuse and as weapons of precision against specific practices. The suggestion that the debate over miracle and magic operated around the principle of 'what I do is miracle, what you do is magic' is plausible and attractive in its simplicity, but it does not do justice to the complexity of the ideas involved or the intellectual rigour of the debate.[8] Richard Kieckhefer's article here on the specific rationality of medieval magic presents an informative introduction to these controversies. Kieckhefer uses Valerie Flint's analysis of early medieval magic, and her assertion that it was the very irrationality of medieval magic that imbued it with value, as the starting point for a broader examination of the rationality in magic across a broad time period. Flint's assumptions about the nature of medieval magic, and the role of the Church in using rational judgements to condone less than rational practices by imbuing them with a positive value, have come under pressure from the association of magic with the foundation and rise of experimental science, debated and analysed in Lynn Thorndike's multivolume study, and Frances Yates' examination of Giardano Bruno and the hermetic tradition.[9] The 'irrationality' of magic has also been challenged from the other side by Tambiah and others who would argue for a necessary distinction between magic and science but an internal rationality that underpinned both magic and religion as systems of belief that ordered reality on the basis not of causation (science) but participation. Kieckhefer, in a similar vein, presents magic in the Middle Ages as something that appeared to be rational in the eyes of those who used it; such rationality was evident in the assertion of evidence that magic both worked and worked by principles that could be articulated. The imprecision with which the label 'magic' was applied, particularly in a polemical context in which the term was used to disparage the beliefs or wonders associated with rivals, clouds this rationality but does not preclude it. Even as a derivative and pejorative term, magic still assumed a shared meaning and understanding; as Keickhefer notes, Lollard and other critics of late medieval religion who characterized Catholicism as magic were not redefining magic but rather recategorizing certain religious beliefs and observances by redrawing the boundary between miracle and conjuring or religious ritual and magic. The close association between religion and demonic magic is not to be underestimated. While natural magic could, in theory, sit relatively comfortably alongside religious activity, demonic magic was, depending on the individual's viewpoint, either religious or irreligious but certainly not neutral. Such modelling of the potential common ground between the two explains, in part, the difficulty in establishing a workable and enduring delineation of the boundary between miracle and magic. Whether there existed a clerical distinction between religion and magic is only part of the question; it is also necessary to consider the extent to which, if it existed, this distinction was communicated and understood by the laity. In this respect, Kieckhefer's analysis is more positive than some others; he concludes that it is plausible to assume that the lay Christians of medieval Europe were well aware of the difference between the invocation and agency of God, a demon or the occult properties of nature.[10]

The value of Kieckhefer's approach is borne out in the emergent constructive analysis of the medieval supernatural that is not predicated upon the assumption that clerical and popular beliefs were born out of ignorance, irrationality or credulity. The picture of medieval attitudes to miracle and magic painted in recent scholarship must depict human activity and understanding that would be recognizable to those represented in it rather than simply one that is comprehensible to those who approach it from a modern academic 'rational' perspective. It is possible to explain away unusual or disturbing events using scientific method or terminology drawn from modern psychology; bleeding hosts are not the fractured body of Christ but the fungus *micrococcus prodigiosus*, and prophetic visions are the consequences of over (or under) consumption of food.[11] A belief in supernatural causation emerges from this reductionist narrative as evidence of ignorance and suggestibility rather than as an accepted part of existence. A useful recent corrective comes in the form of Robert Bartlett's *The Natural and the Supernatural in the Middle Ages*, which encourages the examination of the medieval supernatural derived from the categories that were used at the time to think about such phenomena.[12] There was, he argues, no single, uniform belief system within which these ideas and events operated, but neither is there any particular value in an examination of the supernatural that follows the agenda set by debates over learned and popular culture. Rather, the attempt to explain the world, categorize its peoples and understand its natures became increasingly complex, deriving its terminology from scholastic theology but applying the vocabulary of *miracula* and *mirabilia* in a rather more flexible fashion that reflected parallel and conflicting systems of belief and a range of new experiences and encounters. Tales of miracles and wonders, and advice on how they might be productively interpreted, reflect a multifaceted dialogue between official dogma and local custom and the views of churchmen and their congregations. Bartlett's analysis accepts that the past, and particularly the discussion of the supernatural, was rarely neatly ordered and uses this discordance to construct a more nuanced image of medieval belief. The diversity of belief that might be accommodated within the 'economy of the sacred' need not be seen as evidence of incomprehension and superstition but as an indication of the existence of a vibrant and accommodating late medieval piety.[13] Far from serving as mere entertainment, by situating medieval encounters with the supernatural and explaining these events within their cultural and historical context, it is possible to identify and understand their purpose and interpretation by successive generations.

This process of reinterpretation of the supernatural is equally evident in the discussion of the miracles of the saints in the literature of the Reformation. In the pages of Protestant histories and polemic, such miracles were held up for ridicule and mockery, as a reflection of deception and gullibility, but also, and more significantly, as part of a broader conspiracy to undermine the foundations of the Christian faith and construct a false and fragile ecclesiastical edifice from traditions, legends and false wonders. The iconoclasm of the reformers extended beyond the images and relics of the saints into their *vitae* and miracles; miracles did not disappear from the post-Reformation mental landscape but were rather imbued with an alternative meaning and interpretation that was infinitely more destructive. The second article in this part, 'Lying histories fayning false miracles' examines the handling of the Catholic miraculous by English evangelicals and explores the extent to which the debate over doctrinal truth and falsehood in the present was conducted on the battlefield of the past. Accounts of false and feigned miracles enabled the characterization of the Catholic Church as the 'false' Church and the depiction of the saints not as holy men and women but as conjurers, invoking devils and demons in order to perform wonders that would deceive the faithful.[14] The argument that the age of miracles had ceased was repeated regularly in reformed sermons, treatises and anti-Catholic polemic but the debate over the nature and presence of 'false wonders' in the life of the medieval Church ensured that the miraculous would occupy a central role in the fashioning of new confessional identities. At a basic level, and perhaps inadvertently, the continued discussion of the false miracles of the saints ensured that the memory of these legends and accounts also remained part of religious memory; for all the vigour with which Protestant writers attacked the saintly miraculous, in so doing, they presented for public consumption a detailed narrative of these events that could well be read with a more sympathetic eye. 'Lying wonders', 'egregious impostures' and 'Ignatian fables' that might otherwise have disappeared from view were thus preserved in Protestant print, and miracles remained a potent symbol and component in debate.[15] This agenda and its consequences was not unique to the English context. Philip Soergel's recent study of miracles and the Protestant imagination addresses both the issue of definition and identification of 'miracle' (Wunderzeichen) and the interaction of writing on miracles with the burgeoning genre of Wunderzeichenbücher (wonder-sign books) in Lutheran Germany.[16] Such debates and narratives were informed by a changing, and increasingly hazardous, political and confessional (and even climatic) context – a context in which the theological message might well be submerged by the preoccupations of the reader, the entertainment of the narrative and the tendency for the regulation of belief and interpretation to reinforce that which it sought to undermine.

Far from suppressing the miraculous and the magical, the impact of the Reformation was to reinvigorate debate over its presence and meaning in the life of the Christian community. As Soergel suggests, 'in the history of religion and culture, there are no sudden changes, no revolutions that alter everything in their wake', and the debates of the Reformation owed much to the attitudes and arguments of an earlier age.[17] The third article in this part, Lorraine Daston's study of 'marvellous facts', engages with such evolutions in the meaning and function of facts and evidence, including wonders and miracles, across the medieval and early modern debates. Miracles, she argues, were (albeit briefly) a form of evidence that was both patent to the senses and, crucially, dependent upon intention; in contrast, prodigies might be presented as the ancestor of scientific fact. The shifting focus and concerns of medieval and early modern natural philosophy and theology located such supernatural events within an altogether different context, and Daston charts the evolution of perception and classification, alongside questions of evidence, in the face of change. Patristic and medieval attempts to define miracle and magic and establish a workable barrier between the two had utilized and modelled a vocabulary of the natural, preternatural and supernatural causation which came under pressure in the aftermath of the Reformation. By the seventeenth century, the 'preternatural' category had become more closely tied to nature to the point where prodigies and portents lost their status as 'signs' and became conceptually neutral facts. At the same time, debates over miracles focused less upon the evidence that they might present and more upon evidence for their existence. The heterogeneity of the Christian miracle, and the continued influence of the analytical models of Augustine and Aquinas into the sixteenth century, had contributed to a blurring of the boundary between miracle and marvel which was highly unsatisfactory in the sight of Protestant writers. The naturalization of the 'preternatural' in the seventeenth century reflected the evolution of this category from the demonic associations that it had acquired in the era of the Reformation, just as the allegation that miracles might be feigned or constructed eroded the assumption that as a pure form of evidence they required no interpretation.

Such an analytical approach and its conclusions sit readily amid the range of recent scholarship on miracles, wonders, signs and providences in the early modern period. Alexandra Walsham has explored in its full potential the assumption in Calvinist theology that the Christian God was 'an assiduous, energetic deity who constantly intervened in human affairs', examining the desire in post-Reformation England to find meaning in disaster and explain the apparently inexplicable.[18] In its providentialism, English Protestantism showed itself to be capable of contextual adaptation and of a syncretic approach to the supernatural that allowed seemingly 'superstitious' events to act as a vehicle for the transmission of a moral and theological meaning. The persistence of the wonder in the culture of English Protestantism was not evidence of 'failure' in the Reformation assault on magic and miracle but rather evidence of the extent to which a new theology might be transmitted effectively through a familiar medium.[19] In this manner, traditional beliefs and models were slowly divested of their original meaning and new levels and layers of interpretation superimposed until the original foundations for belief and understanding were almost invisible.[20] Protestant interventions in the debate over magic and miracle imbued the controversy with a new rhythm and agenda and located it firmly within an evolving religious context. Providence neither shattered belief in the capacity of supernatural forces to shape events nor negated the obligation to interpret the meaning that inhered in such occurrences.

Notes

1. Lampe, G. W. H. (1965), 'Miracles in the acts of the apostles', in C. F. D. Moule (ed.), *Miracle*. London: A. R. Mowbray & Co., p. 212; Justin Martyr, *Apology*, 30.1 and *Dialogue with Trypho* 69.7.

2. Murray, A. (1992), 'Missionaries and magic in dark-age Europe', *Past and Present* 136, 186–205. See also Russell, J. (1994), *The Germanisation of Early Christianity*, New York, NY: Oxford University Press; Brown, P. (1996), *The Rise of Western Christendom. Triumph and Diversity 200–1000 AD*. Cambridge, MA: Harvard University Press.

3. Rider, C. (2012), *Magic and Religion in Medieval England*. Chicago, IL: University of Chicago Press; see also Bailey, M.D. (2001), 'From sorcery to witchcraft: clerical conceptions of magic in the middle ages', *Speculum*, 76, 960–90; Boureau, A. (2006), 'Demons and the Christian community', in M. Rubin and W. Simons (eds), *The Cambridge History of Christianity, 4: Christianity in Western Europe, c.1100–c.1500*. Cambridge: Cambridge University Press, pp. 420–32; Peters, E. (1978), *The Magician, the Witch and the Law*. Hassocks: The Harvester Press.

4. Rau, R. (1968), *Bonifatii epistulae, willibaldi vita bonifatii*. Darmstadt wiss. *Buchges*, 5, 19.

5. Augustine (1966–72), *City of God Against the Pagans*, W. Green (ed and trans.), 7 vols. Cambridge, MA: Harvard University Press, III. 308.

6. Ward, B. (1982) *Miracles and the Medieval Mind*. London: Scolar Press, pp. 3–7.

7. Oderic, *Historia Ecclesia*, 6, pp. 434–5.

8. Neusner, J. (1989), 'Science and magic, miracle and magic in formative judaism', in J. Neusner, E. S. Frerichs and P. McCracken Flesher (eds), *Religion, Science and Magic*. New York, NY: Oxford University Press, p. 63.

9. See also Hansen, B. (1986), 'The complementarity of science and magic before the scientific revolution', *American Scientist*, 74(2), 128–36; Styers, R. (2004), *Making Magic: Religion, Magic and Science in the Modern World*. Oxford: Oxford University Press; Eamon, W. (1983), 'Technology as magic in the late middle ages and renaissance', *Janus*, 70, 171–212; Pinto, L. (1973), 'Medical science and superstition: a report on a unique medical scroll of the eleventh-twelfth century', *Manuscripta*, 17, 12–21; Scragg, D. G. (ed.) (1989), *Superstition and Popular Medicine in Anglo-Saxon England*. Manchester: Manchester Centre for Anglo-Saxon Studies; Weston, L. M. C. (1995), 'Women's medicine, women's magic: the old english metrical childbirth charms', *Modern Philology*, 92, 279–93; Henry, J. (2012), *Religion, Magic and the Origins of Science in Early Modern England*, Aldershot: Ashgate.

10. Such questions are not unique to the study of medieval magic and popular religion. For a consideration of lay understanding of the boundary between magic and religion in the early modern period, see Gentilcore, D. (1992), *From Bishop to Witch. The System of the Sacred in Early Modern Terra D'Otranto*. Manchester: Manchester University Press; Klaniczay, G. (1990), *The Uses of Supernatural Power. The Transformations of Popular Religions in Medieval and Early Modern Europe*. Princeton, NJ: Princeton University Press; Gurevich, A. (1990), *Medieval Popular Culture: Problems of Belief and Perception*, János M. Bak and Paul A. Hollingsworth (trans.). Cambridge: Cambridge University Press; Ginzburg, C. (1992), *The Cheese and the Worms. The Cosmos of a Sixteenth Century Miller*. Baltimore, MD: Johns Hopkins University Press; Monter, W. (1983), *Ritual Myth and Magic in Early Modern Europe*. Athens, OH: Ohio University Press.

11. Ciobanu, E. A. (2012), *The Spectacle of the Body in Late Medieval England*. Iasi: Editora Lumen; Matteoni, F. (2008), 'The jews, the blood and the body in late medieval and early modern Europe', *Folklore*, 119(2), 182–200; Walker Bynum, C. (1988), *Holy Feast and Holy Fast: The Religious Significance of Food to Medieval Women*. Berkeley, CA: University of California Press; Bell, R. (1987), *Holy Anorexia*. Chicago, IL: University of Chicago Press.

12. Bartlett, R. (2008), *The Natural and the Supernatural in the Middle Ages*. Cambridge: Cambridge University Press.

13. Scribner, R.W. (1987), 'Cosmic order and daily life: sacred and secular in pre-industrial German society', and 'Ritual and popular belief in Catholic Germany at the time of the Reformation', both reprinted in his *Popular Culture and Popular Movements in Reformation Germany*. London: Hambledon, pp. 1–16, 17–47; Finucane, R. C. (1977), *Miracles and Pilgrims: Popular Beliefs in Medieval England*. London: Palgrave Macmillan; Duffy, E. (1992), *The Stripping of the Altars: Traditional Religion in England, c.1400–c.1580*. New Haven, CT: Yale University Press.

14. Parish, H. L. (2002), 'Lying histories fayning false miracles: magic, miracles and medieval history in reformation polemic', *Reformation and Renaissance Review*, 4(2), 230–40; Parish, H. L. (2005), *Monks, Miracles and Magic. Reformation Representations of the Medieval Church*. London: Routledge; Marshall, P. (1995), 'The rood of boxley, the blood of hailes and the defence of the henrician church', *Journal of Ecclesiastical History*, 46, 689–96; Marshall, P. (2003), 'Forgery and miracles in the reign of Henry VIII', *Past and Present*, 178, 39–73.

15. For a fuller discussion of these ideas, see Walsham, A. (2003), 'Miracles and the counter reformation mission to England', *Past and Present*, 46(4), 782; Watt, T. (1991), *Cheap Print and Popular Piety 1550–1640*. Cambridge: Cambridge University Press. For a discussion of the repetition of the vision of Bernard of Clairvaux in Protestant ballads: Collinson, P. (2002), 'John Foxe and national consciousness', in Christopher Highley and John N. King (eds), *John Foxe and His World*. Aldershot: Ashgate, pp. 31–34; Collinson, P. (1997), 'Truth, lies, and fiction in sixteenth-century protestant historiography', in Donald R. Kelley and David Harris Sacks (eds), *The Historical Imagination in Early Modern Britain: History, Rhetoric and Fiction, 1500–1800*. Cambridge: Cambridge University Press, pp. 55–7.

16. Soergel, P.M. (2012), *Miracles and the Protestant Imagination: The Evangelical Wonder Book in Reformation Germany*. New York, NY: Oxford University Press.

17. Soergel, *Miracles and the Protestant Imagination*, p. 182.

18. Walsham, A. (1999), *Providence in Early Modern England*. Oxford: Oxford University Press, p. 2.

19. See also Walsham, A. (1994), ' "The fatall vesper": providentialism and anti-popery in late jacobean London', *Past and Present*, 144, 36–87; Walsham (1999), 'Vox piscis: or, the book fish: providence and the uses of the reformation past in caroline Cambridge', *English Historical Review*, 114, 574–606; Walsham, (2012), 'History, memory and the english reformation', *Historical Journal*, 55 899–938; Lake, P. and Questier, M. (eds) (2002), *The Antichrist's Lewd Hat: Protestants, Papists and Players in Post Reformation England*. New Haven, CT: Yale University Press; Hall, D. (1990), *Worlds of Wonder, Days of Judgement. Religious Popular Belief in Early New England*. Boston, MA: Harvard University Press; Parish, *Monks, Miracles and Magic*; Scribner, *Popular Culture and Popular Movements in Reformation Germany*.

20. Scott Dixon, C. (1996), *The Reformation and Rural Society: The Parishes of Brandenburg-Ansbach-Kulmbach, 1528–1603*. Cambridge: Cambridge University Press, pp. 201–2.

CHAPTER 4

'LYING HISTORIES FAYNING FALSE MIRACLES': MAGIC, MIRACLES AND MEDIEVAL HISTORY IN REFORMATION POLEMIC

Helen Parish

In the mid 1540s, an English priest attempted to demonstrate to his congregation the veracity and reality of the teaching of the pre-Reformation church on the theology of the Eucharist. Nicholas Germes, by John Bale's account of the incident, a 'popysh priest', pricked his fingers with a pin at the moment of the consecration to give the illusion of Christ's blood on the altar.[1] The visible eucharistic miracle had been a common feature of late medieval devotional literature, but in the context of the Henrician Reformation of the 1530s and 1540s the exposition of a false miracle of this kind had an even stronger polemical purpose and effect. Conservative clergy such as Germes might well have viewed such a wonder as a powerful tool of propaganda and persuasion, and in the standard medieval *exampla* the miracles surrounding the host had often involved a sceptic or critic. The most famous illustration on the eve of the Reformation was perhaps the 'Mass of St Gregory', in which the pope convinced a doubting woman of the truth of Catholic teaching with the sight of 'raw flessch bleedyng'. However the experience of such miracles was not a clerical monopoly, and tales and legends of eucharistic wonders had a powerful and popular resonance in late medieval devotion.[2] For this reason, a miraculous fraud that deluded and deceived the faithful, such as that perpetrated by Germes could be an equally potent weapon in the hands of evangelical propagandists such as Bale. The false miracle, the pious fraud was not just an act of meaningless mendacity which could be mocked and derided in humorous polemical exchanges. In the eyes of evangelical writers, the feigned wonder became a fundamental feature of the false church across the historical ages, and the re-evaluation of the miracles of the medieval church was to be an important part of the shaping of a historical identity for the nascent Protestant church. Miracles that were not of divine origin were recast as the work of the devil, with the result that the history of the medieval church and the marvels of its saints acquired a fresh and vital significance in the literature of the reformation.

Under the influence of Gregory the Great and St Augustine, miracles had become the connection between the material world of man and the mystical world of the divine, a sign of the continuing influence of the divine in the material, and a fleeting glimpse of the heavenly powers.[3] The saint not only embodied another world but, in the promise of miracles, allowed the faithful access to it. While the number of pilgrims to the great medieval shrines in England was declining on the eve of the Reformation, the saints and their miracles still occupied a central role in popular piety and perceptions of the church. At a local level, the position of the saint as beneficent patron with miraculous powers was all the more important given the material proximity of the relics of the saint to the community: as Aron Gurevich suggests the saint 'found a much easier path to the consciousness of the common people than did the idea of a distant, invisible and awe-inspiring God'.[4] Although the canonised saint might have been the embodiment of heroic feats of holiness, it was the image of the saint as miracle worker which was to have the most immediate relevance for those who called upon holy men and women in times of need. The collection of miracle stories at the shrines of the saints, and the emergence of hagiographical stereotypes which placed miracles at the heart of the *lives* of the saints ensured that the wonderworking capacity of the saints lay at the heart of their cults.

Pope Urban VIII's decrees at the start of the seventeenth century recognised this close relationship between sanctity and the supernatural, and located intercessory miracles and heroic virtue at the heart of the ecclesiastical definition of sainthood. However as Weinstein and Bell have indicated there was little scientific objectivity in the evaluation of claims to the miraculous, and the impetus for canonisation often came from the local community rather than the institutional church.[5] While the Church demanded evidence of doctrinal purity to ensure a uniformity of faith within the community of the saints, the *lives* of the saints focused upon heroic virtue and purity of life. It was this evidence of heroic virtue that separated bona fide miracles from false wonders, and enabled the church and the faithful to make the all-important distinction between the supernatural power of the saints and demonic frauds or magic. Scriptural examples ranging from the Moses' encounter with Pharaoh's magicians, to Saul's congress with the witch of Endor, to the efforts of Simon Magus to lay claim to the miraculous powers of the apostles presented a model in which those who enjoyed divine favour triumphed, but also held up the real and potent power of magic.

In the first Christian centuries, missionaries relied upon this distinction between miracle and magic to demonstrate the superiority of the supernatural power of the church over that of the pagan gods, but the separation of miracle and magic was highly subjective. Gregory the Great had permitted the use of miracles as a tool of conversion, but when King Aethelbert first encountered Augustine, he insisted that their meeting take place outside, fearing that the papal missionary was to resort to harmful magic.[6] Keith Thomas has argued that the dependence of the early church upon miracles as a means of persuasion saddled the medieval church with the conviction that there was a relationship between its control over the supernatural and its role as custodian of doctrinal truth. The miracles of the saints, therefore, were a crucial component of what Thomas referred to as the 'magic of the medieval church' which came under threat from the evangelical reassertion of the distinction between magic and religion in the sixteenth century and beyond.[7]

Medieval hagiography attributed almost every conceivable kind of miracle to the holy men and women of the church, but such literature had a remarkable capacity to become self-validating. The medieval *lives* of the saints established the conformity of their subjects to accepted biblical patterns of holiness and access to the supernatural, using the authority of the past to buttress the claims of the present. Perceptions of holiness were far from static, and the *lives* of the saints embodied not only their own actions but also the expectations of others; as Pierre Delooz has suggested, saints are 'remodelled to collective mental representations'.[8] The seeds of the medieval image of sanctity had been sown in the record of the life of Christ and the lives of the apostles and martyrs as recounted in Scripture. Thomas Becket turned water into wine, St Martin raised the dead to life, and saints did battle with demons as Christ withstood temptation in the desert.[9] Thus the *life* of a saint recorded the deeds of the individual, their miracles, and the growth of their cult, but it also became one link in the historical chain that both brought back to life the champions of the past and helped to cast the heroes of the future by lending historical legitimacy to their actions. However this self perpetuating quality of medieval hagiography would only endure as long as the assumptions on which it was predicated continued to have a hold on the imagination of the faithful and, more particularly, those who recorded and studied the *lives* of the saints. The repetition of key themes in traditional hagiography had created an image of sanctity that was built upon the supposition that virginity, chastity, monasticism, miracles and the defence of the liberties of the church were the defining characteristics of the saint. For an emerging evangelical church that looked to Scripture rather than tradition, words rather than wonders for its historical identity, these traditional ecclesiastical heroes were all too often the embodiment of powers and principles that were diametrically opposed to those of early Protestantism. The chronicles of the medieval church and the lives of the saints, John Foxe claimed, were 'lying histories faining false myracles', and the reconstruction of these histories, and the exposition of the false miracles of the medieval church, were a necessary part of the search for Protestant historical identity.

The reputation of the medieval saints faced a powerful and devastating challenge from the Protestant Reformation. As the names of the saints were deleted from service books and statues removed from churches, so the recorded *lives* of the saints were broken apart and reconstructed, with the heroes of the medieval past portrayed as villains of the present. The supernatural wonders associated with the saints were re-examined, and their miracles recast as magic, worked by the power of the devil and testimony to the growing presence of Antichrist within the historical and institutional church. At the heart of this rejection of the miraculous powers of the saints was the assertion that the age of true miracles had passed.[10] The miracles of the apostles had ensured that the roots of the church would be firmly planted, it was argued, but once the church had been established, such wonders were not necessary.[11] In his commentary on Matthew (1535) Martin Luther had distinguished between the ongoing and enduring miracle of faith, and the historical miracles of the flesh, and concluded that the expectation of further miracles of this kind was tantamount to putting God to the test.[12] The 'doctors which planted the church watered it with miracles', William Tyndale argued, but this was not a legitimation for the use of miracles to support doctrinal innovation: the miracles of the saints, he argued, were no proof of doctrine, but served only to confirm Thomas More's 'false imagination'.[13] Richard Sheldon, in his *Survey of the Miracles of the Church of Rome* quoted Gregory to hammer home the same point, 'therefor for the greatest part signes of miracles and virtues shall be withdrawen from the faithfull in the holy Church'.[14] The words of Scripture and the writings of the Fathers, he claimed 'tell vs that after the planting of the church and establishing the Gospell … the ordinarie vse of miracles should cease'. For defenders of Catholic miracles to claim otherwise, he argued, was to admit that their faith was new, and that it was a lack of historical continuity in the Roman Church which left it in need of miracles.[15] The precise point at which the church had ceased to require miraculous support was uncertain, with estimates ranging from the end of the apostolic period, to the conversion of Constantine,[16] to the expansion of the missionary effort to England in the sixth century.[17] There was certainly no obvious date at which ecclesiastical miracles should have ceased: the promise made by Christ to the apostles (Mark 16, John 14:12) did not suggest that the capacity to work wonders would be withdrawn. The apparent lack of scriptural support for the evangelical position fuelled the suspicion in the mind of Catholic writers that their opponents were simply searching for a justification for the absence of miracles in their own church, and the paucity of wonders associated with their heroes. Bellarmine argued that the lack of Protestant miracles was clear evidence that the reformed churches did not enjoy divine favour, and contrasted the numerous miracles of Francis Xavier with Martin Luther's failure to even resuscitate a fly.[18]

However there was rather more to the Protestant assertion that the age of miracles had passed than the simple denial of the powers of the saints. William Tyndale argued that the wonders associated with the medieval saints were not simply frauds, but rather a demonstration that the church of Rome was the fulfilment of the prophecy of Christ that 'deceivers shall come with miracles'.[19] William Perkins' rejection of Catholic miracles was fuelled by the familiar contention that the age of divine miracles had ceased, but culminated in the conclusion that 'the miracles of the Popish Church at this day are indeed either no Miracles, or false and deceitful wonders'.[20] These false and deceitful wonders were more than a simple sleight of hand. The apparent consensus among writers on both sides of the religious divide in the sixteenth century that the devil could and did work wonders before the faithful made possible a more negative and damaging interpretation of the *lives* and miracles of the saints. In his *Answer* to Thomas More, William Tyndale claimed that the prophecy of Paul (2 Thess 2) could be applied to the medieval church, arguing that 'unto them that love not the truth hath God promised by the mouth of Paul to send them abundance and strength of false miracles, to stablish them in lies and to deceive them'.[21] However the assumption that the devil could and did work wonders invited speculation as to which miracles and wonders attributed to the saints deserved to be seen as 'true' miracles, and which should be dismissed as devilish deceptions. John Bale hoped that the history of the English church outlined in his *Actes of the Englysh Votaries* would enable the reader 'to iudge false miracles, that they be no more deuylishly deceyued'.[22] Bale did not doubt that St Augustine had worked miracles as part of his missionary work in England, but concluded that the wonders associated with the Gregorian mission merely confirmed that Augustine and his monks were the fulfilment of the prophecy of Matthew 24. The miracles of the saints, which had been promoted as the antithesis of pagan magic, were condemned by Bale and other evangelical writers as frauds and wonders perpetrated by the devil, and dismissed as the fruits of magic, conjuring, and even necromancy.

The Reformation depiction of the miraculous *topoi* of the past as demonic frauds and wonders had far reaching implications. The parallels drawn in hagiography between the miracles of the saints and the miracles of Christ and the Apostles had not been lost on evangelical writers. 'You compare your miracles with those of Christ and his Apostles', Richard Sheldon wrote, 'wherein you shew yourselues to bee of Antichrist, for both hee and his shall doe the same, pretending the name of Christ and power of the Lambe'.[23] Sheldon noted that even the 'superstitious viscount of Sussex' had laughed at the legend of St Francis, but complained that the defenders of Catholicism were afraid to concede that even one miracle might be false, as once one miracle was proven to be a false illusion, it would be legitimate to ask more far reaching questions about not just the individual saint, but about the whole construct of sanctity that underpinned the cult of the saints. The mockery of medieval miracles, and the representation of individual saints as the agents of the devil not only discredited the individual – as in the Henrician assault on Thomas Becket – but also broke a link in the hagiographical chain that linked the heroes of the past with the apostles and with the church of the present.

The attack on the miracles of the saints was both sweeping and specific. Richard Sheldon dismissed the whole of the Golden Legend as a collection of 'copper fables', but also presented his reader with a selection of tales from the legends of the saints that he believed bordered on the ridiculous.[24] Indeed Sheldon complained that the *lives* of the saints contained such fooleries that it was impossible to abstain from laughter. Among the highlights from medieval hagiography that he appeared to find especially amusing, Sheldon included an incident from the *life* of St Hyacinth in which a cow was brought back to life by the intercession of the saint, and the description in the *life* of St Anthony of fish listening attentively to the saint's preaching, and even responding to his words.[25] John Foxe protested that numerous 'fabulous miracles' had been recorded in the *lives* of several medieval saints, from St Cuthlake, whose 'fables and lying miracles' included enclosing the devil in a boiling pot, and compelling evil spirits to build houses, to Bishop Adelm, who according to William of Malmesbury had given the power of speech to a nine year old child and restored to its original form a broken altar stone brought from Rome. Reflecting on the miracles, and the apparent gullibility of William of Malmesbury, Foxe concluded that 'father experience hath taught the worlde now adaies more wisdom in not beleuing such practices'.[26]

The volume of similar incidents recounted in evangelical literature might suggest that the finger-pricking priest in Surrey was not the only individual to have perpetrated a fraudulent eucharistic miracle for polemical purposes. Miracles, or feigned miracles, such as this were almost inevitably the target of evangelical writers, given the close association between miracles and doctrinal truth in the mind of their Catholic opponents. Where 'miracles' such as that claimed by Germes, appeared to support theological statements that were antagonistic to the evangelical interpretation, it was vital that such wonders be discredited. Bale's account of Germes' actions simply sought to expose a practical and physical explanation for the events, and Richard Sheldon adopted a similar approach, arguing that the blood associated with eucharistic miracles was usually dark and decaying, unlike the blood of Christ, that would be living and fresh.[27] The English investigation into the Blood of Hailes in the 1530s came to much the same conclusion, with the relic being dismissed as gum, duck blood, or bird-lime.[28] However, as Keith Thomas has suggested, it was the Mass, more than the other sacraments of the medieval church, that became most closely entwined with popular attitudes to magic and the miraculous. The recitation of the prayers of the Mass was believed to work 'like a charm upon an adder', and Thomas concluded that despite the good intentions of the theologians, it was the 'magical notion' that uttering the words of consecration brought about the transformation of the bread and wine which had the strongest hold upon the laity.[29] William Perkins denounced the Catholic clergy as conjurers, who used magic and sorcery to effect the eucharistic miracle, a choice of words that no doubt had a powerful popular resonance with those for whom the function of the priest was most readily defined using terminology more closely associated with the realm of magic.[30]

This association between the Mass and the magical was ruthlessly exploited by John Bale and by John Foxe in their assessment of the legend and the miracles of St Odo, the tenth century Archbishop of Canterbury. In Bale's account, Odo had presided at a debate over the true interpretation of the eucharist, at which a party of monks had argued strongly that at the consecration the bread and wine did indeed become the body and blood of Christ. Strong opposition to this standpoint, Bale claimed, and a lack of scriptural foundation for their opinions, had left the monks at the point of defeat, until Odo, 'by a cast of legerdemayne' had effected a real and physical transformation of the elements into flesh and blood, presenting to the assembled congregation a bleeding and broken host.[31] John Foxe echoed Bale's condemnation of this, and other, miracles of Odo, 'as where they imagine that he shuld see from heauen a sword fall into the scabberd of kyng Ethelstan … and also where he should turn the bread of the aultar … into lyuely flesh and fro[m] flesh into breed agayne: to confirme the people which before doubted in the same.'[32] The miracles associated with Odo, Foxe claimed were but 'idle stories', and such 'lying histories' of his life 'make him indeed to seem worse than he was' – strong praise for a tenth century archbishop from the sixteenth century martyrologist![33] For both Bale and Foxe, the miracle of Odo proved nothing except that there were divisions within the tenth century church over the theology of the eucharist. Odo's miracle was not an indication of divine sanction for the teaching of the Catholic church, but rather a sign of the shaky foundations of Odo's reputation for sanctity, and for the doctrine of the Mass, which now appeared as an error, supported only by magic and manipulation.

It was this link between magic and miracles which was to prove the most destructive. Where Foxe had criticised the frauds associated with Odo, Bale had brought out the full implications of the association of frauds with diabolic deceptions, and chose to focus on the issue of magic and 'legerdemayne'. Odo was not the only victim of Bale's assault on the magic of the medieval church and its clergy. The magical learning of Elmer, a monk of Malmesbury, Bale claimed, enabled him to fly, Archbishop Oswald was as learned in sorcery as the magicians of Pharaoh, and St Dunstan used his skills in necromancy to make images speak.[34] Ecclesiastical magicians were to be found among the occupants of the chair of St Peter, with Silvester II and Gregory VII emerging as the favoured targets of evangelical writers. Silvester, it was alleged, had secured his election as pope by necromancy, and Gregory VII, according to Bale, had used his knowledge of magic to impose celibacy upon an unwilling clergy, and to work false miracles, including the transformation of communion bread into a finger.[35] However other popes were equally suspect. Bale claimed that Benedict IX's artifice had first secured the accession of his father and uncle to the papal throne, and then 'by his magicke [Benedict] brought to passe that he succeeded them'. Benedict's advisers, Lawrence and John Gratian were both 'notorious coniurers', educated in the magical arts by Pope Silvester.[36] Boniface VIII's conflict with secular authority in the form of Philip of France was unlikely to endear him to English evangelicals keen to secure the subordination of the church to the king, but Boniface was also condemned as a magician and necromancer, perhaps reflecting his ethereal visitations to his predecessor, in the attempt to secure his resignation.[37] It was not only the medieval popes who came under scrutiny. The pontificate of Paul III (1534–1549) revealed that certain Renaissance popes continued the apparently traditional practice of papal magic and necromancy. Bale described Paul as 'very conning in astrologie, southsaying, and coniuring … an astrologian, a Magician, a wyzard' who had in his service a number of individuals who were 'raysers of euyl spirites in the bodies of dead men', employed to cast his nativities and destiny by the stars.[38] By 1611, John Napier had identified some twenty two popes who were 'abhominable Necromancers'.[39] Medieval saints, and occupants of the See of St Peter emerged from Bale's rewriting of history as a dynasty of conjurers and necromancers, installed as popes not by apostolic succession but by their skills in demonic magic.

The apparent presence of wonder-working saints and papal soothsayers in the Roman church allowed evangelical propagandists to represent Catholicism as a false religion, a church preaching doctrines that were shaped by magic, venerating as heroes saints whose reputation rested on their ability to work false and diabolic wonders, and headed by conjurers and necromancers. The false miracle was not an innocuous deception, but rather an indication of the power of the devil and his agents within the Roman church, and the search for feigned wonders and legerdemaynes in the medieval church became a crucial part of the separation of personalities of the past into adherents of true and false religion. Where the medieval biographers of the saints had turned to the heroes of the past to ensure that their subjects conformed to accepted patterns of holiness, Protestant history writers looked for evidence of divergence, deviation, and diabolic influence in the effort to shatter both the traditional image of sanctity and the historical harmony of sainthood. The miracles of the saints, which had been the building blocks of much of medieval hagiography, were turned by Protestant writers into a defining characteristic of the false church, with the result that the legends of the saints, or the reconstructed legends, became a central feature of the emerging historical identity of the reformed churches. Despite the Reformation appeal to the authority of Scripture and the church of the Apostles, evangelical writers recognised the importance of reclaiming the middle ages from the pages of 'lying histories fayning false miracles'.[40]

Notes

1.   J. Bale, *The first two partes of the Actes of the Englysh Votaries* (Antwerp, 1551), Pt 1 sig.Gvi^v.

2.   E. Duffy, *The Stripping of the Altars. Traditional Religion in England 1400–1580* (New Haven & London, 1992), pp. 102–7.

3.   B. Ward, *Miracles and the Medieval Mind. Theory, Record and Event 1000–1215* (Aldershot, 1982), p. 216.

4.   A. Gurevich, *Medieval Popular Culture. Problems of Belief and Perception* (Cambridge, 1990), p. 43.

5.   D. Weinstein and R.M. Bell, *Saints and Society. Western Christendom 1000–1700* (Chicago & London, 1982), p. 141.

6.   B. Colgrave, R.A.B. Mynors ed., *Bede's Ecclesiastical History of the English People* (Oxford, 1992), I. 25.

7.   K. Thomas, *Religion and the Decline of Magic* (London, 1991), pp. 28, 58.

8.   P. Delooz, *Sociologie et Canonisations,* (Liege, 1969).

9.   Ward, *Miracles.,* pp. 168–9.

10.   D.P. Walker, 'The Cessation of Miracles', in I. Merkel, A.G. Debus eds., *Hermeticism in the Renaissance. Intellectual History and the Occult in Early Modern Europe* (Washington, 1988), pp. 111–24.

11.   J. Calfhill, *An Answer to John Martiall's Treatise of the Cross,* ed R. Gibbins (Parker Society, Cambridge, 1846), p. 333; J. Mason, *The Anatomie of Sorcery wherein the wicked impietie of charmers and such like is discouered and confuted* (London, 1612), sig E1r.

12.   Walker, 'Cessation', p. 112.

13.   W. Tyndale, *Answer to Sir Thomas More's Dialogue,* ed., H. Walter (Parker Society, Cambridge, 1850) p. 130–1.

14.   R. Sheldon, *A Survey of the miracles of the Church of Rome, prouing them to be Antichristian* (London, 1616), sig. C1r.

15.   ibid., sig.R1r-v.

16.   Mason, *Anatomie of Sorcerie,* p. 7.

17. Walker, 'Cessation', p. 111; Sheldon, *Miracles* sig.R1r.

18. R. Bellarmine, *Disputationes de Controversiis,* in Walker, 'Cessation', p. 118. For a discussion of some of the miracles later associated with Luther see R.W.Scribner, 'Incombustible Luther: The Image of the Reformer in Early Modern Germany', in Scribner, *Popular Culture And Popular Movements in Reformation Germany* (London, Ronceverte, 1987), pp. 323–353.

19. Tyndale, *Answer,* p. 130.

20. W. Perkins, *A Discourse on the damned art of witchcraft* (Cambridge, 1608), Epistle dedicatory.

21. Tyndale, *Answer,* p. 129.

22. Bale, *Votaries,* pt.1, sig.Av^v.

23. Sheldon, *Miracles,* sigs.Y3r-v.

24. Sheldon, *Miracles,* sig. I3v.

25. Sheldon, *Miracles,* sigs Ff3v-Ff4v.

26. J. Foxe, *The Actes and Monumentes of these latter and perillous dayes* (London, 1570) pt. I, fol.167–168.

27. Sheldon, *Miracles* N1v.

28. P. Marshall, 'The Rood of Boxley, the Blood of Hailes, and the defence of the Henrician Church', *JEH* 46 (1995), pp. 689–696.

29. Thomas, *Religion and the Decline of Magic,* pp. 36–7.

30. W. Perkins, 'A Reformed Catholike', in I. Breward ed., *The Work of William Perkins* (Courtenay Library of Reformation Classics, Abingdon, 1970), p. 574.

31. Bale, *Votaries,* pt.1 sigs.G6r-v.

32. Foxe, *AM* pt.I fol.199.

33. ibid., fol.199.

34. Bale, *Votaries,* pt.2, sigs.C7r-D2r; Pt.1, sig.I3r, Pt.2 sig.I1r; H.L.Parish, 'Impudent and Abhominable Fictions', *Sixteenth Century Journal* (forthcoming).

35. Bale, *A Mystery of Iniquitye conteyned within the heretycall Geneaologye of Ponce Pantolabus* (Antwerp, 1545), p. 16; *Acta Romanorvm Pontificum a dispersione discipulorum Christi* (Basle, 1558), sig K8v, I1v;*Votaries* Pt. 2 sigs.B1r, D6v; Foxe, *AM* pt.I, pp. 217–8, 228; M. Judex & J. Wigand, *Ecclesiastica Historia* (Basle 1560–74), Cent X col.547–8; T. Swinnerton, *A Mustre of the Schismatyke Bysshoppes of Rome* (1534), sig. A6v.

36. J. Bale (tr.J.Studely), *The Pageant of Popes* (London, 1574), fol.75–6; Foxe, *AM* pt.1 fol.218–9.

37. ibid., fol.125ff.

38. ibid., fol.231.

39. J. Napier, *A Plaine discovery of the whole revelation of St John* (Edinburgh, 1611), fols.56–8.

40. Foxe, *AM* pt.I fol.199.

CHAPTER 5
MARVELOUS FACTS AND MIRACULOUS EVIDENCE IN EARLY MODERN EUROPE

Lorraine Daston

Introduction: Facts versus evidence

According to a commonplace view, facts are evidence *in potentia:* mustered in an argument, deduced from a theory, or simply arranged in a pattern, they shed their proverbial obstinacy and help with the work of proof and disproof. However, in modern usage facts and evidence are nonetheless distinct categories, and crucially so. On their own, facts are notoriously inert – 'angular,' 'stubborn,' or even 'nasty' in their resistance to interpretation and inference. They are robust in their existence and opaque in their meaning. Only when enlisted in the service of a claim or a conjecture do they become evidence, or facts with significance. Evidence might be described as facts hammered into signposts, which point beyond themselves and their sheer, brute thingness to states of affairs to which we have no direct access: the clues pertaining to a crime committed without witnesses, the observations testing a theory about the true configuration of the solar system or the workings of the mind, the ruins of a civilization that vanished millennia ago, the indices that predict the future.

On this view, facts owe no permanent allegiance to any of the schemes into which they are impressed as evidence. They are the mercenary soldiers of argument, ready to enlist in yours or mine, wherever the evidentiary fit is best. It is exactly this fickle independence that makes them so valuable to a certain view of rationality, one that insists upon the neutrality of facts and staunchly denies that they are 'theory-laden.' Were facts to be frozen into any one evidentiary scheme, fixed signposts forever pointing in the direction of a single conjecture, they would lose their power to arbitrate between rival arguments or theories.

Implicit in this conventional distinction between facts and evidence is that in order for facts to qualify as credible evidence, they must appear innocent of human intention. Facts fabricated as evidence, that is, to make a particular point, are thereby disqualified as evidence. Nature's facts are above suspicion, because presumed free of any intention, but many man-made facts also qualify: the blood-stained weapon found at the scene of a murder counts as incrimating evidence as long as it was not planted there with the intention of incriminating; the unaffected simplicity of the witness adds weight to testimony as long as it was not feigned with the intention of persuading. Similarly, many methodological precautions in contemporary science, such as the double-blind clinical trial and the fixing of statistical significance levels before the experiment, were instituted to thwart the intention, however unconscious, to confirm a pet hypothesis. Note that the planted weapon, the affected testimony, the skewed empirical results lose neither their status as facts nor their potential to serve as evidence for conjectures *other* than those intended: so long as they do not point in the intended direction, these fabricated facts can be made to point somewhere else with no loss of evidentiary force. It is the distinction between facts and evidence that is at issue, not the reality of the facts per se, nor their quality as evidence in general.

I have sketched the well-known distinction between facts and evidence not to defend or attack it (as does a vast literature in the history and philosophy of science), but rather as a preface to a key episode in the history of the conceptual categories of fact and evidence. My question is neither, 'Do neutral facts exist?' nor 'How does evidence prove or disprove?' but rather, 'How did our current conceptions of neutral facts and enlisted evidence, and the distinction between them, come to be?' How did evidence come to be incompatible with intention, and is it possible to imagine a kind of evidence that is intention-laden?

It is my claim that partial answers to these questions lie buried in the sixteenth- and seventeenth-century literature on prodigies and miracles. I shall argue that during this period prodigies briefly became the prototype for a new kind of scientific fact, and that miracles briefly exemplified a form of evidence patent to the senses and crucially dependent on intention. Both conceptions diverge sharply not only from current notions of facts and evidence, but also from medieval views on the nature of prodigies and miracles. Prodigies were originally closely akin to portents, divine signs revealing God's will and things to come; miracles were more intimately associated with the private experience of grace than with the public evidence of the senses. Prodigies were transformed from signs into nonsignifying facts, and miracles into compelling evidence, as part of more sweeping changes in natural philosophy and theology in the mid-seventeenth century.

My account of both transformations and the context in which they occurred is divided into five parts. I first outline the patristic and medieval distinctions between marvels and miracles, and the related distinctions between natural, preternatural, and supernatural causation. Part 2 traces the gradual naturalization of the preternatural in the early modern period. I then examine in part 3 how prodigies and portents became the first neutral facts in the reformed natural philosophy of the mid-seventeenth century, losing all status as signs. In part 4, I turn to controversies over the definition and meaning of miracles both in Protestant England and Catholic France in the latter half of the seventeenth century, arguing that for some theologians, miracles briefly became 'pure' evidence, requiring neither interpretation nor further corroboration. In the fifth, concluding part, I show how the debate over the evidence *of* miracles became a debate over the evidence *for* miracles in the early eighteenth century.

Natural, preternatural, and supernatural

In the early sixteenth century the received views on miracles, marvels, and their relationship to the natural order still derived principally from the teachings of Augustine, and, especially, from those of Thomas Aquinas. These authorities were sometimes difficult to square with one another. Augustine praised all of nature as a miracle, and complained that familiarity with such marvels as the individuality of each and every human being had unduly blunted our sense of wonder. Since nature was simply the will of God realized, it made no sense to speak of miracles as *contra naturam*: 'For how can anything done by the will of God be contrary to nature, when the will of so great a creator constitutes the nature of each created thing?'[1] Marvels shaded into miracles without a sharp break for Augustine, for both testified to how far the power of God exceeded that of human understanding. This is why Augustine parried the objections of pagan philosophers to Christian miracles like the resurrection by listing natural wonders – the wood of a certain Egyptian fig tree that sinks rather than floats, the Persian stone that waxes and wanes with the moon, the incorruptible flesh of the dead peacock – that also defied explanation: 'Now let those unbelievers who refuse to accept the divine writings give an explanation of these marvels, if they can.'[2] However, certain events deserved to be singled out from the perpetual wonder of nature as true miracles because of the message they bore. The miracles of the early Christian church were of this sort, consolidating faith and unity by a wave of conversions, and, at least in later life, Augustine was also willing to credit miraculous cures performed by saintly relics and also those performed on behalf of his side of the Donatist controversy as serving the same special ends.[3]

Aquinas treated miracles within an Aristotelian framework that made nature considerably more orderly and autonomous than Augustine's profusion of marvels, ordinary and extraordinary, had allowed. Dividing causes into a higher and lower order, Aquinas contended that God's miracles transgressed only those of the lower order, which exist by God's will, not by necessity.[4] Miracles are of three kinds, and each kind admits of degrees, depending on how far the ordinary powers of nature are surpassed: miracles of substance [*miracula quoad substantiam*] overcome an absolute impossibility in nature (for example, two bodies in the same place at the same time); miracles of subject [*miracula quoad subjectum*] accomplish what nature can do, but not in that body (for example, speech in a cat); miracles of mode [*miracula quoad modum*] accomplish what nature can do in that subject, but not by those means (for example, a sudden cure effected by a holy relic).[5]

Yet according to Aquinas we recognize miracles by their subjective effect on us rather than by their objective causes:

The word miracle is derived from admiration, which arises when an effect is manifest, whereas its cause is hidden. ... Now the cause of a manifest effect may be known to one, but unknown to others. ... : as an eclipse is to a rustic, but not to an astronomer. Now a miracle is so called as being full of wonder; as having a cause absolutely hidden from all: and this cause is God. Wherefore those things which God does outside those causes which we know, are called miracles.[6]

God performs miracles for an audience, which credits them in proportion to the wonder they excite, which wonder in turn measures the magnitude of the audience's ignorance. Miracles convert and convince by their psychological effects; they are God's oratory.

Like Augustine, Aquinas often blurred the boundary between the marvelous and the miraculous, albeit for different reasons. For Augustine, especially in his earlier writings, there existed in principle no sharp distinction between the marvelous and the miraculous (and for that matter, the natural as well), for all sprang directly from God. Augustine was largely unconcerned with how God brings about these effects, much less with orders of causation.

Aquinas, in contrast, drew a principled distinction between the truly supernatural (God's unmediated actions) on the one hand, and the natural (what happens always or most of the time) and the preternatural (what happens rarely, but nonetheless by the agency of created beings), on the other. Marvels belong, properly speaking, to the realm of the preternatural:

> For the order imposed on things by God is in keeping with that which is wont to occur in things for the most part, but it is not everywhere in keeping with what always occurs: because many natural causes produce their effects in the same way usually, but not always; since sometimes, though seldom, it happens otherwise, whether on account of a defect in the power of an agent, or through the indisposition of the matter, or by reason of a stronger agency: as when nature produces a sixth finger in a man.[7]

Not only unaided nature, but created spirits such as angels and demons can produce preternatural effects, although these fall short of true miracles on ontological grounds: spirits must work 'through the local movement of a body,' for God alone can 'induce any form into corporeal matter, as though matter were in this obedient thereto.' However, we humans are hard put to separate the supernatural wheat from the preternatural chaff, for both excite wonder when we are ignorant of the causes, and wonder is the hallmark of the miraculous.[8]

As one might expect in a body of beliefs discussed and elaborated over a millennium, medieval views on the relationships between the natural, preternatural, and supernatural were by no means monolithic, and it is possible to find many variants on and exceptions to both the Augustinian and Thomist views, not to mention tensions between the two. The medieval Christian doctrine of miracles was further complicated by the heterogeneity of the category: not only scriptural miracles, but also the miracles of saints and their shrines and relics, the miracles of the sacraments, the miracles of judicial ordeals (at least until their abolition by the fourth Lateran Council in 1215), the historical miracles recounted by the chronicles, and the 'jocular' miracles inserted in sermons all had to be subsumed therein, and the conceptual integrity of the category suffered accordingly.[9]

Nonetheless, the general outlines of the doctrine as it crystallized in the thirteenth and fourteenth centuries can be discerned with some clarity. First, there was a tendency, always present among theologians and increasingly pronounced after the Aristotelian synthesis of the thirteenth century, to segregate the natural and the preternatural from the supernatural, having recourse to the latter only as a last resort. Second, although theologians followed Aquinas in principle by defining miracles by the abrogation of the lower order of causes, they also followed him in practice by making universal wonderment the actual criterion. Third, despite the ensuing practical difficulties of distinguishing between the preternatural marvel and the supernatural miracle, theologians nonetheless continued to insist on the theoretical distinction between the two.

This distinction was fortified in the sixteenth century, when the preternatural came to be ever more closely associated with the dubious and possibly demonic activities of magic and divination.[10] Because of these demonic associations some historians have assumed that medieval theologians deemed theurgy to be supernatural, but this does not do justice to the nicety of the conceptual distinctions that reserved the supernatural for God alone. Although demons, astral intelligences, and other spirits might manipulate natural causes with superhuman dexterity and thereby work marvels, as mere creatures they could never transcend from the preternatural to the supernatural and work genuine miracles. Well into the seventeenth century and beyond, sober thinkers warned against the counterfeit miracles of Satan, who 'being a natural Magician … may perform many acts in ways above our knowledge, though not transcending our natural power.'[11]

Theology cemented the barrier between the preternatural and the supernatural; scholastic natural philosophy erected a similar barrier between the preternatural and the natural. The natural order itself was a matter of nature's habitual custom rather than of nature's inviolable law, what usually rather than what infallibly happened.[12] Although *scientia* properly so called dealt in demonstration and therefore in what must be the case, it did not pretend to be comprehensive. There were pockets of experience that defied necessity, and therefore scientific treatment. Magnetism, the virtue of coral to ward off lightning, the antipathy between elephant and dragon – few doubted the existence of such phenomena, but because their occult (that is, 'hidden') causes were inaccessible to sense and reason, they formed no part of natural philosophy.[13]

Indeed, particulars and a fortiori singularities of all kinds, whether ascribed to occult causes or to chance, were not readily susceptible to scientific explanation, which trafficked in universals and regularities: Aquinas thought the study of singulars in ethics, alchemy, and medicine might at best approximate but never attain scientific certitude.[14] Thus even strange or singular phenomena without the slightest whiff of the demonic were effectively excluded from the natural, by dint of being excluded from natural philosophy. Although preternatural phenomena were in theory difficult to distinguish from natural events (since they belonged to the same, lower order of causation), and in practice difficult to distinguish from supernatural events (since they evoked the same astonishment and wonder), they nonetheless constituted a third ontological domain until the late seventeenth century.

It might be argued that the inherent conceptual instability of the category of preternatural phenomena predestined it for collapse into the sturdier categories of the natural and supernatural. However, the preternatural was very long in meeting its doom, not only resisting attempts to absorb it into the natural and into the supernatural, but also expanding in extent and intellectual importance throughout the sixteenth century. Fifty years before its demise around the turn of the eighteenth century, the preternatural preoccupied theologians and natural philosophers more urgently than ever before.

The early modern vogue for the preternatural arose from a confluence of circumstances: Marsilio Ficino's revival of magic, both natural and demonic, imbued scholarly Neoplatonism with a strong affinity for the occult;[15] the new printing centers north and south of the Alps spewed out edition after edition of books of secrets retailing household recipes, virtues of herbs and stones, tricks of the trades, and 'natural magic';[16] the witchcraft trials concentrated theological and legal attention on the precise nature of demonic meddling in human affairs;[17] the voyages of exploration brought back tales and trophies of creatures and landscapes more marvelous than anything in Pliny or Mandeville;[18] the religious and political upheavals set in motion by the Reformation also triggered an avalanche of crude broadsides and learned Latin treatises that anxiously interpreted comets, monstrous births, rains of blood, and any number of other strange phenomena as portents.[19] Although portents were the very prototype of signifying events, spectacular and unsettling messages sent by God to herald triumph or catastrophe, it was this last category of portents and prodigies that ultimately supplied reforming natural philosophers of the seventeenth century with a new kind of fact that signified nothing at all.

The naturalization of the preternatural

Not all preternatural events qualified as portents or prodigies. Medieval chroniclers enlivened their accounts with comets, earthquakes, monstrous births, and the like, and often, but not always, speculated on their significance. For example, Gerald of Wales in his *Topographia hibernia* (ca. 1185) allows that some strange events may be portents, such as a large fish with three gold teeth caught two years before the arrival of the English, which might 'prefigure the imminent conquest of the country,' but he records many others – a ship-swallowing whirlpool, a Limerick woman with a beard and a mane – without interpretation.[20]

The difficulty in interpreting preternatural events as divine signs was twofold: first, their ambiguous status between natural and supernatural; and second, theological distrust of divination as most likely demonic. Although *bona fide* miracles were always missives from God – signs of divine power, intent, approval or disapproval – establishing their *bona fides* was in practice a delicate matter of balancing theological context against admittedly incomplete natural knowledge. This balancing act became increasingly precarious in the early modern period, when heterodox sects, reformed natural philosophy, and fear of demonic deception forced a reexamination of the definition and function of miracles.

Both context and the possibility[21] of a natural explanation determined which preternatural events counted as signs: in a time of plague, war, or religious schism, the two-headed cat or shooting star that might have otherwise aroused only mild interest as a wonder provoked anxious interpretations as a portent. The interpretations of portents also teetered dangerously close to divination, which (except for predictions based on natural signs – for example, a red sky in the morning presages a storm at sea) was regularly and emphatically condemned from the twelfth century on by the Catholic church as a usurpation of God's perogative to foretell the future. Prodigies were in principle exempt from the ban on divination, as were visitations from God, angels, or saints in dreams, but in practice the distinction was difficult to maintain.[22]

In the latter half of the sixteenth century religious and political turmoil combined with an intense intellectual interest in the preternatural, first, to magnify the portentous associations of strange events and, second, to provoke ever more concerted attempts to distinguish genuine (that is, divine) portents from demonic counterfeits and superstitious divination. (That portents never fully merged with miracles can be seen by the lively interest that Protestant theologians took in their interpretation, however firmly they insisted that miracles per se had ceased after the early Church.)[23] In general, the former trend was fed by the popular press, broadsides, and vernacular tracts, and the latter was sustained by more scholarly writings, although there was some crossover.[24] This distinction in audiences was to play an important role in late seventeenth-century attempts to discredit the ominous significance of portents, and, ultimately, to belittle the importance of miracles.

In the late sixteenth century, however, scholars like Jean Bodin, hack writers like Pierre Boaistuau, and the composers of broadside ballads saw eye-to-eye on the proliferation and meaning of portents in general, even if they differed in their interpretations of specific cases. Bodin took Aristotle to task for claiming that nothing was truly unnatural: 'For as to monsters and signs, which occur out of the order of nature [*outre l'ordre de nature*], one cannot deny that they carry some signification of the wrath of God, which he gives to men to make them repent and convert to Him.'[25] Boaistuau and the several other authors of the enormously popular *Histoires prodigieuses* (1567) argued that God sometimes sent 'signs and prodigies, which are most often the heralds, trumpets, and advance couriers of justice.'[26] Stephen Batman advertised his 1581 compendium of 'the strange Prodigies hapned in the Worlde' with the promise to reveal 'divers secrete figures of Revelations tending to mannes stayed conversion towardes God';[27] countless broadsides preached, in the words of a 1619 broadside printed in Augsburg on the occasion of a comet, that: 'War and blood are in the door/Hunger and rising prices draw near/Pestilence hovers in the air/This we have earned by great sin and our godless living.'[28] Strange events – monstrous births, oddly shaped fish and animals, apparitions of armies in the clouds, rains of iron and blood, bleeding grape vines, comets, flood tides, swarms of insects and vermin – all became grist for the interpreter's mill, and were as often as not pressed into service as propaganda on one or another side of the raging religious controversies of the day.[29]

However, the printed collections of prodigies, learned and lay alike, did not saddle every prodigy they reported with a portentous interpretation. Some might be signs either of impending events (an invasion of Turks, an outbreak of plague, the coming of the Messiah), or religious heresy, or more generally of God's wrath and power – but not all. Bodin believed only comets and monsters to be true portents, and took care to distinguish these from superstitious and impious divination.[30] Boaistuau and his coauthors blithely related prodigies that testified to 'the excellence of man' (a man who slept for thirty years, another who washed his face and hands with molten lead, women who had borne litters of children, a prodigiously obese man) and to the fecundity of nature (stones that could render brackish water sweet, nereids and tritons, volcanoes), rather than to divine judgements and messages. Even the German broadsides, generally the gloomiest of a gloom-and-doom genre, sometimes published simple descriptions, without interpretations.

In these collections of strange events, popular and learned, the genuinely intermediate character of the preternatural, that twilight zone between the natural and supernatural, stubbornly asserted itself, whatever the declared orientation of the author. Avowedly naturalist accounts could not expunge the numinous association that clung to Siamese twins or an aurora borealis; avowedly supernaturalist accounts were equally unable to resist the temptation to include patently unportentous natural wonders such as hot springs and petrified forests. The cabinets of curiosities, those museums of the preternatural, contained a great many objects, secular as well as religious, that can only be described as relics – for example, the Ashmolean Museum in Oxford had among its holdings St. Augustine's pastoral crook.[31]

Analogously, churches had long displayed curiosities of no particular religious significance, such as a giant's bones, ostrich eggs, and unicorn horns, alongside splinters of the true cross and other more conventional objects of devotion.[32] Pious authors heaven-bent on assembling instances of divine providences padded their account of remarkable deliverances at sea and blasphemers struck down by lightning in mid-oath with tales of a man who had voided a serpent seven ells long and kidney stones in the shape of 'divers sorts of Animals.' No pretense was made of drawing religious lessons from these latter 'prodigious and astonishing' things.[33] Until the late seventeenth century the category of the preternatural retained a certain phenomenological homogeneity – wondrous objects and events not unambiguously miraculous in the strict sense – that defied tidy attempts to divide it in half down the line of natural versus supernatural causes. Preternatural events always qualified as wonders, but only sometimes as signs.

Sixteenth-century demonology briefly reinforced this phenomenological homogeneity with a causal unity of sorts. Increasingly, preternatural events were attributed not just to any remarkable conjunction of natural causes, but to conjunctions of natural causes cunningly wrought by demons. The effect of such demonic attributions was to weaken ties not only with purely natural explanations but also with purely supernatural ones. Indeed, the latter tendency was the more pronounced, for the religious peril of becoming a dupe to a counterfeit miracle, staged by the devil to trap the unwary, loomed large in an imagination haunted by the terrors of heresy, demonic magic, and witchcraft.[34] Alert to this peril, writers on the demonic preternatural actually tended to emphasize the natural character of preternatural events, in order to steal the devil's thunder. Thus Sir Thomas Browne accused Satan of 'distorting the order and theory of causes perpendicular to their effects,' deluding the credulous into taking stars and meteors as portents: 'Thus hath he [Satan] also made the ignorant sort believe that natural effects immediately and commonly proceed from supernatural powers.'[35] William Fleetwood, recalling St. Paul's warning about the 'lying wonders of Satan' (2 Thess. 2:9), denied demons the power of working true miracles, although he did 'not deny but that Spirits may foresee many Events that lye hid in their Natural Causes, which are concealed from *Us* but not from *Them*; because I do not know the extent of their intellectual Powers' (*EM*, p. 108).

Nor were these worries about how to distinguish preternatural, demonic wonders from supernatural, divine miracles confined to English Protestants: a Sieur de Sainte-Foy (possibly the pseudonym for the Jesuit Père Annat) insinuated that the Port-Royal miracle of the Sacred Thorn was a false miracle, the work of demons manipulating subtle natural causes in order to mislead good Catholics into the Jansenist heresy.[36] French Catholic writers on demonic imposture, however, did tend to concentrate more on superstitions like divination than on portents, possibly because they were saddled with the additional task of keeping sacramental as well as revelatory miracles pure from the taint of demonic imposture.[37]

The proximate impact of these warnings was to discredit preternatural phenomena as true signs from on high; they were rather to be rejected as forgeries from below. The ultimate impact was to naturalize almost all of them, even when natural explanations for specific cases were wanting, as was the rule rather than the exception. The writings of the demonologists show that it was not sufficient simply to posit natural causes for preternatural phenomena in order to naturalize them fully; it was also necessary to rid nature of demonic agency. To simplify the historical sequence somewhat: first, preternatural phenomena were demonized and thereby incidentally naturalized; then the demons were deleted, leaving only the natural causes. This two-step process should not be insisted on too adamantly: there were plenty of respectable theologians, both Protestant and Catholic, who invoked demonic plots well into the eighteenth century. In general, however, the activities and autonomy of the devil declined steadily in the last quarter of the seventeenth century, for reasons I shall discuss in part 5. The overall thrust of attempts to demonize preternatural phenomena was to discredit them as true signs. Counterfeit portents and false miracles pretended to a status they did not deserve, namely, that of the 'signs and wonders' (Heb. 2:4) that truly announce God's will and doctrine.

While miracles became ever more closely associated with evidence, especially in the writings of late seventeenth-century Protestant theologians, preternatural phenomena became ever less so. The English Hebraist John Spencer, writing in 1665, condemned the belief that prodigies were portents as 'a very Vulgar and Pernicious Error,' endangering philosophy by inhibiting the search for natural causes, corrupting divinity by allowing 'a liberty for men to bring into it what Divine signs they please without warrant from Scripture or reason,' and undermining the state by giving 'every pitiful Prodigy-monger … credit enough with the

People' to gainsay authority 'by telling them that heaven frowns upon the laws, and that God writes his displeasure against them in black and visible Characters when some sad accident befals the complyers with them.' Spencer did blame the devil for fobbing off prodigies as miracles in an attempt to deceive the gullible, but he was at least as concerned about the human manipulation of such alleged signs for nefarious purposes.[38] Meric Casaubon was willing to allow for sincere (though mistaken) claims to the power of divination, suggesting that 'many natural things before they come to that passe, as to be generally known or visible, have some kind of obscure beginnings, by which they be known by some long before.' People or animals with unusually acute senses may indeed foretell coming events by these 'natural foregoing signes.'[39] Although these indicators were in Casaubon's view genuine signs, they were neither supernatural nor preternatural, but prosaically natural – for example, the throbbing bunions that precede a storm.[40]

From signs to facts

Thus did preternatural phenomena lose their religious meaning as signs. But they did not cease to be of interest for learned as well as for lay audiences. Not only did vernacular collections of prodigies, now frankly advertised as 'pregnant with pleasure and delight,' continue to spill forth from the presses in multiple editions; the annals of the fledgling scientific academies and other journals serving the Republic of Letters also devoted many pages to monstrous births, celestial apparitions, cyclones, diamonds that glowed in the dark, and other strange phenomena. These entries in the *Philosophical Transactions of the Royal Society of London*, the *Journal des Savants*, the *Histoires et Mémoires de l'Académie Royale des Science*, and other new journals concerned primarily with natural philosophy testify to a new status for preternatural phenomena. Long marginal to scholastic natural philosophy, and now stripped of their religious significance, they had become the first scientific facts. The very traits that had previously unfitted them for use in natural philosophy, and which had then disqualified them from use in theology, made this new role possible.

I have shown elsewhere in detail how this transformation came about in mid-seventeenth-century natural philosophy;[41] here, I shall very briefly rehearse the main lines of this argument, as it relates to early modern views about the meaning of preternatural phenomena. As we have seen, preternatural phenomena, even when free of many portentous associations, had been in principle excluded from scholastic natural philosophy: *scientia,* properly speaking, was the corpus of demonstrated, universal truths, and preternatural phenomena were by definition exceptions to 'that which is always or of that which is for the most part.'[42] Neither Aristotle nor his medieval followers denied the existence of such oddities, but they did deny that anomalies resulting from chance and variability could form the subject matter of true science, for 'there can be no demonstrative knowledge of the fortuitous.'[43] Nicole Oresme's *De causis mirabilium* (ca. 1370) shows how it was possible for Scholastic philosophers to simultaneously maintain that individual prodigies were wholly natural but nonetheless not susceptible to scientific explanation: 'Therefore these things are not known point by point, except by God alone, who knows unlimited things. And why does a black hair appear on the head right next to a white one? Who can know so small a difference in cause?'[44] Well into the seventeenth century, natural philosophy continued to restrict its investigations to common experience.[45]

Aristotelian natural philosophy shunned not only singular events, but all particulars, however commonplace, unless these led to generalizations and the discovery of causes.[46] The proper domain of particulars, of facts, as they came to be called, was history, not philosophy: 'The register of *Knowledge of Fact* is called *History*. Whereof there be two sorts: one called *Naturall History*; which is the History of such Facts, or Effects of Nature .... The other is *Civill History*; which is the History of the Voluntary Actions of men in Common-wealths.'[47] History could contribute the raw materials and illustrations to natural philosophy – thus Aristotle's *History of Animals* was to prepare the way for a philosophical zoology – but by itself it was an inferior sort of knowledge, subordinated to the study of universals in philosophy or poetry.[48] Jurisprudence, like history, also relied predominantly on facts and inferences from them, rather than on universals and demonstrations about them. However, this was simply proof positive of the inferiority of legal reasoning, even in the view of the jurists themselves.[49]

This does not mean that Aristotelian philosophy was not empirical, only that its empiricism was not that of facts, in the sense of deracinated particulars untethered to any theory or explanation. Examples drawn from daily experience pepper the pages of Aristotelian treatises in natural philosophy, but they are just that – examples, and mundane ones at that. Examples illuminate or illustrate a general claim or theory; counterexamples contradict these claims only when an alternative universal lies ready at hand. Examples do not float free of an argumentative context;[50] they are, in our parlance, evidence rather than facts. To have served up particulars, even prosaic ones, without an explanatory sauce would have thereby demoted natural philosophy to natural history. To have served up preternatural particulars would have added insult to injury in the view not only of orthodox Aristotelians but also of innovators who, like Galileo or Descartes, still upheld the demonstrative ideal of science.[51]

Only a reformer intent on destroying this ideal, as well as specific claims of Aristotelian natural philosophy, would have been able to embrace preternatural particulars with open arms, and such was Francis Bacon. Impatient with Scholastic logic and scornful of the syllogism as an instrument for the investigation of nature, Bacon also challenged the validity of the axioms on which Aristotelian demonstrations were grounded. Human nature being what it is, we rashly generalize our axioms from an experience too scanty to reveal the true rules and species of nature.[52] Bacon prescribed a cautionary dose of natural history to correct these prematurely formed axioms. Nor would ordinary natural history of what happens always or most of the time ('nature in course') suffice, for common experience does not probe nature deeply enough. Natural philosophers must also collect '*Deviating* instances, such as the errors of nature, or strange and monstrous objects, in which nature deviates and turns from her ordinary course' (*NO*, 14:138/ii. 29). In short, natural philosophy would have to take not only particulars, but preternatural particulars seriously.

Bacon's grounds for studying the preternatural were metaphysical as well as epistemological. Although he still spoke the language of 'nature in course' and 'nature erring,' he also initiated a unified and thoroughgoing determinism. Dissolving the ontological barriers between natural and artificial, and between natural and preternatural, Bacon insisted that natural philosophy explain all such phenomena, and all by appeal to the same kind of causes. In particular, marvels and prodigies were no longer exempted from scientific explanation: 'Nor should we desist from inquiry, until the properties and qualities of those things, which may be deemed miracles, as it were, of nature, be reduced to, and comprehended in, some form or certain law; so that all irregularity or singularity may be found to depend on some common form' (*NO*, 14:137/ii. 29). A due attention to preternatural phenomena would also act as an epistemological brake to over-hasty axioms and, Bacon further believed, offer privileged insights into the essential but often hidden workings of nature; they would 'reveal common forms' as well as 'rectify the understanding in opposition to common habit' (*NO*, 14:138/ii. 29).

Baconian facts were new not because they were particulars, nor even because they were preternatural. Particulars were the stuff of history, natural and civil, and expressly preternatural particulars had been a staple of both sorts of history since Herodotus and Pliny.[53] They were new because they now belonged to natural philosophy, expanding its realm beyond the universal and the commonplace. Within natural philosophy they supplemented the empiricism of examples used to confirm and instruct with a collection of counterexamples that were a standing reproach to all extant theories. Indeed, Baconian facts were handpicked for their recalcitrance, anomalies that undermined superficial classifications and exceptions that broke glib rules. This is why the first scientific facts retailed in the annals of the Royal Society of London and the Paris Académie des Sciences were often such strange ones, for natural philosophy required the shock of repeated contact with the bizarre, the heteroclite, and the singular in order to sunder the age-old link between 'a datum of experience' and 'the conclusions that may be based on it'; in other words, to sunder facts from evidence.

Thus in the course of the sixteenth and seventeenth centuries preternatural phenomena swung from the almost-supernatural extreme of portents to the almost-natural extreme of Baconian facts. They began as signs par excellence and ended as stubbornly insignificant. The crucial step in this astonishing transformation was the naturalization of preternatural phenomena. However, it would be a mistake to conclude that Spencer, Casaubon, and others who attacked the portentous interpretation of prodigies were always or even usually asserting the autonomy and inviolability à la David Hume. First, these so-called naturalizers countenanced the most unnatural of natural causes in their attempts to debunk false miracles. Pietro Pomponazzi's *De naturalium effectuum causis; sive, De incantationibus* (1556) explained putative miraculous cures and apparitions by causes almost as wondrous: occult virtues of animals, plants, and humans; astral influences; the power of the imagination on animate and inanimate bodies.[54] Bacon was equally willing to grasp at the imagination as a natural alternative to a supernatural explanation. Reviewing stories about corpses bleeding anew in the presence of their murderers, he commented: 'It may be, that this participateth of a miracle, by God's just judgment, who usually bringeth murders to light: but if it be natural, it must be referred to imagination.'[55]

Second, the structure of natural causes was not always mechanical or even deterministic. Spencer, for example, invoked the metaphor of natural law, but so literally that nature, like human legislators, was granted considerable freedom to make exceptions: 'the more private and common Laws of Motion' only hold until superseded by 'some more catholick and indispensable Laws … as the Statutes and Customs of private Corporations take place, till their power be suspended by some more catholick and inforcing Law of State' (*DCP*, p. 5). Similarly, when he likened nature to clockwork, it was a mechanism whose 'blind and decaying Powers must be managed and perpetually woond up by an Hand of Power and Counsel, or they will either stand still, or perform their motions without time and method' (*DCP*, p. 136).

Thirdly, a natural explanation did not always preclude a preternatural or supernatural one. The cause of a monstrous birth might be both the bestiality of the parents *and* divine displeasure at such sinful acts.[56] The doctrine of providence was based on the assumption that primary and secondary causes sometimes worked in tandem to 'bring about striking accidents or coincidences.'[57] Natural philosophers from Jean Buridan through John Evelyn believed that comets were due to natural causes *and* foretold the death of kings. Since God controlled the natural and moral orders, there was no reason for him not to synchronize them.[58] Thus sixteenth- and seventeenth-century naturalism was synonymous neither with strict mechanical materialism nor with ironclad determinism nor with the autonomy of secondary causes. The impulses that eventually made it so were as much political and theological as philosophical, as the debate over the evidence of miracles reveals.

The pure evidence of miracles

The idealized miracle of the seventeenth-century theologians takes place in the pages of Bacon's unfinished Utopia, *The New Atlantis.* The governor of the island of Bensalem explains to his shipwrecked guests how the islanders were converted to Christianity by 'a great pillar of light,' topped by a still-brighter cross at sea, which one of the wise men of Solomon's House certified as a genuine heavenly sign with the following prayer:

> 'Lord God of heaven and earth, thou hast vouchsafed of thy grace, to those of our order, to know thy works of creation, and the secrets of them; and to discern, as far as appertaineth to the generations of men, between divine miracles, works of nature, works of art, and impostures and illusions of all sorts. I do here acknowledge and testify before this people, that the thing which we now see before our eyes, is thy finger, and a true miracle; and forasmuch as we learn in our books, that thou never workest miracles, but to a divine and excellent end, for the laws of nature are thine own laws, and thou exceedest them not but upon great cause, we most humbly beseech thee to prosper this great sign, and to give us the interpretation and use of it in mercy; which thou dost in some part secretly promise by sending it unto us.'[59]

This fictional (and atypical, since unrelated to healing) miracle includes almost all of the elements that preoccupied seventeenth-century writers on miracles. First, the miracle is a public rather than a private sign, on display for all the people of Bensalem to inspect and wonder at. Traditionally, private revelations, particularly sudden conversions, had counted as miracles, and many biblical miracles were directed at select persons or groups.[60] However, many seventeenth-century theologians, particularly Protestant theologians intent on discrediting sacramental miracles, insisted on 'a public and visible demonstration.'[61] Second, experts (here the members of the House of Solomon) are needed to distinguish the supernatural from the preternatural, natural, and artifical, and to guard against fraud. Since the members of the House of Solomon actually experiment with 'all manner of feats of juggling, false apparitions, impostures, and illusions' that might be disguised 'to make them seem more miraculous,'[62] we may assume that Bacon himself was primarily concerned with human fraud. His contemporaries, however, also warned against demonic fraud, though still achieved by manipulation of natural causes. Third, God ideally delivers the proper interpretation of the miracle on the spot, in the form of revealed doctrine (the Bensalemites receive a box containing the Old and New Testaments, plus an explanatory letter from St. Bartholomew), which forestalls conjecture and dispute. These three elements – publicity, inspection for fraud, and interpretation in light of doctrine – defined the seventeenth-century concept of the miracle as evidence. I shall discuss each in turn, showing how all three tended to shift the focus of seventeenth-century debate from the evidence *of* miracles to the evidence *for* miracles.

It is striking that those seventeenth-century writers most exercised by the topic of miracles were those who insisted that miracles had long ago ceased. Protestants challenged by Catholics to produce miracles in attestation of their reformed faith retorted that there was no need for God to confirm the revelations of Christianity anew, for the Protestants meant to reinforce, not break with the teachings of the Bible.[63] Although there was some internecine wrangling as to exactly when miracles had ceased,[64] that they had done so many centuries ago was above dispute for Protestant authors. Edward Stillingfleet inquired rhetorically, 'What imaginable necessity or pretext can there be contrived for a power of miracles, especially among such as already own the *Divine revelation* of the *Scriptures?*' It would be otiose for God to heap miracle on miracle in order to re-prove the proven, 'meerly for satisfaction of mens *vain curiosities*.'[65] John Tillotson had a similarly parsimonious interpretation of God's miracle-working: 'when the end is obtained, the means cease; and the wise God, who is never wanting in what is necessary, does not use to be lavish in that which is superfluous.'[66]

Yet their very preoccupation with explaining why miracles could no longer be expected drove Protestant theologians to develop a new view of miracles as evidence: if miracles were proofs, how and what did they prove? Many medieval miracles were probative, certifying the sanctity of persons and the authenticity of relics.[67] Many others, however, presupposed and confirmed faith rather than compelling it.[68] Biblical miracles sometimes converted the skeptical as well as confirmed the faithful, but their evidence was not irresistible, for some remained unconvinced or at least unresolved – not all who witnessed Christ's miracles and those of the martyrs became Christians, and even Christ's disciples deserted him at his trial and execution. What I shall call the evidentiary school of seventeenth-century Protestant theology narrowed the function of miracles to that of providing irrefragable evidence for the truth of Christian revelation.[69] Some argued that miracles were only part of the evidence for the truth of Christianity,[70] but the general tendency was to concentrate ever more exclusively on the evidence of miracles, if only because '*an extraordinary message to the world, in the name of, and by commission of God*' demanded 'more then ordinary *evidence* of such *authority*' (*OS*, p. 142). At the same time that preternatural events were losing all their evidentiary associations, supernatural events were strengthening theirs.

Not just any kind of evidence would do: a miracle was a 'supernatural Effect evident and wonderful to Sense' (*WJT*, 2:495). Tillotson offered this definition with an eye toward excluding the sacramental miracles of the Catholics; later writers such as Stillingfleet also used it to exclude the private revelation of the fanatic or enthusiast: 'this *inward sense* can be no *ground* to another person to *believe* his *doctrine divine*, because … it is impossible to another person to distinguish the *actings* of the *divine Spirit* from strong *impressions* of *fancy* by the *force* and *energy* of them' (*OS*, p.143). Thus sudden conversions and other inward visitations of grace ceased to be miraculous by the new evidentiary criteria. John Toland went so far as to brand all such secret miracles as false.[71]

However, the evidence of miracles was more than a spectacular appeal to the senses. Ideally, it was pure evidence, unequivocal in its interpretation, and irresistible in its persuasive power. The evidence of miracles straddled the distinction between the 'internal' evidence of things and the 'external' evidence of testimony, a distinction that was to dominate later debates over the evidence for miracles in the late seventeenth and early eighteenth centuries.[72] The evidence of miracles was internal, insofar as it was a thing or event. Moreover, its internal evidence, read off from the very nature of the event, was of a special sort, pointing unmistakably to supernatural agency, just as fingerprints point to a certain hand. At the same time, the evidence of miracles was external, a form of testimony from God that the miracle-worker's message was an authentic revelation. In both cases, the evidence of miracles was saturated with intention, God's intention to suspend the natural order to certify his messenger, and God's intention to establish certain doctrines. Because miracles accompanied doctrine, their meaning was clear; because God was the author of miracles, they proved beyond a shadow of a doubt.

However, the faith in pure evidence was short lived. The evidentiary theologians soon became preoccupied with the question, 'What distinguished a true miracle from a false one?' Definitions of miracles proliferated in the late seventeenth century, as theologians and natural philosophers groped for some clear-cut criterion. The very number and diversity of these definitions testifies to their failure to find such. Almost every imaginable position found a supporter; a few examples from major writers suffice to suggest the breadth of opinion and the lack of agreement.

Tillotson asserted a miracle must be a 'supernatural Effect,' but admitted that since angels and demons can 'exceed any natural Power known to us,' their works would often be indistinguishable from those of God (*WJT*, 2:496). Casaubon eluded the problem of distinguishing supernatural and natural effects by reasserting the Augustinian position that there was nothing so ordinary 'but, if looked into Philosophically, did afford me a miracle,' in the sense of being inexplicable.[73] Joseph Glanvill confronted the difficulty head-on, and pronounced it irresoluble,

> for we are ignorant of the *Extent* and *Bounds* of *Natures Sphere,* and possibilities; and if this were the *Character* and *essential Mark* of a Miracle, we could not know what was *so;* except we could determine the *Extent* of Natural causalities, and fix their *Bounds,* and be able to say to *Nature, Hitherto canst thou go, and no farther.*

Hence Glanvill required that putative miracles not only exceed the known powers of nature but also be performed by 'Persons of Simplicity, Truth, and Holiness, void of Ambition, and all *secular Designs*' (*ST*, p. 52). Fleetwood thought it was enough that miracles violated the 'setled Laws of Nature,' these latter being observationally defined as 'Operations that are constant, certain, and expected' (*EM*, p. 2). Samuel Clarke was more cautious than Fleetwood in qualifying 'the Course of Nature' as the 'perfectly *Arbitrary*' workings of divine will, 'as easie to be *altered* at any time, as to be *preserved*,' but also opted for a rarity criterion: ''tis only *usualness* or *unusualness* that makes the distinction.'[74] John Locke faced these epistemological difficulties squarely, and retreated to the subjective appreciation of the miracle, defined as a 'sensible operation, which, being above the comprehension of the spectator, and in his opinion contrary to the established course of nature, is taken by him to be divine.'[75]

These definitions were always convoluted and often circular or self-contradictory to boot. Only the intensity of the desire for such a hard-and-fast criterion can explain the willingness to wrestle with definitions that could not command internal consistency, much less consensus. What drove these writers into the definitional quagmire was the threat of false miracles; what altered in the course of the debate was not the fear of being deceived, but rather the identity of the suspected deceiver.

Increasingly in the last quarter of the seventeenth century, the enemy was the enthusiast rather than the devil. In the middle decades of the seventeenth century, the devil was still a force to reckon with: Browne contended that Satan counterfeited miracles to spread idolatry and superstition;[76] Pascal was deeply disquieted by the Jesuit insinuation that the Port-Royal miracle of the Sacred Thorn was a demonic imposture;[77] Glanvill warned that witches and evil spirits could simulate miracles with 'wonderful Combinations of *natural Causes*' (*ST*, p. 52). But already in the 1660s the devil had yielded the title of Great Deceiver to enthusiasts, both sincere and feigned. Long before Shaftesbury called on a witness in favor of a 'new Prophesying Sect' and its purported miracles to prove himself 'wholly free of melancholy, and ... incapable of all Enthusiasm besides,'[78] portents and miracles had become associated among the learned with 'all the common causes of deceit, *Superstition, Melancholy, natural weakness of sight, softness of imagination*' and other flaws of body and soul (*DCP*, p. 183). To judge from Clarke's 1705 Boyle lectures, even Christ was in some circles suspected of baneful enthusiasm (see *D*, p. 373).

The deep-seated anxiety about imposture, both diabolical and human, was simply the obverse of the emphasis on miracles as evidence. For the evidentiary theologians, the truth of Christian revelation was chiefly supported 'by the many infallible *Signs and Miracles,* which the Author of it worked publickly as the Evidence of his Divine Commission' (*D*, p. 372).[79] Miracles were God's signature, 'the greatest testimony of *Divine authority* and *revelation*' (*OS*, p. 139). However, in contrast to most testimonial evidence, what must be proved is not the trustworthiness but rather the identity of the witness, for once God's identity was established, absolute trustworthiness followed necessarily for seventeenth-century theologians.[80] Since belief in revelation and, conversely, rejection of heresy was in their view the gravest of human duties, no pain should be spared in distinguishing divine signatures from forgeries. Fleetwood went so far as to make the miracle itself subsidiary to the signature, advising his readers that 'you are under no obligation of Necessity, to believe all that a Man shall say, who works Miracles, without declaring he is sent of God, and telling you, that God has given him that miraculous Power, in order to obtain Credit with you' (*EM*, p. 117). Confident that God always provides 'sufficient marks' for the 'impartial Enquirers after Truth' to distinguish true from false miracles (*WJT*, 2:499), the theologians sought the signs that would validate the 'Signs and Wonders.' The claim that miracles were irrefutable evidence thus led willy-nilly to the demand for still further evidence that the miracles in question were genuine.

The clinching evidence for the authenticity of an ambiguous miracle was doctrinal. As we have seen, both the objective criterion of supernatural causation and the subjective criterion of wonder dissolved under the scrutiny of seventeenth-century theologians: too little was known of nature to locate the boundary between natural and supernatural causes, an uncertainty exacerbated rather than mitigated by the discoveries of the new natural philosophy; too much was known of the uncritical human tendency to wonder at the wrong objects to lodge much confidence in admiration and astonishment. Their solution was to let doctrine certify the miracle, just as miracles certified the doctrine: 'For it is my Opinion, that the Doctrine, in general at least, should always be first laid down, and then the Miracle be wrought to give the Messenger Authority and Credit to establish it in People's Minds; which would prevent all manner of Abuses of any Accidental Miracles' (*EM*, p. 63).[81]

The evidentialists were well aware of the potential circularity of this criterion, but insisted that the tautology was only apparent. Pascal summed up the problem in a laconic 'Regie': 'One must judge doctrine by miracles, and one must judge miracles by doctrine. All of this is true, but not contradictory. For it is necessary to distinguish the times [*distinguer les temps*].'[82] The English evidentialists wriggled out of the difficulty by arguing that it was only the *kind* of doctrine which had to pass muster, not the specifics of its content. The doctrine must be inaccessible to human reason, for otherwise it need not be vouchsafed as revelation; moreover, it must not tend to promote idolatry and other impieties: '*If* the Doctrine attested by Miracles, be in it self *impious,* or manifestly *tending to promote Vice;* then without all question the Miracles, how great soever they may appear to Us, are neither worked by God himself, nor by his Commission' (D, p. 382). However, the elasticity of the term *impious,* which could be stretched to encompass all that contradicted a particular orthodoxy, blurred the boundary between kind and content of miracles that the evidentialists had hoped would protect them from tautology.

In cases of contested doctrine, the evidentiary import of the miracle, even one universally acknowledged to be genuine, was effectively neutralized by competing interpretations. When for example Pascal's niece was cured of a lachrymal fistula by contact with a thorn from the crown of Jesus on 24 March 1656, even the most bitter opponents of the Port-Royal Jansenists submitted to the official decision certifying the miracle as authentic. But whereas Pascal and his allies took the miracle as a divine vindication, their Jesuit critics argued that it was a divine warning to forsake their heresy.[83] The miracle remained a divine sign, but an inscrutable one.

The end result of the doctrinal criterion was to weaken dramatically the evidentiary force of miracles. Miracles alone, no matter how public and palpable to the senses, no longer sufficed to prove a doctrine or messenger heaven-sent. Further proof, in the form of harmony with preexisting doctrine, was required to establish divine credentials. If the doctrine was disputed, miracles could no longer settle the issue, for they then became signs without clear signification. A miracle unannounced by doctrine was no miracle at all, even if not under suspicion of fraud. Glanvill quoted with approval the Reverend Doctor R. Dean's opinion that the cures performed by Greatrakes, the 'Irish Stroker,' were 'more than *ordinary*' but 'not miraculous': for not only did Greatrakes's patients occasionally suffer relapses, 'He pretends not to give *Testimony* to any *Doctrine*' (ST, p. 53). Although Locke shook his head over the credulity of the ancients, who accepted their religion without any evidence – that is, without miracles – he was quick to rule out any mission inconsistent with 'natural religion and the rules of morality,' however wondrous its works.[84] In seventeenth-century evidentiary theology, miracles began as 'the principal external Proof and Confirmation of the Divinity of a Doctrine'; they ended as themselves requiring 'Proof and Confirmation' from doctrine.

Conclusion: Naturalization and the reassertion of authority

Even after miracles had lost their peculiar evidentiary power to compel belief unambiguously and automatically in early eighteenth-century theology, they did not immediately wither away. It took some forty years before the likes of Hume and Voltaire could discuss the problem of miracles as if it were one of the evidence *for* miracles, as opposed to the evidence *of* miracles.[85] However, evidentialist theologians did unintentionally prepare the way for this shift. First, by depriving miracles of evidentiary autonomy, they also deprived them of their ostensive function. If miracles require the evidence of doctrine, who needs the evidence of miracles? Among orthodox British theologians, not to speak of Deists like Toland and Anthony Collins, portents and miracles played an ever more modest role in Christian apologetics. Although none of them would have thought of denying their existence or importance in the early Church, late seventeenth-century theologians assumed an ever more condescending tone toward their predecessors for requiring such a vulgar sort of proof. Whereas Christ had been forced by his motley audience to address 'the lower faculties of the Soul, phancy and imagination' with showy miracles, nowadays 'all things are to be managed in a more sedate, cool, and silent manner,' by invoking 'steady and calm arguments' (*DCP*, p. 27–28). Just because miracles were 'such sensible Demonstrations,' they penetrated even 'the *weakest* Judgments and *strongest* Imaginations,' but the enlightened had no need of them (*D*, p. 403).[86]

This lofty manner points to the second unintentional contribution evidentialist theology made to the frontal attack on the very existence of miracles. By associating miracles with the bumptious and unlettered, they anticipated Hume's guilt-by-association argument that wonders proliferated most among the ignorant and barbarous. Thus Casaubon thought it necessary to apologize for St. Augustine's credulity in matters marvelous as unbecoming an educated man: 'It may be, *St. Augustine* may be thought by some, to have been somewhat more credulous in this point of strange relations, then became so wise, so Learned, and judicious a man, as certainly he was: neither do I think my self bound to believe all things in this kind, which he may be thought by his words to have believed.'[87] More dangerously, miracles had come to be linked with rabble-rousing enthusiasts, who sincerely or maliciously pretended to a divine mission in order to undermine the powers-that-be. This was one of Stillingfleet's most telling arguments for the cessation of miracles, for otherwise public order would be at the mercy of 'an innumerable company of *croaking Enthusiasts* [who] would be continually pretending *commissions* from heaven' (*OS*, p. 109).

Although Catholic theologians in principle did not subscribe to the doctrine of the cessation of miracles, nor to the claim that miracles must be palpable to the senses, they were in practice as concerned about the destabilizing effects, theological and political, of alleged miracles as their Protestant colleagues. The Council of Trent stiffened the evidentiary requirements for miracles, and placed the responsibility for a thorough investigation in the hands of the local bishop, with the intent of reining in the deviations of popular religion.[88] Both the reasoning behind and the execution of the new regulations closely paralleled Protestant developments. Catholic reformers emphasized the need to distinguish between true religion and superstition, and since they further contended that superstitions were the work of the devil, the problem boiled down to distinguishing genuine miracles from demonic counterfeits. So rigorous were the diocesan investigations that the number of certified miracles in France declined precipitously in the second half of the seventeenth century.[89] Those that did pass through the fine sieve of official scrutiny were backed by so much legal and medical evidence that historian Jean de Viguerie has argued that they are among the best-documented historical facts of the early modern period.[90] However, as for Protestants, doctrine steered Catholic deliberations over evidence, no matter how solid and copious the latter. Hume noted that the healing miracles performed in the Parisian parish of Saint-Médard in 1731 were immeasurably better confirmed than those of Christ and his disciples,[91] but after a meticulous investigation the Archbishop Vintimille condemned the Saint-Médard cures for fostering Jansensism and 'subvert[ing] the natural, established order of the Church.'[92] De facto if not de jure, the Catholic church also subscribed to the doctrine of the cessation of miracles, and for much the same reasons that John Calvin had, namely, that miracles 'could disturb and arouse doubts in a mind that would otherwise be tranquil [*en repos*].'[93]

The reaffirmation of political and religious authority reflected in the official dismissal of unsettling portents and miracles on both sides of the Channel had its theological analogue in the centralization of divine power, especially in Protestant writings. Both the natural and, particularly, the preternatural domains lost territory as a result. Robert Boyle attacked natural philosophers who granted nature an unseemly amount of autonomy by endowing it with plastic powers and capricious deviations; nature was simply brute, passive matter set in motion and sustained by God.[94] Neither mechanistic nor Newtonian natural philosophy necessarily promoted nature's independence and the inviolability of natural law. As Clarke put it in his Boyle lectures of 1705, 'what Men commonly call the *Course of Nature,* or the *Power of Nature*' is simply the '*Will of God*' which 'is as easie to be *altered* at any time, as to be *preserved*' (*D*, p. 377).

The preternatural had depended crucially on insubordination to divine decree, both nature's and the devil's, and therefore virtually disappeared as a result of God's new, tightened regime. Although few went so far as to deny the devil's existence, he was, like nature, put on a very short leash. Clarke thought God could at least partially restrain evil spirits (see *D*, p. 391), and Fleetwood essentially demoted the devil to God's lieutenant, 'for his Power or Impotence, it depends entirely on God, how far he will restrain or limit him' (*EM*, p. 50). By granting God a monopoly on agency in the universe, late seventeenth-century Protestant theologians, at least English ones, radically simplified ontology as well. Spinoza's pantheistic critique of miracles was a scandal because it merged God with nature, but the simplifying ontological tendencies of the *Tractatus theologico-politicus* (1670), as well as the contempt for the low understanding of the 'masses,' were echoed in numerous, more orthodox works.

There were early eighteenth-century voices, most famously Leibniz's, that called for a more aloof relationship between God and his creation, insisting on the integrity of the 'laws of nature, and the beautiful pre-established order.'[95] Were it not for Newton's equally famous objection to Leibniz, it would be tempting to ascribe this vision of a determined, immutable nature wholly to the successes of late seventeenth-century natural philosophy, most notably to those of Newton himself. However, the impulse for naturalization had other sources besides natural philosophy, or even metaphysics.[96] The motives behind excluding miracles in principle, as Leibniz and many eighteenth-century philosophes did, and excluding them in practice, as many devout Protestant and Catholic theologians did, sometimes converged in a form of naturalization. Pierre Bayle, ridiculing portentous interpretations of the comet of 1682, argued that the ordinary laws of nature were sufficient to show the will and benevolence of God, whereas natural phenomena cried up as portents merely misled the people into superstition and idolatry.[97] In addition to the usual naturalizing maxims that, in Thomas Burnet's words, to shift explanations from God's ordinary to his extraordinary providence was 'but, as the Proverb says, to rob *Peter* to pay *Paul*,'[98] Bayle contended that a naturalized religion was also a sounder religion.

In view of the often subversive uses to which portents and miracles were often put, it is not surprising to find more candid arguments that a naturalized religion was a safer, more pleasant one as well. Spencer complained that a religion rife with portents was incompatible with 'the peace and tranquility of common life,' for '*how can a man, as he is councelled, eat his bread with joy, and drink his wine with a chearful heart* (Eccles. 9.7); *if every strange accident must perswade him that there is some sword of vengeance hanging over his head*' (*DCP*, fig. A4v). Stillingfleet ruled out the possibility of new revelations, supported by new miracles, on grounds of inconvenience: 'For if *God* may still make new *articles of faith,* or constitute new *duties* by fresh *miracles,* I must go and enquire what *miracles* are wrought in every *place,* to see that I miss nothing that may be *necessary* for me, in order to my happiness in another world' (*OS*, pp. 147–48). A hankering for peace and quiet was by no means the only reason for promoting the naturalization of marvels and miracles, but it was a powerful one. A great deal of the rhapsodizing over law-abiding, commonplace nature that filled the writings of the natural theologians appealed to the desire for a calm religious life, free from nasty surprises and inspired upstarts.

Scientific facts also became more regular and more commonplace, although the transition from bizarre singularities to mundane universals was a gradual and uneven one.[99] However, even after scientific facts had been domesticated, the distinction between facts and evidence remained part of the conceptual framework of natural science, often contested (starting with Descartes and continuing to the present day) but never completely extirpated. Long after scientific facts ceased to be the anomalies and exceptions Bacon used to destroy Aristotelian axioms and natural kinds, they retained their reputation for orneriness. The portentous-sign-turned-scientific-fact left deeply etched traces in our way of thinking about evidence. In contrast, the contributions of the evidentiary miracle were not so long lived. Before worries first over demonic counterfeits and later over human enthusiasm reduced miracles to rubber-stamping extant doctrine, miracles seemed the purest form of evidence: their meaning was patent to all who had eyes to see, and they compelled belief as irresistibly as a mathematical demonstration – indeed, more so, since they required neither the training nor the concentration of a mathematician. Miracles were God's privy seal and letters patent, certifying a doctrine as divine and thereby convincing onlookers of its truth. Ideally, miracles were transparent, requiring no interpretation, and were as satisfying to the senses and to the imagination as to reason.

This dream of pure evidence evaporated with the division of evidence into the internal evidence of things and the external evidence of testimony, which division structured the debate over the evidence *for* miracles.[100] The pure evidence of miracles, at least as conceived in the mid-seventeenth century, straddled the line between internal and external evidence: as sensible events miracles belonged to the realm of things, but as supernatural events they also bore witness. They were the last form of evidence compatible with intention, in this case divine intention, and it is ironic that suspicions of human intention – that is, the intent to feign miracles in order to usurp political and religious authority – ultimately deprived them of evidentiary value.

Notes

1. Augustine, *De civitate Dei,* trans. W. M. Green, 7 vols. (Cambridge, Mass., 1972), 7:51.
2. Ibid., 7:29.
3. See Peter Brown, *Augustine of Hippo: A Biography* (Berkeley, 1967), pp. 413–18.

4. See Thomas Aquinas, *Summa theologica,* trans. Fathers of the English Dominican Province, 3 vols. (New York, 1947), 1: 520.

5. See Aquinas, *Summa contra gentiles,* trans. English Dominican Fathers, 4 vols. (London, 1928), vol. 3, pt. 2, pp. 60–61.

6. Aquinas, *Summa theologica,* 1:520.

7. Aquinas, *Summa contra gentiles,* vol. 3, pt. 2, p. 57.

8. Ibid., vol. 3, pt. 2, pp. 65–66.

9. On shrines and relics, see Jonathan Sumption, *Pilgrimage: An Image of Mediaeval Religion* (London, 1975), pp. 22–44. On the trial by ordeal, see Robert Bartlett, *Trial by Fire and Water: The Medieval Judicial Ordeal* (Oxford, 1986). On sacramental and jocular miracles, see Benedicta Ward, *Miracles and the Medieval Mind: Theory, Records, and Event, 1000–1215* (Philadelphia, 1982), pp. 13, 213. For a general survey of theological views on miracles, see Bernhard Bron, *Das Wunder: Das theologische Wunderverständnis im Horizont des neuzeitlichen Natur und Geschichtsbegriffs* (Göttingen, 1975).

10. See Jean Céard, *La Nature et les prodiges: L'Insolite au XVIe siécle, en France* (Geneva, 1977), pp. 111–15.

11. Thomas Browne, *Pseudodoxia Epidemica,* in *The Works of Sir Thomas Browne,* ed. Charles Sayle, 3 vols. (Edinburgh, 1912), 1:188. See William Fleetwood, *An Essay upon Miracles,* 2d ed. (London, 1702), p. 108; hereafter abbreviated *EM*; and Joseph Glanvill, *Sadducismus Triumphatus: Or, A full and plain Evidence, Concerning Witches and Apparitions* (London, 1682), p. 52; hereafter abbreviated *ST.*

12. On the medieval notion of 'natural,' see Bert Hansen, *Nicole Oresme and the Marvels of Nature: The 'De causis mirabilium'* (Toronto, 1985), p. 64.

13. On occult causes, see Keith Hutchison, 'What Happened to Occult Qualities in the Scientific Revolution?' *Isis* 73 (June 1982): 233–53.

14. See Eileen Serene, 'Demonstrative Science,' in *The Cambridge History of Later Medieval Philosophy: From the Rediscovery of Aristotle to the Disintegration of Scholasticism, 1100–1600,* ed. Norman Kretzmann, Anthony Kenny, and Jan Pinborg (Cambridge, 1982), p. 506n.

15. See D. P. Walker, *Spiritual and Demonic Magic: From Ficino to Campanella* (Notre Dame, Ind., 1975).

16. See William Eamon, 'Arcana Disclosed: The Advent of Printing, the Books of Secrets Tradition and the Development of Experimental Science in the Sixteenth Century', *History of Science* 22 (June 1984): 111–50.

17. See Stuart Clark, 'The Scientific Status of Demonology,' in *Occult and Scientific Mentalities in the Renaissance,* ed. Brian Vickers (Cambridge, 1984), pp. 351–74.

18. See Mary B. Campbell, *The Witness and the Other World: Exotic European Travel Writing, 400–1600* (Ithaca, N. Y., 1988).

19. See Katharine Park and Lorraine Daston, 'Unnatural Conceptions: The Study of Monsters in Sixteenth- and Seventeenth-Century France and England,' *Past and Present* 92 (Aug. 1981): 20–54.

20. Gerald of Wales, *The History and Topography of Ireland,* trans. John J. O'Meara (Harmondsworth, 1982), p. 65. On Gerald's treatment of marvels and miracles, see Bartlett, *Gerald of Wales, 1146–1223* (Oxford, 1982).

21. It is possibility in principle, not the actual availability of a natural explanation that counted here. Nicole Oresme's attempts to 'show the causes of some effects which seem to be marvels and to show that the effects occur naturally' (Hansen, *Nicole Oresme and the Marvels of Nature,* p. 137) almost never provide a specific explanation of an individual case; indeed, Oresme despaired of ever being able to provide such explanations: see, for example, his denial that monstrous births are portents (p. 247); also see p. 227 concerning explanations of individual cases. This kind of

promissory naturalism, based more on metaphysical faith than scientific competence, remained typical of attempts to naturalize marvels and miracles well into the eighteenth century. See, for example, [John Toland], *Hodegus; proving the pillar of fire, that guided the Israelites in the wilderness, not miraculous, but ambulatory beacons* (London, 1753), and Conyers Middleton, *A Vindication of the Free inquiry into the miraculous powers, which are supposed to have subsisted in the Christian church & c. from the objections of Dr. Dodwell and Dr. Church* (London, 1751).

22. On the importance of signs and divination in sixteenth-century learned culture, see Céard, *La Nature et les prodiges.*

23. See, for example, Calvin's cautious declaration that 'cependant je ne nie pas, lors que Dieu veut estendre sa main pour faire quelque jugement digne de memoire au monde, qu'il ne nous advertisse quelquefois par les cometes: mais cela ne sert de rien, pour attacher les hommes et leur condition à une influence perpetuelle du ciel' ['however, I do not deny that when God wants to extend his hand to make some judgment worthy of the memory of the world, that he sometimes advertises (it) to us by comets: but that in no way serves to attach men and their condition to a perpetual influence of the heavens'](quoted in ibid., p. 130).

24. See Park and Daston, 'Unnatural Conceptions,' concerning mutual learned/popular borrowing.

25. Jean Bodin, *De la démonomanie des sorciers* (1580; Hildesheim, 1988), fol. 48, r/v.

26. Pierre Boaistuau, *Histoires prodigieuses* (Paris, 1567), p. 5. For a full account of the various volumes of the *Histoires prodigieuses* and their publishing history, see Céard, *La Nature et les prodiges,* chap. 13.

27. Stephen Batman, *The Doome warning all men to the Judgemente. Wherein are contayned for the most parte all the straunge Prodigies hapned in the Worlde, with divers secrete figures of Revelations tending to mannes stayed conversion towardes God* (London, 1581).

28. *Wahrhafte Neue Zeitung von dem neuen Cometstern… welcher zu Augspurg und in vilen Landen ist gesehen worden* (Augsburg, 1619).

29. See Park and Daston, 'Unnatural Conceptions,' pp. 27–34.

30. See Bodin, *De la Démonomanie des sorciers,* fol. 49 r/v.

31. See R. F. Ovenell, *The Ashmolean Museum, 1683–1894* (Oxford, 1986), p. 37. On the composition of the cabinets, see *The Origins of Museums: The Cabinet of Curiosities in Sixteenth- and Seventeenth-Century Europe,* ed. Oliver Impey and Arthur MacGregor (Oxford, 1985).

32. See Julius von Schlosser, *Die Kunst- und Wunderkammern der Spätrenaissance: Ein Beitrag zur Geschichte des Sammelwesens* (1908; Braunschweig, 1978), and David Murray, *Museums: Their History and Their Use* (Glasgow, 1904).

33. Increase Mather, *An Essay for the Recording of Illustrious Providences* (1684; New York, 1977), chap. 9. On the background to collections of providences, see Keith Thomas, *Religion and the Decline of Magic* (New York, 1971), chap. 4.

34. See Jean Delumeau, *La Peur en Occident, XIVe–XVIIIe siècles, une cité assiégée* (Paris, 1978). See also Walker, *Spiritual and Demonic Magic,* and Clark, 'The Scientific Status of Demonology,' on the growing fear of demons in the sixteenth century.

35. Browne, *Pseudodoxia Epidemica,* 1:193.

36. See Tetsuya Shiokawa, *Pascal et les miracles* (Paris, 1977), p. 112.

37. See, for example, Jean-Baptiste Thiers, *Traité des superstitions qui regardent les sacrements,* 4th ed., 4 vols. (Paris, 1741), and Pierre Le Brun, *Histoire critique des pratiques superstitieuses* (Paris, 1702).

38. See John Spencer, preface, *A Discourse concerning Prodigies,* 2d ed. (London, 1665); see also pp. 59–60; hereafter abbreviated *DCP.*

39. Meric Casaubon, *A Treatise Concerning Enthusiasme, As it is an Effect of Nature: but is mistaken by many for either Divine Inspiration, or Diabolical Possession* (London, 1655), p. 42.

40. On natural divination, see also Céard, *La Nature et les prodiges,* pp. 115ff., and Thiers, *Traité des superstitions qui regardent les sacrements,* pp. 294–95.

41. See Daston, 'Baconian Facts, Academic Civility, and the Prehistory of Objectivity,' *Annals of Scholarship* (forthcoming), and 'The Factual Sensibility,' review of *The Origins of Museums,* ed. Impey and MacGregor, *Tradescant's Rarities: Essays on the Foundation of the Ashmolean Museum, 1683,* ed. MacGregor, and *The Ashmolean Museum, 1683–1894,* by Ovenell, *Isis* 79 (Sept. 1988): 452–67.

42. Aristotle, *Metaphysics,* 1027a20–27.

43. Aristotle, *Posterior Analytics,* 87b19–20.

44. Hansen, *Nicole Oresme and the Marvels of Nature,* p. 279.

45. See Peter Dear, '*Totius in verba:* Rhetoric and Authority in the Early Royal Society,' *Isis* 76 (June 1985): 145–61, and 'Jesuit Mathematical Science and the Reconstitution of Experience in the Early Seventeenth Century,' *Studies in History and Philosophy of Science* 18 (June 1987): 133–75, on the transformation of the scholastic conception of experience.

46. See Aristotle, *Parts of Animals,* 639a13–640a10.

47. Thomas Hobbes, *Leviathan,* ed. C. B. Macpherson (1651; Harmondsworth, 1981), p. 148.

48. See Aristotle, *Poetics,* 1451b1–7.

49. See, for example, Jean Domat, *Les Loix civiles dans leur ordre naturel,* 2d ed., 3 vols. (Paris, 1696–97), 2:346–47.

50. I owe this view of scholastic empiricism to a paper by Joan Cadden on Albertus Magnus, to my knowledge never published.

51. See Daston, 'Baconian Facts, Academic Civility, and the Prehistory of Objectivity.'

52. See Francis Bacon, *Novum organum,* in *The Works of Francis Bacon,* ed. Basil Montagu, 17 vols. (1620; London, 1825–34), 14:34/i. 28, 73–74/i. 104; hereafter abbreviated *NO.*

53. See Charles William Fornara, *The Nature of History in Ancient Greece and Rome* (Berkeley, 1983), pp. 96–97.

54. See Pietro Pomponazzi, *De naturalium effectuum causis; sive, De incantationibus* (1556; Hildesheim, 1970).

55. Bacon, *Sylva Sylvarum: or, A Natural History in Ten Centuries* [1627], in *The Works of Francis Bacon,* 4:516–17.

56. See Ambroise Paré, *Des monstres et prodiges,* ed. Céard (1573; Geneva, 1971), p. 4.

57. Thomas, *Religion and the Decline of Magic,* p. 80.

58. Ibid., p. 91.

59. Bacon, *New Atlantis* [1627], in *The Works of Francis Bacon,* 2:336.

60. See Romano Guardini, 'Das Wunder als Zeichen,' in *Studien und Berichte der Katholischen Akademie in Bayern,* Heft 17, *Wunder und Magie* (Würzburg, 1962), pp. 75–93.

61. See John Tillotson, 'Jesus the Son of God Proved by His Resurrection,' *Tillotson's Sermons,* ed. G. W. Weldon (London, 1886), p. 372.

62. Bacon, *New Atlantis,* 2:375.

63. Although this view had Augustinian antecedents, it was vigorously revived by Calvin during the reformation: see Jean Calvin, 'Epistre,' *Institution de la religion chrestienne* (n. p., 1541).

64. See, for example, William Whiston, *Account of the exact time when miraculous gifts ceas'd in the church* (London, 1749).

65. Edward Stillingfleet, *Origines sacrae, or a Rational Account of the Grounds of Christian Faith, as to the Truth and Divine Authority of the Scriptures, And the matters therein contained* (London, 1663), pp. 140, 147; hereafter abbreviated *OS.*

66. Tillotson, 'The General and Effectual Publication of the Gospel by the Apostles,' *Tillotson's Sermons*, p. 236.

67. See Sumption, *Pilgrimage*, pp. 39, 70.

68. See Campbell, *The Witness and the Other World*, pp. 31–33.

69. For a full account of the evidentiary school of British theology as background to the later debate over the existence of miracles, see R. M. Burns, *The Great Debate on Miracles: From Joseph Glanvill to David Hume* (Lewisburg, Pa., 1981).

70. See Tillotson, *The Works of the Most Reverend Dr. John Tillotson*, 3d ed., 2 vols. (London, 1722), 2:501; hereafter abbreviated *WJT*; and Casaubon, *Of Credulity and Incredulity in Things Divine and Spiritual* (London, 1670), p. 116.

71. See Toland, *Christianity Not Mysterious* (1696; Stuttgart-Bad Canstatt, 1964), p. 155. On Toland's ambiguous position on miracles, see Robert E. Sullivan, *John Toland and the Deist Controversy: A Study in Adaptations* (Cambridge, Mass., 1982), pp. 128, 223.

72. The *locus classicus* of the distinction is Antoine Arnauld and Pierre Nicole, *La Logique, ou l'art de penser*, ed. Pierre Clair and Francois Girbal (1662; Paris; 1965), p. 340. On the significance of the distinction for seventeenth-century conceptions of evidence, see Ian Hacking, *The Emergence of Probability: A Philosophical Study of Early Ideas about Probability, Induction and Statistical Reference* (Cambridge, 1975), chaps. 1–5. On its role in the later debate over miracles, see Daston, *Classical Probability in the Enlightenment* (Princeton, N. J., 1988), chap. 6, sect. 3.

73. Casaubon, *Of Credulity and Incredulity in Things Divine and Spiritual*, p. 107.

74. Samuel Clarke, *A Discourse Concerning the Being and Attributes of God, the Obligations of Natural Religion, and the Truth and Certainty of the Christian Revelation* [Boyle lectures of 1705], 8th ed. (London, 1732), pp. 377, 375; hereafter abbreviated *D*.

75. John Locke, *A Discourse of Miracles*, in *The Works of John Locke*, 10 vols. (London, 1823), 9:256.

76. See Browne, *Pseudodoxia Epidemica*, chaps. 10–11.

77. See Blaise Pascal, 'Le Miracle de la Sainte Epine,' in *Oeuvres complètes*, ed. Fortunat Strowski, 3 vols. (Paris, 1923–31), 2:434–50.

78. [Shaftesbury], *A Letter Concerning Enthusiasm, to My Lord ****** (London, 1708), pp. 68–69.

79. See also *WJT*, 2:498, and *OS*, pp. 138–39.

80. Sometimes, however, theologians entertained the possibility that God might allow false prophecies to be fulfilled to 'try the People's Faith and Constancy' (*EM*, p. 57).

81. See *D*, p. 387; *WJT*, 2:498; and Casaubon, *Of Credulity and Incredulity in Things Divine and Spiritual*, p. 120.

82. Quoted in Shiokawa, *Pascal et les miracles*, p. 162.

83. See ibid., pp. 128–29, 136–37.

84. Locke, *A Discourse of Miracles*, 9:261.

85. See Voltaire, 'Miracles,' *Dictionnaire philosophique*, in *Oeuvres complétes* (1764; Paris, 1783), 42:88–113, and David Hume, 'On Miracles,' *Essays Moral, Political and Literary* (1741–42; London, 1963).

86. See also Casaubon, *Of Credulity and Incredulity in Things Divine and Spiritual*, p. 10.

87. Ibid., p. 116.

88. See Delumeau, *Un Chemin d'histoire: Chrétienté et christianisation* (Paris, 1981), p. 194.

89. See Jean de Viguerie, 'Le Miracle dans la France du XVIIe siécle,' *XVIIe siècle* 35 (July–Sept. 1983): 313–31.

90. Ibid., p. 316.

91. See Hume, 'On Miracles.'

92. B. Robert Kreiser, *Miracles, Convulsions, and Ecclesiastical Politics in Early Eighteenth-Century Paris* (Princeton, N. J., 1978), p. 370.

93. Calvin, 'Epistre.'

94. Robert Boyle, 'A Free Inquiry into the Vulgarly Received Notion of Nature,' in *Works of the Honourable Robert Boyle,* ed. Thomas Birch, 5 vols. (1685; London, 1744), 4:398.

95. *The Leibniz-Clarke Correspondence,* ed. H. G. Alexander (1717; Manchester, 1970), p. 12.

96. The metaphysical grounds were most powerfully argued in Benedict Spinoza, *A Theological-Political Treatise* [*Tractatus theologico-politicus*], in *The Chief Works of Benedict de Spinoza,* trans. R. H. M. Elwes, 2 vols. (New York, 1951), 1:84.

97. See Pierre Bayle, *Pensées diverses, écrites à un docteur de Sorbonne, á l'occasion de la comète qui parut au mois de décembre 1680* (Rotterdam, 1683), pp. 256–57, 700–708.

98. Thomas Burnet, *The Sacred Theory of the Earth* (1691; London, 1965), p. 221.

99. On this transition, see Daston, 'The Cold Light of Facts and the Facts of Cold Light: Luminescence and the Transformation of the Scientific Fact 1600–1750,' paper presented to the workshop on 'The Technologies of Objectivity,' University of California, Los Angeles, February 1990.

100. On the early eighteenth-century debate in general, see Burns, *The Great Debate on Miracles.* On the role played by the distinction between internal and external evidence, see Daston, *Classical Probability in the Enlightenment,* pp. 323–30.

CHAPTER 6
THE SPECIFIC RATIONALITY OF MEDIEVAL MAGIC
Richard Kieckhefer

In her important recent study of early medieval magic, Valerie Flint argues that the sheer nonrationality of magic, kept within bounds, gave it positive value: 'There are forces better recognized as belonging to human society than repressed or left to waste away or growl about upon its fringes... Many of our forebears knew this.' She applauds early medieval churchmen for encouraging an 'unreason deeper than... reason.' To be sure, when magic outlived its usefulness, it could become superstitious and irrational, 'that is, damagingly upheld,' but Flint does not recognize this decay as arguing against the benign nonrationality of magic in the early Middle Ages, the era following the initial missionary efforts in Western and Northern Europe.[1]

The rationality of magic is a classic problem in both history and anthropology. Lynn Thorndike's *History of Magic and Experimental Science* sought to show a historical link between magic and science, and Frances Yates argued that the occult sciences played a significant role in the early modern scientific revolution.[2] While Thorndike and Yates suggest elements of continuity between magic and modern scientific thought, more recent writers have proposed that magic represents an alternative form of rationality. Thus, writing on the magical songs of Marsilio Ficino, Gary Tomlinson argues for an unbridgeable divide between the rationality Ficino perceived in his magic and any rationality we might seek in it: we can view Ficino's magic from a 'dialogical space' between his world and ours, but we 'cannot cross over to his side.' Even to ask precisely how his magical songs functioned, expecting an answer in terms of our own mental categories, is unwarranted.[3] Similarly, Stanley Tambiah sees magic and religion as forms of rationality distinct from that of science – as ordering reality according to participatory rather than causal principles.[4] Many cultural anthropologists see magic not as causally efficacious but as symbolically expressive. In this interpretation, magic is not meant to work but to express wishes, or to encode in symbols a perception of how things do or should work. This is not to say that magic is *ir*rational but perhaps rather that it is *non*rational, or not grounded in a rational correlation of means and ends – a perspective close to that of Flint.[5]

I intend to argue that the people in medieval Europe who used the term 'magic' thought of it as neither irrational nor nonrational but as essentially rational. To conceive of magic as rational was to believe, first of all, that it could actually work (that its efficacy was shown by evidence recognized within the culture as authentic) and, secondly, that its workings were governed by principles (of theology or of physics) that could be coherently articulated. These principles need not always have been fully articulated or always articulated in the same way: conceptions of magic varied in their degree of specificity and in the specific types of principle they invoked. But the people in medieval Europe who used, feared, promoted, or condemned magic, and who identified magic as such, not only assumed it worked but could give (or assumed that authorities could give for them) reasonably specific explanations of how it worked. Not all those who shared these assumptions were rational in the sense of being bookish, given to abstraction, or even particularly deliberative, yet they normally used words in ways that had reasonably specific meaning, and their language reflected the way the world made cognitive sense to them.

I will begin by reviewing briefly the rational principles seen as underlying the operation of magic.[6] Then I will examine Flint's notion that magic was recognized, tolerated, even encouraged and taken over into official usage as a nonrational practice. Finally, I will suggest that, while the rational principles seen as explaining the operation of magic might be variously articulated in relatively specific or unspecific terms, the basic principles were widely shared in medieval culture; thus distinctions between 'popular' and 'elite' conceptions of magic must be significantly qualified.

Some recent historians of magic in antiquity have emphasized the rhetorical force of the term 'magic,' suggesting that it merely expressed disapproval for the rituals of alien cultures and that its force was emotive rather than conceptual. John Gager has argued that the label 'magician' tells us little more than that the speaker views the person so labeled as 'powerful, peripheral, and dangerous,' while Jacob Neusner formulates the position concisely: 'What I do is miracle; what you do is magic.'[7] But while 'magic' obviously served as a polemical term, even its polemical usage presupposed a shared understanding of magic as a cluster of countercultural rituals worked privately for the magicians' personal ends or those of their clients. The term 'magic' was sometimes used for the rituals of insiders (even members of elites) as well as outsiders or for the rites of people who became defined as outsiders only because they used magic.[8] To brand a Christian, a pagan, or a Jew as a magician was to use a word with prior and independent meaning and to give it abusive, polemical application.

The terms *magia, magica,* and *ars magica* were standard in educated language throughout the Middle Ages. This point requires emphasis, because it has been argued that in medieval Europe various specific terms were current ('enchantment,' 'necromancy,' 'conjuration,' or 'sorcery') but that the generic term 'magic' was not common until the sixteenth century.[9] To be sure, collections of charms do not present these formulas as magical, and the records of the witch trials may refer to curses and sorcery rather than magic. But Augustine and Isidore of Seville had discussed the concept of magic at some length, and educated writers throughout the Middle Ages routinely used these generic terms when the context required them. The *Index scientiarum occultarum* in J. P. Migne's *Patrologia latina* shows amply that *magia* and related terms remained in common use.[10] Rather than importing anachronistic definitions of magic into the study of medieval culture, it would seem appropriate to examine how medieval writers themselves used this language.

'Magic' could be used as a polemical term in medieval Europe as well as in antiquity. When Thomas Becket was reported working posthumous miracles, his adversaries 'spread it around everywhere that the monks of Canterbury did these things by magical incantations and by such devilish arts that they seemed rather than were miracles.' When heretics claimed to perform miracles, orthodox propagandists called their deeds magic.[11] The heretics were quite capable of returning the compliment: Lollard critics referred to Catholic practices as magical, not thereby redefining the concept of magic but suggesting instead that Catholics were engaged in wicked and even diabolical practices.[12] (There is certainly no evidence that Lollards or anyone else thought of rites as magical simply because they were said to work *ex opere operato*.[13]) Yet these derivative applications of the standard pejorative language presuppose a shared understanding of what 'magic' normally meant.

Because the meaning of 'magic' was never absolutely uniform or constant, and because the same concept could be expressed by various terms, it is perhaps most accurate to speak of parallel histories of words and concepts. The notion of demonic intervention in the natural order on behalf of those who invoked demons was deeply rooted in the religious and theological literature of Christianity; the idea of occult powers and processes within the natural order was firmly established and variously developed in philosophical and scientific writings from antiquity through the early modern era. Parallel to this history of concepts ran the history of the term *magia,* which usually referred in medieval usage to one or both of these concepts. In some contexts, *magia* and related terms could have less specific reference, analogous to that of *superstitio,* but as a rule of thumb *superstitio* implied irrational and improper religious practice, while *magia* suggested more often either a sinister or an occult rationality.[14] In early medieval writings, the theory of demonic intervention was articulated in far more specific terms than that of occult natural processes, and only demonic intervention was commonly called magic. After the twelfth century, when the notions of occult processes received more specific articulation, the term *magia* could equally apply to these. While the word remained highly connotative and could easily devolve into an abusive and polemical label, it was primarily a term of learned discourse whose semantic development closely paralleled that of the concepts of demonic intervention and occult natural process.

The conception of demonic intervention on behalf of conjurers was rooted in New Testament notions of apocalyptic conflict with demonic forces, but it received fuller articulation in early apocryphal literature such as the *Clementine Recognitions* and in hagiography,[15] and it found its definitive formulations in the West in Augustine's *De civitate Dei* and in Isidore of Seville's *Etymologiae.*[16] Even when Augustine and his early medieval successors did not give the term explicit definition, their use of *magia* makes clear that, for them, operation through demons was the only factor consistently found in all magical and no nonmagical transactions. Underlying this notion was a conflict model of spiritual process: the life of a Christian might be one of spiritual ascent, and it might involve a quest for purity, but most fundamentally it was a life of conflict with unseen, malevolent spirits. This assumption pervades the New Testament and retained its cogency until the Enlightenment.[17] For writers who conceived the life of the spirit essentially in terms of conflict with demons, magic was the most explicit form of collaboration with the enemy. Magic might accomplish the same effects as prayer or natural techniques; its distinguishing feature lay not in its effects but in the causal principle it invoked, the intervention of demons.[18]

When Christian writers referred to magic as entailing the aid of demons, they were in part reflecting a Christian equation of pagan deities and lesser *daimones* with fallen and malign spirits.[19] Many pagan writers would have agreed that magic had been invented and imparted by the gods, without accepting this characterization of their deities.[20] The idea that magic was devised, taught, and worked by demons would have seemed reasonable to anyone who read the Greek magical papyri or the *Sefer-ha-Razim* and found that healing magic appeared alongside rituals for killing people, gaining wealth or personal advantage, and coercing women into sexual submission.[21] A long tradition in the West from Augustine to the *Malleus maleficarum* and beyond specified in considerable detail how demons could conjecture the future, delude the mind and senses, manipulate physical objects by processes such as locomotion, and exploit occult virtues within nature (at which point natural and demonic magic intersect).[22] Doubts about the possibility of such demonic intervention in nature led the secular Aristotelians of fifteenth-century Italy, and Pietro Pomponazzi in the early sixteenth century, to dismiss the notion of demonic magic as philosophically unsupportable. Even if they nonetheless ultimately accepted the idea on faith, they called into question the claim that demonic magic was a rational concept.[23] In this respect, they distinguished themselves sharply from the great majority of their predecessors and contemporaries.

From the scientific literature of Greco-Roman antiquity, Christian writers inherited the alternative notion of occult powers and processes within the natural order. The category of natural magic differed from that of demonic magic in various ways: it often implied approbation, it was rooted in philosophical and scientific (rather than theological) discourse, its history was discontinuous, and it met frequently with skepticism from those who doubted that magic could be natural. Pliny the Elder had recounted the wondrous powers within nature that magicians claimed they could exploit: a tiny fish called the *echeneis* could cause a mighty ship to stop dead in the water;[24] the blood of a goat could crack a diamond; animals, plants, and minerals of all sorts were repositories of strange powers. Galen had alluded to occult virtues that could not be explained by the physical properties of a medicine's ingredients but were attributable rather to the 'whole substance' of a remedy. The Arabic tradition of occult sciences furnished ideas about astral emanations gathered and available in natural objects or extraordinary processes involving the human imagination.[25] All such occult (which is to say hidden, or non-manifest) powers and processes operated within the natural rather than supernatural order. Augustine recognized the reality of such processes, although he did not theorize in detail concerning them as Thomas Aquinas and others would later do; Roger Bacon took them as heralding a brighter technological tomorrow.[26] In medieval Europe, such phenomena were often called marvels or wonders *(mirabilia)* rather than magic,[27] but educated writers from the thirteenth century on increasingly cited these phenomena as works of natural magic, in effect reclaiming a classical sense of the term 'magic.' William of Auvergne in the thirteenth century was among the first Western writers to develop explicitly the notion of natural magic as a 'part of natural science.'[28] He and others, interested in probing the capacities of nature and extending the scope of natural science, reclaimed for such inquiry many phenomena that had appeared to be supernatural.[29] By the time Chaucer referred to 'magyk natureel,' the notion was well established,[30] and in the sixteenth and seventeenth centuries it became the subject of extensive discussion and debate.[31]

For those who accepted it, the concept recognized the limitations of ordinary scientific models and allowed for alternative explanatory paradigms within the natural order.

While the translation of Arabic texts in the twelfth and thirteenth centuries vastly increased Western knowledge about occult processes and their interpretation, the same Arabic culture that gave powerful impetus to the recognition of natural magic also furnished ample material that could call into question the nondemonic nature of this allegedly natural art.[32] Thus the claim that some magic was natural aroused deep suspicion, and defenders of this notion such as Jacques Lefévre d'Etaples sometimes grew suspicious of their own claims,[33] while other writers argued that all natural magic was merely demonic magic in disguise.[34] For those who accepted the reality of natural magic, it represented a distinct form of magical process alongside the demonic variety (whose reality few seriously doubted). For those who did not accept the notion of natural magic, the two conceptions represented not distinct forms of magic but rival interpretations of the same process, properly seen as always demonic. While there was thus no consensus in medieval culture regarding the notion of natural magic or its relationship to demonic magic, these were the chief conceptions of magic available to pre-modern Europeans. If educated people had been asked what magic was, they would have given something very much like one or both of these definitions.

Demonic magic entailed a complex interplay of wills: that of the magician, attempting to constrain the demons; that of the demons, seeking to deceive and ensnare the magician; that of God, whose permission was required for any magical effect; at times, that of a client, who secured the magician's service; and that of the victim, who might have some power to resist the magic.[35] Natural magic could be equally complex in its workings but was less fraught with personality. The powers it exploited were impersonal ones within the natural order. This is not to say that the use of these powers was necessarily mechanical; they exerted a greater or lesser (and perhaps indeterminate) influence, less like a machine than like a drug, which is assumed to affect the course of a disease whether or not it effects a cure.

To say that an effect was caused by occult powers and processes could in some cases be a programmatic assertion without the backing of a specific explanatory framework, but the writers who from the thirteenth century on reclaimed the term 'natural magic' also developed highly specific ideas that explained not only the general operation of these processes (through occult virtues, sympathies and antipathies, astral forces, and psychological powers) but, in addition, the specific working of particular forms of magic. In other words, they could explain not only why the carving of astral images might be effective but why an image for a particular planet could have its specific efficacy. Marsilio Ficino, who drew his explanations from sources as early as Plotinus and as recent as Thomas Aquinas, represents a high point in this effort at specific explanation.[36] Nicole Oresme explained the workings of natural magic in alternative terms, as the result of properties or 'configurations' inherent in sublunary objects and verbal formulas.[37] While such writers were perhaps exceptional in the level of the specificity of their explanations for natural magic, they shared with most of their contemporaries the conviction that various occult processes within nature were rational, in the sense that they worked and that their workings could in principle be explained. Theorists differed from other people not so much because they interpreted magic according to rational principles but because they had more specific rational explanations of how magic worked.

Anthropology has accustomed us to conceive of magic as distinct from both religion and science.[38] In a medieval context, however, the question is not so much the relationship between magic and either science or religion but its relationship to approved religion and to ordinary science: demonic magic is itself essentially religious (or perhaps irreligious but at least not nonreligious), while natural magic could easily be combined with devotional practice. The terms 'magic' and 'religion' were both current in medieval discourse, but they would not usually have been viewed as opposites or even as essentially distinct categories.[39] The distinction between 'magic' and 'miracle' would have seemed more familiar to medieval Europeans. Both were extraordinary phenomena, inexplicable solely by the known laws of nature, and in each case the defining feature was the operation of exceptional forces: demonic intervention, occult virtues within nature, or divine intervention. Ordinary science, natural magic, approved religion, and demonic magic could all be rationally explained but by appeal to different types of causal principle.

Valerie Flint sees magic (and believes that medieval churchmen saw it) as a nonrational practice with essentially psychological efficacy; she thus cannot believe it was fundamentally different from any other rite with similar efficacy. For her, the churchmen's efforts to distinguish between what they condemned as magic and what they condoned as legitimate ritual mask a more basic similarity between the two. Yet it seems clear that Augustine and his successors viewed magic as a rationally explicable practice with objective efficacy – as a means for securing the aid of demons or (in later interpretation) for exploiting occult virtues in nature. When they branded rituals as magical, it was because they saw these rites as relying on demonic causality that was ultimately harmful, even if apparently helpful. When they encouraged or tolerated other rituals, it was because they perceived their causality as nondemonic. Considerations of power no doubt helped to give direction to these concerns; prior cause for enmity obviously made it easier to perceive another person as a magician. But Flint's book provides ample evidence that condemnation of magic was not in any simple sense an assertion of cultural hegemony: churchmen were willing to tolerate various forms of unofficial ritual so long as these did not transgress vitally important boundaries, and the thickest line of demarcation was that traced by early Christian demonology.

Flint wrote *The Rise of Magic* largely in response to the notion that medieval churchmen were unable to discern and prevent the seepage of superstition and pagan magic into Christian culture.[40] Reacting against this 'faintly condescending colonialism in history', she argues that early medieval compromises with pagan magic were deliberate, the product of 'a delicate social sensitivity or extended reasoning at the highest levels'. Churchmen tolerated and even encouraged certain magic, to avoid conflict with existing traditions and leaders or to appropriate for their own religion the consolations, loyalties, devotional habits, and spiritual aspirations associated with non-Christian magic. They valued this magic 'above some of the manifestations of "reason" they saw about them'.[41] Rational judgment thus lent its approval to nonrational practice. Flint herself clearly values and wishes to defend a culture not yet affected by disenchantment, a culture still appreciative of the 'mystery, miracle, and magic' that so offended sixteenth-century reformers.[42] She sees the landscape of medieval culture as a land of grace, filled with diverse manifestations of extraordinary power. The historians she criticizes argue in effect that irrational medieval Christian rituals were equivalent to magic and just as bad; Flint revises this judgment, maintaining that nonrational medieval Christian rituals were equivalent to magic and just as good.

Ultimately, she views the distinction between approved and disapproved ritual as a distinction without a real difference. She insists repeatedly that many approved rituals were magical, even if churchmen said otherwise. But this ahistorical use of the word 'magic' blurs distinctions vitally important to those who made them. In her attempt to defend early medieval churchmen and their acceptance of 'magic', Flint seems to ascribe to them a kind of theoretical incoherence, a sacrificing of principle to practical necessity. She argues that in spite of their own protestations, what they were defending and perpetrating was also a kind of magic; they tried to distinguish between magic and approved ritual, but their distinctions were not cogent. Flint's effort to avoid condescension and recognize the integrity of early medieval Christianization might be more successful if she recognized more fully how and why medieval writers used the term 'magic' as they did. In speaking of the church's own magic, Flint is on common ground with the historians she sets out to oppose, who refer to 'the magic of the medieval Church' as if that phrase were unproblematic.[43] She thus concedes too much to the opposition, allowing them to define the primary terms for discussion. The task for early churchmen was, to be sure, one of negotiating cultural differences, but these churchmen conceived of magic and its relation to approved ritual in ways that made more coherent sense than Flint assumes and that did not compromise their theological principles.

Flint is aware of using the term 'magic' more broadly than early medieval writers did: she admits that these writers distinguished explicitly between their rituals and magic.[44] Yet in cases where early medieval writers speak of miracles, wonders, mysteries, and grace, and even where they expressly contrasted such processes with magic, Flint wishes to correct this medieval usage and to speak of approved forms of magic. She defines magic as 'the exercise of a preternatural control over nature by human beings, with the assistance of forces more powerful than they,' thus arbitrarily absorbing much official and approved religious practice into the capacious sponge of magic.[45] She sees religion and magic as lying along a spectrum: in a cautious nod toward Frazerian categories, she writes that religion 'at its best' requires 'reverence, an inclination to trust, to be open and to please, and be pleased by, powers superior in every way to humankind,' while magic 'may wish to subordinate and to command these powers.'[46] By her criteria, however, much (perhaps most) religious practice would then be magical.

I do not wish to argue that historians must always be restricted to a historical use of language, but it seems particularly unhelpful to use a historical term in a way that not only differs from but actually conflicts with its historical usage.[47] To say that certain rituals constituted magic even though medieval writers specifically excluded these rites from the category of magic as they defined it is to distract from the specific rationalities assigned to magic and to nonmagical practice within the historical culture. Flint uses her extremely broad definition of magic to highlight what she sees as the unacknowledged similarity, indeed, the functional equivalence, between magic and much Christian ritual. She sees the veneration of relics, the consultation of oracles, the use of charms and ligatures (medical use of magical objects bound to the patient), the devotion to holy wells, and the invocation of spirits all as salutary forms of nonrationality, and she classifies them as 'magic.' To observers in medieval Europe, however, these practices would have been grounded in fundamentally distinct rational assumptions. Invoking malign spirits might be illicit, but an observer who granted that demons exist and that they can be persuaded to serve human purposes could not think of such invocation as nonrational. Relying on the miraculous powers of saints might or might not be encouraged, but a contemporary who recognized the efficacy of the saints' intercession could by no means classify such recourse as nonrational. Wearing a gem or an herb to ward off evil influences might seem futile to some observers, but those who credited the gem or herb with occult powers were ascribing rationality to the practice. All three operations were practiced and defended because they were perceived as rational, yet the assumed causality that made them so was not the same: the intervention of demons, the intercession of saints, and occult powers within nature were causal factors in principle distinct from each other, each having its specific rationality, even if in some cases they could be combined or confused. It is only on the modern assumption that all these operations are irrational or nonrational that they can be grouped together as manifestations of 'magic.'

Flint sees the mainstream ecclesiastical policy (after the initial wave of conversion) as one of benign toleration, even encouragement, of pre-Christian ritual. Her articulation of this argument, which echoes earlier work, is on the whole convincing.[48] She maintains that the incorporation of pagan rites into the Christian culture of the early Middle Ages was not an accidental or grudging accommodation to the missionized populace but rather the result of conscious choice by monks and other churchmen who ascribed a positive value to the magic thus incorporated.[49] The initial effort of missionaries may have been to erase all vestiges of pagan culture, but (Flint argues) churchmen soon recognized that subtler and often gentler approaches were needed, and they came to value the skills of pagan magicians. The practices taken over by medieval Christianity, Flint insists, were not merely 'pagan survivals.' They were vitally important elements deliberately absorbed into a new cultural mélange.[50] Flint does not argue that official attitudes toward Christianized magic were uniformly benign but recognizes a spectrum ranging from hearty approval to severe condemnation.[51] She finds evidence of tension, for example, at the monastery of San Pedro de Montes, where a seventh-century abbot accused the monks of receiving magicians and other malefactors and charged the local priest as well with participating in orgiastic 'nocturnal forest rites.' Flint plausibly suggests that these were ancient and innocent rituals which the monks and priest, unlike the abbot, were eager to accommodate.[52] On balance, she finds more evidence of genteel toleration than of repudiation. She presents an image of a kinder, gentler Middle Ages, in which the relationship between shepherds and sheep, even black ones, was less conflictual than cooperative.[53]

While Flint seems at times to overstate the case for toleration,[54] she has enriched our understanding of the long-range dynamics of conversion, the process by which European peoples over several generations developed and adopted a new type of Christianity. In response to a critique inspired ultimately by Protestant polemics, she shows how the official representatives of Christianity engaged in a process of reasonable negotiation with pagan tradition. I sympathize with Flint's effort to approach medieval Christianity on its own terms; if on certain points my reading of the sources differs from hers, the disagreement is thus largely intramural and perhaps less significant than our common goal of contextual understanding, although the differences are nonetheless real and not negligible.

The best evidence for both toleration and systematic condemnation of unofficial rituals comes not from the chief period of missionary activity in Western and Central Europe but from roughly the ninth through the eleventh centuries. Why was it that many churchmen of the Carolingian and Ottonian ages could make accommodations that their predecessors and successors found problematic? Flint argues that these churchmen had come to recognize a positive value in the paganism and magic they encountered, and they realized that they could more effectively retain their following by exercising moderation. It would be useful to inquire further into the types of people to whom Flint refers and the circumstances in which they found themselves. The churchmen she has in mind came after the period of embattled polemics and heroic early missionary ventures[55] but before the period in which educated clerics (such as R. I. Moore's twelfth-century *clerici* or even later firebrands such as Bernardino of Siena) sought to reform Christendom according to abstract ideals.[56] They found themselves in a hiatus between two forms of zealotry. Essentially ecclesiastical functionaries, from a social and institutional viewpoint they resemble those Chinese bureaucrats of Philip A. Kuhn's *Soulstealers* who thwarted prosecution for charges of magic that they could not quite take seriously.[57] The clerics surely accepted the principle that the work of demons must be suppressed, but they could not persuade themselves that ordinary charms and ligatures were demonic. They were disinclined to see demons lurking behind every herb. These churchmen may indeed have been genteel and urbane in the ways that Flint suggests; Stephen Jaeger has argued that it was within their circles that ideals of courtliness first arose.[58] But we may be permitted to suspect that this urbanity manifested itself more in a sense of proportion, a recognition that certain problems are less vital than others, than in any positive valuation of pagan magic.

Flint's notion that early medieval clerics approved magic for largely pragmatic reasons shows affinity with other recent studies on magic. Much recent historical and anthropological work interprets magic as an expression of desire that has psychological rather than physical efficacy: it gives and sustains confidence or perhaps enhances the magician's sense of well-being; it serves as an emotional outlet and a means of emotional support for the practitioner, the client, or both.[59] This understanding of magic is central to Flint's work,[60] and it serves as a warning against a rationalist repudiation of magic: while the rationalist takes magic to be contemptible because it offends against reason, Flint and other writers in effect suggest that magic deserves sympathetic consideration because it is psychologically and socially useful. But to assume that magic either has power to coerce external forces or else has nothing but subjective efficacy is to create a false disjunction. It is indeed likely that people who practiced magic or had it practiced on their behalf experienced a powerful emotional reaction, which could be positive or problematic depending on the circumstances. But that this emotional effect was the reason for their practice remains highly doubtful, and writers such as Augustine, Isidore, and Hincmar of Reims certainly neither defended nor attacked magic because of its subjective effects. Isidore's category of ocular illusion (*praestigium*) might be seen as pointing in this direction, but he argues that *magi* are also called *malefici* because of the magnitude of their presumably real accomplishments of disrupting the elements, disturbing people's minds, and killing with charms alone, without poison. Reference to early medieval magic as a quest for 'enrichment of human life' seems suspiciously anachronistic.[61]

Flint shows that much of the ritual tolerated or encouraged by medieval clerics resembled in certain ways what these clerics called magic and that these rites may have been derived from the ritual practice of pre-Christian culture. Indeed, on these points, further evidence might readily be added.[62] Yet Flint does not adequately explain why rituals that to us seem similar to magic were not so defined within medieval culture or on what grounds medieval writers distinguished between these rituals and those they did call magic.

If, as Flint suggests, early medieval churchmen could not recognize magic as such, why was this so? She argues that for them the term 'magic' was too negative a term to be used for rituals they wished to condone.[63] They thus used the term only for rites practiced for unacceptable ends, or by inappropriate persons, or with reprehensible techniques. As she rightly shows, the distinction between beneficent and maleficent ends was crucial in the Theodosian Code. When saints were accused of using 'diabolical enchantments,' they could be defended on the grounds that their results were good, although the implication here *prima facie* is not that laudable ends excused diabolical means but that the means could not have been diabolical. Flint quotes Augustine as recognizing that magicians and good Christians 'may do similar things'; the difference 'lies in their means and ends.' She takes this to be the message in stories about Simon Magus, who is criticized for using magic 'in unacceptable ways and for unacceptable ends.' But when she refers to illegitimate means, Flint seems to suggest that it was essentially a matter of good taste that made certain ritual means legitimate and others not: ligatures and magic potions were disgusting and therefore reprehensible. When she refers to means as a criterion for distinguishing legitimate from illegitimate ritual, she seems to have in mind chiefly the immediate, concrete means: potions that aroused disgust were thought reprehensible. Citing the council of Rome in 494, the *Admonitio generalis* of 789, and early ninth-century capitularies, Flint writes that the invocation of angels was sometimes condemned because it was 'over-enthusiastic.'[64]

Flint sees the Christianization of pagan ritual as essentially cosmetic.[65] At times, her assertions of similarity seem particularly forced.[66] Thus her chief specimen of 'Christian love magic' is the 'ecclesiastical medicine' recommended by Hincmar of Reims for impotence: confession with contrite heart and humbled spirit, alms, prayer and fasting, and exorcisms. Flint views these as techniques 'of a quite clearly magical kind.'[67] But, if so, then the entire sacramental system is equally magical – a conclusion that could only be drawn outside the context of medieval sacramental thinking. Elsewhere, to be sure, especially in hagiography, the alleged similarities are more convincing: when magicians accomplished nothing with herbs and incantations, oil and wax from St. Martin's tomb were immediately effective.[68] In such cases, the Christian rituals as reported appear closely similar in form and function to the magic of non-Christian culture. It does not seem frivolous to argue here that what looks like magic and sounds like magic must surely be magic. Even in these cases, however, we are left with the question why contemporaries did not perceive the similarities Flint wishes to underscore. The answer to this question, I would contend, is that medieval churchmen differed from modern historians in their distinctions between central and marginal concerns. From the perspective of Hincmar of Reims or Rabanus Maurus, to rewrite a charm and substitute Christ for Odin was not to make a slight adjustment. Even if a story originally told about Odin was retained as part of the charm, its transference to Christ made a substantial difference.[69] The adjustment did not result in a Christian type of magic; rather, it involved editing out the magical elements.[70] Flint seems concerned mainly with the outer forms and results of the rituals in question; what concerned medieval churchmen more deeply was the question *how* a ritual worked, the specific rationality assigned to it.

At one point, Flint tellingly refers to early medieval writers 'associating demons with the magic they condemned.'[71] This way of phrasing the point seems precisely backward, analogous to speaking of health inspectors associating rats with the restaurants they condemn. There may be corrupt, prejudiced, irrational, or even arbitrary inspectors who close down restaurants and use rat infestation as their excuse, but normally one trusts that the presence of vermin is the reason and not merely a rationalization for condemning restaurants. So, too, Christian writers did not argue that 'magic is evil and therefore involves the intervention of demons' but that 'magic involves the intervention of demons and therefore is evil.'[72] Doubtless, certain classes of people were repeatedly singled out for condemnation (especially women, Jews, and political adversaries), and in individual cases hostile treatment may well have been rationalized by allegations of magic. But such accusations could be recognized as cogent precisely because the society shared a deep anxiety about collaboration with demons.

Flint sees pagan magic as an alternative form of religious practice and the magicians as alternative priests. Religious systems are not altogether interchangeable, however: they may promote different values, perform different functions within a culture, and involve different types of organizational structure. Without meaning to perpetuate a naïve equation of Haitian folk religion (vodun) with magic, Lawrence E. Harrison has recently argued that this religion has served as 'a highly conservative force,' has aided in isolating Haitians from progressive ideas, and has encouraged dysfunctional norms of behavior that are partly responsible for Haiti's political and economic problems.[73] The medieval critique of magic, like Harrison's critique of vodun, assumed that different cultural systems rest on distinct and potentially incompatible norms. Cultural conflict may arise from a failure to perceive shared values, but it may also emerge from a realistic perception of conflicting values. Medieval magic was not simply the religious ritual of a rival culture; it gave ritual (and therefore practical) expression to a system of values whose eradication was a basic goal of Christian missionary work and later preaching. It encouraged a privatization of numinous and dangerous powers, a removal of the spiritual process away from the public sphere and into a relationship of independent practitioners to their clients that was guaranteed to arouse suspicion.

Individual rituals taken in isolation may indeed suggest a close similarity between pagan and Christian rituals, and it may be tempting to construe the practitioners as pagan priests, analogous to Christian clergy. The 'wizards' who appear in the legendary accounts of Celtic hagiography may indeed be distant reflections of historical Druids,[74] and the magicians confronted in the first flush of missionary effort in a particular region may well have been priests, such as Coifi the *primus pontificum* in Anglo-Saxon England.[75] But the later the period, the more likely it is – particularly by the Carolingian and Ottonian eras, from which Flint draws most of her evidence of accommodation – that the magicians were professional or semi-professional healers and diviners who worked privately, for a fee, on behalf of their clients, closer to Keith Thomas's 'cunning men' than to Coifi. There is no evidence that such practitioners were expected to serve as community leaders, to teach, or to set any sort of moral example for people under their charge. Not being thought of as priests, they did not really have followers for whose care they were regularly responsible. Granted, one should not overestimate the official or supralocal character of Christian priesthood in the early Middle Ages[76] or the possibility that Christian priests might practice what their own Christian culture defined as magic.[77] But in early medieval Europe, priests were at least in principle intended to exercise a public and regular ministry for a community,[78] and the role of magician (or local healer and diviner) was in this respect different. The ecclesiastical perception of magicians as diabolical agents who worked harm when they could and healed only to cause ulterior harm obviously cannot be taken as objective truth. But these distortions rested on realities that lent themselves easily to such interpretation: magicians in many if not most cultures are feared and distrusted even by those who employ them, and there is little reason for surprise if officialdom casts a suspicious eye on such practitioners.

This is not to argue with Marcel Mauss that religion is essentially official and magic unofficial;[79] much of the unofficial ritual practiced by medieval laity and lower clergy was tolerated, however grudgingly, as nonmagical, provided their rituals appealed to the same spiritual forces that orthodoxy recognized as legitimate.[80] Yet private practitioners using unofficial rituals for personal ends readily fell under the suspicion that what they were doing was fundamentally and not just circumstantially different: that they were in fact invoking demons. Unofficial healers and diviners were not inherently reprobate, but their status was ambiguous and they came easily into disrepute.

But is it not the case that people in medieval Europe would have *experienced* magic and approved ritual similarly, even if these were explained in different terms? Is it not legitimate to use 'magic' as what Flint calls a 'sounding word,' suited to evoke the experience of various rituals?[81] We can analyze hermeneutically how medieval people made cognitive sense of their experience, but how can we know about the unreflective, intuitive experience itself? It is interesting and not implausible to suppose that on an experiential level what churchmen called magic and what they called blessings or sacramentals had similar effects: that the two systems evoked similar feelings of contact with the mysterious or the numinous and that all the effort to define distinct areas of licit and illicit ritual on a cognitive map was in large part a strategy to gain a sense of control over dangerous terrain. Yet this is supposition; we are faced here with that barrier to historical understanding that Gary Tomlinson warns of. We can only intuit what medieval people might have intuited – but we may come to know what they claimed to know, although we will know it differently, because we cannot share the intuitions in which their knowledge was grounded.

It could be argued that, in accepting the definitions of magic used by the educated in medieval society, I am presenting a distorted picture of medieval thought about magic. C. John Sommerville has contended in a different context that accepting the definitions of historical elites 'robs dissent of its true voice and its nuance' and cloaks popular mentalities, whereas substituting 'the sort of generic definition refined by anthropologists ... avoids prejudging what we might uncover.'[82] Indeed, while educated clerics thought of magic as a rational activity (in the sense specified above), it might well be argued that questions of rationality would not have occurred to most of the population. The evidence cited so far has come chiefly from clerical writings, in which notions of magic were formally articulated. It is not unreasonable to ask whether clerical distinctions were too subtle for the populace at large. On this point, the position of Aron Gurevich may represent something of a historical consensus: 'To the majority of the population the difference between amulets, which were strictly forbidden by the clergy, and holy relics was not too clear ... Magic was admitted by the church into its practices and rituals; the border dividing Christian magic from what was condemned as *maleficium* was indefinite and surely unclear to the parishioners.'[83]

It might seem less prejudicial to use modern, anthropological definitions that do not commit us to the bias of any historical class and do not blind us to the perceptions of the illiterate. But when we attempt to use anthropological definitions of magic, we quickly find that they fit the historical material awkwardly at best,[84] and it is not obvious that medieval peasants are well served by conceptions imported on their behalf from Africa or Melanesia or by anachronistic redefinition of terms used by their learned contemporaries. If, for comparative purposes, we need terms that are free of specific historical associations, it is surely best to use genuinely neutral terms such as 'unofficial ritual,' rather than to invest historical words such as 'magic' with anachronistic neutral meaning.[85]

It could well be argued that 'magic' must simply be recognized as chiefly a term of literate discourse. But, even so, how different were 'popular' perceptions in this area from those of the theological and scientific writers? I have argued elsewhere that the distinction between 'popular' and 'elite' cultures can usefully be subordinated to a more nuanced and fluid distinction between 'common tradition' and various specialized traditions; once this basic distinction is established, it becomes possible to see diverse 'high' and 'low' cultures as forms of specialized culture related in complex and shifting ways to common culture.[86] Much of the culture at any time was common: not universal or uniform but sufficiently diffused that it cannot be assigned to any specific subgroup and expressive more of solidarity than of either hegemony or dissent. Magical gems, for example, were primarily found in courtly circles that could afford such luxuries, but the use of image magic for bodily harm and sexual attraction seems to have been part of the common culture of medieval Europe, used by people of various positions in society and feared (to different degrees) by virtually all, even if its details and interpretation varied considerably.[87] Similarly, the basic idea of conjuring demons seems to have been widely enough diffused to count as part of common culture, although the fully developed methods of necromancy were practiced chiefly in a clerical underworld. When we hear accusations of diabolism (involving the witches' Sabbath and related phenomena), the voices we are hearing seem to be those of a theologically informed elite, at least in the early stages of the witch trials.[88] The question, then, is not whether 'popular' notions of magic can be distinguished from 'elite' conceptions but the extent to which the articulated understanding of magic found in educated circles rests on an understanding of magic that was 'common,' or widely shared.

It is only rarely that we have anything like direct access to the mental world of the nonliterate, and when we do find words for specific actions and objects (curses, wax images) more often than generic terms suggesting a broad conception of magic. It is possible, however, to speak about the relationship between the Latin and the vernacular words with broadest application. The terms *magia* and *ars magica*, and related terms such as *nigromantia*, were themselves taken over by the vernaculars yet retained their character as essentially learned parlance; when Chaucer's Franklin uses 'magyk natureel,' there is no reason to think that the term meant anything different from *magia naturalis*. Native vernacular terms, however, such as *sorcellerie* and *wiccecræft*, had meanings that overlapped yet differed from that of *magia*. Without pretending to provide a full analysis, let me make two suggestions: first, these vernacular words, more than *magia* and *ars magica*, were used mainly for harmful and secretive magic; but, second, like the Latin terms, these vernacular expressions referred to activities that drew on either sinister or occult sources of power.

In vernacular texts such as the Icelandic sagas, for instance, sorcery appears primarily as a mysterious and unfair way of attacking one's adversaries.[89] Rather than approaching them openly with force that can be seen and confronted, the sorcerer attacks secretly, with a force that is unknown and thus not confrontable. Sorcerers tap into a hidden source of dark power disproportionate to their operations: it is not the carving of runes per se that works wondrous effects but the invocation of a mysterious power through the runes. Ultimately, it was this disproportion between means and effects that was puzzling and disturbing. Educated observers might try to make sense of the disproportion by speaking of occult virtues deriving perhaps from astral influence or by explaining magical rites as signs to the demons who carry out the magician's will. In giving these explanations, however, the elite observers were expressing a perception that surely did not differ greatly from that of any observer; they were rationalizing a sense of disproportion that aroused varying mixtures of wonderment and fear in anyone who suspected the workings of magic. Fear of magicians was widespread in medieval society; villagers and townspeople in the early as well as the late Middle Ages accused as sorcerers those of their neighbors who over several years had gained a reputation for working harm, even if many also served as healers and diviners. There is nothing extraordinary about this simultaneous fear of the practitioner and interest in the practice; it was found in the pagan culture of antiquity, and it would be surprising not to find it in medieval Europe.

The practitioners of magic, whether educated or not, also shared conceptions of magic at least broadly similar to those of the clerical interpreters of magic. Allegations of *wiccecræft* in Anglo-Saxon England, for example, make clear that people at all levels of society saw it not merely as a venting of wishes or frustrations but as effective.[90] The person who observed ritual taboos in gathering herbs, or who used a charm with *voces mysticae,* or who imbibed pulverized vulture kidneys to restore sexual potency clearly recognized that there was occult virtue in these actions, formulas, and substances. In somewhat the same way that *sorcellerie* and *wiccecræft* were most distinctly marked off from other forms of activity when perceived as maleficent, it is probably the case that in non-learned circles substances were more likely to be perceived as having occult natural power when they were repugnant and taboo: late medieval trials for sorcery, for example, suggest that such materials as menstrual blood, excrement, or dead animals could easily be seen as bearing mysterious and extraordinary power.[91] Among the educated, the idea of natural magic might be given more specific articulation as the result of astral influences or other forces within nature. The educated and the populace at large seem to have shared alternative explanations having to do with sympathy and antipathy, the powers of elves, and symbolic resemblances. At any rate, the fundamental notion of exploiting secret powers in nature was part of a common culture that scientists and philosophers shared with practitioners and observers generally.

The basic ideas of demonic magic also belonged to this common tradition. The magicians of late antiquity who conjured *daimones* may not have understood them as specifically fallen spirits, but they, like Christian theologians, recognized that such magic worked through the deliberately sought intervention of spirits willing to collaborate in murder, seduction, and personal aggrandizement.[92] The clerical necromancers of the later Middle Ages sometimes claimed to be conjuring neutral spirits but often explicitly identified their *spiritus maligni* with the demons of Christian theology.[93] Uneducated magicians seem also at times to have dabbled in similar forms of conjuration.[94] Once again, the ideas of practitioners, observers, and theorists about what was occurring were recognizably similar, even if the theologians had more specific notions of how demonic magic worked. The basic rational principles ascribed to magic were part of a common culture, even if the theological formulation of those principles was part of a specialized subculture. The concepts of magic here in question were not simply expressions of a hegemonic culture: even when prosecution for magic served as a means of asserting or establishing social or political control, it was effective largely because its legitimating conceptions were widely shared and thus elicited collaboration and built coalitions that cut across social and cultural lines.[95]

As for Gurevich's notion that most people would not have distinguished ecclesiastical rituals from magic, much depends on precisely what is being asserted. One might argue that people without occasion to explore very deeply the rational assumptions entailed in the use of vulture kidneys or the rational postulates implied in making the sign of the cross might readily confuse or conflate these systems of behavior. But Gurevich seems to posit an implausible degree of cultural impenetrability. There is nothing conceptually difficult in the basic distinction between appeal to God, invocation of demons, and exploitation of mysterious powers within nature. To assume that the majority of the population was unable to grasp such principles is to underrate the capacity of the lay mind. Anthropologists have found distinctions no less subtle than these in nonliterate cultures worldwide. And even if many people were nonreflective about these various forms of ritual, it would be more accurate to say that the conceptual relationship between the ritual systems simply was not an issue for these people. One cannot then assert that such observers categorized both forms of ritual (use of vulture kidneys and making the sign of the cross) as magic; one must maintain simply that they saw no need to locate either behavior in a system of abstract categories.

Some might still argue that on an intuitive level most people would have experienced the church's rituals and magical acts similarly. When historians rely on arguments of this sort, however, one suspects that they are expressing their own intuitions. It may well be that if members of the historical profession were to perform arcane rituals with hoopoe hearts, they would be unable to distinguish these from the rites performed in churches.[96] But if so, is this a fact of real historical significance?

Notes

1. Valerie I. J. Flint, *The Rise of Magic in Early Medieval Europe* (Princeton, N.J., 1991), 12, 4, 406, see also 83 and following, 203 and following. For a highly illuminating review article of Flint's book, see Alexander Murray, 'Missionaries and Magic in Dark-Age Europe,' *Past and Present,* 136 (August 1992): 186–205. See also the review by R. I. Moore, *Times Higher Education Supplement* (December 20, 1991): 21.

2. Lynn Thorndike, *The History of Magic and Experimental Science*, 8 vols. (New York, 1923–58); Frances A. Yates, *Giordano Bruno and the Hermetic Tradition* (London, 1964); and Yates, *The Occult Philosophy in the Elizabethan Age* (London, 1979). See more recently Brian Vickers, ed., *Occult and Scientific Mentalities in the Renaissance* (New York, 1986); and Ingrid Merkel and Allen G. Debus, eds., *Hermeticism and the Renaissance: Intellectual History and the Occult in Early Modern Europe* (Washington, D.C., 1988).

3. Gary Tomlinson, *Music in Renaissance Magic: Toward a Historiography of Others* (Chicago, 1992), esp. chap. 8, pp. 247–52.

4. Stanley Jeyaraja Tambiah, *Magic, Science, Religion, and the Scope of Rationality* (New York, 1990). This characterization greatly simplifies Tambiah's dialogue with numerous alternative views. Magic and science, conceived as alternative rational systems, can presumably coexist not only within a culture but even within a single mind: for example, T. M. Luhrmann, in *Persuasions of the Witch's Craft: Ritual Magic in Contemporary England* (Cambridge, Mass., 1989), examines the magical practices of modern-day English witches, seeking to explain how magic makes rational sense even to sophisticated people with scientific education.

5. On this issue, see especially Hans H. Penner, 'Rationality, Ritual, and Science,' in Jacob Neusner, Ernest S. Frerichs, and Paul V. McCracken Flesher, eds., *Religion, Science, and Magic in Concert and in Conflict* (New York, 1989), 11–24; and Robin Horton, 'African Traditional Thought and Western Science,' *Africa*, 37 (1967): 50–71, 155–87, reprinted in highly abridged form in Max Marwick, ed., *Witchcraft and Sorcery* (Harmondsworth, 1970), 342–68.

6. In this section, I will in part be extending certain arguments of my book, *Magic in the Middle Ages* (Cambridge, 1989). The function of this book as a concise survey did not permit extended discussion of potentially controversial issues.

7. John G. Gager, ed., *Curse Tablets and Binding Spells from the Ancient World* (New York, 1992), 25; Jacob Neusner, 'Science and Magic, Miracle and Magic in Formative Judaism: The System and the Difference,' in Neusner, *et al., Religion, Science, and Magic*, 63. See also R. M. Grant, *Gnosticism and Early Christianity*, 2d edn. (New York, 1966), 93.

8. Gager recognizes this fact in *Curse Tablets*, 39, n. 119.

9. Keith Thomas, 'An Anthropology of Religion and Magic,' *Journal of Interdisciplinaiy History*, 6 (Summer 1975): 91–109 (esp. 94 and following), relying on Robert-Léon Wagner, 'Sorcier' et 'Magicien': Contribution a l'histoire du vocabulaire de la magie* (Paris, 1939), 26 and following. (Wagner does recognize the use of *magia* as a generic term in theological discussion.)

10. J. P. Migne, ed., *Patrologia latina*, vol. 221, especially the *sectio prima* of this index, cols. 443–49.

11. Benedicta Ward, *Miracles and the Medieval Mind: Theory, Record and Event, 1000–1215* (London, 1982), 12 and following.

12. Keith Thomas, *Religion and the Decline of Magic* (New York, 1971), 62, cites one clear indication that Lollards as early as 1395 were rejecting orthodox rituals as tantamount to a kind of magic: the Twelve Conclusions of 1395 refer to the 'exorcisms and hallowings, made in the Church' as 'the very practice of necromancy, rather than of the holy theology … For by such exorcisms creatures be charged to be of higher virtue than their own kind, and we see nothing of change in no such creature that is so charmed, but by false belief, the which is the principle of the devil's craft.' Note, however, that the reasoning in this polemic does *not* imply that orthodox ritual is 'magical' because it is coercive; the point is simply that such 'false belief' is diabolical and thus belongs to the 'devil's craft' of necromancy. While the rituals themselves are branded as necromantic at the outset, and the reference to false imputation of superior 'virtue' could suggest an allusion to the *virtutes occultae* of natural magic, it is false belief regarding them that is ultimately condemned as diabolical. The language was equally unspecific when Lollards spoke of Mary as the 'witch of Walsingham' (p. 62) and when lay people (according to Reginald Pecock) held sacraments 'to be points of witchcraft and bindings' (p. 74). It would be misleading to suggest on the basis of this evidence that the Lollards were proposing a new concept of magic and more accurate to say that they were using received notions of magic abusively to vilify the established church.

13. Sacraments were thought to function independently of subjective disposition, or *ex opere operato,* but only because God had ordained that he should operate through them in this manner, and in medieval theology it was the divinely ordained and accomplished efficacy of the sacraments – rather than assumed automatic efficacy – that was their defining feature. Thomas Aquinas discusses such questions in *In IV Sententiarum*, 2.1.4d ra. 2 and 4.3.2c ra. 1, in *Opera omnia*, Robertus Busa, ed., vol. 1 (Stuttgart-Bad Cannstatt, 1980), 429 and 441; in the latter passage, he speaks of baptism as effective 'ex opere operato, quod est opus dei.' See further the complex formulations of Thomas Aquinas in the *Summa theologiae*, iii.64. Aquinas's distinctions would obviously not have been replicated in the lay understanding of ritual; but, just as obviously, the basic idea that certain rituals were occasions for divine action was one that could be grasped by virtually everyone.

14. Dieter Harmening, *Superstitio: Überlieferungs- und theoriegeschichtliche Untersuchungen zur kirchlich- theologischen Aberglaubensliteratur des Mittelalters* (Berlin, 1979), 33–42, traces the history of the word's meaning. Thomas Aquinas defined superstition as divine worship, rendered *deo vero, modo indebito* (in the wrong manner) or *ei cui non debet exhiberi* (to the wrong subject), in *Summa theologiae*, II-II, q. 92, art. 2; either form could presumably include magical practice *per accidens* without being essentially identified with magic. Johann Hartlieb, *Das Buch aller verbotenen Künste, des Aberglaubens und der Zauberei*, Falk Eisermann and Eckhard Graf, ed. and trans. (Ahlerstedt, 1989), illustrates the complexities of medieval usage: he routinely calls the 'forbidden arts' superstitious and virtually never magical, although he clearly builds on a tradition of antimagical literature going back to Isidore, and he ascribes the efficacy of these arts to demonic agency. Augustine, *De doctrina Christiana*, iii. 19–29, makes no clear distinction between *superstitio* and *artes magicae*. George Ferzoco, 'Historical and Hagiographical Aspects of the Religious World of Peter of Morrone,' in W. Capezali, ed., 3. *Pietro del Morrone Celestino V nel medioevo monastico: Atti del Convegno storico internazionale L'Aquila, 26–27 agosto 1988*, 227–37, argues that clerics in Pope Celestine V's entourage found his blessings dangerously magical, but they would more probably have raised the question of *superstitio*. For an example of prosecution of a priest for defending superstition, see Robert E. Lerner, 'Werner di Friedberg intrappolato dalla legge,' in *La parola all'accusato* (Palermo, 1991), 268–81. The distinction between magic and superstition was not critical when the question was simply what sorts of practice should be allowed, and writers thus mingled these concerns in giving specific criteria for legitimate blessings or charms: see Heinrich Kramer (Institoris), *Malleus maleficarum 1487 (Hexenhammer): Nachdruck des Erstdruckes von 1487*, G. Jerouschek, ed. (Hildesheim, 1988), ii.2.6, 86v; and

Johannes Nider, *Praeceptorium divinae legis*, in Henry Charles Lea, *Materials toward a History of Witchcraft*, Arthur C. Howland, ed., 3 vols. (Philadelphia, 1939), 1: 269.

15. The *Clementine Recognitions* are translated in Alexander Roberts and James Donaldson, eds., *The Ante-Nicene Fathers*, vol. 8 (Buffalo, N.Y., 1886), 75–211. The best compilation of relevant hagiographic material is probably one devoted specifically to Byzantine materials: H. J. Magoulias, 'The Lives of Byzantine Saints as Sources of Data for the History of Magic in the Sixth and Seventh Centuries A.D.: Sorcery, Relics and Icons,' *Byzantion*, 37 (1967): 228–69; but see also, for example, Roy J. Deferrari, ed., *Early Christian Biographies* (Washington, D.C., 1952), 44 and following, 258–61.

16. Augustine, *De civitate Dei*, viii–x (Turnholt, 1955), 216–314; Isidore of Seville, *Etymologiae*, viii. 9, in *Patrologia latina*, 82, cols. 310–14.

17. See Neil Forsyth, *The Old Enemy: Satan and the Combat Myth* (Princeton, N.J., 198); Elaine Pagels, 'The Social History of Satan, the "Intimate Enemy": A Preliminary Sketch,' *Harvard Theological Review*, 84 (April 1991): 105–28; Jeffrey Burton Russell, *Satan: The Early Christian Tradition* (Ithaca, N.Y., 1981); and, for an important fifteenth-century example built on traditional formulations, Alisa Meyuhas Ginio, 'The Conversos and the Magic Arts in Alonso de Espina's *Fortalitium Fidei*,' *Mediterranean Historical Review*, 5 (December 1990): 169–82.

18. See especially Origen, *Contra Celsum*, ii.51, H. Chadwick, trans. (Cambridge, 1953), 105. Francis C. R. Thee, *Julius Africanus and the Early Christian View of Magic* (Tübingen, 1984), gives a useful systematic survey of Christian attitudes toward magic, pp. 316–448.

19. The clearest exception is the euhemerism of Snorri Sturluson, on which see Anthony Faulkes, 'Pagan Sympathy: Attitudes to Heathenism in the Prologue to *Snorra Edda*,' in Robert J. Glendinning and Haraldur Bessason, eds., *Edda: A Collection of Essays* (Winnipeg, 1983), 283–314, esp. 301–05.

20. Christopher A. Faraone, *Talismans and Trojan Horses: Guardian Statues in Ancient Greek Myth and Ritual* (New York, 1992), 28.

21. Hans Dieter Betz, ed., *The Greek Magical Papyri in Translation, Including the Demotic Spells*, 2d edn. (Chicago, 1992); Michael A. Morgan, trans., *Sepher-ha-Razim: The Book of Mysteries* (Atlanta, Ga., 1983); see also Chester Charlton McCown, *The Testament of Solomon, Edited from Manuscripts at Mount Athos, Bologna, Holkham Hall, Jerusalem, London, Milan, Paris and Vienna* (Leipzig, 1922).

22. See, for example, Augustine's *De divinatione daemonum*, in *Patrologia latina*, 40, cols. 581–92, and Saint Augustine, *Treatises on Marriage and Other Subjects*, Roy J. Deferrari, ed. (New York, 1955), 421–44. A further mechanism is hinted at by Nicholas of Cusa: demonic magic was essentially futile, but at times the magician, assimilated as he was to the devil (in a parody of a mystical union with Christ), could actually accomplish results by his 'faith,' meaning presumably his imagination; see Jasper Hopkins, *Nicholas of Cusa on Learned Ignorance: A Translation and an Appraisal of De Docta Ignorantia*, iii.11 (Minneapolis, Minn., 1981), 152 and following. For the spirits' mastery of occult virtues, see, for example, Daniel Driscoll, trans., *The Sworn Book of Honorius the Magician* (Berkeley Heights, N.J., 1983), 4 and following. Stuart Clark, 'The Scientific Status of Demonology,' in Vickers, *Occult and Scientific Mentalities in the Renaissance*, 351–74, argues that sixteenth-century demonologists saw demons as bound to the use of occult virtues in nature, so that demonic magic becomes conflated with the natural variety. These demonologists' purpose, however, is to show that demons cannot work genuine miracles; demons' capacity to use non-occult natural processes (such as locomotion) is assumed. In any event, demonic and natural magic could be collapsed only in their instrumentality; demonic magic remained distinct in its recourse to an agent not employed in strictly natural magic.

23. See Martin L. Pine, *Pietro Pomponazzi: Radical Philosopher of the Renaissance* (Padova, 1986), 235–74; Brian P. Copenhaver, 'Astrology and Magic,' in *The Cambridge History of Renaissance Philosophy*, Charles B. Schmitt, gen. ed. (Cambridge, 1988), 264–300 (esp. 267–74); and Brian P. Copenhaver, 'Did Science Have a Renaissance?' *Isis*, 83 (September 1992): 387–407.

24. Brian P. Copenhaver, 'A Tale of Two Fishes: Magical Objects in Natural History from Antiquity through the Scientific Revolution,' *Journal of the History of Ideas*, 52 (July–September 1991): 373–98.

25. See Brian P. Copenhaver, *Magical Objects: The Foundations of Magical Belief in Western Philosophy and Medicine* (Cambridge, forthcoming).

26. Pliny, *Natural History*, vol. 10, D. E. Eichholz, trans. (Cambridge, Mass., 1962); Augustine, *De civitate Dei*, xxi.4–6, pp. 261–68; Joseph Bernard McAllister, *The Letter of Saint Thomas Aquinas De Occultis Operibus Naturae Ad Quemdam Militem Ultramontanum* (Washington, D.C., 1939); *Roger Bacon's Letter Concerning the Marvelous Power of Art and of Nature and Concerning the Nullity of Magic*, Tenney L. Davis, trans. (Easton, Pa., 1923); E. J. Dijksterhuis, *The Mechanization of the World Picture*, C. Dikshoorn, trans. (Oxford, 1961), 156–60; and Bert Hansen, 'Science and Magic,' in David C. Lindberg, ed., *Science in the Middle Ages* (Chicago, 1978), 483–503.

27. *The Book of Secrets of Albertus Magnus of the Virtues of Herbs, Stones and Certain Beasts, also A Book of the Marvels of the World*, Michael R. Best and Frank H. Brightman, eds. (Oxford, 1973). Jacques Le Goff, *The Medieval Imagination*, Arthur Goldhammer, trans. (Chicago, 1988), 27–44, discusses the relationship between the categories *mirabilis, magicus*, and *miraculosus*.

28. Guillelmus Alvernus, *De universo*, i. 1.43, in *Opera omnia*, 1 (1674; rpt. edn., Frankfurt am Main, 1963), 648 ('in ea parte naturalis scientiae, quae vocatur magica naturalis').

29. Thorndike, *History of Magic and Experimental Science*, 2: 338–71 (William of Auvergne), 517–92 (Albertus Magnus), 616–91 (Roger Bacon). See also Lynn Thorndike, 'Some Medieval Conceptions of Magic,' *The Monist*, 25 (January 1915): 107–39, for the general development of views on magic in the high Middle Ages.

30. Chaucer, *Canterbury Tales*, Franklin's Tale, v. 397.

31. Paola Zambelli, 'Le probleme de la magie naturelle á la Renaissance,' in *Magia, astrologia e religione nel Rinascimento* (Wroclaw, 1974), 48–79; Wayne Shumaker, *Natural Magic and Modern Science: Four Treatises, 1590–1657* (Binghamton, N.Y., 1989); *Magia naturalis und die Entstehung der modernen Naturwissenschaft: Symposium der Leibniz-Gesellschaft Hannover … 1975* (Wiesbaden, 1978).

32. See especially David Pingree, ed., *Picatrix: The Latin Version of the 'Ghāyat Al-Hakim'* (London, 1986).

33. Eugene F. Rice, Jr., 'The *De Magia Naturali* of Jacques Lefevre d'Etaples,' *Philosophy and Humanism: Renaissance Essays in Honor of Paul Oskar Kristeller*, Edward P. Mahoney, ed. (New York, 1976), 19–29.

34. Petrus Garsías, *In determinationes magistrates contra conclusiones apologales Ioannis Pici Mirandulani Concordie Comitis proemium* (Rome, 1489); Thorndike, *History of Magic*, 4: 497–507.

35. Jean Vincent, in Joseph Hansen, ed., *Quellen und Untersuchungen zur Geschichte des Hexenwahns und der Hexenverfolgung im Mittelalter* (Bonn, 1901), 228, discusses various complications involving conflicts of wills, including the question whether bewitchment performed with the power of one demon can be overcome by another witch with the power of another demon.

36. Marsilio Ficino, *Three Books on Life*, Carol V. Kaske and John R. Clark, ed. and trans. (Binghamton, N.Y., 1989), 236–393. See also Copenhaver, 'Astrology and Magic,' 274–85; Brian P. Copenhaver, 'Scholastic Philosophy and Renaissance Magic in the *De Vita* of Marsilio Ficino,' *Renaissance Quarterly*, 37 (Winter 1984): 523–54; D. P. Walker, *Spiritual and Demonic Magic from Ficino to Campanella* (London, 1958); and Ioan P. Couliano, *Eros and Magic in the Renaissance*, Margaret Cook, trans. (Chicago, 1987).

37. Nicole Oresme, *Nicole Oresme and the Marvels of Nature: A Study of His 'De causis mirabilium,'* Bert Hansen, ed. (Toronto, 1985). See also Thorndike, *History of Magic*, 3: 424–39; and Eugenia Paschetto, *Demoni e prodigi: Note su alcuni scritti di Witelo e di Oresme* (Turin, 1978).

38. William A. Lessa and Evon Z. Vogt, eds., *Reader in Comparative Religion: An Anthropological Approach*, 4th edn. (New York, 1979), 332–79.

39. Jean-Claude Schmitt, 'Der Mediävist und die Volkskultur,' in Peter Dinzelbacher and Dieter R. Bauer, eds., *Volksreligion im hohen und spaten Mittelalter* (Paderborn, 1990), 34, points out that the concept of religion is especially inappropriate, paradoxically, in research on societies that from our viewpoint appear thoroughly penetrated by religion. But while the Latin *religio* often referred to a mode of religious life or to a religious order, it had other meanings as well. In patristic and medieval writings, it was argued that Christianity, unlike Roman paganism, represented a true *religio*, and in this context the word had something like its modern meaning: true *religio* combined proper worship of the true God with correct beliefs about God. See, for example, Augustine, *De vera religione*, i.l (Turnholt, 1962), 189, and *De civitate Dei*, ii.27, p. 63. In medieval usage, 'religion' often meant 'piety' or 'devotion,' not a system of beliefs and practices; see, for example, Erich Heck, *Der Begriff Religio bei Thomas Aquin: Seine Bedeutung für unser heutiges Verständnis von Religion* (Munich, 1971).

40. The works in question are Thomas, *Religion and the Decline of Magic*; and J. H. G. Grattan and Charles Singer, *Anglo-Saxon Magic and Medicine, Illustrated Specially from the Semi-Pagan Text 'Lacnunga'* (London, 1952).

41. Flint, *Rise of Magic,* 404, 394 and following, 397.

42. On the 'mystery, miracle, and magic' of medieval Christianity that the reformers repudiated, and on the theological implications of the shift in world view, see Peter L. Berger, *The Sacred Canopy: Elements of a Sociological Theory of Religion* (Garden City, N.Y., 1967), 111 and following.

43. Thomas, *Religion and the Decline of Magic*, chap. 1, deals with 'the magic of the medieval Church' and has done much to make such notions fashionable. In his exchange with Hildred Geertz, 'An Anthropology of Religion and Magic,' p. 97, Thomas even goes so far as to suggest that the key distinction is between 'those religions which, like medieval Catholicism, credited their rituals with physical efficacy' and 'those which, like eighteenth-century deism, did not,' and seems to mean by this that any religion using petitionary prayer of any sort is to that extent magical. But this makes the term 'magic' a clumsy analytical tool indeed: if the only religion that counts as nonmagical is an extreme version of deism, then virtually all religion – Protestant as well as Catholic, insofar as Protestants also make use of petitionary prayer for physical well-being – is conflated with magic.

44. Adamnan insisted that while competing with sorcerers St. Columba did not himself practice sorcery, and a Cotton Caligula manuscript maintains that its formulas are 'no sorcery' but divinely bestowed knowledge (Flint, *Rise of Magic*, 326, 323).

45. Flint, *Rise of Magic,* 1.

46. Flint, *Rise of Magic,* 8. Thomas, in *Religion and the Decline of Magic*, 41, uses more explicitly Frazerian definitions of magic and religion, while Leander Petzoldt, 'Magie und Religion,' in Dinzelbacher and Bauer, *Volksreligion im hohen und späten Mittelalter*, 467–85, retains this mode of definition as a heuristic construct. On Frazer and other theorists of magic, see Lessa and Vogt, *Reader in Comparative Religion*, 332–62. For more recent theories on religion and magic, see the materials collected in Leander Petzoldt, ed., *Magie und Religion: Beitrage zu einer Theorie der Magie* (Darmstadt, 1978).

47. Thus, while I am using 'rationality' in a context different from that of the medieval *rationalitas,* I would maintain that my usage does not conflict with medieval usage, first because no one could reasonably assume that I am claiming to articulate a medieval sense of that term, and second because my usage does not require me to take issue with medieval usage or to suggest that medieval writers were somehow wrong or incoherent. For discussion regarding the related issue of 'emic' and 'etic' terms in anthropology, see Marvin Harris, *The Rise of Anthropological Theory: A History of Theories of Culture* (New York, 1968), 568–604.

48. On the theme of missionary accommodation to pre-Christian ritual, see Richard E. Sullivan, 'The Carolingian Missionary and the Pagan,' *Speculum*, 28 (October 1953): 705–40; and R. A. Markus, 'Gregory the Great and a Papal Missionary Strategy,' in G.J. Cuming, ed., *The Mission of the Church and the Propagation of the Faith* (Cambridge, 1970), 29–38.

49. Thus men such as Gregory the Great, Wilfrid, Cuthbert, and Bede cannot be seen as having 'confused, all unwittingly, pagan echoes with Christian truths.' Flint, *Rise of Magic,* 310.

50. Flint, *Rise of Magic,* 74, 79, 71, see also 310, 324. Alexander Murray, 'Missionaries and Magic,' 199–201, reformulates Flint's argument, emphasizing not so much the strength of the new cultural amalgam as the dissolution of the old culture.

51. Flint, *Rise of Magic*, for example, 204.

52. Flint, *Rise of Magic,* 207.

53. Flint's views are paralleled in the fictional work of Brian Bates, *The Way of Wyrd: The Book of a Sorcerer's Apprentice* (New York, 1984).

54. Peter Damian surely did not mean to encourage the practices he described, and the existence of love charms in a monastic manuscript is no indication that they gained wide approval in monastic circles (see Flint, *Rise of Magic*, 298 and 312, on 'encouraged magic'). The source is too sketchy to show that St. Vaast refrained from hostility because he felt 'friendly association' with pagan magicians (p. 78). Flint speaks of compromise or accommodation where nothing was conceded from a traditional Christian viewpoint, as in the use of saints' relics for healing or in natural astrology (pp. 28, 99, 128–46). Ecclesiastical punishments were usually more lenient than the secular equivalents but not specifically in the case of magic, and thus ecclesiastical penalties do not show a sympathetic and protective stance toward magicians (pp. 56–58, 296 and following): ecclesiastical penalties were generally less harsh than those of secular courts, largely because in principle they were penitential, even when they were also judicial, and because their formal purpose was not primarily to restore social order but to save the souls of penitents. Agobard of Lyon (p. 82) protected the victims of lynch prosecution not because he sympathized with their magic but because he believed the charges against them were false. (In discussing Agobard's stance, Flint begins by using the term 'supposed' magicians, then silently transforms them into real magicians.) Flint argues that blaming demons for the effects of magic could be a way of reducing the magicians' own culpability (pp. 148, 156); but when magicians associated with demons, they did so knowingly and willingly, and the spiritual company they kept compounded rather than reduced their guilt. Flint does not show that magicians who wittingly consorted with demons were treated more leniently because they had been misled by these demons. A possessed nun was not blamed for associating with demons but was clearly perceived as a victim (p. 154); however, this fact has little bearing on the status of magicians, whose dealings with demons were voluntary.

    Flint finds corroboration of her thesis in what she takes to be historical and anthropological parallels, in manifestations elsewhere of an intelligent sensitivity to 'the social advantage of competing magic deliberately transferred' (pp. 404 and following). She adduces the Greek magical papyri, in which magic from Hellenistic, Egyptian, and other cultures mingles. But the churchmen of early medieval Europe, unlike the magicians of late ancient Egypt, were committed in principle to a monotheist doctrine of exclusive validity. Even when they borrowed from other traditions, they had to find some way of rationalizing this borrowing in terms of their own exclusivism. Their monotheist commitment could lead them either to reject magic or to transform it and deprive it (to their satisfaction) of its original character; in either case, magic was problematic for them in a way that it was not for late ancient magicians. Furthermore, the purposes served by magic should have been (and generally were) more problematic to Christian clerics than to authors of the Greek magical papyri.

55. To be sure, missionary fields were still being opened in Northern and Eastern Europe, but the time Flint calls one of growing accommodation was one in which Christian structures had long been established in the parts of Europe she discusses.

56. R. I. Moore, *The Formation of a Persecuting Society: Power and Deviance in Western Europe, 950–1250* (Oxford, 1987); on Bernardino, see Kieckhefer, *Magic in the Middle Ages,* 181, 194 and following.

57. Philip A. Kuhn, *Soulstealers: The Chinese Sorcery Scare of 1768* (Cambridge, Mass., 1990), 187–222, 230–32.

58. C. Stephen Jaeger, *The Origins of Courtliness: Civilizing Trends and the Formation of Courtly Ideals, 939–1210* (Philadelphia, 1985).

59. Penner, 'Rationality, Ritual, and Science.'

60. Flint sees the quest of emotional satisfaction as not simply an unintended result of magic but as the specific reason for encouraging magical practice: 'many people' in early medieval Europe 'became increasingly convinced' that magical practices should be preserved, 'in pursuit precisely of the enrichment of human life with which some today are inclined to link the word *magic*' (p. 3). Not hesitating to write as cultural critic, Flint applauds this policy of cultivating 'this form of energy' (p. 4). Use of preexisting magic lent an 'emotional force' that was needed especially for a religion 'weak or in its infancy' and thus unable to eradicate its rivals (p. 9).

61. Flint, *Rise of Magic*, 3.

62. G. Ronald Murphy, 'Magic in the Heliand,' in Murphy's translation of *The Heliand: The Saxon Gospel* (New York, 1992), 205–20, shows, for example, that Christian formulas could be interpreted on the model of pagan magic: the letters in the words 'Pater noster' were seen as combat runes in the Anglo-Saxon *Dialogues of Solomon and Saturn*, and *The Heliand* also suggests such interpretation – although Murphy's use of 'spell' (pp. 4, 48, 49, 59, 67, 80, 81, 87, 126, 142) has the effect of giving uniform magical meaning to a term that surely has greater fluidity and in many contexts does not connote magic. Even more could be said about the healing and protective charms that Hugh of St. Victor included under the category of *maleficia* and that many later medieval writers listed under the rubric of natural magic. Clearly, these often mingled Christian formulas indiscriminately with pagan material; see Irmgard Hampp, *Beschwörung, Segen, Gebet: Untersuchungen zum Zauberspruch aus dem Bereich der Volksheilkunde* (Stuttgart, 1961); and Karen Louise Jolly, 'Magic, Miracle, and Popular Practice in the Early Medieval West: Anglo-Saxon England,' in Neusner, *et al., Religion, Science, and Magic*, 166–82.

63. Flint, *Rise of Magic*, 5, see also 31.

64. On these issues, see Flint, *Rise of Magic*, 25, 31, 33, 163, 185, 240–53, 302 and following, 339.

65. She suggests that 'slight adjustments' were deliberately made, rendering the magical procedures acceptable to all concerned, preventing opposition from other churchmen, while keeping the audience from losing interest *(Rise of Magic*, p. 398). She refers to Augustine as sharing an openness toward 'something very like the ancient magia,' as approving wonders and miracles that 'undeniably … contain magic of a kind,' and as indirectly giving legitimacy to practices 'very similar to the magical ones that had been outlawed' (pp. 31, 33, 301). Similar comparisons abound throughout the book (for example, pp. 185, 283, and 284).

66. She compares the apostles' powers of binding and loosing to pagan defixion and the gospel declarations of the insolubility of marriage to the binding magic of the Greek magical papyri (p. 289 and following). But the power of binding and loosing seems to have involved essentially the authority to decide the spiritual and ecclesiastical consequences of actions; it was surely never construed, like pagan defixion, as a power literally to constrain actions against the will of the actors. And the gospel statements on marriage have the form and force of moral injunctions (which can, of course, be violated), not of magical spells. Elsewhere (p. 259 and following), Flint suggests that the blood-soaked cross in *The Dream of the Rood* may have recalled necromantic rites involving blood and that the unguent of Mary Magdalene on the Ruthwell cross may have reminded viewers of magical ointments. Flint takes a spontaneous vision warning of a subdeacon's fraud as 'a Christianized and very studied type of thief divining,' largely because both acts involve use of a chalice (p. 282). Morton Smith, in *Jesus the Magician* (San Francisco, 1978), pursues a more radical version of Flint's argument.

67. Flint, *Rise of Magic*, 290–96. Similarly, she seems to think of pagan holy places that became Christian shrines as magical per se, whatever use was made of them (pp. 254–73).

68. Flint, *Rise of Magic*, 60. See also the cases involving St. Junianus the Confessor (p. 61), St. Odile of Hohenburg (p. 266), and St. Monegunde (p. 302 and following).

69. Rudolf Kriss, 'Grundsatzliche Betrachtung zum 2. Merseburger Zauberspruch,' *Oberdeutsche Zeitschrift für Volkskunde*, 6 (1932): 114–19. Hampp, *Beschwörung, Segen, Gebet*, 110–15, deals more generally with the relationship between the 'pagan form' and the 'Christian content' of charms.

70. Karen Louise Jolly, 'Anglo-Saxon Charms in the Context of a Christian World View,' *Journal of Medieval History*, 11 (December 1985): 279–93, argues persuasively that most Anglo-Saxon charms were so thoroughly Christianized that the users would have thought of them as essentially Christian and would even have been conscious of their pagan elements. The crucial question is not whether Christian or pagan material was quantitatively more significant but rather what categories the culture offered for interpreting the inevitable blend of pagan and Christian elements. Jolly cites the sermons of Aelfric as allowing for an intermediate space between magic and miracles – a space that would later be identified with 'natural magic.' Aelfric took demonic agency as the defining characteristic of magic, and he regarded medical practices such as the charms as neither magical nor miraculous but a tertium quid. Nor was Aelfric atypical in his use of these Augustinian assumptions and categories.

71. Flint, *Rise of Magic*, 152. Flint points out in this passage that these writers did believe this magic was real, but she does not seem to believe that for the early medieval writers its demonic source was its defining character, rather she seems to regard this as an afterthought. She repeatedly uses the phrase 'rescue' of demons (esp. pp. 105 and 146–57), by which she seems to mean that the concept of demons was salvaged because of its utility. But she does not make it clear from what peril demons needed to be rescued; the cruelest of all fates, oblivion, surely never threatened them.

72. For example, Isidore of Seville, *Etymologiae*, viii.9, in *Patrologia latina*, vol. 82, col. 313, on the varieties of magic: 'In quibus omnibus ars daemonum est ex quadam pestifera societate hominum, et angelorum malorum exorta. Unde cuncta vitanda sunt a Christiano, et omni penitus exsecratione repudianda atque damnanda.'

73. Lawrence E. Harrison, 'Voodoo Politics,' *Atlantic Monthly* (June 1993): 101–07.

74. See Charles Plummer, ed., *Vitae sanctorum Hiberniae*, 2 vols. (Oxford, 1910), 1: clviii–clxvii.

75. Bede the Venerable, *Historia ecclesiastica gentis Anglorum, Bedes Ecclesiastical History of the English People*, Bertram Colgrave and R. A. B. Mynors, ed. and trans. (Oxford, 1969), ii. 13, 182–85. Bede does not portray Coifi as the sort of person likely to engage in magic.

76. On shifting roles of the lower clergy, see Patricia A. DeLeeuw, 'The Changing Face of the Village Parish: The Parish in the Early Middle Ages,' in J. A. Raftis, ed., *Pathways to Medieval Peasants* (Toronto, 1981), 311–22; and Joseph W. Goering, 'The Changing Face of the Village Parish: The Thirteenth Century,' *ibid.*, 323–34.

77. A twelfth-century field-blessing in Godfrid Storms, *Anglo-Saxon Magic* (The Hague, 1948), 172–87, involves clearly pagan and magical elements, including invocation of a pagan deity, but it seems to have been intended for use by a rural priest in Christian orders. Storms proposes that the practitioner was a pagan priest, but the celebration of Masses and use of other Christian ritual indicates that he was a Christian priest borrowing elements of non-Christian ceremony. Even in the later Middle Ages, the loosely controlled lower clergy functioned at times also as magicians, analogous to the wandering monks Kuhn mentions in *Soulstealers* (pp. 105–18) as magicians or suspected magicians in China. In each of these cases, the magician-priests or magician-monks belonged to an ambiguous border category, sharing the spiritual powers but not subject to the same controlling structures as the higher religious elites.

78. Joyce E. Salisbury, *Iberian Popular Religion, 600 B.C. to 700 A.D.: Celts, Romans, and Visigoths* (New York, 1985), 116–60, emphasizes the mediatory role of parish priests in the early Middle Ages. Compare Henry G. J. Beck, *The Pastoral Care of Souls in South-East France during the Sixth Century* (Rome, 1950), 43–91.

79. Marcel Mauss, *A General Theory of Magic*, Robert Brain, trans. (London, 1972).

80. Adolph Franz, *Die kirchlichen Benediktionen im Mittelalter,* 2 vols. (Freiburg i. Br., 1909), deals in principle with 'ecclesiastical' blessings, but his compendious study includes a considerable amount of material that was not in any clear sense official.

81. Flint concedes that her use of 'magic' is 'terminologically difficult,' yet she finds it helpful as a 'sounding word' for exploring that 'hopeful belief in preternatural control' in early medieval Europe; she uses the term 'as one way into a time, and as one approach to sensibilities that were preoccupied to an extraordinary degree with the preternatural' (p. 5 and following).

82. C. John Sommerville, in a debate with John Edwards, 'Religious Faith and Doubt in Late Medieval Spain: Soria *circa* 1450–1500,' *Past and Present*, 128 (August 1990): 153.

83. Aron Gurevich, *Medieval Popular Culture: Problems of Belief and Perception,* János M. Bak and Paul A. Hollingsworth, trans. (Cambridge, 1988), 62. See also Robert W. Scribner, 'Magie und Aberglaube: Zur volkstümlichen sakramentalischen Denkart in Deutschland am Ausgang des Mittelalters,' in Dinzelbacher and Bauer, *Volksreligion im hohen und spaten Mittelalter,* 253–74.

84. For example, George M. Foster, 'Disease Etiologies in Non-Western Medical Systems,' *American Anthropologist,* 78 (December 1976): 773–82, represents personalistic healing as indistinguishably religious or magical and naturalistic medicine as scientific – which seems to imply that leaping over a grave as an aid in childbirth, curing lunacy by suspending clovewort from the patient's neck under specified astral conditions, or bearing an opal on one's body to become invisible are not magical acts, while praying to God for a cure is magical.

85. Alan F. Segal, 'Hellenistic Magic: Some Questions of Definition,' in R. van den Broek and M.J. Vermaseren, eds., *Studies in Gnosticism and Hellenistic Religions* (Leiden, 1981), 350 and following, argues forcefully that 'no definition of magic can be universally applicable' because the meanings vary from one context to another. Richard C. Trexler, *Public Life in Renaissance Florence* (New York, 1980), prefers the relatively neutral term even within his historical context.

86. Kieckhefer, *Magic in the Middle Ages,* 56 and following.

87. See Richard Kieckhefer, *European Witch Trials: Their Foundations in Popular and Learned Culture, 1300–1500* (Berkeley, Calif., 1976), 50–53, 59. Having recognized this basic distinction, we can then discuss how the specialized cultures related to the common culture, what pressures there were to diffuse specialized practices, and what safeguards arose (such as the alchemists' vaunted secrecy) to thwart this diffusion. See *Magic in the Middle Ages,* 140–44, and literature there cited. While the pretense of secrecy cannot always be taken seriously, many practitioners of the occult arts did make an effort to resist the popularization of these arts.

88. Kieckhefer, *Magic in the Middle Ages,* 153–56; and Kieckhefer, *European Witch Trials.*

89. See Konrad Jarausch, 'Der Zauber in den Islandersagas,' *Zeitschrift für Volkskunde,* n.s. 1 (1929–30): 237–68; and Kieckhefer, *Magic in the Middle Ages,* 48–53.

90. Jane Crawford, 'Evidences for Witchcraft in Anglo-Saxon England,' *Medium Aevum,* 32 (1963): 99–116.

91. See Kieckhefer, *European Witch Trials,* 53 and following, 57 and following.

92. See Betz, *Greek Magical Papyri in Translation, passim*; and Gager, *Curse Tablets.*

93. Kieckhefer, *Magic in the Middle Ages,* 169 and following.

94. See, for example, J. Hansen, *Quellen und Untersuchungen,* 524–26, 553–55.

95. For a detailed study of a case of political intervention by a centralizing city-state, see Arno Borst, 'Anfänge des Hexenwahns in den Alpen,' in Andreas Blauert, ed., *Ketzer, Zauberer, Hexen: Die Anfänge der europäischen Hexenverfolgungen* (Frankfurt am Main, 1990), 43–67; for examples of how witch trials could be instigated from either above or below, see Andreas Blauert, *Frühe Hexenverfolgungen: Ketzer-, Zauberei- und Hexenprozesse des 15. Jahrhunderts* (Hamburg, 1989), 87–109.

96. See Kieckhefer, *Magic in the Middle Ages,* 6 (n. 4) and 142 (n. 31).

PART III
GHOSTS AND APPARITIONS

INTRODUCTION: GHOSTS AND APPARITIONS IN LATE MEDIEVAL AND EARLY MODERN EUROPE

> I am thy father's spirit,
> Doomed for a certain term to walk the night,
> And for the day confined to fast in fires,
> Till the foul crimes done in my days of nature
> Are burnt and purged away.

(*Hamlet* 1.5)

Ghosts were, it is suggested, the disorderly dead. They are largely absent from the documentation of the living, and, with the honourable exception of the example above, received little treatment in the polemic and literature of the time. They are afforded little space in traditional histories of the Reformation in England, or indeed writing on the social history of death in the early modern period.[1] However, a burgeoning interest in the cultural context of the Reformation, and the impact of the Reformation as an agent of cultural change, has revealed the extent to which the 'problem' of ghosts reflected the priorities of the reformers, and the obstacles that stood in the way of the construction of a new culture of belief. The 'untimely dead', Scribner argues, had little reverence for the confessional conflicts of early modern religion and seemed almost oblivious to the theological changes that threatened their very existence.[2] The precise nature and function of the ghostly apparition had been far from constant in medieval religious culture, but the early modern ghost was to become, albeit unwillingly, the focus of a more vibrant and vigorous debate about the theology and geography of the afterlife, the nature of death and the interpretation of apparitions. Protestant polemical and pastoral literature on ghosts drew upon the vocabulary and imagery of scripture and the literature and thought of medieval churchmen to explain and explain away the apparently ongoing appearances of the dead in the land of the early modern living. The rejection of purgatory should, in theory, have meant that ghosts, the purgatorial dead, would cease to present themselves before the eyes of the believer. And yet, they continued to do so, and such appearances formed the basis of a lively body of controversial literature. Ghosts, it was argued, were not what they seemed but rather frauds perpetrated at the hands of popish priests to deceive the people. 'Sowles departed do not come again and play boo peape with us' wrote Robert Wisdom, and the faithful were counselled to put aside their ignorance in order to alleviate their fears of the walking dead.[3]

The simplicity of such statements, read alongside the apparent reluctance of the living or the dead to co-operate with this new model, has received more substantial treatment in recent years as ghosts and other apparitions have been recognized as an instructive field of study for those seeking to establish a better understanding of the religious cultures of the medieval and early modern periods. Historians, anthropologists and folklorists have shared and developed the methodologies of their disciplines in their analyses of ghosts, fairies, angels and other supernatural phenomena, and in doing so have also added new layers to ongoing debates about the interaction of lay and learned culture, official and popular religion, Catholicism and Protestantism, and the natural and supernatural. Ghosts and other such phenomena have infiltrated histories of religion, culture, society, literature and language, as their role as both the arbiters and creators of tensions and conflicts has been recognized. The Protestant abolition of purgatory, it has been argued, did not succeed in removing ghosts from the mental and physical landscape of early modern Europe precisely because the argued non-existence of purgatory created a vacuum in which ghosts were able to exist. 'No canon dealt with the laying of unquiet spirits or the clearing of haunted places, presumably because there was nothing to discuss; there were no such things as ghosts. However, as time went on, it became obvious that the ghosts themselves were oblivious to official opinion and continued to come and go at their own sweet will.'[4] The efforts of Protestant reformers to explain away these ghostly appearances was insufficient to counter belief entirely. The image of the ghost was not destroyed, but, in the era of reformation as throughout its history, modelled itself upon the language of the day. Early modern views of ghosts were often syncretic, blending traditional ideas about the origins and role of the medieval ghost, with more practical and pastoral concerns that grew out of a search for comfort and security and the more overtly Protestant model of the providential functions served by intrusions of the supernatural into the human world.[5] This syncretism reflected more than just the confessional tensions of Reformation. Medieval ghost lore had displayed a similar heterogeneity and fluidity, and ghosts and apparitions had always been malleable constructs. Interpretations and interactions with the dead are, almost in their entirety, reflective of the needs and concerns of the living, and therefore perpetually subject to the shifting sands of cultural, personal and doctrinal priorities. The continued existence and presence of ghosts was, in some respects, an open and almost insurmountable challenge to the evangelical assertion, repeatedly articulated, that there was no productive interaction between the living and the dead; the prayers and intercessions of the living could not influence the fate of the soul, and the dead had neither the ability nor the motivation to intervene in the affairs of the living. The fact that the place of the dead continued to be debated and contested, and the lack of uniformity in its interpretation, reflected the theological and emotional hold that the dead, and their memory, exercised over the living. Such contradictions, complexities and conflicts, Marshall suggests, are a vital part of any meaningful understanding of the religious culture of any age.[6]

Both continuity and change in the perceptions of ghostly apparitions are evident in Ronald Finucane's *Appearances of the Dead: A Cultural History of Ghosts*, and in Owen Davies' recent analysis of the social history of ghosts.[7] The permeability of the apparition, and the intermingling of images and interpretations from past and present is perhaps most evident in the portrayal of the ghost on stage. Shakespeare's ghosts, in *Hamlet* and *Macbeth*, are among the most frequently studied, in both their dramatic and confessional contexts. Ghosts from the past, and particularly those from antiquity, are seen to reappear on the early modern stage and in print, while medieval ghost stories with their images of purgatorial suffering and intercession have been mapped onto early modern drama.[8] Ghosts were possessed of a recognizable social meaning, even if their form and meaning was adjusted under pressure from conflict and controversy and the early modern ghost might well have recognized something of himself in his medieval ancestors.

Richard Bowyer's discussion of the role of the ghost story in medieval Christianity, the first article in this section, provides a useful introduction to the form and function of the ghost, integral to medieval Christianity and, he argues, largely taken away by the Reformation. The historian of the medieval ghosts encounters both a wealth of information and a range of problems, not the least of which is language; our modern work 'ghost' lacks a firm counterpart in the lexicon of the men of the Middle Ages. The modern ghost, it is suggested, seems more terrifying, sitting on the far reaches of belief, but the ghost of the Middle Ages occupied a much more central role in a well-ordered and substantially accommodating spiritual world. Ghosts were reported and recorded at the moment of death, confirming the veracity of Christian teaching and reinforcing the demarcation of saint and sinner. Visions of the dead in the afterlife form a second model of ghost-story; the soul of an individual is taken on a journey through the horrors of hell, the torments of purgatory and the blissful rewards of heaven. Such narratives were informed both by the reading and writing of purgatory in the land of the living and by the cultural transmission of models from the ancient past and classical literature, and served to call the sinner to repentance and reinforce the teachings of the Church. Bowyer concludes with discussion of a third model of ghost story, that of the revenant, in which the ghost returns to the world of the living to offer miraculous assistance, to motivate and energize the unrepentant and to educate the faithful in their obligations to provide for the dead. With the advent of the reformation, when 'the church formally severed diplomatic relations with the Other World', the Church triumphant and militant ceased to exist, and man stood alone between God and the devil. Ghosts, as a result, appeared in a rather different guise, sometimes frightening, sometimes sorrowful and often contested. But, significantly, they still appeared.[9]

Ghosts were not the only form of apparition to survive the Reformation. Less directly affected by the abolition of purgatory in Protestant Europe, but still subject to scrutiny and criticism in reformed culture, angels were both present and problematic. Angels were dually seen and unseen, present in heaven and on earth, perpetually present in the Christian mentality. For the theologians of the medieval Church, angels were both an explanation and in need of explanation; their existence and appearance had roots in debates that were both pastoral and ontological.[10] Angels were no less present in the early modern world, and the sixteenth-century angel, like its medieval counterpart, could reflect and create tensions and invite multiple, sometimes conflicting interpretations. Angels were both contingent and ubiquitous, their appearance tied to the immediate context but reflecting and directing their presence on a vast geographical, historical and confessional stage. The restoration of angels to the forefront of scholarship has established their position amid the panoply of signs, wonders and spirits present in religious culture and popular belief and as a result has added a new dimension to an already rich scholarship on these topics. Angels survived the Reformation either because they were too deeply rooted to cast aside or because, like ghosts, their image remained in many respects powerful enough to repulse the iconoclastic approach of the Protestant reformers.

Reformation Europe remained a world of signs and wonders – one in which angels, demons, ghosts, fairies and other spirits engaged in dialogue with mankind and in which the understanding and interpretation of the natural world was enhanced by its interactions with the supernatural. Such signs and symbols offer insights into the fears and preoccupations of those who perceived them; however such events and wonders were to be interpreted, there were few who would deny the meaning that might inhere within them.[11] The assumption that there was something to be learned from apparitions and signs in the earth and heavens is explored in the second article in this section, Alexandra Walsham's illustrated discussion of these 'sermons in the sky'. Such signs might include multiple rainbows, distortions of the sun, blood mingled with rain, or more striking visions of swords, armies, crucifixes and fiery pillars appearing in the sky. The hand of God at work in the heavens was the most commonly articulated and widely shared interpretation of these phenomena as a sign of God's impatience with the sins of men, and a set of visible footsteps that were imprinted along the path to the end of the world. There was a solid biblical foundation for such images and their interpretation, with both Old Testament and New Testament prophecies of the end of time involving supernatural signs that presaged upcoming catastrophes. The Reformation, Walsham contends, 'did nothing to arrest the tendency to read divine meaning into strange aberrations of nature'; indeed the fragmentation of religious culture in the face of confessional conflict reinforced just such a sense of apocalyptic urgency. Prodigies and apparitions of any kind remained a contested and controversial category in Reformation thought, one which required new interpretation and reflection. Indeed, it is possible to see a cyclical relationship between portents and doctrinal instability, as one reinterpreted and remodelled the other. Ghosts, angels and armies in the sky were not only individual in their message and meaning but also shared an inception and interpretation that moulded and was modelled by medieval and early modern religious cultures.

Notes

1. Marshall, P. (2002), *The Disorderly Dead. Ghosts and Their Meanings in Reformation England*. Oxford: Oxford University Press; see also Maxwell-Stuart, P. G. (2006), *Ghosts: A History of Phantoms, Ghouls, and Other Spirits of the Dead*. London: Trafalgar Square; Newton, J. (ed.) (2002), *Early Modern Ghosts*. Durham: Centre for Seventeenth-Century Studies.

2. Scribner, R.W. (1994–5), 'Elements of popular belief', in T. Brady, H. Oberman and J. Tracey (eds), *Handbook of European History 1400–1600*. 2 vols. Leiden, The Netherlands: Brill, p. 237.

3. Marshall, *The Disorderly Dead*, p. 245.

4. Brown, T. (1979), *The Fate of the Dead. A Study in Folk-Eschatology in the West Country after the Reformation*. Ipswich, Suffolk: D.S. Brewer, pp. 8, 83.

5. For a fuller discussion, see Lewis, B. (2002), 'Protestantism, pragmatism and popular religion: a case study of early modern ghosts', in J. Newton (ed.), *Early Modern Ghosts*. Durham: Centre for Seventeenth Century Studies, p. 85; Bath, J. (2002), ' "In the divells likeness", interpretation and confusion in popular ghosts belief', in J. Newton (ed.), *Early Modern Ghosts*. Durham: Centre for Seventeenth Century Studies, pp. 70–78. Gaskill, M. (2000), *Crime and Mentalities in Early Modern England*. Cambridge: Cambridge University Press examines the interesting role played by ghosts in the mediation and facilitation of justice; rather like bleeding corpses in murder trials, the ghost might point the (providential) finger of blame at the guilty.

6. See, for example, Marshall, P. (2002), *Beliefs and the Dead in Reformation England*. Oxford: Oxford University Press; Marshall, P. and Gordon, B. (2000), *The Place of the Dead*. Cambridge: Cambridge University Press; Marshall, P. (2002), 'Old mother leakey and the golden chain: context and meaning in an early stuart haunting', in J. Newton (ed.), *Early Modern Ghosts*. Durham: Centre for Seventeenth Century Studies, pp. 93–109; Marshall, P. (2002), 'Deceptive appearances: ghosts and reformers in Elizabethan and jacobean England', in Helen Parish and William G. Naphy

(eds), *Religion and Superstition in Reformation Europe*. Manchester: Manchester University Press, pp. 188–209; Marshall, P. (2009), *Mother Leakey and the Bishop: A Ghost Story*. Oxford: Oxford University Press; Marshall, P. (2010), 'Transformations of the ghost story in post-reformation England', in H. Conrad-O'Briain and J. A Stevens (eds), *The Ghost Story from the Middle Ages to the Twentieth Century*. Dublin, Ireland: Four Courts; Edwards, K. (2008), *Leonarde's Ghost: Popular Piety and 'The Appearance of a Spirit' in 1628*, ed. and trans. in collaboration with Susie Speakman Sutch, Kirksville, MO: Truman State University Press; for discussions of the relationship between ghosts and witchcraft, see Bennett, G. (1986), 'Ghost and witch in the sixteenth and seventeenth centuries', *Folklore*, 96, 3–14; Hutton, R. (1995), 'The English reformation and the evidence of folklore', *Past and Present*, 148, 89–116; Gowing, L. (2002), 'The haunting of susan lay: servants and mistresses in seventeenth-century England', *Gender and History*, 14, 183–201.

7. Finucane, R. (1984), *Appearances of the Dead; A Cultural History of Ghosts*. London: Junction Books; Davies, O. (2007), *The Haunted: A Social History of Ghosts*. Basingstoke, Hampshire: Palgrave Macmillan; for the later period see also Handley, S. (2005), 'Reclaiming ghosts in 1690s England', in J. Gregory and K. Cooper (eds), *Signs, Wonders, Miracles: Representations of Divine Power in the Life of the Church*. Woodbridge, VA: Boydell and Brewer, pp. 345–55; Hunter, M. (2005), 'New light on the "drummer of tedworth". Conflicting narratives of witchcraft in restoration England', *Historical Research*, 78, 311–53.

8. See for example Battenhouse, R.W. (1951), 'The ghost in hamlet: a catholic "linchpin"'? *Studies in Philology*, 48, 161–92; Greenblatt, S. (2001), *Hamlet in Purgatory*. Princeton, NJ: Yale University Press; Hunter West, R. (1939), *The Invisible World. A Study of Pneumatology on the Elizabethan Stage*. Athens, GA: Georgia University Press.

9. For a further discussion of the medieval ghost, see Caciola, N. (1996), 'Wraiths, revenants and ritual in medieval culture', *Past and Present*, 152, 3–45; Caciola, N. (2002), 'Spirits seeking bodies: death, possession and communal memory in the middle ages', in Bruce Gordon and Peter Marshall (eds), *The Place of the Dead*. Oxford: Oxford University Press; Schmidt, J-C. (1998), *Ghosts in the Middle Ages*. Chicago: Chicago University Press; Walters, G.M. (1992), 'Visitacyons, Preuytes and Deceytys'. Unpublished University of Cambridge Ph.D.

10. Recent studies of angels include Marshall, P. and Walsham, A. (eds) (2006), *Angels in the Early Modern World*. Cambridge: Cambridge University Press; Copeland, C. and Machielson, J. (2012), *Angels of Light. Sanctity and the Discernment of Spirits in the Early Modern Period*. Leiden, The Netherlands: Brill; Raymond, J. (ed.) (2011), *Conversations with Angels*. Basingstoke, Hampshire, PalgraveMacmillan; Gordon, B. (2000), 'Malevolent ghosts and ministering angels: apparitions and pastoral care in the Swiss reformation', in Bruce Gordon and Peter Marshall (eds), *The Place of the Dead. Death and Remembrance in Late Medieval and Early Modern Europe*. Cambridge, Cambridge University Press, pp. 87–109; Patrides, C.A. (1959), 'Renaissance thought on the celestial hierarchy: the decline of a tradition', *Journal of the History of Ideas*, 20, 115–66; Mohamed, F.G. (2004), 'Renaissance thought on the celestial hierarchy: the decline of a tradition?' *Journal of the History of Ideas*, 65, 559–82; Mayr-Harting, H. (1998), *Perceptions of Angels in History*. Oxford: Oxford University Press.

11. Marshall, P. (2009), 'Protestants and fairies in early modern England', in S. Dixon, D. Freist and M. Greengrass (eds), *Living with Religious Diversity in Early-Modern Europe*. Aldershot, Hampshire: Ashgate; Walsham, A. (2010), 'Invisible helpers: angelic intervention in early modern England', *Past and Present*, 208, 77–130; Cressy, D. (2000), *Agnes Bowker's Cat. Travesties and Transgressions in Tudor and Stuart England*. Oxford: Oxford University Press; Wilson, D. (1993), *Signs and Portents: Monstrous Births from the Middle Ages to the Enlightenment*. London: Routledge; Crawford, J. (2005), *Marvellous Protestantism: Monstrous Births in Post-Reformation England*. Baltimore, MD: Johns Hopkins University; Thomas, K. (1983), *Man and the Natural World: Changing Attitudes in England 1500–1800*. Harmondsworth: Penguin; Hall, D. (1989), *Worlds of Wonder, Days of Judgment: Popular Religious Belief in Early New England*. New York: Knopf; Niccoli, O. (1990), 'Menstruum quasi monstruum: monstrous births and menstrual taboo

in sixteenth and seventeenth century England', in E. Muir and G. Ruggiero (eds), *Sex and Gender in Historical Perspective*. Baltimore, MD: Johns Hopkins University Press; Brammall, K.M. (1996), 'Monstrous metamorphosis: nature, morality and the rhetoric of monstrosity in tudor England', *Sixteenth Century Journal*, 27, 3–21; Park, K. and Daston, L. (1991), 'Unnatural conceptions: the study of monsters in sixteenth and seventeenth century France and England', *Past and Present*, 92, 20–54; Edwards, K. (ed.) (2002), *Werewolves, Witches, and Wandering Spirits: Folklore and Traditional Belief in Early Modern Europe*. Kirksville, MO: Truman State University Press; Scribner, R.W. (1986), 'Incombustible luther: the image of the reformer in early modern Germany', *Past and Present*, 110, 38–68; Durston, C. (1987), 'Signs and wonders and the English civil war', *History Today*, 37(10); Edwards, K. (2007), 'And blood rained from the sky': creating a burgundian identity after the fall of Burgundy', in Christopher Ocker et al. (eds), *Defining and Redefining Early Modern History: Old Paradigms and New Directions*. Leiden, The Netherlands: Brill, pp. 344–57; Walsham, A. (1999), *Providence in Early Modern England*. Oxford: Oxford University Press; Walsham, A. (1999), 'Vox piscis: or, the book fish: providence and the uses of the reformation past in caroline Cambridge', *English Historical Review*, 114, 574–606.

CHAPTER 7
SERMONS IN THE SKY: APPARITIONS IN EARLY MODERN EUROPE

Alexandra Walsham

One September night in 1583 inhabitants of the city of London were greatly puzzled and troubled by a series of 'wonderfull straunge sightes' in the sky. Between eight o'clock and midnight the heavens were lit up with fiery constellations, 'watery elements' the colour of brimstone and blood, and shafts of light resembling arrows and spears. Fifteen years later frightened residents of the Cumbrian town of Cockermouth watched a fierce battle between regiments of soldiers take place in the elements above them. A similar vision of a spectral army seen over Berkshire one spring evening in 1628 was accompanied by the sound of heavy artillery and the semblance of a man steadily beating a drum. Many of those who witnessed this 'miraculous' apparition apparently 'fell on their knees, and not only thought, but said, that verily the day of Judgement was come'. Triple suns and inverted rainbows perturbed observers in Sussex the following decade, and when a flaming sword appeared over several parts of Devon in 1638 an Axminster Justice of the Peace solemnly recorded it in his diary as a sinister portent of impending calamity.

Mysterious celestial sights of this kind were extremely common in sixteenth- and seventeenth-century England. The stuff of rumour and gossip and the subject of dozens of pamphlets and broadside ballads reporting strange and sensational news, they also filled the pages of chronicles, technical treatises, and popular anthologies of prodigies and wonders. Fascination with such phenomena was not confined to the credulous poor. Attested to by 'worthy magistrates', distinguished divines and respected men of letters, interest in heavenly spectacles transcended the barriers erected by wealth, education and social rank.

Nor was it limited to the British Isles. Early modern Europe was awash with accounts of bizarre and eerie apparitions. Phantom armies appeared high above hundreds of continental cities in the course of the period. Charging cavalry were discerned in the firmament near Nuremberg in 1554 and over Croatia in 1605, while a vision above Poland in January 1581 incorporated an ominous funeral procession of hooded black figures. Wittenberg was the scene of an apparition of a bloody sword and a cannon mounted on wheels in 1547; fourteen years later people at Eisleben saw an enormous crucifix, a rod and two fiery pillars. The 'likeness' of Atlas bearing the world on his shoulders and crying 'Vigilate & Orate, (Watch and Pray)' was perceived in the sky over Montpellier in 1573. Angels brandishing dangerous weapons proclaimed 'woe, woe' above Normandy and Picardy on several occasions in the late 1590s and the ghastly image of a wild man threatening vengeance terrified members of a community near Frankfurt around 1600. Visions of bears, lions and serpents fighting in the sky were also widespread: an account of two dragons which clashed over Ghent in 1579 was one of the many foreign news pamphlets London publishers had translated for the edification of their readers.

From a modern perspective, reports of such apparitions may seem like an acute form of collective delusion. There is a temptation to explain them away 'scientifically', as peculiar cloud formations, manifestations of the aurora borealis, or other meteorological anomalies. And yet to dismiss them as symptoms of 'superstitious' ignorance and quaint relics of a primitive mentality is to risk overlooking their historical and cultural significance. Like more recent sightings of flying saucers and extraterrestrial objects, the astonishing images early modern men and women saw projected in the air provide us with a unique glimpse of their deepest fears and anxieties. Close scrutiny of how contemporaries interpreted these intriguing visions reveals much about the underlying assumptions and pre-occupations of post-Reformation English and European society.

According to lay and clerical commentators alike, apparitions were sermons inscribed by the finger of God in the sky. They were 'heralds' and 'trumpeters' of His wrath and indignation, alarm bells alerting mankind to the punishments which the Almighty would shortly be inflicting upon it, 'most apparent prints' and 'visible footsteps' of His growing impatience with sin. Since the exhortations of godly ministers were scorned and ignored, the Lord had ordained 'the Pulpit of the Heavens to be a Preacher of Repentance' to His people on earth. Constant reiteration of this commonplace may help to explain why parishioners of the German village of Holzhausen were convinced that they had seen an image of Martin Luther hovering above them in June 1548! Along with monstrous babies, sixteen-headed cabbages, deformed animals and downpours of wheat, such prodigies warned of terrible plagues and proclaimed that the end of the world was imminent. Preaching before the House of Commons in 1628, Jeremiah Dyke, vicar of Epping, described them as 'John Baptists of Judgement'. Like the handwriting which had appeared on the wall during King Belshazzar's feast, they too prophesied doom and destruction.

These beliefs had ancient Christian and classical roots. The Old and New Testaments supplied ample proof that God used the natural world as a medium for communicating with and admonishing humanity: from the amazing signs shown to the Israelites in the wilderness, to the wonders listed in the Gospels as forerunners of Christ's Second Coming. The books of Daniel and Revelation encouraged the idea that occult phenomena would prefigure the overthrow of the Antichrist and the advent of the millennium, while the Jewish historian Josephus's famous account of the blazing comet, bright lights, and aerial battles which preceded the siege of Jerusalem in AD 70 further cemented the link between celestial marvels and future catastrophes. The same premise underpinned the many astrological prognostications which circulated in the late Middle Ages, in which peculiar sights in the heavens, along with unusual conjunctions of the planets and stars, were likewise interpreted as harbingers of political and social upheaval, auguries of the death of princes and the collapse of kingdoms. Revived during the Renaissance, the writings of Greek and Roman historians and natural philosophers, such as Livy and Pliny, also contained many remarkable omens and portents. All of these sources of influence converged to make speculation about the significance of prodigies a central component of late medieval popular culture.

The Reformation has often been represented as a movement which comprehensively rejected and violently disrupted the settled patterns of traditional piety. However, although Protestantism initiated a break with many aspects of the Roman Catholic past, it did nothing to arrest the tendency to read divine meaning into strange aberrations of nature or to undermine the notion that the universe was a sensitive gauge of human misconduct and moral disorder.

Indeed, if anything, it seems to have reinforced it. Protestant theology placed renewed emphasis on the sovereignty and majesty of God and his constant providential intervention in temporal affairs. It also heightened apocalyptic expectancy, fostering the belief that contemporaries were living in the Last Days, when the cosmic battle between good and evil would reach a dramatic and cataclysmic conclusion. As historians have recently stressed, these observations cast doubt on Max Weber's claim that the Reformation was a major watershed in the process of secularisation which he called 'the disenchantment of the world'.

For Martin Luther and his successor Philip Melanchthon scrutiny of 'visual impressions', together with other signs and wonders, was a form of pious contemplation, a legitimate method of investigating the arcane purposes of the Almighty. John Calvin (1509–64) was more cautious, insisting that the Lord's ways were beyond human comprehension and that it was presumptuous for mere human beings to 'peep into the Ark of divine secrets' and to seek to unravel the riddles of His Creation. Although they gave lip-service to this caveat, in practice Calvinists were no less inclined than Lutherans to regard nature as 'God's great book in folio' and to analyse its irregularities as meticulously as they might do difficult passages in the Bible.

All over Europe ministers and pastors were at the forefront of efforts to record and interpret apparitions and other inexplicable phenomena. The second half of the sixteenth century saw the publication of many extensive collections of wonders such as Job Fincelius's Wunderzeichen (1556), Conrad Lycosthenes's Prodigiorum ac ostentorum chronicon (1557), and The Doome Warning all Men to the Judgemente (1581) compiled by Stephen Batman, chaplain to Archbishop Matthew Parker of Canterbury. The cumulative effect of these encyclopedias of the preternatural was to intensify fear that God would soon send His vengeance and to enhance anticipation that the Apocalypse was nigh.

Like other prodigies, celestial visions were a problematic category in Protestant thought. Their status was fraught with ambiguity. Reformation theologians insisted that miracles had ceased and that God no longer chose to override or operate in defiance of nature. But they still had to account for the many events which appeared 'miraculous' in the eyes of the average layman. There were several ways of tackling this challenge. One was to acknowledge that apparitions might be optical illusions created by elaborate tricks with mirrors or other 'cunning devices'. A second was to suggest that spectral sights were sometimes the by-product of psychological disturbance or of a physical illness which interfered with and distorted the senses. Thirdly, they could be identified as diabolical in origin: false wonders wrought by that master magician, Lucifer, 'stratagems of Satan' designed to lead the innocent astray. This was a favourite way of discrediting prodigious visions exploited by the papists as propaganda for their cause – idolatrous visions of the Virgin Mary and the saints like those reported regularly in sixteenth-century Spain.

But the fourth explanation was the one most frequently invoked. All too often, it was argued, people without a detailed understanding of the normal workings of nature were simply unable to discern the hidden secondary causes of strange phenomena. Drawing on the theories of Aristotle and Pliny, scholars demonstrated that apparitions were the consequence of vapours and exhalations rapidly inflaming and cooling in the upper regions of the air. In his Certaine Secrete Wonders of Nature (1569), the Frenchman Pierre Boaistuau explained that mock suns were merely reflections projected onto clouds heavily laden with droplets of rain, while the Cambridge divine William Fulke devoted a section of his treatise on meteors, A Goodly Gallery with a most Pleasaunt Prospect, into the Garden of Naturall Contemplation (1563), to proving that a vision of a *draco volans* or fire-breathing dragon seen over the Thames on May Day 1547 was 'nothing else' but a curious configuration of 'clouds and smoke'. As for menacing luminous impressions of aerial battles, these too were simply the unusual side effects of particular atmospheric conditions.

And yet none of these writers regarded enquiry into the natural causes of apparitions as incompatible with the notion that they were ambassadors sent by the Lord 'to declare his power and move us to amendment of life'. They sharply criticised those of 'Gallileo's temper' who sought to push the deity out of the picture completely. After all, it was axiomatic that 'not so much as one Sparrow falleth to the ground, without God's providence'. He simply used the elements as the couriers and executioners of His just punishments. In this sense, religious speculation stimulated rather than restrained scientific investigation – and vice versa. In striving to understand the natural world, Protestants like William Fulke and Philip Melanchthon were glorifying the Almighty. And in their attempts to decipher the cryptic messages enshrined in Creation they were also contributing to the expansion of botanical, zoological, astronomical and meteorological knowledge.

This, then, was the intellectual framework within which contemporaries interpreted celestial spectacles. It is now time to analyse the contents of these visions in a little more detail. Apparitions of angels wielding sabres and devils with forked tails and cloven feet tell us of a culture in which good and evil spirits were believed to be ever present, while the naked but hairy figure of the wildman which haunted German villagers around 1600 alerts us to the mythology surrounding creatures which hovered on the boundary between human and beast.

And just as reports of UFOs highlight late twentieth-century fears of invasion by aliens from other galaxies, so too do the sinister visions of violence and bloodshed seen in early modern England and Europe give graphic expression to the events that filled contemporaries with greatest horror and dread. As one writer explained, 'Battles in the Air were most lively pictures of the same to be seen on earth'. They were premonitions of the tragedy about to engulf those who were witnesses to them.

Not surprisingly, such apparitions proliferated significantly in contexts of political and religious instability. On the fringes of Eastern Europe communities often saw the characteristically crescent-shaped blades used by the Ottoman Turks – ominous symbols of the threat Islam presented on the frontiers of Christendom. In the period between the invasion by the French king Charles VIII and the sack of Rome by the troops of the Holy Roman Emperor Charles V in 1527, Italians observed many visions of hideous confrontation in the air. So too did the French amid the turmoil, hatred and destruction generated by the protracted Wars of Religion between the Catholics and Huguenots in the second half of the sixteenth century. They were likewise a common sight in the young and still vulnerable Dutch Republic. The conflicts which had racked the Holy Roman Empire in the 1540s and 50s were also accompanied by many extraordinary apparitions: a few days before one crucial battle between Maurice, Duke of Saxony, and Albert, Marquis of Brandenburg, for instance, the image of a huge man dripping blood and emanating sparks of fire appeared in the heavens. Such visions multiplied during the Thirty Years' War between 1618 and 1648, when confessional tension and discord culminated once more in prolonged military confrontation.

Continental prodigies of this period were widely publicised in England in translations of foreign newsbooks and compilations like Captain L. Brinkmair's *The Warnings of Germany* (1638). Fascinated and appalled by the similarity between these portents and strange phenomena seen on their own side of the Channel, many observers became increasingly convinced that God was sending advance notice that the English, too, would soon taste the cup of affliction. John Everard, an outspoken lecturer at St Martin in the Fields, for example, saw a disturbing connection between the appearance of three suns above the Cornish market town of Tregony in December 1621 and comparable signs observed prior to the Catholic massacre of Swiss Protestants at Valletelline in July 1620. Surely, thundered dozens of preachers, this sinful nation could not hope to be spared the horrors which had been endured by countries abroad for a whole generation? The Angel of the Lord had 'poured out his viall of red wine' on Germany and France, proclaimed Daniel Featley in the late 1620s, 'our sins as it were holler to him to stretch his hand over the narrow sea, and cast the dregs of it on us, who have been long settled upon our lees: and undoubtedly this will be our potion to drink'.

Predictably, in the decade preceding the breakdown of relations between Charles I and Parliament in 1642, reports of spectral armies clashing in the firmament sprang up in large numbers. Just as visions of huge navies of ships had indexed expectations of the 'invincible' Spanish Armada in the mid- and late-1580s, so the Civil War was clearly no surprise when it came: it had already been the theme of scores of God's sermons in the sky. We may even wonder if the anxieties which they enshrined played a part in helping to bring it about.

Once the fighting broke out, there were many sightings in the vicinity of key battlefields such as Edgehill in Northamptonshire. At Aldeborough in Suffolk in August of 1642 muskets and ordnance were heard discharging in the air for over an hour, at the end of which appeared a group of angels with stringed and wind instruments playing melodious music. According to the puritan schoolmaster John Vicars, who described this 'Masterpiece of Wonderment' in his Prodigies and Apparitions or Englands Warning Pieces (1642–43), it signalled that 'the terrible storm of wars and woes' stirred up by 'Papists, Atheists, and Profane Malignants' would eventually make way for 'a glorious peace and perfect reformation and for the setting up of Christ's throne'.

Vicars's millenarian reading of this vision reflects the fact that by the mid-seventeenth century the interpretation of prodigies had become dangerously politicised. Indeed his entire tract was designed to demonstrate divine displeasure at the policies pursued by Archbishop William Laud in the 1630s. But those who supported the Stuart king proved equally adept at harnessing aerial spectacles as evidence that God was on their side. A striking case in point is the report that the headless body of the royal martyr Charles had been seen hovering over the place of his execution in Whitehall in 1649. Blatantly exploited as propaganda by Royalists and Parliamentarians throughout that decade, prodigies were also utilised as powerful weapons of faction in the early Restoration. In a series of three tracts with the title Mirabilis Annus published in 1661 and 1662, the beleaguered Nonconformists assembled a collection of signs and wonders in support of their cause. In one of the many celestial apparitions they cited, armed men had been seen thrusting preachers from their pulpits above East Sussex – an obvious manifestation of the Lord's displeasure at the ejection of so many Dissenting ministers from their church livings. It was significant that the editors of the treatise felt it necessary to ward off suggestions that some of the examples they included were merely 'feigned' and fabricated for the occasion. In the long run the appropriation, embellishment and perhaps even the invention of such spectacles for sectarian ends probably contributed to discrediting them and to fostering scepticism towards manifestations of the supernatural. After 1700 many learned lay and clerical observers began to condemn belief in omens and portents as a form of 'vulgar superstition' and irrational 'enthusiasm'.

But in the preceding period this development, though important, was still embryonic. Throughout the century between the Reformation and the Civil War the consensus of opinion endorsed the traditional interpretation of visions and other prodigious phenomena as providential messengers which had been central to medieval cosmology. Powerfully reinforcing the idea of a moralised universe, Protestantism served to encourage the predisposition of contemporaries to invest celestial sights with eschatological significance. Notwithstanding growing awareness that such spectacles could be explained in terms of 'natural causes', in England, as in Europe as a whole, both the elite and the lower orders continued to see them as perturbing signs of divine indignation. We may see them as symptoms of profound political, ecclesiastical and social disequilibrium.

CHAPTER 8
THE ROLE OF THE GHOST-STORY IN MEDIAEVAL CHRISTIANITY
R. A. Bowyer

I originally suggested this paper under the title 'The Role of the Ghost in Mediaeval Christianity', but, having now written the paper, I realise what a more appropriate (and only slightly less ambitious) title would be 'The Role of the Ghost-Story in Mediaeval Christianity', for the purpose of this paper is to introduce something of the richness of mediaeval Latin ghost-literature, and to suggest some of the various contexts – theological, social, literary and folkloric – in which these ghost-stories can be studied.

I will be including as 'ghosts' any supernatural apparitions of the dead, whether they belong in hell, purgatory, or heaven, whether they are restless sinners or benevolent saints. This is, I admit, an unusually broad definition, but I think my subject forces it upon me: the men of the Middle Ages did not share our concept of the 'ghost', and indeed there is no mediaeval word which means quite the same as our modern word 'ghost', with all its associations of distressed or malevolent 'revenants'; the Middle English word 'ghost' means merely 'spirit' (it translates and is translated by the Latin *spiritus*) and both the English and Latin words are of very general application, carrying no particularly sinister or spine-chilling nuances. The stories I shall be discussing are all about 'spirits', but spirits of every kind: for while the modern 'ghost' appears in a psychological vacuum, terrifyingly isolated from our normal, everyday experience, the mediaeval 'ghost' or 'spirit' appears as an integral part of an immense and ordered spiritual world which includes not merely tormented sinners and devils, but also guardian angels and benevolent saints.

Ghost-stories, then, in this broad sense, are abundant in all forms of mediaeval literature; in this paper I shall be concentrating almost entirely on mediaeval Latin literature, although much of my argument might equally well be applied to the vernacular literatures of the period. The stories I shall be discussing come from all kinds of texts – histories of the world, chronicles of contemporary life, theological and even scientific treatises, lives of saints and the remarkable *Libri Exemplorum*, – preachers' manuals of edifying and usually miraculous tales for use in sermons. Different as the various genres sound, the material is in fact surprisingly homogeneous, and we may note three qualities common to them all. Firstly, they were all written by men who, whether English or German, French or Italian, all shared the same common literary culture – the Bible, the Church Fathers, the Lives of the Saints, and a few of the classics. This literary culture was by our standards extremely small – a hundred books would have been regarded as a very substantial academic library. Thus inevitably, all our writers betray the influence of the same models; indeed we often find exactly the same story told in exactly the same words in perhaps half a dozen different texts. Secondly, all our stories were written down by churchmen; some of them, like the preaching exempla, were written with an overtly didactic purpose; but all of them, directly or indirectly, serve to confirm the teachings of the mediaeval church: they confirm that righteousness will be rewarded and wickedness will be punished; they confirm the church's teachings about heaven, hell, and purgatory; they confirm the efficacy of the church's prayers and masses for the dead, and of its absolutions for sins committed. Thirdly, we must remember that the idea of prose-fiction in the modern sense did not exist in the Middle Ages – all these stories, without exception, were told as being absolutely and historically true.

In this paper I want to illustrate three kinds of typical mediaeval ghost-story, distinguished by the three situations in which the ghost can appear: firstly, the departing ghost, seen, usually at the moment of death, making its way from this world to the next; secondly, the ghost seen actually within the confines of the next world; and thirdly, the returning ghost or 'revenant'. Here of course the breadth of my definition makes itself felt, for to most of us today, the world 'ghost' conjures up specifically the third kind of story, the 'revenant': but as I have said, the Middle Ages did not share our idea of the 'ghost', and all three kinds of apparition were regarded as the same kind of experience of that spiritual world which was integrated into the life and theology of the mediaeval church.

The departing ghost

I would like to begin with a story from Pope Gregory the Great, for he is undoubtedly the most influential single figure in the development of the mediaeval ghost-story. Gregory's *Dialogues,* written at the end of the sixth century, contain dozens of curious and incredible ghost-stories, which remained incredibly popular throughout the Middle Ages[1]; they were told and retold, translated even into Anglo-Saxon, and served as models for many similar stories. Moreover, Gregory's work was treated with a respect similar to that accorded to Holy Scripture, and was frequently adduced as the theological justification for the whole ghost tradition. Indeed, we often find the mediaeval chroniclers telling some very tall ghost-story, and then warning their readers 'Let no man doubt that this story is true: for something very similar is related in Gregory's *Dialogues…*'

Gregory tells many stories of departing ghosts, and here is a tale from the *Dialogues* concerning Theodoric the Goth, the Arian and Barbarian ruler of Italy in the early sixth century:

When I was living in a monastery, there was a man called Julian who used to visit me, to share with me godly and profitable conversation. One day he told me this story: Back in the days of King Theodoric my father-in-law's father had been serving in Sicily, and was sailing back to Italy when his ship was cast up on the Isle of Lipari. Now there was a certain hermit, a man of great sanctity, who dwelt on that island, so while the sailors were making repairs to the ship, my father-in-law's father decided to pay a visit to that holy man and ask to be remembered in his prayers. When the hermit met him and his companions, he asked, among other things, whether they knew that King Theodoric was dead. 'But that is impossible,' they replied, 'he was alive when we left and we have heard no news of his death.' But the man of God replied: 'He is dead indeed; yesterday at the ninth hour he was led along between Pope John and Symmachus the Senator, barefoot and ungirded, with gyves upon his wrists, and thrown into the mouth of the nearby volcano.' When they heard this, they made a careful note of the date, and when they arrived back in Italy, they found that Theodoric had died on the very day when the holy hermit of Lipari had been shewn his passing and his punishment.[2]

This story is typical of many in Gregory's *Dialogues*: I do not know whether Gregory's tales can rightly be called 'folk-tales', but they can certainly be studied, like folk-tales, in terms of recurring structures and recurring motifs: thus at least four elements of the story – the holy mermit gaining news by super-natural means, the mouth of the volcano as place of punishment, the written note of the time which later proves accurate, and even the fact that Gregory claims to have the story from a reliable source – are all motifs which occur elsewhere in the *Dialogues,* and also in the many later mediaeval writers who were familiar with Gregory's work.

The purpose behind Gregory's story of the death of Theodoric is obvious enough: it confirms Christian teaching about the existence of life after death; it warns the sinner that wickedness will be punished; it comforts the oppressed with the knowledge that the oppressors, be they kings or princes, will be judged and punished according to their works. It also demonstrates a favourite point of Gregory's, that clairvoyance – in this case the hermit's ability to see the ghost – is a natural grace of the ascetic or monastic life.

The ghost being thrown into hell or purgatory is but one form of the story of the departing ghost: the other, of course, tells of the ghost being carried up to heaven, and Gregory tells many such stories too. Both kinds of story are a commonplace of the saints' lives of the later Middle Ages, adduced to demonstrate the saintliness of the saint and the sinfulness of the sinner. Indeed the two kinds of story parallel each other very closely: the saint is carried upwards by angels, the sinner dragged downwards by devils; the saint is accompanied by heavenly music and sweet fragrance, while the sinner departs amidst hellish screams, and leaves behind a choking sulphurous stench.

If we wish to be cynical, we may attribute something of the enormous popularity of such tales in mediaeval literature to their polemical possibilities: what better way to prove the rightness of one's own cause, than to tell how its champions had been seen received into heaven; what better way to demonstrate the wickedness of one's enemies' cause, than to tell how its misguided adherents had been seen dragged down to hell by the cackling demons who had beguiled them in their lives? The ghost-story can thus take on a political aspect; a delightful example occurs in the late mediaeval *Chronicle of Scotland,* which records British history from an aggressively Scottish point of view. According to the Chronicle, when Edward I, the 'Hammer of the Scots', died, his ghost was seen carried off to hell by a crowd of jubilant demons armed with whips, who chanted a chorus:

En Rex Edwardus, debacchans ut leopardus,
Olim dum vixit populum Domini maleflixit.
Nobis viae talis comes ibis, care sodalis,
Quo condemneris, ut daemonibus socieris.
Te sequimur voto prorsus torpore remoto.

– which E.C. Brewer rendered into equally diabolical English verse:

> Behold Edwardus rex O, once wont the church to vex so,
> As raging leopard now sir, to the infernal slough sir,
> Where demons fleer and titter, with us dear friend you'll flitter,
> And company for ever, henceforth we will not sever.

But, the *Chronicle of Scotland* records, when William Wallace, the great Scottish patriot, died, a certain holy hermit (notice again the clairvoyant hermit) saw his ghost borne up to heaven by angels, in company with innumerable souls released from Purgatory by the merits of that most glorious martyrdom![3]

The ghost in the other world

One very familiar genre of mediaeval ghost-story tells of the man whose body lies for some time dead or in a deathlike trance, while his spirit is given a guided tour of the Other World, where he sees the ghosts of the dead suffering grotesque and horrible punishments in the fires of hell and purgatory, or enjoying sweet music and ineffable fragrance among the flowery meadows of heaven. The story, and many of its motifs, are older than Gregory the Great, but it was he who was most responsible for disseminating the tradition throughout the Christian world. One of Gregory's stories, again from the *Dialogues,* is too delightful not to be quoted:

> There was a man called Stephen, who died and was taken to hell, where he saw devils and sinners tormented for their sins; but when Stephen was presented to the Judge, the Judge declared to the devils 'This is the wrong Stephen: it was Stephen the blacksmith, not this Stephen, that I ordered you to bring before me!' – And at that very instant, Stephen found himself back in his body, alive again; but at the same moment, Stephen the blacksmith, who lived next door, suddenly passed away.[4]

Gregory claims to have heard this story from Stephen himself, but in fact – as the non-Christian image of the judgment taking place in hell indicates – the story has a classical origin, and can be found in Plutarch and Lucian as well as in Saint Augustine.

The development of the tradition of the Other World Journey – from Gregory the Great, through Bede and Celtic versions like the Fis Adamnain, to the most elaborate and sadistic forms of the High Middle Ages, Tindale, Turchill, Alberic, Orm and the monk of Eynsham, and ultimately to the literary creation of Dante's *Divine Comedy* – is of course well beyond the scope of this modest paper. I would like merely to make the rather obvious point that all these visions encourage the reader to think of the dead as continuing their existence in apparently physical bodies in an apparently physical world; and while certain theologians[5] doubted whether these visions could be taken literally, it is clear that for the majority of mediaevel men, the next world was conceived as a mode of existence barely different from this life. All these visions place the Other World within the confines of the physical universe: thus heaven is somewhere above the earth, purgatory somewhere just below the surface of the earth, and hell deep in the bowels of the earth. This belief was held even by educated and articulate men: Caesarius of Heisterbach, a thirteenth century Cistercian who wrote a *Dialogue of Miracles* modelled in part on the *Dialogues* of Gregory the Great, is asked 'Ubi est purgatorium?' (Where is purgatory?) and replies, without batting an eyelid, 'Quantum ex variis colligitur visionibus, in diversis locis huius mundi'. (As far as can be gathered from the various visions, in different places in this world.) He goes on to enumerate some of the places: Saint Patrick's Purgatory in Lough Derg, Mount Etna, Mount Geber, and various volcanoes, like the one into which Theodoric was thrown in my first story. If the educated classes held such primitive ideas, we can only speculate on the beliefs of the illiterate peasantry.

Like the visions of the departing ghost, the visions of the ghost within the Other World may be concerned with heaven, purgatory, or hell; but it is perhaps a reflection of an inherent imbalance in mediaeval Christianity that it is the accounts of purgatory and of hell that are the most frequent, the most detailed, and the most memorable; the *Inferno,* for example, has always been the most popular book of Dante's trilogy. Somehow the elaborate torments of hell, in which the punishment is exquisitely made to fit the crime, stir the imagination rather more than the flowery meadows and rarefied delights of heaven; but there was also a feeling that heaven, of its very nature, beggared all description, and a number of theologians taught that while accounts of hell could be taken literally, all descriptions of heaven – even those in Scripture – could only be taken metaphorically.[6] This emphasis on hell and purgatory rather than on heaven is most lyrically evoked in the vision of one fourteenth century monk, who reported:

> I saw souls descending into hell like a raging blizzard; I saw souls going into purgatory like a fine, fine shower; but I only saw three souls entering heaven.[7]

Most of these visions of ghosts in the Other World are too long and too repetitive to be worth quoting in detail; but I would like to refer specifically to two visions, to illustrate particular points of interest – firstly about the nature of the ghost itself, and secondly about the way in which these stories might be used as aids to preaching.

Saint Barontus was an eighth-century French monk who one day collapsed after mattins and lay in a death-like trance for several days, during which time he was given a guided tour of heaven, hell, and purgatory. His vision is interesting not so much for the details of what he saw (which are pretty conventional), as for his quite unconventional explanation of the mechanics of the out-of-body experience: Barontus relates that while he was lying in his trance, two devils appeared, to take him to hell; but the archangel Raphael also arrived, to rescue him; there ensued a long altercation between Raphael and the devils, each side laying claim to possession of Barontus' soul. Eventually, after a whole day's wrangling, they reached a compromise, and agreed to take the matter to divine arbitration: they will leave his *spirit* in his body, and take his *soul* to the judgment-seat of God. This distinction between the soul and the spirit is most unusual, and even in the eighth century might well have been regarded as heretical.[8] Anyway, this is how Barontus describes his soul being removed from his body:

> The archangel Raphael stretched forth his finger and touched my throat, and immediately I felt my poor soul being wrenched out of my body. I will tell you what it looked like: it seemed about as small as a newly-hatched chick when it emerges from

the shell, but tiny as it is, it still has head and eyes and all other members, and carries with it all the five senses – sight, hearing, taste, smell, and touch; but it cannot speak until it arrives at the judgment, where it receives a new body, made of air, identical to the one it left behind.[9]

So detailed an explanation of the process of leaving the body is very rare, and Barontus' account of his separable spirit, his homunculus-soul, and his ghostly body made of air, have few parallels in comparable Christian literature.

As a final example of ghosts seen within the confines of the Other World, I would like to quote a text to illustrate how these tales might be used as aids to preaching. The story is from a thirteenth century *Liber Exemplorum* or preacher's manual, compiled by a Franciscan preacher in Ireland; this book, incomplete as the only surviving manuscript is, contains over two hundred stories, most of them miraculous, and many of them encompassing, in the broadest sense, the activities of ghosts. The stories are conveniently arranged alphabetically, under the various themes on which the preacher might be called to preach: thus 'accidy', 'advocates', 'avarice', 'baptism', 'charity' 'clerks', 'evil', and 'cogitations, carnal'. This story comes under 'gluttony', and is taken from Bede, but the story itself is by no means as interesting as advice which the compiler of the manual gives to accompany it:

This exemplum is found in Bede's Ecclesiastical History, and goes like this: I knew a certain monk who was in an excellent monastery, but who lived a most disgraceful life: he was often taken to task by the senior monks, but he never took any notice; nevertheless they used to put up with him on account of his job, for he was a skilled craftsman. But he was much addicted to drink and to other vices, and he was much happier lazing about in his workshop night and day instead of going to chapel with the other monks to say the offices. One day he fell ill, and summoning the brethren to his bedside, told them, with tears in his eyes and the look of a condemned man, how he had seen hell open, and seen Satan wallowing in the depths of the Underworld, and Caiaphas too, and the Jews who crucified Our Lord. 'In the midst of these,' he said, 'I saw a place prepared for me.' When the monks heard this, they urged him to repent of his sins; but he replied: 'There is no time for repentance now, the judgment is already passed against me'. And so he died, without even receiving the last sacraments. Here ends the exemplum. As you see, the story concerns a monk who was a slave of the above-mentioned vices, but it is hardly a good idea to tell such stories about monks to the laity; so if you are preaching to a lay congregation, it is advisable to refer to him merely as a certain drinker – for such indeed he was – and to refer to the other monks merely as men – for such indeed they were; so the whole story can be told without mentioning monks, but the truth of the story will in no way be compromised. If on the other hand you are preaching to monks, then you can tell the story as it stands.[10]

The passage is a rather amusing comment on one aspect of mediaeval preaching; but whether he was addressing the religious or the laity, the preacher's message was the same, a simple message for simple hearts: repent and lead a right life, for the pains of hell are real and horrible.

And so to our final category.

The returning ghost

As we have seen from the stories I have told so far, communications between the living and the dead seem to have been fairly easy throughout the Middle Ages; and just as the departing ghost, and the ghost within the Other World, may be associated with heaven, purgatory, or hell, so the returning ghost may appear from any of the three places. Having defined the word 'ghost' as 'any supernatural apparition of the dead', I now find myself obliged to say that the largest single class of mediaeval ghost-story is the tale of the spirit which returns from heaven to earth to give miraculous help in an hour of need, in fact, the saint who answers the prayers of the faithful by a direct and personal intervention – like Saint George appearing at the siege of Antioch during the First Crusade and spurring on the Christian forces to victory over the Saracens. Of course, this kind of story is not what we usually understand by a 'ghost-story', but as I have said, the Middle Ages did not share our concept of the 'ghost'. The story of the saint intervening in human affairs is so well known as a genre that I hardly need quote further instances; I mention this kind of story merely to emphasise one important point: that the idea of a spirit returning from the Other World did not necessarily mean to the men of the Middle Ages, as it does for us, something sinister, malevolent, or frightening, but could equally well mean something holy, joyful and benevolent. We shall bear this in mind as we glance at some other stories of returning ghosts.

There are quite a number of accounts of people actually arranging before their death that they would return from the dead, to bring news of the Other World. Thus the Irish Franciscan preachers' manual from which I quoted the story of the bibulous monk also tells a story, under the heading 'Joys of Heaven', of how two monks made a pact with each other, according to which whoever should die first was to return from the dead, if God should permit, and tell the other what had happened to him beyond the grave. One of the monks duly died, and six months later appeared to his surviving brother in a blaze of light, and informed him that the joys of heaven were greater than men had ever dreamed of.[11]

About the same time as the preachers' manual was being compiled in Ireland, another Franciscan, Fra Salimbene, in Italy, was including similar stories in his diary-cum-chronicle of contemporary life. I cannot resist telling one of his delightful, if grisly, cameos of the mediaeval world:

Brother Leo, one of our order, heard the last confession of the governor of the Milan hospital, a man of good name who had a reputation for holiness. When he was at the point of death, Brother Leo made him promise that after his death he would return to him, with news of what became of him in the Other World; and the governor of the hospital willingly promised to do this. That evening the word went round the town that he had died; so Brother Leo asked two of his most trusted companions to sit up and watch with him that night, in the gardener's cell in the corner of the monastery garden. As they watched together that night, Leo dozed off to sleep, telling his companions to wake him if they heard or saw anything. Then, all of a sudden, they heard something coming, with wild screams of anguish, and they saw what looked like a ball of fire falling out of the sky onto the roof of the cell, like a hawk swooping on its prey. The noise and the shock started Leo from sleep: the voice wailed out 'Alas, alas.' 'What has become of you?' asked Leo. The voice replied that he was damned, because when foundling children were abandoned at the hospital, he used to let them die without baptism, in order to save the hospital from the expense of keeping them. When Brother Leo asked him why he had never confessed the sin, the voice replied that he had forgotten about it, or didn't think it worth confessing. So brother Leo said: 'Then you have nothing to do with us: depart from us and go your way.'[12]

The story is beautifully told, and gains something of its dramatic force from being in a way a parody of the more familiar form of the story – like the one I quoted from the preachers' manual – in which the ghost returns with news of the joys of heaven: Salimbene deliberately leads his readers to expect that the respected public figure would likewise return with news of heaven, and then gives us an unpleasant shock when the truth is revealed. The story also illustrates, incidentally, that the ghost did not always appear in human form, but sometimes, as here, as a ball of fire: the motif is an international one – Japanese ghosts occasionally appear as globes of light, and West Indian witch-doctors transform themselves into fireballs.

Ghosts whose return is pre-arranged are of course in a minority; if we leave aside saints who appear from heaven, we find that the majority of mediaeval ghosts appear from purgatory, and return to earth with a very specific purpose: to escape from purgatory into heaven as quickly as possible. The transition from purgatory to heaven is usually effected by the normal sacramental means: thus ghosts return to earth to request a certain number of masses for the repose of their souls; excommunicate ghosts return to ask for their excommunications to be revoked; unshriven ghosts were even known to return from purgatory to buy indulgences for themselves. Ghost-stories like these remained popular with the church from the time of Gregory the Great until the Reformation, for such stories offered a 'living' proof of the validity of the church's sacraments and the truth of the church's teaching.

Rather less frequently, ghosts return to make direct amends for the crimes they have committed in this life, and stories like these can reflect quite closely the social concerns of the day: thus many stock characters – the licentious priest, the oppressive lord, the dishonest tradesman – can all appear as repentant revenants. One particular social injustice of the Middle Ages was the enclosure of land for hunting reserves – with no pity or compensation for the evicted tenants. A story originally told by Thomas Walsingham in his *Historia Anglicana* (s.a. 1342) illustrates the point well:

In this same year died Harry Burwake (Burghersh), Bishop of Lincoln. And when he was dead, he appeared unto one of his squires, with a bow, arrows, and horn, in a short green coat, and said unto him: 'Thou knowest well when I made this park I took many poor men's lands, and closed them in; therefore go I here, and keep this park with full muckle pain. I pray thee, go to my brethren canons of Lincoln, and pray them that they restore the poor men to their land, break down the hedges, make plain the dykes, and then shall I have rest.' Then by the common assent of the chapter of Lincoln, they sent a canon, clept William Bachelor, and he fulfilled all this restoring.[13]

The bow, arrows, and horn, and the short green coat, are of course the uniform of a huntsman or gamekeeper; but they also suggest the garb of the fairies: is it conceivable that the bishop was biding his time with the fairy-folk, the fallen angels who were not wicked enough to fall

all the way to hell? Perhaps the most remarkable aspect of the story is the fact that the canons actually did restore the land to the poor men, simply on the strength of this apparition: we see here a sociological dimension to the ghost-story – the supernatural as a means by which the oppressed could assert their interests.

****

So we have looked at three kinds of mediaeval ghost-story: the departing ghost, the ghost in the Other World, and the returning ghost. We have seen *that the* mediaeval church not only tolerated a belief in ghosts, but was active in disseminating the belief, and the ghost-story had an important role in the church's system of instruction – especially instruction of the populace, whose attention could more easily be caught by a good ghost-story than by a fine distinction from Thomas Aquinas. The mediaeval world accepted ghosts within its wide embrace, for the mediaeval church conceived itself as a great triangle of inter-dependent groups: the church militant, the church suffering, and the church triumphant. The church on earth supplied the membership of the church in purgatory and in heaven, and relied on the help and intercession of the latter, while the souls in purgatory looked to the church on earth for prayers and masses to expedite their promotion to heaven, whence they in turn would offer assistance to the church on earth. The ghost-stories we have been discussing can all be seen as embodying in concrete images this mystical communion between the church in this world and the church in the next world. Thus the mediaeval ghost fits into and confirms the mediaeval world-view; and while the mediaeval ghosts are often unpleasant, they are not usually terrifying in the same sense as their modern counterparts: they are a part of the world-order, and they obey the rules – they can be released from torment by prayers and masses, they can be held at bay by the sign of the cross or by a handful of holy relics.

When the Reformation came to northern Europe, the picture changed drastically: the church formally severed diplomatic relations with the Other World, ceasing to invoke the aid of the saints in heaven, and ceasing to recognise its responsibility towards the souls of the dead in purgatory. The church triumphant and the church suffering effectively ceased to exist, and the church militant was left starkly alone, between God and the Devil. The church also ceased officially to believe in ghosts, and ascribed all such apparitions to the malevolent wiles of the Devil. This did not mean that ghosts ceased to appear, but merely that the church abdicated its authority over them, and renounced the sacramental means of laying or exorcising the ghost.

It was perhaps this change in the church's position which fostered our modern concept of the 'ghost' – a word which has come to mean not the diversity of mediaeval apparitions which we have been discussing, but rather one specific type of apparition – the sinister revenant, an unknown outsider who represents a vague threat to our world-view, who is laid by no prayers or ceremonies.

A word inextricably linked with our modern concept of the ghost is the verb 'to haunt'; there is no mediaeval word which means the same as the modern English 'haunt', and indeed, the concept is strikingly absent from our mediaeval ghost-stories: the mediaeval ghosts almost invariably appear for a specific purpose, and having achieved their end, go, or are sent, away – they do not hang about for centuries, rattling chains and worrying the visitors. An interesting corollary of this is that, unlike modern ghost-stories, mediaeval ghost-stories are rarely associated with particular places: the idea of mediaeval castles and houses having their own resident ghosts belongs to the Gothic Novel rather than to mediaeval literature itself.

We may perhaps sum up the history of the ghost-story in the history of the English word 'ghost': the Middle English 'ghost' means simply 'spirit', and can refer to one's own soul, to God himself, or to a spirit returning from beyond the grave; the multiple use of the word itself indicates the solidarity of the spiritual world, it places the 'ghost' in the context of an integrated natural and supernatural order. The modern English 'ghost', on the other hand, has taken on more specific connotations, to mean the apparition of a dead person, almost invariably sinister and frightening; this restricted use of the term embodies the isolation of the modern 'ghost' from the rest of the modern world-order.

The substance of this paper can thus be formulated in the words of my title: the characteristic of the mediaeval ghost-story, as of the mediaeval ghost itself, is that it does indeed have an integral role in mediaeval Christianity – a role which, for good or ill, was to be taken away from it at the Reformation.

Notes

1. Gregory's authority was not discredited until the Reformation; Lewes Lavater, for example, wrote 'As touching St. Gregory's Dialogues, I cannot hide (which many have noted before me) that many things are contained in them that are nothing true, but altogether like old wives' tales. Not because the holy father hath written these things of malice, but for that he being too credulous hath put many things into his books, rather upon other men's report, than that he himself knew them certainly to be true.'

2. Latin text in Migne, PL 77, 369.

3. Fordun and Bower, *Scotichronicon*, sub annis 1307, 1305; Brewer's *Dictionary of Miracles*, page 460.

4. Latin text in Migne, PL 77, 384; *cf.* Delehaye, *Legends of the Saints*, pp. 186–7.

5. e.g. Hugh of Saint Victor, Migne, PL 176, 584.

6. e.g. Richard of Saint Victor, Migne, PL 196, 12–3.

7. Latin text in *Eulogium Historiarum* (Rolls Series 9), vol. I, page 284.

8. *cf.* Gennadius, Migne, PL 58, 985; Isidore, Migne PL 82, 398.

9. Latin text in *Acta Sanctorum* March III, p. 571.

10. Latin text in *Liber Exemplorum* ed. A.G. Little (1908), pp. 94–5.

11. *Ibid.,* page 91.

12. Latin text in Salimbene, *Chronica,* sub anno 1233. (MGH Scriptores in Folio 32, page 74.)

13. The English version quoted is from Capgrave's *Chronicle of England* (Rolls Series 1) page 210. (spelling modernised).

PART IV
WITCHCRAFT

INTRODUCTION: WITCHCRAFT AND WITCH BELIEFS IN MEDIEVAL AND EARLY MODERN EUROPE

Few areas of academic study have witnessed such a prodigious output of publications as the recent history of European witchcraft. Research into witches, witch trials and the intellectual context in which demonologists and persecutors operated has covered a vast landscape in its geographical scope, conceptual range and methodological approaches. Recent studies of early modern witchcraft have been local, regional, national and pan-European and have focused upon the trials of witches, the popular perceptions of witchcraft and learned demonology.[1] Questions have been posed about the role of the Church, the early modern state, religious change, social dislocation and women and gender in shaping the ebb and flow of persecution and in constructing the image of the witch itself. Witchcraft beliefs have been located much more firmly within their political, intellectual, social and cultural milieu: a more substantial effort has been made to examine both 'popular' belief in witchcraft and the views of the learned, historians have engaged with the work conducted in other disciplines and a vigorous debate has been conducted about the position of gender in the understanding of early modern witchcraft.[2]

The scope and scale of research has created an interpretation of witchcraft that is both more complex and more nuanced than half a century ago, reinforcing the assertion that there might be 'many reasons' underpinning the recognition and prosecution of witchcraft – reasons shaped and moulded by local contexts and conflicts and the interaction and interplay of a diverse range of ideas and realities.[3] The mental constructs that made possible, even necessary, the prosecution of witchcraft are best understood within the context of the literature of witchcraft and the methodologies of anthropological and folklore research. The reasons why neighbour might accuse neighbour are best explored against the broad backdrop provided by an awareness of the functioning of the early modern community and, perhaps, the role of gender within it. It is hard to make sense of the process by which witches were brought to trial without the contextual apparatus provided by an understanding of early modern religion, politics, economy and ideas.

For this reason, the best starting point for those new to the study of witchcraft is still perhaps to be found in those broad studies that cover a substantial physical and mental geography. The most enduring among these remains Brian Levack's *The Witch Hunt in Early Modern Europe*, but other recent contributions to the expanding bibliography of witchcraft highlight the pace at which historiography continues to evolve.[4] The significant and sometimes divergent regional and national contexts of witch trials and prosecutions have become evident in a wealth of recent studies that situate both witches and the fear of witches firmly within their local context. On a national scale, Christina Larner's work still exerts a powerful influence over the study of witchcraft in Scotland, both in her identification of some 3,000-plus cases that made up the Scottish witch hunts and in her interpretation of these cases as evidence that the best explanation for witchcraft accusations lies in the intersection of conflict between peasant neighbours and the determination of the godly elite to impose a cultural and moral uniformity.[5] Levack's analysis of the Scottish trials within their British context presents the case for a modification of Larner's conclusions, arguing that law, politics and religion all had a pivotal role to play in the dynamics of the prosecutions.[6] The North Berwick witch trials of 1590–1 have been the subject of substantial analysis and the Bargarran trial, a century later, likewise. Julian Goodare's investigation of the Aberdeenshire trials has established their importance on the map of Scottish witchcraft.[7] Stuart MacDonald's recent study of witchcraft in Fife has adapted and corrected Larner's records of the trials, arguing for the critical role of the presbytery in organizing the prosecution of witches. The stereotypical witch that emerges from the study is female, elderly and economically marginalized, and the accusations brought against her primarily in the field of *maleficia*, reflecting local concerns rather than intellectual trends.[8] The historiography of witchcraft in England still owes much to the methodologies and conclusions of Alan Macfarlane and Keith Thomas. Macfarlane's approach prioritized the relationships of the accused to their accusers and concluded that on the basis of the evidence of the Essex witch trials, issues of charity, especially in relation to the elderly members of the community, were highly significant.[9] His close analysis of the records of local trials has exerted a powerful influence over subsequent work on the English trials, and the influence of the techniques of anthropology is increasingly apparent in the scholarship of the 1970s and 1980s.[10] The focus upon the social and community context behind the English trials underpins Malcolm Gaskill's study of the Kent witch trials, James Sharpe's treatment of English witchcraft as a whole and Anne de Windt's investigation of the role of the village community in initiating and shaping accusations.[11] The most substantial witch-hunt in England, which took place in East Anglia in the mid-1640s, has also been subjected to close scrutiny, most recently by Malcolm Gaskill.[12]

Witchcraft in the imperial lands has been debated by a series of local and regional studies which highlight both the unique circumstances that underpinned individual trials and the common ground shared by inquisitorial inquiry and popular belief. Witchcraft emerges, once more, as a multifaceted and complex problem, shaped by legal structures, polemical and pastoral concerns and local pressures. Dillinger's analysis of the 'evil people' of Swabia and Trier examines the role and position of women in the witch trials, concluding that the fear of witchcraft was such that even apparently insubstantial evidence might form the basis of a prosecution. Such fear, and the negative perception of women and their agency in the trials, is also evident in Jonathan Durrant's discussion of *Witchcraft, Gender and Society in Early Modern Germany*.[13] Further, geographically defined but conceptually wide-ranging studies cover witchcraft prosecutions in Rothenburg, Bavaria, Langenberg, Nordlingen and south-western Germany.[14] Significant contributions have also come in the form of discussions of the role of religion, weather, natural disaster, print culture and the drive to enforce political and social order in shaping the fear and prosecution of witchcraft in central Europe.[15] Similar approaches can be seen in the history of witchcraft in France and Switzerland, with understanding enriched by an analysis of trials, court records and learned and popular belief at a local and regional level.[16]

In recent years, debate over the influence of late medieval and early modern demonology and intellectual ideas about witches has acquired a more central position in witchcraft scholarship, in no small part as a result of Stuart Clark's magisterial survey, *Thinking with*

Demons. Clark examines what he refers to as the emergence of 'elemental' features of early modern witchcraft (for example, ritual dedication to Satan, infanticide, anthropophagy, a threat to Christian society) alongside an analysis of a rapidly expanding learned literature on witchcraft and demonology in the early modern period. A close reading of a wide range of texts – not just the staple of the *Malleus Maleficarum* – reveals the gradual construction and evolution of a standard image of the witch and of standard questions that are to be asked of witchcraft. Can, for example, a witch control the weather? Is it possible for witchcraft to cause disease? Can witches transform their shape? What is apparent from these texts is evidence of both the existence of an intellectual belief in witchcraft, and of the ongoing struggle to come to terms with this model. By the mid-sixteenth century, this tension was being heightened in a more sceptical stance among both authors of demonological treatises and the inquisitors who were charged with the investigation of witches. Weyer, Scot, Alciati and Pomponazzi articulated concerns, often naturalistic, about the reality of witchcraft while in many respects remaining committed to some of the traditional imagery, particularly that of the female witch. Clark contends that this scepticism was accompanied by the publication, and in some cases republication, of tracts that affirmed the reality of witchcraft, encouraging a kind of synthesis of belief and unbelief that is evident in the works of the French demonologists Remy and Boguet. This sense that later demonologists had neither broken away from the past nor learned much from its debates rings true in Christina Larner's analysis Scottish witchcraft tracts.[17]

The persistence of belief in the reality of witchcraft and the threat that it posed, Clark argues, was in part the consequence of the transformation of witchcraft into a crime of conscience in the aftermath of the Protestant and Catholic Reformations, which spawned a flurry of new writing on the subject from the pens of Pierre Crespet, Juan Maldonado and Martin del Rio, among others. It was this intensification of the debate that fed into and fuelled the witch trials that took place in Europe in the century after 1550.[18] Scepticism, such as it was, focused around practical questions (was there evidence that justified the prosecution of witchcraft?), legal questions (did witchcraft deserve the status of a 'crimen exceptum'?) and demonological issues (was witchcraft a crime for which people might legitimately be held responsible?). The content of learned writing on witchcraft in the early modern period, Clark contends, is best understood if demonology is placed firmly within its intellectual context. The adoption of a sociological or anthropological approach to witchcraft has yielded substantial benefits but perhaps at the price of a fuller understanding of the meaning of witchcraft in this period – a meaning that is apparent once the texts are located more firmly within the milieu of Renaissance thought and debates over authority, politics and images of order.

Clark's agenda has been shared by other scholars who have sought to understand more clearly the substance and the shape of early modern demonology. Nowhere is this more apparent than in the analyses of the *Malleus Maleficarum*, the fifteenth-century treatise that set out what a witch did, how to find one, and what to do with a witch once apprehended. Seen on occasion as the spark that lit the powder keg of the early modern witch hunts, the *Malleus* has been recently republished in a substantial and scholarly English translation by Chris Mackay.[19] Debate over the agenda and influence of the *Malleus Maleficarum* has been conducted over a substantial time-period, and spawned some significant contributions that have fed into the broader history of late medieval and early modern witchcraft.[20] Alongside studies of the *Malleus Maleficarum* sit more general overviews of the literature of witchcraft, the role of the devil and the representation of the witches' Sabbath in demonological writing. The position of the *Malleus Maleficarum* as a result has moved from centre stage, in favour of a rather broader cast of authors who attempted to set out what witchcraft was and what it meant to those who wrote about it.[21]

The most evident interaction between the intellectual world of the demonologist and the popular perception of witchcraft is often argued to lie in the prominent position of women among those accused of witchcraft. The second two articles in this part approach the problem of women and witchcraft, or gender and witchcraft, from different perspectives, both of which reflect the way in which the debate over the 'anti-feminist' stance that some argue to be apparent in the European witch trials has developed. One of the most significant aspects of this development has been the incorporation of debates about women and witchcraft into the mainstream historiography. While most of the early studies of the issue, even in the 1970s and 1980s, were written outside either discipline of history, or outside academia, by the 1990s historians had come to recognize the potential benefits of a more thoughtful analysis of the role of gender in the construction of witchcraft. Significant strides in this direction were taken by Lyndal Roper in *Oedipus and the Devil*, which broadened the scope of the debate to reflect questions of society, fertility, motherhood alongside and within the literature of witchcraft.[22] Further significant contributions came from Dianne Purkiss, Marianne Hester, Merry Wiesner and others, who examined the gendering of witchcraft in print and in reality and the role of women as victims and accusers in individual trials.[23] As a result, the association of women with witchcraft has become recognized without being seen as a given and explored without being assumed to be readily explicable.

The second article in this part, Edward Bever's exploration of witchcraft, female aggression and power reflects some of the significant strides taken but also the multiplicity of interpretations and uncertainties that have ensued in this vibrant debate. Recent scholarship, Bever contends, has established gender and gender and witchcraft as a vital area of study but has perhaps taught us rather more about the role of women in society than about witchcraft itself. Although the majority of those accused of witchcraft were indeed women, it is important to remember that the 20 per cent of cases that involved men should not be removed from the picture; as Larner argued, it is perfectly plausible that early modern witchcraft was gender related without this meaning that it was gender specific. Demonological writing, important to any analysis as we have seen, might have included a discussion of the role and character of women, but it was not entirely devoted to the construction of the image of a female witch. Bever's analysis derives from his research into patterns of witchcraft and prosecution in the duchy of Wurttemberg, where accusations, and the character of those accused, both reflect commonly held assumptions but also encouraged a more cautious approach; the women who were accused of witchcraft in Wurttemberg were, for example, not all drawn from among the economically poor. Bever poses a series of questions arising from the general context of the women and witchcraft debate and the specific example of Wurttemberg. Were the women involved in the trials, he asks, stirring up conflict in the community, and was there a logic to the accusation that women and witches were capable of causing harm after the breakdown of societal relations? Did the reputation of women have a role to play in accusations, and is there evidence to suggest that accusers and witnesses were willing to retroactively interpret incidents in the past once an accusation was made? What role did physical violence play in shaping accusations? Over a broader time period, Bever also reflects upon the extent to which the accusations and trials might themselves have exerted an influence over female behaviour, perhaps contributing to a process of the disarmament and domestication of women in the early modern period.[24]

The benefits of giving due consideration to those men who were accused of witchcraft in early modern Europe are apparent in recent scholarship on masculinity, gendered-categorization and witchcraft across the period. Often, the trials of men for witchcraft were highly localized; William Monter's analysis of the male witches of Normandy concludes with a telling reminder that the patterns of witchcraft in this part of France were far removed culturally and practically from those of the Channel Islands, its geographical neighbour. Individual case studies of the image and the reality of male witchcraft in different parts of Europe have restored the 20 per cent of witches who were men to the broader debate over witchcraft but also feed into a better understanding of the female witch. Rolf Schulte's discussion of the male witches of central Europe, for example, sets their trials within the context of the prosecution of female witches and applies to the trials of men the same questions as are commonly asked of female witchcraft trials, particularly those relating to the age, social status and conduct of the accused.[25] A more theoretical context is provided by a number of scholarly studies of the gender in the early modern period and its relationship to and with witchcraft accusations and trials. Alison Rowlands' *Witchcraft and Masculinities*, for example, considers the groups of men who were at greatest risk of being accused of witchcraft in early modern Europe and the extent to which ideas about masculinity underpinned the mentality of those involved in the prosecution of witches. To what extent were beliefs about magic in theory and practice gender related, and to what extent did gender shape the experience of demonic possession and belief in werewolves? Why did some regions persecute more men as witches than others?[26]

William Monter's discussion of the witches of Normandy reflects and shapes these debates. Despite the deeply rooted image of the female, elderly and marginalized witch, Monter argues, the archetypal witch in Normandy was male, probably a shepherd, possibly a priest and either elderly or still a teenager. These witches were feared because their spells used toad venom and their magic was performed with a stolen Host. In Normandy, the pattern of witchcraft prosecutions suggests a belief and a fear that was endemic rather than epidemic, and trials were conducted carefully and methodically, with the invocation of harsh penalties for those found guilty. The role of the shepherd and priest in these accusations reveals the extent to which models of witchcraft were deeply rooted in the local context and challenges the assumption that there was of necessity a predictable or predominant role played by women in early modern witchcraft. The three essays that follow, Monter's included, are in some respects a drop in the ocean of recent scholarship, but all three reflect the vibrancy of the academic study of witchcraft in the late twentieth and early twenty-first centuries, and the sophisticated and challenging picture of the crime, context and conflicts that shaped the trials.

Notes

1. Ankarloo, B. and Henningsen, G. (eds) (1990), *Early Modern European Witchcraft: Centres and Peripheries*. Oxford: Oxford University Press; Hutton, R. (2004), 'Anthropological and historical approaches to witchcraft: potential for a new collaboration', *Historical Journal*, 47, 413–34; Behringer, W. (2004), *Witches and Witch-Hunts: A Global History*. Cambridge: Cambridge

University Press; Thomas, K. (1970), 'The relevance of social anthropology to the historical study of English witchcraft', in Mary Douglas (ed.), *Witchcraft Confessions and Accusations*. London: Routledge, pp. 47–81; Macfarlane, A. (1970), *Witchcraft in Tudor and Stuart England*. London: Routledge, pp. 211–53; Cohn, N. (1975), *Europe's Inner Demons*. London: Chatto and Windus, pp. 220–3; Geertz, H. and Thomas, K. (1975), 'An anthropology of religion and magic: two views', *Journal of Interdisciplinary History*, 6, 71–110; Crick, M. (1973), 'Two styles in the study of witchcraft', *Journal of the Anthropological Society of Oxford*, 4, 17–31; Rowland, R. (1990), ' "Fantasticall and devilishe persons": European witch-beliefs in comparative perspective', in Bengt Ankarloo and Gustav Henningsen (eds), *Early Modern European Witchcraft*. Oxford: Oxford University Press, pp. 161–9; Hutton, R. (2002), 'The global context of the Scottish witch-hunt', in Julian Goodare (ed.), *The Scottish Witch-Hunt in Context*. Manchester: Manchester University Press.

2.   The best recent overviews of the field are Barry, J. and Davies, O. (eds) (2007), *Witchcraft Historiography*. Basingstoke: Palgrave Macmillan; Levack, B.P. (2006), *The Witch-Hunt in Early Modern Europe*, 3rd edn. Harlow: Longman; Ankarloo, B., Clark, S. and Monter, W. (2002), *Witchcraft and Magic in Europe: The Period of the Witch Trials*. London: Athlone; Scarre, G. and Callow, J. (2001), *Witchcraft and Magic in Sixteenth- and Seventeenth-Century Europe*. 2nd edn. Basingstoke: Palgrave; Briggs, R. (1996), *Witches and Neighbours. The Social and Cultural Context of European Witchcraft*. London: Harper Collins. On witchcraft and gender see Roper, L. (1994), *Oedipus and the Devil. Witchcraft, Sexuality and Religion in Early Modern Europe*. London: Routledge; Purkiss, D. (1996), *The Witch in History*. London: Routledge; Willis, D. (1995), *Malevolent Nurture. Witch Hunting and Maternal Power in Early Modern England*. Ithaca, NY: Cornell University Press; Rowlands, A. (ed.) (2009), *Witchcraft and Masculinities in Early Modern Europe*. New York, NY: Palgrave/St. Martin's Press; Apps, L. and Gow, A.C. (2003), *Male Witches in Early Modern Europe*. Manchester: Manchester University Press; on the location of demonology within its cultural context, the most significant contributions are Clark, S. (1997), *Thinking with Demons. The Idea of Witchcraft in Early Modern Europe*. Oxford: Clarendon Press, and Clark, S. (1980), 'Inversion, misrule and the meaning of witchcraft', *Past and Present*, 87, 98–127.

3.   Briggs, R. (1996), ' "Many reasons why": witchcraft and the problem of multiple explanation', in Jonathan Barry, Marianne Hester and Gareth Roberts (eds), *Witchcraft in Early Modern Europe: Studies in Culture and Belief*. Cambridge: Cambridge University Press.

4.   The *Athlone History of Witchcraft and Magic*, for example, under the editorship of Clark and Ankarloo covered period from antiquity to present; see also Barry, J., Hester, M. and Roberts, G. (eds) (1996), *Witchcraft in Early Modern Europe*. Cambridge: Cambridge University Press; Klaits, J. (1985), *Servants of Satan: The Age of the Witch-Hunts*. Bloomington, IN: Indiana University Press; Barstow, Anne L. (1994), *Witchcraze: A New History of the European Witch Hunts*. San Francisco, CA: Pandora; Briggs, ' "Many reasons why" '; and Behringer, W. (2004), *Witches and Witch-Hunts. A Global History*. Cambridge: Polity Press; Gaskill, M. (2010), *Witchcraft: A Very Short Introduction*. Oxford: Oxford University Press; Zika, C. and Kent, E. (eds) (1998), *Witches and Witch-Hunting in European Societies. A Working Bibliography*. Melbourne: University of Melbourne Press; Pearson, J. (2007), 'Writing witchcraft: the historians' history, the practitioners' past', in Jonathan Barry and Owen Davies (eds), *Palgrave Advances in Witchcraft Historiography*. Basingstoke: Palgrave Macmillan, pp. 225–41; Burke, P. (1993), 'The comparative approach to European witchcraft', in B. Ankarloo and G. Henningsen (eds), *Early Modern European Witchcraft*. Oxford: Clarendon Press, chapter 18; Midelfort, H.C.E. (1968), 'Recent witch-hunting research, or where do we go from here?' *Papers of the Bibliographical Society of America*, 62, 373–420; Monter, W. (1971–2), 'The historiography of European witchcraft: progress and prospects', *Journal of Interdisciplinary History*, 2, 435–51.

5.   Larner, C. (1977), *Sourcebook of Scottish Witchcraft*. Glasgow: Glasgow University Press; Larner, (1981), *Enemies of God: The Witch Hunt in Scotland*. London: Chatto and Windus.

6.   Levack, B.P. (2008), *Witch-Hunting in Scotland: Law, Politics, and Religion*. New York, NY: Routledge.

7. Normand, L. and Roberts, G. (eds) (2000), *Witchcraft in Early Modern Scotland: James's* Demonology *and the North Berwick Witches.* Exeter: University of Exeter Press; Cowan, E.J. (1983), 'The darker vision of the Scottish renaissance: the devil and Francis Stewart', in Ian B. Cowan and Duncan Shaw (eds), *The Renaissance and Reformation in Scotland.* Edinburgh: Scottish Academic Press; Maxwell-Stuart, P.G. (1997), 'The fear of the king is death: James VI and the witches of East Lothian', in W.G. Naphy and Penny Roberts (eds), *Fear in Early Modern Society.* Manchester: Manchester University Press; McLachlan, H. and Swales, K. (2002), 'The bewitchment of christian shaw: a reassessment of the famous Paisley witchcraft case of 1697', in Yvonne G. Brown and Rona Ferguson (eds), *Twisted Sisters: Women, Crime and Deviance in Scotland since 1400.* East Linton: Tuckwell; Goodare, J. (2001), 'The aberdeenshire witchcraft panic of 1597', *Northern Scotland*, 21, 17–37.

8. Macdonald, S. (2002), *The Witches of Fife: Witch-hunting in a Scottish Shire 1560–1710.* East Linton: Tuckwell.

9. Macfarlane, A. D. J. (1970), *Witchcraft in Tudor and Stuart England.* New York, NY: Harper and Row Publishers.

10. See for example Thomas, K. (1971), *Religion and the Decline of Magic.* New York, NY: Scribner; Geertz and Thomas, 'An anthropology of religion and magic'; Barry et al., *Witchcraft in Early Modern Europe*, especially introduction; c.f. Favret-Saada, J. (1980), *Deadly Words: Witchcraft in the Bocage.* Paris: Gallimard.

11. Gaskill, M. (1996), 'Witchcraft in early modern Kent: stereotypes and the background to accusations', in J. Barry et al (eds) *Witchcraft in Early Modern Europe*; Sharpe, J. (1996), *Instruments of Darkness. Witchcraft in England 1550–1750.* London: Hamish Hamilton; Sharpe, J. (2001), *Witchcraft in Early Modern England.* Longman, Harlow; de Windt, A. (1995), 'Witchcraft and conflicting visions of the ideal village community', *Journal of British Studies*, 34, 427–63; Gibson, M. (1999), *Reading Witchcraft. Stories of Early English Witches.* London: Routledge.

12. Sharpe, J. (1996); Gaskill, M. (2005), *Witchfinders. A Seventeenth-Century English Tragedy.* Cambridge, MA: Harvard University Press, chapter 2; Timber, F. (2008), 'Witches' sect or prayer meeting?: Matthew Hopkins revisited', *Women's History Review*, 17(1), 21–37; Gaskill, M. (2008), 'Witchcraft and evidence in early modern England', *Past & Present*, 198, 33–70; Purkiss, D. (1997), 'Civil war and its deformities: fantasies of witchcraft in the English civil war', *Journal of Medieval and Early Modern Studies*, 27(1), 103–32; Jackson, L. (1995), 'Witches, wives, and mothers: witchcraft persecution and women's confessions in seventeenth-century England', *Women's History Review*, 4(1), 63–83.

13. Dillinger, J. (2009), *'Evil people': A Comparative Study of Witch Hunts in Swabian Austria and the Electorate of Trier.* Laura Stokes (trans.). Charlottesville, VA: University of Virginia Press; Durrant, J. (2007), *Witchcraft, Gender and Society in Early Modern Germany.* Leiden: Brill.

14. Rowlands, A. (2003), *Witchcraft Narratives in Germany: Rothenburg, 1561–1652.* Manchester: Manchester University Press; see also Rowlands, A. (2001), 'Witchcraft and old women in early modern Germany', *Past and Present*, 173, 50–89; Midelfort, H.C.E. (1981), 'Heartland of the witchcraze: central and Northern Europe', *History Today*, 31(2), 27–31; Behringer, W. (1997), *Witchcraft Persecutions in Bavaria. Popular Magic, Religious Zealotry and Reasons of State.* Cambridge: Cambridge University Press; Midelfort, H.C.E. (1972), *Witch-Hunting in South-Western Germany 1562–1684.* Stanford, CA: Stanford University Press; Robisheaux, T. (2009), *The Last Witch of Langenburg. Murder in a German Village.* London: W.W. Norton & Co.; Friedrichs, C.R. (1979), *Urban Society in an Age of War: Nördlingen 1580–1720.* Princeton: Princeton University Press.

15. Scribner, R.W. (1990), 'Witchcraft and judgement in reformation Germany', *History Today*, 12–19; Lehmann, H. (1988), 'The persecution of witches as the restoration of order: the case of Germany 1590–1650', *Central European History*, 107–21; Roper, L. (2004), *Witch Craze. Terror and Fantasy in Baroque Germany.* New Haven, CT: Yale University Press; Walinski-Kiehl, R. (2002), 'Pamphlets, propaganda and witch-hunting in Germany, c.1560–c.1630', *Reformation*, 6, 49–74.

16. Monter, W. (1976), *Witchcraft in France and Switzerland: The Borderlands during the Reformation*. Ithaca, NY and London: Cornell University Press; Briggs, R. (2007), *The Witches of Lorraine*. Oxford: Oxford University Press; Briggs, R. (1989), *Communities of Belief: Cultural and Social Tensions in Early Modern France*. Oxford: Oxford University Press; Briggs, R. (1984), 'Witchcraft and popular mentality in Lorraine, 1580–1630', in Brian Vickers (ed.), *Occult and Scientific Mentalities in the Renaissance*. Cambridge: Cambridge University Press, pp. 337–50; Clark, S. (1991), 'The gendering of witchcraft in French demonology: misogyny or polarity?', *French Studies*, 5, 426–37; Favret-Saada, *Deadly Words*; Golden, R. M. (1997), 'Satan in Europe: the geography of witch hunts', in M. Wolfe (ed.), *Changing Identities in Early Modern France*. Durham: Duke University Press, 216–47; Klaits, J. (1982), 'Witchcraft trials and absolute monarchy in alsace', in Richard M. Golden (ed.), *Church, State, and Society under the Bourbon Kings of France*. Lawrence, KS: Coronado, pp. 148–72; Monter, W. (1980), 'Witchcraft in France and Italy', *History Today*, 30, 31–35; Muchembled, R. (1984), 'Lay judges and the acculturation of the masses (France and the southern low countries, sixteenth to eighteenth centuries)', in Kaspar von Greyerz (ed.), *Religion and Society in Early Modern Europe, 1500–1800*. London: Allen and Unwin, pp. 56–65; Pearl, J. (1985), 'Demons and politics in France, 1560–1630', *Historical Reflections*, 12, 241–52; Pearl, J. (1983), 'French catholic demonologists and their enemies in the late sixteenth and early seventeeth centuries', *Church History*, 52, 457–67; Sluhovsky M. (1996), 'A divine apparition or demonic possession? female agency and church authority in demonic possession in sixteenth-century France', *Sixteenth Century Journal*, 27(4), 1039–55.

17. Larner, C. (1977), 'Two late Scottish witchcraft tracts', in Sydney Anglo (ed.), *The Damned Art: Essays in the Literature of Witchcraft*. London: Routledge. On the influence of James VI and his writings, see Clark, S. (1977), 'King James's *daemonologie*: witchcraft and kingship', in S. Anglo (ed.), *The Damned Art*. London: Routledge; Wormald, J. (2000), 'The witches, the devil and the king', in Terry Brotherstone and David Ditchburn (eds), *Freedom and Authority: Scotland, c.1050–c.1650*. East Linton: Tuckwell; Dunlap, R. (1975), 'King James and some witches: the date and text of the *daemonologie*', *Philological Quarterly*, 54, 40–6.

18. For a fuller discussion of the relationship between religious change and witchcraft in this period and beyond see Davies, O. (1997), 'Methodism, the clergy and the popular belief in witchcraft and magic', *History*, 82, 252–65; Ginzburg, C. (1991), *Ecstasies: Deciphering the Witches' Sabbath*. Raymond Rosenthal (trans.). New York, NY: Pantheon Books; Graham, M.F. (1996), *The Uses of Reform: 'Godly Discipline' and Popular Behaviour in Scotland and Beyond, 1560–1610*. Leiden: Brill; Goodare, J. (1999), *State and Society in Early Modern Scotland*. Oxford: Oxford University Press, ch. 8; Todd, M. (2002), *The Culture of Protestantism in Early Modern Scotland*. New Haven, CT: Yale University Press.

19. Mackay, C. (2009), *The Hammer of Witches*. Cambridge: Cambridge University Press.

20. Anglo, S. (1977), 'Evident authority and authoritative evidence: the *malleus maleficarum*', in S. Anglo (ed.), *The Damned Art*. London: Routledge & Kegan Paul, pp. 1–31; Bailey, M. D. (2006), 'The disenchantment of magic: spells, charms and superstition in early European witchcraft literature', *The American Historical Review*, 111(2), 383–404; Broedel, H. P. (2003), *The Malleus Maleficarum and the Construction of Witchcraft: Theology and Popular Belief*. Manchester: Manchester University Press; Broedel, H. P. (2002), 'To preserve the manly form from so vile a crime: ecclesiastical anti-sodomitic rhetoric and the gendering of witchcraft in the *malleus maleficarum*', *Essays in Medieval Studies*, 19, 136–48; Stephens, W. (1998), 'Witches who steal penises: impotence and illusion in the *malleus maleficarum*', *The Journal of Medieval and Early Modern Studies*, 28, 495–529; Brauner, S. (1995), 'The Malleus Maleficarum: Witches as Wanton Women', in *Fearless Wives and Frightened Shrews. The Construction of the Witch in Early Modern Germany*, Amherst, MA: University of Massachusetts Press, pp. 31–49.

21. O'Connor, P. J. (1996), 'Witchcraft pamphlets in renaissance England: a particular case in which the tale was told', *The Midwest Quarterly*, 37, 215–27; Roper, *Witch Craze*; Oplinger, J. (1990), *The Politics of Demonology: The European Witch-Crazes and the Mass Production of Deviance*.

Selinsgrove, PA, Susquehanna University Press; Scholz Williams, G. (1995), *Defining Dominion. The Discourses of Magic and Witchcraft in Early Modern France and Germany*. Ann Arbor, MI: University of Michigan Press; Stephens, W. (2002), *Demon Lovers. Witchcraft, Sex, and the Crisis of Belief*. Chicago, University of Chicago Press; on the sabbath more particularly see Muchembled, R. (1998) 'Satanic myths and cultural reality', in B. Ankarloo and G. Henningsen (eds), *Early Modern European Witchcraft*. Oxford: Clarendon Press, ch. 5; de Blécourt, W. (2007), 'The return of the sabbat: mental archaeologies, conjectural histories or political mythologies', in J. Barry and O. Davies (eds), *Witchcraft Historiography*. Basingstoke: Palgrave Macmillan, pp. 125–45; Ginzburg, C. (1998), 'Deciphering the sabbath', in B. Ankarloo and G. Henningsen (eds), *Early Modern European Witchcraft*. Oxford: Clarendon Press, ch. 4.

22. Roper, *Oedipus and the Devil*; see also Roper, *Witch Craze*.

23. Purkiss, *The Witch in History*, particularly chapter 7; Hester, M. (1996), 'Patriarchal reconstruction and witch-hunting', in J. Barry et al (eds), *Witchcraft in Early Modern Europe*. Cambridge: Cambridge University Press, ch. 11; Hester, M. (1992), *Lewd Women and Wicked Witches: A Study of the Dynamics of Male Domination*. London: Routledge; Wiesner, M.E. (1993), *Women and Gender in Early Modern Europe*. Cambridge: Cambridge University Press, pp. 218–38; Karlsen, C. (1988), *The Devil in the Shape of a Woman. The Witch in 17th-Century New England*. New York, NY: Norton, pp. 179–99; Holmes, C. (1993), 'Women, witnesses and witches', *Past and Present*, 140, 45–78; Ehrenreich, B. and English, D. (1974), *Witches, Midwives and Nurses: A History of Women Healers*. London: Compendium; Willis, *Malevolent Nature*; Martin, L. (2002), 'Witchcraft and family: what can witchcraft documents tell us about early modern Scottish family life?' *Scottish Tradition*, 27, 7–22; Anderson, A. (1978), 'Witchcraft and the status of women – the case of England', *British Journal of Sociology*, 29, 171–84; Brauner, 'The Malleus Maleficarum'; Thomson, J.A. (1993), *Wives, Widows, Witches and Bitches: Women in 17th Century Devon*. New York, NY: Peter Lang Publishers; Hodgkin, K. (2007), 'Gender, mind and body: feminism and psychoanalysis', in J. Barry and O. Davies (eds), *Witchcraft Historiography*. Basingstoke: Palgrave Macmillan, pp. 182–202; de Blecourt, W. (2000), 'The making of the female witch. reflections on witchcraft and gender in the early modern period', *Gender & History*, 12(2), 287–309; Rowlands, *Witchcraft Narratives in Germany*, especially chapter 5.

24. For a further discussion of this theme see Hester, M. (1996), 'Patriarchal reconstruction and witch hunting' in J. Barry et al. (eds), *Witchcraft in Early Modern* Europe. Cambridge: Cambridge University Press. Hester argues that witchcraft did become sex-specific in this period, 'serving as one means of maintaining and reconstructing male dominance and male power vis-à-vis women' (p. 305); Amussen, S. (1988), *An Ordered Society*. Oxford: Oxford University Press; Klaits, *Servants of Satan*, p. 52.

25. See for example Ankarloo and Henningsen, *Early Modern European Witchcraft*, particularly the sections on Iceland, Finland and Estonia; Gaskill, M. (1998), 'The devil in the shape of a man: witchcraft, conflict and belief in jacobean England', *Historical Research*, 71, 142–71; Schulte, R. (2009), 'Men as accused witches in the holy Roman Empire', in A. Rowlands (ed.), *Witchcraft and Masculinities*. Basingstoke: Palgrave Macmillan, pp. 52–73; Schindler, N. (2002), *Rebellion, Community and Custom in Early Modern Germany*. Cambridge: Cambridge University Press, pp. 236–92; Kivelson, V. (2003), 'Male witches and gendered categories in seventeenth-century Russia', *Comparative Studies in Society and History*, 45(3), 606–31; Zguta, R. (1977), 'Witchcraft trials in seventeenth-century Russia', *American Historical Review*, 82(5), 187–207; Walinski-Kiehl, R. (2004), 'Males, "masculine honour", and witch hunting in seventeenth-century Germany', *Men and Masculinities*, 6(3), 254–71.

26. Apps and Gow, *Male Witches*; Rowlands, *Witchcraft and Masculinities*; Labouvie, E. (2002), 'Men in witchcraft trials: towards a social anthropology of "male" understandings of magic and witchcraft', in U. Rublack (ed.), *Gender in Early Modern German History*. Cambridge: Cambridge University Press; Roper, L. (1991), 'Stealing manhood: capitalism and magic in early modern Germany', *Gender and History*, 3(1), 4–22.

CHAPTER 9
TOADS AND EUCHARISTS: THE MALE WITCHES
OF NORMANDY, 1564–1660
William Monter

The province of Normandy was the most notable region of masculine witchcraft in western Europe, and it was also the epicenter of witchcraft prosecutions by French parlements. Each feature helps explain the other: putting men at the center of witch trials apparently prodded French appellate judges into handing down unusually harsh sentences for the crime of *sortilège.* The Normans' concentration on types of witchcraft practiced by men rather than women changed some of the ordinary features of the crime. In Normandy, the archetypical witch was not an old woman, but a shepherd who might be either an old man or a teenager; the most feared witches' spells were likely to involve toad venom; and the most powerful witches' magic was performed with stolen Eucharists. But the practice of forbidden forms of diabolic magic was called by the same name throughout the French kingdom, and *sortilège* was feared and punished wherever possible.

With respect to trials for *sortilège,* the Parlement of Rouen stands out in a French context in four ways: trials were unusually regular; punishments were unusually severe; the crime was remarkably masculinized; and such trials lasted longer there than anywhere else in France. Those peculiarities are probably interdependent. Normandy displays a clear pattern of endemic rather than epidemic witch-hunting: rarely does one find more than three or four defendants in one place at one time, although by the 1590s there was plenty of talk about witches' sabbaths. Relative to the size of its district or *ressort,* the Parlement of Rouen confirmed a larger number of death sentences for *sortilège* than any of its French peers. It held at most one-eighth the population of the *ressort* of the Parlement of Paris, and its criminal records are less complete than those for Paris, yet both appellate courts condemned about a hundred witches to death– and no other French parlement except Toulouse, also with a much larger judicial district than Rouen, condemned as many as fifty. Alfred Soman has shown that over half of the 1,300 witchcraft defendants judged by the Parlement of Paris after 1565 were men, a much higher ratio than in samples from Provence;[1] but at nearby Rouen, almost three-fourths of the 380 known witchcraft defendants between 1564 and 1660 were men.

The oldest and firmest bit of conventional wisdom about witch trials in early modern Europe insists that the people accused of witchcraft were overwhelmingly women. The links between women and witchcraft have been at or near the center of witchcraft scholarship for the past quarter century, tightly interwoven with the rise of women's history and gender studies.[2] Thousands of cases from Germany, Scotland, and other centers of the great witch-hunts repeat basically the same statistical story: at least four-fifths of those tried and executed for witchcraft in sixteenth- and seventeenth-century Europe were women. If scholars still argue about which kinds of women were most likely to be put on trial and quarrel noisily about how many women were tried and how many were executed, no one denies that most accused witches were women. Exceptions to this generalization have been few and far between and have hitherto come only from the remotest margins of Latin Christendom. To date, the most glaring exception to the formula 'witches = women' has been found in the most remote corner of all, namely seventeenth-century Iceland, where all but one of the twenty-one people known to have been executed as witches were men. The Duchy of Normandy, however, lies near the heart of northern and western Europe.

Normans drank cider rather than wine, but otherwise behaved as ordinary subjects of the king of France. An unremarkable province, Normandy entered the age of western Europe's great witch-hunts in the late sixteenth century dowered with typically French institutions. Criminal justice was administered by the courts of seven royal *bailliages,* each with several subdistricts (lieutenancies). Numerous seigneurial courts, including the sizable district covered by the duchy of Longueville and the smaller principality of Yvetot, still pronounced capital punishments. But after 1515, both the *bailliages* and the seigneurial courts came under the appellate jurisdiction of the Parlement of Normandy, which closely supervised both civil and criminal justice throughout this province of three thousand parishes from its magnificent Gothic palace in the center of Rouen.[3] Normans retained a few legal peculiarities that looked strange to other Frenchmen. For example, they retained both the medieval *clameur de haro,* a kind of citizen arrest, and the Privilege of St. Romain, an annual contest conducted by the cathedral canons of Rouen to pardon the most deserving criminal in their city's jails.[4] However, these peculiarities had no visible impact on the way Normans conducted witch trials; no accused witch was ever arrested by *clameur de haro* (usually directed at thieves or seducers), and, as one should expect with an unpardonable offense, none was ever pardoned at the festival of St. Romain.

Normandy participated fully in the witch-hunting era during the confessional century, although there is little early evidence for its unusual record after 1560. We have only a few shadowy traces in the Middle Ages, apart from the ambiguous case of Joan of Arc. Two shepherds (one of them only fourteen years old) from the southeastern *bailliage* of Gisors were executed for sacrilege at Rouen in 1540; they had been caught stealing Hosts on behalf of a *sorcier et enchanteur* who was never found. Two years later, Laurens de Limoges was sentenced to be hanged for *sortilège* and his body burned by the deputy *bailli* at Les Andelys, on the Seine south of Rouen. He appealed; the parlement ordered an additional investigation of the defendant's character, and a month later it ordered him banished for five years from the *bailliage* of Gisors.[5] His case follows the first Parisian intervention of 1540, but precedes other known cases from southern France, and the Rouen Parlement's ruling fits its general pattern. The unusual feature is that all three early defendants were men, two of them shepherds charged with magical misuse of the Eucharist. In this respect, Norman witchcraft would change but little between the reigns of François I and Louis XV.

After the religious wars got under way, the Parlement of Rouen was not the first in the kingdom to confirm a death sentence for witchcraft: Toulouse did so at least three times in 1562; Paris began to do so in 1568. At Rouen, there is no record of the parlement's hearing another appeal of a lower-court death sentence for *sortilège* until 1564, and no record of its confirming such a sentence until 1574; in both instances, the defendants were women from the *bailliage* of Evreux, west of Rouen.[6] (It is worth noting that, in contrast to the documentary record of most subsequent periods, fewer than half the criminal *arrêts* of the Rouen Parlement from 1564 to 1574 have been preserved.)

The next death sentences for *sortilège* to be confirmed by the Parlement of Rouen, in 1577, were inflicted on two shepherds (as in 1540) from the *bailliage* of Gisors. They were originally tried at Vernon, just south of the site of the 1542 case. Both were 'accustomed to bewitching, causing deaths of people and animals for twenty years'; both had previously been tortured for the crime after appealing to the parlement.[7] A careful search reveals that men outnumbered women fifteen to ten among recorded defendants for *sortilège* tried by the Parlement of Rouen between 1564 and 1579, although women composed half of the twelve defendants appealing death sentences. The pattern whose outlines can be vaguely discerned in this early and fragmentary evidence would be strikingly confirmed across the next half century: there was a sizable majority of male defendants in witchcraft cases, becoming almost a male monopoly after 1625.

The endemic rather than epidemic pattern of Normandy's preserved witchcraft trials is not an illusion. The preserved criminal decisions or *arrêts* of the Parlement of Rouen, complemented by its sizable series of *plumitifs* or interrogations of prisoners, offer the richest set of records anywhere outside Paris for studying how appellate courts actually judged this offense. Table 1 shows that Rouen's *arrêts* and *plumitifs* together cover 90 percent of the period 1585–1630 when witch trials were most common throughout western Europe.[8] The small variations, both in rates of preservation and rates of death sentences appealed from lower courts, inspire confidence in the accuracy of the general picture of witchcraft cases judged by the Parlement of Rouen. The figures from 1590–93 reflect conditions of civil war, with two rival parlements in operation, and they illustrate the huge decrease in all forms of judicial business at the time. The endemic nature of Norman witch trials is evident from the fact that, even with some lacunae and apart from two of the worst war years (1591 and 1592), the Norman Parlement judged at least one death sentence for witchcraft every year from 1582 to 1619. Its severity is evident from the fact that it confirmed at least one such death sentence every year between 1585 and 1609 and again between 1611 and 1615 (again excepting the war years 1591–93). Yet at the same time, there were few statistical peaks in the series: ten death sentences for witchcraft were appealed in 1605, and a maximum of twelve was reached

Table 1 Witchcraft Cases at Rouen Parlement, 1580–1630

Years	Months of decisions preserved (%)	Sentences appealed (Avg.)
1580–84	37/60 (62%)	1.2/yr.
1585–89	56/60 (93%)	5.4/yr.
1590–93	43/48 (89%)	0.5/yr.
1594–99	65/72 (90%)	5.0/yr.
1600–1609	117/120 (98%)	5.0/yr.
1610–19	103/120 (86%)	3.5/yr.
1620–29	98/120 (82%)	3.4/yr.

Source: ADSM, IB 3185–3314, 5719–5729, 3021–3030.

Note: From 1590–93 the Norman Parlement, like nearly all the others in France, was divided into a royalist branch (sitting at Caen) and a Ligueur branch (sitting in Rouen). Records from the Ligueur branch appear to be complete, but records from the royalist branch show a ten-month lacuna. Therefore five months are missing from the four-year span, and the figure in the table is a composite average from the divided parlement.

in 1609. Apart from Rouen, only Paris shows the same annual continuity in death sentences for witchcraft appealed. However, other provincial parlements eclipsed Rouen's single-year totals: Dijon, for example, judged twenty-three death sentences for witchcraft in 1633, and Bordeaux, its jails full of Basques tried by De Lancre, must have judged more than twenty in 1609–10. Year in, year out, witchcraft cases comprised between 5 and 10 percent of the Rouen Parlement's criminal business under Henri IV and remained significant under Louis XIII. Yet there is no sign of any panic concerning witchcraft in Normandy.

Our only usable Norman source comes from an appellate court, and only those prisoners who appealed their original sentences were ever heard by it. How complete was the Rouen Parlement's grasp? Did it reach with equal alacrity into all corners of Normandy? Dewald's sampling suggests that most of its mid-sixteenth-century cases originated in the *bailliage*. of Rouen, although by 1600 they came from all parts of Normandy. Witch trials, as we have seen, began to appear in the 1560s, mainly from areas south and west of Rouen. Indeed, the geographical distribution of the province's first two dozen witchcraft cases during the Wars of Religion, judged between 1564 and 1578, partially confirms Dewald's findings. Ten cases, and two of the three deaths, came from two river villages, Les Andelys and Vernon, in the southeastern *bailliage* of Gisors. The *bailliage* of Evreux, west of Rouen, produced six cases and the remaining death. The local *bailliage* of Rouen, which Dewald found dominating the parlement's criminal case load at mid-century, generated only five defendants charged with witchcraft before 1580, none of whom was executed. Of the remaining four cases, two were tried in Caudebec, seat of the *bailliage* of Caux, on the Seine north of Rouen, while the other two came from relatively distant Alençon, on Normandy's southern frontier. Given Normandy's size, no part of the province was more than four or five days distant from Rouen, even under sixteenth-century conditions. But many regions that would be most heavily represented during the apogee of Norman witch trials (1585–1615), including the northern and eastern portions of the large *bailliage* of Caux, were absent from the first sample. More important, so was the whole of lower Normandy, most of it comprising the two large western *bailliages* of Caen and Cotentin.

When did witch trials first appear from the most distant region of Normandy, the far western *bailliage* of Cotentin? Interestingly, they began only during the final phase of the Wars of Religion, when the royalist parlement sitting at Caen had solidified its control over the westernmost corner of the province. A widow had been condemned to death at Avranches 'pour sortilèges et ensorcellements' in the summer of 1593, but the parlement evoked the case because the defendant had not been informed of her rights, and a week later they reduced her sentence to perpetual banishment from the kingdom. A month later they received another appeal from a woman who had been condemned to death for *sortilège* at Carentan; after further investigation, she was ordered released in February 1594.[9] Only when it sat temporarily in Caen, the capital of lower Normandy and much closer to Cotentin, did the parlement intervene to control witch trials in the far west. However, it is worth pointing out that death sentences for infanticide were appealed to Rouen from the *bailliage* of Cotentin at least as early as 1564, when the series of witchcraft appeals begins.[10] After 1593, Cotentin brought many cases of witchcraft to the reunited parlement, including the most elaborately documented and hotly argued case until the time of Madeleine Bavent in the 1640s.

The earliest recorded witchcraft cases from Cotentin, unlike the earliest cases from the Seine valley, involved women, including one who had not been informed of her rights of appeal. Historians sometimes object that women tend to be underrepresented in appellate cases because they appeared in courts only as witnesses or defendants; being less familiar with legal practice than men, they were less likely than men to appeal. In Normandy, women–or men–were never required to appeal a death sentence for witchcraft, unlike the vast district of Paris or, later, Languedoc and Burgundy. However, the process of appeal was extremely simple and cost the appellant nothing. How often did people convicted of witchcraft in Normandy fail to appeal their condemnations? Historians wonder, rightly, about the 'dark figure' of trials and executions for witchcraft that left no tracks in the official records. But there are good reasons for accepting the Norman appellate-court figures as reasonably close approximations to the complete numbers of Norman witch trials; the lacunae in the parlement's records present a more serious problem than their incompleteness. Those sources, 90 percent complete for the peak years of witch trials, reveal scarcely ten instances where people accused of witchcraft were known to have been executed without making any recorded appeal. Moreover, most of those few 'passive' or 'hidden' victims from Normandy were men. In other words, the evidence about witch trials in Normandy seems relatively complete and unusually reliable compared to that from most other regions of France, apart from Paris, or indeed compared to most regions of western Europe.

It is worth looking at the 'hidden' executions in more detail. In the first instance, Alison Hocquart, tortured on 7 February 1585 at Vernon just prior to her execution, accused a large number of 'accomplices,' three of whom appealed (two had been sentenced to death; all had been ordered tortured). Three days later, the parlement widened its net to include everyone she had charged: three more people had been condemned to death, one to banishment, and three others were ordered to be tortured. There were ten defendants in all, by far the largest cluster of witchcraft cases yet heard in Rouen. Only three of them, including one of the original three who had appealed, were women. After examining the evidence, the parlement upheld one man's death sentence and sent a shepherd to the galleys for life; at Vernon, he had been ordered to be burned alive. It further ordered two women to be tortured (both were subsequently banished) and simply released six suspects, including two who had been sentenced to death but had successfully withstood torture.[11] This incident marked a significant departure in two ways. First, it began a surge of recorded witchcraft trials that lasted until Normandy became politically paralyzed by the royalist-*ligueur* wars in 1589. Second, the unusually large number of suspects involved suggests that Alison Hocquart may have been the first Norman witch who admitted attending a sabbat–although most of the people she denounced were men.

The next 'hidden' execution for witchcraft, that of Mariette Damoise, occurred at Essay in the southwestern *bailliage* of Alençon in autumn 1597. Unlike Alison Hocquart at Vernon, she was the first person from her district to be *convaincue de sortilège*. Damoise accused two other women, both of whom were condemned to death but promptly appealed. After a procedural delay because their original sentences had not accompanied them to Rouen, the parlement upheld both sentences in December.[12] Although the first two witches executed without appealing to the parlement were women, the next three we learn about were men. Robert Martin, 'exécuté à mort pour ledit crime [sortilège]' at the end of 1600, lived in the *bailliage* of Gisors, as did Alison Hocquart. He accused two brothers, both shepherds, who promptly appealed to Rouen. The parlement ordered one of them executed and sent the other, who withstood torture, to the galleys for life in January 1601.[13] It is probably worth noting that no 'hidden' executions occurred during the peak years of witchcraft appeals during the first decade of the seventeenth century, when the surviving evidence is unusually complete. The next such instance occurred in autumn 1612, when Laurens Harnas and Jean Le Vigoreulx were 'executez à mort' for witchcraft at Arques, in the northeastern corner of the *bailliage* of Caux near Dieppe. They accused a shepherd whose death sentence was upheld on appeal at Rouen in November.[14]

The next three incidents occurred relatively close to Rouen, but apparently originated in seigneurial courts rather than local branches of royal courts. Jean Crevier, 'exécuté à mort le vingt-six septembre [1618] pour le crime de sortilège' at Rouen, accused six people of attending sabbats with him at Londiniéres. Crevier apparently confirmed his confession under supervision by the parlement; but one of his victims (another shepherd) had his death sentence reduced on appeal to perpetual service in the galleys.[15] In 1627, a woman named Jeanne Conart, apparently 'executée à mort,' similarly accused several people of attending sabbats with her; one woman appealed her death sentence, and the parlement ordered that all recent witch trials from the seigneurial court of La Londe be examined.[16] Next year, the confessions about people seen at sabbats made by Guillemette Picard ('ceste putaine de Picard' to one of her victims) fueled several arrests just south of Rouen; one man's death sentence was subsequently upheld by parlement, which ordered three other men to be banished.[17]

The next traceable instance probably reflects someone who did appeal to the Rouen Parlement, but at a time when its criminal decisions have disappeared. Bernard Borral, whose widow was being tried for witchcraft at Louviers in 1634, 'was executed to death in this city [Rouen] for witchcraft three years ago.'[18] Our final 'hidden' execution for witchcraft involves a man named Jobillard, who in 1647 accused a tailor of attending the sabbat with him near Evreux.[19] Contrary to expectations, therefore, only two of the nine people presumably executed for witchcraft in Normandy after 1600, but whose appeals cannot be traced, were women. At least one of the men, Borral (and perhaps Crevier), probably did appeal. Since appeals of death sentences for witchcraft were pouring into Rouen even from seigneurial courts in the most distant parts of Normandy by 1600 and since the parlement's records seem relatively complete until 1630, there is good reason to believe that these instances represent most of the witches executed without recorded scrutiny from the Rouen Parlement.

Moreover, in only one of these seventeenth-century instances did the Rouen Parlement find any significant irregularities in the conduct of witch trials by lower courts. Here and there, legal mistakes were noticed. Early in 1605, for example, a woman sentenced to be hanged and her corpse burned for witchcraft by *Maître* Adrien Blanchart, lieutenant of the *bailli* of Alençon at Moulins, appealed. The parlement discovered that the judge had improperly employed *censures ecclésiastiques* to ensure her conviction; the prisoner was quickly released and the judge summoned to Rouen for questioning.[20] But such instances remained rare: justice in Normandy normally followed its routines carefully, even (or especially) when conducting witch trials.

If witch trials in Normandy were handled on a regular, frequent, and generally careful basis, it is also true that Norman judges, from the parlement down, made relatively severe decisions. Despite the absence of major witchcraft panics, Normandy stands out as the French province with the largest known number of witches executed. Between the Wars of Religion and Louis XIV, one finds 97 death sentences for witchcraft confirmed (excluding Crevier's and Borral's) among 219 death sentences appealed: a rate of 44 percent, much higher than that for the Parlement of Paris, which upheld fewer than 25 percent of the death sentences for witchcraft appealed to it.[21] Since the Parlement of Paris has virtually complete records of its criminal decisions between 1565 and 1648 (only the decisions of the royalist Parlement of Tours from 1589–94, which ordered some witches executed, are missing), its 112 confirmed deaths for witchcraft or magic are probably matched by Rouen's known figure of 97, given the lacunae in the Norman evidence.[22] Let us examine the rate of death sentences for witchcraft upheld by the Parlement of Rouen across time (see Table 2). Two peak periods emerge clearly from this table: the first occurred in 1585–89, years of the Catholic apogee, institutionalized by the Holy League in Normandy and elsewhere in France, a time when large numbers of witchcraft prosecutions were also being appealed to the Parlement of Paris. After the wars, Normandy's witchcraft prosecutions accelerated once again. In the first decade of the seventeenth century, they had returned to the levels of 1585–88: on average, five death sentences appealed per year, three executions upheld per year. After Henri IV's death, the number of witchcraft deaths being appealed declined, although the previous severity remained (almost 60 percent of the deaths upheld). After 1620, the number of witchcraft deaths appealed held steady for a decade, although the parlement's severity declined sharply (fewer than one death per year upheld after appeal). After 1629, the evidence suddenly dwindles; apart from a two-year period (November 1633–October 1635), there is little usable surviving evidence from 1630 until 1647, when the famous cases of Madeleine Bavent's bewitchers were finally decided. Between 1636 and 1645, the Parlement of Rouen was deeply compromised by the revolt of the Nu-Pieds and its aftermath. It was abolished for a few years; its routines were badly upset, and it probably handled very few criminal appeals.[23] The Bavent cases, deservedly famous, were finally judged by a restored parlement amid a swirl of pamphlets. Not surprisingly, the episode provoked a brief flurry of witch trials across the next few years.[24]

By a curious coincidence – or is it more than coincidence? – the surviving criminal decisions of the Rouen Parlement are most complete precisely during these periods of greatest apparent severity, but there is no reason to doubt the general accuracy of the picture. For example, in a six-year early period (1574–79) during which Rouen's criminal *arrêts* are over 95 percent complete, one finds only nine defendants appealing convictions for witchcraft; only six of them – one per year – were appealing death sentences. By the 1650s, when Rouen's criminal *arrêts* finally become somewhat less fragmentary than for previous decades, we again

Table 2 Witchcraft Death Sentences by the Rouen Parlement, 1560–1660

Years	Sentences/upheld (%)	Arrêts conserved (%)
1564–84	16/3 (19%)	48%
1585–89	26/16 (62%)	93%
1590–93	2/1 (50%)	89%
1594–99	30/13 (43%)	90%
1600–09	50/32 (64%)	98%
1610–19	35/20 (57%)	86%
1620–29	34/7 (21%)	82%
1650–59	9/1 (11%)	78%

Source: ADSM, IB 3155–3374, 3021–3045.
Note: See Table 1, note.

find an average of only one person per year appealing a death sentence for witchcraft. If the surviving criminal decisions from the Rouen Parlement are not quite a random sample, they seem slightly biased in favor of preserving most of the actual evidence from the peak years of witch-hunting in Normandy. We therefore possess abundant and relatively complete evidence about both the rise and the decline of witch-hunting in Normandy.

To grasp the Rouen Parlement's behavior in judging cases of witchcraft, let us examine its actions in detail at a moment of unusual severity. Across the whole period, two years in particular stand out as candidates for examination in this respect. The peak year for recorded witchcraft appeals was clearly 1609, with sixteen episodes involving a total of twenty-one defendants, seven of whom were ultimately sentenced to death. But the year of greatest severity came four years previously, in 1605: eleven appeals involving a total of sixteen defendants, nine of whom were ultimately sentenced to death. No other year produced more than five known death sentences upheld for witchcraft, although as we have seen, at least one person was ordered executed for this crime every year but one between 1585 and 1615, except in wartime.[25]

In 1605 the parlement's witchcraft business began early. On 13 January, the first defendant, an eighty-year-old widow from the remote port city of Granville in Cotentin, sat on the *sellette*, the three-legged stool where prisoners were interrogated by a panel of judges. The judges already knew the testimony against her from eight men (two of them priests) and no fewer than thirty women. Her lengthy interrogation touched upon many cases of bewitchments, including the nephew of a prominent local gentleman; some of them were apparently cured the same way they were inflicted, simply by being touched by the alleged witch. The old woman explained that she had been imprisoned for five months and that the local *bailli* had her whipped. Four days later her original sentence was upheld and duly recorded: a public apology (*amende honorable*) at the cathedral of Coutances, then hanging and the burning of her corpse.

The next case opened in mid-March. A fifty-year-old shepherd, who had exercised this profession for over thirty years, protested that he had been illegally arrested the previous June by the *vibailli* of Caux at Montivilliers (near Le Havre) after refusing to cure some of this official's relatives; he had also been beaten with a stick by a local nobleman for the same reason. The parlement, after questioning him on the *sellette*, agreed that his death sentence of the previous November may have been dictated by a highly partisan judge. But there was also serious material evidence involved: a venomous toad had been found among his belongings. The Rouen judges therefore ruled 'that he will be judged by the ordinary method,' reviewed the evidence from fourteen men and five women next day, and promptly convicted him. He was returned to Montivilliers to be tortured to elicit the identity of his accomplices, and then hanged.

A few days later came a defendant whose procedural irregularities made her appeal extremely successful. Françoise Le Poyne, a married woman from a remote southern corner of the *bailliage* of Alençon, had been condemned to death in January by a local judge who had illegally ordered the clergy to collect information against her through public appeals (the *monitoire*, or *censures ecclésiastiques*). The judges immediately overturned her condemnation, without even putting her on the *sellette*, and summoned the judge who had convicted her to Rouen for a reprimand. Another case a month later revealed the same kind of procedural flaw. A day laborer from a suburb of Rouen had been condemned to six years in the galleys for *sortilège,* but the parlement learned, as soon as he began to testify on the *sellette,* that he had quarrelled with the wife of his local *lieutenant-criminel,* whose husband thereupon ordered a *monitoire* against him in the parish church. Although there was testimony against this defendant from more than twenty witnesses and although he admitted that he had tried to lift spells laid on horses, he too was immediately released.

The next witchcraft defendant actually sat on the *sellette* three days sooner, on the same day his case was decided. Jacques Godevent was a priest from Briquebec in the northern peninsula of Cotentin, who gave his age as forty-one. He had been ordained five years earlier by the bishop of Avranches. In June 1603 he had been ordered defrocked by the bishop of Coutances, who had forced him to resign his benefice after various scandals, *Maître* Godevent admitted to his judges that he 'had visited the fortuneteller, for which he begged the court's forgiveness and had already performed formal penance.' The parlement heard testimony from twenty-eight laymen, ten priests, and five women (one of them a noble) about his fornications and about his habit of finding missing objects by means of a magical mirror. Some of them described a booklet with twelve or fifteen pages of recipes for curing spells, which he apparently kept in a missal that he refused to hand to his successor. The most damning piece of evidence, however, was that he had been caught red-handed with some magical 'characters inscribed on virgin parchment, on which are written words of invocations' of devils. After three days of hearings the parlement upheld his original sentence – that he perform an *amende honorable* at Carentan, then that he be hanged and his body burned – but they omitted the requirement that he be formally defrocked (*dégradé*) beforehand.

Two shepherds sat on the *sellette* in May, appealing death sentences for witchcraft. The first was only twenty years old, but already a recidivist who had been banished from the district of Moulins in the *bailliage* of Alençon in December 1603 because of his *sortilèges.* This time the *bailli* of Argennes and Saint-Gabriel, east of Caen, sentenced him to be hanged and burned for various 'execrable blasphemies of the name of God'; five of the twenty-nine witnesses in his trial were priests. The parlement noted his plea for clemency by reason of age ('avoir esgard à sa jeunesse') and reduced his sentence a bit; he was ordered to make a formal apology in court for his blasphemies and sent to the galleys for life. The second shepherd was married, fifty years old, and lived at Chiroville in the district of Saint-Silvin, an enclave near Caen belonging to the *bailliage* of Alençon. A man named Dany, previously 'condemned for *sortilège*,'[26] accused him of making a 'pact with the enemy of the human race,' which he denied. He denied he knew how to set wolves on a flock, but admitted 'that he knows well how to protect his flock from wolves by a prayer that he recited.' The parlement ordered surgeons to inspect him for the Devil's mark. The next day they reported that 'a great number of marks had been found on all parts of his body'; when pricked, 'a large part had been found to be sensitive,' but one spot on his left side was pricked four times without any sign of pain. Since he was also charged with stealing sheep, the parlement decided to uphold his conviction after hearing the surgeon's report.

In early June, an unusually rowdy wedding at the Rouen parish church of Sainte-Croix-des-Pelletiers led to the arrest and conviction of two men. The shepherd Guillaume Beuse performed the famous impotence spell, the ligature ('a noué l'esguillette'), in public at his sister's marriage; his partner, a pharmacist named Etienne Moreau, then pretended to undo the spell with another magic ritual. Moreau had been arrested 'in possession of a bad book containing many recipes and magical signs,' a paper covered with odd symbols, and 'four pieces of virgin parchment containing invocations of evil spirits.' The bride's brother had been ordered to make a public apology, watch the book and papers burn in public, and serve ten years in the galleys. The parlement upheld his sentence, adding a stiff fine of 150 livres and five years' banishment from the *bailliage* of Rouen for the druggist; the book and papers used in their prank were burned in court.

In September, a husband and wife appealed their sentences from the seigneurial court of Condé-sur-Noireau, deep in lower Normandy; she had been sentenced to death, he to life in the galleys. Claudine Brevet, who gave her age as forty, admitted 'that she had formerly been imprisoned for this crime.' She had been rearrested because a noblewoman claimed that Claudine had bewitched her. After denying that she had a devil's mark, she couldn't remember what she might have said about the Devil 'when she was full of anger.' Her day-laborer husband, aged somewhere between thirty-five and forty, was asked first 'if his wife hadn't taught him something.' He defended her staunchly throughout his interrogation, pointing out that they had been married for twenty years. But the evidence, from fifteen men including a priest and twenty-two women, was substantial. The judges voted to uphold both sentences on 22 September and pronounced them the following day.

That same day, 23 September, the parlement heard testimony against four people from La Haye-du-Puis in the Cotentin peninsula, all condemned to death for witchcraft by another seigneurial court. Twice as many defendants as in the previous case, twice as much testimony to digest from forty-eight men (including four priests) and thirty-two women. The lone man among the accused admitted that 'the sick addressed themselves to him to be cured' and that he generally advised them to find and burn whatever objects had been used to bewitch them. His wife admitted that she was also in the business of healing but insisted that 'it is wrong that she is reputed a sorceress.' An older woman nicknamed *la Josette* admitted that she had been 'diffamée' as a witch twenty years ago, but, she insisted, 'wrongly.' The final woman, Michelle Pontrain, denied that she ever performed magical cures and refused to accuse the married couple who did ('doesn't know if Lubé and his wife are witches'). The parlement upheld the convictions of the first three, but deferred judgment on Pontrain, asking for supplementary evidence. Four months later, they commuted her sentence to perpetual banishment from France.[27]

The final witchcraft case heard by the Rouen Parlement in 1605 followed only two days after this group. An old man, who gave his age as sixty-six, with two children, one living at home and the other in the king's service, had been accused by seven men and had been sentenced to torture by the royal court at Cany in the northeastern corner of Normandy. He had been caught with a dangerous-looking box holding some toads and mysterious powders. Although he tried to explain that the toads were really only some 'frogs that had been given to him to eat' and 'denie[d] having any Mark on his right shoulder and that he felt it clearly when he had been pricked,' the Rouen judges remained unimpressed by such disingenuous disclaimers. They aggravated his sentence, ordering him to be tortured to learn his accomplices and then hanged.

When the judicial year ended in early November, the Rouen Parlement had judged six women condemned to death for witchcraft in 1605 and upheld four convictions. Only five men had appealed death sentences for the same crime; but more men than women were ultimately executed, because the judges upheld four of them and raised another man's sentence into a fifth death penalty. The parlement also sentenced three men to the galleys, two of them for life – the harshest punishment it could inflict below death, but one that could not be given to women. Their mildest punishments ordered one man and one woman banished, although they also released a man and a woman because the evidence against them had been obtained illegally. The considerations that weighed most heavily with them can best be glimpsed in their interrogations of prisoners. Apart from a previous conviction (whether of a young man or an old woman), they focused first on any kind of pertinent material evidence. Those pieces of virgin parchment with spells written on them decided the fates of the priest from Bricquebec and the two pranksters from Rouen. Animals could provide equally decisive evidence. A box full of toads and powders caused them to surpass a local court and impose a death sentence; a live toad persuaded them to uphold a death sentence that they admitted had been pronounced by a prejudiced judge. A less certain type of material evidence, much in vogue in 1605, was the Devil's mark; the shepherd from Chiroville was executed only after it was finally confirmed. Indispensable, but least satisfactory in judging matters of life and death, was the prisoner's local reputation, usually measured in dozens of depositions, normally including one from his local parish priest. It helped, of course, if prisoners like the couple from La Haye-du-Puis readily admitted that they habitually cured magical spells for a great many people. Usually, under the intense pressure of the *sellette* if not before, some kind of decisive information would emerge to shape the judges' rulings.

The first witch executed by the Rouen Parlement in 1605 was an old woman from the far western *bailliage* of Cotentin. Like all the other women who appealed death sentences that year, she came from deep in lower Normandy, well west of Caen. The geographical distribution of the Norman women condemned for witchcraft was far from random. Cotentin saw far more female witches executed than any other region of Normandy, but relatively few male witches (despite the unfortunate priest and the professional healer of 1605, both of whom lived in the distant Cherbourg peninsula). The far western rim of Normandy was therefore the only part of the province that even approximated the ordinary western European pattern of witchcraft as a crime ordinarily charged to women. Moreover, our evidence from Cotentin fits fairly well with that offshore corner of Normandy under British rule, the Channel Islands, where witch trials were remarkably thick between 1560 and 1660. Indeed, several witches tried in Guernsey or Jersey had been born in the Cotentin;[28] conversely, a well-known Norman witch, executed at Rouen in 1617, had been born on the small island of Alderney.[29] But east and south of Cotentin, women witches become much rarer; only the far southern *bailliage* of Alençon shows a majority of women among its few known executions for witchcraft. It borders the Perche, the one district in the Paris Parlement's vast *ressort* where witches were almost exclusively female.[30]

If we compare and contrast Normandy's witchcraft cases with a capital crime whose defendants were exclusively female, infanticide, we find a geographical pattern that partially corroborates the prominence of far-western Cotentin. In the late sixteenth and early seventeenth centuries, the Rouen Parlement judged approximately as many death sentences for infanticide as for witchcraft; across the fifty-year span 1575–1634 we can locate about two hundred instances of each.[31] Despite the distance from Rouen, about two-thirds of the infanticide cases came from lower Normandy, the western half of the province. Before 1630, the Parlement of Rouen reduced only a handful of death sentences for infanticide. Although Cotentin was heavily represented with forty-six deaths for infanticide upheld during this period (while fewer than a dozen women from Cotentin were executed for witchcraft), the center of infanticide prosecutions was clearly the *bailliage* of Caen, which furnished over one-fourth of Normandy's totals. But only two women from the *bailliage* of Caen ever appear among witchcraft defendants at Rouen, and neither was executed.[32] Conversely, executions for infanticide were virtually unheard-of in the southeastern *bailliage* of Gisors (only one death in fifty years), the region where Normandy's prosecutions for witchcraft began. Overall, in Normandy more than six times as many women were executed for infanticide as for witchcraft during the apogee of witch-hunting.

The second witchcraft execution approved by the Parlement of Rouen in 1605 condemned a shepherd from the *bailliage* of Caux, the region forming Normandy's northern border east of the Seine. His case was even more representative than that of the old widow from the Cotentin peninsula. Men composed a large majority of Normandy's accused witches; shepherds composed a majority of Norman men charged with witchcraft whose occupations can be identified; and men from the *bailliage* of Caux outnumbered those from any other Norman region after 1594. Three tribunals near the northern coast offer a remarkable composite picture. Together, the local royal courts at Arques (near Dieppe) and Montivilliers (near Le Havre), and the principal court of the autonomous Duchy of Longueville (south of Arques) condemned forty-one people for witchcraft between 1595 and 1635. Exactly three of them, all tried at Longueville, were women. Three other local royal courts in the Pays de Caux, at Cany (near the coast), Neufchâtel (an eastern district), and Caudebec (on the Seine, the capital of Caux) add fourteen men and two women convicted of witchcraft; seigneurial courts at Lillebonne, Maulevrier, and Londiniéres (all near the Seine) add five more men to the totals. In all, the Parlement of Rouen ordered seventeen men from Caux – and one woman – executed for witchcraft, not counting the two 'hidden' executions at Arques in 1612. The region as a whole produced five women and fifty-nine men who were tried for witchcraft during Normandy's main phase of witch-hunting. Here, in the Pays de Caux, lay the epicenter of male witchcraft in western Europe.

How many of the men from the Pays de Caux were shepherds? Nearly half (twenty-eight of fifty-nine) are clearly identifiable as such from either the *arrêts* or the *plumitifs*. Conversely, almost half the shepherds found in Norman witch trials lived in the Pays de Caux. After 1594 this region produced many more shepherd-witches than the southeastern *bailliage* of Gisors (nine cases) or the *bailliage* of Rouen (twelve men). Guilt by association did not extend to their spouses in the Pays de Caux. However, seigneurial courts in southeastern Normandy twice put a shepherd's wife on trial with him and would do so again in 1692. Considering the obvious connection between shepherds and wolves, it is interesting to note that the only man charged with turning himself into an animal lived in the Pays de Caux, near Longueville; but he identified himself as a farmer and shoemaker, not a herdsman, and he was released by the parlement without punishment.[33]

West of the Seine, one finds four shepherds tried for witchcraft in a triangle southeast of Caen formed by the *seigneurie* of Argences and Saint-Gabriel, Saint-Silvin (an enclave of the *bailliage* of Alençon), and Orbec (at the western edge of the *bailliage* of Evreux). But no shepherd appears among the other accused witches of lower Normandy: none from anywhere in Cotentin, none even as far west as Caen, none along the southern border of Normandy until one approaches the Seine. The fascinating geography of Normandy's shepherd-witches needs to be understood in the context of the province's economic history as well as its folklore, but given the paucity of reliable studies on either subject, the phenomenon can be identified far more easily than it can be explained.

Apart from shepherds, the second most prominent category among Normandy's male witches in 1605 appears to consist of clergymen. We can assert with complete confidence that this situation was typical not just of several regions in Normandy, but throughout the kingdom of France. If geography helps us isolate Normandy's shepherd- witches, chronology is more instructive here. Until the Edict of Nantes ended the French Wars of Religion, only one or two Italian clerical magicians ran afoul of the French judiciary, including the Parlement of Paris; Soman notes that women were as likely as men to be condemned to death for illicit magic until 1600. In Normandy, the first priest condemned to death for witchcraft by a secular court was turned over to the jurisdiction of the bishop of Avranches by the reunited parlement in May 1594. But by December 1598, the parlement ordered two priests, appealing convictions for *sortilège* by a royal court at Falaise in the *bailliage* of Caen, to be hanged at Rouen. Like their unfortunate colleague who was later executed in 1605, they had been caught in possession of 'a book of diabolical invocations and incantations, with figures, kept inside the breviary', in addition to some 'small pieces of paper written with diabolical invocations'. The parlement remarked scornfully of the older priest, who had run the parish of Saint-Jean at Basson for seven years, that 'one doesn't know of what religion he is', adding that 'he had made his house into a brothel and had had five or six bastards'. They were unimpressed by his flat denials (in the face of much testimony) that he engaged in 'magic, witchcraft and invocation of devils, something execrable, evil, and abominable before God', and proceeded to rid the earth of such clerical black sheep without hesitation.[34]

The same royal court at Falaise condemned another priest to death for *sortilège* less than two years later, but the parlement reduced his sentence to perpetual banishment from Normandy, entailing the loss of his benefice. This pattern was repeated at least five times across the following decade, with royal courts in five of Normandy's seven regional *bailliages* pronouncing death sentences against clerics and the Rouen Parlement usually commuting their sentences to perpetual banishments.[35] Two other parish priests were hanged in 1607 and 1608. The first was a cause célèbre that began after the accused made 'execrable blasphemies in a sermon… against God and the Virgin Mary' in February 1606 and grew to involve a book of divination plus two letters in Latin. The parlement first approved the curé's trial in June 1606 at the royal court of Saint-Lô, but by October they ordered a change of venue to Valognes, located in a district less infested with Huguenots. By May 1607 the defendant had appealed his conviction, and he was tried by the Grand-chambre rather than the usual criminal court. They gave him the stiffest punishment ever handed out to a Norman priest: a public apology at the cathedral of Rouen, afterward 'to have his tongue pierced by a hot iron', then 'the fire to be shown to his face three times' before he was hanged and his body burned. The other curé had been condemned by the deputy *bailli* of Caen at Falaise as a notorious witch whose spells had caused the deaths of several people and animals and who frequently performed the spell of ligature.[36]

Only once, in 1616, did the Parlement of Rouen commute a priest's death sentence for *sortilège,* to life in the galleys. The defendant was relatively young (he gave his age as thirty and specified that he had been ordained eight years earlier) and a wretchedly underpaid chaplain in the little village of Quillebeuf along the Seine. He too was caught red-handed in possession of magical recipes (in Latin) for curing horses and seducing women and was charged in addition with sacrilege and fraud. His age and his attitudes caused the parlement not to transfer him to episcopal jurisdiction, but also to spare his life.[37] Afterward, the list of Normandy's clerical sorcerers condemned to major punishments resumes thirty years later with the famous cases at Louviers, following the equally famous Norman revolt of the Nu-Pieds.

Six Norman priests, plus one of their servants and the cadaver of a deceased priest, were executed for sorcery by order of the Rouen Parlement between 1598 and 1647. They form a much smaller share (about 10 percent) of the executed male sorcerers than the shepherds of upper Normandy, but priests were more numerous than any other occupational category, and they came from many different regions of the province. In fact, the only other occupation that was clearly overrepresented among Normandy's male witches was blacksmithing. This group, all from the same regions of upper Normandy which also produced nearly all of the shepherd-witches, appealed five sentences of death and two of life in the galleys between 1598 and 1628. Two deaths and one galley sentence were confirmed; three blacksmiths were banished.[38] Like shepherds, blacksmiths were frequently involved in illicit forms of veterinary medicine; they were usually charged with bewitching (and/or magically curing) the most valuable animals of all, horses.

From the outset, the Rouen Parlement judged more men than women on charges of witchcraft. The male majority among accused witches increased over time (see Table 3). The comparisons between the first (1564–78) and last (1646–59) samples are especially instructive. In both instances, we find fewer than two people per year tried for witchcraft and only a handful of executions (three in the early sample, four in the latter). But in the first sample, 40 percent of the accused witches were women, while in the last sample their share had fallen below 10 percent. After 1615, women were seldom put on trial for witchcraft in Normandy and almost never convicted. A woman was executed for witchcraft by order of the Rouen Parlement as late as 1635, long after the last such instance in Paris. However, hers was the last such case in Normandy until a female magician was hanged at Rouen in 1684 and a shepherd's wife was executed ten years later.[39]

The famous Madeleine Bavent had made and several times confirmed a full confession of witchcraft that led to the condemnation and execution of two priests and she had been sentenced to death by her original judge in 1644. But she was never condemned for witchcraft by the parliamentary judges who executed her male associates in 1647. Five years later she was still rotting in the episcopal prison of Evreux, writing her autobiography and repeating her stories to her Capuchin confessor, who published a huge book about her case at Rouen; but still the parlement refused to confirm her sentence.[40] No matter what she said or how often she repeated it, no woman was executed for witchcraft by order of the Parlement of Rouen for half a century after 1635. But those same judges condemned and sometimes executed men for *sortilège* throughout those years.

Table 3 Gender Distribution of Accused Witches in Normandy, 1560–1660

Years	Men tried	Women tried	Proportion of men to women	Cases/yr.
1564–78	15	10	1.5	1.6/yr.
1581–94	45	21	2.1	5.2/yr.
1595–1614	137	56	2.4	9.7/yr.
1615–35	60	14	4.3	5.0/yr.
1646–59	21	2	10.5	1.7/yr.

Source: ADSM, IB 3155–3374, 3021–3045.

To take a closer look at Norman witchcraft during its 'masculinized' phase, let us review the parlement's interrogations of witchcraft defendants during 1627, the last year when as many as four people were executed for witchcraft in Normandy.[41] The first appellant, judged in early January, seems an archetypical Norman witch: a sixty-year-old shepherd from the Duchy of Longueville in the Pays de Caux, appealing a death sentence based largely on the charge that he had stolen a pot containing four toads; testimony from twenty witnesses accused him of bewitching four horses and a woman. But the parlement believed most of his denials and reduced his sentence to nine years of banishment from Normandy. The next case, in February, seems equally archetypical: a woman sentenced to death by a seigneurial court near Rouen because she had been seen at the sabbat by another woman who had already been executed. The parlement simply ordered that all recent witch trials from that court be brought for inspection; and there is every likelihood that the defendant, who stoutly denied 'that she had killed a baby with her kiss' or 'that she has any mark of the Devil', was ordered banished for a short term.

The third case, decided in mid-May, is far more interesting. An old man, who gave his age as an unusually precise seventy-seven, appealed a death sentence from the district court of the *baitti* of Alençon at Essay (he was the first known male witch tried by that court). On the *sellette,* he began by denying everything, although more than two dozen witnesses had testified against him: 'Nobody had found a Devil's mark on him.... he hadn't said that he had been to the sabbat and adored the Devil.... he hadn't named any people as witches.... he doesn't know how to perform the ligature [*nouer l'esguilette*].' But he began to stumble just a bit and 'confessed that he had said that the Devil's name was Leviathan,' because he recalled that 'at the midnight Mass he had heard all the Devil's names.' Soon he admitted having once said, 'I'm a real witch [*je suis vray sorcier*],' adding immediately 'that it was crazy stupidity [*qu'il estoit fol ignorance*].' When the judges started questioning him about another reported statement, he cracked. 'They asked if he had not said that he had seen the Devil say Mass with his back turned, and piss in his shoes to be distributed like holy water?' and he broke down. 'He said several times,' notes the interrogation record, '*mon Dieu misère*, and confessed to having attended the sabbat.' He then reported a huge jumble of details, providing one of the richest descriptions of a witches' sabbath anywhere in Norman records. Of course, the judges upheld his death sentence.

In June, a teenager appealed his death sentence from the royal district court at Orbec, on the western edge of the *bailliage* of Evreux. The circumstances were classic. The most important of the ten witnesses against him, the parish priest at Beaumesnil, charged that 'after having received the Sacrament of the Altar, he took it out of his mouth,' doubtless to use it afterward to perform some spell. Once the judges learned that 'he had been a shepherd for one year,' his fate was sealed and his sentence upheld.

The next month came a forty-seven-year-old woman from the same *bailliage,* heavily charged. Although she stonewalled the judges ('didn't say that she would rather be a devil... didn't keep a toad in her house'), she was apparently undone by one piece of circumstantial evidence that she could not deny. She had given some milk to a bewitched woman, 'who then gave it to some animals who died miserably, although the woman herself was soon cured.' Her sentence was upheld, and she became the penultimate woman known to have been executed for witchcraft by the Parlement of Rouen until after the so-called decriminalization of witchcraft in 1682. In August, a middle-aged woman of forty-nine appealed her death sentence from the *bailli's* court at Lisieux. The essential charge was exactly the same as with the youth at Orbec two months earlier, but she did a much better job of defending herself on the *sellette* by proving that she had made a proper confession on Good Friday and pointing out 'that she had not been caught with anything [of a compromising nature].' The parlement, uncertain, ordered her to be tortured at Rouen. Like nearly everyone else, she withstood it successfully; whereupon they ruled that she be imprisoned for a year and a day at Orbec and then released, unless further substantial evidence could be produced against her.

The final five witchcraft defendants of 1627 were men. A fifty-year-old blacksmith tried at Les Andelys, on the Seine south of Rouen, although accused by almost sixty people, escaped a death sentence because no devil's mark was found on him. The judges noted drily that 'when he was examined [for the mark], it was said that he cried out too loudly'; they confirmed his condemnation to the galleys, but omitted the preliminary public apology decreed by the local royal court. The next man, sentenced to nine years in the galleys, had been tried by the royal court at Breteuil (*bailliage* of Evreux) as much for theft as for *sortilège*. He pointed out that he had already been whipped on these charges and had 'neither cast nor lifted the spell of ligature' on his main accuser, a woman. His sentence was also upheld.

The final cases from 1627 involved men sentenced to death at Saint-Lô in eastern Cotentin. They all had unusual occupations for accused witches: a dry-goods merchant aged forty-two; a weaver aged thirty-three; and a young man of twenty-three who had been 'captured with several drugs and wearing a double-layered cloak [to conceal them].' Their witchcraft took the unusually deadly form of 'having sent the plague through spells and conjurations and causing the death of many people thereby.' The merchant was heard first, in October. He denied having a pact with the Devil, nor did he 'cure the plague with medicines.' But during a very long interrogation he could not satisfactorily answer the charge that he had bought a book from an Italian at Reims in Champagne, teaching how to cure the plague. It was 'full of conjurations,' but he had burned it just before his arrest. Finally he confessed that, like Doctor Faustus, he had made a pact with the Devil, who promised that he 'would make him perform many admirable things.' The parlement therefore aggravated his death sentence by having him 'feel the fire three times' before having him garroted and his corpse burned.

The other men were heard in December. The weaver never broke during his long interrogation, insisting at its very end that he 'denie[d] having been at the sabbat.' His death sentence was reduced to nine years in the galleys. The youngest man sounds like a genuine sorcerer's apprentice. He was accused of making alchemical distillations, of 'asking a student for a book by Agrippa,' of owning a *grimoire,* of reading a book about a sorceress from the Channel Islands, of boasting 'that he would go to Paris in order to study magic.' The local prosecutor demanded a death sentence; but the parlement evoked the case, questioned him closely over three days, and finally banished him from Normandy for five years.[42]

By 1627, therefore, Rouen judges were deciding witchcraft cases not just on the basis of physical evidence, but also on information about witches' sabbaths and pacts with the Devil. The sabbat and the pact did not, however, multiply witchcraft executions in Normandy. Paradoxically, the judges at Rouen, like the Paris Parlement, reduced executions for witchcraft during the seventeenth century while simultaneously paying increasing attention to the witches' apostasy to the Devil. Both the judges' preoccupation with the sabbat and their reluctance to confirm death sentences for witchcraft occurred earlier and more decisively in the capital than in Normandy. At Paris, an official sentence labeled the sabbat an 'illusion' in an official decree as early as 1610.[43] At Rouen, such an opinion was literally unthinkable. If someone volunteered a full description of the sabbat or admitted a Faustian pact with the Devil, the Norman judges handed down a death sentence; and both situations occurred at Rouen in 1627.

We know that Norman witchcraft became increasingly masculinized after 1615, and increasingly concerned with the witches' apostasy. But how do these aspects fit together? How did the shepherds' *maleficia* with toad venom and spells to keep wolves away from flocks or blacksmiths' trickery with the health of horses (both very much present in cases from 1627) fit with these fabulous nocturnal rituals, to which women had been flying on broomsticks ever since the late Middle Ages? It is easy enough to see that the principal physical aspect of the diabolical pact, the insensible Devil's mark, was not gender-specific. When examined by responsible surgeons commissioned by royal judges, men were as likely as women to display such anesthetic spots. Evidence from the 1605 trials shows the importance of testing men for the Devil's mark; but there is no evidence that the Rouen judges questioned anyone, not even the group of four from Cotentin, about the sabbat. It was difficult to accommodate beliefs about the orgies at the witches' sabbath to a predominantly male population of witches. Consequently, the traces of the witches' sabbath among the records of the Rouen Parlement remained relatively meager. Its effect on multiplying trials was probably small, particularly since our few detailed descriptions of witches' sabbaths in Normandy report very small numbers of people in attendance.

The first sensational confession about a witches' sabbath encountered in the Rouen *plumitifs* came from a woman. In 1599, the parlement's jailer sent a memorandum of a prisoner's voluntary confession, made to another prisoner who had wrongly claimed that her life would be spared if she confessed everything. The prisoner, who admitted 'that she hadn't confessed it to her judge,' thereupon told the full classical story of seduction by the Devil and described a sabbat she attended afterward with three other women and a priest. The provocateur then put her on oath and persuaded her to repeat her story to three other prisoners, one of whom the judges summoned. The woman was then summoned and duly repeated her confession a third time, repeating her detailed charges against two women and a priest, whom the parlement promptly ordered arrested. She offered many details about the physical appearance of the Devil, but gave no information about any rituals or orgies.[44]

On the other hand, the first man to describe a sabbat on the *sellette* at Rouen said nothing about how he got there, but spent some time explaining what happened there: 'He saw the Devil dressed in gray in the form of a woman.... said Devil requested that he give himself to her... there was eating and dancing.' Although he claimed to have refused to perform any ritual homage and denied that he had been marked, he admitted 'having had the [sexual] company of the succubus or the [female] Devil,' but specified that the experience gave him less pleasure than with his wife! He had been sentenced to be burned alive; the parlement, which never inflicted that punishment on anyone, ordered that he smell the fire before being strangled. A woman arrested with him, whom he saw at the sabbat three years earlier, confirmed to her Rouen judges that she had indeed been present. Like the first woman, she offered no details about what went on there.[45]

By 1601, one finds two women treated with extreme leniency by the parlement when appealing sentences based on accusations about sabbats, but without any concrete *maleficia*. One denied vigorously that her mother had taken her, flying on a greased stick, to a sabbat; the judges cut her testimony short and ordered her released. The other, who had been sentenced to be shaved and tortured 'in order to confess more precisely the manner and fashion of the carnal copulation which she had with the evil spirit,' was inspected by physicians and quickly released by the parlement, who evidently felt they could distinguish a psychologically disturbed person from a criminal. They ordered her sent first to the local archiepiscopal court 'in order to receive some consolation from M. le Penitentier,' and then turned over to Rouen's charity hospital for medical treatment, donating twelve *écus* (to be repaid from the next fines they collected) to pay her expenses. Hers was literally a sentence of unprecedented charity among Rouen's witchcraft cases.[46]

Usually, the Rouen judges finessed the problems associated with men at the sabbat by spending a relatively small share of their time asking prisoners about it, unless the issue lay unavoidably at the center of the evidence. In 1627, for example, they never seem to have raised the issues of the diabolical pact or the sabbat when questioning the young sorcerer's apprentice. Nor did they order him, or anyone else, to be checked for the Devil's mark by surgeons. Ordinarily the Rouen judges paid relatively little attention to discourse about the witches' sabbath, because it was impossible to corroborate through physical evidence. Since it placed little reliance on torture as a means to elicit truth, the Parlement of Rouen generally avoided using it against suspected witches. Chains of denunciations formed by other witches seen at sabbats were usually brief and easily broken. Only exceptional circumstances like the outbreak of plague at Saint-Lô in 1627 led to multiple arrests in situations where men rather than women formed the majority of the 'usual suspects.' Overall, then, the witches' sabbath and the diabolical pact do not emerge as major concerns of the Rouen judges, and they certainly cannot help us explain why Normandy put mainly male witches on trial.

If the witches' sabbath or the pact, issues that provoked the execution of two men for witchcraft in 1627, provide the wrong way to approach the Norman judges' concentration on male witches, the principal cause of the third man's death proves more helpful. A young shepherd was executed because he had sacrilegiously preserved the consecrated Eucharist instead of swallowing it. His technique may have been slightly different, but his essential crime, the reason for his execution, was identical with the very first case we hear about in Normandy. Both involved sacrilegious use of the Eucharist for magical purposes, principally by shepherds trying to protect their flocks against disease or wolves. A woman (who was obviously not a shepherdess) narrowly escaped execution in 1627 on an identical charge. The thread that connects the two main occupational categories among Rouen's numerous male witches, the shepherds and the priests, also helps explain the parlement's unusual severity toward both of them. The common element, and the link, is sacrilege, particularly when it involved misuse of the Eucharist. Occasionally the complicity between priest and shepherd was direct. In the vicinity of Rouen, one finds a priest directly associated with a shepherd in misuse of consecrated objects for magical purposes.[47] Various consecrated objects could be used for magical purposes by shepherds or others. In 1662, five shepherds from the region around Vernon were charged with stealing a chalice 'to use it for a profane purpose,' almost certainly magical. In 1684, a woman was hanged at Rouen and her corpse burned for 'profanations, impieties and sacrilege,' specifically 'making use of magic, written pacts made with the Devil, and notes in the form of invocations' to find hidden treasures, 'win at games of chance, and make people sick.' On the same day, the Rouen Parlement sentenced shepherds for 'so-called *sortilège* and poisoning animals,' and one of them was sent to the galleys.[48]

The most serious Norman cases, from 1540 until late in the reign of Louis XIV, involved shepherds illegally obtaining consecrated Hosts. A notorious case was also heard on appeal by the Rouen Parlement in 1684. A thirteen-year-old boy, making his first communion during a Jubilee, was observed letting the wafer drop from his mouth and then putting it in his pocket. He had done this at the request of two shepherds (one of whom escaped from jail), 'to make use of it with certain words in order to seduce girls, and with other words to protect their flocks.' The Rouen Parlement ordered all three of them, including an effigy of the fugitive, burned. The shepherd who did not escape proceeded to accuse five other shepherds before he died; one of them, arrested a month later, was ultimately executed at Rouen in 1687 for 'profanations and *sortilèges*' after testimony from no fewer than 253 witnesses.[49] Nor was he the last such instance. In 1692 the Rouen Parlement upheld death sentences against a shepherd and his wife (once again, residents of the region near Vernon) for sacrilegious magic performed with consecrated Hosts that the shepherd had avoided swallowing while taking communion. As late as 1703, the Rouen Parlement condemned three more shepherds to death for 'having broken down a church door at night and carried off some Hosts from the tabernacle as well as holy water from the baptismal fonts'; one of them admitted the deed, explaining that the Hosts had been stolen to cure their animals.[50] Seldom is the French proverb 'The more things change, the more they remain the same' better illustrated than by the sad sacrilegious tale of Norman shepherds and the Eucharistic magic that they performed on their flocks.

The judges of Rouen inflicted such severe punishments on those shepherds, especially the boy making his first communion in 1683, not because they were magicians, but because they profaned the Eucharist, the body of Christ. Our most important clue to explain why a crime associated to an unusual degree with men, above all with shepherds, was treated with such unusual severity in Normandy, over such an unusually long period, lies in Eucharistic theology. In one significant respect, Normandy's judges treated male witches in much the same way as they had treated male heretics before 1561. The 'burning question' was profanation of the Eucharist. Protestant 'sacramentarians' denied transubstantiation; the shepherds (apparently Catholics to a man; none came from regions of Normandy where Protestantism flourished) believed in it fervently. But one of the surest ways to prod the Rouen judges into burning someone at the stake was to convince them that a prisoner might have given a consecrated Host to an animal. It made no difference whether one was trying to demonstrate a theological point experimentally or trying to inoculate animals. In God's eyes, and therefore in those of the judges, the offense was equal. Shepherds were a rough lot, charged with plenty of crimes other than *sortilège*, capable of desperate remedies. Toad venom was one element of the Norman shepherd's arsenal that the judges frequently encountered in witch trials; the Eucharist, its polar opposite, was another.

In the context of French appellate justice, the Parlement of Rouen seems unusually severe in its handling of *sortilège*. But this impression depends upon which neighboring system one chooses to compare it with. Up the Seine sat the Parlement of Paris. Its judges could blandly describe the sabbat as an illusion in a public statement as early as 1610, and its witchcraft defendants, at least until 1680, included a relatively small share of shepherds. It seems a far gentler and kinder court than its downstream neighbor. The relatively small size of Normandy compared to the vast judicial district of the Parlement of Paris underlines the peculiar severity of the former with respect to witchcraft. At its most severe, between 1580 and 1610, the Parlement of Paris upheld about 30 percent of the death sentences for witchcraft appealed to it, while the Parlement of Rouen upheld more than half of its share between 1585 and 1615. Paris failed to confirm any such executions for a very long time after 1625; Rouen upheld some death sentences for witchcraft more than twenty years later.

Why were Norman judges so much more severe than their Parisian counterparts during the worst phase of witch-hunting? Part of the explanation is that Parisian judges, who seem every bit as severe toward accused witches as the Normans until 1585, discovered at least two types of gross abuses in witch trials not long thereafter – and Norman judges never encountered either. Soman described how the Paris Parlement (quietly helped by its *ligueur* enemy, the cardinal of Lorraine) had to punish more than twenty local officials in 1587–88 for illegally 'ducking' suspected witches to see if they floated and lynching many of them without proper trials. Fifteen years later, the Parisians caught a horribly successful professional witch finder, the public hangman of Rocroi, who had helped convict no fewer than 274 witches for personal profit, and sent him to the galleys for life.[51] In our abundant Norman evidence there is no trace of professional witch finders or of the superstitious water ordeal, both of which were directed almost exclusively against women. Because it never confronted serious procedural irregularities in the hundreds of witch trials it handled, the Parlement of Rouen saw no reason to supervise them with a critical eye.

In the final cycle of French witch trials, the Norman Parlement started up again much earlier than Paris, in 1670, and kept going longer, until after 1700. There are a few signs, in the margins of the Affair of the Poisons (1678–82) and its immediate aftermath, that the Parisian judges of Louis XIV's reign could be almost as frightened of toad venom and dangerous shepherds in the upper Seine basin as were their Norman neighbors. The two final death sentences for *sortilège* (now officially described as 'so-called *sortilège*') were upheld against shepherds at Paris in 1691; the last two at Rouen, against a shepherd and his wife, were upheld two years later. But it was nonetheless fair for Louis XIV's sarcastic German sister-in-law to write in 1718 that 'at Paris people don't believe in witches and we hear nothing about them; at Rouen they believe that witches exist, and there one always hears about them.'[52] Seen from Paris, Normandy was a singularly superstitious place, preoccupied with hanging shepherds for sorcery. Within the kingdom of France, the Parlement of Rouen fully deserves this opinion. It took sorcery very seriously partly because so many of the sorcerers it found were men, and sometimes women, with solid physical evidence (e.g., written spells or live toads) against them. The Norman Parlement also finessed as much as possible the legal difficulties of proving physical attendance at the sabbat, concentrating instead on *maleficia* performed against humans and especially animals.

Moreover, the French province of Normandy and its Parlement at Rouen seem like models of judicial restraint in witch trials when compared to the part of Normandy outside French control. The deservedly obscure Channel Islands, firmly under English control but speaking no English in this era, hold the dubious distinction of being, proportionate to their size, the witch-hunting capital of Atlantic Europe. Between 1562 and 1661, the Channel Islands – whose archives contain at least as many gaps as those of the Rouen Parlement – record 167 people tried for witchcraft. Over half of them were hanged and their corpses burned.[53] Executions there began in 1562 by order of the royal court on Jersey, and in 1563 by order of the *bailli* of Guernsey. Each sovereign court, Jersey's and Guernsey's, held jurisdiction over scarcely a dozen parishes. All together, the Channel Islands held at most fifteen thousand people. They earned their living from livestock as well as from fishing, as the names of today's major breeds of cattle attest. They had wide powers of self-government. Jersey, with an elaborate multilayered jury system, executed two of every three witchcraft defendants (43 of 65). Guernsey, with a more centralized system of trial by nine jurats and the *bailli*, executed slightly under half of its witchcraft defendants (47 of 102), but put even more on trial. Witches' sabbaths can be glimpsed in the very first trials, at least on Guernsey, which helps explain why island trials involved a relatively small share of male witches. Overall, men composed exactly one-sixth of the witches executed in the Channel Islands, a much smaller share than in the closest mainland region of Cotentin (which, as we have seen, was the most 'feminized' zone of witchcraft in Normandy). The importance of sabbats in Channel Islands witchcraft also helps explain why one finds occasional clusters of executions there (for example, five on Jersey in 1585 and eight on Guernsey in 1617). But the really significant conclusion about witch trials in the Channel Islands, when compared to evidence from the Parlement of Rouen, is that it confirms more clearly than anywhere else in western Europe the decisive importance of appellate courts in judging witchcraft. The disproportion is grotesque: on one side, ninety recorded deaths in a few islands with scarcely two dozen parishes but complete judicial autonomy; on the other, slightly over a hundred recorded deaths in a province of over two thousand parishes. If the difference in severity of witchcraft prosecution between the Parlements of Paris and Rouen is arithmetical, that between the Parlement of Rouen and the Channel Islands is geometrical. The ultimate grotesque statistic is that more than twice as many women were executed for witchcraft in the Channel Islands as in the Duchy of Normandy. In the history of Norman witchcraft, the real nightmares lay offshore, and the archetypical witches were once again female.

Notes

1   Alfred Soman, *Sorcellerie et justice criminelle (16e–18e siécles)* (London, 1992), 798–99, first revealed a slight masculine majority among more than a thousand witchcraft defendants judged by the Parlement of Paris in an essay first published in 1977. Samples from the Parlement of Provence (1580–1628) show thirty men and seventy-three women tried for witchcraft; samples from the Parlement of Burgundy (1580–1642) show eighty-three men and seventy-six women tried for witchcraft. No other usable comparative data have yet been found from other parlements.

2   Including several items written by me, for example, 'The Pedestal and the Stake,' in *Becoming Visible: Women in European History,* ed. Renate Bridenthal and Claudia Koonz (Boston, 1974), 138–54. Sometimes the link between women and witchcraft supports an entire attempt at synthesis, e.g., Joseph Klaits, *Servants of Satan* (Bloomington, Ind., 1986).

3   The old account by Amable Floquet, *Histoire du Parlement de Normandie,* 7 vols. (Paris, 1840–45), 5:615–766, remains fundamental. See also Jonathan Dewald, *The Magistrates of the Parlement of Normandy in the Sixteenth Century* (Berkeley, Calif., 1980).

4   See the remarkable account by Amable Floquet, *Histoire du Privilege de Saint Romain,* 2 vols. (Rouen, 1835).

5   See Floquet, *Parlement de Normandie,* 5:618: Archives Departementales Seine-Maritime (hereafter ADSM), IB 3124 (1 Sept. 1542).

6   ADSM, IB 3170 (14 Jan. and 8 Feb. 1574). Christine Coquerel, wife of Thomas Harel of Ste. Croix dcs Baulx, charged 'pour estre sorcière et avoir empoisomié et faict mourir de poison et sort plusrs personnes' – but she was also charged with prostituting young girls 'et estre larron-esse ordinaire' and had been sentenced by the *bailli* of Evreux to be 'brulee vive.' Following its usual procedure,

the parlement ordered a further character investigation on 14 Jan.; upon learning (8 Feb.) that she had thrown a pot at a guest during the wedding feast for her stepson, they ordered her to be hanged at Evreux.

7   ADSM, IB 3179 (12 Sept. 1577): Lazare Boyvin and Thomas Bourdet, convicted of 'avoir usé de sortilège et fait mourir plusrs personnes et bestes avec leur sort, puys vingt ans.' The figure of twenty years of maleficient activities may be conservative. Their previous trial is in IB 3162 (21 Aug. 1567), when the parlement upheld a sentence of torture against both shepherds who had 'fait mourir plusrs personnes et bestes de leur sort puys vingt ans et d'estre coustumyere de ensorceller.'

8   The Parlement of Normandy, like most others in France, was split during the wars of the League. A royalist court met in Caen between July 1589 and April 1594. Its criminal *arrêts,* now at ADSM, IB 5719–29, lack nine months (Aug.–Dec. 1591 and Sept.–Dec. 1593); those of the League Parlement at Rouen are officially complete for 1589–94 (ADSM, IB 3215–18), although by 1590 it controlled much less territory than its rival.

9   See ADSM, 1B 5728 (3 and 11 Aug. 1593), case of Jehanne Poret; 1B 5729 (25 Feb. 1594), case of Mariette Hue alias 'la Cocquette,' whose condemnation of 30 Aug. 1593 was appealed 24 Sept. and the further investigations then ordered were completed on 29 Nov. 1593.

10 For the first known case of infanticide from Cotentin appealed to Rouen, see ADSM, IB 3155 (12 June 1564: a widow tried at Coutances and ordered to be hanged and her corpse burned had her sentence confirmed by the parlement); for the first cases of infanticide from the *bailliage* of Caen, see IB 3156 (6 Apr. 1565, a death sentence upheld); IB 3159 (11 Mar. 1566, from Bayeux, death sentence also upheld).

11 ADSM, IB 3199 (11 Feb., 14 Feb., and 12 Mar. 1585). At least two of the men, including the only one sentenced to be burned alive (Richard Neslé), were shepherds.

12 ADSM, IB 3229 (26 Nov. and 13 Dec. 1597: Maryne Marcheguey and Françoise Bigot, a widow who had 'faict mourir ung petit enffant et jectélé sort sur des vaches').

13 ADSM, IB 3239 (23 and 26 Jan. 1601, Robert and Thomas Agasse). Their *plumitifs* in IB 3014 (19 Jan. 1601) never mention Martin's accusations.

14 ADSM, IB 3272 (26 Nov. 1612, Guillaume Regnárt).

15 ADSM, 1B 3288 (17 Oct. 1618, Jean de Renti).

16 ADSM, IB 3030 (*plumitifs* of 10, 11, and 12 Feb. 1627, Thomasse Thiboult).

17 ADSM, 1B 3031 (*Plumitifs* of 31 July, and 1, 2, 4, 6, 9, and 11 Aug. 1628). Guillaume Busquet, who together with Thomas Le Sueur had appealed a death sentence for *sortilège* as early as February, was ultimately executed on 6 Aug.; Le Sueur and Philippe Paller (who called Guillemette Picard a whore under oath) were perpetually banished from France, and Claude Picard was banished for nine years, on 11 Aug.

18 ADSM, IB 3033 (*plumitif* of 9 Mar. 1634, Adrienne Lestrange). Parlement sentenced his widow, condemned to death at Louviers, to perpetual banishment from Normandy.

19 ADSM, IB 3037 (*plumitif* of 29 May 1647, Pierre Guiffart).

20 ADSM, IB 3251 (22 Mar. 1605).

21 The Paris Parlement upheld a relatively large share of the earliest death sentences for witchcraft judged on appeal, most of which were against women. From 1564 to 1580, for example, it upheld thirteen of thirty-eight such sentences (over one-third), while Rouen upheld only three of its first sixteen. The rate of death sentences for witchcraft upheld on appeal at Paris hovered close to 30 percent until 1610, but dropped rapidly thereafter: see Soman, *Sorcellerie et justice,* 35, table.

22 See ibid., 793, graph, which shows a pattern quite similar to Rouen's, except that the Parlement of Paris reached its peak of witchcraft deaths appealed before 1600, rather than during the following decade.

23 Between 1630 and 1646, only two years of *plumitifs* (IB 3034–35) survive, although they again cover nine of the eleven years after 1646. None of the parlement's criminal *arrêts* between 1630 and 1633 is extant. From 1636 to 1646, this series survives at a rate of only 44 percent (IB 3316–31 covers a total of 58 months out of 132), or approximately the same level as the mid-sixteenth century. In other words, from 1630 until the famous Louviers demonic-possession cases, we know fewer than one-third of the Rouen Parlement's criminal decisions. For the manifold troubles of the Rouen Parlement during the Nu-Pieds revolt, see Floquet, *Histoire du Parlement,* vol 4.

24 For the Bavent case, ending with one priest executed in person, another in effigy, and a futile struggle to extradite a prominent woman from Paris, see the classic treatment by Robert Mandrou, *Magistrats et sorciers en France au XVIIe siècle* (Paris, 1968), 219–26, 284–96. The Rouen Parlement judged four other death sentences for *sortilège* in 1647 and upheld two other executions: ADSM, IB 3037, *plumitifs* of 5 Apr., 29 May, 4 June and 18 Dec. 1647.

25 Another reason for choosing 1605 over 1609 is that our evidence happens to be unusually complete in the former year; the criminal *arrêts* survive for all twelve months (IB 3251–53) in addition to the *phmitifs* of interrogations (IB 3018). We have complete *plumitifs* for 1609 (IB 3026), but no *arrêts* for the first nine months (gap between IB 3263 and 3264). Thus 1605 was not only more severe in its decisions, but they were also more comprehensively recorded.

26 Dany is not included among the 'hidden' executions for witchcraft because the *plumitif* describes him as 'convicted,' but does not specify 'executed.' They ordinarily noted testimony about accomplices seen at sabbats that was not revoked when the witch was being executed; Daily accused Guillaume Saffrey of making a pact with the Devil (and therefore of being marked), but there is no trace of a sabbat here.

27 See ADSM, IB 3254 (3 Feb. 1606), for the final decision on Michelle Poutrain.

28 On witchcraft in the Channel Islands, see G. R. Balleine, 'Witch-Trials in Jersey,' *Société jersiaise: Bulletin annuel* 13 (1939): esp. 394–98 (nos. 51, 52, and 61), for witches born in Normandy, banished in 1626 and 1649. For Guernsey, see S. Carey Curtis, 'Trials for Witchcraft in Guernsey,' *La Société guernesaise: Reports & Transactions* 13 (1937): 109–43 (nos. 43, 44, and 57), for witches born in Normandy, banished in 1619 and 1622.

29 ADSM, IB 3283 (11 Jan. 1617): Jeanne Taffin ('la Pillemortiére'), 'native de l'isle d'Orrigny' (i.e., Alderney). Ten years later, a man from Saint-Lô was asked whether he owned a book entitled *LaDevineresse d'Aurigny*: IB 3031, *plumitif* of Jean le Francois (13 Dec, 1627).

30 See Soman (above, n. 1), chap. XIII, 'Trente Procès de sorcellerie dans Le Perche (1566–1624).' In all, only five women (including the 'hidden' case from 1597 mentioned above, n. 13) and three men from the oddly shaped *bailliage* of Alençon were known to have been executed for witchcraft.

31 The exact figures are 208 infanticide deaths confirmed by the Rouen Parlement between 1575 and 1635, and fewer than ten reduced; during the same period, approximately half of the 182 death sentences for witchcraft were reduced.

32 The women from the *bailliage* of Caen include the following: ADSM, IB 3248 (2 June 1604): Jeanne Baillehache, a widow, death sentence from the seigneurial court of Argences/St. Gabriel, 20 Feb. 1603, finally upheld. Two trials, IB 3241 (12 July 1601) and IB 3245 (20 Feb. 1603), both deal with the same woman, Marie de Lange, a fortune-teller from the Falaise district whose death sentences were twice commuted to banishments.

33 ADSM, IB 3027 (13 and 15 Mar. 1624): Pierre Grandin, aged thirty-five, appealing a death sentence, was released by the parlement: werewolves were no problem in Normandy.

34 ADSM, IB 3219 (19 May 1594); IB 3233 (2 Dec. 1598, plus the interrogations in IB 3011 on 27 Nov. 1598). One of their parishioners, tried with them, naively remarked that 'he did not know that his priest was a sorcerer'; his attitude earned him a round of torture alongside his spiritual guides, but the parlement ultimately accepted his plea for mercy and reduced his original sentence of banishment to a whipping and a huge fine of forty *écus*.

35 ADSM, IB 3242 (27 Sept. 1601, curé of Chefdeleau, *bailliage* of Rouen); IB 3262 (24 Apr. 1608, curés of Mesnil-le-Barbery and Grainville, both *bailliage* of Caen); IB 3021 (30 Mar. 1609, curé of Sauchey-Ie-Bas, *bailliage* of Caux); IB 3265 (2 Apr. 1610, vicar of Tilleul-Lambert, *bailliage* of Evreux). The last case included abuse of the sacrament of confession with a married woman and physical evidence of recipes for invoking demons, but the priest exhibited a written 'absolution obtained by him from our Holy Father, Pope Paul V' and a subsequent rehabilitation by the Official of Evreux. The next such case occurred ten years later: IB 3294 (8 Oct. 1620: priest at Saite-Opportune, in the Cotentin district of Saint-Sauveur-Lendelin).

36 ADSM, IB 3259 (27June 1607): *Meître* Pierre Baudel, curé of Vahais, *bailliage* of Cotentin; his servant, Michel Toutain, was executed with him. For the two priests whose death sentences were upheld in 1608, see IB 3262 (24 Apr. 1608).

37 ADSM, IB 3024 (*plumitifs* of 23, 27, 28, and 29 Jan. 1624): *Maître* jean Goubert, appealing from the royal court at Pontaudemer, *bailliage* of Rouen.

38 For blacksmiths as witchcraft defendants, see ADSM, IB 3010 (31 July 1598: Francois Helot, aged forty, 'a esté mareschal' near Rouen); IB 3016 (28 Aug.1605, Etrepagny, aged forty- five); IB 3021 (4 Aug.1609, Les Andelys, aged seventy, executed); IB 3274 (20 Apr.1613, near Rouen); IB 3277 (13 May 1614, Charleval, executed); IB 3293 (28 Apr.1620, Evreux); IB 3030 (9 Sept.1627, Les Andelys, aged fifty, perpetual galleys); IB 3031 (6 Aug.1628, Jonas Helot, aged fifty-three, Rouen, judgment unknown).

39 See ADSM, IB 3035 (26 Sept.1635): Anne Marye, a spinster from Condé-sur-Noireau, released after her first trial but rearrested and convicted after making threats against those who had originally caused her arrest. See below, nn. 48 and 50, on the two women executed in Normandy for crimes of magic and *sortilège* after Louis XIV supposedly decriminalized witchcraft.

40 Both Floquet, *Histoire du Parlement,* who gave the first full account of Bavent's case, and Mandrou, *Magistrats et sorciers,* who gave the best recent account. note without commentary that her case was never decided, although her guilty testimony provided the basis for condemning two priests and ordering the arrest of a prominent Parisian nun, whose extradition was blocked by the monarchy and the Parlement of Paris. Rauen's treatment of Bavent offers a curious foretaste of Louis XlV's behavior in the Affair of the Poisons, where many of the most loquacious prisoners who made the most spectacular charges were never publicly executed, but simply left to rot in obscure prisons.

41 ADSM, IB 3030.

42 The cluster of trials at Saint-Lô for diabolical witchcraft connected with spreading the plague spilled over intoJanuary 1628, when the Rouen Parlement heard three more appeals from death sentences, all of which they reduced: a weaver was banished for ten years, another weaver was freed, and a woman was banished for five years. See ADSM, IB 3031 (6, 9, and 31 Jan. 1628).

43 Alfred Soman, 'Le Sabbat des sorciers: Preuve juridique,' in *Le Sabbat des sorciers en Europe, XVe-XVIIIe siècles,* ed. Nicole Jacques-Chaquin and Maximc Préaud (Grenoble, 1993), 85–100.

44 ADSM, IB 3011 (26 May 1599); see also her *arrêt* in IB 3235 (27 May 1599).

45 ADSM. 1B 3012 (21 Feb. 1600): Guillaume Berney. from the *bailliage* of Evreux.

46 ADSM, IB 3014 (17 Jan.1601); 1B 3239 (*arrêt* of l8 Jan. 1601); 1B 3015 (23 Nov. 1601) and 1B 3242 (*arrêt* of 24 Nov. 1601).

47 See ADSM, IB 3242 (27 Sept. 1601) and the *plumitifs* in IB 3014 (28 Sept. 1601): the priest, dressed in clerical garb, burned incense to protect a flock from wolves; he probably lent his chalice to the shepherd to perform some ritual, although he claimed the shepherd stole it; a witness saw a copy of the famous *Key of Solomon* in the priest's possession.

48 On the 1663–64 cases, see ADSM, 1B 5522, dossier A. The *arrêts* of the female magician of 1684, Catherine Marie Moissan, and the shepherds are in ADSM, 1B 3372 (22 Mar., 15 and 18 Apr. 1684).

49 See Claude Lannette, 'Les Pratiques magiques dans la vallée de la Risle sous Louis XIV: Enquête et répression judicaires,' in *Actes du 107e Congrès national des Sociétés savantes, Brest, 1982; Section d'histoire moderne et contemporaine* (Paris, 1984), 1:313–37.

50 For the 1692, 1694, and 1703 executions, see Mandrou, *Magistrats et sorciers,* 507–11.

51 See Alfred Saman, 'La Décriminalisation de la sorcellerie en France,' *Histoire, économie et société* 4 (1985): 183–84, 189–95; idem, 'Decriminalizing Witchcraft: Does the French Experience Furnish a European Model?' *Criminal Justice History* 10 (1989): 15.

52 Liselotte von der Pfalz, *Briefe* (Ebenhausen, 1958), 297, 311, quoted by Wolfgang Behringer, *Hexen und Hexenprozesse,* 3d ed. (Munich, 1995), 449.

53 Balleine, 'Witch-Trials in Jersey'; Curtis, 'Trials for Witchcraft in Guernsey.' Forty-three were executed on Jersey, forty-seven on Guernsey.

CHAPTER 10
WITCHCRAFT AND MAGIC IN EARLY MODERN CULTURE
Stuart Clark

This essay looks at manifestations of witchcraft and magic in the broader culture of the period by considering three of these contexts. The first concerns the beliefs and practices associated with magic and fear of *maleficium* among the broad mass of the European population. The last concerns a kind of magic far more restricted both in appeal and historical occurrence – the 'high' or intellectual magic that attracted many Renaissance and late-Renaissance European thinkers and their patrons by its promise of universal wisdom. In between, is sandwiched an account of what might be called the textual life of witchcraft – its representation in the literature known as 'demonology' between the fifteenth and eighteenth centuries. At first sight, these aspects of our subject may well seem as bizarre and irrational as the witch trials themselves, and such, indeed, has been their reputation in the past. The aim in what follows is to dispel this impression by showing that witchcraft and magic had a culturally and historically based rationality of their own. Even if they were always contentious matters, this too arose from circumstances internal and intrinsic to early modern culture.

Popular magic

Magic at work

In 1517, a Castilian by the name of Alonso González de la Pintada presented himself to inquisitors in the diocese of Cuenca concerning a cure he had always used against haemorrhoids:

> Take the sick person to a certain fig tree and have him kneel facing the east with his hat off. Then you bless him, saying, 'In nomine patris et filii et spiritu sancti, what do I cut?' The sick one then says, 'The piles of so-and-so', and recites devoutly a Pater Noster and an Ave María, while you recite them as well. Together you recite the prayers three times, while you cut off nine figs from the fig tree. Then you take the figs to a place where neither sun nor smoke can get at them. While the figs dry out, the piles are cured.

González was punished as a Judaizer, but attempting to heal by sympathetic magic cannot have helped his cause (Nalle 1992: 14–15). In mid-sixteenth-century Rome, the prostitute Lucrezia the Greek was also using magic to gain customers and political allies in the city and to tap into the amatory powers of her rivals. In 1559, she was investigated by the governor's court on suspicion of making a young servant recite over and over again an incantatory 'prayer' addressed to an image of St Daniel. The prayer asked the saint, acting for God, the Virgin Mary and all the other saints 'of the sky, of the earth, of the air, fire, and water [to] work magic on one messer Giovanni Maria, a [domestic] servant of the pope, to make him love Lucrezia'. It had been bought for five scudi from a woman friend who had in turn inherited it from her mother. Another servant reported that Lucrezia also 'went to cut the cords of the bells and that she had them burnt in a lamp with oil and holy water so that messer Giovanni Maria might love her, and that she had earth taken from in front of the doors of the famous courtesans and brought to her house, saying that in such a way she would have good fortune come to her house' (Cohen and Cohen 1993: 190).

Thirty-five years later the people of an entire German district – Wiesbaden in the county of Nassau-Wiesbaden (Hesse) – were described by church visitation officials as habitual users of 'spells' and 'incantations' in every conceivable situation:

> To wit: when they are in pangs of childbirth, when an infant is picked up or laid down (to guard him against sorcery), when a child is taken to be baptized (at which time they bind amulets or bread crumbs into the baby's swaddling cloths to ward off enchantment), when cattle are driven out or brought home or are lost in the fields, when they shut their windows in the evening, and so on; also against all manner of sickness or misfortune. Whenever something has been mislaid, when a person feels sickly or a cow dries up, they make straightway for the soothsayer ... to find out who has stolen the object or put a bad spell on the animal, and to procure from him some charm to use against the offender.

Names, words and rhymes were 'mumbled' or written on scraps of paper and then eaten or worn as amulets. 'Outlandish' signs and gestures accompanied strange deeds with 'roots, herbs, mandrakes, and Saint-John's-wort'. Every action, it was said, had its 'special day, hour, and secret place' (Strauss 1978: 304; cf. for Catholic Germany, Forster 1992: 236).

The early seventeenth-century inhabitants of Lower Brittany were apparently no different. The Catholic priest Michel Le Nobletz described a whole series of magical rituals practised during his 'missionary' work among them around 1610. Women swept dust from chapel floors and threw it into the air to secure the safe return of their fishermen husbands and sons. Objects with magical significance were strewn in fields to keep wolves away from straying livestock, and local fountains were given sacrificial offerings and used for divination. 'The people', he wrote, 'offered these fountains as many pieces of bread as there were persons in their families, and drew conclusions, from the way the bits they had thrown in in their name floated or not, as to who would die during the coming year' (Delumeau 1977: 162). Half a century later, in another part of Europe again, the peasants of the parish of Maarja-Magdaleena in Estonia were doing much the same kind of thing, but with fire rather than water. On Midsummer Eve 1667, they built a fire near a ceremonial stone and then set about healing their various afflictions:

> the sick come, who have internal ailments, and must take bandages with wax and tie one around their bodies and also pick up a dipper of ale, go around the fire three times and while doing this they must bow to certain places of the stone while saying 'O help us, St John.' Having done this, they remove their bandages and hand them to the same old

woman who holds it before the patient's mouth to be kissed. Then the bandage will be burned on the stone, the sick will drink from the dipper and pass it to the woman who will make the sign of the cross three times on the dipper and say, 'Help, dear St John, through these healing drugs this person', saying the sick person's name and ailment; afterwards she drank from the dipper and let the two widows drink also.

Other similar 'sacrifices' using wax and candles were prescribed for headaches and external injuries (Kahk 1990: 279–80).

These are not isolated or untypical instances – quite the contrary. During the early modern centuries, as in those before and after, individual men and women throughout Europe could draw on a very wide and versatile repertoire of communally shared practices of this sort (Wilson 2000). But, in addition, there were countless local experts in magic who provided extra help and resources when occasion demanded. In the Netherlands, for example, a region whose professional magicians have been much studied, one of them, Dirck Pieters, was banished from the province of Holland in 1550 for practising as a cunning man and conjuror. A century later, in Kampen, Jannigien Clinckhamers was likewise exiled for expelling ghosts, blessing cattle, and putting charms under thresholds and giving them to sick horses. And another century on, physicians in Amsterdam were complaining about a healer from Germany, Johann Christoph Ludeman, who, despite his university diploma, was still using many of the same 'cunning' techniques in the 1720s (Waardt 1993: 33–41; Waardt 1997: 142–5; Blécourt 1993: 52). In the 1570s and 1580s, the parishioners of the German margravate of Brandenburg-Ansbach-Kulmbach were travelling from a 35 mile radius to the village of Baiergrűn to visit Margaretha Hohenberger, who treated sicknesses, provided abortions, recovered stolen goods and practised general soothsaying and divination. Meanwhile, in Ergersheim in Rothenburg ob der Tauber, the local cunning man Georg Kissling was being punished for using a crystal ball to find stolen goods and herbal protections for animals (Dixon 1996: 179–81; Rowlands 1996: 111–12).

In the Italian city of Modena in 1595, a 60-year-old healer called Antonio Coreggi confessed to local inquisitors that he had treated hernias for half a century without realizing that his special cure for the condition was sinful. It was performed at daybreak, either on the feast of St John the Baptist or on Good Friday. The sufferer had to be passed three times through an opening in a freshly split nut tree to readings from John's Gospel. A fellow healer, Diamente de Bisa, also from Modena, reported that her cure for worms involved the sign of the cross and the saying: 'On Holy Monday, Holy Tuesday, Holy Wednesday, Holy Thursday, Holy Friday, Holy Saturday, Easter Sunday, the worm dies and decays' (O'Neil 1987: 93, 97). And in 1632, in Kõlleste in Estonia, the authorities from Tartu indicted a popular sorcerer called Pudell for using spells and magical objects, including a stick, a coin, rings, and pieces of yarn and moss (Madar 1990: 268).

In England, and in the British Isles generally, cunning men and women were just as plentiful and just as popular. An Elizabethan cunning man from Dorset, John Walsh, was examined and tried in 1566 (as a suspected sorcerer) for a range of magical practices that included finding lost goods and consulting fairies (Thomas 1971: 215, 634; Gibson 2000: 25–32). In North Moreton in Oxfordshire in 1604, the 20-year-old Anne Gunter, seemingly bewitched, was seen by John Wendore of Newbury, 'being a person supposed to be cunning in matters concerning witchcraft', and by another cunning man called Blackwall, and her case was discussed with a third named Palliser. All of them were well known in the area. A doctor summoned to examine her, Roger Bracegirdle, even recommended that her family seek 'some cunning men to do [her] good'. Anne's neighbour, Alice Kirfoote, who was similarly afflicted, received 'a little bag' to hang around her neck and 'a little green vial glass' with liquid in it to drink, both supplied by Goodwife Higgs of Ashampstead, who had a reputation for helping bewitched cattle. 'Few settlements', says James Sharpe, 'could have lain more than five miles from the residence of one of these good witches' (Sharpe 1999: 72, 57–9, 46). On the borders of Sussex and Kent, in the town of Rye around the same time, the widow Anne Bennett and her daughter Anne Taylor were both well known as 'cunning folk' and the daughter attended their neighbour Susan Swapper who was afflicted by spirits in 1607, only to be accused herself (and acquitted) of practising witchcraft (Gregory 1991: 35–8). In 1634, the JPs in Lancashire investigated the activities of one Henry Baggilie, who used charms and spells to heal clients despite becoming ill with the same afflictions himself (Sharpe 1996: 67). Across the Pennines in Yorkshire, assize depositions mention the general services of charmers and healers such as Joan Jurdie (1605), Elizabeth Hodgson of Scarborough (1651) and a 'widow Gransley' (1655) (Sharpe 1992: 13–14). Such individuals even appeared in the imaginative literature of the period, another telling indication of their place in English culture. At the conclusion of George Gifford's fictional yet documentary book, *A Dialogue Concerning Witches and Witchcraftes* (1593), a character meant to capture the essence of local Essex expertise in magic, 'Good Wife R', enters the debate and attempts to confound its main arguments. The dramatist and poet Thomas Heywood even wrote a play called *The Wise-Woman of Hogsden* (1638), in which its central figure describes herself as a fortune-teller and a dealer in 'Physick and Fore-speaking, in Palmistry, and recovering of things lost', as well as a pimp and abortionist (Beier 1987: 29).

Individually identified magicians like these are scattered in great abundance through the ecclesiastical records of early modern Europe. But a whole typology is also evident in the collective terms that contemporaries used to describe them. Magic was a recognized ingredient in the rituals of Italian healers such as the *benandanti* of Friuli, the wandering *pauliani* (who specialized in snakebite cures) and the *ciarlatani,* as well as of those cunning folk known in the kingdom of Naples under the names *janare, magare* and *fattucchiare* (Burke 1987: 209, 213–17; Gentilcore 1998: 22–3). In Hungary, the equivalents of the western European magical practitioners were the *táltos,* men and women who were treasure seekers, fortune-tellers and enemies of witches, as well as healers. But Hungarians also knew the seer (*néző*), the wise man (*tudományos*) and the soothsayer (*javasasszony*) (Dömötör 1980; Klaniczay 1990: 254). French magicians were known as *devins, conjureurs* and *leveurs de sorts,* while in Portugal it was the *saludadores,* men with innate powers, who dominated rural magic (especially the healing of livestock) and the 'sorcerers', usually women, who dealt with the management of love and marriage by divination, often in urban environments. In some Portuguese cities there were even informal networks of sorcerers – 23 of them in Alcácer do Sal and 62 in Évora (Bethencourt 1990: 421–2). In early eighteenth-century Debrecen in Hungary – and no doubt in many other early modern communities – fierce rivalries broke out between the 'wise women' who made up a substantial proportion of those accused of witchcraft in the city (Kristóf, 1991/92: 107–9). In the Netherlands, and in Finland and Iceland, men have been found to predominate among the 'cunning folk'; in Modena, most of those investigated by the Inquisition for magical healing were women.

We can already see from many of the examples given so far what sort of actual techniques made up the magical practices of both private individuals and specialists. To attempt a comprehensive survey of them would be an endless task and not especially enlightening. To some extent – greater, perhaps, than one might imagine in the context of oral transmission – the techniques were uniform. All over Europe, men and women practised divination with scissors and sieves, or books and keys, or by peering into the flat surfaces made by water or mirrors or 'crystals'. They scrutinized the natural fluids of humans and animals, especially urine, they cast lots, they read 'signs' in the heavens and in nature, they consulted with the dead and with spirits, they spoke conjurations over crops or dwellings and they diagnosed illnesses and even cured them by measuring the bodies of the sick. The psychological skills of professional magicians in articulating the fears, suspicions and diagnoses of their clients also seem similar wherever they practised; so too do many of their practical ones. On the other hand, there was seemingly no limit to the words and things deemed to have special powers or to the ingenuity shown in manipulating them for magical gain. In Zwickau in the early sixteenth century a healer applied fried onions and incantations to a patient's head in order to cure him. A peasant from Saint-Dié in Lorraine offered to heal a neighbour's dislocated hip 'by begging manure from nine different stables, filling the peasant's breeches which he had been wearing at the time of the accident with it', and then hanging them up in the church of St Benedic in Brecklange. Jesuit visitors to Untergrombach in the bishopric of Speyer in the later seventeenth century were shocked to discover a traditional cure that involved the sick person saying a sacrilegious prayer and walking naked round the church altar (Karant-Nunn 1987: 201; Delumeau 1977: 163; Forster 1992: 236). Mary O'Neil reports of eight prostitutes tried in Modena in 1593–4 that they 'knew scores of devices to induce passion in another person'. One of them was a love charm calling on St Martha to go

> to that wood where Our Lord Jesus Christ baptised with his twelve Apostles .... Cut three branches of fire and flame and for love of me send them to the heart of N.N. Send them through the veins of the heart, of the head, of the lungs, through the marrow of the bones, the flesh of the legs, with such love that it beats and scourges, so that for my love he should suffer incessantly .... For love of me, take away from him drink, food, sleep, power that he might not go or stay, nor ride nor drive nor walk, nor have relations with any woman, until he should come to me to satisfy all my desire and do all that which I will ask of him. (O'Neil 1987: 102)

In Tallinn in 1526, less glamorously, three people were ordered to be whipped for 'stealing clothes off a hanged man, which they believed would improve their sale of beer' (Madar 1990: 259).

In addition, one can sense that particular professions and particular regions knew their own types of magic. Love magic, for example, was not unnaturally a speciality of prostitutes and courtesans in their attempts to attract and keep their clients and lovers (Ruggiero 1993: 24–56, 88–129). Although 'signing' (using *segnamenti*) was current in many places in Italy and elsewhere, the Modenese Inquisition archives studied by O'Neil reveal a fascinating local form of it in cases of healers' cures for *mal di pediga*. This was the potentially fatal sickness of the missing or 'lifted' footprint, thought to be caused by malefice (itself often in response to suspected theft). The sick person had to be measured, using thread freshly spun by a virgin.

Should one leg turn out to be longer than the other, or if ashes stuck to the sole of the sick person's foot, a 'lifting' of the footprint by magic had occurred. The missing footprint was replaced in the following manner:

> The healer would have the sick person place his foot on some ashes, creating a new footprint. These ashes were then gathered with a silver coin, placed in a piece of new cloth, and taken outside, where the bundle was thrown backwards into a well or running water. In some accounts, the person throwing the bundle was instructed to run away before it hit the water to avoid hearing the sound of the impact. One client who could not travel even managed to have her footprint lowered at a distance; she sent her shoe to the healer, and [?] ashes were sent back to be thrown in the water.

Once a person was cured, he or she then acquired the power and the legitimacy (and the technique, of course) to make the same cure for others (O'Neil 1991/92: 128–9; for similar details of magical practices from the late medieval archives in Lucca, see Meek 2000; for Terra d'Otranto, see Gentilcore 1992: 211–17).

The meaning of magic

The habit of describing all these social phenomena as 'magical' is now virtually universal – and I have obviously conformed to it. But what the label actually designates remains highly elusive, since neither social scientists nor social historians have succeeded in defining it. This is because what magic has signified has varied from age to age and context to context. It is a classic example of a concept whose meaning and application are always a function of local circumstances. The reason for this is that magic has most often been something disapproved of, and 'magical' a term of refusal. This is especially true in the sphere of religion, where magic has invariably been a concept employed either to stigmatize competitor faiths or to proscribe beliefs or behaviour deemed to be irreligious – both these uses being widespread among early modern churchmen. It is in this sense that magic has been the 'other' of Judaeo-Christian religious tradition from biblical times through to the present day. Western science has also had a major part in investing magic with oppositional meanings, in this case between the cogency and rationality of orthodox scientific or medical practice on the one side and the error and irrationality of the magician on the other. Here, magic has mostly been bad or pseudo-science, as defined by the scientific establishment of the day.

We shall see in the last section that this last point has to be qualified in the light of the enthusiastic endorsement of a certain kind of magic – *magia* and natural magic – by the scientists (the 'natural philosophers') of the early modern period *themselves*. But for the time being the point holds – and, certainly, the popular magic we have just been considering has usually been condemned in the name of 'higher' forms of knowledge as popular error (see, for example, in the field of medicine, Joubert 1989). Naturally, modern scholars too have indulged in the same labelling. The early academic history of anthropology, for example, was marked by the adoption of distinctions between magic and religion and between magic and science that were almost entirely stipulative and dismissive of the practices of other cultures. More recently, historians of religion have been charged with the same fault, in their case one of categorizing large swathes of pre-Reformation and early modern lay piety as 'magical', without thought to the condescension that this implies (Davis 1974; Frijhoff 1979: 71–88; Clark 1983; Bossy 1985: viii; Scribner 1993).

In general, then, magic has invariably been thought of in terms of what it is *not,* varying in direct relation to whatever its positive counterpart is taken to be. This is even true of the definition still most often adopted, which continues to distinguish magic from religion; the latter is characterized by 'human dependence on, and deference toward, the divine' and its supernatural power, the former by 'human attempts to appropriate divine power and apply it instrumentally' (Scribner 1993: 477, drawing on Flint 1991: 3). At present, it is probably best to assume that describing an aspect of any culture, past or present, as 'magical' runs the risk of begging serious questions. Indeed, we have come to see magic as a cultural construction, there being nothing in our attitudes to ourselves or to the world that is inherently 'magical'. In the case of Renaissance Europe there is even a suggestion that it fails to designate anything distinctive. Of the world of healing practitioners and their practices, for example, Katherine Park has written that the boundaries between 'medicine', 'magic' and 'religion' 'often did not correspond to modern ones, and in many cases are hardly to be discerned at all' (Park 1998: 132). In these circumstances, the task of the historian becomes that of understanding how such constructions have come about and been utilized and discussed in various sociocultural settings. In this particular essay, they continue to be adopted for the sake of conformity rather than from conviction, and in full awareness of all the pitfalls that have been indicated.

Perhaps the most obvious question begged by the terms 'magic' and 'magical' has to do with the issue of efficacy. All too often in the past it has been assumed that magic is a false belief in the sense that magical techniques are completely incapable of producing the effects they aim at. This, indeed, has been the principal reason for calling them 'magical' in the first place. In religion, they were 'superstitions', in science, falsehoods. In classic anthropology – as well as in the anthropologically influenced history of the 1970s – magic was the use of ineffective techniques to allay the anxiety caused by the absence of effective ones (Thomas 1971: 668).

Yet historians, at least, no longer feel that they have to take up a position of their own on this issue before writing about the history of magic. Instead, they prefer to leave the issue in the hands of those they study. In the case of the early modern centuries, there was in fact a lively debate among contemporaries about the efficacy of what they called magic. This, however, only reinforces the need for neutrality, since to decide now whether magic was efficacious or not is to take sides in the very thing being studied.

The sheer ubiquity of magic alone suggests that those who used it assumed, in principle, that it worked – in this important sense it was not a false belief at all. It was resorted to in all types of situation, by every kind of person and with a regularity that made it endemic. 'No man or woman', wrote the Hessian church visitors, 'begins, undertakes, does, or refrains from doing, desires or hopes for anything without using some special charm, spell, incantation–'. Every action, we recall, had its 'special day, hour, and secret place' (Strauss 1978: 304). Professional specialists in magic were known and could be found, if not in the next house, then in the next street, village or district. 'Their sheer numbers and ubiquitous presence', writes Robin Briggs, 'at once sustained the world view they represented and clogged any official attempt at repression' (Briggs 1996: 174). In recent years, indeed, the historiography of early modern magic has typically been concerned not just with individual specialists but with whole networks of them – not only among the urban sorcerers of Portugal but, for example, in Essex (Macfarlane 1970), in the regions of France (Briggs 1989: 21–31), in Lorraine (Briggs 1996), in the rural parishes of Germany (Dixon 1996: 181–3), and in the province of Holland (Waardt 1991).

The purposes for which magical techniques were adopted do certainly fall into a pattern. They were used typically to find lost or stolen goods, buried treasure, and missing persons, to heal a wide variety of ailments and illnesses in animals as well as humans, to procure or inhibit love and affection and to influence family affairs, to 'divine' or otherwise foretell the future, and to diagnose and counteract witchcraft. But this too hardly suggests a useless or futile resource. These were often matters of vital importance and urgency to those involved and they can hardly have given so much time and energy to magical solutions unless they expected – and, indeed, received – a positive outcome from them. Sheer need drove many 'cunning folk' to offer their services for a small fee or a gift of food but, even so, the sense that they were pressured by a large and demanding clientele is strong. It is not the absence of more effective (and to modern eyes more rational) services that led to magic's popularity but a combination – certainly in some contexts – of the absence of much else and its own effectiveness. Where different levels and types of healing practice *were* available, for instance, magic simply took its place alongside these other versions in an eclectically employed 'hierarchy of resort' (Park 1998: 133). The argument that magic is a substitute for real technology is no longer plausible in its anthropological form, and there seems to be little reason to go on accepting it in its historical form either.

Many magical techniques possessed their own kind of general rationality, quite apart from the intricate rules for performing them individually. In a famous review of Keith Thomas's *Religion and the Decline of Magic*, criticizing him for failing to see this, Hildred Geertz wrote: 'These practices are comprehensible within the framework of a historically particular view of the nature of reality, a culturally unique image of the way in which the universe works, that provides a hidden conceptual foundation for all of the specific diagnoses, prescriptions, and recipes that Thomas describes' (Geertz 1975: 83; *cf.* Thomas 1975). Neither anthropologists nor historians spend as much time as they used to working this rationality out, but Jean Delumeau, for example, has spoken of an underlying animism and a resort to the three laws of contact, similarity and contrast (contagion, sympathy and antipathy in other versions). It is not difficult to see the first of these in the use made of earth collected from a courtesan's doorstep or the dust swept from a chapel floor. The second is just as clearly at work in Alonso González de la Pintada's imitative rite for curing haemorrhoids or in Antonio Coreggi's for treating hernias. It is tempting, again, to think of the efficacy here as symbolic, but, as Robin Briggs has recently remarked, contemporaries must have believed the actions involved 'to have direct physical effects, through the principles of sympathy which permeated their vision of the natural world' (Briggs 1996: 181).

Magic also depended on other principles that evidently made as good sense, such as the idea that the cure for an illness consisted of the inverse of its cause (also found in the more traditionally learned medicine of the period) and the supposed equivalence of healing and harming (to which we shall return). Thus, the successful diagnosis of *mal di pediga* depended on the view that the foot's contact with the ground represented 'a strategically located, magical opening in the body ... through which its vitality was drained', while the successful cure for the condition by 'lowering' of the footprint was simply the opposite of the original 'lifting' (O'Neil 1991/92: 129, 134). Other ingredients in magic's 'ontology' have been said to be a blurring of the natural and supernatural, a resistance to neutrality (in the sense that everything becomes potentially significant), the use of reversals of causality and the organization of time into auspicious or inauspicious moments rather than linear directions (Geertz 1975: 85, following Thomas). Above all, magic rested on the perceived power of words. Those who believed in this power did not necessarily have to think that there was a causal connection between words and their referents; they may simply have been exploiting the expressive capacities of language in a technological context heightened by ritual (Tambiah 1985). Nonetheless, the assumption that words, simply by virtue of being uttered, had a mechanical power at least to assist in the causation or prevention of events seems to have been an intrinsic element of many of the procedures we noted earlier. The most important instrument of supernatural power in early modern Iceland, according to Kirsten Hastrup, was words: 'Words were the main vehicles of magic influence, whether expressed in love-poetry, defamatory prose, or in secret codes' (Hastrup 1990: 387).

In most cases, as the earlier examples also show, the words spoken or written for magical purposes were religious in origin and character – blessings, prayers, Pater Nosters, Ave Marias and so on. Living at a time when religions gave sacred words a kind of agency, the users of them might be forgiven for taking this more literally than was intended. But this raises another vexed question in the history of magic – its relationship to the religious belief-systems that condemned it (Scribner 1984: 61–77). Many of the other things that made up magic – objects, rituals, occasions and places – were also derivations from (or, as Delumeau called them, 'folklorizations' of) religious practice. Lucrezia the Greek's love magic involved a prayer, a blessed candle, an image of a saint, holy bells and holy water, while the charm of the Modenese prostitutes was to be said 'kneeling and fasting for nine mornings with nine Pater Nosters, [and] nine Ave Marias…' (O'Neil 1987: 102). Among the borrowings of religious metaphors in the love magic of Venice was one which gave new meaning to the consecration 'For this is my body' and another that appealed to Christ on the cross: 'I bind and pierce the hands and feet of you N. with my love just as were bound the holy hands and feet of Our Lord Jesus Christ so that you cannot love another person in the world excepting M.' (Ruggiero 1993: 93, 105). The spell-casters of Wiesbaden mixed 'the names of God, the holy Trinity, some special angels, the Virgin Mary, the twelve apostles and the three kings, also with numerous saints, with the wounds of Christ and his seven last words … with gospel verses and certain prayers' (Strauss 1978: 304). In Lower Brittany, saints' statues were whipped, the Lord's Prayer was addressed to the moon and the devil was propitiated as a cereal-god. In Portugal, the *saludadores* mimed Catholic rites of blessing and aspersion and mixed this with popular motifs: 'Their procedure was usually based on the miraculous blessing of water in a bowl with a cross of salt, together with an invocation of the Holy Trinity or, sometimes, of demons; this water was then sprinkled over the "damned livestock" with a branch of spurge-laurel' (Bethencourt 1990: 410). Again, these instances could be multiplied endlessly from the literature. Across Europe, throughout the centuries we are discussing, magic often seems indistinguishable from religion.

The clergymen whose task it was to make the distinction knew exactly where it lay, as we shall see later. At least some of their colleagues, particularly in the lower ranks of the Church, did not, making the cleric who behaved like a wizard or magical healer by no means a rarity at the time (Waardt 1993: 36–8, for a comparison of techniques; *cf.* Briggs 1989: 23; Bethencourt 1990: 409; Gaskill 2000: 56). The very first user of magic we came across, Alonso González de la Pintada, turns out to have been a 'beato' and a lay Franciscan for 40 years (Nalle 1992: 14–15). None of this, however, allows *us* to say where religion ended and magic began, unless we are simply to adopt the definitions of theologians arguing 400 years ago. Hildred Geertz's other main charge against Thomas was that he had imposed a conceptual language of his own on magic that made it less comprehensive, less organized and less coherent than religion and more concerned with utilitarian ends – with 'practical solutions to immediate problems' (Geertz 1975: 72). But it remains the case today that virtually any criterion that we settle upon to separate these two cultural forms – major institutional and financial considerations apart – turns out to yield statements that are equally true of both of them (Scribner 1993).

With so many reservations about the very identity of something called 'magic', it might be thought better to dispense with the term altogether – to regard it, as Geertz did in her exchange with Thomas, as an entity only in the ideological weaponry of the past (Geertz 1975: 88). If, for its users, magic was efficacious, then it can presumably be dissolved without residue into its various practical purposes and be called simply 'healing', 'cultivation', 'household management', 'forecasting' and so on. What then would the addition of the predicate 'magical' – as in 'magical' healing, 'magical' cultivation, etc. – indicate, except our own ignorance of how these practices were thought to work?

> For a person to employ a certain procedure that is conventionally considered by all around him to be the acceptable thing to do in his situation, does not necessarily indicate that he is motivated by an attitude of self-deception and wishful distortion of reality, even though others, contemporaries or historians, may term that procedure 'magical'. (*ibid.* 1975: 82)

If, on the other hand, 'magical' relates not to efficacy in general but to the precise methods and techniques used by magicians – sympathy, antipathy, contagion, and so forth – then what is to separate these from the procedures warranted by any knowledge system?

What might prove a helpful guide in this context is the vocabulary used at the time to describe what we habitually refer to as 'magic'. One of the striking consequences of magic's role as a term of attribution is that it can be quite difficult to find anyone in the past who accepted it as a correct description of what they thought or did, let alone who called themselves a 'magician'. Significantly, perhaps, the labels most generally adopted in the sixteenth and seventeenth centuries to describe what we are discussing were simply 'cunning' or 'knowledge' – a usage first made generally known to modern scholars by Alan Macfarlane (Macfarlane 1970: esp. 115–34). In Iceland, according to Hastrup, the boundary between wisdom and magic was 'totally absent in the category of "knowledge"', while the literal meaning of the category used for witchcraft (*fjölkyngi*) was 'much knowledge' (Hastrup 1990: 387–8). In the 1640s, Jannigien Clinckhamers from Kampen in the Netherlands spoke of her power to charm and bless as 'the art' (Blécourt 1993: 52). Other contemporaries caught up in investigations of their 'magic' talked (or at least were reported to have talked) of simply having 'skill'. Of course, they may just have been evading the more dangerous word or simply dressing up their actions as a kind of mysterious speciality. Nevertheless, what seems to have been implied here was a more than usually difficult, or powerful or effective way of doing things, based on special wisdom and technique, but not one that was necessarily different in kind from the way they were usually done.

It is important not to exaggerate the case for the coherence of popular magic, to rationalize it excessively, or otherwise overcompensate for its poor reputation hitherto. One of the foremost current scholars of the subject, Robin Briggs, prefers to describe it as 'a flexible and polymorphous vision of the world, whose internal logic was often rickety or non-existent'. Everyday events were assumed to have many possible meanings and the world was full of significance and power for those who could understand and use it. But to the extent that this meant 'super- enchantment', it was, he adds, 'quite impossible as a permanent context for ordinary life' (Briggs 2001: 176). Yet flexibility was also a marked feature of those contemporary beliefs and practices with which magic most closely competed – notably those of religion and medicine. The health strategies of the pre-modern world were particularly marked by improvisation and choice. And magical practices do seem to have enjoyed an integral place in the culture of fortune and misfortune that made up so much of popular life at this time. It was, it seems, pluralism and eclecticism that marked people's attitudes to the vagaries of existence and how to react to them, and magic was obviously well suited to this way of seeing things (on magic and medical pluralism in particular, see Park 1998; Gentilcore 1998).

Maleficium and magic

One of the key reasons for the popularity of magical practices was that they were deployed to detect and counteract the harmful effects of witchcraft. Only the curing of illnesses occupied as important a place in the tasks for which magic was singled out – and, of course, many of these were attributed to *maleficium* anyway. Indeed, so intimate was the relationship between protective (or remedial) magic and malevolent witchcraft that historians have come to see them more and more as the two inseparable halves of the world of popular culture in this period. Gábor Klaniczay remarks that the 'two poles of the popular magical universe – the beneficial [in which Klaniczay includes religion] and the harmful, or the positive and the negative – have in fact always developed in relation to each other.' According to Mary O'Neil too, the merit of studying counter-witchcraft (and the counter witch) is that it puts witchcraft back into its original context, where it comprised 'only one half of a more elaborate system of beliefs'. And, more recently, Robin Briggs has spoken of the 'symbiosis' of witches and witch doctors, two categories that always accompanied each other and were always liable to be reversed (Klaniczay 1990: 240–1; O'Neil 1991/92: 123, *cf.* 137, 139; Briggs 1996: 171; *cf.* O'Neil, 1987: 104).

There was, moreover, a precise sense in which magical healing and maleficent harming were linked in the popular mind – they were equivalents. It was assumed as a matter of course that those with the special power to heal by magic must know how to harm by the same means. To reverse the effects of witchcraft was to understand how it worked in the first place. The idea crops up in many witchcraft trials, where defendants charged with *maleficium* often returned the plea allegedly made by Ursley Kempe to Grace Thurlowe in the Essex village of St Osyth sometime before 1582: that 'though shee coulde unwitche shee coulde not witche' (Gibson 2000: 78). Nor was this association made only by the unlettered; we find it even among Lutheran church visitors and inquisitors of the Holy Office. The former reported indiscriminately of the people of Wiesbaden that their 'signs' and 'spells' were employed 'to inflict harm or do good to men, women, animals, and crops, to make things better or worse, to bring good or bad luck on themselves and their fellow creatures' (Strauss 1978: 304). In Modena in 1601, an inquisitor told a healer of *mal di pediga,* who had presumably protested her innocence of witchcraft in much the same terms as Kempe, that her statement lacked 'verisimilitude, for those who know how to lower one [i.e. a footprint], also know how to lift one'. In a later example from 1624, Maria Priora was similarly warned 'to beware of lies because it is the sad and common rule among witches "that who knows how to heal, knows also how to harm"' (O'Neil 1991/92: 131, *cf.* 126–8, 134).

If the arts of healing and harming were themselves equivalent, the principle of transference likewise encouraged the idea that no bewitchment was removed without the *maleficium* being shifted elsewhere. Furthermore, those healers whose magical remedies for illness failed to bring relief or made things worse were naturally likely to be suspected of witchcraft. In Modena, where accusations of *maleficium* were invariably against healers, the pressure to see things this way came mostly from client-witnesses who thereby hoped to turn cases almost into suits for malpractice (O'Neil 1987: 95, 97). The Italian inquisitors did not share this priority, but in the Lorraine archives Robin Briggs has discovered several examples of 'witch doctors' who ended up at the stake for this reason (Briggs 1996: 171; Briggs 2001). In general, historians have found it impossible to agree over the question of how many of the accused in witchcraft cases had previously practised as 'cunning folk' of one kind or another in their communities. But the correlation is sufficiently strong to suggest that those who practised 'cunning' ran a definite risk in this respect, even if they were never remotely in a majority. What can be agreed upon, given the cultural values current among the general population of the time, is that there was an ambiguity intrinsic to what they did (Blécourt 1994: 288–98, for the best discussion).

Such cultural values have recently become much more central to the historiography of witchcraft than they once were. As long as prosecutions were deemed to be inspired by government institutions or churches, the views of the general population were not thought to matter. But as William Monter emphasized at the outset, study after study has now shown that it was pressure from the communities to which alleged witches belonged that lay behind a great deal of 'witch-hunting', with the institutions of central government, the higher ranks and appellate courts of the judiciary and the church courts – especially the Inquisition – usually acting far more cautiously. Summarizing the work of historians such as Walter Rummel, Eva Labouvie and Rainer Walz, Wolfgang Behringer has written:

> The major shift in German witchcraft studies in recent years has been the recognition of a massive desire for persecution stemming from the general population. One apparent peculiarity of Central Europe is the role of communities, the self-appointed protagonists of witchcraft persecutions who placed their superiors under massive pressure to conduct them. (Behringer 1996: 88–9)

Remarkable instances of this have been discovered in the village committees, notably in the region around Trier, elected by communities to organize the detection and persecution of witches (Briggs 1996: 340–51; Monter). Further evidence of pressure 'from below' of this sort is offered by the findings of Al Soman concerning local justice in the regions of France (Soman 1992). Clearly, what seems to have mattered in the initial stages of a witchcraft case was, above all, the personal conviction on the part of victims that *maleficium* was something very real and that they were genuinely afflicted by it. This applied equally throughout the many thousands of episodes that never came to trial at all, as well as to those which carried on generating both accusations and protective counter-measures after the decriminalization of witchcraft altogether. In the Netherlands, for example, where the last execution took place in 1608, the resort to specialists in counter-witchcraft and the defamation suits brought by those still popularly accused of the crime bear witness to the long continuance of the belief in *maleficium* and its practitioners. The case notes of the English astrological physician Richard Napier likewise reveal sincerely expressed accusations of bewitchment on the part of hundreds of his patients (Sawyer 1988/89).

What witchcraft *meant* to most ordinary people, after all, was that it caused misfortune, not that it led to devil-worship. What was important was the harm it could do to themselves, their livelihoods and their families and communities. Witches disrupted the weather, wasted crops, ruined the production of beer and butter and, above all, brought sickness and death. This was not usually traced to demonic agency – except perhaps in the case of the English belief in witches' 'familiars' – nor was the witch automatically thought of as a servant of Satan. The detailed ethnography of these convictions, inspired originally by *Religion and the Decline of Magic,* is still being worked out. While malevolence itself and the often poisonous social rivalries that accompanied it were hardly rarities in early modern communities, to identify it as the inspiration for *witchcraft* required a particular set of cultural traits. While by no means unique to this period of European history, these traits were manifested in terms of witchcraft's association with particular individuals, occasions and misfortunes. However, establishing just *which* individuals, occasions and misfortunes were most likely to be selected is proving to be more and more difficult, as historians break down the stereotypical expectations about witchcraft (both among contemporaries and among modern scholars) and substitute a picture that is marked by the 'complexities, contingencies and ambiguities' of everyday experience (Gaskill 2000: 50). The process by which a person became a witch was itself long and complex, involving many intricate judgements about behaviour and reputation over a period of time. In the past, the sorts of interpersonal conflicts that occasioned accusations were found by anthropological historians to be concerned with indigence and the exercise of charity (Thomas 1971: 535–69; Macfarlane 1970: 147–207). More recently, feminist historians and historians of gender have linked them to the management of the household and the anxieties of motherhood (Roper 1994: 199–248; Purkiss 1995; Willis 1995: 27–81). The latest analysis of the English cases speaks more broadly of 'competition for power and resources' (Gaskill 2000: 55).

The means allegedly used by witches for harming their neighbours were likewise intelligible in terms of popular beliefs about such things as the maleficent powers of language and of bodily gestures, notably touching and looking (Thomas 1971: 435–49; Bethencourt 1990: 414–15). Certain kinds of misfortunes, and particularly certain kinds of illnesses, were more likely to be attributed to witchcraft than others. If a sickness was not immediately recognized or otherwise thought to be 'unnatural', if it was slow and lingering and failed to respond to treatment, if it occurred suddenly or violently in a previously healthy person, then *maleficium* was its likely cause (Briggs 1989: 29–31). Napier's patients, for example, complained typically of being 'strangely or sorely afflicted' by disturbances of the mind, fits, swoonings, tremblings and convulsions (especially in children), and lameness, pining and consuming (Sawyer 1988/89: 468–9). Provided such ailments coincided with an 'episode' involving a neighbour thought to be a witch and the resulting suspicions were confirmed by (as Briggs 1996: 171 has termed them) those 'key figures in the whole nexus of belief and practice' – the cunning folk – then an accusation of witchcraft was likely to make sense.

These features of the experience of witchcraft – in thought and practice alike – were subject to an infinite number of variations across the expanses of Europe. Yet a fundamental constant can still be asserted: whatever we may think about the social realities behind these episodes, discovered by historians looking 'through' them to features that contemporaries themselves may not have grasped, their ingredients took the form they did as the consequence of the consciously shared assumptions and expectations that circulated in the cultures of the time. As far as illness is concerned, it has been said that accusations of witchcraft were 'ineluctably connected to the purposeful action and behaviour of patients who were actively seeking care for their afflictions' (Sawyer 1988/89: 466). We may talk here of a 'popular mentality' of witchcraft, or speak of 'cultures of misfortune'. What we cannot any longer say is that the accusations were made out of ignorance – ignorance of the real causes of disease, or of bad weather, or of poverty or of poor human relationships. On the contrary, the world of witchcraft accusations was a world of *knowledge* – indeed, a world rich in the particular forms of knowledge that allowed diagnosis, identification of those responsible and therapy all to take place, as they undoubtedly did, without any form of legal prosecution whatsoever.

Religious reformation and popular magic

Unfortunately, the wardens of ordinary people's culture at the time – the clergy – did not agree. For them these were indeed forms of ignorance. They were lamentable displays of the lack of real religion and faith in God. Maria Priora, the Modenese healer, was told by her inquisitors that her skill had to involve a demonic pact, 'because ashes or flour do not of themselves have the power to heal the sick, especially those *in extremis*'. If, according to their own testimony, her clients were healed nevertheless, either God or the devil must have intervened, and 'since God holds superstitions in abomination, it is necessary to affirm that it was done by the power of the devil'. Antonio Coreggi was dealt with in the same terms as an apostate 'from God to the devil' for misappropriating holy words and holy days for 'superstitious' purposes – that is, purposes without efficacy (O'Neil 1991/92: 132; O'Neil 1987: 93–4). Such cases, and such opinions, multiplied in thousands of similar instances, represent, at grassroots level, the impact on popular magic of the most fundamental and most sustained of all the changes experienced in the early modern centuries – those wrought by religious reformation. For while 'Reformation' has long been known as a far-reaching doctrinal, liturgical and ecclesiastical phenomenon, those involved also saw it as the refashioning of other equally fundamental aspects of human piety to do with day-to-day conduct and moral discipline. These embraced such things as sexual behaviour and the regulation of families, the proper use of language and speech codes, sabbath observance, and all the other matters that came under the heading of 'manners'. But they also included lay attitudes to fortune and misfortune, since securing the one and avoiding the other, and dealing with misfortunes when they came, raised issues that went to the heart of contemporary spirituality. Popular attitudes to magic and *maleficium* thus entered into Reformation debate from the outset as an urgent clerical priority. They became caught up in the process already described by William Monter (Part 1, above) whereby confessional rivalry turned the major European faiths into competing vehicles for the expression of religious zeal.

In essence, what reformers did with these matters was to spiritualize them – internalizing all their traditional ingredients until they became spiritual problems. For both Protestant and Catholic clerics, the real significance of witchcraft, as of all misfortunes, was not the immediate, this-worldly harm that it brought but the way the victim was give an opportunity for introspection and spiritual improvement. Misfortunes were a test or a punishment, sent by God, and the proper response to them was to reflect patiently on faith and sin, move on to repentance and then seek divine, clerical and eventually other approved forms of help. To think in terms of *maleficium* and to blame witches was therefore to miss the point. An affliction by witchcraft was not really a case of misfortune at all; it was a case of conscience – and, indeed, witchcraft turns out to be included in a great many early modern discussions and collections of 'cases of conscience'.

Popular *counter*-witchcraft, moreover, was itself superstitious and, so, idolatrous. People who resorted to magic were not merely ignoring the spiritual significance of fortune and misfortune, they were themselves appealing – like Maria Priora and Antonio Coreggi – to the devil. It is important to realize that this entire argument was built – as I indicated earlier – on a criterion of natural efficacy. Early modern clerics were being utterly naturalistic in this respect – given that their naturalisms were not ours. In the cultural milieu they inhabited, magic was specious in the sense that it attributed to persons, or places, or times or things causal properties that had no existence in nature (as well as no warrant in orthodox religious practice) and could therefore have no natural effects. If natural effects did nevertheless occur, then – as Maria and Antonio were told – it was the devil who had stepped in to bring them about. A demonic pact that was at least implicit was necessarily involved. As we shall see in a moment, magic was in this sense both 'superstitious', which was the term for inefficacy in this context, and also idolatrous, which meant an appeal to a false God. In love magic, in addition, the theological objection (in Italy, for example) was to the coercing of the victim to commit sin by subverting his or her free will. Many churchmen therefore came to think that what was done by magic – ostensibly a beneficial practice – to avoid or respond to misfortune, and especially to *maleficium,* had much more serious implications than maleficent witchcraft itself. The fact (as we saw earlier) that so many magical practices involved the use – or rather, misuse – of orthodox religious language and practice only served to make it more hateful. For all these reasons, nothing less than the general spiritual welfare of the laity seemed to be at stake in its widespread adoption.

These clerical arguments and opinions can be traced and illustrated in many forms and idioms of Reformation literature (Clark 1997: 445–525; Delumeau 1974). Churchmen of both the major faiths published sermons and treatises on the proper response to witchcraft that placed equal emphasis on its providential purpose, its key role in the economy of faith, sin and redemption and the duty of Christians to act like Job when faced by *maleficium.* Job's attitude to tribulation was so crucial to the argument that the Book of Job may be regarded as its spiritual cornerstone. The German Lutheran Johann Brenz preached in this manner in 1539 in a well-known sermon on hailstorms (Midelfort, 1974: 213–19) and so too did other pastors in later sermon-series on witchcraft – for example, Joachim Zehner in Thuringia, Daniel Schaller in Brandenburg and Hermann Samson in Riga. The Geneva pastor Lambert Daneau said typically that it was the duty of the bewitched to 'patiently abyde and looke for ye helpe of God, and depende onely upon his providence' (Daneau, 1575: sig. Lii^r). English Calvinists like William Perkins and George Gifford likewise devoted whole books to replacing popular views about the sources of misfortune with arguments that gave witches the least significant role, the devil a more important one and God the only one that really mattered (Macfarlane 1977: 140–55).

Among the Catholic providentialists who shared this aim with their Protestant opponents – sharing also an enthusiasm for St Augustine in the process – were the nominalist Martin Plantsch, the Freiburg theologian Jodochus Lorichius and the suffragan bishop of Bamberg Friedrich Förner (Oberman 1981: 158–83; Midelfort 1972: 60–1; Clark 1997: 453–4). It seems that in this respect the two competing religions had exactly comparable evangelistic aims.

The same is true of their reactions to popular magic itself – to the sorts of things we began this chapter by considering. If Job was one biblical model to be commonly deployed against ordinary notions of misfortune, King Saul – for resorting to the 'witch' of Endor (a pythonness or Old Testament cunning woman) – was another. The perception of an unbridgeable gulf between *what they saw as* religion and magic came to dominate the sensibilities of churchmen and their evangelical efforts. Indeed, their hostility to the malevolent, devil-worshipping witch of the classical stereotype often seems to have been quite overshadowed by their hatred of her benevolent counterparts – the professional magicians and 'cunning folk' – towards whom greater severity was often shown (for examples of this from Germany, Denmark and Hungary, see Rowlands 1996; Johansen 1991/ 92; Kristóf 1991/92). This, of course, is because these too were regarded as witches, and of a more insidious and dangerous kind. Over and over again in the literature we find the term 'witch' being applied to *anyone* who practised the 'cunning' arts, whether as private individual or professional expert. Gifford, for example, explained that the conjuror, the enchanter, the sorcerer and the diviner were all 'compassed' by it. His *A Dialogue Concerning Witches and Witchcraftes* was largely taken up with the role in Essex villages of what he revealingly called the 'other sort of Witches, whome the people call cunning men and wise women' – that is, local experts in healing, divination, theft-detection and counter witchcraft. His fellow Englishman William Perkins was even more explicit; 'by Witches', he wrote, 'we understand not those onely which kill and torment: but all Diviners, Charmers, Juglers, all Wizzards, commonly called wise men and wise women … and in the same number we reckon all good Witches, which doe no hurt, but good, which doe not spoile and destroy, but save and deliver' (Gifford 1587: sig. Bii^r; Gifford 1593: sig. A3^r; Perkins 1610: 255). Such sentiments must have been shared in the Calvinist Low Countries, where cunning men and women continued to be targets of clerical disapproval long after the cessation of trials for malevolent witchcraft (Gijswijt-Hofstra 1989; Blécourt 1993: 49–55).

This means that 'witchcraft' turns out to have been an interest of many reformers not usually thought of as 'demonologists', Luther and Calvin among them (Haustein 1990; Jensen 1975), and in many countries, like Wales and Portugal, not normally associated with the diabolical witchcraft of the sabbat or where it was treated with scepticism. Quite simply, reformers saw witchcraft and demonism in many other contexts than those we normally associate with the terms, notably among the traditional resources favoured by ordinary people in need. Instead of Exodus 22:18 ('Thou shalt not suffer a witch to live'), or perhaps in addition to it, they turned to Deuteronomy 18:10–11 ('There shall not be found among you any one that maketh his son or his daughter to pass through the fire, or that useth divination, or an observer of times, or an enchanter, or a witch, Or a charmer, or a consulter with familiar spirits, or a wizard, or a necromancer'). This again can be illustrated from treatises denouncing magic by Lutheran clergymen and theologians such as Conrad Platz of Biberach in Württemberg, Bernhard Albrecht of Augsburg and Niels Hemmingsen of Copenhagen, or from the Calvinist demonology of English ministers such as Henry Holland and Richard Bernard. The Catholic Reformation's contribution to the anti-magical polemic was enormous. By 1679, when the

Jansenist abbé Jean-Baptiste Thiers started to publish his *Traité des Superstitions (Treatise on Superstitions),* he was able to list countless official denunciations of divining, astrology, soothsaying and magical healing by the central and regional institutions of the Church all over Europe. Catholic casuistry found ample space for these sins and there were many individual monographs on the subject, for example by the Spaniards Martín de Arles and Pedro Ciruelo and the Netherlanders Jacob van Hoogstraten and Johannes David. Pierre Massé's *De L'Imposture et tromperie des diables (On the Trickery and Deceit of Devils)* (1579) was an extended discussion of the *devins* and astrologers, the wearers of amulets and the interpreters of dreams who (in his view) seemed to be as popular in sixteenth-century France as in pagan times. Ciruelo spoke for all these, and many other authors, when he wrote that the folk healers of Spain were 'enchanters' (*ensalmos*) who destroyed the souls of those they cured even while they removed their bodily afflictions: 'Since this is true, any man or woman who seeks a cure through spells tacitly accepts a return to health with the aid of the devil and thus makes a pact of friendship with the enemy of God and man' (Ciruelo 1977: 208).

Two other features of this cross-party campaign indicate its extent and its seriousness. One is the way in which popular magic was classed as a 'superstition', a word that implies trivialization in our language but was far more ominous at the time. A 'superstition' could be many things in early modern theology, including an exaggerated, superfluous or otherwise incorrect devotion, but when applied to magic it meant natural inefficacy – the appeal to cause and effect relationships that were spurious in nature. As we have already seen, it was this inefficacy in magic that made it demonic; an appeal to magical causation was always necessarily an appeal to demonic causation as well, since it was only the devil who made magic actually work. Gregorius de Valentia, author of a set of *Commentariorum Theologicorum (Theological Commentaries)* published at Ingolstadt in 1591–7, wrote that an implicit demonic pact occurred 'whenever anyone employs, as capable of effecting something, such means as are in the truth of the matter empty and useless' (Valentia 1591/97: iii: col. 1985). This made magic a kind of witchcraft (hence 'white' witchcraft) but it also made it a form of idolatry, one of the major categories of superstition, and allowed the classifying of many of its practices as either *divinatio/divination* or *vana observantia / vain practice,* idolatry's two theological subdivisions. But superstition, we should always remember, was the reformers' main target where the laity was concerned – it was the most serious of religious transgressions, religion's 'opposite' – and endlessly debated and discussed throughout the dogmatics and casuistry of the Protestant and Catholic Reformations. Magic's assimilation to it thus meant the rejection of whole areas of popular life and thought as fundamentally illicit. By means of the notion of an implicit pact, an extraordinarily wide application of demonism to lay culture occurred. Given this, one is almost surprised by how little witch-hunting there was in Reformation Europe, not how much.

What there was may well be partly attributed – at least as far as its religious significance is concerned – to a second feature of the reformers' campaign against magic. This is their classification of magic as a sin against the First Commandment. Again, this recurs throughout the literature of the two great Reformations but it is particularly noticeable in the catechisms and guides to using them (and to confessing and hearing confessions) that multiplied in Europe in the period. Examples can be found in the Decalogue writings of Luther himself and the Marburg Lutheran Andreas Gerhard, in the Heidelberg catechism of 1563, in the highly popular confessors' manual by the French Franciscan Jean Benedicti, the *Somme des pechez (A Summation of Sins)* (1584) and in the individual catechisms written by English Calvinists like Alexander Nowell and John Mayer and continental Catholics like Peter Canisius and Robert Bellarmine. The growing dominance of the Decalogue in the 'moral system' of western Europe in this period has been argued by John Bossy (Bossy 1988), who stresses that, once the obligation to worship God correctly was put at the summit of Christian ethics, and idolatry was made a prime offence, witchcraft became a far more serious matter than it had been when still subsumed under one or other of the Deadly Sins. But Reformation catechisms and Decalogue treatises were not directed at witches who flew to sabbats and worshipped the devil in a ritualized antireligion. From Luther's *A Short Exposition of the Decalogue* onwards, the witchcraft, magic and superstition that occur in them were the sorts that were supposed to lie covertly in the way ordinary people regulated their lives – in their use of charms and talismans, in their resort to healers, blessers, diviners and exorcists in sickness or loss, in their appeals to the treasure seekers and procurers of love.

In these ways and by these means, then, the patterns of thought and behaviour we started out with – calling them 'magic' out of habit, rather than conviction – became one of the major cultural battlegrounds of the early modern period. 'Magic', labelled and defined by clerics as spurious and irreligious, was at the heart of what many have seen as the most concerted attempt there has ever been to standardize the lives and ideas of ordinary Europeans – and by no means just the uneducated or unlettered among them. In texts disseminated on a gigantic scale, written by some of the leading reformers of the time, magic and religion were redefined in confrontation and opposition, as belonging to incompatible belief structures. Whether they did indeed belong to such different belief structures – or whether popular magic was rejected simply as a version of religion that clerics could not control – are different issues which this chapter has tried to leave open for debate.

It is not clear, in any case, that practice followed suit – that clerics successfully prosecuted their moral campaign in the church courts or in the consciences of individuals. Certainly, most of what we know about the magic we began with arises from the reports of hostile clerical witnesses or investigations; the Inquisition, in particular, became far more concerned with magic and superstition towards the last third of the sixteenth century. But even if it proved to be impractical and ineffective, the campaign succeeded in reaffirming one of the abiding distinctions on which European modernity and its sense of its origins have been built.

Demonology

The literature of witchcraft

Alongside the legal prosecutions described earlier, Europe witnessed an equivalent upsurge of intellectual interest in witchcraft. As witches were being questioned in hundreds of courtrooms, so their crimes were being interrogated in as many texts. It is as if the trial took place of theories about witchcraft, as well as of those actually accused of it. The result was a literature of witchcraft – a demonology – spanning the fifteenth to eighteenth centuries, in which educated contemporaries explored and debated the complexities of the subject and its implications for their lives and culture. From the Council of Basel to the publication of the *Encyclopédie,* theologians and clerics, philosophers and moralists, lawyers and physicians argued about how to come to terms with it. Here, then, lies a further opportunity to consider the history of witchcraft and magic as a matter of beliefs.

The important role of demonology in early Christian and medieval theological and ecclesiastical thought is clear. Indeed, one of the striking things about reading the texts from the early modern era is realizing how dependent they were on concepts of the devil elaborated by Church Fathers such as Augustine and philosopher-theologians such as Thomas Aquinas. Nevertheless, as Edward Peters also shows, it is possible to date the first textual accounts of witchcraft as a devil-worshipping cult with remarkable precision to the 1430s. In that decade a series of five texts, recently brought together in a new Latin–French edition by Martine Ostorero and her colleagues at the University of Lausanne, described the elemental features that came to dominate representations of the cult. Witches were now associated with ritual dedication to Satan, the practice of infanticide and anthropophagy, the aim of destroying Christian society and attendance at their notorious assemblies or 'sabbats' (Ostorero *et al.* 1999; Peters 2001: 231–3). Single works on demonology and witchcraft multiplied from this point onwards, with titles like *Lamiarum sive Striarum Opusculum (A Brief Work on Lamia or Witches), Flagellum Maleficorum (The Lash Against Those Who Commit Maleficia),* and *Quaestio de Strigis (An Investigation of Witches)* – titles which in themselves indicate the development of a genre. A good example of this emerging pattern and of the typical questions that were addressed is *Tractatus de Pythonicis Mulieribus (Treatise Concerning Women Who Prophesy),* published in 1489 by Ulrich Molitor, a legal professor at Constance. The work takes the form of an imaginary conversation between the man who commissioned it, Archduke Sigismund of Austria, Molitor himself and a magistrate of Constance, Conrad Schatz. The topics they discuss rapidly became standard in early modern demonology: Do witches have powers over the weather? Can they cause diseases and sexual impotence? Can they transform others or be transformed themselves into animals? Are they physically transported to their sabbats and are these real events? How do demons assume human shape and act as incubi? Can procreation take place between demons and witches? Can demons and witches predict the future? (Lea 1939/1957: 348–53; Maxwell-Stuart 2001: 32–41). Apart from the question of the sabbat, these were the sorts of issues that dominated what has come to be seen as the summary work of this period, *Malleus Maleficarum (Hammer of Witches),* a modern perspective produced in part by the tendency of modern commentators to read this text and little else. Certainly its authors had already encountered opposition to their views and jurisdiction when attempting to put both into practice, and the work itself was also much less immediately influential than has often been supposed.

The fact that Molitor cast his treatise in the form of a *debate* is particularly significant. So, too, is the asking of questions deemed to be answerable in contradictory ways (although this was, in fact, a habit of scholastic discourse). From the very outset, one gets the overwhelming impression that witchcraft was regarded as a controversial and difficult topic, on which many reservations and doubts might be expressed. Indeed, to say simply that early modern intellectuals *believed* in it is to miss the way in which they invariably struggled to come to terms with it. Those who did, on the whole, accept its reality always knew that there were serious objections that had to be overcome. Central to this first phase of the literature, for example, were many attempts to interpret the ninth-century capitulary known as the canon *Episcopi* which had stated,

that some wicked women, perverted by the Devil, seduced by illusions and phantasms of demons, believe and profess themselves, in the hours of the night, to ride upon certain beasts with Diana, the goddess of pagans, and an innumerable multitude of women, and in the silence of the dead of night to traverse great spaces of earth, and to obey her commands as of their mistress, and to be summoned to her service on certain nights. (Peters 1978: 73; Peters 2001: 201–2)

The experience was in fact imposed on their minds, said the canon, by 'the malignant spirit' who transformed himself into the 'species and similitudes' of various people and exhibited other delusory things to them while they were asleep.

Discussions of the canon *Episcopi,* focusing on the nocturnal flight (or 'transvection') of witches to their sabbats, are common in this first phase of early modern demonology and seem almost to have dominated it. If the canon applied to the new fifteenth-century witches as much as to earlier ones, it made their crimes illusory; but if the latest sect was unlike the previous ones, then the text could be disregarded. Questions like these were frequently asked in the period between Johannes Nider's *Formicarius (The Antheap),* dating from around 1437 and Bernard of Como's *Tractatus de Strigibus (Treatise on Witches),* written around 1510. The Franciscan Samuel de Cassini and the Dominican Vincente Dodo clashed over the canon's implications in the first decade of the sixteenth century, and another cycle to the debate occurred in the 1520s between Paolo Grillando (*Tractatus de Sortilegiis (Treatise of Witchcrafts),* written *c.* 1525, published in 1536), who argued that sabbats and sabbat attendance were real and not the product of 'illusion in dreams', and Gianfrancesco Ponzinibio (*Tractatus de Lamiis (Treatise of Witches)),* who took the opposite view (Lea 1939/ 1957: 260–5, 366–7, 367, 370–3, 395–412, 377–82; for de Cassini and Dodo, see also Max 1993).

From the 1560s onwards, the literature of witchcraft may be said to have entered a fresh phase, marked by two developments. On the one hand, scepticism regarding the reality of the crime became even more systematic. To the reservations based on the canon *Episcopi,* which focused on the possibility of wholesale self or demonic delusion, the early and mid-sixteenth century added various forms of more general doubt regarding witchcraft. Considerable philosophical damage was inflicted (at least in theory) on the whole principle of demonic agency by a demon-free treatment of the power of incantations by the Padua-trained, purist Aristotelian thinker, Pietro Pomponazzi, in his *De Naturalium Effectuum Causis, sive de Incantationibus (On the Causes of Natural Effects, Or of Incantations),* which first appeared in 1520. This was a form of naturalism that later had a powerful appeal to the English witchcraft sceptic Reginald Scot. Another Italian, the lawyer Andrea Alciati, managed to achieve a Europe-wide reputation as a witchcraft sceptic as a result of just one memorable sentence reported in his *Parergon Juris (A Law Supplement)* (1538). Asked by an inquisitor for an opinion regarding the burning of witches in the Italian Alps, he had answered that they ought to be purged not with fire but with hellebore – the treatment for diseases of the mind (Lea 1939/1957: 374–5). Even inquisitors themselves could express the most serious doubts on the subject, as revealed by a letter issued in 1538 by the Inquisition in Madrid suggesting that not everything in the *Malleus Maleficarum* should be accepted as true (Henningsen 1980: 347). Above all, perhaps, there were the general cautions regarding occultism and 'superstition' and the punishment of heretics that one associates with the name of Erasmus and with Erasmians across Europe. Later in the century these were to be powerfully supplemented by a revival of interest in ancient philosophical scepticism among European intellectuals. Under its influence, Montaigne denounced the credulity of witchcraft believers in his 1588 essay *Des Boîteux (Of*

Cripples), and the Spanish humanist Pedro de Valencia argued that witchcraft was a crime that it was impossible either to prove or disprove (for Montaigne, see Kors and Peters 2001: 402–6; for de Valencia, see Henningsen 1980: 6–9).

Nevertheless, it was with the publication of the first version of Johann Weyer's *De Praestigiis Daemonum (On the Tricks of Devils)* in 1563 (it was considerably expanded in later versions) that early modern scepticism about witchcraft found its first major voice. Weyer was the court physician to the Duke of Cleve-Mark, Jülich and Berg between about 1550 and 1578 and he worked in a political environment whose culture was thoroughly Erasmian. He also cited Erasmus extensively in attacking the prosecution of witches (Margolin 1974; Béné 1979). Essentially, Weyer explained witchcraft away in accordance with a medicine of gender. While admitting that men (*magi infames*) could deliberately and rationally co-operate with devils to perform feats of magic (not necessarily real ones), he insisted that every case in which *women* claimed or were accused of the same thing should be rejected as legally invalid. The women themselves were mad, senile or ill and thus a prey to wholesale demonic delusion, to which Weyer attributed both the witches' pact and their sabbats. As for the 'bewitched', they were afflicted by illnesses that were either purely natural or caused by demons using natural causes. To prosecute in these circumstances was a travesty of justice, since the defendants lacked 'the rational spirit required for "offending" ' (Weyer 1991: 572). Instead, confessing 'witches' should be offered spiritual counselling and medical treatment. Weyer had, in effect, introduced the insanity defence into cases of witchcraft, in so doing 'fundamentally altering the terms of legal discourse' (Midelfort 1999: 196, see also 196–213; Clark 1997: 198–203; extracts from Weyer in Kors and Peters 2001: 280–9).

Weyer's audacious attempt to exempt all except poisoners from the charge of witchcraft was built on the physical powers of demons and (what he saw as) the physical weaknesses of women – to this extent he was a traditional demonologist (and misogynist). Much later in the debate, it was said that he had tried 'to load the Divell as much as he [could], his shoulders being more able to bear it, and so to ease the Haggs' (More 1653: 133). Twenty years after Weyer, a member of the Kentish farming gentry, Reginald Scot, took witchcraft scepticism that much further by picking up on Pomponazzi's arguments and giving demons no agency whatsoever in the physical world. In a 'Discourse on Divels' added to his *The Discoverie of Witchcraft* (1584) he assigned them a purely non-corporeal status, making physical collusion with human beings – men or women – an impossibility. With perhaps understandable lack of clarity, Scot spoke of demonic spirits only as 'ordeined to a spirituall proportion', the exact nature of which was unknown. This pseudo-Sadduceeism left him free to explain away all the phenomena associated with witchcraft in non-demonic terms. 'Witches' were either innocent victims of ignorance and legal barbarity or they were deluded by their own illnesses and senility, by their imaginations or by their Catholicism. A great deal of witchcraft was no more than 'prestigious juggling', by which Scot meant the creation of optical or other illusions by human trickery, and the rest was attributable to strange but ultimately natural causes. The only people who took it seriously were 'children, fools, melancholic persons [and] papists' (Scot 1584: 472; on Scot, see Anglo 1977b; West *c.* 1984; Estes 1983; and extracts in Kors and Peters 2001: 394–401).

The arguments of Weyer and Scot systematized the grounds for *not* believing in witchcraft that had been in existence from the beginning. But the second development that marked the literature of witchcraft after the 1560s was the publication, and republication, of a far greater number of texts asserting the general reality of the crime and the need to eradicate it from European society. These claims were still not always made uncritically, devoid of all qualification or discrimination. On the contrary, most authors opted for a middle way between credulity and scepticism – between accepting too much and accepting too little. They were thus usually as ready to question as to affirm and knew the dangers of misattributing phenomena when trying to assign them to natural, preternatural or supernatural causes. Most authors continued to disavow aspects of witchcraft that contravened either theological or natural philosophical propriety, like the supposed metamorphosis of witches into animals or the possibility of miscegenation involving witches and demons. Both of these were invariably treated as popular misconceptions and explained away. Most, while insisting on demonic agency, restrained it within the bounds of nature, although all were agreed that demons could *seem* to go beyond these limits by means of various delusions of the external or internal senses. The actual arts of witchcraft – words and gestures, ceremonies and rituals – were universally thought to be inefficacious in themselves, though not if they were linked with genuinely natural effects by, for example, the use of poisons. The culpability of the witch was therefore thought to consist in the implicit or explicit collusion with devils that was needed to intrude the additional causes that made these arts seem to work. The mere pronunciation of words, for example, was never granted the power to cause physical *maleficium* but, instead, seen as a sign (literally a sacrament) for the devil to step in and bring about the intended effect by natural means. All this meant that most defenders of the reality of witchcraft knew that individual confessions could nevertheless contain things that were not real. Indeed, distributing the subject across a grid of possibilities and impossibilities seems often to have been the major purpose of their texts.

But if belief was always combined with scepticism in demonology, this still left plenty of scope for the vigorous denunciation of witches and the demand that they be punished. Probably the best-known group of writings in this respect comprised the books published by magistrates or judges in witchcraft trials who wished to pass on their experiences and reflections to their legal colleagues and the reading public (Houdard 1992). From the French-speaking lands – based on trials in the duchy of Lorraine, in Burgundy and in Labourd (the French Basque country) respectively – came Nicolas Rémy's *Daemonolatreiae Libri Tres (Three Books of Demonolatry)* (1595), Henri Boguet's *Discours des Sorciers (A Discourse on Witches)* (1602) and Pierre de Lancre's *Tableau de l'Inconstance des Mauvais Anges et Démons (A Display of the Inconstancy of Evil Angels and Devils)* (1612). These texts offered the by now standard arguments concerning the full range of witchcraft issues – the act of apostasy, the powers of demons and spirits, *maleficium,* travel to the sabbat and its ceremonies, banquets and dances, sexual dealings between witches and devils, the possibility of metamorphosis and so on – citing all the time individual cases purporting to come from the judicial archives. Even the legally trained Jean Bodin, who had little to do with any actual trials and whose demonology was vastly more abstract and philosophical, opened his *De la Démonomanie des Sorciers (On the Demon-Mania of Witches)* (1580) with the case of Jeanne Harvillier, executed at Ribemont in 1578. The largely unoriginal and rather unphilosophical work entitled *Daemonologie,* published by James VI of Scotland in 1597, falls into the same category. It originated in trials in Edinburgh in 1590–1 at which James himself had partly officiated, reportedly saying that God himself had made him 'a King and judge to judge righteouse judgmente' (*Calendar of State Papers Relating to Scotland etc., x, 1936:* 521–5; text in Normand and Roberts 2000: 353–426; extracts from Rémy and Bodin in Kors and Peters 2001: 322–9, 290–302; abridged trans. of Bodin in Bodin 1995).

Naturally, all these writings expressed religious convictions as well as judicial experience. But it is also helpful to think of other contributions to this later phase of the witchcraft debate in confessional and clerical terms. The Protestant and Catholic reformers, for example – whose work we have already seen impacting on popular magic – tended to see maleficent witchcraft through the same evangelical and spiritualizing lens. In attempting to turn *maleficium* into a case of conscience they played down the physical damage done by witches and saw their crime much more as an act of apostasy – a crime of which, as we have also seen, those who practised *counter*-witchcraft might be equally guilty. For Protestant writers in particular – men like William Perkins and George Gifford – secular laws that stressed the doing of harm by witchcraft were, therefore, somewhat wide of the mark. This meant that, while they often lamented the vengefulness of witchcraft victims and pointed to legal abuses and the convicting of innocent people, they would undoubtedly have strengthened the witchcraft legislation had they been able to. In this sense, religious reform contributed to the belief in the reality of witchcraft and the pressures to prosecute it that developed from the 1560s onwards (on Protestant demonology, see Clark 1990).

A further substantial contribution was made by Catholic intellectuals committed to the aims and programmes of the Counter-Reformation. In this category were prominent bishops, like the two suffragans Pierre Binsfeld of Trier, whose demonology appeared in 1589, and Friedrich Förner of Bamberg, who published 35 sermons on superstition, magic and witchcraft in 1625. So also were the Catholic theologians who wrote on witchcraft – men such as Martín de Azpilcueta, Gregory Sayer and Francisco de Toledo. The orders were well represented, particularly those with a keen sense of the Church in danger and the need for a militant response to lay indifference or error. The Dominicans had been prominent among witchcraft theorists from the beginning (including Johannes Nider, Johannes Vineti, Girolamo Visconti, the authors of *Malleus Maleficarum,* Bartolommeo Spina, Jacob van Hoogstraten and Silvestro Da Prierio), and in demonology's heyday they were represented by the eventual vicar- general of the French order, Sebastien Michaëlis. Other Frenchmen in this category included the Benedictine René Benoist, the Celestine Pierre Crespet and the Franciscan Jean Benedicti (whose views on witchcraft appeared in a popular confessors' manual). It was, however, the Jesuits who contributed most in this later period, men who, according to Marjorie Reeves, 'saw the world as the battlefield of two mighty "opposites", under whose banners of good and evil the whole of humankind was encamped' (Reeves 1969: 274). They included Juan Maldonado, and Martin Del Río, whose huge study of magic and witchcraft, the *Disquisitionum Magicarum Libri Sex (Six Books of Disquisitions on Magic)* appeared first in Louvain in 1599. Such men were absolutely central to the intellectual strategy and direction of the Counter-Reformation. Maldonado had studied at Salamanca and taught at both the Jesuit College in Rome and at the Collège de Clermont in Paris, and was a highly respected Aristotle scholar (Lohr 1978: 562–3). The colleges and universities where Del Río spent a lifetime of study were among the most active and influential in the new Catholic Europe – the Collège de Clermont, Douai, Louvain, Salamanca and Graz. Significantly, such men saw the spread of witchcraft throughout Europe as an inevitable accompaniment of Protestant heresy (for Del Río on this theme, see Kors and Peters 2001: 331–4; on Catholic demonology, Caro Baroja 1990).

The combined impact of all these publications must have been to encourage witchcraft prosecutions, or at least to justify and explain them – even if the nature of the relationship between texts and events remains elusive. It is striking, for example, how the intensification of discussions of witchcraft in print from the 1560s onwards coincides with the opening of the period chosen by William Monter as the key century of witchcraft trials. But if intellectual disbelief in witchcraft seems more muted in this period it was certainly still an important option (Lehmann and Ulbricht 1992). Many of Weyer's arguments were endorsed in Germany in the 1580s and 1590s, notably by the Lemgo preacher Jodocus Hocker, the Bremen physician Johann Ewich and the Heidelberg Greek and mathematics professor Hermann Witekind, whose book on witchcraft (published under the pseudonym 'Augustin Lercheimer') was scathing in its attack on popular credulity and clerical zeal. A particularly effective advocate of legal caution and the need for discrimination between real crimes and those which (as he said) 'never existed in nature' was Johann Georg Godelmann, a law professor at Rostock, whose lectures on witchcraft appeared in 1591 as *Tractatus de Magis, Veneficis et Lamiis deque his Recte Cognoscendis et Puniendis (A Treatise on Magicians, Poisoners, and Witches and How Properly to Identify and Punish Them)*. In Trier in 1593, Cornelius Loos, a Catholic priest and theologian who sympathized with Weyer, was also forced to recant what seems to have been a more extreme denial of the physical existence of devils (Lea 1939/1957: 602–3).

Scepticism and opposition to witchcraft trials had come to take a variety of forms by this stage, each varying in its effectiveness (Clark 1992: 15–33). Firstly, as we have already seen, doubt could be strictly demonological in nature. Here the main issue was whether witchcraft was a crime for which any human agent could be held responsible. Did witches have the powers to commit the actions of which they were accused or were they caused directly by devils? Were they the victims of complex delusions brought about by illness and demonic deception? Could a natural explanation be given of the phenomena associated with them that precluded demonic agency? And most fundamental of all, did devils have a physical presence in the world to match their spiritual existence? These were questions about the very nature of witchcraft and what it was possible and impossible for witches and devils to do in the real world. Essentially, they fell within the realms of theology and natural philosophy.

Second, scepticism could also take what may be called a methodological form. Here criticism was directed at the evidence cited in support of the reality of witchcraft and the need to prosecute witches. Was it right to use episodes from the poetry of the ancient world as authority on matters of fact? Did the Bible really contain unambiguous references to demonic witchcraft or had translators misconstrued the Hebrew words for such things as 'poisoning' and 'divining'? Were any of the reports and narratives of witchcraft acceptable as testimony, or were they all corrupted by hearsay? These were questions about the reliability and interpretation of sources; in effect, they were questions about texts. As such they became the concern of exegetics and literary scholarship. A further considerable section of Weyer's *De Praestigiis Daemonum* was devoted to applying the findings of Hebrew scholars to various biblical labels for the black arts and showing that the usual conversions into Latin were mistranslations. In this he was followed extensively by Scot and, to a lesser extent, by Robert Filmer, whose sceptical tract *An Advertisement to the Jury-men of England, Touching Witches* appeared in 1653, in the wake of witchcraft executions at Maidstone in Kent the year before, with the subtitle: 'A Difference Betweene an English and Hebrew Witch'. It is noticeable, too, that a humanist attention to the construction and interpretation of historical texts is at the heart of Gabriel Naudé's attack, published in 1625, on the misattribution of the term 'magician' to many of the great figures of the European intellectual tradition – including Pythagoras, Socrates, Roger Bacon and Giovanni Pico della Mirandola (Naudé 1625).

Finally, there were legal forms of doubt, such as those voiced by Godelmann. Here scepticism was aimed at the whole conduct of witchcraft investigations and trials. Did not the fact that witchcraft was supposedly *crimen exceptum,* an exceptional, even unique, crime, imply stricter limits to the professional discretion of judges and greater control over the influence of clerics? Could the use of torture ever yield results that were not prejudicial to the accused? Was not the protection of the innocent more important as a judicial criterion than the punishment of the guilty? And should not many of those convicted of witchcraft suffer milder penalties than was customary? These were questions concerning rules of criminal procedure and points of law and their terms of reference were evidently those of jurisprudence. At a time when prosecutions were reaching a new peak in Germany, Godelmann himself complained of basic miscarriages of justice brought about by inexperienced judges who actually neglected or were ignorant of the correct laws relating to witchcraft and who therefore sent many innocent 'witches' to their deaths without proper evidence or proof. On matters of detail, he denounced the search for the witch's mark and the use of the water ordeal (as did many other legal theorists and theologians), demanded that the character and motives of hostile witnesses be scrutinized and that the accused be given copies of the charges and evidences against them and insisted that *corpus delicti* be conclusively established. Godelmann clearly believed that judges should always remember that defendants needed defending.

It was undoubtedly these legal scruples that made the greatest headway in the early to mid-seventeenth century – so much so that Brian Levack cites judicial scepticism and procedural caution as 'the starting point for any investigation of the decline of witch-hunting' (Levack 1999: 7). This is probably because it was perfectly possible to take a radically questioning position concerning the legal issues while remaining much more orthodox or indifferent with regard to the demonological ones. A string of published works critical of the handling of witchcraft cases (works that Levack also considers) emerged in this period, notably from the German opponents of witch trials (none of them lawyers), Adam Tanner, Paul Laymann, Friedrich Spee von Langenfeld and Johann Meyfart. Each paid at least lip-service to the possibility of witchcraft and, thus, of true convictions while virtually ruling out guilty verdicts as unjust in the present legal circumstances. Spee's *Cautio Criminalis seu de Processibus Contra Sagas (A Warning on Criminal Justice, or About the Trials of Witches),* published anonymously in Rinteln in 1631, and Meyfart's *Christliche Erinnerung (A Christian Reminder),* which appeared in Schleusingen in 1636 (the one by a Jesuit who experienced the prosecutions at Würzburg as a confessor to the condemned, and the other by a Lutheran who saw them at Coburg in Franconia), have come down to us as among the most passionate and eloquent denunciations of excessive religious zeal and barbaric legal procedures from this period – themselves built, said Spee, on 'popular superstition, envy, calumnies, back-bitings, insinuations, and the like' (Kors and Peters 2001: 425). These were men who thought that witchcraft *trials,* not witches, were demonic. Moreover, their reservations were gradually absorbed by the legal professionals themselves, such that we find them repeated or matched by jurists like Hermann Goehausen of Rinteln and Justus Oldekop of Hildesheim.

Demonological scepticism, by contrast, was much less clear-cut. It was much more difficult for critics to distance themselves intellectually from orthodox demonology than to attack trial procedures and investigative techniques such as torture. If restricted to the relative powers (and responsibilities) of witches and devils and the role played by trickery and delusion, the arguments could seldom be decisive, since no believer in witchcraft ever thought witches *themselves* had occult powers or denied that they could be deceived. In this way, negative arguments were already anticipated among the positive ones. The same was true of the naturalistic alternatives proffered for witchcraft phenomena; since devils were acknowledged by all to be inside nature and natural causation, to give a natural explanation for witchcraft effects was not as damaging as it might now seem. To get rid of devils altogether, or at least their physical powers in the physical world, would certainly have delivered a knockout blow to the acceptance of witchcraft but was far too radical a step for most to take, opening the door, as it was perceived to do, to atheism. Across the European intellectual community the aphorism voiced by the Englishman Henry More in 1653 held good throughout the seventeenth century: 'assuredly that Saying was nothing so true in Politicks, No Bishop, no King; as this is in Metaphysicks, No Spirit, no God' (More 1653: 164).

Yet even if legal criticisms were easiest to mount and most effective overall, notable individual attempts to sweep witchcraft beliefs away by restricting or reconceptualizing the powers of demons did multiply in this final period too. In England, where Scot's arguments were in abeyance for about three-quarters of a century, they were eventually taken up again by the physician Thomas Ady in the 1650s, by the one-time religious radical John Webster in the 1670s and by Francis Hutchinson in 1718. By 1690, when Balthasar Bekker began publishing his complete repudiation of witchcraft, *De Betoverde Weereld (The Enchanted World)*, it was possible for this Dutch Calvinist pastor to combine all the misgivings previously felt about miscarriages of justice and misreadings of texts with a radical demonology that left no place for a devil who made a mockery of Providence. The same was true of the total scepticism of Christian Thomasius, the Prussian jurist, whose *De Crimine Magiae (On the Crime of Magic)* appeared in 1701. In a later work of 1712, his *Historische Untersuchung vom Ursprung und Fortgang des Inquisitions Prozesses (Historical Investigation into the Origins and Continuation of the Inquisitorial Trial)*, Thomasius even went so far as to demolish the very genre that was demonology by treating every one of its canonical texts as critically unsound.

Witchcraft and intellectual history

As Thomasius clearly understood, then, the history of early modern witchcraft beliefs is in one sense a story of individual texts and the specific ideas and arguments their authors wielded against each other. It is indeed the history we have just been tracing. But there is another way to approach it that seems ultimately more rewarding, in the sense that it reveals much more about the very possibility of witchcraft belief and its limitations and makes interpreting the texts less a matter of giving a blow-by-blow account of their contents and more a search for the congruities and incongruities that characterized early modern thought as a whole. Even identifying the texts themselves becomes less predictable and more open-ended. For this different approach we need to think more broadly about the intellectual and cultural history of Europe in the early modern period and, indeed, about intellectual and cultural history *itself* as a way of accessing early modern meanings.

What constituted the crime of witchcraft and the culpability of those charged with it were undoubtedly key issues in the long history of demonology. But witchcraft was able to raise issues across a much wider terrain, making demonology an unusually revealing guide to early modern intellectual and cultural values in general. For this reason, historians of witchcraft are now beginning to take a fresh look at it after a long period of relative neglect. In the 1970s and 1980s, at a time when witchcraft studies were being generally modernized, traditional intellectual history was in decline and the study of pure ideas discredited. Witchcraft historians also looked back with disapproval to a much earlier phase of study when conditions on both sides of the Atlantic led to a concentration on demonology and little else. The culture wars of mid- and later nineteenth-century Germany had turned the scholarship of pioneers like Wilhelm Gottlieb Soldan, Johann Diefenbach and Nikolaus Paulus not just into battles of books but into battles *about* books. In America, progressivists like Andrew Dickson White and George Lincoln Burr (and later rationalist historians like Henry Charles Lea and Rossell Hope Robbins) again saw the essence of what they deplored in witchcraft as the ideas expressed about it in writings. It seemed typical of these men that the 'materials toward a history of witchcraft' left behind by Lea in 1909 and first published by Arthur Howland in 1939 should have comprised notes taken almost entirely from demonological texts – the same texts collected by White while he was Cornell University's first President and by Burr his librarian, so that scholars might rid the world of intolerance and superstition by reading them (they are now in the magnificent rare books collection in Cornell's John M. Olin Library; Crowe 1977). As late as 1978 Robert Muchembled was complaining of what he called the 'intellectual' view of witchcraft, which he associated with Robert Mandrou (1968) and Hugh Trevor-Roper (1967), on the grounds that it privileged the opinions of a cultural élite remote from the social experiences of those most directly concerned with the crime (Muchembled 1978a). By this time, indeed, historians of witchcraft everywhere were refocusing on such things as the magical elements in popular culture, the social pressures and tensions behind witchcraft accusations in small communities and the fact that most of the accused were women. Their adoption of sociological and anthropological perspectives, some of them highly functionalist in character, also led to less and less attention being given to what demonology was best at revealing – the meaning of witchcraft.

Witchcraft studies today are an exciting blend of many innovative approaches and no one would wish to return to the days when what contemporaries wrote about witches was taken to be the key to everything else about them. On the other hand, neglect has not been good for the study of demonology either. For too long it remained unreformed, out of date and subject to misreadings and misinterpretations. Trevor-Roper himself expressed a crude form of rationalism in which the witchcraft beliefs of intellectuals were seen as 'hysterical', 'lunatic' and so much 'rubbish'. In a survey published in 1972, the American scholar Wayne Shumaker spoke similarly of 'delusions', 'stupidities', insanity and the lack of 'hard intellectual argument' in early modern demonology (Trevor-Roper 1967: 97; Shumaker 1972: 61, 101–2). Until very recently, educated concepts of witchcraft, especially those expressed by magistrates and clergymen, were still regarded as little more than rationalizations for 'witch-hunting'. Relatively few texts were well studied – a complaint made by Sydney Anglo in one of the first modern attempts to remedy the situation (Anglo 1977a: vii, 1–3) – and disproportionate attention was given to the sceptics and opponents of witch trials, presumably on the, again rationalist, grounds that they merited more attention than those writers who supported prosecution. Shumaker spoke typically of their 'healthy tough-mindedness' (Shumaker 1972: 61). Finally, it was usually assumed (and often still is) that 'demonologists' discussed only witchcraft – and only the classic, highly stereotyped diabolism of the sabbat – and studied it to the exclusion of anything else.

For, above all, Renaissance demonology has been read out of context – its *Renaissance* context. Modern readers have had difficulty in appreciating that educated beliefs about witchcraft were not held in isolation but were dependent on other intellectual commitments, as well as on a whole series of social and institutional practices. This is not just a matter of intellectual processes and styles of argument and scholarship – the kinds of mental habits that made the Bible, the Ancients and the Fathers authoritative (and cumulative) sources of belief and the 'argument from authority' itself a form of proof and persuasion in every Renaissance field (Shumaker 1972: 70–85, 100–2; Anglo 1977a: 6–14). Rather, it is a matter of substance. Most 'demonologists' were not interested exclusively in demonology and if the label implies that they were it ought to be used only with caution or not at all. Take, for example, the Spaniard Maldonado, whom we have already noted as one of the leading Jesuit intellectuals of the Catholic Reformation – a philosopher, theologian and an authority on Aristotle; or the Englishman William Perkins, the most prolific and influential of the 'Puritan' authors of the Elizabethan age, who wrote on every aspect of Calvinist theology and morality; or the Swiss intellectual Thomas Erastus, holder of the chair of philosophy, theology and medicine at Heidelberg University, author of a classic refutation of Paracelsus and immortalized as a proponent of 'Erastianism' in Church–state relations. It would be wrong to think of these men as 'demonologists' simply because Maldonado's lectures in Paris gave rise to a *Traicté des anges et demons (Treatise on Angels and Demons),* published posthumously in 1616, because some of Perkins's hundreds of sermons were turned into one of England's best-known witchcraft tracts, *A Discourse of the Damned Art of Witchcraft,* which also appeared posthumously in 1608, and because, in addition to denouncing Paracelsus, Erastus also denounced Johann Weyer and defended witchhunting in his *Repetitio Disputationis de Lamiis seu Strigibus (A Renewed Examination of Lamiae or Witches)* (Basel 1578). To do so would run the risk of isolating their interest in demonology from their other pursuits – in fact, from precisely the things that help to explain why they were interested in demonology at all.

There were others, of course, who do seem to have written (or at least published) little besides demonology and who may well have been preoccupied by it. Examples might be the *procureur général* of the duchy of Lorraine, Nicolas Rémy, or his magistrate colleague at Saint-Claude in Franche-Comté, Henri Boguet, or, again, Bishop Peter Binsfeld from the city of Trier, all of whom were mentioned earlier as authors of specific works. But we still cannot read their books on magic and witchcraft without being struck by the way their demonology was linked conceptually to other aspects of their thinking – for example, their views about the natural world, about the course of human history, about the nature of legal and political authority and so on. Here, too, we need to treat educated witchcraft beliefs in a rounded way, resituating them among the other beliefs with which they were associated and which made them seem rational to those who held them. Most illuminating of all, in fact, are those occasions when we find extensive discussions of witchcraft in texts that are concerned with precisely these other ingredients of Renaissance belief – and which for this very reason have invariably been missed by witchcraft historians. The material on witchcraft in Book 5 of Johannes Nider's fifteenth-century treatise, *Formicarius,* has often been analysed, but there is just as much embedded in the Decalogue theology contained in his *Praeceptorium Legis sive Expositio Decalogi (Instruction in the Law, or an Exposition of the Decalogue),* written a few years later in about

1440. There is a substantial demonology in the French political theorist Pierre Grégoire's tract on government, *De Republica (On Government)* (1578), and another in the section on 'occult' diseases in a textbook for physicians by the leading medical authority in early seventeenth-century Wittenberg, Daniel Sennert. Casuists on both sides of the religious divide, like the Benedictine Gregory Sayer or the irenicist François Baudouin, included extensive sections on witchcraft and magic in their guides to the perfect conscience. In the same way, the Würzburg Jesuit Gaspar Schott inserted a great deal of witchcraft material into the natural philosophical discussions he published in 1662 entitled *Physica Curiosa, sive Mirabilia Naturae et Artis (A Curious Physics, or The Wonders of Nature and Art)*. The question 'what is witchcraft doing in these books?' may be prompted initially by the false expectation that it ought not to be present in any of them. But it is still a question well worth considering, if by answering it we are able to place witchcraft in its true intellectual surroundings.

Another reason why this wider context has often been missed is the tendency to relate witchcraft beliefs *solely* to witchcraft trials, as if these were their only point of reference. Naturally, many witchcraft texts did originate either in specific episodes or in waves of prosecutions, provoked into being by reflection on or the desire to justify what had occurred in the courtroom. The magistrates who acted in trials and later wrote books based on their experiences are obvious cases in point, with Boguet's *Discours des Sorciers* actually concluding with 70 'articles' of advice about how other judges should proceed in trying witches. In his contribution, William Monter makes clear how the writings of Binsfeld and Förner were intimately related to the 'superhunts' in Trier and Franconia which they helped to co-ordinate. Many adverse reactions to witch prosecutions, like those of Scot, Godelmann, Spee and Filmer already mentioned, arose likewise in response to individual cases or longer episodes of witch-hunting that struck these critics as grossly unjust. Conversely, there are numerous examples of individual witchcraft texts being brought into play during the course of prosecutions. This happened most often when lawyers sought help with legal technicalities directly from professional manuals or indirectly from the legal faculties of neighbouring universities in the form of what in Germany was called *gutachten* (e.g. Lorenz 1995). Many other general forms of guidance and advice could be found in demonologies should judges and magistrates choose to consult them – as, for example, they were invited to do by the English preacher Thomas Cooper and by Pierre Nodé in France. Indeed, for this reason, there has even been an assumption among modern historians that demonology was one of the principal causes of witchcraft prosecutions and that its profile as a scholarly genre rose and fell exactly as they did in seriousness and frequency.

Yet discussions of witchcraft in print also had a life that was independent of the trials (Closson 2000). They flourished in some contexts – in the Dutch Republic in the 1690s or in England on the eve of the repeal of the witchcraft legislation in 1736, for example – where prosecutions had actually ceased. They appeared in texts – texts such as catechisms or published university dissertations or biblical commentaries – whose primary purpose had little to do with either encouraging or reflecting upon the legal process. And they were written by authors – authors like Joseph Glanvill and Henry More in English philosophical circles – who showed little interest in apprehending and punishing witches. Throughout the European scientific community, indeed, witchcraft excited a theoretical interest that bore little relation to the practice of witch-hunting. At the same time, works that we habitually identify as witchcraft texts turn out to contain many other things, to which witchcraft was nevertheless thought at the time to be integrally linked. A work like Del Río's ranges over a truly vast intellectual terrain that quite outreaches anything as focused as a witchcraft trial. On many occasions, then, one has the impression that the subject of witchcraft was being used as a kind of intellectual resource – as a means for thinking through problems that originated elsewhere and had little or nothing to do with the legal prosecution of witches. What witchcraft scholars are currently looking for in demonology has much to do with these various features. At the same time, intellectual and cultural history itself has also changed, insisting on far less – if any – segregation between the sorts of things that used to be pigeon-holed as 'religion', or 'science' or 'politics' and, at the same time, ready to acknowledge the strangeness that marked many aspects of the early modern world, not just its witchcraft beliefs.

The politics of witchcraft belief

If Renaissance witchcraft belief is to be made intelligible in its original intellectual surroundings, a good place to begin is with the political (and linked religious) ideologies of the age. A number of recent studies have shown how demonology could never be merely a set of abstract theories about witchcraft or 'demonologists' a group of ideologically disinterested or unattached observers of the crime – or simply members of some undifferentiated 'élite'. Attitudes to witchcraft were always mediated by the complicated and fluctuating allegiances of dominion and faith, party and faction, and in turn help to reveal these to us historically. In later sixteenth-century and early seventeenth-century France, for example, those who were most zealous about witch-hunting were deeply committed – through conviction and connection alike – not just to Tridentine Catholicism but to the Holy League of the 1580s and 1590s and to the *dévot* party thereafter. 'Their point of view', says Jonathan Pearl, 'was not just a worldview or religious inclination, but a party allegiance in a time of bitter sectarian violence.' At their heart was a group of Jesuits, heavily influenced by Maldonado's lectures on witchcraft in Paris in the 1570s, who in their demonologies went on to write propaganda for a cause, rather than anything that had a direct influence on the pace or severity of French witchcraft trials. Indeed, the latter better reflected the moderation of the Gallican lawyers and magistrates who staffed France's parlements, both in Paris and in the provinces. In the end, Pearl has argued, the zealots, their impact already blunted by their very factionalism, were gradually marginalized as a minority of extremists in a political culture increasingly given over to *politique* values (Pearl 1999: 6 and *passim*; cf. Soman 1992).

A similar analysis of attitudes to witchcraft in England in the same period has yet to be completed, although an approach based on mapping the ideological significance of believing in or denying witchcraft for particular groups caught up in the ever-changing flow of national and local affairs has been sketched (Elmer 2001). What has been clear for some time is that, in France and England alike, both the theoretical debates about possession and exorcism and also the unfolding of individual episodes were heavily factionalized in terms of the complex religious and political controversies of the time. This was an aspect of the demonic that was linked to witchcraft through accusations that witches or sorcerers had caused possessions in the first place and could therefore be denounced by their victims during exorcism. It was not just that possession and exorcism were contentious subjects dividing Protestants from Catholics; they divided the faiths *internally* as well, together with the political configurations of faction and party. In Elizabethan England, the credibility of specific cases involving Jesuit and

Puritan exorcists and the ideological capital that could be gained (and lost) when they were proved genuine or fraudulent became central to the fortunes of the settlement and survival of religious consensus (Walker 1981: 43–73, 77–84; *cf.* MacDonald 1991). In France, the case of the demoniac Marthe Brossier in 1598–9 was caught up in exactly the same way in the public fortunes of the Edict of Nantes, after she disclosed that Satan himself approved of tolerating Huguenots. To the Catholic opposers of the Edict, especially the Capuchins, she was genuinely possessed and, thus, of great propaganda value; to Henri IV and the *Parlement* of Paris she was emphatically not (Mandrou 1968: 163–79; Ferber 1991; Walker and Dickerman 1991). Perhaps the best illustration of this point – and undoubtedly the most brilliant exposition of it by a modern historian – lies in Michel de Certeau's account of how the conduct of the exorcisms of the possessed Ursulines of Loudun in the 1630s and the resulting trial of Urbain Grandier were affected by the intervention of the French government, with its royalist and centralist aims, in the form of a commission from Richelieu to the *intendent* Jean Martin, baron de Laubardemont. De Certeau best makes the point that emerges from all such cases, and from the world of witchcraft beliefs in general – that it was the very reality of the phenomena (what it was possible to believe or disbelieve, accept or reject), and not merely what action to take, that was determined by ideological positioning. The diabolical, he says, became 'the metaphor of politics'; political conflicts organized the 'vocabulary' of the Loudun episode, revealed themselves in it, used it and then moved on (Certeau 2000: 65 and *passim*).

To talk this way about 'use' seems too reductive, perhaps. Even so, evidence of how the political use of the idioms and vocabulary of witchcraft – indeed, their *overuse* – eventually damaged the credibility of witchcraft and led to its ideological appeal becoming exhausted comes in the form of the most sophisticated and original of all recent histories of early modern demonology, Ian Bostridge's *Witchcraft and Its Transformations c.1650–c.1750* (1997). One aim of this study is to account for witchcraft's resonance in England long after it is usually supposed to have been in inevitable decline – indeed, Bostridge seeks to avoid the assumption of inevitability altogether. The other is to achieve this by tracing witchcraft's place in public life as a function (even the creation) of political debate, its fortunes being much more dependent on this political context than on abstract intellectual arguments (in the case of scepticism, broadly unchanged since Reginald Scot) or the onset of the rationalism and the science of the Enlightenment – or, once again, the actual occurrence or intensity of prosecutions. The book is a series of case studies, reaching from the Civil Wars and Interregnum, through the Restoration and the 'rage' of party, to the repeal of English witchcraft legislation in 1736. Bostridge pits the covenantal witchcraft of Perkins against the politics of the Arminian and absolutist Filmer, the political theology of demonology against the Church–state relations envisaged by Hobbes, the royalist traditionalism of Meric Casaubon against the radicalism of John Webster and the freethinking Hobbism of John Wagstaffe, and the *Spectator* of Joseph Addison against the *Review* of Daniel Defoe. Party narrowly defined is not necessarily seen as the key to these differences of view, though the trial of Jane Wenham in 1712, when she was found guilty by the jury and reprieved by the judge, did lead to a spate of pamphleteering in which the High Church Tory Francis Bragge asked for conviction and his Whig respondents the opposite. After her pardon, writes Bostridge, she became 'part of the Whig mythology of Tory superstition' (Bostridge 1997: 135).

What these various studies reveal, then, are examples of the specific contexts in which writers and others positioned themselves with regard to witchcraft in relation to the major public issues of their times. But even if we recede somewhat from the intricacies and practicalities of public affairs to the more abstract patterns of argument discernible in demonology itself – that is to say, even if we recede from contingency to theory – we can still detect correlations between attitudes to witchcraft and particular styles or languages of political commitment. In fact, these may very well be the more general correlations that lay behind the ideological choices made by individuals in the particular situations they confronted. It was always impossible, after all, to arrive at a theory about witchcraft and its treatment by public officials without some kind of attention to political values of one sort or another. Conversely, any formulation of a theory of government necessarily implied a view about what kind of social and moraldis order it was designed to secure and what kind of social and moral disorder it was expected to prevent. Demonology and ideology, we might say, were always mutually entailed, whatever the level of generality we approach them at.

Speaking in very broad terms, we can identify three major traditions of political theorizing in the sixteenth and seventeenth centuries. The first, the most familiar and predictable, consisted of defences of theocratic absolutism and the 'divine right' of rulers. Here, authority was said to originate in – and 'descend' from – a divine gift of grace that made it literally charismatic. Political forms stemmed directly from God and were bestowed on men as divine favours via the temporal authority of rulers acting in his image and as his lieutenants or viceregents. Rulership in fact lay wholly outside the intentions of human agents, its force and ability to command depending solely on supernatural qualities and powers. Far removed from this way of theorizing, and in many ways diametrically opposed to it, were attempts to demystify politics by offering naturalistic accounts of its supposed supernaturalisms, and justifying all political actions in terms of pragmatism and rational calculation. One important strand of this was derived from Machiavelli's account of the social and political functions of religious belief in ancient Rome, which openly or surreptitiously was then extended to cover the political utility of Christianity itself. Another was the political vocabulary of what Richard Tuck has described as the 'new humanism', combining scepticism with Stoicism and stressing the importance of prudence, necessity and *raison d'état*. What emerged was an unscrupulous, instrumentalist ethic – almost an anti-ethic, says Tuck – which permitted citizens and their princes to concentrate on their own interests, effectively self-preservation, at the expense of traditional norms. Notoriously, religion, along with laws and constitutions, might be subordinated to the demands of political necessity (Tuck 1993: 31–119). Midway between these two traditions – rejecting the Augustinianism of the first and the individualism and relativism of the second – lay the kind of politics that has come to be called 'constitutionalist'. Here the main stylistic trait was to place political responsibility in the community, whether as the originator of power or as one of its participants. Actual rulers were said to be hedged about with legal and institutional, and not merely moral, other-worldly restrictions – their power was 'limited'. Constitutionalism often spoke the language of social contract and of popular sovereignty. It was committed to the normative value of human institutions and traditions, and owed much to the rehabilitation of human reason. Political society and its forms of domination came about, hypothetically, when men, living in a state of natural liberty, and acting for reasons of utility, freely agreed to delegate their sovereignty to rulers while yet reserving the collective right to remove them if they were not conducive to the public good.

It is difficult to see how a crime like witchcraft could have meant the same thing in these three very different theoretical contexts (Clark 1997: 596–612, 668–82, from which much of this present discussion is taken). And, indeed, the varying significance attached to witchcraft by those who wrote directly about it – the authors of the demonological texts we have been discussing – seems to bear this out. Those who took it most seriously did so in terms of the first political tradition, adopting its concepts of government and magistracy. Here, witchcraft assumed the terrible proportions of a threat to cosmological order. Service to the devil and the disorder that it produced were heinous criminal offences to those who assumed that God was the direct author of political forms. Witchcraft appealed to a source of authority which parodied the type that God had actually created in his own image, and it reverberated with all manner of damaging implications for the sense of order and hierarchy on which divine politics ultimately rested. A special enmity – even a kind of symmetry – could be said to exist between magistrates conceived of as agents of divine authority and justice and the witches they tried; they were similar vehicles of antithetical powers. This is the reason why so many witchcraft theorists could plausibly claim that magistrates were actually immune from *maleficium* – inviolable to direct assaults on their authority by the devil or his agents (Clark 1997: 572–81).

Mainstream demonology is full of these ideas and sentiments. But we can now also see why standard witchcraft theory found a natural place in a work like Grégoire's *De Republica*, which argued that 'since the king was no less than the actively inspired agent of the Deity, the people had no choice but to give reverence to their ruler as to the divine majesty itself' (Church 1941: 247–8). The best illustration of all lies in the absolute congruity between Jean Bodin's two major publications of the late 1570s, his *Six Livres de la République* (*Six Books of the Commonwealth*) (1576) and his *De La Démonomanie des Sorciers* (1580), making them virtually one book and explaining, in particular, Bodin's harsh and punitive attitude to witches.

In stark contrast, witchcraft played almost no role at all in the arguments of those who were so cynical – or at least instrumentalist – about politics that they turned supernaturalism into a useful form of statecraft and relativized religious orthodoxy to the needs of policy. Mystical and quasisacerdotal views of magistracy were absent from the writings of Machiavelli and those of 'new humanists' like Montaigne, Lipsius and Charron, relying heavily as they did on models of power drawn from Tacitus and Seneca. For them the charisma of princes was a product of artifice and superstition, leading, in the words of Gabriel Naudé (who, significantly, was deeply sceptical about such things as the witches' sabbat; Mandrou 1968: 124, 298–301, 310–11, 336) to 'feigned Dieties [*sic*], pretended Conferences, imaginary Apparaitions … to lay a surer foundation of future Empire' (cited by Clark 1997: 597). As a crime defined in antithesis to mystical rulership, witchcraft made no sense in this non-mystical context. The awfulness of witches ceased to be inherent in their deeds and became a political construction. Mostly, then, they were either ignored in this way of talking about politics, or laughed at as crude attempts to frighten people into compliance. This is why we can see witches being dismissed as serious deviants by the most important 'new' political humanist of the sixteenth century, Montaigne (in the essay *Des Boîteux*, mentioned earlier), and in a book by the later seventeenth-century English 'libertine' thinker John Wagstaffe, entitled *The Question of Witchcraft Debated* (1669, 1671).

On the one hand, a summation of everything that was evil in the world; on the other, the product of dreams and trickery. But was there a midway position on witchcraft and did it correspond to the third form of political theorizing – constitutionalism? This is a more difficult question to answer, given the current state of research. In the context of man-made politics, witchcraft could never assume the importance given it by the political theology of divine right, but there was no reason for it to disappear altogether. It became a different crime – less portentous, certainly, and less Mosaic – but still a real one. In a commonwealth erected to ensure the citizens' security and well-being, its seriousness depended on the threat it posed to these goals. Witchcraft lost the overtones of rebelliousness and antimonarchism and became primarily a menace to life and property. What mattered were not the symbolic overtones of apostasy and the devil worship of the sabbat but the actual harms caused by *maleficium*. That these could still occur through demonically inspired actions – without being reduced entirely to non-demonic causes – meant a continued belief in witchcraft's reality as a phenomenon, if not in its more sensational aspects.

We can see the political weighting at work here in the way English Royalists of the 1640s turned to the subject of witchcraft – and in particular to the biblical verse in 1 Samuel 15:23; 'For rebellion is as the sin of witchcraft' – in order to bring out the awfulness of armed opposition to the king. This, indeed, exemplifies again witchcraft's relationship to the first of the three political traditions we have been examining here – as does the use made of this text by other Crown supporters in the seventeenth century, from Isaac Bargrave in 1627 defending the 'forced loan' of Charles I, to the tracts and sermons concerned with the Exclusion Crisis and Monmouth's rebellion in the 1680s. But what is especially striking is the contrast drawn by the royalists of the 1640s between their own linking of demonology with politics and the way their constitutionalist opponents made the connection. The suggestion was that those who defended the parliamentarian cause in terms of the notion of popular sovereignty were comparable to those who were sceptical about the reality and seriousness of witchcraft. Diminishing the significance of witchcraft was like diminishing the significance of resistance to Charles I.

Searching for overt constitutionalism in demonologies that did indeed play down the seriousness of witchcraft while still regarding it as a crime is a task that has hardly begun. But a good indication of what to look for comes in another text that was mentioned earlier, Godelmann's *Tractatus de Magis, Veneficis et Lamŭs*. Clearly, this work contains the main elements of the midway position on witchcraft – in particular, a concentration on the inflicting of actual harm, a concern to distinguish real *maleficium* from crimes that were illusory and fictitious (the term 'witchcraft' itself being reserved, in this case, for the latter), and a distaste for the public disorder and judicial abuses of trials and ordeals conducted by poorly qualified and 'superstitious' magistrates. Many other German jurists came to share some or all of Godelmann's misgivings; so too did the magistrates of the Parlement of Paris, and so too did many Protestant clergymen through Europe (Godelmann himself was a Lutheran), inviting the question as to what role constitutionalist leanings may have played in this. But in Godelmann's own case, endorsement was given to his arguments by a fellow jurist who went on to enunciate a political theory that became synonymous with constitutionalism. At the conclusion of Part 1 of the *Tractatus* there is a 'Warning to the Judge', contributed by Johannes Althusius, at the time a teacher in the law faculty of the Calvinist academy of Herborn, and later the author of *Politica Methodice Digesta (Politics Methodically Set Forth)*, published in 1603. This juxtaposition of identical views expressed by an intellectual normally thought of as a demonologist and one normally thought of as a political theorist itself invites the kinds of questions we have been considering about the, at least cognitive, relationships that existed between the two fields. But more precisely it allows us to match the mainly legal reasons for questioning witchcraft trials with the kind of politics that was congruent with them (Clark 2000).

Languages of witchcraft

Congruence and incongruence are in fact the key to the kind of intellectual history of demonology that is being proposed here. If we move beyond politics to religious ideology and to views about the Church and about salvation; if we move beyond these to conceptions of history, of historical time, agency and process; and if we move beyond these to questions about natural causation and physical reality; if, indeed, we reconstruct the issues raised by demonology in each of these other overlapping areas of early modern thought, the same general pattern keeps recurring – the belief in witchcraft was congruent with particular styles of religious, historical and scientific thinking and incongruent with others. Those who, on the whole, believed in witchcraft and wanted it eradicated derived their view of religious deviance from a providential interpretation of misfortune, a pastoral and evangelical conception of piety and conformity and a preoccupation with sins against the First Commandment. This is why there is so much demonology stored up in texts such as catechisms and casuistical treatises. They were not supporters of what Ernst Troeltsch called the 'sect–type' churches of Anabaptists and other independents or of their spiritualist and antinomian theologies – churches which paid much less or little attention to the physical presence of devils and to the association of witchcraft with heresy. Hence, by contrast, the significance of the links which the two most radical witchcraft sceptics in England *do* seem to have had with this kind of religious radicalism, Scot with the Familists and Webster with the Anabaptists and antinomians (Wootton 2001: 119–38; Elmer 1986, 2–12).

Again, with regard to their views about history, believers in witchcraft (and demonic possession) espoused a linear, apocalyptic and prophetic understanding of the past and the demonic events of their own times, derived from Revelation, which gave a prominent place to the Antichrist. To cleanse societies of their witches (and to exorcise demoniacs) was to prepare the way for the end of the world, an incentive to witchcraft prosecution whose powerful appeal has only recently begun to be recognized (Behringer 1997: 113, 115–21; Crouzet 1990: ii. 340–1; Boyer and Nissenbaum 1974: 174–5). However, this view of history was rivalled in the sixteenth and seventeenth centuries by the quite different style of Renaissance Ciceronianism, with its more cyclical, more secular concentration on human motivation and the provision of lessons for the conduct of public life. This was the sort of humanistic history-writing we associate with the Florentines Leonardo Bruni, Machiavelli and Francesco Guicciardini, with de Thou in France, and with Francis Bacon and the Earl of Clarendon in England. The contrast here is equally instructive; eschatological history found a natural, intelligible place for witchcraft but could we imagine any of the humanist historians paying serious attention to devils, the Antichrist and witches as agents of historical change?

Finally, those who believed in witchcraft operated with a natural philosophy that blended in a flexible way the up–to–date Aristotelianism of the European universities and the theory and practice of natural magic, of which demonic magic – the physical means by which the devil produced witchcraft effects – was considered the exact analogue (on natural magic, see Chapter 3 below). But their acceptance of demonic intervention in natural events rested on notions of causation that purists of both the Aristotelian and corpuscularian philosophies would have liked to rule out. Once again, then, we are presented with a situation in which demonology matched up with one version of things but not with others – in this case, one account of nature and natural knowledge rather than the alternatives on offer at the time. Of the purist Aristotelians, the most threatening to witchcraft belief – as we saw earlier – was Pomponazzi; among the corpuscularians were philosophers like Marin Mersenne and Pierre Gassendi. For René Descartes and Thomas Hobbes, nature consisted entirely of matter in motion, and incorporeal causes and preternatural effects were physically impossible. Although many English admirers of this 'mechanic' philosophy found it hard to do without spirits (or witches), no pure Cartesian would have been expected to defend the physical reality of demonism and witchcraft.

Relating witchcraft belief much more broadly to the intellectual and cultural history of Europe in this manner helps us to grasp two important features of it. On the one hand, we can better see the reasons for its strength and resilience between the fifteenth and eighteenth centuries. Its essential congruence with so many other ways of thinking explains its appeal and the nature of its coherence and rationality for contemporaries. On the other hand, congruence also helps to account for the rise and decline of witchcraft belief. It became possible to 'think' witchcraft as and when the intellectual positions that were allied to demonology themselves became available as options for intellectuals to adopt. It ceased to be possible when they lost their appeal, to be replaced by others with which witchcraft belief was *incongruent*. Bostridge, for example, speaks of the eventual loss of witchcraft's ideological roots in religion and politics, notably with the waning of commitment to the ideal of divine order in Church, state and society. More importantly, he indicates a kind of ideological exhaustion at work in early eighteenth-centuiy Britain, whereby the habitual association of witchcraft with transparently 'party' passions acted to discredit its very authenticity, especially at the time of the trial of Jane Wenham in 1712 (Bostridge 1997: 108–38).

This, of course, is a modern historian's insight. But among the most interesting features of early modern writings on witchcraft are the, first occasional and then ever-growing, indications that contemporaries grasped this idea too – first, identifying in the acceptance of witchcraft a specific ideological position and then using this very partiality as a reason for scepticism. Probably, this could not happen before the Protestant Reformation introduced radical religious partisanship into European intellectual life. Indeed, the earliest example of this sort of scepticism seems to be the Protestant Johann Weyer's accusation that many of the things witches were supposed to do were merely anti-*Catholic* transgressions – that is, things that no one but Catholics could take seriously (Weyer 1991: 177–9). Further impetus was given by the emergence of so-called 'libertinism' in early seventeenth-century France and by the adoption of *cui bono* arguments among intellectual radicals and freethinkers in mid- to later seventeenth-century England. Following Hobbes, 'policy' came to be urged as a reason for creating and maintaining the fear of witches, with John Wagstaffe, in particular, explaining demonology away as a politically useful tool (Hunter 1995). Eventually, Francis Hutchinson was to repeat Weyer's point but in a now all-embracing manner, remarking that 'the Numbers of Witches, and the suppos'd Dealings of Spirits with them', increased or decreased according to 'the Laws, and Notions, and Principles of the several Times, Places, and Princes'. For him (writing in 1718), 'a Hebrew Witch, a Pagan Witch, a Lapland Witch, an Indian Witch, a Protestant Witch, and a Popish Witch [were] different from one another' (cited by Clark 1997: 144). Today we would say that Hutchinson was seeking to destroy the belief in witchcraft by turning it into a cultural construction. But this form of relativism had begun at least 150 years before.

Intellectual magic

'The greatest profoundnesse of natural philosophie'

The two preceding chapters have been very much concerned with the twin questions of reputation and interpretation, and this last one continues the theme. We saw firstly how, in recent years, popular magic has had to be rescued from various kinds of rejection at the hands of both contemporaries and modern scholars; and then, in the last chapter, how demonology, likewise, has suffered in the past from the depredations of rationalism and historical isolation and only now is being read in a context that begins to make sense of it. In the case of popular magic, those who accepted it and used it left litte record of their reasons for doing so, let alone their way of conceptualizing it; the sense it undoubtedly had for them has largely to be inferred. Indeed, as was noted earlier, it can be difficult in this context to find anyone in the early modern period who would have agreed that 'magic' was the best (or, certainly, the safest) description of what he or she did or who would have called him/herself a 'magician'. With learned witchcraft beliefs (though not, of course, the beliefs of those actually accused of witchcraft) the case is quite different. We have an abundance of published statements about why it was important to take witchcraft and its legal prosecution seriously, and in this sense there is no silence in the historical record or lack of self-confessed 'demonologists'.

The subject of this last chapter – the intellectual magic of the Renaissance centuries – has also experienced wild fluctuations in fortune and so its history too must, in part, be the history of a reputation and the problems of interpretation this has caused. But unlike its popular counterpart it was certainly not lacking a voice of its own. As the name usually given to it suggests, it was a theory and practice of magic enunciated by intellectuals. Like demonology, indeed, it was described and debated in a multitude of texts – sometimes, the same texts. Initially, at least, there is no need for inference in discovering what it was. Before considering its reputation, therefore, it will be best to let the intellectual magicians of Renaissance Europe speak for themselves.

A good place to start is with a work known throughout the period as a kind of encyclopaedia of intellectual (or 'high') magic, *De Occulta Philosophia Libri Tres (Three Books Of Occult Philosophy)* by Heinrich Cornelius Agrippa (1486–1535) (the work is described and discussed by Yates 1964: 130–43, and by Shumaker 1972: 134–56). Agrippa was a student and teacher of philosophy, theology and medicine (which he also practised, for a time at the French court), who moved between France, Italy, Switzerland, Germany and the Low Countries in the course of a lifetime of study. For a while, the witchcraft author Johann Weyer served as his assistant. In *De Occulta Philosophia,* which appeared between 1531 and 1533 and in manuscript long before that, Agrippa gave a definition of magic that was widely shared by his contemporaries:

> Magic is a faculty of wonderful power, full of most high mysteries. It contains the most profound contemplation of things which are most secret, together with their nature, power, quality, substance and virtues, and the knowledge of the whole of nature. It instructs us in the way things differ and agree with each other and thus it produces wonderful effects by applying the virtues of one thing to another and thus uniting them. It also joins and knits firmly together compatible inferior objects by means of the powers and virtues of superior bodies. This is the most perfect and principal branch of

knowledge, a sacred and more lofty kind of philosophy, and the most absolute perfection of every most excellent philosophy. (Maxwell-Stuart 1999: 116)

This definition repays close attention since it refers to many of the key features of intellectual magic and captures its characteristic mentality. Self-congratulatory as it may sound, this kind of magic was always described as the summation of knowledge and wisdom, as something 'high' and 'more lofty'. It was not just another kind of science, but its apogee ('the most perfect and principal branch of knowledge'). In another work, Agrippa described it as 'the greatest profoundnesse of natural Philosophie, and absolutest perfection therof'. Francis Bacon, tracing it like everybody else to the ancient Persians and their word *magia,* explained that they regarded it as 'a sublime wisdom, and the knowledge of the universal consents of things' (cited by Clark 1997: 216).

Generally, many contemporaries shared this notion of the seriousness, the importance and the stature of intellectual magic. However we may think of it, it was certainly not regarded as routine, everyday knowledge. One reason for this, as we shall see in a moment, was that it was all-embracing; it was 'the knowledge of the whole of nature' – indeed, of the whole of creation. Another was that it dealt with the most profound and mysterious aspects of the created world, those 'which are most secret'. In many ways, intellectual magic was synonymous with the attempt to grasp what was hidden – literally 'occult' (Latin = *occulta)* – about nature's workings. It specialized, in particular, in uncovering what were known as 'occult virtues', whose remarkable effects were manifest to experience in the form of natural marvels but whose causes remained beyond the reach of human intellect, and so could not be rationally explained. In the third part of his *De Vita Libri Tres (Three Books on Life),* the Italian Neoplatonist (and high magic's greatest Renaissance theoretician), Marsilio Ficino, spoke about the example of talismanic stones whose power depended not just on 'the qualities recognized by the senses, but also and much more on certain properties … hidden to our senses and scarcely at all recognized by reason' (cited by Copenhaver 1984: 525). Another Italian humanist, Giovanni Pico della Mirandola, described the magician's craft as to bring forth 'into the open the miracles concealed in the recesses of the world, in the depths of nature, and in the storehouses and mysteries of God, just as if she herself were their maker' (cited by Grafton 1990: 111). Agrippa himself explained that, in addition to the qualities of the four elements, there were natural 'virtues' that could be admired but not seen or known. Of all these occult agents, perhaps the most discussed were the sympathies and antipathies that drew natural things together in 'friendship' and drove them apart in 'enmity' ('the way things differ and agree with each other'). Magicians hoped, above all, to master these universal inclinations in things, hoping thereby to manipulate artificially the interactions that resulted.

Also considered crucial among them were the relationships between the 'inferior' and the 'superior'. Intellectual magic had a hierarchical notion of causation and influence, captured elsewhere in *De Occulta Philosophia* by the statement: 'It is clear that all inferior things are subject to higher and (as Proclus says) in a certain fashion each is present inside the other, i.e. the highest is in the lowest and the lowest in the highest' (Maxwell-Stuart 1999: 96). Later in the sixteenth century, another Italian philosopher, Giambattista della Porta, renowned as an exponent and promoter of this kind of magic, quoted Plotinus to the effect that the study had only originated at all 'that the superiors might be seen in these inferiors, and these inferiors in their superiors; earthly things in heavenly … likewise heavenly things in earthly' (cited by

Clark 1997: 218). Obviously, this was the ultimate rationale that guaranteed the workings of astrology in all its various manifestations.

Finally, Agrippa's definition speaks of producing 'wonderful effects', another aspiration central to intellectual magic and which also explains its elevated self-image and its considerable appeal. This kind of magic was intensely utilitarian as well as intensely cerebral. The magician – the *magus* – was one who could imitate and manipulate nature's most fundamental and challenging operations in order to create powerful and dazzling works of his own. Something of this is captured in the subtide which della Porta gave to his highly influential book on magic, which first appeared at Naples in 1558 – *Magiae Naturalis, sive de Miraculis Rerum Naturalium* (*Natural Magic, or the Miracles of Natural Things*).

With an illustrious pedigree stretching back to ancient Persia, therefore – and, in addition, to a mythical Egyptian philosopher, Hermes Trismegistus, and a series of very real Neoplatonists that included Proclus, Porphyry and Plotinus – magic signified the pursuit by adepts of a highly elevated and esoteric form of wisdom based on the perceived presence in the world of secret patterns and mysterious intelligences possessing real efficacy in nature and human affairs. In the *De Occulta Philosophia,* as well as in the writings of Ficino, this causation was seen in terms of an organically related hierarchy of powers divided into three levels. Influences descended from the highest level of the angelic or intellectual world of spirits, to the stellar and planetary world of the heavens, which in turn governed the behaviour of earthly things and their physical changes. The magician was, in consequence, someone who sought to ascend to knowledge of these superior powers and then accentuate their normal workings by drawing them down artificially to produce amazing effects. 'The Agrippan Magus', writes Frances Yates, 'aims at mounting up through all three worlds … and beyond even that to the Creator himself whose divine creative power he will obtain' (Yates 1964: 136). In effect he needed three sets of abilities and achieved three kinds of insight. Agrippa's definition continues in this way:

> So whoever wishes to study this faculty must be skilled in natural philosophy in which is to be found the qualities of things and the hidden properties of everything which exists. He must also be expert in mathematics, and in the aspects and figures of the stars, upon which depends the sublime virtue and property of everything; and in theology in which are manifested those immaterial substances which regulate and administer all things. Without these, he cannot possibly be able to understand the rationality of magic. (Maxwell-Stuart 1999: 116)

Natural philosophy; mathematics and astrology; theology and religion. Magic's claim to be the highest form of wisdom depended on its ability to embrace all three aspects of the world order, elementary, celestial and supercelestial, and all forms of access to its truths. At the highest level, it became as much an act of mystical illumination as a piece of science. Here, the magician aimed at a priest-like role and his wonders competed with the miracles of religion. Indeed, another of the characteristic features of intellectual magic is its invariably intense religiosity and sense of piety, even if this was often construed as misplaced or superstitious. It liked to trace its doctrines to ancient sages (or *prisci theologi*) and contemporaries of Moses, of whom Hermes, who himself was both natural philosopher and priest, was only one (a tendency shared by Isaac Newton: McGuire and Rattansi 1966). Its conception of the world that it struggled to comprehend and master was always as a religious entity – something created by a divine intelligence that was the ultimate model for the magician's own creative intelligence. Agrippa himself thought that the mysteries of the angelic intelligences above the stars could only be grasped by rites – by what he called in Book 3 of the *De Occulta Philosophia* 'Ceremonial Magic'. Herein lie some of the most notorious and esoteric aspects of intellectual magic, captured particularly in the cabbalistic principle of the power lying encoded in the names of God and in holy language in general. 'The Kabbalah', wrote the German humanist Johannes Reuchlin in 1517, 'is the reception, through symbols, of a divine revelation handed down so that we may contemplate, to our salvation, both God and the individual Forms' (Maxwell-Stuart 1999: 139).

However, 'ceremonial magic' and cabbala were always less prominent in intellectual magic than the study of the two lower levels of Agrippa's tripartite world – that is to say, 'Celestial Magic' and 'Natural Magic'. Communing with angels and tapping their knowledge and powers were very different and vastly more dangerous than dealing with the properties of terrestrial things or the effluvia of the planets and stars, and it was with these joint inquiries that magic was mostly occupied and in which it made its biggest impact. They were joint because of the relationship between 'superior' and 'inferior' things on which magic, as we have seen, was fundamentally based. Magic, said many commentators, was the 'marrying' of heaven and earth. Besides astrology, the key ingredient of 'Celestial Magic' was mathematics, linked to artificial and mechanical marvels and to numerology. Book 2 of *De Occulta Philosophia* dealt accordingly with the creation of 'living' statues and other marvellous mechanical feats (classed as mathematical), the virtues of single numbers and of arrangements of them (more like numerology), universal harmony and the effects of music, images for 'talismans' corresponding to the planets and zodiacal signs and the nature and powers of incantations and 'Orphic' hymns. In Book 1, reserved for 'Natural Magic', Agrippa turned correspondingly to 'those things which are in the world', identifying in particular the studies of medicine and physics. These terrestrial matters were to be taken up above all with the four elements and their mixtures, the nature of the occult virtues of things, the idea of signatures stamped upon objects corresponding to their stars and the manipulation of sympathies and antipathies and other 'stellar virtues in natural objects' (Yates, 1964: 132).

None of these three 'levels' of magic was, or was intended to be, separate from the others; quite the contrary. The universe of virtues, powers and influences, whether these were deemed to be earthly, heavenly or spiritual, was organically and hierarchically integrated. One of the reasons why we tend to miss this point is that we have a much more exclusive understanding of the category of nature and feel that some of these topics do not belong in natural science at all. But in this respect we are largely inheritors of trends that post-dated the kind of knowledge that Agrippa sought. For him and many other Neoplatonists, the relationship between objects in the lower or material world and the celestial powers that ruled their behaviour was a genuinely natural relationship. When Ficino adoped the *spiritus mundi* as the link between the two, he was thinking of something substantial. The occult virtues that governed so many of nature's secret processes and produced so many of its wonderful effects stemmed from the natural powers of the heavens; Agrippa, like Ficino, derived occult events from the *spiritus mundi* and the rays of the heavenly bodies. The idea of signatures also contained the argument that the heavens stamped particular characteristics and uses onto natural things from above. Talismans could only be thought to work if pneumatic links were assumed between *spiritus* and *materia* and if the characters and figures placed on them were capable of natural activity.

Even incantations and songs could draw down stellar influences through the channel of the *spiritus* – and there are wonderful accounts in Ficino of how this astrological music was to be achieved (Walker 1958: 12–24). Thus, despite Agrippa's restriction of the label 'natural magic' to the first or elementary level of the world, his depiction of its relationship to the second, celestial level – and of that level's relationship to the first – is entirely in what he conceived of as naturalistic terms. The angelic powers of the highest level of magic might be truly spiritual things, and only something like a religious discipline could engage with them. But everything else about magic was natural – it was *all* 'natural magic'. Besides its grandly astrological and mathematical foundations and its broad commitment to physics and medicine, the sorts of individual scientific fields that Agrippa associated with the marrying of heaven and earth were arithmetic, music, geometry, optics, astronomy and mechanics.

It has to be said, too, that down-to-earth naturalism is present in many of magic's individual pronouncements, no matter what we may think of the concepts and causalities that underpinned them. In 1608 we find Oswald Croll plotting out the various correspondences that existed between the microcosm and the macrocosm and suggesting, for example, that 'the generation of epilepsy in the lesser world is the same as that of storm and thunder in the greater'. In 1650 we find Athanasius Kircher explaining reports that fishermen captured swordfish in the Straits of Messina by talking to them by saying that 'whenever a sound meets an object with which it is in correspondence and harmony, it disturbs only this object and leaves other things, no matter how many there may be, undisturbed because there is no correspondence between it and them' (Maxwell-Stuart 1999: 150–1, 129–31). Agrippa himself accounted for occult properties, their medical uses and 'magical rites' in similar terms:

> Anything which has within it an excess of any quality or property, such as heat, cold, audacity, fear, sadness, anger, love, hate or any other passion or virtue … these things especially prompt and provoke a similar quality, passion or virtue. So fire occasions fire, water occasions water, and a bold quality occasions boldness. Physicians know that a brain helps the brain and a lung helps the lungs. Thus they say that the right eye of a frog cures inflammation of the right eye, when hung round one's neck in a piece of undyed cloth, while its left cures the left eye … Therefore if we want to perform magical rites with a view to provoking some property or virtue, let us seek out living things, or other things in which such properties conspicuously exist, and from them let us take for ourselves the part in which such a property or virtue is most pre-eminently strong. (Maxwell-Stuart, 1999: 125–6)

Love was thus provoked by taking from particularly affectionate animals (pigeons, doves, swallows) the parts of them (hearts, genitals) where desire was most strongly concentrated at a time when their sexual appetites were at their height. Like its popular counterpart, intellectual magic clearly had a logic that guaranteed its practical efficacy in the eyes of its users and defenders.

There were those who sought out the highest forms of gnostic, theurgical enlightenment in magic, at Agrippa's third level. A recent study by Deborah Harkness of the Elizabethan *magus,* John Dee, for example, accounts for his attempts to talk to angels in terms of this kind of magic, set nevertheless in the context of an improved – indeed, a kind of ultimate – natural philosophy. Dee emerges from this book as very much a man of his age, sharing in its intellectual traditions. Despairing of conventional natural philosophy, convinced that the world was coming to an end and imbued with large doses of prophetism, perfectionism and universalism (and supported intermittently by powerful patrons), he sought to bridge the terrestrial and the supercelestial and ascend to true wisdom by means of divine revelations from angelic intermediaries and messengers. His was a science conducted as revealed theology and via spirit experiments. For him the world was an opaque holy text to be read in the light of the language that had originally created it and given it power – the true cabbala of nature. Dee tried literally to learn this language from the angel Raphael; he tried, that is, to speak God's language, hoping thereby to transform human knowledge and the declining world simultaneously. As another of his angels put it to him, this was 'to talk in mortal sounds with such as are immortal'. Predictably enough, God's language turned out to conform to no known rules of grammar, syntax or pronunciation, and to be utterable only as the world did actually end (Harkness 1999; *cf.* Clulee 1988).

Nevertheless, Neoplatonic magic was, on the whole, of more modest and more practical ambitions. Magicians mostly claimed to practise only natural magic – or *magia naturalis* – and concentrated on the understanding of material forms and the production of this-worldly effects. This cautious and restrained approach, often profoundly empirical and observational in character, gave their work a powerful appeal in early modern scientific circles (survey in Copenhaver 1988; Shumaker 1989, is a study of four typical discussions of natural magic between 1590 and 1657). It was a dominant influence on Paracelsus and on his seventeenth-century followers and adaptors, including Daniel Sennert and Joan Baptista van Helmont, and it served to give coherence to the polymathic thinking of Girolamo Cardano which embraced the fields of medicine, natural philosophy, mathematics and astrology. In England it informed many of the projects associated with the circle of Samuel Hartlib during the 1640s and was one of the many tributaries feeding into the thought and activities of the Royal Society (Webster 1975; 1982). Both its range and its essentially operative and mimetic – that is to say, naturalistic – qualities are seen, above all, in the recognition given it by Francis Bacon. Bacon certainly criticized elements of the magical approach to knowledge, attacking Paracelsus, Cardano and, indeed, Agrippa as he did so. But his dislike was more of the way things had hitherto been done, not of the concept of magic itself, which he called 'ancient and honourable', placing it in the 'most excellent tier' of natural philosophy. Indeed, his understanding of it was, in Agrippan terms, as 'the science which applies the knowledge of hidden forms to the production of wonderful operations; and by uniting (as they say) actives with passives, displays the wonderful works of nature' (cited by Clark 1997: 222). Bacon built many of the ideals of magical intellectual enterprise into his depiction of the ideal scientific community in his *New Atlantis* (1624); he incorporated many individual natural magical enquiries and speculations into his *Sylva Sylvarum* (1624); and he even projected (but did not complete) a 'natural history' of sympathies and antipathies (on the magical elements in Bacon, see especially Rossi 1968: 11–35).

Intellectual magic and the scientific revolution

The case of Bacon – and, indeed, of other 'mainstream' natural philosophers who adopted high magical concepts and procedures – raises questions about the relationship between the history of intellectual magic and those transformations in scientific knowledge and practice conventionally known as the 'Scientific Revolution'. Such questions need not be seen as inevitable, however. We might choose instead to discuss the world of science in the sixteenth and seventeenth centuries, with all its many fluctuations and changes, without invoking the concept of 'revolution' and simply talking about the various loose conceptual schemes – Aristotelian, mechanistic and, yes, magical – that, competing or mingling, allowed individual thinkers to ground their explanations of phenomena in a preferred cosmology. Alternatively, should we wish to preserve the notion of a 'Scientific Revolution' in some form or other, we might still write an entirely convincing account of what was truly new and radical in early modern science without finding much space in it for intellectual magic (see, for example, Shapin 1996). Nevertheless, it has been the case historiographically that magic has most often been related to the yardsticks supposedly provided by the 'Scientific Revolution' – just as that revolution has been identified, in part, in terms of its capacity to disenchant the world. On the one hand, magic's reputation has varied according to whether it is seen to have advanced or retarded 'modern science'; on the other, 'modern science' itself has been variously judged in terms of its rejection or retention of magical elements. Inevitable or not, therefore, there seems to be a need to relate the magic we have been describing to the science we have come to recognize as definitional of early modern intellectual change (Henry 1997).

The process started immediately with the revolutionizers themselves, many of whom dismissed, or at least criticized, elements of the magical tradition. An essay by Roy Porter describes how this process continued throughout the period of the European 'Enlightenment' and, indeed, helped 'enlightened' thinkers and writers to establish their own intellectual and social identity (Porter 1999). During the following centuries of the ascendancy of modern science, magic was neglected altogether, even by historians, except as a misguided obstacle in the way of true knowledge. Between the two World Wars, especially in the work of Lynn Thorndike (Thorndike 1923–58), this approach began to be challenged, and then in the 1960s it was completely rejected by the historian Frances Yates – so much so that, for a time, the attempt to rehabilitate intellectual magic became known as the 'Yates thesis'. Yates conducted pioneering fresh research on central figures of the magical tradition, notably Giordano Bruno (Yates 1964), but it was in an essay edited by Charles Singleton (Yates 1967) that she made her central claims on behalf of the 'Hermetic tradition' as, if not scientific modernity itself, then an essential preparing of the ground. What distinguished the 'new science' of the seventeenth century, in her view, was the ideal of human intervention in, and dominion over, nature, an attitude prefigured by the aims of the *magus* set forth in the *Corpus Hermeticum (Hermetical Works)* translated by Ficino and in Agrippa's *De Occulta Philosophia* and also anticipated in the magical enthusiasm for mathematics and mechanics. As a manifesto for the 'advancement of learning' Yates preferred not Bacon's work of that name but the astrologer and 'conjuror' John Dee's preface to his edition of Euclid, although she did recognize in the *New Atlantis* an immensely influential rationalization and remoralization of the Hermetic ideals. She concluded:

If one includes in the [Hermetic] tradition the revived Platonism with the accompanying Pythagoro-Platonic interest in number, the expansion of theories of harmony under the combined pressures of Pythagoro-Platonism, Hermetism, and Cabalism, the intensification of interest in astrology with which genuine astronomical research was bound up, and if one adds to all this complex stream of influences the expansion of alchemy in new forms, it is, I think, impossible to deny that these were the Renaissance forces which turned men's minds in the direction out of which the scientific revolution was to come. (Yates 1967: 273)

Thus, the 'Scientific Revolution', in her view, had two phases; first, the magical and animistic phase, and then the mathematical and mechanical one, each interlinked with the other.

Frances Yates herself – together with others who were prepared to suggest a more central role for the 'occult' sciences, like Allen G. Debus (on Paracelsianism: Debus 1966; on magic generally: Debus 1978), P. M. Rattansi, Charles Webster (especially Webster 1982) and Betty Jo Teeter Dobbs (on Newton and alchemy: Dobbs 1975; 1991) – succeeded in reassessing the significance of magic in the history of science in a manner that will never be altogether reversed. Nevertheless, the 'Yates thesis' itself is no longer thought to be convincing and has now been superseded by an approach to the history of early modern natural philosophy that stresses its eclecticism and heterogeneity and, thus, the lack of any 'single coherent story' to be told about it (Shapin 1996: 10). Partly, the problem was with Yates's own sometimes exaggerated arguments – particularly so in the case of her attribution to Rosicrucianism of a number of key seventeenth-century intellectual and cultural developments (Yates 1972; Vickers 1979). Another difficulty lay with the differences in kind that seemed to persist whenever intellectual magic and the new science were strictly compared, overruling the affinities that Yates had successfully identified. There is, after all, something conceptually irreconcilable between a nature seen as alive and purposive and a nature seen as inert and machine-like – yet the machine metaphor was at the very heart of what many new scientists thought they were trying to achieve. To this fundamental incompatibility may be added others; between the magical (and cabbalistic) idea that 'sounds and words have efficacy in magical operation because that by which Nature works magic first and foremost is the voice of God' (Giovanni Pico della Mirandola, cited by Maxwell-Stuart 1999: 147) and the opposite principle that language is related to the world only arbitrarily by human convention and agreement – adopted by Marin Mersenne, Robert Boyle, Thomas Hobbes, John Wilkins and John Locke; between treating analogy as a way of grasping actual relationships in the universe and seeing it as an heuristic tool, 'subordinate to argument and proof'; between saying that metaphor 'is not just a trope, but reality' and saying it 'is not reality, but only a trope' (Vickers 1984: 95–163, esp. 95, 135). To view the world as a work of art, full of mysteries and capable of surprise, was just not the same as viewing it as driven by regularity and predictability.

Above all, perhaps, it is now realized that appeal does not have to be made solely to the 'Hermetic tradition', or to Neoplatonism more generally, in order to account for the presence in early modern natural philosophy of a widespread enthusiasm for natural magic. It was discussed and evaluated by many whose cosmology and epistemology was still Christian Aristotelian and Thomist. The study of preternatural and artificial marvels had always complemented the study of nature's normal processes in scholasticism, since the latter allowed for the presence of occult qualities in nature of exactly the sort described by Ficino and Agrippa. For Aristotelians the sorts of things that governed normal natural processes were the four qualities of hot and cold, and wet and dry. Preternatural phenomena (events and behaviour that were 'beyond' or 'above' ordinary nature) were often caused by other qualities, not accessible to the senses, that operated in a secret manner. Because they were insensible they were unintelligible in Aristotelian terms – their effects could not be deduced from the perceptible (or manifest) qualities of the objects or creatures in question. But the effects *themselves* embraced some important natural phenomena that could clearly not be ignored. They included gravitation, magnetism, the generation of lower animal forms, the ebbing and flowing of the tides, the effects of electricity, the workings of poisons and their antidotes, and the strange behaviour of many individual plants, minerals and animals. In addition, Aristotelianism also allowed for (indeed, was built upon) purpose and appetite in nature and could therefore readily embrace 'sympathies' and 'antipathies' (as, for example, in the work of Girolamo Fracastoro, an astronomer and physician trained in Padua).

There was, therefore, what Bert Hansen has called a 'scholastic magic', more sober, perhaps, than its Hermetic counterpart, but still dedicated to investigating nature's innermost secrets, to manipulating actives and passives and to producing rare and wonderful effects (Hansen 1978; 1986). In this guise it crops up regularly in the pronouncements – and, indeed, the textbooks – of the early modern Aristotelians who still dominated university education in physics well into the seventeenth century. The occult causes of diseases were also widely discussed by the orthodox medical theorists and practitioners of the age, together with the commentators on Galen. Here, writers like Jean Fernel, who was physician to the French king Henri II, Levinus Lemnius, a physician in the province of Zeeland in the Low Countries, and Daniel Sennert, the leading professor of medicine in Lutheran Germany in the early seventeenth century, published important works with titles like *De Abditis Rerum Causis (Of the Secret Causes of Things)* and *De Miraculis Occultis Naturae (Of the Hidden Wonders of Nature)*.

In a sense, natural magic was an attempt – shared, as we have just seen, by early modern 'Hermeticists' and Aristotelians alike – to deal more satisfactorily with the epistemological difficulties created by occult qualities. It tried to account for occult causes and effects and render them less mysterious, less unintelligible. In this respect it contributed to an intellectual enterprise, identified by Ron Millen as the 'manifestation' of occult qualities, that formed one strand of contemporary scientific innovation and which he describes as 'a serious effort … to bring occult qualities within the scope of natural philosophy' (Millen 1985: 190). Among the most prominent figures involved were Pomponazzi, Fracastoro, Cardano, Fernel, Bacon and Sennert. The overall aim was to break the connection between insensibility and unintelligibility – in effect, to retain the occult as a category of investigation, but to make manifest its features. In this way, science and natural magic would no longer be merely complementary but identical. We can see this happening in the many sixteenth- and seventeenth-century scientific textbooks that presented natural magic simply as a branch of physics and also in the popularity of natural magic as a subject for the dissertations defended by examinands in Europe's universities.

Occult causes could still be attacked and derided by the spokesmen of the newest, 'mechanical' approaches to natural philosophy, for whom they represented intellectual evasion as well as philosophical nonsense. 'Sympathy' and 'antipathy', in particular, were ridiculed as things that could not possibly cause motion between inert, insentient corpuscles of matter. But another striking argument by a historian of science – in this case John Henry – is that the onset of the mechanical philosophy did not necessarily mean the end of occult qualities anyway. Purely mechanical explanations for things like 'spring' (the supposed elasticity of air), the cohesion of matter and magnetism were extremely clumsy and implausible, and for the cause of weight a mechanical explanation could not be provided at all. Even transference of motion itself remained inexplicable to many, without the existence of active principles. In the end, Isaac Newton himself could only come to terms with gravitational forces by arguing that there must be 'occult active principles in the world to initiate and preserve motions' (Henry 1986: 339). For this he was attacked by Leibnitz, who said in a famous accusation that Newton's gravity was a 'chimerical thing, a scholastic occult quality'. Henry suggests not only that Newton was able to distance himself from the kind of unintelligibility attached to the scholastic version of occult qualities, but that his stance on the whole issue had been anticipated by a series of natural philosophers among his older contemporaries. English new scientists, in particular, were able more and more to accept the fact that such qualities were not accessible to the senses as it became apparent that *many* natural qualities were insensible and that it was only their effects that needed to be accessible to empirical investigation. Insensibility was, after all, at the heart of the corpuscularian conception of matter. Many exponents of the new science were thus able to reconcile the idea of occult properties with mechanical explanations of phenomena – including Robert Boyle, Henry More, Robert Hooke, Walter Charleton and William Petty. They were helped in this by a desire, felt throughout the scientific circles of Restoration England, to develop a natural philosophy that would protect traditional Anglican theology and the orthodoxies that went with it. In this respect, the principles of activity and immateriality that were allied with occult aetiology represented important protections against atheism and subversive sectarian enthusiasm. What seems to have happened, then, was a continuation of a very old intellectual preoccupation by other means, rather than an abandonment of it. 'The mechanists of the seventeenth century', George MacDonald Ross has written, 'had a considerable problem if they wanted to maintain that they were different in kind from the magicians of old, and were not simply the first generation of *successful* magicians' (MacDonald Ross 1985: 102, author's emphasis; *cf.* Henry 1986; Hutchison 1982; Millen 1985: 186).

These are admittedly complicated matters to do with the intricacies of early modern natural philosophy – and they are still being researched by historians. But they do give a good idea of how scholars currently view the issues that Frances Yates was the first to raise openly. Essentially, there is now an unwillingness simply to confront the 'Hermetic tradition' with the 'Scientific Revolution' – let alone 'magic' with 'science' – or to think in terms of a single narrative of change. Instead, historians tend to talk much more about the multiple and diverse ways in which the natural world might be confronted and explained and to concentrate not on conceptual monoliths but on overlapping thematic strands that illuminate the conflicting, changing and essentially eclectic interests of the age. Two recent studies have made a considerable impact in this respect and will provide final examples of how some of the preoccupations of intellectual magic are now being related to their cultural and social contexts. William Eamon's book *Science and the Secrets of Nature,* published in 1994, traces the many collections of 'secrets' published in the sixteenth and seventeenth centuries, which embraced not only nature's spontaneous productions but also the recipes of the arts and crafts, medical remedies and mechanical devices. These works, he argues, impinged greatly on the general development of natural philosophy by presenting the secret as a tested and classified experiment with practical and theoretical applications, by suggesting that scientific knowledge was characterized by the pursuit and disclosure of things hidden in the world, and by contributing to the emergence of rigorous analysis and attention to detail. A more recent book of 1998 by Lorraine Daston and Katharine Park, entiled *Wonders and the Order of Nature,*

1150–1750, looks at both wonder itself as a collective scientific sensibility – as something felt – and at the things that medieval and early modern scientists found wonderful – monsters, gems that shone in the dark, petrifying springs, celestial apparitions and so on. The two authors suggest that natural magic was crucial to the way naturalists of all sorts envisioned their own activity and divided up the natural world into various orders of being and causation (Eamon 1994; Daston and Park 1998).

Natural magic and demonic magic

In stressing the successful reception of magical ideas and practices and their appeal to many early modern intellectuals engaged in natural philosophy, we should not forget the very strong lobby directed *against* them on religious and moral (rather than philosophical) grounds. Quite simply, intellectual magic was denounced as demonic as frequently as was its popular counterpart. The attack came from many quarters – indeed, from anyone sufficiently sceptical of the intrinsic powers of words and signs, or of amulets and talismans, to think that demons must be involved in their workings. It came especially from those whom D. P. Walker memorably called the 'evangelical hard-heads' of the age (Walker 1958: 145–85, discussing Gianfrancesco Pico della Mirandola, Johann Weyer and Thomas Erastus). In general, we can say that the religious reformers who belonged to the main churches of the period, together with a vast number of conservative moral and social commentators, were always likely to express opposition to 'high' magic. Sometimes it was denounced in its entirety; more usually it was said to have declined from its original integrity and purity in the ancient world, becoming corrupt and evil in its present form. In 1580, the French witchcraft writer (though not a church reformer) Jean Bodin defined the magician simply as 'someone who knowingly and deliberately tries to achieve something by diabolical means' (Maxwell-Stuart 1999: 122). Magicians were often said to be constantly teetering on the very edge of respectability, always liable to topple over it into outright devil-worship. Although perhaps an extreme case, it is hardly surprising that John Dee's 'angel diaries' should have been published by Meric Casaubon in 1659 with the aim of exposing them as records not of conversations with heavenly spirits but of consultations with 'false lying' ones – with demons. But even the more routine and naturalistic aspects of magic could attract the charge of demonism, since any attempt to trace and manipulate nature's most hidden processes in order to produce amazing effects smacked intrinsically of aid by extra-human powers. In this respect, the boundary between miracles and wonders (*false miracles*) was seen to be in need of constant redrawing. Additionally, occult disciplines like alchemy and astrology were subject to sustained criticism, as both irreligious and subject to charlatanry.

Mostly, these were aspects of the religious quarrels and divisions of the times, revealing only the (admittedly very important) extent to which the acquisition and distribution of knowledge about the natural world was subject to ideological interventions. However, probably the most common position was to distinguish natural magic and demonic magic as the two parallel expressions of a single *magia,* and this does have a number of important implications for the way we look back on the history of witchcraft and magic now (Zambelli 1988). The Portuguese Jesuit and inquisitor Benito Pereira is a typical example. In a treatise 'against the false and superstitious arts' he said that all forms of magic were of two sorts: 'The first is Natural Magic in which wonders are created by the individual artifice of certain people who make use of things which are natural. The second is Unnatural Magic which invokes evil spirits and uses their power for its operation' (Maxwell-Stuart 1999: 117). This statement, and hundreds of others like it, contained two implied comparisons. Most obviously, it expressed the cautions we have just noted; it allowed for a genuine form of magic but set it in proximity to a false version. In this way, it acted as a warning against 'the false and superstitious arts'. Less obviously, but just as significantly, it also placed the powers of evil spirits in proximity to those of magicians. In doing this it revealed an attitude to demonism, very common in the sixteenth and seventeenth centuries, in which the devil became the analogue of the natural magician.

In every Christian society the devil has meant different things to different people. In the Renaissance period he was the serpent of the Garden of Eden in the Old Testament, the roaring lion of the New Testament, the force behind the Antichrist, the model for tyrants, the figure who tempted Faustus, the ruler of the demons who ran through the streets at carnival time and many more besides. But if we restrict ourselves solely to natural philosophical questions, the devil *had* to be a natural magician. According to orthodox Christian theology, the devil had to be both a supremely powerful figure and at the same time inferior to God. He had to be able to achieve marvellous things in the created world but without ever rivalling God's own interventions; in other words, he too had to be able to perform wonders not miracles. In natural philosophical terms this made him the exact equivalent of the natural magician, who also specialized in preternature. A physician from Ferrara wrote in 1605 that magic was 'a single thing' and that the devil only worked through natural secrets just as the natural magicians did. In 1658 a colleague in Seville wrote similarly that diabolic magic was 'the ape of natural magic' (cited by Clark 1997: 234). Another way to put this is to say that the difference between Pereira's 'Natural Magic' and his 'Unnatural Magic' was one of intention, not one of substance. The same kinds of natural processes were manipulated in each case, but for completely opposite purposes; 'unnatural' magic was still natural, even if it was evil.

In the demonology we surveyed in the last chapter, portrayals of the devil as a natural magician, albeit a supremely gifted one, were actually quite precise. The theologian Hieronymus Zanchy said that there was 'in herbs and stones, and other natural things a marvellous force, although hidden, by which many strange things can be performed. And this force is especially well marked and perceived by the devil.' According to King James VI of Scotland, the devil was 'far cunninger than man in the knowledge of all the occult properties of nature'. Nicolas Rémy wrote that devils had 'a perfect knowledge of the secret and hidden properties of natural things' (all cited by Clark 1997: 245). Perhaps the best statement of all comes from the Elizabethan Puritan writer and preacher, William Perkins:

> Whereas in nature there be some properties, causes, and effects, which man never imagined to be; others, that men did once know, but are now forgot; some which men knewe not, but might know; and thousands which can hardly, or not at all be known: all these are most familiar unto [the devil], because in themselves they be no wonders, but only misteries and secrets, the vertue and effect whereof he hath sometime observed since his creation, (cited by Clark 1997: 246–7)

What then are the implications for historians of this early modern way of relating and comparing natural and demonic magic? One of them takes us back to witchcraft beliefs and to questions about opposition to them and their decline – questions that were raised in the previous chapter. For if natural magic and demonism were exact analogues, notably in terms of their causation, could not natural magic have posed a powerful threat to witchcraft beliefs? Could it not have accounted successfully for the puzzling effects blamed on witches by giving a non-demonic explanation of them that was just as causally complete? It was Hugh Trevor-Roper in his famous 'European witch-craze' essay who first suggested that natural magicians like Agrippa and Cardano and alchemists like Paracelsus and Van Helmont were among the enemies of witchcraft trials, while those who attacked Neoplatonism, Hermetic ideas and Paracelsian medicine were often keen defenders of them (Trevor-Roper 1967: 132). And it does make sense to assume that a demonic cause for witchcraft could have been made redundant – and the witchcraft itself explained away – if all the mysterious phenomena at issue were given purely natural explanations. What better source for this than the science that specialized in accounting for mysterious phenomena in terms of the secrets of nature?

There is undoubtedly evidence that supports this possibility but it is not decisive (see Clark 1997: 235–50 for a full account). Agrippa did indeed defend a peasant woman accused of witchcraft in 1519 and was said to mock the very idea of witchcraft as a delusion and a dream (Zambelli 1988: 137–8; *cf.* Zambelli 1974). Paracelsus, Cardano and Van Helmont all tried to give non-demonic accounts of witches' powers and Cardano (whose views were later borrowed by Johann Weyer) said that witchcraft could only be believed by those who were ignorant 'of natural causes and effects' (for Cardano on witchcraft see Maxwell-Stuart 1999: 174–6). The classic natural magician of the sixteenth century, della Porta, reported in the first edition of his *Magiae Naturalis* an experiment with the ointment that witches were supposed to smear on themselves to enable them to fly. He had tested it by physically beating an old woman after she had used it and fallen into a trance, so that he could show her the bruises when she regained consciousness. She still insisted that she had flown to the witches' sabbat but he was able to prove that she had dreamed the whole experience under the influence of the narcotics in the ointment. The outstanding English witchcraft sceptic of the seventeenth century, John Webster, drew heavily on the natural magical tradition and, once again, insisted that there was 'no other ground or reason of dividing Magick into natural and Diabolical, but only that they differ in the end and use'. If both were worked by natural agency, then men might do 'without the aid of devils whatsoever they can do' (cited by Clark 1997: 239).

When looked at more closely, however, the witchcraft beliefs of the magicians turn out to be ambiguous. Johannes Trithemius, to whom Agrippa presented a first draft of *De Occulta Philosophia,* discussed witchcraft in terms reminiscent of *Malleus Maleficarum,* and both Paracelsus and Cardano made remarks that suggest uncertainty rather than outright rejection. In any case, as we saw in Chapter 2, scepticism about witchcraft could derive from things that had little to do with 'high' magic – the widespread attribution of witchcraft phenomena to the condition known as 'melancholy' and to dreaming, or doubts about the legal procedures employed in witch trials, for example. In the cases of Reginald Scot and John Webster, it seems to have been unorthodox, even radical, theology that mattered more than the attempt to explain witchcraft away in terms of natural magical findings. Johann Weyer, who disbelieved in witchcraft altogether, also denounced the entire magical and Neoplatonic traditions, despite his time as Agrippa's servant and assistant; he is thus a major exception to Trevor-Roper's generalization. There is, too, the wider question of whether, in comparing the powers of devils to the powers of magicians, early modern writers were not *strengthening* the credibility of witchcraft, rather than weakening it. Witchcraft authors may, if anything, have been helped in their portrayals of the demonic efficacy that lay behind witchcraft by their increasing familiarity with its natural magical counterpart.

We cannot be sure, then, whether natural magical explanations sustained witchcraft beliefs or undermined them. But what is clear is the sheer level of interest shown in witchcraft matters by exponents of 'high' magic – and, indeed, by many natural philosophers who made a special study of the occult aspects of the natural world. Here we have another example of an aspect of demonology and witchcraft that was also discussed in the last chapter – the capacity of these subjects to arouse interest in a wide range of intellectual contexts *other than* the legal prosecution of witches. They obviously appealed to some of the brightest scientific talents of the day who showed a theoretical interest in them that bore little relation to witch-hunting. Whether these men ended up believing more or less in witchcraft than they would otherwise have done therefore seems less important than their use of the subject as a kind of intellectual resource.

What a statement like William Perkins's suggests is that the devil posed a particular epistemological challenge to the theorists – the challenge of accounting for both his knowledge of natural things and his capacity to operate in the natural world in terms of the concepts and categories of natural magic. As Girolamo Cardano said: 'No discussion is as difficult or as excellent as that which concerns demons.' But this meant that witchcraft too, which, after all, was one of the things the devil actually brought about with his occult powers, became a suitable subject for natural philosophers to analyse. Indeed, it was an especially revealing subject to analyse since it was full of precisely the sorts of phenomena that gave natural magic its reputation as the most demanding and yet most revealing branch of scientific inquiry. It was defined, as we have already seen, as the practical application of abstruse natural knowledge to produce wonderful effects. In the case of witchcraft, there were several demonically caused effects that conformed exactly to this definition – known both generally in terms of traditional expectations and, more precisely, from the confessions that were emerging from witchcraft trials. These effects were all quite clearly bizarre and abnormal in relation to nature's usual workings. But they were nevertheless still natural rather than supernatural or miraculous; they were, again, preternatural phenomena. How then were they brought about? And what light did this shed on the natural world?

Let us look at some examples. First, there was the question of how witches were able to travel vast distances to their meetings (or 'sabbats') by flying. When they were also reported to be at home in their beds at the time, did this mean that they attended the sabbat in spirit only or did it mean that they merely dreamed that they were there? The natural philosophers and the demonologists gave an unhesitatingly naturalistic answer; they either travelled really to the sabbat, 'transvected' through the air at an enormous speed by the devil's prodigious (that is to say, natural magical) powers, or they were deluded about going altogether. Sometimes the devil put counterfeit bodies in their beds to confuse the issue, but, in general, transvection was either a true preternatural phenomenon or a product of dreams – for which, of course, preternatural explanations were likewise possible. Then there was the further question, also linked to the sabbat, of whether or not witches who had sex with devils could then bear demonic children. Again the answer was naturalistic; the devil had no procreative power but could borrow human semen and use it to inseminate witches so that they gave birth to human children. Monstrous demons might be instantly substituted for the babies delivered to pregnant witches but this was still a secondary complication, with no effect on the main claim. A third topic was metamorphosis; could witches turn themselves or their victims into animals, particularly wolves? With few exceptions no one accepted this as a real phenomenon. For the most part it was attributed to the strange effects of the human imagination, especially when inflamed by melancholy. Alternatively, the devil might replace lycanthropic humans with real wolves so quickly that transmutation appeared to occur, or represent illusory wolves to the senses either by 'wrapping' real humans in the required shape or condensing the air between eye and object in such a way as to produce a suitable effigy. But these illusions were allowed for as part of the devil's natural powers and so a consistently naturalistic explanation for lycanthropy was maintained. A yet further debate concerned the possibility of demons causing strange diseases, an idea accepted by most physicians of the period. The diseases included melancholy, epilepsy, paralysis and contortions, the vomiting of bizarre objects, impotence and the inflammation of all the human passions to the point of pathological disturbance. Finally, there was the issue of the apparently malevolent efficacy of words – whether witches could achieve their *maleficium* merely by the pronunciation of curses or charms. Once more, an apparently very bizarre form of causation was denied on the grounds that language was merely a human convention for conveying meanings and its apparent efficacy was explained as a demonic intervention. When witches cursed, the words themselves caused nothing; they were, instead, signs to the devil to step in and bring the desired misfortune about by natural means.

It is quite extraordinary how often these five topics were analysed, not merely in the pages of those who wrote directly on witchcraft but more generally in the field of early modern natural magic. We therefore have to ask ourselves what scientific purposes these analyses served. At one level, obviously, they were simply ways of accounting for witchcraft – of explaining it in accordance with the scientific criteria of the age. They were ways of answering doubts about the very possibility of witchcraft as a real activity with real effects. But there is, in addition, a deeper purpose in these discussions, a purpose indicated by a remark of Francis Bacon in his *The Advancement of Learning,* in the course of his defence of natural magic as a scientific field of interest. Arguing for a new study of natural marvels, he asked that the arts of witchcraft be included in it:

> from the speculation and consideration of them (if they be diligently unravelled) a useful light may be gained, not only for the true judgement of the offences of persons charged with such practices, but likewise for the further disclosing of the secrets of nature, (cited by Clark 1997: 254)

What Bacon was saying was that stories of witchcraft were not merely evidence in a legal sense – they were evidence in an empirical sense as well, what he called elsewhere 'experiments of witchcraft'. They contained the moral deviations of men and women but also the physical deviations of a nature under demonic control. Like the other marvels and prodigies, the secrets and wonders that preoccupied the natural magicians of Bacon's Europe, they afforded privileged access into nature's innermost workings. This is the reason why Giambattista della Porta included his witchcraft experiment in (at least the first edition of) his book on natural magic. The way we might put this today would be to say that the subject of witchcraft had become particularly rich in thought-experiments. Experimenting with it in any practical way was obviously not advisable – beyond the beating up of old ladies – but all manner of insights might be gained by imagining what would have to follow for such strange phenomena as transvection or metamorphosis or the instrumental power of words to be true and what needed to be the case for them to be false. What was at stake, it seems, was the issue of scientific intelligibility *itself*, and the various criteria by which it was achieved in a particular scientific community at a particular time in European history.

Magic and politics

In every such scientific community, there are those who want to work at the very limits of the discipline, even if the paradigmatic constraints classically described by Thomas Kuhn act as a brake in this respect. This, after all, is the most demanding, the most innovative and frequently the most rewarding kind of science to do. This is especially true in periods of rapid change in scientific thought and practice, when Kuhn's 'paradigms' are at their least effective. By its very nature, early modern natural magic provided such an opportunity, and this chapter has sought to explain why. Magic's very concentration on occult causes made it particularly challenging from an intellectual point of view, while its promise of marvellous effects made it exciting as an observational and empirical practice and offered material rewards as well as renown. It was also thought to be especially enlightening from a religious point of view, giving access to the most fundamental aspects of God's creation and improving closeness to the Creator himself. All these attractions were summed up in what the word 'magic' meant to those intellectuals who saw in it the sum of wisdom and insight.

What has also become apparent in the most recent research on intellectual magic and the occult sciences in general is that they also had considerable political appeal, especially in the circles in which many magicians moved and received patronage. For although one thinks of figures like Agrippa and Paracelsus as almost physical and intellectual nomads, many of the intellectuals who defended or practised high magic were linked to specific monarchical or princely courts and aristocratic households. This is a pattern recognizable in Ficino's relationship with the Medici, John Dee's with Elizabeth I and her courtiers and della Porta's with Luigi d'Este and Federico Cesi (on della Porta, see Eamon 1991: 39–40). We thus arrive finally at a politics of high magic to match – and in part explain – the politics of witchcraft belief that we looked at earlier. In one way, this discovery is not at all surprising. Magic could offer a vocabulary for rulership and the exercise of authority (even for Elizabethan imperialism, in the case of Dee), just as it provided a pattern for science. The powers and attributes of rulers were often seen in divine and mystical terms in Renaissance Europe and their ability to provide solutions to political problems was regarded as thaumaturgical and charismatic, as much as administrative and logistical (aspects of governing that could rest on very shaky foundations). Monarchs and princes who liked to think of themselves as removed from the scrutiny of their subjects and in possession of absolute or semi-absolute 'prerogatives' were, in many ways, *magus*-like figures. Just as the latter worked in secret ways and on secret matters, so did princes in the realm of *arcana imperii* (secrets of state). Just as the latter sought to achieve wonderful effects in the field of natural philosophy, so the magician-ruler – like Mercury with his caduceus, it has been suggested (Brooks-Davies 1983) – aimed at *mira* in the sphere of government. Religiosity, ritualism and even hints of hoped-for infallibility were common to both. This, after all, is the age in which French and English monarchs cured those suffering from 'scrofula' by means of the 'royal touch', a politically inspired miracle that repeatedly had to be distinguished from magical forms of healing that were otherwise identical to it in form (Bloch 1973).

Many modern commentators have remarked on the way in which court festivals and pageants – notably masques – embodied such ideals. In a ritual setting, they celebrated the magical power and aura of the ruler and his or her court by means of stage effects and other spectacles that were themselves marvels of hidden invention and technology (Parry 1981; Kogan 1986; Greene 1987). Often they pitted royal figures against evil forms of magic and witchcraft – *theurgia* versus *goetia* – in a manner that suggests ritual disenchantment (Clark 1997: 634–54). In another illustration of the links between magic and politics, it has also been noted how the processes of alchemy, in particular, were often applied allegorically to the problems of maintaining order and harmony in societies divided by religious and other conflicts (classically Yates 1972; Moran 1991b; recent reappraisal by Mendelsohn 1992). In the world of early modern literature there is, perhaps, no more effective portrayal of these various aspects of the political occult, including its ambiguity, than the figure of Prospero in Shakespeare's last play *The Tempest*. In some respects, Prospero is a Baconian figure, a natural magician seeking knowledge and control of nature's secret powers; he nevertheless renounces magic before returning to power as the Duke of Milan.

The fictional Prospero, according to Stephen Orgel, is a royal scientist and masque-maker who exemplifies Walter Raleigh's definition of magic as 'the connection of natural agents … wrought by a wise man to the bringing forth of such effects as are wonderful to those that know not their causes' (Orgel 1987: 20). But even a real king could be fêted as a magician. Bacon addressed James I as a Hermetic figure, at once a ruler, priest and *magus*; the royal dedication of Robert Fludd's *Utriusque Cosmi … Historia* (*The History of Both Worlds*) (1617) comes almost as close. Bacon thought highly of the ancient Persian practice of always training would-be governors in natural magical philosophy, and designed his own Utopian *New Atlantis* (which appeared in eight editions between 1626 and 1658) as a society ruled by *magi* who combined the functions of politicians, priests and natural philosophers. Yet another illustration of these associations and the patronage they created is the sustained interest shown in the magical and occult sciences at the court of the Emperor Rudolf II in Prague between 1583 and 1612 (Evans, 1973; *cf*. Evans 1979: 346–80). At the Danish court, the best-known Danish Paracelsian, Petrus Severinus, was supported by Frederik II (Shackelford 1991: 86). According to Bruce Moran, the court of the German landgrave, Wilhelm IV of Hessen-Kassel, 'stands out as a sort of scientific research institute at the end of the sixteenth century' (Moran 1991b: 170).

In this broad context, the more specific links between natural magic and court society – noted, for example, by Eamon – take on considerable significance. In his view, the idea of scientific discovery as a *venatio*, a hunt, mirrored the courtly self-image much more than the idea of knowledge acquired via the university and scholastic disputation. Curiosity and virtuosity likewise became common aims, and reputation a way of measuring importance. Marvels and secrets became the currency of courtly science. Natural magic helped to promote the keen interest in the setting up of *Wunderkammern* (cabinets of curiosities) that typified courtly and aristocratic notions of power and knowledge in this period. The political purpose of all this was to represent the prince 'as a repository of praeternatural, superhuman secrets, and as the rightful heir to a tradition of esoteric and hidden wisdom' that provided authority and control. The kinds of scientists who flourished in such an environment were those 'whose contributions were formerly considered to be only ancillary to natural philosophy, including engineers, craftsmen, and mathematicians, as well as those whose activities formerly carried the stigma of the forbidden arts, alchemists, magicians, and investigators of the occult sciences'. The key figure in Italy, for example, was della Porta and his ideal of natural magic 'the courtly science *par excellence*'. Like Bacon at the court of James I, della Porta thought that the understanding brought by natural magic had a direct bearing on the government of kingdoms and societies. The commonwealth of the whole world and the commonwealth of men and women operated according to the same principles, and the prince and *magus* were thus exactly alike in their powers and roles (Eamon 1991: 37, 28, 40; *cf.* Henry 1997: 46; Moran 1991a). We seem to have come a long way from the pronouncements of Agrippa in the 1530s but, in fact, we have not travelled any distance at all. The principles that ruled all affairs, natural and political alike, were, not unintelligibly, those of 'sympathy' and 'antipathy'. Friendship and enmity were indeed the universal inclinations of all things.

Bibliography

Anglo, S. (1977a) 'Preface' and 'Evident authority and authoritative evidence: the *Malleus Maleficarum*', in Anglo, ed. *The Damned Art: Essays in the Literature of Witchcraft* (London): vii–viii, 1–31.

Anglo, S. (1977b) 'Reginald Scot's *Discoverie of Witchcraft*: scepticism and sadduceeism', in Anglo, ed. *The Damned Art: Essays in the Literature of Witchcraft* (London): 106–39.

Ankarloo, B. and Henningsen, G., eds. (1990) *Early Modern European Witchcraft: Centres and Peripheries* (Oxford).

Behringer, W. (1996) 'Witchcraft studies: Austria, Germany and Switzerland', in J. Barry, M. Hester, and G. Roberts, eds. *Witchcraft in Early Modern Europe: Studies in Culture and Belief* (Cambridge): 64–95.

Behringer, W. (1997) *Witchcraft Persecutions in Bavaria: Popular Magic, Religious Zealotry and Reason of State in Early Modern Europe*, trans. J. C. Grayson and D. Lederer (Cambridge).

Beier, L. M. (1987) *Sufferers and Healers: The Experience of Illness in Seventeenth-Century England* (London).

Béné, C. (1979) 'Jean Wier et les procès de sorcellerie, ou l'érasmisme au service de la tolérance', in P. Tuynman, G. C. Kuiper, and E. Kessler, eds. *Acta Conventus Neolatini Amstelodamensis* (Munich): 58–73.

Bethencourt, F. (1990) 'Portugal: a scrupulous Inquisition', in Ankarloo and Henningsen, eds. (1990): 403–22.

Blécourt, W. de (1993) 'Cunning women, from healers to fortune tellers', in H. Binneveld and R. Dekker, eds. *Curing and Insuring: Essays on Illness in Past Times: The Netherlands, Belgium, England and Italy, 16th–20th Centuries* (Hilversum): 43–55.

Blécourt, W. de (1994) 'Witch doctors, soothsayers and priests: on cunning folk in European historiography and tradition', *Social History*, 19: 285–303.

Bloch, M. (1973) *The Royal Touch: Sacred Monarchy and Scrofula in England and France*, trans. J. E. Anderson (London).

Bodin, J. (1995) *On the Demon-Mania of Witches*, trans. R. A. Scott, intro. J. L. Pearl (Toronto).

Bossy, J. (1985) *Christianity in the West, 1400–1700* (Oxford).

Bossy, J. (1988) 'Moral arithmetic: seven sins into ten commandments', in E. Leites, ed. *Conscience and Casuistry in Early Modern Europe* (Cambridge): 214–34.

Bostridge, I. (1997) *Witchcraft and Its Transformations c. 1650–c. 1750* (Oxford).

Boyer, P. and Nissenbaum, S. (1974) *Salem Possessed: The Social Origins of Witchcraft* (London).

Briggs, R. (1989) *Communities of Belief: Cultural and Social Tensions in Early Modern France* (Oxford).

Briggs, R. (1996) *Witches and Neighbours: The Social and Cultural Context of European Witchcraft* (London).

Briggs, R. (2001) 'Circling the Devil: witch-doctors and magical healers in early modern Lorraine', in Clark, ed. (2001): 161–78.

Brooks-Davies, D. (1983) *The Mercurian Monarch: Magical Politics from Spenser to Pope* (Manchester).

Burke, P. (1987) *The Historical Anthropology of Early Modern Italy: Essays on Perception and Communication* (Cambridge).

Caro Baroja, J. (1990) 'Witchcraft and Catholic theology', in Ankarloo and Henningsen, eds. (1990): 19–43.

Certeau, M. de (2000) *The Possession at Loudun*, trans. M. B. Smith (Chicago and London); originally published 1970.

Church, W. F. (1941) *Constitutional Thought in Sixteenth-Century France* (Cambridge, MA).

Ciruelo, P. (1977) *A Treatise Reproving All Superstitions and Forms of Witchcraft Very Necessary and Useful for All Good Christians Zealous for Their Salvation*, trans. E. A. Maio and D'O. W. Pearson, ed. D'O. W. Pearson (London).

Clark, S. (1983) 'French historians and early modern popular culture', *Past and Present*, 100: 62–99.

Clark, S. (1990) 'Protestant demonology: sin, superstition, and society (*c.* 1520–*c.* 1630)', in Ankarloo and Henningsen, eds. (1990): 45–81.

Clark, S. (1992) 'Glaube und Skepsis in der deutschen Hexenliteratur von Johan Weyer bis Friedrich Von Spee', in Lehmann and Ulbricht, eds. (1992): 15–33.

Clark, S. (1997) *Thinking with Demons: The Idea of Witchcraft in Early Modern Europe* (Oxford).

Clark, S. (2000) 'Johannes Althusius and the politics of witchcraft', in L. M. Andersson *et at.*, eds. *Rätten: En Festskrift till Bengt Ankarloo* (Lund): 272–90.

Clark, S., ed. (2001) *Languages of Witchcraft: Narrative, Ideology and Meaning in Early Modem Culture* (London).

Closson, M. (2000) *L'Imaginaire démoniaque en France (1550–1650): Genése de la littératuré fantastique* (Geneva).

Clulee, N. H. (1988) *John Dee's Natural Philosophy: Between Science and Religion* (London).

Cohen, T. V., and Cohen, E. S., eds. (1993) *Words and Deeds in Renaissance Rome: Trials before the Papal Magistrates* (Toronto, Buffalo, and London).

Copenhaver, B. P. (1984) 'Scholastic philosophy and Renaissance magic in the *De Vita* of Marsilio Ficino', *Renaissance Quarterly*, 37: 523–54.

Copenhaver, B. P. (1988) 'Astrology and magic', in C. B. Schmitt, ed. *The Cambridge History of Renaissance Philosophy* (Cambridge): 264–300.

Crouzet, D. (1990) *Les Guerriers de Dieu: la violence au temps des troubles de religion*, 2 vols (Paris).

Crowe, M. J., ed. (1977) *Witchcraft: Catalogue of the Witchcraft Collection in Cornell University Library*, intro. R. H. Robbins (Millwood, NY).

Daneau, L. (1575) *A Dialogue of Witches*, trans. attrib. to T. Twyne (London).

Daston, L., and Park, K. (1998) *Wonders and the Order of Nature 1150–1750* (New York).

Davis, N. Z. (1974) 'Some tasks and themes in the study of popular religion', in C. Trinkaus and H. A. Oberman, eds. *The Pursuit of Holiness in Late Medieval and Renaissance Religion* (Leiden): 307–36.

Debus, A. G. (1966) *The English Paracelsians* (New York).

Debus, A. G. (1978) *Man and Nature in the Renaissance* (Cambridge).

Delumeau, J. (1974) 'Les réformateurs et la superstition', in *Actes du Colloque l'Amiral Coligny et son temps* (Paris): 451–87.

Delumeau, J. (1977) *Catholicism between Luther and Voltaire: A New View of the Counter-Reformation*, intro. J. Bossy, trans. J. Moiser (London).

Dixon, C. S. (1996) *The Reformation and Rural Society: The Parishes of Brandenburg-Ansbach-Kulmbach, 1528–1603* (Cambridge).

Dobbs, B. J. T. (1975) *The Foundations of Newton's Alchemy: Or, 'The Hunting of the Greene Lyon'* (Cambridge).

Dobbs, B. J. T. (1991) *The Janus Faces of Genius: The Role of Alchemy in Newton's Thought* (Cambridge).

Dömötör, T. (1980) 'The cunning folk in English and Hungarian witch trials', in V. Newell, ed. *Folklore Studies in the Twentieth Century* (Woodbridge): 183–7.

Eamon, W. (1991) 'Court, academy, and printing house: patronage and scientific careers in late-Renaissance Italy', in Moran, ed. (1991a): 25–50.

Eamon, W. (1994) *Science and the Secrets of Nature: Books of Secrets in Medieval and Early Modern Culture* (Princeton).

Elmer, P., ed. (1986) *The Library of Dr. John Webster: The Making of a Seventeenth-Century Radical, Medical History*, suppl. 6 (London).

Elmer, P. (2001) 'Towards a politics of witchcraft in early modern England', in Clark, ed. (2001): 101–18.

Estes, L. L. (1983) 'Reginald Scot and his *Discoverie of Witchcraft*: religion and science in the opposition to the European witch craze', *Church History*, 52: 444–56.

Evans, R. J. W. (1973) *Rudolf II and His World: A Study in Intellectual History 1576–1612* (Oxford).

Evans, R. J. W. (1979) *The Making of the Habsburg Monarchy, 1550–1700: An Interpretation* (Oxford).

Ferber, S. (1991) 'The demonic possession of Marthe Brossier, France 1598–1600', in C. Zika, ed. *No Gods Except Me: Orthodoxy and Religious Practice in Europe, 1200–1600* (Melbourne): 59–83.

Flint, V. I. J. (1991) *The Rise of Magic in Early Medieval Europe* (Oxford).

Forster, M. R. (1992) *The Counter-Reformation in the Villages: Religion and Reform in the Bishopric of Speyer, 1560–1720* (Ithaca, NY, and London).

Frijhoff, W. Th. M. (1979) 'Official and popular religion in Christianity: the late middle ages and early modern times (13th–18th centuries)', in P. H. Vrijhof and J. Waardenburg, eds. *Official and Popular Religion: Analysis of a Theme for Religious Studies* (The Hague): 71–116.

Gaskill, M. (2000) *Crime and Mentalities in Early Modern England* (Cambridge).

Geertz, H. (1975) 'An anthropology of religion and magic', *Journal of Interdisciplinary History*, 6: 71–89.

Gentilcore, D. (1992) *From Bishop to Witch: The System of the Sacred in Early Modern Terra d'Otranto* (Manchester).

Gentilcore, D. (1998) *Healers and Healing in Early Modern Italy* (Manchester and New York).

Gibson, M. (2000) *Early Modern Witches: Witchcraft Cases in Contemporary Writing* (London and New York).

Gifford, G. (1587) *A Discourse of the Subtill Practises of Devilles by Witches and Sorcerers* (London).

Gifford, G. (1593) *A Dialogue Concerning Witches and Witchcraftes* (London).

Gijswijt-Hofstra, M., (1989) 'Witchcraft in the northern Netherlands', in A. Angerman *et al.*, eds. *Current Issues in Women's History* (London): 75–92.

Grafton, A. (1990) 'Humanism, magic and science', in A. Goodman and A. MacKay, eds. *The Impact of Humanism on Western Europe* (London and New York): 99–117.

Greene, T. M. (1987) 'Magic and festivity at the Renaissance court', *Renaissance Quarterly*, 40: 636–59.

Gregory, A. (1991) 'Witchcraft, politics and "good neighbourhood"', *Past and Present*, 133: 31–66.

Hansen, B. (1978) 'Science and magic', in D. C. Lindberg, ed. *Science in the Middle Ages* (Chicago): 483–506.

Hansen, B. (1986) 'The complementarity of science and magic before the Scientific Revolution', *American Scientist*, 74: 128–36.

Harkness, D. E. (1999) *John Dee's Conversations with Angels: Cabala, Alchemy, and the End of Nature* (Cambridge).

Hastrup, K. (1990) 'Iceland: sorcerers and paganism', in Ankarloo and Henningsen, eds. (1990): 383–401.

Haustein, J. (1990) *Martin Luthers Stellung zum Zauber- und Hexenwesen* (Stuttgart).

Henningsen, G. (1980) *The Witches' Advocate: Basque Witchcraft and the Spanish Inquisition (1609–1614)* (Reno, NV).

Henry, J. (1986) 'Occult qualities and the experimental philosophy: active principles in pre-Newtonian matter theory', *History of Science*, 24: 335–81.

Henry, J. (1997) *The Scientific Revolution and the Origins of Modern Science* (London).

Houdard, S. (1992) *Les Sciences du diable: quatre discours sur la sorcellerie* (Paris).

Hunter, M. (1995) 'The witchcraft controversy and the nature of free-thought in Restoration England: John Wagstaffe's *The Question of Witchcraft Debated* (1669)', in M. Hunter, *Science and the Shape of Orthodoxy: Intellectual Change in Late 17th-Century Britain* (Woodbridge): 286–307.

Hutchison, K. (1982) 'What happened to occult qualities in the scientific revolution?', *Isis*, 73: 233–54.

Jacques-Chaquin, N., and Préaud, M., eds. (1993) *Le Sabbat des sorciers en Europe (XVe–XVIIIe siècles)* (Grenoble).

Jensen, P. F. (1975) 'Calvin and witchcraft', *Reformed Theological Review*, 34: 76–86.

Johansen, J. Chr.V. (1991/92) 'Witchcraft, sin and repentance: the decline of Danish witchcraft trials', *Acta Ethnographica Hungarica*, 37: 413–23.

Joubert, L. (1989) *Popular Errors*, trans. and ed. G. D. de Rocher (Tuscaloosa and London).

Kahk, J. (1990) 'Estonia II: the crusade against idolatry', in Ankarloo and Henningsen, eds. (1990): 273–84.

Karant-Nunn, S. C. (1987) *Zwickau in Transition, 1500–1547: The Reformation as an Agent of Change* (Columbus, OH).

Klaniczay, G. (1990) 'Hungary: the accusations and the universe of popular magic', in Ankarloo and Henningsen, eds. (1990): 219–55.

Kogan, S. (1986) *The Hieroglyphic King: Wisdom and Idolatry in the Seventeenth-Century Masque* (London).

Kors, A. C., and Peters, E. (2001) *Witchcraft in Europe 400-1700: A Documentary History*, 2nd edn. (Philadelphia).

Kristóf, I. (1991/92) ' "Wise women", sinners and the poor: the social background of witch-hunting in a 16th–18th century Calvinist city of eastern Hungary', *Acta Ethnographica Hungarica*, 37: 93–119.

Lea, H. C. (1939/1957) *Materials toward a History of Witchcraft*, ed. A. C. Howland, intro. G. L. Burr, 3 vols (New York and London).

Lehmann, H., and Ulbricht, O., eds. (1992) *Vom Unfug des Hexen-Processes: Gegner der Hexenverfolgung von Johann Weyer bis Friedrich Spee* (Wiesbaden).

Levack, B. P. (1999) 'The decline and end of witchcraft prosecutions', in B. Ankarloo and S. Clark, eds. *Witchcraft and Magic in Europe: The Eighteenth and Nineteenth Centuries* (London): 1–93.

Lohr, C. H. (1978) 'Renaissance Latin Aristotle commentaries: authors L–M', *Renaissance Quarterly*, 31: 532–603.

Lorenz, S. (1995) 'Zur Spruchpraxis der Juristenfakultät Mainz in Hexenprozessen: Ein Beitrag zur Geschichte von Jurisprudenz und Hexenverfolgung', in G. Franz and F. Irsigler, eds. *Hexenglaube und Hexenprozesse im Raum Rhein-Mosel-Saar (Trierer Hexenprozesse, 2)* (Trier): 73–87.

MacDonald, M., ed. (1991) *Witchcraft and Hysteria in Elizabethan London: Edward Jorden and the Mary Glover Case* (London).

MacDonald Ross, G. (1985) 'Occultism and philosophy in the seventeenth century', in A. J. Holland, ed. *Philosophy: Its History and Historiography* (Dordrecht): 95–115.

Macfarlane, A. (1970) *Witchcraft in Tudor and Stuart England: A Regional and Comparative Study* (London), 2nd edn. 1999, ed. J. A. Sharpe.

Macfarlane, A. (1977) 'A Tudor anthropologist: George Gifford's *Discourse* and *Dialogue*', in S. Anglo, ed. *The Damned Art: Essays in the Literature of Witchcraft* (London): 140–55.

McGuire, J. E., and Rattansi, P. M. (1966) 'Newton and the "Pipes of Pan" ', *Notes and Records of the Royal Society of London*, 21: 108–43.

Madar, M. (1990) 'Estonia I: werewolves and poisoners', in Ankarloo and Henningsen, eds. (1990): 257–72.

Mandrou, R. (1968) *Magistrats et sorciers en France au XVIIe siècle: un analyse de psychologie historique* (Paris).

Margolin, J.-C. (1974) 'La politique culturelle de Guillaume, due de Clèves', in F. Simone, ed. *Culture et politique en France à l'époque de l'humanisme et de la Renaissance* (Turin): 293–324.

Max, F. (1993) 'Les premières controverses sur la réalité du sabbat dans l'Italie du XVIe siècle', in Jacques-Chaquin and Préaud, eds. (1993): 55–62.

Maxwell-Stuart, P. G. (1999) *The Occult in Early Modern Europe: A Documentary History* (London).

Maxwell-Stuart, P. G. (2001) *Witchcraft in Europe and the New World, 1400–1800* (Basingstoke).

Meek, C. (2000) 'Men, women and magic: some cases from late medieval Lucca', in C. Meek, ed. *Women in Renaissance and Early Modern Europe* (Dublin): 43–66.

Mendelsohn, J. A. (1992) 'Alchemy and politics in England 1649–1665', *Past and Present*, 135: 30–78.

Midelfort, H. C. E. (1972) *Witch Hunting in Southwestern Germany, 1562–1684: The Social and Intellectual Foundations* (Stanford).

Midelfort, H. C. E. (1974) 'Were there really witches?', in R. M. Kingdon, ed. *Transition and Revolution* (Minneapolis): 189–226.

Midelfort, H. C. E. (1999) *A History of Madness in Sixteenth-Century Germany* (Stanford).

Millen, R. (1985) 'The manifestation of occult qualities in the Scientific Revolution', in M. J. Osler and P. L. Farber, eds. *Religion, Science, and Worldview: Essays in Honour of Richard S. Westfall* (Cambridge): 185–216.

Moran, B. T., ed. (1991a) *Patronage and Institutions: Science, Technology, and Medicine at the European Court, 1500–1750* (Woodbridge).

Moran, B. T. (1991b) 'Patronage and institutions: courts, universities, and academies in Germany; an overview', in B. T. Moran, ed. (1991a): 169–83.

More, H. (1653) *An Antidote Against Atheisme* (London).

Muchembled, R. (1978) *Culture populaire et culture des élites dans la France moderne (XVe–XVIIIe siècles)* (Paris); trans. by L. Cochrane, *Popular Culture and Elite Culture in France, 1400–1750* (Baton Rouge and London, 1985).

Muchembled, R., ed. (1994) *Magie et sorcellerie en Europe du Moyen Age a nos jours* (Paris).

Nalle, S. T. (1992) *God in La Mancha: Religious Reform and the People of Cuenca, 1500–1650* (Baltimore and London).

Naudé, G. (1625) *Apologie pour tous les grands personnages qui ont esté faussement soupçonnez de magie* (Paris).

Normand, L., and Roberts, G. (2000) *Witchcraft in Early Modern Scotland: James VI's Demonology and the North Berwick Witches* (Exeter).

Oberman, H. A. (1981) *Masters of the Reformation: The Emergence of a New Intellectual Climate in Europe,* trans D. Martin (Cambridge).

O'Neil, M. (1987) 'Magical healing, love magic and the Inquisition in late sixteenth-century Modena', in S. Haliczer, ed. *Inquisition and Society in Early Modern Europe* (London): 88–114.

O'Neil, M. (1991/92) 'Missing footprints: maleficium in Modena', *Acta Ethnographica Hungarica*, 37: 123–42.

Orgel, S., ed. (1987) *The Tempest (The Oxford Shakespeare)* (Oxford).

Ostorero, M., Bagliani, A. P., and Tremp, K. U., eds. (1999) *L'Imaginaire du sabbat: édition critique des textes les plus anciens (1430c.–1440c.)* (Lausanne).

Park, K. (1998) 'Medicine and magic: the healing arts', in J. C. Brown and R. C. Davis, eds. *Gender and Society in Renaissance Italy* (London): 129–49.

Parry, G. (1981) *The Golden Age Restor'd: The Culture of the Stuart Court, 1603–42* (Manchester).

Pearl, J. L. (1999) *The Crime of Crimes: Demonology and Politics in France 1560–1620* (Waterloo, Ontario).

Perkins, W. (1610) *A Discourse of the Damned Art of Witchcraft* (Cambridge).

Peters, E. (1978) *The Magician, the Witch, and the Law* (Brighton).

Peters, E. (2001) 'The medieval church and state on superstition, magic and witchcraft: from Augustine to the sixteenth century', in B. Ankarloo and S. Clark, eds. *Witchcraft and Magic in Europe: The Middle Ages* (London): 171–243.

Porter, R. (1999) 'Witchcraft and magic in Enlightenment, Romantic and Liberal Thought', in B. Ankarloo and S. Clark, eds., *Witchcraft and Magic in Europe: The Eighteenth and Nineteenth Centuries* (London): 191–282.

Priester, P., and Barske, A. (1986) 'Vervolging van tovenaars(en) in Groningen, 1547–1597', in Blécourt and Gijswijt-Hofstra, eds. (1986): 50–76.

Purkiss, D. (1995) 'Women's stories of witchcraft in early modern England: the house, the body, the child', *Gender and History*, 7: 408–32.

Reeves, M. (1969) *The Influence of Prophecy in the Later Middle Ages* (Oxford).

Roper, L. (1994) *Oedipus and the Devil: Witchcraft, Sexuality, and Religion in Early Modern Europe* (London).

Rossi, P. (1968) *Francis Bacon: From Magic to Science*, trans. S. Rabinovitch (London).

Rowlands, A. (1996) 'Witchcraft and popular religion in early modern Rothenburg ob der Tauber', in R. Scribner and T. Johnson, eds. *Popular Religion in Germany and Central Europe, 1400–1800* (London): 101–18.

Ruggiero, G. (1993) *Binding Passions: Tales of Magic, Marriage, and Power at the End of the Renaissance* (New York).

Sawyer, R. C. (1988/89) ' "Strangely handled in all her lyms": witchcraft and healing in Jacobean England', *Journal of Social History*, 22: 461–85.

Scot, R. (1584) *The Discoverie of Witchcraft* (London).

Scribner, R. (1984) 'Ritual and popular religion in Catholic Germany at the time of the Reformation', *Journal of Ecclesiastical History*, 35: 47–77.

Scribner, R. (1993) 'The Reformation, popular magic and the 'disenchantment of the world'', *Journal of Interdisciplinary History*, 23: 475–94.

Shackelford, J. (1991) 'Paracelsianism and patronage in early modern Denmark', in Moran, ed. (1991a): 85–109.

Shapin, S. (1996) *The Scientific Revolution* (Chicago and London).

Sharpe, J. A. (1992) *Witchcraft in Seventeenth-Century Yorkshire: Accusations and Counter Measures*, University of York Borthwick Institute of Historical Research, Paper 81 (York).

Sharpe, J. A. (1996) *Instruments of Darkness: Witchcraft in England 1550–1750* (London).

Sharpe, J. A. (1999) *The Bewitching of Anne Gunter: A Horrible and True Story of Football, Witchcraft, Murder, and the King of England* (London).

Shumaker, W. (1972) *The Occult Sciences in the Renaissance* (London).

Shumaker, W. (1989) *Natural Magic and Modern Science: Four Treatises 1590–1657* (Binghamton, NY).

Soman, A. (1992) *Sorcellerie et justice criminelle: le Parlement de Paris (16e–18e siècles)* (Bath).

Soman, A. (1993) 'Le sabbat des sorciers: preuve juridique', in Jacques-Chaquin and Préaud, eds. (1993): 85–99.

Strauss, G. (1978) *Luther's House of Learning: Indoctrination of the Young in the German Reformation* (London).

Tambiah, S. J. (1985) 'The magical power of words', in S. J. Tambiah *Culture, Thought, and Social Action: An Anthropological Perspective* (London): 17–59.

Thomas, K. V. (1971) *Religion and the Decline of Magic: Studies in Popular Beliefs in Sixteenth and Seventeenth Century England* (London).

Thomas, K. V. (1975) 'An anthropology of religion and magic', *Journal of Interdisciplinary History*, 6: 91–109.

Thorndike, L. (1923–58) *A History of Magic and Experimental Science*, 8 vols (New York).

Trevor-Roper, H. R. (1967) 'The European witch-craze of the sixteenth and seventeenth centuries', in H. R. Trevor-Roper, *Religion, the Reformation and Social Change* (London): 90–192.

Tuck, R. (1993) *Philosophy and Government 1572–1651* (Cambridge).

Valentia, G. de (1591/97) *Commentariorum Theologicorum*, 4 vols (Ingolstadt).

Vickers, B. (1979) 'Frances Yates and the writing of history', *Journal of Modern History*, 51: 287–316.

Vickers, B. (1984) 'Analogy versus identity: the rejection of occult symbolism, 1580-1680', in B. Vickers, ed. *Occult and Scientific Mentalities in the Renaissance* (Cambridge): 95–163.

Waardt, H. de (1991) *Toverij en Samenleving: Holland 1500–1800* (The Hague): 335–9, English summary.

Waardt, H. de (1993) 'From cunning man to natural healer', in H. Binneveld and R. Dekker, eds. *Curing and Insuring: Essays on Illness in Past Times: The Netherlands, Belgium, England and Italy, 16th–20th Centuries* (Hilversum): 33–41.

Waardt, H. de (1997) 'Breaking the boundaries: irregular healers in eighteenth-century Holland', in M. Gijswijt-Hofstra, H. Marland and H. de Waardt, eds. *Illness and Healing Alternatives in Western Europe* (London and New York): 141–60.

Walker, A. M., and Dickerman, E. H. (1991) ' "A woman under the influence": a case of alleged possession in sixteenth-century France', *Sixteenth Century Journal*, 22: 535–54.

Walker, D. P. (1958) *Spiritual and Demonic Magic from Ficino to Campanella* (London).

Walker, D. P. (1981) *Unclean Spirits: Possession and Exorcism in France and England in the Late Sixteenth and Early Seventeenth Centuries* (London).

Webster, C. (1975) *The Great Instauration: Science, Medicine and Reform 1626–1660* (London).

Webster, C. (1982) *From Paracelsus to Newton: Magic and the Making of Modern Science* (Cambridge).

West, R. H. (*c.* 1984) *Reginald Scot and Renaissance Writings on Witchcraft* (Boston).

Weyer, J. (1991) *Witches, Devils, and Doctors in the Renaissance: Johann Weyer, De praestigiis daemonum*, ed. G. Mora, trans. J. Shea (Binghamton, NY).

Willis, D. (1995) *Malevolent Nurture: Witch-Hunting and Maternal Power in Early Modern England* (London).

Wilson, S. (2000) *The Magical Universe: Everyday Ritual and Magic in Pre-Modern Europe* (London and New York).

Wootton, D. (2001) 'Reginald Scot / Abraham Fleming / The Family of Love', in Clark, ed. (2001): 119–38.

Yates, F. A. (1964) *Giordano Bruno and the Hermetic Tradition* (London).

Yates, F. A. (1967) 'The Hermetic tradition in Renaissance science', in C. S. Singleton, ed. *Art, Science, and History in the Renaissance* (Baltimore): 255–74.

Yates, F. A. (1972) *The Rosicrucian Enlightenment* (London).

Zambelli, P. (1974) 'Le problème de la magie naturelle à la Renaissance', in L. Szezucki, ed. *Magia, Astrologia e Religione nel Rinascimento* (Warsaw): 48–82.

Zambelli, P. (1988) 'Scholastic and humanist views of Hermeticism and witchcraft', in I. Merkel and A. G. Debus, eds. *Hermeticism and the Renaissance: Intellectual History and the Occult in Early Modern History* (London): 126–53.

CHAPTER 11
WITCHCRAFT, FEMALE AGGRESSION, AND POWER IN THE EARLY MODERN COMMUNITY
Edward Bever

Introduction

Almost a generation ago the study of European witchcraft was revolutionized by a 'paradigm shift', as Wolfgang Behringer has termed it, that involved the adoption of anthropological and sociological methodologies, a greater attention to archival sources, and an interest in focusing on history 'from below.' [1] Part of the larger shift to social, and more recently cultural, history, it has led to the emergence of a broad consensus on many aspects of the topic over the past three decades. The early modern discourse on witchcraft, it is generally agreed, developed out of the interplay of Europe's learned and popular cultures.[2] Individual trials, too, involved an interplay between government officials and local communities; while some spectacular hunts may have been driven by officials obsessed with a diabolical conspiracy, most trials took place because of complaints brought to the authorities by ordinary peasants and townspeople – rumors uncovered in local or church courts, requests that such rumors be quashed, or outright accusations.[3] These complaints manifested both long-standing folk beliefs and the hard times that stemmed from population pressures, socioeconomic change, and the climatic downturn of the 'Little Ice Age.'[4] Once started, witch trials took on a life of their own because the tortured testimony appeared to validate the discourse as the victims constructed narratives corresponding to the expectations of their interrogators.[5] Sometimes torture resulted in an ever-expanding chain of denunciations, however, and as the accusations spread farther and farther from the stereotyped suspects and closer and closer to the magistrates and their families, the elite suffered a crisis of confidence that brought the trial to an end. On a larger scale, a similar sort of 'crisis of confidence' is thought to have been at work as well, supported and stimulated by growing legal concerns, religious scruples, and an increasing propensity to medicalize the problem. The resultant decline in prosecutions reflected not a sudden denial that witchcraft was possible but a gradually increasing skepticism within the elite about its power and importance. While the traditional belief in malevolent (as opposed to diabolical) witches survived among the peasants, the change began a more fundamental paradigm shift that set the basic framework for educated understanding of witchcraft down to today.[6]

Women and witchcraft in historical understanding

The existence of this broad consensus naturally has not precluded new investigations to develop new angles of interpretation, and marked disagreement about certain issues remain. One area that has remained particularly controversial is the role of gender in the witch discourse and trials.[7] The advocates of the trials asserted that 'the fragile feminine sex ... feebler in both mind and body' was particularly prone to witchcraft, and their skeptical opponents used this very predominance of 'poore, sullen, superstitious' women to argue against them.[8] Historians thereafter have taken the association pretty much for granted, and a large number of local studies during the last generation have confirmed that most of the time women did in fact predominate heavily among the suspects.[9] While in some regions and certain trials men predominated, overall women constituted about 80% of the people tried.[10]

Most of the earlier historians acknowledged the special association of women and witchcraft without making it a significant part of their discussion, either ignoring it in constructing their explanations or dismissing it as a product of late Medieval clerical misogyny.[11] The first social and anthropological historians offered some tentative hypotheses about how gender relations and the changing circumstances of women contributed to the trials, suggesting that increasing numbers of widows and spinsters threatened a society based on patriarchal family units, or that people increasingly resisted helping to support poor elderly women in the village.[12] Women's historians moved gender relations into the forefront of explanations for the persecutions by drawing on the insight that the trials were part of a larger campaign by governments to Christianize the countryside (and in the process expand their own authority), and linking them to a general strengthening of patriarchy during the same period.[13] Some feminist accounts, seizing on an estimate of 9 million victims, cast the trials as 'the persecution of a whole sex ... the second phase of the patriarchal seizure of power at the beginning of the bourgeois era,' while others pointed more specifically to midwives and 'wise women' as the chief targets of persecutions, and drew a connection to the specific interests of a particular male group, doctors.[14] Subsequent local studies have found that neither midwives nor wise women played an especially prominent role in most areas, however, while syntheses of local studies now suggest that the figure of nine million deaths is two orders of magnitude too large, but historians of women nevertheless give the persecutions an important place in women's history as part of the larger campaign to erect an increasingly patriarchal society and culture in early modern Europe.[15] Europe's male leaders considered patriarchal families to be the foundation of society, and used their administrative powers and the power of the pulpit to build it up.[16] 'Assertive and aggressive' women challenged this order, and could be beaten by their husbands, punished for moral offenses ranging from scolding to adultery, or, at the extreme, burned for witchcraft.[17]

This view of witchcraft is generally acknowledged to convey some important truths about the evolving position of women in early modern society, but historians of witchcraft have recently begun bridling at the implications this interpretation has for our understanding of witchcraft itself.[18] Noting that 20% of the suspects in the trials were *not* women, and that in certain times and places men outnumbered women by a wide margin, some historians of witchcraft point to Christina Larner's statement that the witch hunts were gender related, but not gender specific, arguing that while the witch trials may have hit women particularly hard, they were 'not some complicated mechanism for persecuting women.'[19] Different historians have pointed out that the witch literature did not generally emphasize the role of women, that the laws tended to be written in gender-neutral language, that torture and execution were common elements of criminal trials which affected men far more often than women, and that women played a significant role in formulating and supporting accusations.[20] Stuart Clark has gone so far as assert that the view that 'witch-hunting was in reality women-hunting,' and social-functionalist explanations in general, do not show, 'and given their logic...cannot show...why the accusations should have concerned witchcraft...[for] there is no necessary link between being anomalous and being a witch.'[21] Clark's criticism can be extended to the most recent direction in feminist interpretation, which links witchcraft suspicions to tensions within the female sphere.[22] While the variants of this interpretation shed interesting light on why and how the female witch stereotype was applied once it existed, it does not really explain how or why the image of the evil magician came to be feminized in the first place.

For his part, Clark proposes that the explanation for the association of women and witchcraft lies in the 'linguistic structures of contrariety;' the 'dualism characterizing early modern thought,' as Allison Coudert put it.[23] Early moderns linked a whole series of polar opposites like men and women, 'public/private, dominant/subordinate, aggressive/passive' and so on. Women, presumably because they weren't the ones devising the system, simply ended up on the wrong side of the divide.[24] Clark's critique of functionalist explanations has considerable merit, but his own explanation has some problems itself. For one thing, Heidi Wunder has asserted that '"man" and "woman" were defined...in terms of comparative differences...not...dichotomies,' while Manuel Simon has disputed the notion that the witch and the dutiful housewife were considered a pair of opposites, since they also stood in relation to the virgin on one side and the 'disobedient and disorderly woman' on the other.[25] For another, early modern dichotomous thinking is inadequate to explain the popular element in witchcraft belief.[26] The popular association of woman and witchcraft was both ancient and widespread, common to many cultures worldwide and far back into antiquity, and popular concern was not with the nature of evil or even the danger of the Devil, but rather with specific harms attributed to a neighbor's malefic powers.[27] The learned theologians who wrote the witch tracts drew from several sources, but the association of women with witchcraft, in particular, came from experience in the field.[28] The most fundamental question is not why early modern male elites thought women were particularly susceptible to the Devil's blandishments, but why early modern common people – female as well as male – thought women were particularly likely to use magical powers against them.

Women and violence in early modern society

To begin answering this question, we will first look in more detail at current treatments of the relationship of women and witchcraft in popular culture and then evaluate them in light of both a systematic sample of cases drawn from the archives of the Duchy of Württemberg and a recent reassessment of the most common form of malefic magic associated with witchcraft.

To begin with, recent investigations have emphasized that the women most likely to be accused of witchcraft tended not to be poor, marginal outsiders, but integral members of their communities: married, not single; part of the broad middling peasantry, not the poorest of the poor.[29] Certainly some witch accusations stemmed from conflicts between poor old widows and their better-off neighbors, but others involved well-to-do women accused by poorer villagers, and still others, probably the majority, involved people of roughly equal station. The conflicts were often economic, but they could arise 'from a wide variety of interpersonal conflicts.'[30] Indeed 'nearly every human relationship which went wrong might lead to a charge of witchcraft.'[31]

Furthermore, these conflicts were not isolated incidents; they were part of a pervasive pattern of interpersonal conflict that permeated early modern village society. Crowded, riven by increasing economic inequalities, 'characterized by constant positioning for control of, and access to, resources, and by unwritten rules governing intra-group behavior ... acrimony, fractiousness, "existential jealousy," and conflict were endemic.'[32] Modes of conflict included gossip, insults, scolding, threats, curses, ritual magic, legal action, and various forms of physical assault.[33] Early modern village life certainly included warm friendships and peaceful coexistence, but any attempt to understand early modern witchcraft must start by recognizing that the 'internal viciousness of village interactions ... and the brutality of interpersonal conflict' drove some members 'to pursue personal quarrels with a degree of persistence and ruthlessness' that might 'harass an enemy even unto death.'[34] In this 'community of terror,' as Reiner Walz has termed it, women played as important a role as men.[35] However, Walz's research has cast doubt on the conventional understanding of what that role was.[36] Most accounts have assumed that women specialized in verbal combat and have treated witch accusations as the culmination of an escalating series of interactions in which the woman moved from scolding to threats to curses, and was denounced when one of these was coincidentally followed by some harm supposedly associated with witchcraft. Walz has studied witch accusations in the context of all judicial activity in a set of German villages, however, and surprisingly found that far more men ended up in court as a result of verbal exchanges, and that eventual witch suspects were seldom among the women.[37] The reason for the low number of women among verbal abusers is unclear – it could be that women were less verbally abusive, or it could be that women simply did not move from verbal exchanges to litigation as readily as men, – while the absence of witch suspects suggests that either people suspected women who were actually fairly passive or that village roles were relatively stratified, that some people were known as yellers, while others were suspected of more dangerous things.

Walz favors the passive interpretation, arguing that once a suspect was identified, people retroactively interpreted incidents to support the new accusation.[38] The sampled trials from the Duchy of Württemberg, however, do not support this conclusion. While some people undoubtedly did alter their memories and stories as Walz suggests, many of the prior incidents and suspicions mentioned had left some public record or involved some explicit comment at the time.[39] Given the well-known importance of reputation in defining a witch, the history of suspicions going in many cases back years or even decades, it seems more likely that suspects had not been in court for verbal excesses either because it was not their style or because people were already too fearful to tangle with them in a situation where the victory would be minor and the consequences could, in their minds anyway, be deadly.[40]

The village witch, then, appears to have been a different role than the village scold.[41] Both roles, however, could bestow real power. A scold could get her way by wearing people down, while a suspected witch could gain considerable deference by scaring them.[42] Reginald Scot, for example, reported how 'these miserable wretches are so odious unto their neighbors, and so feared, as few dare offend them, or denie them anie thing they ask.'[43] Another English observer reported that one reputed witch 'had so powerful a hand over the wealthiest neighbors about her, that none of them refused to do anything she required, yea, unbesought they provided her with fire, and meat from their own tables.'[44] In France, 'even substantial *laboureurs* who crossed a suspected witch were liable to be reproached by their own kin for running unnecessary risks,' while in Germany 'women, who were known as sorceresses' were equally feared for their readiness to 'use their magical powers as weapons in conflicts' with their neighbors.[45]

That some people accepted or even cultivated a reputation for possessing 'magical powers' has long been recognized, although its importance has generally been minimized. Trevor-Roper spoke of 'a scattered folk-lore of peasant superstitions … universal, in time and place,' while William Monter speculated about solitary women's need 'to rely on magical means of revenge for their injuries because nothing else was open to them … and perhaps to introduce, in a drugged sleep, some excitement into their monotonous and wretched lives.'[46] More recently, however, historians have begun to treat peoples' witch beliefs more seriously, and put more emphasis on the lengths to which people would go in acting out the role of sorcerer or witch.[47] Clark Garrett, for example, has recounted an incident where a cunning man identified a shepherd as the cause of animals' deaths, and 'the authorities found books of magic and quantities of arsenic and other drugs in the home of the suspect.'[48] In another example, from the Vorarlberg region of Germany, Hubert Vogel reported on a suspect whose home was searched, and the authorities found, among other things, a variety of herbs, powders and salves; 'an old sealed case with an old communion Host in it;' a 'horseshoe nail bound in a handkerchief;' a small 'locket' in which was 'a lump of wax in the middle of which a piece of wood was stuck;' a small pillow with various things sewn into it, including 'human skin;' and 'a small wooden horse, whose hindquarters were bound together with string.'[49] Ingrid Ahrendt-Schulte has made one of the strongest arguments along these lines, based on her research in the city of Horn. 'When general or gender-based inequalities blocked legal possibilities for protection' of women's interests, 'malefic magic could take their place.'[50] She acknowledges that women had a broad range of magical means of attack according to contemporary culture, but she focuses on poisoning, arguing that 'the word for magical means is "*Vergift*," or in the language of the protocols, "*venenum*." '[51] Her focus on poison emphasizes that witchcraft was not just some sort of idle fantasy or imaginary compensation, but an active assertion of power; poisons could be used to kill an abusive husband or, in one specific case she discusses, a powerful male relative involved in a property dispute.[52]

Ahrendt-Schulte's focus on poison is seconded by the example of Giovanna Bonanno, an 'old Vinegar lady' who has been shown to have supplied poison to a number of dissatisfied wives in Palermo, and by the cases contained in the sample of small trials in Württemberg as well.[53] Allegations of poison were, in fact, the most common accusation leading to these trials, and they also comprised a number of supporting denunciations registered once a trial had begun. In some cases the allegations appear to have been spurious, and in a few the 'poison' was actually a remedy or herbal potion offered for its beneficial effect, but in many the accusations were plausible, and in some the suspect's intentions were clear. In one example, a young boy, Jakob Endris, fell ill after eating a soup prepared by his step-grandmother, Maria Schneider, the mother of his father's second wife.[54] A doctor 'found … that something wrong had been given to him in his food,' and Jakob said that Maria had earlier threatened to 'feed him lye.' When the officials questioned her, 'at first she did not want to admit any knowledge of a soup' at all. Confronted by the testimony of other witnesses showing up this lie, she 'finally … acknowledged her guilt.' The problem with focusing on poisoning and other explicit forms of sorcery, however, is that they were factors in only a minority of cases. Among the sampled trials from Württemberg, of the 94 accusations that were made, 73, over 75%, alleged malefic crimes, crimes that involved a specific injury, while 21, one-quarter, involved diabolism, Devil-worship not involving a specific harm to a specific victim.[55] However, while poisoning was the single most frequent allegation precipitating a trial, it accounted for only seven of the 22 primary accusations involving maleficium, and only six of the 51 secondary (supporting) accusations involving it. Allegations of ritual magic or cursing were even less significant numerically: just two trials involved allegations of some sort of ritual action, while only three accusations involved some sort of explicit verbalization.[56] Among the 24 allegations of harm to animals, two specified poisoning as the form and three some sort of occult influence, so the total allegations of malefic crimes that specified poisoning and sorcery came to 23 of the total of 73, or about one third.[57] In addition to these means of attack, though, the records from Württemberg contain evidence of other, less formal, forms that were also associated with witchcraft. One of these was physical assault, which accounted for another ten of the 73 allegations. The one case that was precipitated by an assault occurred after Katharina Masten, a 71 year old wife of a carter and citizen of the village of Metzingen, went to a neighbor's house to collect a debt he owed.[58] Since he was not home, she tried to take food as compensation. A servant girl in the household, Catharina Baitinger, stopped her, and the next day, when Catharina was walking alone on a secluded path in the woods, Katharina approached her, demanding the money once again. Catharina said that she would get it after her chores were done, but Katharina became angry and began to berate and hit her, knocking her down. When the magistrates investigated, Katharina denied that the incident had taken place, but witnesses placed her at the scene of both the argument and the subsequent assault, while a smith reported that 'she had told him she had given the girl what she deserved.' In the other nine instances the assaults were recounted during the course of trials that started for other reasons.

In addition to physical assaults against people, physical violence could also be directed against animals. Farmsteads in Württemberg's villages, as in many other agricultural societies, were often crowded together, and it was impossible to lock the animals away or keep them under constant supervision.[59] Most peasants could afford to support at most a few animals, so the death or injury of one was a major economic blow. In a minority of cases, as we have seen, allegations specified sorcery as the means by which damage was supposed to have been inflicted, and Ahrendt-Schulte argues that poisons were the primary means by which witches might have injured animals. However, as many of the 24 sampled allegations specified mechanical injury as chemical, the great majority of the allegations did not attempt to explain how the damage had been done at all.[60] Of course, some of the alleged injuries, like some of the human illnesses blamed on witchcraft, were undoubtedly naturally contracted, but the earliest of the sampled cases involved a confession rather than an accusation, which showed that attacks on animals did, in fact, take place.[61] In this instance, an elderly woman named Magdelena Horn spontaneously confessed that she had injured her neighbors' pigs and a cow, and when the magistrates investigated, the people confirmed that the animals had sickened at the time Magdelena said, although they said they had not suspected her.[62] She also claimed to have struck a boy so hard he subsequently died, and, when asked, his mother confirmed that he had complained of this before he expired.

Another case from the duchy's archives provides even more remarkable evidence that some suspects had deliberately inflicted injuries, and that simple physical violence was as likely as (and less complicated than) some sort of poison. The case is contained in the transcript of the tortured testimony of Margretha, Jung Michael Stainer's wife from Rosenfeld. While Carlo Ginzburg has advocated 'teasing' the reality out of such testimony by searching for anomalies and Lyndal Roper has used tortured testimony to explore the interplay of the interrogators' expectations and the suspects' psychocultural repertoire, no such subtlety is needed here, for the magistrates checked into the 27 malefic acts she confessed to and noted the results of their investigation in the margins of the transcript.[63] They also followed the more routine practice of reviewing her confessions with her after the torture session and noting which she confirmed and which she retracted. She claimed to have killed and lamed eleven horses, three cows and one goose, specifying that she hit many with a stick or a stone, poisoned one teenage girl, hit three children so hard that they died, caused three more children to die by kissing or blowing on them, slew one woman by throwing a stone at her head, and killed two other people. In many of these instances, she described the specific motives that led her to perpetrate these acts: a man 'refused to carry her wood' in his wagon; a woman dishonored her by asserting that she had 'had born a bastard child;' an employer had 'beat her badly.'

Outside of the torture chamber, Margretha retracted six of her stories: the last three she confessed to, two of the injuries to animals, and one other. When the magistrates investigated the stories she left standing, most of the people interviewed confirmed the conflicts and the damages. A few confirmed some but not all the details, while in one instance the person denied any knowledge of what she said. Some of the people said that they had suspected her at the time, but others reported that they 'had no idea it was her.' Margretha also confessed to a number of stereotyped details of contact with the devil, use of a salve, and participation in a witches' dance, but in the realm of malefic crimes the combination of partial retraction and partial confirmation, substantial corroboration but sporadic disagreement, lack of prompting on the part of the interrogators, detailed discussions of motives, and simple, for the most part directly physical violence set in the context of what we know about the intensity of conflict that was possible in early modern villages, makes it likely that Margretha did in fact do many of the things she said she did.

Occult injury and psychosocial factors in disease

Most of Margretha's confessions specified very mundane mechanical means by which she inflicted injuries, but what are we to make of her claim to have killed children by kissing or blowing on them? We could just take the position that it doesn't matter whether magical attacks had any intrinsic efficacy, that all that matters is just that the people involved thought they did. However, this position is inadequate, because it marginalizes what was for the participants the very heart of the matter, the conviction that these cases involved an extraordinary malevolent power.[64] On the one hand, the demonologists (and, following them, generations of historians) may have emphasized the pact with the Devil, but in general the law put equal emphasis on harmful magic, while commoners, as already noted, were far more interested in this aspect of the crime than its theological implications.[65] On the other hand, early modern people – commoners as well as the elite – understood that use of poisons did not necessarily involve a pact with the Devil or other witchcraft, and prosecuted some people for the secular crime alone even as they prosecuted others as witches. Similarly, they knew that assault and battery need not involve some sort of magical power to cause harm and accused some of their neighbors for the physical act alone, yet accused other batterers of witchcraft.[66] And some people were accused of manifesting this malevolent power quite independent of any specific physical contact. A few were accused of manifesting it through some ritual or verbal means, while others were accused of simply manifesting it.

Twenty-three of the 73 malefic accusations in the sampled trials, almost one-third, concerned some sort of occult bewitchings, ailments attributed to people without any physical medium being specified.[67] While a few were vague enough that a physical means may have been assumed but not mentioned, most imply that some sort of intangible force, some extraordinary malevolent power, was at work.[68] In one example, a woman named Anna Rueff said another woman, Catharina Ada, stood 'to her right side [and] without a word' ripped a loaf of bread in half, which caused her 'head to hurt somewhat [and] the next day' she 'became lame on her right side' and hurt so badly that she seemed to be losing her mind.[69] In a second example, a young man claimed that at his wedding an older woman named Anna Gebhard made lewd comments and grabbed his trousers, until 'suddenly such a fright came over him,' that 'he lost his manhood and thereby became impotent.'[70] In a third case, a man named Andreas Leichten said that his elderly neighbor Agnes Langjahr 'frequently' harassed his family, distressing his daughter so much that she refused to go out and eventually died.[71]

In all three cases, there is good evidence that, intentionally or not, the suspects' actions may well have played an important role in the maladies blamed on them. In the first case, both the timing and nature of Anna Rueff's symptoms suggest that they were caused by her distress over Catharina Ada's actions. Pain and paralysis are common forms of conversion disorder, and 'there is a strong association between somatic symptoms and psychological distress,' so it seems suggestive that Anna's symptoms appeared while Catharina was with her and on the side where she stood.[72] In the second example, the fact that Konrad ascribed his impotence to the 'fright' that 'came over him' is very significant, for according to modern psychologists men's 'erectile problems' are a psychophysical reaction which 'tend to be associated with fear.'[73] If he just made up the story to save face, it seems more likely that he would have talked about a spell or curse rather than his own, dishonorable, fear. In the third example, the girl's refusal to go out of the house suggests that Agatha's harassment had bothered her a great deal, and the stress this engendered could have contributed to a fatal cardiac arrhythmia, or, more likely for a young girl, reduced her immune competence and thereby made her more vulnerable to some other disease.[74]

The accusers in these cases may well have had psychological or organic problems that also contributed to their distress, but their allegations that the maladies were caused or at least strongly influenced by disturbed interpersonal relations were not unreasonable in light of the circumstances described in the trial records. These and many other alleged occult bewitchings appear to have been manifestations of the considerable power of interpersonal relations on physical health.[75] This is the effect popularly referred to as 'psychosomatic,' although physicians have abandoned the term because of its connection with Freudian and neo-Freudian psychodynamics, which have not been supported by experimental evidence or clinical experience in this respect.[76] In their place, current medical understanding includes four primary means by which psychological processes influence physical health.[77] The first, somatoform disorders, involves somatic symptoms that either cannot be attributed to organic disorder or whose severity cannot be accounted for by organic damage. The second, psychophysical disorders, are fully organic disorders that are nevertheless strongly affected by emotional and psychosocial influences. These disorders usually result from the physiological effects of prolonged stress, which also cause the third form of psychological influence on physical health, suppression of the immune system. Finally, psychological processes can cause actions that lead to somatic harm, including, most significantly in regard to witchcraft, misjudgments that result in accidents.

We cannot conclusively diagnose diseases from old trial records, of course, but since psychological distress does have a real potential to contribute to a wide range of maladies, accusers often did have some real basis for their suspicion that the suspects' actions or attitudes had caused or contributed to their ailments. Naturally, in some cases the psychological influences that affected their bodily health were probably generated purely by their own internal psychological processes, but in others it seems probable that interpersonal conflict triggered the psychologically mediated physiological effects. Furthermore, while in some cases interpersonal tensions probably exacerbated the accuser's pre-existing psychological or physiological problems, in other cases interpersonal conflict could have had an independent effect, for pre-existing psychological or physiological problems are not necessary in order for physiological effects to occur.[78] Nor is it necessary for a person to have a cultural expectation that other peoples' actions can affect their health to be affected, although such an expectation can naturally contribute to psychological distress.[79] Similarly, the other party in the conflict does not have to intend to cause injury or even believe that this is possible to trigger the stress reaction, and her actions do not even have to cause fear, for any negative feelings that are strong enough – fear, anxiety, anger, depression, despondency, resentment, or frustration – will do.[80]

The key words here are 'strong enough,' for this would seem to be the source of the malevolent power in many witchcraft cases. Deliberately or inadvertently, it appeared that a threshold had been crossed when interpersonal antipathy burst forth in physiological symptoms. This was true not only of the explicitly occult accusations, but of most of the assault cases and at least some of the allegations of poison as well.[81] Most instances of assault result in cuts and bruises, but these sorts of injuries seldom led to witch accusations. Instead, accusations resulting from physical contact generally involved some sort of paralysis, severe pain, or, in one of the sampled cases, such intense distress that the person killed herself. It is possible in some of the cases of paralysis the damage resulted from purely mechanical trauma since the suspects were young adults, and one was male, but even these instances most likely involved a significant psychosocial component, and most of the injuries caused by the other physical attacks almost certainly resulted primarily from the victim's stress response rather than the direct bodily effect of the suspect's action.

In some instances, the accusation did not even involve a blow, but instead some sort of touch, grabbing or stroking of the victim. In these cases, physical trauma is unlikely or impossible, so psychological factors would seem to be paramount. However, during some trials the possibility was raised of a powder or ointment that witches were said to rub onto their victims. One suspect, Anna Maria Rothin, was said to have smeared Conrad Herwick's wife with something that caused her to become lame and then die, for example.[82] Another woman, Agatha Weil, confessed to having smeared people with an ointment that caused them to become lame and even to die, and when the magistrates investigated people confirmed most of the injuries. The hallucinogenic ointments that people in the region are known to have used on themselves included alkaloids that block neurotransmitters in both the central and peripheral nervous systems, so they or something similar could have been used to cause a loss of sensation and possibly control of a limb.[83] Their chemical effects in such a limited, local, and topical application would not likely have caused death, however, so the frightening effects of the perceptual and motor distortions on unwitting victims must have also played an important part. In the same way, the victim's fears appear to have played an important role in some of the poison cases as well.[84] The effects of salves and poisons, like many other somatic disorders, probably involved a complex interplay between physiology, psychology, and cultural expectations. A final type of accusation in which the psychophysical connection appears to have played an important role was harm to animals. Ahrendt-Schulte ascribes these cases, to the extent that they were founded, to the use of poisons, and we have seen that they could also involve physical blows.[85] Some accusations, however, specified an occult influence, as when one suspect was said to have used 'her witchcraft,' to cause a horse to throw its rider, and when another suspect was said to have cured a cow by grabbing its horns and saying 'up, up,' and then later killing it by throwing 'a bucket of water on it.'[86] The idea that a person could affect an animal so strongly may seem implausible, but it is supported by recent studies of animal psychology and of farm animals' relations with humans. Animals have been used as subjects in many of the experimental investigations of psychological factors in disease, and these have shown that the dynamics of their social groups can affect a variety of types of animals' health.[87] It has even been demonstrated that dominant animals can cause sudden death through cardiac arrhythmias in submissive animals by harassing them.[88] Humans' influence on the health and behavior of animals has not been as well studied, but a growing number of investigations indicate 'that farm animals may be very fearful of humans, with adverse consequences for the animals.'[89] This would explain the occult powers some suspects were reported to have exercised over animals, and also clarify the dramatic consequences of some physical assaults on animals which, like some of the physical assaults on people, do not seem to have left noticeable bruises or cuts. Margretha Stainer's attacks on her neighbors' animals, for example, may have worked not purely or even primarily through their physical force, but instead through their psychological power, their exploitation of animals' subordinate place in the farmyard dominance hierarchy.

Ahrendt-Schulte has raised an important issue by pointing to the reality of poisonings as a source of belief in and fear of witches. The analysis here suggests that her insight should be extended dramatically, for poisoning was only the most obvious, and far from the most frequent, form of aggression associated with witchcraft. Assault, occult injury, and harm to animals accounted, along with poisoning, for the great bulk of accusations, though, and as we have seen they were just as real dangers to early modern people as poisoning. Furthermore, the residual accusations among the sampled cases in Württemberg, theft and arson, were equally mundane.[90] The more exotic accusations against witches like causing storms, keeping butter from churning, and the like obviously present a different problem of interpretation, one which the classic understanding of magic as the rationalization of inexplicable misfortune seems more on point, but even where these forms of maleficium were reported, they were either far less significant than the types of health-related issues encountered in the sampled cases in Württemberg or, in the case of weather magic, played a prominent role only temporarily, in special circumstances.[91] For the most part, witchcraft fears centered on problems of health and disease (including accidents), and far from being the misguided rationalization of inexplicable misfortune, they were in many cases reasonable if not necessarily correct attempts to specify the source of a malady. The charge of witchcraft was certainly abused, both cynically and naively, but the fear not only that malefic magic was being practiced, but also that malevolent power was in fact being projected, was not inherently unreasonable. It was perfectly consistent with a full understanding of both the role of magic in early modern popular culture and the actual interplay of interpersonal relations, psychology, and physiology in human health and well being.

Ahrendt-Schulte and others' insistence that poisonings and other acts of sorcery were real acts which conferred real power on women has opened the way for a new, more realistic understanding of witchcraft, but because these explicit acts were only practiced by a minority of suspects, they remained secondary in our understanding of the phenomenon, overshadowed by the need to explain the majority of 'implausible' accusations.[92] Recognizing that many of these were not implausible at all shifts the emphasis in what needs to be explained: not why people believed in an impossible set of crimes, but why their belief in this set of possible crimes got so out of hand, causing greater social problems than the crimes themselves appear to have done in the first place.

While many of the traditional explanations for the witch trials – the importance of elite demonology, the self-validating nature of torture, the cynical manipulation of a vague and elusive set of beliefs by self-interested parties, and the subconscious reversal of guilt by people who felt guilty – work at that level, this revised understanding contains in itself a new insight that helps explain it as well, for it not only broadens the range of offenses that potentially caused people harm, it also broadens the range of people who could have caused it. Just as a person does not have to believe in witchcraft or magic for their stress reaction to be triggered by other peoples' displays of hostility, a person does not have to consciously intend to cause harm in order to cause it. Poison and sorcery require premeditation, and verbal curses require a conscious articulation of a desire for harm, but a look, gesture, or inarticulate exclamation of rage can be made with no conscious, or even unconscious, thought of its effect on its recipient, and even physical blows can be made without a serious expectation that they will be traumatic or fatal.[93] This aspect of the connection between interpersonal relations, psychology, and physiology – what E.E. Evans-Pritchard distinguished as 'witchcraft' as opposed to deliberate acts of 'sorcery' – helped make the early modern judicial process so potentially damaging, for it came to include not just people who appeared to be practitioners of harmful magic, but also people who were seen to have exerted a spontaneous harmful power.[94] The phrase 'came to' is used deliberately here, for the witch hunters generally thought they were dealing with diabolical sorcerers and sorceresses, but by their use of torture compelled people who had never practiced sorcery to admit to it.

The commoners who brought charges were generally reacting to specific incidents in which they perceived that specific harms had been done. Most of the time, they perceived that women were the ones who caused harms through the mechanisms associated with witchcraft. More specifically, they perceived that women more frequently took that extra step, crossed the threshold in their relations, where consciously or unconsciously, through some covert action or through the spontaneous expression of emotion they manifested their anger in a way that caused physiological damage to their antagonist.[95] Stuart Clark has suggested that 'we may be faced with nothing more significant than a correlation between the sex of most "witches" and the sex of most of the practitioners,' of sorcery and the present analysis indicates that he may be right on the money, but with one caveat.[96] The suspects did not have to practice sorcery more, but instead could just manifest baleful interpersonal power more. The crucial question about the relationship of women and witchcraft may not be why early modern women practiced harmful magic more often than men, but why they seemed to manifest the malefic power ascribed to witches more often than men.

285

Female aggression in cross-cultural and biological perspective

The sampled trials in Württemberg, as research elsewhere, give plenty of evidence that some women did consciously practice sorcery, while other women did act in ways that spontaneously expressed their anger so vehemently that it caused physical harm to other people. However, it is difficult to tell from the early modern records alone whether women acted in these ways more often than men, or whether they were just expected to act these ways more often than men.[97] We know that women were involved in far fewer violent crimes than men, but this leaves open the question of whether they were simply less aggressive, or whether they acted out their aggression in different ways, in ways associated with witchcraft.[98] Therefore, we will turn to cross-cultural psychology and biology to see if they can shed any light on the issue.[99] They cannot by themselves provide solid answers, but they can provide context and highlight broader human tendencies that can make one answer more probable than another.

I have already examined the connection between old age and witchcraft in an earlier article, and in it I found evidence from the historical record, from cross-cultural sociological and anthropological studies, and from the biology of aging that the stereotyped old woman as witch did correspond to cross-cultural patterns of behavior, which were rooted in the interplay of sociocultural and biological influences during the life transition known as the climacteric.[100] Elderly women were beset by socioeconomic problems like poverty and marginality and frustrated by sociocultural restrictions like limited legal rights and restricted outlets for sexuality. Across cultures, women tend to exhibit irritable and other socially disruptive behaviors during this phase of life due to the combination of psychological and biological adjustments the end of reproductive potency triggers, and in the conditions of early modern Europe some elderly women accepted and even cultivated these patterns of behavior in order to enforce respect and obedience.

However, elderly female witches had the same relationship to female witches that female witches had to witches: they made up a majority, but there was a significant minority who also must be taken into account. Furthermore, the statistics on age tend to reflect the point at which a woman was tried, but witch suspicions built up over years, so the statistics exaggerate the median age of suspected witches in the community.[101] Significantly, the *Malleus Maleficarum* discussed the supposed reasons why older women were especially prone to witchcraft, but it also discussed the reasons why younger women were attracted to it as well.[102] The particular problems of elderly women in early modern Europe, and the general characteristics of elderly women, were important, but they do not account for the overall association of women and witchcraft.

Early cross-cultural psychological studies of female aggression concluded that women are less aggressive than men, a conclusion that fit comfortably with the prevailing Western notion of 'natural' female character at the time.[103] Critics, however, have suggested that the studies' definition of aggression was biased toward male forms, and more recent studies suggest that both genders have similar capacities for aggression, but that they manifest them rather differently.[104] Across cultures, males are more likely than females to use direct physical aggression; the two genders tend to be roughly equal in their propensity toward verbal aggression; and females are more likely than males to use indirect aggression: spreading gossip, manipulating surrogates, and other forms of covert attack.[105] When women do commit acts of direct aggression, like murder, they tend to use surreptitious means that minimize the actual violence, like poison or battery against a sleeping foe, although when they have power and think they are unobserved (as when they care for children and aged people) they are less reticent about resorting to direct physical violence.[106] While the correspondence between these modern findings and early modern suspicions about witches is not exact – the witches were thought to, and in some trials were shown to, use more direct violence (poisons, ritual magic, and battery) than the females in the modern studies, the parallels are certainly suggestive.[107] Furthermore, on the other side of the gender equation, the propensity for direct physical violence of early modern men documented by Württemberg's court records is strikingly consistent with the general patterns observed for men.[108] On balance, the cross-cultural evidence seems to support the conclusion that early modern witch fears did reflect a real tendency for women to engage in witch-related practices and exhibit witch-like behaviors more often than men.[109]

The reasons for these different styles of aggression are discussed in many of the cross-cultural studies, and there is general agreement that sociocultural forces play a strong role.[110] Modern studies emphasize modern women's greater degree of social integration to account for both their reluctance to openly aggress and their reliance on indirect means, while early modern historians discuss the importance of women's social space as the arena in which witch-related activities took place.[111] However, it is becoming clearer that the either-or division between sociocultural influences and biology, nature and nurture, is an oversimplification; sociocultural and biological factors interact in complex ways to influence human behavior, including gendered behavior.[112] And while they sometimes exist in tension or conflict, sociocultural structures 'commonly' reinforce or exaggerate biological differences.[113] This seems to be the case in regards to aggressive behaviors, for while women tend to utilize indirect and covert aggression in part because they have internalized sociocultural images of appropriate female behavior, they also do this because of a conscious or unconscious recognition that they are at a disadvantage physiologically in confrontations with men, because men on average are larger and heavier and have more muscle-mass in their upper bodies.[114] On the one hand, this difference in biology to some degree underlies the difference in sociocultural images, for males have specialized in hunting and physical combat since Paleolithic times, and have augmented this basic biological difference with individual training in fighting, the use of increasingly complex and lethal weapons, and an expanding scale of group cooperation, further magnifying the differential coercive power of men and women.[115] It seems significant that in many simple societies men and women are thought to have similar, if not always the same, propensities to use magical powers, while in Western civilization, dominated by male violence, male government, and male religion, females have come to be seen as particularly likely to rely on occult forms of power. On the other hand, this difference in biology is itself in part a product of social forces, for it was the existence of effective social groups that enabled human beings to evolve specialized physiologies to this degree.[116]

The role of gross anatomical differences between women and men in predisposing them to certain modes of aggression, both directly, through conscious or unconscious calculation of optimum conflict strategies, and indirectly, through sociocultural expectations and restrictions, would seem relatively unproblematic. Other, more subtle, biological differences are more controversial, but also seem to play a role. The best known gender difference in behavior directly linked to physiological differences is the effect of male sex hormones (androgens) in stimulating aggression in men.[117] While recent research has challenged the simplistic notion that surges of testosterone cause uncontrollable fits of aggression in males, it is well established that prenatal exposure to androgens produced in response to the presence of the Y chromosome causes the hypothalamus to develop differently in males than females.[118] Because of this difference, testosterone affects males' brains differently than females' brains, and while some researchers argue that it simply makes men more capable of violence rather than compelling them to it, in either case this difference does appear to be a biological contributor to the differential levels of direct aggression observed across cultures.[119] The absolute levels of violence manifested by both sexes vary widely from one culture to the next, but the relatively greater readiness of males to resort to overt violence appears to be a constant, and appears to be attributable to this genetic and hormonal difference as well as to gross anatomical differences and differences in social roles and acculturation.[120]

While the different prenatal development of females makes them less responsive to the influence of androgens, it would be a mistake to conclude that their behavior is simply a reflection of their lack of something males have. In the first place, the presence of estrogen has been shown to promote composure, even in men, so women's greater restraint also reflects their possession of something men lack (or at least have far less of).[121] Furthermore, the evidence suggests that the forms of aggression women do tend to favor are positive adaptations that maximize their natural strengths. Specifically, across cultures women have been shown to be on average more emotionally responsive, more socially attuned, and more verbally gifted than men.[122] While socialization undoubtedly accounts for much of that difference, both because girls are encouraged to foster these skills in order to take on their role as nurturers and because subordinate groups in society generally cultivate a greater awareness of the nuances of behavior and expression than dominant groups, the evidence suggests that the tendency has biological roots as well.[123] One study, for example, has shown newborn girls to be more responsive to sounds of other peoples' distress than newborn boys, while another has shown that at four months girls are already better at recognizing faces than boys.[124] Furthermore, women appear to be biologically equipped to hear better, see better in the dark, have better visual memories, differentiate tastes better, and smell more acutely than men.[125] Women's brains are structurally different from men's: they are 15% smaller (even accounting for differences in body size), with proportionately the same number of neurons, but more tightly packed.[126] There is some evidence that the corpus callopsum, the nerve bundle that connects the right and left hemispheres, is bigger in women than men, and it has been suggested that this enables women to integrate the cognitive activities of the two hemispheres more quickly than men.[127] More solidly established is that women process emotion in more regions of the brain than men; both hemispheres of women's brains recognize the emotional content of visual messages, whereas only the right hemisphere of a men's brains do.[128] As a consequence some of women's emotional processing is located in the same hemisphere as the areas responsible for verbal activity, which suggests a reason why women may express emotions more readily than men, in whom emotional processing and verbal activity occur in different halves of the brain.[129] Furthermore, women's verbal dexterity may be further enhanced by the fact that their language centers are consolidated in one region of the brain, while men's are scattered.[130] Finally, there is some evidence that estrogen plays a role in the full development of verbal fluency, memory, and the recognition of emotion in faces.[131] Indirect aggression (the infliction of harm through the manipulation of third parties) and the infliction of harm through verbal or gestural emotional signaling are thus conflict strategies that exploit abilities that women tend to be good at while, like covert violence, they avoid contests women tend to be less well equipped for.[132]

None of these physiological attributes impels women to behaviors associated with witchcraft, of course; what the cross-cultural and biological evidence suggests is not that some or all women have some innate drive to act like witches, but instead that they have innate characteristics that make them more likely than men to adopt conflict strategies in violent cultures or moments of anger that are characterized as witchcraft (or, more specifically, malefic magic).[133] Early modern women certainly lived in a society permeated by violence, and the cross-cultural and biological evidence suggests that it is no wonder that some of them acted in ways that made them seem like witches to their neighbors, particularly in the increasingly difficult demographic and socioeconomic circumstances of the late sixteenth and early seventeenth centuries. Even then, most women, like most men, lived either non-violently or within socially acceptable bounds of aggressiveness, but some early modern women, like some early modern men, aggressed beyond acceptable limits. The difference was, the men tended to aggress with fists or knives, while the women tended to aggress with poisons, rituals, or raw emotional onslaughts.[134] In so doing, they were manifesting both their culture's expectations and their own psychophysical endowments.[135]

Consequences of the witch trials for early modern women

Psychological studies have shown that not only does the absolute amount of aggression displayed by both genders vary tremendously according to culture, but also that it can vary within a culture over time.[136] One study in Finland, for example, has shown a measurable increase in aggressiveness in girls over the past few decades, presumably because of some combination of changes in social circumstances and in cultural values.[137] This finding is particularly important for a consideration of witchcraft in early modern Europe, because it points to a relatively neglected aspect of the early modern witchcraft persecutions: their results. Traditional discussions of the witch persecutions uniformly ended on a note of relieved discontinuity, implying that for all their horror and violence, the main result of the trials was to discredit magical beliefs by taking them to their extreme. The first historians to work in the new paradigm gave the trials a role in the process of modernization, enabling prosperous citizens to repudiate the obligations of communal charity, and in the growth of the state, asserting that they gave the central government entree into local affairs. An extension of this last argument was to portray them as a form of acculturation, part of the larger process of confessionalization by which elite culture attempted to assert its dominance over popular culture. Feminist historians redirected this line of reasoning by portraying the trials as part of the larger process of the construction of patriarchy, but, as noted above, their assertion that they were used to suppress women's traditional medical knowledge and practices has been substantially discredited by recent studies showing that trials generally did not target midwives or beneficent healers, while the larger assertion that the trials were used to punish women who strayed beyond the boundaries prescribed for their sex has been subjected to the criticism that the need for this roundabout approach has not been demonstrated. Furthermore, the exact mechanism by which essentially arbitrary accusations and punishments were supposed to have changed the status and activities of women, and exactly what the nature of those changes was, have never been systematically explained.

Some critics have gone so far as to question whether acculturation worked at all. Gerald Straus has said that if the 'central purpose' of the Reformation 'was to make people ... think, feel, and act as Christians … it failed.'[138] Heidi Wunder says that 'the endless repetition of gender norms...makes it doubtful whether authorities were really so successful,' while Susan Karent-Nunn has claimed that preachers' exhortations got people to 'pay lip service' but questions if they 'won a significant amount of conformity.'[139]

Nevertheless, there is a significant body of evidence suggesting that both exhortation and repression can be a powerful forces in reshaping 'not only behavior but feeling as well.'[140] Norbert Elias first pointed to them as a part of the early modern 'civilizing process,' and Po-Chia Hsia has cited specific evidence that in Calvinist territories assaults declined while suicides increased, suggesting that that religion's insistence on self control succeeded in redirecting people's aggression, even if it could not eliminate it altogether.[141] Mary Elizabeth Perry cites the power of 'consciousness of shame' as the source of 'sexual control over women' in Seville, for 'women imposed it on themselves,' while Ajay Skaria asserts that Indian witchcraft beliefs cause 'most women' to take 'routine precautions to reduce the chance of being identified.'[142] Reiner Walz has reported his impression that the suspects in the earliest cases from the villages he studied exhibited 'a particular threatening power' that was lacking in later suspects, and there is evidence from Württemberg that the trials there exerted a real influence on women's aggressiveness as well.[143]

It must be acknowledged at the outset that this evidence is not conclusive, for demonstrating that behaviors as diverse and diffuse as those associated with witchcraft changed over time because of specific legal and social pressures, and then generalizing across a much larger cultural area, is beyond the scope of this article. However, given the insight that the analysis in this paper gives into the connection between gender specific traits and witchcraft beliefs in general, and the logic of a specific connection between the intensifying struggle for resources in the late sixteenth and early seventeenth centuries and an increased reliance on witch-like behaviors by some women as one stimulus to the intensifying concern about witchcraft, it seems worth considering the possibility that along with the usual explanations for the decline in the persecutions – improvements in Europe's socioeconomic situation and changes in attitudes toward tortured testimony, confessions by marginal social actors, the power of the Devil, the proper response to misfortune, and the plausibility of supernatural causation in ordinary affairs, – the persecutions led to changes in women's behavior and attitudes that also contributed to the decline in concern about witchcraft.[144] The early suspects from Württemberg, from before 1660, in any case, did include a significant number of women whose words and behavior were quite violent. As we have seen, in 1603 Margretha Stainer confessed to numerous acts of violence that were confirmed by investigation. In another case we have seen, in 1621 Katharina Masten physically assaulted a servant girl, and in 1628 Maria Schneider poisoned her step-grandson. Another sampled suspect, Magdelena Kochen, was tried in 1629 after hurling abuse at those who denied her favors, and Magdelena Horn freely confessed in 1563 to harming the animals of those who rebuked her.[145] Agatha Sacher threatened her ex-boyfriend's fiancée in 1611, while Catharina Ada assaulted people, cursed, them, and carried out a ritual attack on a neighbor in 1628. Her daughter, Margaritha, followed in her footsteps. Few of the later suspects manifested such overtly violent behavior. To be sure, change was gradual, and some exhibited strong anger, but these women appear to have been more retrained and they constituted a smaller proportion of the suspects. None of the later sampled suspects was initially denounced for assault, for example, and only a few of the secondary allegations involved physical contact, with as many alleging stroking or grabbing as hitting. Overall, only three out of the fourteen late suspects exhibited the quickness to express anger that had characterized about half of the earlier ones.[146]

More indirect evidence of the change in women's behavior is suggested by the rising concern for male violence during the late seventeenth century, precisely the time when official concern about female violence was waning. In Württemberg, 'some time around the middle of the seventeenth century there was more concern about husbands behaving badly' than there had been before.[147] By the eighteenth century, the provincial church court 'distanced itself from the notion that women were intrinsically evil, that they harbored hidden malice which could erupt at any time,' and 'on the whole ... judges were more inclined to see marital violence grow out of the impetuousness and willfulness of men then out of the anger of women.'[148] Peasant women, in fact, came to be seen as 'strong proponents of disciplined behavior,' an attitude that also characterized the pietist movement that also, significantly, spread widely, particularly among women, in the region during the same period.[149] Finally, in literature, it has been noted that 'only in the last decades of the [seventeenth] century do we find increasing reference to women's "softness."'[150]

The role of the witch persecutions in this process is suggested by considering the way the majority of trials were conducted. Close analysis of the conduct of trials has revealed that in general they focused on one or at most a few individuals and they essentially constituted their selective punishment by ordeal.[151] Relatively few suspects were actually put to death. Rather more underwent excruciating torture, and still more had time to contemplate these fates while languishing in jail. Others were banished, fined, or confined in poor houses. Still others escaped torture, conviction, and incarceration, but lived for the rest of their lives under the watchful eyes of local notables and neighbors. And beyond those drawn into the legal process, a much larger circle of women lived amid vague rumors and unspoken suspicions. These threats remained long after the torture and executions ceased, and affected women in areas that never saw mass panics or even many small trials. Far more insidious than a homicidal pathology, the early modern witch persecutions constituted a wide-ranging and multifaceted repression of individuals exhibiting certain behaviors and attitudes, basically women who exhibited strong sexual, physical, or psychological aggressiveness.[152]

In simple behaviorist terms, the witch persecutions constituted a schedule of negative reinforcement for disapproved patterns of female behavior.[153] In many areas, at least three successive generations lived amid pervasive suspicions and periodic trials, which could be expected to have had a profound impact on popular practices by creating a sharp discontinuity between those who existed before, and those who came after.[154] For example, a woman born in Württemberg in 1567, the year the government adopted its statute against witchcraft, would have grown up amid the stirring of concern, and would have lived her entire adult life surrounded by a rising tide of persecutions. Her daughter, born just before 1600, would have grown up during the first height of the persecutions, and she would have lived her whole life in the shadow of the stake. The formative experience of her daughter, the third generation, born around 1630, would have been the relative tranquillity of the 1640s, when land was plentiful, grain prices were high, and trials for witchcraft infrequent, but the belief remained, and as economic conditions worsened and the government increased its policing of public morals, the witch persecutions rose to a new height that would have dominated her middle years.

The fourth generation, a great-granddaughter born in 1660, would never have known the grim cruelty of the government's prosecutions, but she would have grown up amidst widespread popular concern and frequent rumors and accusations. She might, at age eight or fourteen, have been caught up for a brief spell in one of the late, child-centered trials, the result of a child's fantasy or bad dream. While she was likely to have gotten off with no more than a scare and a scolding, the incident would likely have had a significant influence on the girl and on other girls in the community, warning them of sanctions against women who acted in ways that brought to them suspicion of witchcraft.

The fact that the persecutions took the form of both generations of suspicions and small trials and occasional mass panics could be expected to have heightened their effect. The suspicions, rumors, and small trials focused on a particular type of woman and specific forms of behavior, and everyone knew who and what was particularly suspect. Yet, suspicions and small trials could easily involve quite innocent women, and panics engulfed them by the dozens. The persecutions combined a relentless specificity with sudden, blind generality that might force any woman to confront the asocial, immoral side of being human. This dual focus meant that one type of female suffered endless persecution, while all other women lived in danger that the small ways in which they acted or felt like that type might lead to ostracism, jail, the torture chamber, or even the stake.

Thus, it seems reasonable to suggest that the persecutions declined in the later part of the century in part because of their very success.[155] Educated men in the mid-sixteenth century could look around and see numerous women who seemed to act like witches, openly practicing magic or expressing their anger without restraint; a century later their great-grandsons could see only isolated and furtive examples of these behaviors, a residuum that scarcely warranted the violence and disruption of the witch trials. Peasant beliefs could survive their crisis of confidence in the witch demonology and the end of the legal persecutions because they were sustained by the power of even subtle, unconscious expressions of anger to cause harm (as well as their usefulness in explaining misfortune and victimizing enemies), but the days when village women openly coerced their neighbors through unbridled spontaneous displays and consciously deployed magic rituals and articles were over. The change was not total or complete, of course, affecting the middle and upper classes of provincial society and women in towns more strongly than women on the land, and women in the core areas of the witch persecutions more strongly than those in the peripheral ones, but it seems that a critical turning point had been reached in the evolution of European culture, and the next two centuries would see substantial extension and consolidation of this 'civilizing process.'[156] Certainly there were many forces during this time contributing to the process by which European women went from being a feared source of violence and disorder to a presumptive fount of gentle succor, but the repression of witchcraft – official and unofficial; protracted, brutal, and pervasive – would seem to have been on the cutting edge.[157]

Conclusion

The foregoing analysis supports the importance of the witch trials in the history of women, and also reasserts the importance of women in the history of witchcraft. The conscious and unconscious behaviors associated with witchcraft were a source of power, and late Medieval and early modern women utilized that power more readily than men. The power of the behaviors stemmed in part from people's belief in their efficacy, but that belief itself reflected the fact that to a much greater degree than the paradigm inherited from the Enlightenment recognized these behaviors were, in fact, efficacious. Specifically, the entire range of 'magical' attacks on the health and well-being of people and animals, from poisons through curses and symbolic rituals to raw displays of intense emotion, which formed the primary concern of the commoners who denounced witches, had the potential to cause real injury through chemical and/or psychophysical effects. Women were particularly likely to utilize this source of power in part because significant elements of it fell into female social space (food preparation and the tending of social relations), in part because they were at a disadvantage in utilizing other sources of power (overt violence and legal processes), and in part because it played to their innate and learned strengths (sensitivity to and manipulation of emotional signals).[158]

The campaign against witchcraft certainly victimized innumerable women innocent of inflicting harm consciously or unconsciously, but the central dynamic of witchcraft was not this process of victimization.[159] Instead, it was a struggle for power. 'Witches' used the power of the range of behaviors from unconscious expressions of anger to premeditated use of poisons to compel compliance or punish defiance; accusers used the coercive power of the state as the most extreme step in a series of countermeasures that included appeasement and counter-magic to check these tactics or get revenge.[160] Accusers could be women as well as men, but since the suspects were overwhelmingly female, on balance the trials served to diminish women's power and strengthen men's.[161] In fact, it seems that by literally disarming women they helped increase the differential in coercive power between the genders in European society, and thereby may have made a critical contribution to the 'domestication' of women in the early modern period.

Notes

1. Wolfgang Behringer, 'Zur Geschichte der Hexenforschung,' in: *Hexen und Hexenforschung in deutsche Südwesten,* ed. Sönke Lorenz (Karlsruhe, 1994), p. 122.

2. Christina Larner, 'Crimen Exceptum? The Crime of Witchcraft in Europe,' in: *Crime and the Law,* ed. V.A.C. Gatrell, et al. (London, 1980), p. 60; Clive Holmes, 'Popular Culture? Witches, Magistrates, and Divines in Early Modern England,' in: *Understanding Popular Culture in Early Modern Europe from the Middle Ages to the Nineteenth Century,* ed. Stuart Kaplan (Berlin, 1984), pp. 86, 88, 92, 94, 103–4; Eva Labouvie, 'Hexenspuk, und Hexenabwehr: Volksmagie und volkstümlichen Hexenglaube,' in: *Hexenwelt: Magi und Imagination von 16–20 Jahrhunderts,* ed. Richard van Dülmen (Frankfurt a.M., 1987) p. 89; Karl Kramer, 'Schaden- und Gegenzauber in Alltagsleben des 16–18. Jahrhunderts nach Archivalischen Quellen aus Holstein,' in: *Hexenprozesse: Deutsche und Skandinavische Beitrage,* ed. Christian Degen, et al. (Neumünster, 1983), p. 234; William Monter, 'The Pedestal and the Stake: Courtly Love and Witchcraft,' in: *Becoming Visible: Women in European History,* ed. Renate Bridenthal and Claudia Koonz (Boston, 1977), p. 128; Ingrid Ahrendt-Schulte, 'Hexenprozesse,' in: *Frauen in der Geschichte des Rechts: Von der Frühen Neuzeit bis zur Gegenwart,* ed. Ute Gerhard (Munich, 1997), p. 199; Robin Briggs, 'Many Reasons Why: Witchcraft and the Problem of Multiple Explanations,' in: *Witchcraft in Early Modern Europe: Studies in Culture and Belief,* ed. Jonathan Barry, et al. (Cambridge, 1996), p. 59; Gerd Schwerhoff, 'Die Erdichtung der weisen Männer: Gegen falsche Übersetzungen von Hexenglauben und Hexenverfolgungen,' in: *Hexen und Hexenverfolgungen in deutschen Südwest,* p. 405; Robin Briggs, 'Witchcraft and the Community,' in: Robin Briggs, *Communities of Belief: Culture and Social Tension in Early Modern France* (Oxford, 1989), p. 58; Wolfgang Behringer, 'Weather, Hunger, and Fear: Origins of the European Witch-hunts in Climate, Society,

and Mentality,' *German History*, 13 (1995), p. 19; Wolfgang Behringer, 'Witchcraft Studies in Austria, Germany, and Switzerland,' in: *Witchcraft in Early Modern Europe*, p. 89; Rainer Walz, *Hexenglaube und Magische Kommunikation im Dorf der Frühen Neuzeit* (Paderborn, 1993), p. 512. Heidi Wunder, 'Gender Norms and Their Enforcement in Early Modern Germany,' in: *Gender Relations in German History: Power, Agency, and Experience from the Sixteenth to the Twentieth Century*, ed. Lynn Abrams and Elizabeth Harvey (Durham, 1997), p. 47 points out social subdivisions even more complex than this polar divide suggests.

3.   On defamation cases, Peter Rushton, 'Women, Witchcraft, and Slander in Early Modern England: Cases from the Church Courts of Durham, 1560–1675,' *Northern History*, XVIII (1982), pp. 128, 130–2. Critique of state-sponsorship, Briggs, 'Victims,' pp. 440–1; Ulinka Rublack, *The Crimes of Women in Early Modern Germany* (Oxford, 1999), p. 47 describes Württemburg's annual or semi-annual 'Vogtgericht.'

4.   On general conditions, Robert Jütte, *Poverty and Deviance in Early Modern Europe* (Cambridge, 1994), pp. 195–196; Thomas Robischeaux, *Rural Society and the Search for Order in Early Modern Germany* (Cambridge, 1989), pp. 70–72; Rublack, pp. 93, 95; on general consequences for social relations, Bruce Tolley, *Pastors and Parishioners in Württemberg during the Late Reformation, 1581–1621* (Stanford, 1995), p. 3; Malcom Gaskill, 'Witchcraft and Power in Early Modern England: the Case of Margaret Moore,' in: *Women, Crime, and the Courts*, p. 129; for specific link to witch trials Behringer, 'Weather,' pp. 3–5, 7, 14, 18, 26; R. Po-Chia Hsia, *Social Discipline in the Reformation* (London, 1989), p. 160; Edward Bever, 'Witchcraft in Early Modern Württemberg' (Ph.D. dissertation, Princeton University, 1983), pp. 93–95; Jürgen Schmidt, 'Die Kurpfalz, die Hexen und die Frage der Gelehrten, warum der Teufel mehr Weyber in diesem Fall dann Männer versucht und verführet,' unpublished paper presented to the 91st Sitzung of the Arbeitskreis für Landes- und Ortsgeschichte, 3/28/98, p. 34.

5.   H. C. Eric Midelfort, *Witch Hunting in Southwestern Germany*, (Stanford), p. 194; Lyndal Roper, *Oedipus and the Devil: Witchcraft, Sexuality, and Religion in Early Modern Europe* (London, 1994), pp. 227, 230–1.

6.   On survival of beliefs in populous, Ian Bostridge, 'Witchcraft Repealed,' in: *Witch- craft in Early Modern Europe*, p. 311; Willem de Blécourt, 'On the Continuation of Witchcraft,' in: *Witchcraft in Early Modern Europe*, p. 343; David Sabean, *Property, Production, and Family in Neckarhausen, 1700–1870* (Cambridge, 1990), p. 335; Karl Wegert, *Popular Culture, Crime, and Social Control in Eighteenth-Century Württemberg* (Stuttgart, 1994), p. 57 contends that some diabolical elements remained.

7.   Willem de Blécourt, 'The Making of the Female Witch,' *Gender & History* 12 (2000), pp. 289–90.

8.   Heinrich Kramer and James Springer, *Malleus Maleficarum*, trans. Montague Summers (New York, 1971), pp. 41, 44; Susanna Burghartz, 'The Equation of Women and Witches: A Case Study of Witchcraft Trials in Lucerne and Lausanne in the Fifteenth and Sixteenth Centuries,' in: *The German Underworld*, ed. Richard Evans (London, 1988), p. 60 (on Nider); Reginal Scot, *The Discoverie of Witchcraft* (New York, 1972), p. 4; Jean-Michel Sallman, 'Witches,' in: *A History of Women in the West,* vol II, *Renaissance and Enlightenment Paradoxes*, ed. Natalie Davis and Arlette Farge (Cambridge, MA, 1973), p. 457; Manual Simon, *Heilige, Hexe, Mutter: Der Wandel des Frauenbildes durch die Medizin in sechzehnten Jahrhundert* (Berlin, 1993), pp. 45, 50, 136; Ahrendt-Schulte, 'Hexenprozesse,' p. 220.

9.   Elspeth Whitney, 'International Trends: the Witch "She"/The Historian "He,"' *Journal of Women's History* 7 (1995), p. 78.

10.   Brian Levack, *The Witch-Hunt in Early Modern Europe* (London, 1995), pp. 133–5; Richard Godbeer, *The Devil's Dominion: Magic and Religion in Early New England* (Cambridge,1992), p. 20, n. 30 for America.

11.   Sigrid Brauner, *Fearless Wives and Frightened Shrews: The Construction of the Witch in Early Modern Germany*, ed. Robert Brown (Amherst, 1995), p. 13; Burghartz, p. 57.

12. Midelfort, pp. 183–6; William Monter, *Witchcraft in France and Switzerland* (Ithica, 1976), p. 197; Monter, 'Pedestal,' p. 133; Burghartz, p. 66; Brauner, pp. 5, 17; Manfred Tschaikner, 'Also schlecht ist das Weib von Natur: Grundsätzliches zur Rolle der Frau in den Vorarlberger Hexenverfolgungen,' in: *Hexe oder Hausfrau: Das Bild der Frau in der Geschichte Vorarlbergs*, ed. Alis Niederstätter und Wolfgang Scheffknecht (Sigmarungendorf, 1991), p. 71; Barbara Becker-Cantarino, '"Feminist Consciousness" and "Wicked Witches:" Recent Studies on Women in Early Modern Europe,' *Signs* 20 (1994), p. 169. Keith Thomas, *Religion and the Decline of Magic* (New York, 1971), p. 561.

13. Behringer, 'Weather,' p. 23; Diana Purkiss, *The Witch in History: Early Modern and Twentieth Century Representations* (London, 1996), p. 153; Lynn Abrams and Elizabeth Harvey, 'Introduction: Gender and Gender Relations in German History,' in: *Gender Relations*, p. 6; Robin Briggs, 'Women as Victims? Witches, Judges, and the Community,' *French History*, 5, 4 (December, 1991), p. 444 on expansion of judiciary; Beate Popkin, 'Wives, Mothers, and Witches: The Learned Discouse about Women in Early Modern Europe,' *Journal of Women's History* 3 (1997), p. 193.

14. Andrea Dworkin, *Woman Hating* (New York, 1974), p. 149; Silvia Bovenschen, 'The Contemporary Witch, the Historical Witch, and the Witch Myth,' *New German Critique*, 5 (1978), pp. 102, 106; Marianne Hester, *Lewd Women and Wicked Witches* (London, 1992), pp. 199, 115; Gunnar Heinsohn and Otto Steiger, *Die Vernichtung der Weisen Frauen* (Herbstein, 1985), pp. 15, 193.

15. Not midwives or healers: Burghartz, p. 67; J.A. Sharpe, 'Witchcraft and Women in Seventeenth Century England: Some Northern Evidence,' *Continuity and Change*, 6 (1991), pp. 179–80; Walz, 513; Anita Raith, 'Von den bösen Weibern, die man nennt Hexen – Männerphantasie und Frauenverachtung in württembergischen Hexenprozess,' unpublished paper delivered to the 91st Stitzung of the Arbeitskreis für Landes- und Ortsgeschichte, 3/28/98, p. 15; Tschaikner, p. 68; Clive Holmes, 'Women: Witnesses and Witches,' *Past and Present*, 140 (1993), p. 72; Briggs, 'Victims,' p. 439; Richard Horsley, 'Who were the Witches? The Social Roles of the Accused in the European Witch Trials,' *The Journal of Interdisciplinary History*, 9 (1979), p. 709. Role in women's history: Merry Wiesner, *Women and Gender in Early Modern Europe* (Cambridge, 1993), pp. xx, 229; Allison Coudert, 'The Myth of the Improved Status of Protestant Women: the Case of the Witchcraze,' in: *The Politics of Gender in Early Modern Europe*, ed. Jean Brink, et al., vol. XII, Sixteenth Century Essays and Studies, 1987, p 77; Brauner, pp. 113, 117; Rublack, p. 7; Susan Karant-Nunn, '"Fragrant Wedding Roses:" Lutheran Wedding Sermons and Gender Definition in Early Modern Germany,' *German History*, 17 (1999), p. 28; Abrams and Harvey, p. 7; Becker-Cantarino, pp. 153–155. An American variant is presented in Carol Karlsen, *The Devil in the Shape of a Woman* (New York, 1987).

16. Po-Chia Hsia, pp. 138, 146–7; Robischeaux, pp. 96, 105; Bob Schribner, 'The Mordbrenner Fear in Sixteenth Century Germany: Political Paranoia or the Revenge of the Outcast?' in: *The German Underworld*, p. 48; Tolly, p. 87; Wegert, pp. 12, 35–7, 143; Karant-Nunn, 'Weddings,' p. 25.

17. Behringer, 'Geschichte,' pp. 132–3; Alison Rowlands, review of Sabine Alfin and Christine Schedensack, *Frauenalltag im frühneuzeitlichen Münster*, in: *German History*, 16 (1998), p. 249; Stuart Clark, Thinking with Demons: The Idea of Witchcraft in Early Modern Europe (Oxford, 1997), p. 109; Burghartz, p. 68. Thomas Safley, *Let No Man Put Asunder: The Control of Marriage in the German Southwest: A Comparative Study, 1550–1600* (Kirksville, MO, 1984), p. 167; Brauner, pp. 113, 115; Claudia Opitz, 'Hexenvervolgung als Frauenverfolgung? Versuch einer vorläufiger Bilanz,' in: *Der Hexenstreit: Frauen in der frühneuzeitlichen Hexenverfolgung*, ed. Claudia Opitz (Freiburg, 1995), p. 260; Coudert, pp. 63, 78; David Sabean, *Power in the Blood: Popular Culture and Village Discourse in Early Modern Germany* (Cambridge, 1984), p. 109; Abrams and Harvey, p. 7.

18. Opitz, p. 248; Purkiss, p. 92; Elizabeth Reis, *Damned Women: Sinners and Witches in Puritan New England* (Ithica, 1997), p. xi; Holmes, p. 95; Roper, p. 37.

19. Percentage is in Sallmann, p. 450. Quote from Briggs, 'Victim,' p. 443; David Hall, *Witch-hunting in Seventeenth Century New England* (Boston, 1991) uses the phrase p. 7; so does Pieter Sperenburg,

The Broken Spell: A Cultural and Anthropological History of Preindustrial Europe (New Brunswick, NJ, 1991), p. 117; Malcolm Gaskill, 'The Devil in the Shape of a Man: Witchcraft, Conflict, and Belief in Jacobean England,' *Historical Research,* 71 (1998), pp. 161, 170; Clark, p. 110; Stuart Clark, 'The "Gendering" of Witchcraft in French Demonology: Misogyny or Polarity?' *French History,* 5 (1991), p. 427; Larner, 'Crimen,' p. 66; Opitz, p. 251. On some areas involving men more than women, Behringer, 'Witchcraft Studies,' p. 93; William Monter, 'Women and the Italian Inquisitions,' in: *Women in the Middle Ages and the Renaissance: Literary and Historical Perspectives,* ed. Mary Beth Rose (Syracuse, 1986), pp. 80–81; Gaskill, 'Devil,' p. 147; Gustav Henningsen and Bengt Ankarloo, 'Introduction,' in: *Early Modern European Witchcraft: Centers and Peripheries,* ed. Bengt Ankarloo and Gustav Henningsen (Oxford, 1990), p. 13; Tschaikner, pp. 59, 69; Burghartz, pp. 61–4.

20. Gaskill, 'Devil,' p. 159; Ahrendt-Schulte, 'Hexenprozesse,' pp. 209–10 (law); Helga Schnabel-Schüle, 'Frauen im Strafrecht von sechzehnten bis zum achtzehnten Jahrhundert,' in: *Frauen in der Geschichte des Rechts,* ed. Ute Gerhard (Munich, 1997) pp. 190, 198 (law); Sallmann, p. 453 (theory); Clark, pp. 112, 115 (theory); Schmidt, p. 30 (theory); Brauner, p. 38 (theory); Raith, p. 13 (torture); Rublack, p. 51 (torture); Wegert, pp. 12, 94 (torture); Richard Evans, 'Introduction: The "Dangerous Classes" in Germany from the Middle Ages to the Twentieth Century,' in: *The German Underworld,* p. 4 (torture); Heidi Wunder, *He is the Sun, She is the Moon: Women in Early Modern Germany,* trans. Thomas Dunlap (Cambridge, 1998), p. 14 (torture); Wolfgang Behringer, *Witchcraft Persecutions in Bavaria,* trans. J.C. Grayson and David Lederer (Cambridge, 1997), p. 20 (torture); Rublack, p. 81 (death); Schnabel-Schüle, p. 193 (death); Andrew Finch, 'Women and Violence in the Later Middle Ages: the Evidence of the Officiality of Cerisy,' *Continuity and Change,* 7 (1992), p. 29 (punishment). On women making accusations, Sharpe, 'Northern,' p. 189; Wunder, p. 149; Martin Ingram, ' "Scolding Women Cucked or Washed:" A Crisis in Gender Relations in Early Modern England?' in: *Women, Crime, and the Courts in Early Modern England,* eds. Jennifer Kermode and Garthine Walker (Chapel Hill, 1994), p. 67; Ronald Sawyer, ' "Strangely Handled in All Her Lyms:" Witchcraft and Healing in Jacobean England,' *Journal of Social History,* 22 (1989), p. 464; Ahrendt-Schulte, 'Hexenprozesse,' p. 215; Raith, p. 45; Reis, p. 122; Adrian Pollock, 'Social and Economic Characteristics of Witchcraft Accusations in Sixteenth and Seventeenth Century Kent,' in: *Witchcraft, Women, and Society,* ed. Brian Levack (New York, 1992), p. 199; Hugh McLachlan and J.K. Swales, 'Witchcraft and Anti-Feminism' *Scottish Journal of Sociology,* 4 (1980), p. 147; Holmes, 'Women,' pp. 51, 74, 77; Jim Sharpe, 'Women, Witchcraft, and the Legal Process,' in: *Women, Crime, and the Courts,* p. 107.

21. Clark, 'Gendering,' p. 427; see also Walz, p. 515.

22. Diana Purkiss, 'Women's Stories of Witchcraft in Early Modern England: The House, the Body, the Child,' *Gender and History* 7 (1995), pp. 410–11; Lyndal Roper, 'Witchcraft and Fantasy in Early Modern Germany,' *History Workshop Journal,* 32 (1991), pp. 30–1.

23. Clark, p. 122; Coudert, p. 66.

24. Karant-Nunn, p. 37; Coudert, p. 66.

25. Wunder, 'Norms,' p. 43; Simon, p. 136; Ulinka Ruback, 'Gender in Early Modern German History: An Introduction,' *German History,* 17 (1999), p. 5.

26. Holmes, 'Women,' p. 51.

27. On ubiquity of association: Andrew Sanders, *A Deed without a Name: The Witch in Society and History* (Oxford, 1995), p. 95; A.D.J. Macfarlane, *Witchcraft in Tudor and Stuart England* (New York, 1970), p. 230; Burghartz, p. 58; Bovenschen, p. 97; Schmidt, p. 29; Ahrendt-Schulte, 'Hexenprozesse,' p. 214; Schwerhoff, pp. 410–11; Tschaikner, p. 69; Katherine Morris, *Sorceress or Witch? The Images of Gender in Medieval Iceland and Northern Europe* (Lanham, 1991), p. 3; Elizabeth Tucker, 'Antecedents of Contemporary Witchcraft in the Middle Ages,' in: *Popular Culture in the Middle Ages,* ed. Josie Campbell (Bowling Green, 1986), p. 41; Richard Kieckhefer, *Magic in the Middle Ages* (Cambridge, 1990), pp. 29–33, 39; Sallmann, p. 453; Spierenburg,

p. 114; Behringer, 'W. Studies,' p. 80; Behringer, p. 161, n. 176; Ajay Skaria, 'Women, Witchcraft, and Gratuitous Violence in Colonial Western India,' *Past and Present,* 155 (1997), p. 131; Holmes, p. 94; Opitz, p. 259; Kramer, p. 234; Marianne Hester, 'Patriarchal Reconstruction and Witch Hunting,' in: *Witchcraft in Early Modern Europe,* p. 293. On popular concerns, Briggs, 'Victim,' p. 445; Clark, p. 110; Ursula Bender-Wittman, 'Frauen und Hexen – feministische Perspektiven der Hexenforschung,' in: *Hexenverfolgung und Frauengeschichte,* ed. Regina Pramann (Bielefeld, 1993), p. 26; Sawyer, p. 464; Ingrid Ahrendt-Schulte, 'Hexenprozesse als Spiegel von Altagskonflikten,' in: *Hexen und Hexenverfolgungen,* pp. 349, 351; Reis, p. xvi points out that the Puritans explicitly did not cast women as more evil than men, yet still cast women more often as witches; Behringer, pp. 161, n. 176; Behringer, 'Weather,' p. 2; Po-Chia Hsia, p. 160; Annabel Gregory, 'Witchcraft, Politics, and "Good Neighborhood" in Early Seventeenth Century Rye,' *Past and Present,* 133 (1991), p. 32; Burghartz, p. 63; Horsley, p. 693; Labouvie, 'Hexenspuk,' pp. 90–91; Walz, p. 522; Goodare, p. 295. Note that commoners did express some concerns about Devil: Larner, 'Crimen,' pp. 645; Roper, p. 44; Roper, 'Fantasy,' p. 230; Po-Chia Hsia, p. 153; Reis, p. 12; Holmes, p. 92.

28. Ahrendt-Schulte, 'Hexenprozesse,' p. 203; *Malleus Maleficarum,* pp. 41–2; Holmes, 'Women,' p. 67.

29. Clark, p. 111; Labouvie, 'Hexenspuk,' pp. 90–1; Walz, pp. 214, 512–514; Pollock, pp. 202, 205; Spierenburg, p. 118; Bender-Wittman, p. 18; Behringer, 'Witchcraft Studies,' p. 91; Gaskill, 'Power' p. 126; McLachlan & Swales, p. 150; Holmes, p. 95; Reis, p. 7; Malcolm Gaskill, 'Witchcraft in Early Modern Kent: Stereotypes and the Background to Accusations,' in: *Witchcraft in Early Modern Europe,* p. 285.

30. Gaskill, 'Power,' p. 125;

31. Behringer, 'Weather,' p. 13; Gaskill, 'Devil,' p. 165.

32. Wegert, p. 32; Eva Lacour, 'Faces of Violence Revisited,' *Journal of Social History,* 34 (2001), p. 649; Gaskill, 'Kent,' p. 287; Rainer Walz, 'Schimpfende Weiber: Frauen in lippischen Beleidigungsprozessen des siebzehnten Jahrhunderts,' in: *Weiber, Menschen, Frauenzimmer: Frauen in der ländlichen Gesellschaft, 1500–1800,* ed. Heide Wunder and Christina Varija (Göttingen, 1996), p. 190; Po-Chia Hsia, p. 165. On economic gaps widening, Robischeaux, p. 85; Behringer, p. 20. On crowding, Beate Popkin, 'Marriage, Social Discipline, and Identity in Eighteenth Century Württemberg' (Ph.D. dissertation, University of Pittsburg, 1994), p. 58; Wegert, p. 143. On honor as generator of conflict as well, Walz, 'Schimpf,' p. 183. On hatred and anger these engendered, see Walz, p. 521, Walz, 'Schimpf,' pp. 185, 192; Wegert, p. 151; Pocock, pp. 310, 324; Brauner, p 17.

33. On gossip, Walz, 'Schimpf', p. 177; Tolly, p. 94; Rublack, pp. 18–19. On insults and violence, Nichole Castan, 'Criminals,' trans. Arthur Goldhammer, in: *A History of Women in the West,* p. 480; Wegert, p. 32; Walz, pp. 520–521. On violence, Susanna Burghartz, 'Tales of Seduction, Tales of Violence: Argumentative Strategies before the Basel Marriage Court,' *German History,* 17 (1999), p. 55; Wegert, pp. 127–128, 520; Walz, 'Schimpf,' p. 190. On insults, Walz, p. 513; Sabean, 'Property,' pp. 336–8. On scolding, Ingram, pp. 51, 68–69.

34. Behringer, 'Witchcraft Studies,' pp. 90–1; Gaskill, 'Kent,' p. 286; Walz, 'Schimpf,' p. 185.

35. Walz, p. 182; Wegert, p. 86; Sabean, 'Property,' p. 138.

36. Walz, 'Schimpf,' p. 192. On the view his undercuts, see Matalene, p. 61; Gregory, p. 55; Finch, p. 38; Ingram, p. 67.

37. Walz, 'Schimpf,' p. 179; Walz, p. 513. Note that in England and Scotland, scolds were generally women, Goodare, p. 299.

38. Walz, p. 213.

39. Bever, 'Württemberg,' Appendix (especially cases 4, 11, 15, 17, 22, 24, 27); Walz, p. 516 acknowledges this himself.

40. Holmes, 'Women,' p. 55; Jonathan Barry, 'Introduction,' in: *Witchcraft in Early Modern Europe,* p. 13; Sabean, p. 109; Briggs, 'Victim,' p. 449; Wiesner, 'Early Modern,' p. 231. On general reluctance to use courts, Rublack, pp. 27, 31.

41. Ingram, p. 65 notes the difference in age.

42. On scolds' power, Ingram, p. 52; Anne Barstow, *Witchcraze* (San Francisco, 1996), p. 28. On witches', Holmes, 'Women,' p. 52; Wiesner, 'Early Modern,' p. 231; Skaria, pp. 134–135.

43. Pollock, p. 206.

44. Holmes, p. 52.

45. Robin Briggs, 'Ill Will and Magical Power in Lorraine Witchcraft,' in: Briggs, *Communities,* p. 103; Bender-Wittman, p. 27.

46. Trevor-Roper, 91; Monter, pp. 197–200; Robert Muchembled, *Popular Culture and Elite Culture in France, 1400–1750,* trans. Lydia Cochrane (Baton Rouge, 1985), p. 157.

47. Gabor Klaniczay, *The Uses of Supernatural Power: The Transformation of Popular Religion in Medieval and Early Modern Europe,* trans. Susan Singerman (Princeton, 1990), p. 166; Gaskill, 'Power,' pp. 126–7, 129; Hester, 'Patriarchal Reconstruction,' pp. 299, 301; Wunder, p. 150; Evans, p. 5; Skaria, p. 133; Purkiss, p. 145; Edward Bever, 'Old Age and Witchcraft in Early Modern Europe,' in: *Old Age in Preindustrial Society,* ed. Peter Stearns (New York, 1982), p. 177; Gaskill, 'Power,' p. 129; Horsley, p. 713; Wiesner, 'Early Modern,' p. 225; Holmes, 'Women', pp. 53, 57; Opitz, p. 261.

48. Clarke Garrett, 'Witches and Cunning Folk in the Old Regime,' in: *The Wolf and the Lamb: Popular Culture in France from the Old Regime to the Twentieth Century,* ed. Jacques Beauroy, et al. (Saratoga, CA, 1977), p. 59.

49. Hubert Vogel, *Der gro e Schongauer Hexenproze und seine Opfer: 1589–1592,* published by the city of Schongau, 1989, p. 23.

50. Ahrendt-Schulte, 'Hexenprozesse,' pp. 211–212, 200.

51. Ahrendt-Schulte, 'Alltag,' p. 352; on range of magic, Ahrendt-Schulte, 'Hexenprozesse,' p. 200.

52. Ahrendt-Schulte, 'Alltag,' p. 358.

53. Giovanna Fiume, 'The Old Vinegar Lady, or the Judicial Modernization of the Crime of Witchcraft,' in: *History of Crime,* ed. Edward Muir and Guido Ruggiero, trans. Corrada Curry, et al. (Baltimore, 1997), pp. 65, 67, 74; also Sabean, 'Power,' p. 110. The sample is discussed in Bever, 'Württemberg,' pp. 125–6.

54. Bever, 'Württemberg,' p. 263.

55. *Ibid.,* Table 7.1, Appendix. Note that there are slight discrepancies between the numbers given in Table 7.1 and those given in this paper, based on a reassessment of several cases.

56. Ritual action, Württemberg Staatsarchiv Stuttgart, A209, b. 1856, b. 11; verbal harassment, A209, b. 873, b. 1856, b. 852. All archival references are to this source.

57. Poison, A209, b. 1884, b. 11; occult: A209, b. 1856, b. 2096, b. 1431.

58. A209, b. 1223.

59. Rublack p. 126 on the vulnerability of farms generally.

60. A209, b. 782, b. 1884.

61. Rublack, p. 220.

62. A209, b. 719 (1562).

63. Roper, 'Fantasy,' p. 215; A209, b. 1253.

64. Wiesner, 'Early Modern,' p. 225; Gregory, pp. 65–8 on the belief that quarrelsomeness causes misfortune. Briggs, 'Victim,' p. 443; Purkiss, p. 411 for a forceful statement of the agnostic position.

65. Ahrendt-Schulte, 'Hexenprozesse,' pp. 206, 214.

66. Rublack, p. 100.

67. Bever, 'Württemberg,' pp. 209–221, 228, 259, Appendix.

68. Horsley, pp. 695, 701.

69. A209, b. 1856.

70. A209, b. 873.

71. A209, b. 11.

72. Gregory Simon, et al., 'Somatic Symptoms of Distress: An International Primary Care Study,' *Psychosomatic Medicine,* 57 (1996), p. 481.

73. Julia Heiman and John Hatch, 'Conceptual and Therapeutic Contributions of Psychophysiology to Sexual Dysfunction,' in: *Psychosomatic Disorders: A Psychophysiological Approach to Etiology and Treatment,* eds. Stephen Haynes and Linda Gannon (New York, 1981), p. 223.

74. Benjamin Natelson, 'Cardiac Arrythmias and Sudden Death,' in: Haynes and Gannon, pp. 412, 421–2; Brent Hafen, et al., *Mind/Body Health: The Effects of Attitudes, Emotions, and Relationships* (Boston, 1996), p. 71.

75. Edward Bever, 'Witchcraft Fears and Psychosocial Factors in Disease,' *The Journal of Interdisciplinary History,* 30 (2000), pp. 573–90 contains a fuller discussion of the reassessment of the role of 'psychosomatic' ailments in witchcraft fears outlined here.

76. Helmut Adler and Leonore Adler, 'From Hippocrates to Psychoneuroimmunology: Medicine as Art and Science,' in: *Spirit vs. Scalpel: Traditional Healing and Modern Psychotherapy,* ed. Lenore Adler and Runi Mikherji (Westport, CT, 1995), p. 7; C. Richard Chapman and Margo Wyckoff, 'The Problem of Pain: A Psychobiological Perspective,' in: Haynes and Gannon, p. 52; Barbara Walker and Curt Sandman, 'Disregulation of the Gastrointestinal System,' Haynes and Gannon, p. 164; Hafen, p. 105.

77. Bever, 'Fears,' pp. 577–80.

78. Bever, 'Fears,' p. 580; Robin Kowalski, 'Aversive Interpersonal Behaviors: An Overarching Framework,' in: *Aversive Interpersonal Behaviors,* ed. Robin Kowalski (New York, 1997), p. 217 here on power of response to others' aversive behavior; Anita Vangelisti, 'Messages that Hurt,' in: *The Dark Side of Interpersonal Communications,* ed. William Cupach and Brian Spitzberg (Hillsdale, NJ, 1994), p. 53 on power of words to hurt 'in every bit as real a way as physical objects.'

79. Bever, 'Fears,' p. 581; Garrett, 'Old Regime,' p. 61 credits psychological influence on impotence, but only because of 'a belief in the possibility … could easily lead to the fact of impotence.'

80. Bever, 'Fears,' pp. 589, 581.

81. *Ibid.,* p. 586.

82. A209, b. 1486; A209, b. 1258.

83. Bever, 'Württemberg,' pp. 296–7.

84. *Ibid.,* pp. 260–3.

85. Ahrendt-Schulte, 'Alltag,' p. 352.

86. A209, b. 2096; A209, b. 1856.

87. Richard Totman, *Social Causes of Illness* (New York, 1979), p. 91; Herbert Weiner, *Psychobiology and Human Disease* (New York, 1977), pp. 76, 364, 474.

88. Natelson, p. 425.

89. D.H. Hemsworth, et al., 'Fear of Humans and its Consequences for the Domestic Pig,' in: *The Inevitable Bond: Examining Scientist-Animal Interactions,* ed. Hank Davis and Dianne Balfour (Cambridge, 1992), pp. 264–5, 272 (hens), 275–8 (pigs), 274 (cows).

90. Bever, 'Württemberg,' Table 7.1.

91. Ahrendt-Schulte, 'Alltag,' p. 351; Behringer, p. 4 stresses weather magic, but only in major panics.

92. Briggs, 'Why,' p. 57; see also McLachlan and Swales, p. 146; Hester, 'Patriarchal Reconstruction,' p. 300.

93. Wegert, pp. 33 and 86 stresses that popular violence in general was spontaneous rather than premeditated.

94. That this distinction held for early modern Europe, Bender-Wittman, p. 12. An example of this type of malefic power is in Walz, 'Schimpf,' p. 186. Note that Turner, p. 324, critiqued Evans-Pritchard's dichotomy, but he did not dispute widespread recognition of the specific phenomena it describes (innate and learned magical powers), just the artificial imposition of these two categories as overriding organizing principles when 'these components are varyingly clustered and separated' in different cultures.

95. This is why ill-will was one of the defining characteristics of the witch; Briggs, *Witches and Neighbors* (New York, 1998), p. 23, seconded by Gaskill, 'Devil,' p. 170, n. 115. Note that ill-will only an issue, though, when it appeared to be cause harm: Walz, p. 515; Walz, 'Schimpf,' p. 185

96. Clark, p. 110.

97. Brauner, p. 21.

98. Weigert, pp. 122, 124, 137; For other areas, see Walz, 'Schimpf,' p. 189; Abrams and Harvey, p. 7; Finch, pp. 27, 29; Goodare, p. 294. For the corresponding under-representation of women, Schnabel-Schüle, p. 195; Castan, pp. 476, 486–487; Ingram, p. 49.

99. Note that recourse to biology does not imply acceptance of a simplistic bipolar biological division between males and females; for critique of simplistic biological division of sexes, see Marianne van den Wijngaard, *Reinventing the Sexes: Feminism and Biomedical Construction of Femininity and Masculinity, 1959–1985* (Delft, 1991), p. 46; and Thomas Laqueur, *Making Sex* (Cambridge, MA, 1990), esp. p. 243.

100. Bever, 'Old Age and Witchcraft.' The basic cross-cultural patterns and interplay of social and biological factors have been supported by more recent research; see Ellen Holmes and Sowell Holmes, *Other Cultures, Elder Years,* 2nd ed. (Thousand Oaks, 1995); Judith Brown, 'Cross-Cultural Perspectives on Middle Aged Women,' in: *Cultural Constructions of 'Women',* ed. Pauline Kolenda (Salem, WI, 1988).

101. Goodare, p. 300.

102. *Malleus Maleficarum,* p. 97.

103. On greater physical aggression of males, Margot Duley, et al., 'Biology Versus Culture,' in: *The Cross-Cultural Study of Women: A Comprehensive Guide,* ed. Margot Duley and Mary Edwards (New York, 1986), p. 8; Kaj Björkqvist and Pirkko Niemelä, 'New Trends in the Study of Female Aggression,' in: *Of Mice and Women: Aspects of Female Aggression,* ed. Kaj Björkqvist and Pirkko Niemelä (San Diego, 1992), p. 7; Marshall Segall, et al., *Human Behavior in Global Perspective: An Introduction to Cross-Cultural Psychology* (New York, 1990), p. 244; Bjork, Ost, and Kauli, Kaj Björkqvist, Karin Österman, and Ari Kaukiainen, 'The Development of Direct and Indirect Aggressive Strategies in Males and Females,' in: *Mice and Women,* p. 51; Robert Pool, *Eve's Rib: The Biological Roots of Sex Differences* (New York, 1994), p. 54.

104. On flaws in early studies, Sue Rosser, *Biology and Feminism: A Dynamic Interpretation* (New York, 1992), pp. 71–72; Claudia Heyne, *Täterin: Offene und versteckte Aggression von Frauen* (Kreuz), pp. 80–82; Segall, pp. 263–265. On women's equal capacity for aggression, Bjork and Niemala, Björkqvist and Niemelä, p. 14; Adrienne Zihlmar, 'Sex Differences and Gender Hierarchies among Primates,' in: *Sex and Gender Hierarchies,* ed. Barbara Miller (Cambridge, 1993), p. 40; Resser, p. 71; Loraleigh Keashly, 'Gender and Conflict: What Does Psychological Research Tell Us?' in: *Conflict and Gender,* ed. Anita Taylor and Judi Miller (Cresskill, NJ, 1994), pp. 185–186; David Adams, 'Biology Does Not Make Men More Aggressive than Women,' in: *Of Mice and Women,* p. 23 (in mammals generally). On differences in forms of aggression, Bodil Lindfors, 'The Other Sex: How are Women Different? Gender, Dominance, and Intimate Relations in Social Interaction,' in: *Mice and Women,* p. 231.

105. and Ari Kaukiainen, 'The Development of Direct and Indirect Aggressive Strategies in Males and Females,' i n: *Mice and Women,* Björkqvist, Österman, and Kaukiainen, p. 55; Björkqvist and Niemelä, 'New Trends in the Study of Female Aggression,' in: *Mice and Women,* pp. 6–7; Jacquelynne Parsons, 'Psychosexual Neutrality: Is Anatomy Destiny?' in: *The Psychobiology of Sex Differences and Sex Roles,* ed. Jacquelynne Parsons (Washington, DC, 1980), p. 19. On female emotional manipulation, Deborah Blum, *Sex on the Brain: The Biological Differences between Men and Women* (New York, 1997), pp. 80–1; Jacob Rabbie, et al., 'Sex Differences in Conflict and Aggression in Individual and Group Settings,' in: *Mice and Women,* p. 223; Adam Fraczek, 'Patterns of Aggressive-Hostile Behavior Orientation among Adolescent Boys and Girls,' in: *Mice and Women,* p. 111. On females use of indirect aggression, Björkqvist and Niemelä, pp. 8, 14; Björkqvist, Österman, and Kaukiainen pp. 52, 61; Deborah Richardson and Laura Green, 'Circuitous Harm: Determinants and Consequences of Nondirect Aggression,' in: *Aversive Interpersonal Behavior,* pp. 173, 178. On the equal use of verbal aggression by both genders, Anne Moir and David Jessel, *Brain Sex: The Real Difference between Men and Women* (New York, 1991), p. 82.

106. Björkqvist and Niemelä, p. 14; Heyne, pp. 11–12; Miriam Hirsch, *Women and Violence* (New York, 1981), p. 152.

107. That modern Western women are not notable as poisoners, Walter Feulner, *Zum Giftmord und seinem Nachweis* (Inaugural-Dissertation, Medical Faculty of the Free University of Berlin, 1983), p. 106. That early modern women were, Rublack, pp. 227–229, and women are generally: Liselotte Herx, *Der Giftmord, inbesondere der Giftmord durch Frauen* (Emsdetten, 1937), p. 3. Other connections are the importance of conflicts in women's space in early modern Europe and cross-cultural tendency of women to conflict particularly bitterly with other women: Bjork and Niemala, Björkqvist and Niemelä, p. 12; Luise Eichenbaum and Susie Orbach, *Between Women: Love, Envy, and Competition in Women's Friendships* (New York, 1988), p. 137; especially in patrilocal societies like early modern Europe, Ilsa Glazer, 'Interfemale Aggression and Resource Scarcity in Cross-Cultural Perspective,' in: *Mice and Women,* p. 170.

108. Weigert, pp. 122, 124, 137; For other areas, see Walz, 'Schimpf,' p. 189; Abrams and Harvey, p. 7; Finch, pp. 27, 29; Goodare, p. 294. On the corresponding under-representation of women: Schnabel-Schüle, p. 195; Castan, pp. 476, 486–487; Ingram, p. 49. For a caveat that women could be brutal, Schnabel-Schüle, p. 196; Rublack, p. 203; Walz, 'Schimpf,' pp. 190–191 (but not as often as men). For modern studies of violent crime, Pool, p. 54; David Barash and Judith Lystin, *Making Sense of Sex: How Genes and Gender Influence our Relationships* (Washington, D.C., 1997), p. 86; Blum, p. 72 (who reports that chimps show even more sex differentiation in aggression [95:5 male: female vs. 80:20 for humans]).

109. The connection between indirect aggression and witchcraft is drawn specifically for Zapotec women in Douglas Fry, 'Female Aggression among the Zapotec of Oaxaca, Mexico,' in: *Mice and Women,* pp. 194–195. Kowalski, p 216 notes use of aversive interpersonal behaviors to influence others' behavior.

110. Linda Carli, 'Biology Does Not Create Gender Differences in Personality,' in: *Women, Men, and Gender: Ongoing Debates,* ed. Mary Walsh (New Haven, 1997), p. 44; Rabbie, et al., p. 223; Ute Frevert, 'The Taming of the Noble Ruffian: Male Violence and Dueling in Early Modern and Modern Germany,' in: *Men and Violence: Gender, Honor, and Rituals in Modern Europe and America,* ed. Pieter Spierenburg (Ohio State University Press, 1998), p. 37; Segall, p. 266. Anthony Walsh, *Biosociology: An Emerging Paradigm* (Westport, CT, 1995), p. 34, however, argues that metastudies 'did not provide strong evidence for early gender-role socialization.'

111. On modern women's social integration, Rosaldo and Lamphere, pp. 55–56; Nancy Chodorow, 'Family Structure and Feminine Personality,' in: *Women, Culture, and Society,* ed. Michelle Rosaldo and Louise Lamphere (Stanford, 1974), p. 55. On the connection to aggression, Rabbie, et al., p. 225. On women's space: Behringer, 'Witch Studies,' p. 94 (citing Wunder und Labouvie); Briggs, 'Victim,' p. 447; Sharpe, 'Northern,' pp. 120, 187, 188, 192; Opitz, p. 262; Ulinka Rublack, 'The

Public Body: Policing Abortion in Early Modern Germany,' in: *Gender Relations*, p. 62; Ahrendt-Schulte, 'Alltag,' p. 353; Raith, p. 15; Purkiss, p. 414.

112. On interplay of nature and nurture, van den Wijngaard, p. 47; Pool, pp. 109, 200; Robert Lustig, 'Sex Hormonal Modulation of Neural Development in Vitro: Implications for Brain Sex Differentiation,' in: *Males, Females, and Behavior: Toward a Biological Understanding*, ed. Lee Ellis and Linda Ebertz (Westport, CT, 1998), p. 24; June Reinisch, et al., 'Sex Differences Emerge during the First Year of Life,' in: *Women, Men, and Gender*, pp. 37, 42; Leonard Eron, 'Gender Differences in Violence: Biology and/or Socialization?' in: *Mice and Women*, p. 96; Rosser, p. 73; Segall, p. 251–2. On ubiquity of gender specialization but variability of specific roles among primates, Barbara Miller, 'The Anthropology of Sex and Gender Hierarchies,' in: *Sex and Gender Hierarchies*, p. 3. On twin studies measuring role of genetics in masculinity and femininity, Pool, p. 216. A recent account stressing the importance of biology, Moir and Jessel, p. 75. That some recent feminists accept this: Rosser, p. 65. Among historians advancing this view, Roper, p. 48; Peter Weingart, et al., 'Shifting Boundaries between the Biological and the Social: The Social and Political Contexts,' in: *Human by Nature: Between Biology and the Social Sciences*, ed. Peter Weingart, et al. (Mahwah, NJ, 1997), pp. 151–3; Abrams and Harvey, p. 9. For statements defending traditional historical 'sociocultural' exclusiveness see Garrett, 'Old Regime,' p. 56 (on Durkheim); Clark, pp. 6–7; Weingart, et al., p. 66 (quoting Richard Hofstadter); Brauner, p. 21; Schnabel-Schüle, p. 195; Ulinka Rublack, 'Gender in Early Modern German History,' *German History*, 17 (1999), p. 1 states that 'the theoretical question to all research on gender is whether sex differences is socially and culturally constructed, or to some extent rooted in a pre-discursive body.'

113. Reinisch, pp. 41–2.

114. On the role of socialization, Jan-Erik Ruth and Peter Öberg, 'Expressions of Aggression in the Life Stories of Aged Women,' in: *Mice and Women*, p. 144; Thomas Ruble and Joy Schneer, 'Gender Differences in Conflict-Handling Styles: Less than Meets the Eye?' in: *Conflict and Gender*, p. 165; Fraczek, p. 108; Glazer, p. 163; Rabbie, et al., p. 223; Björkqvist and Niemelä, p. 14; Segall, p 243. On the role of gross physical differences, Parsons, pp. 18–19; Heyne, pp. 82–3, 89; David Stoddart, *The Scented Ape: the Biology and Culture of Human Odour* (Cambridge, 1990), p. 214. On the calculation of danger, Richardson and Green, p. 176.

115. Marvin Harris, 'The Evolution of Human Gender Hierarchies,' in: *Sex and Gender Hierarchies*, pp. 60–63, 69.

116. For example, Rhawn Joseph, *Neuropsychiatry, Neuropsychology, and Clinical Neuroscience* (Baltimore, 1996), pp. 66–9.

117. Pool, p. 53.

118. Walsh, p. 87; Pool, p. 108; Moir and Jessel, p. 76; Blum, pp. 42, 43, 74; Freda Newcombe and Graham Ratcliff, 'The Female Brain: A Neuropsychological Viewpoint,' in: *Defining Females: The Nature of Women in Society*, ed. Shirley Ardener (New York, 1978), p. 186; Lustig, p. 23; Barash, pp. 85, 175, 177.

119. On capability vs. compulsion, see Gail Vines, *Raging Hormones: Do They Rule Our Lives?* (Berkley, 1993), p. 79. Segall, pp. 268–268, and David Benton, 'Hormones and Human Aggression,' in: *Mice and Women*, p. 46 reluctantly concede a role to testosterone. Van den Wijngaard, p. 46 endorses the sensitization interpretation.

120. On primacy of culture as predictor of violence of both genders, Björkqvist and Niemelä, p. 6; on consistency of gender roles but variability of magnitude of difference, Segall, p. 250.

121. Moir and Jessel, p. 79. Rosser, p. 74 emphasizes that both sexes have both hormones in body.

122. On emotional responsiveness and social atunement, Walsh, p. 89; Segall, p. 250; Pool, p. 53. On verbal superiority, Pamela Reid and Michele Paludi, 'Developmental Psychology of Women: Conception to Adolescence,' in *Psychology of Women: A Handbook of Issues and Theories*, ed. Florence Denmark and Michele Paludi (Westpot, CT, 1993), p. 204; Newcombe and Ratcliff, p. 194.

123. On social responsiveness, Reid and Paludi, p. 204; Lindfors, p. 230; Walsh, p. 90; Moir and Jessel, p. 19. On role as caregivers and response to subordination, Barash, pp. 189–190. On socialization to social orientation, Segall, p. 244; Brown, 87. On the role of biological factors, Pool, p. 107; Barash, p. 185; Newcombe and Ratcliff, p. 187; Douglas Kerrick and Robert Hogan, 'Cognitive Psychology' in: *The Sociobiological Imagination,* ed. Mary Maxwell (Albany, NY, 1991), p. 183. On the ubiquity of sex differences in appearance and behavior in animals, Lustig, p. 13.

124. On the response to distress, Blum, *Sex on the Brain: The Biological Differences between Men and Women* (New York, 1997), p. 66. On face recognition, Pool, p. 204.

125. According to Blum, p. 67, these differences are not found to the same degree in females with a male fraternal twin (and who were hence exposed to higher levels of androgens in utero than other females); Walsh, p. 88; Moir and Jessel, p. 18. Stoddart, p. 135.

126. Blum, p. 37; Marianne Legato, *Gender-Specific Aspects of Human Biology for the Practicing Physician* (Armonk, NY, 1997), p. 22.

127. Moir and Jessel, pp. 46, 48; Pool, pp. 111, 119.

128. Walsh, p. 89; Newcombe and Ratcliff, p. 189; Moir and Jessel, p. 48.

129. On women's superiority at interpreting facial expressions and body language, Blum, p. 78; Significantly, early modern women were commonly thought to exhibit both greater facility with as well as greater reliance on verbal power; see Brauner, p. 19, Sabean, pp. 137, 142; Pocock, pp. 336, 353; Ingram, pp. 49, 50; Raith, p. 15 (citing Wunder).

130. On women's greater fluency, Pool, pp. 55–56. On regionalization of brain, Moir and Jessel, p. 46; Merrill Hiscock, et al., 'Is There a Sex Difference in Human Laterality? IV. An Exhaustive Survey of Dual-Task Interference Studies From Six Neuropsychology Journals,' *Journal of Clinical and Experimental Neuropsychology* 23 (2001), p. 137.

131. Pool, p. 108.

132. Moir and Jessel, p. 49, quote Sandra Witlesan on women's 'preferred cognitive strategy … [of] playing to your mental strengths.'

133. Similar to lack of specific psychology of poisoners, as earlier psychologists posited, Herx, pp. 112–113; Inge Weiler, *Giftmordwissen und Giftmörderinnen: Eine diskursgeschichte Studie* (Tübingen: Max Niemeyer, 1998), p. 1. On witchcraft as female conflict strategy, Ahrendt-Schulte, 'Hexenprozesse,' p. 213.

134. Pocock, p. 339; Rublack, p. 202; Sabean, 'Property,' p. 317; Ingram, p. 51; Wegert, pp. 137–8; Bender-Wittman, p. 27; Sharpe, 'Northern,' p. 194 citing Larner. Whitney, 'International,' p. 91 on differences in non-violent use of magic and religious symbols.

135. On cultural stereotypes, Ahrendt-Schulte, 'Hexenprozesse,' p. 212; Hester, 'Patriarchal Reconstruction,' p. 298; Schnabel-Schüle, p. 192 on the incorporation of this in the 'Carolina' legal code.

136. Lea Pulkkinen, 'The Path to Adulthood for Aggressively Inclined Girls,' in: *Mice and Women,* p. 113.

137. Viennero, p. 104.

138. Gerald Strauss, *Luther's House of Learning: Indoctrination of the Young in the German Reformation* (Baltimore, 1978), p. 307; 290 extends this conclusion to the Counter-Reformation.

139. Wunder, 'Norms,' p. 50; Karant-Nunn, p. 39; point also stated by Abrams and Harvey, p. 8.

140. Pocock, p. 6; Rublack, pp. 182, 223; Mary Lindeman, *Health and Healing in Eighteenth Century Germany* (Baltimore, 1996), p. 23; Tolley, p. 99; Po-Chia Hsia, p. 165 notes a rise in melancholy in women in late 17*th* century.

141. Pocock, p. 18; Po-Chia Hsia, pp. 163–5.

142. Mary Perry, *Gender and Disorder in Early Modern Seville* (Princeton, 1990), p. 122; Skaria, p. 133.

143. Walz, p. 513.

144. On the late seventeenth century as a transitional period in women's roles, Rublack, p. 259; Simon, pp. 169, 173; Schnabel-Schüle, p. 197. On the general decline in civil violence in Europe during this time, Eric Johnson and Eric Monkjoven, 'Introduction,' *The Civilization of Crime: Violence in Town and Country since the Middle Ages,* ed. Eric Johnson and Eric Monkjoven (Urbana, 1996), pp. 4, 6–8; Monter, 'Pedestal,' p. 134. On the difference in modern from early modern women's attitudes toward violence, Schnabel-Schüle, p. 195 (citing Wunder). See also Behringer, 'Witch Studies,' p. 88; Castan, p. 481; Rublack, p. 15; Becker-Cantarino, p. 173; Goodare, p. 303; Whitney, 'International,' p. 89–all on women's internalization of new norms. Allison Rowland poses this as an 'intriguing question' in her review of Ingrid Ahrendt-Schulte, *Zauberinnen in der Stadt Horn,* in: *German History,* 17 (1999), p. 287. On the displacement or repression of aggressive impulses as alternatives to indirect aggression, Bjork and Niemala, Björkqvist and Niemelä, p. 14.

145. Bever, 'Württemberg,' pp. 385–6.

146. Bever, 'Württemberg,' Appendix; Sabean, 'Property,' p. 133 reports that 18–19ᵗʰ century men almost never complained of their wives' violence; Popkin, p. 38 also notes lack of concern about female violence in the 18ᵗʰ century.

147. Rublack p. 4; Karant-Nunn p. 26, 35–6; Wegert, p. 137; Lacour, p. 660.

148. Pocock, pp. 353–4. This change might reflect simply a growing awareness of male violence as concern about female aggression waned, or it might reflect a rise in male violence in response to women's lessened ability to retaliate; in either case it suggests that the problem of female violence had receded.

149. Popkin, pp. 3, 13, n. 23.

150. N. H. Keeble, *The Cultural Identity of Seventeenth-Century Woman* (London, 1994), p. 71; see also Joy Wiltenburg, *Disorderly Women and Female Power in the Street Literature of Early Modern England and Germany* (Charlottesville, 1992), p. 266.

151. The roots of judicial torture were in the use of ordeal as a means of ascertaining truth; see Wegert, pp. 116–117. In practice the test itself was a punishment; Bever 'Württemberg,' p. 193.

152. On the systematic nature of trials, Wegert, p. 21; Rublack, pp. 41–2, 52; Bever, 'Württemberg,' p. 193; Ahrendt-Schulte, 'Hexenprozesse,' p. 213. On the role of trials as a warning, Brauner, p. 39; Coudert, p. 78.

153. Popkin, p. 17 emphasizes role of fear in the transition from control to self control.

154. Ahrendt-Schulte, 'Alltag,' p. 353 emphasizes the role of oral transmission from individual to individual, a process particularly vulnerable to disruption by generations of persecution. On the importance of role-models in the transmission of aggressive behavior patterns, see Bjork and Niemala, Björkqvist and Niemelä, p. 14; Pappu Viemerö, 'Changes in Patterns of Aggressiveness among Finish Girls over a Decade,' in: *Mice and Women,* p. 105; Blum, p. 80.

155. Wegert, p. 22, citing Marc Raeff, *The Well Ordered Police State* (New Haven, 1983), puts the watershed in social control in general in the 16ᵗʰ century.

156. Rublack, pp. 259–260 on upper and middle class women; Simon, p. 170 on the extension to lower class women.

157. On pervasiveness, Monter, 'Pedestal,' p. 130; Briggs, 'Why,' p. 61. Some historians now emphasize the limitations of the persecutions, Behringer, 'Weather,' p. 2; Clarke Garrett, 'Women and Witchcraft: Patterns of Analysis,' *Signs* 3 (1977), p. 462 (who calls them endemic not epidemic); Sallmann, p. 451. What this point overlooks is that suspicions, rumors, warnings, and so on were far more prevalent than trials; see Walz, p. 515.

158. On poison and food preparation, Schnabel-Schüle, p. 196; Ahrendt-Schulte, 'Alltag,' p. 352; Ahrendt-Schulte, 'Hexenprozesse,' p. 211; Herx, p. 182; Behringer, p. 161, n. 176 (citing Wunder); on women's orientation to social relations, Behringer, 'Witchcraft Studies,' p. 94 (citing Wunder).

159. Critics of victimization theory for its de-emphasis on female agency include Gaskill, 'Devil,' p. 144; Sharpe, 'Northern,' pp. 185, 192; Bender-Wittman, p. 19; Carolyn Matalene, 'Women as Witches,' in: Levack, *Women and Witchcraft*, p. 19; Abrams and Harvey, pp. 4–5; Sallmann, p. 457; Purkiss, p. 170.

160. Gaskill, 'Devil,' p. 168; Bender-Wittman, pp. 13, 23. On other steps, Holmes, 'Women,' p. 57; Walz, p. 516; Labouvie, 'Hexenspuk,' p. 91.

161. Although Gaskill, 'Devil,' p. 144 says more women benefited from the suppression of witches than were hurt by it.

PART V
'DISENCHANTMENT' OF EUROPE?

INTRODUCTION: THE 'DISENCHANTMENT' OF EUROPE?

Max Weber's notion, borrowed from Schiller, of the 'disenchantment of the world' reflected his sense that the roots of the modern world were visible in this process of transformation, not isolated within the realm of religion but extending into the economic and social structures and organizations of modernity. This process of disenchantment, he argued, might best be seen as one in which not just the natural world but all areas of human experience became recognized and understood as somehow less subject to mysterious or magical forces. The supernatural no longer exerted (or was perceived to exert) a transformative effect but rather the operation of the world was subject to the influence of mechanical forces, known, and predictable, even if not yet fully understood. The modern world, and indeed the Protestant world, was human-centred – one in which an intellectualized religion subverted the sacramental magic of the medieval Church and a belief in personal election denied the possibility that supernatural forces might shape the rhythms of day-to-day life. Disenchantment came in various forms but its impact was felt both intellectually and culturally in the 'decline of magic' and the concomitant collapse of axiomatically shared beliefs that had contributed to the construction of a moralized community and universe and politically and economically in the rise of the capitalist model, the expansion of bureaucracy and the nature of policymaking.

Weber's conclusions, and analyses of them, have provided the starting point for numerous essays, academic papers and representations of the cultures of late medieval and early modern Europe.[1] The very notion of 'disenchantment' has been called into question, and the implications of the 'decline of magic' debated and contested. The apparent simplicity of Weber's model makes it both enticing and open to criticism from all sides. As we have seen, there are good reasons to doubt the assumption that magic and supernatural, and beliefs about them, were possessed of any substantive homogeneity in the later Middle Ages. Such a lack of uniformity in perception and impact mitigates against any representation of any assertion of the existence of an epistemically consistent community. Recent interest in those on the margins of medieval and early modern society, the persecuted and the excluded, the critics and the sceptics presents a multiform model of culture and belief in which elements of 'disenchantment' are already present.[2] Similarly, the notion that the magical and mysterious were banished from the mental and physical world by the birth of modern science is too simplistic in its construction to be meaningful as an explanation for the multiplicity of cosmological understandings and interpretations in early modern Europe. Scientific explanations and models were as capable of creating divisions and fragmentations of belief as they were of imposing a uniform and naturalistic elucidation of events. In part, this reflects the pace at which new ideas were disseminated and planted, but further questions need to be asked, and indeed have been, about the extent to which the persistence of 'magical' belief impeded, or at least decelerated, the imputation of a more mechanical world view and an understanding of religion that was devoid of reassuring and/or challenging numinous agents.[3] The image of a smooth, linear progression from an 'enchanted' Europe to one that was 'disenchanted' has been, quite rightly, challenged and undermined. However, there are equal limitations in a model of cultural transformation that assumes a pattern of cultural change that resembles the trajectory of a tennis ball, battered to and fro with a mixture of planning, aggression, defensiveness and misfortune. In the encounter between magic and religion, rationality and superstition, the court was constantly being reshaped and, as new players entered, the vocabulary of debate and its meaning metamorphosed.

These issues are explored in the first article in this section, Michael Bailey's analysis of the 'disenchantment' of magic. The breadth of the debate over the 'disenchantment of early modern Europe' is reflected in the scope of the essay, which ranges from considerations of magic, religious belief and concepts of demonic power to debates over the legitimacy of ritual activity, the meaning of charms and spells, and beliefs about witches and witchcraft in the late medieval and early modern period. The argument about the disintegration of medieval magical and superstitious beliefs, Bailey suggests, needs to be rescued from the misconceptions that arise as a result of the application of post-Reformation vocabulary and understanding to the rituals and cosmologies of pre-Reformation Europe. There is, he concludes, a danger in binding the origins of disenchantment to the era of the Protestant and Catholic reformations; rather, it is important to recognize both the extent to which this debate was already active in the decades, even centuries, before the Reformation and the potent influence that these medieval controversies had upon the ideas and events of the early modern period. An analysis unconfined by rather arbitrary boundaries of periodization can reveal the degree to which post-Reformation religious culture possessed a 'twilight zone' that occupied the ground between sanctioned ritual and witchcraft and the very real presence of disenchantment at the heart of medieval magic.[4] A shift has certainly taken place in recent scholarship from the perception and representation of medieval popular religious culture as derived from a model of the 'magic of the medieval Church' towards one constructed around the existence of a 'system of the sacred'. The culture of late medieval Catholicism has been recognized as both vibrant and 'Christian' rather than intellectually moribund and practically quasi-pagan.[5] Similarly, the impact of the European Reformations upon the form and content of religious belief and practice has emerged as a rather more complex and complicating force.[6] Miracle and magic were argued but not abrogated; ritual and ritual observances were reformed but not rejected; wonder was interrogated but not written out of the world view.

The subtleties of such controversies and their outworkings are evident in the early modern debate over the cessation of miracles. The second article in this section examines this debate in detail, and the extent to which the miraculous had, or should have, ceased to intrude into daily life. The argument that the age of miracles had passed, Walker contends, was both deceptively simple and alarmingly imprecise. Not all questions were easy to answer, and the correct interpretation was often far from self-evident. At what point in Christian history had miracles ceased? Did miracles support doctrine, or did the invocation of the miraculous imply innovation in matters of theology and a deviation from doctrinal truth? A lack of scriptural support for either contention created a context for the debate in which concrete answers were virtually impossible to find, not least given the capacity for controversy over the miraculous to engage with wider debates over false wonders, justifying faith, the nature and limitations of diabolic power, and just what it meant to be 'marvellous in our eyes'.[7] The contested position of the miraculous, like the lexicon of disenchantment, owed much to the discussion of miracle in medieval literature and philosophy. But new challenges and pressures were also brought to bear by the fragmentation of confessional unity in the sixteenth century and the debate over the legitimacy and demonstrable veracity of the miraculous in the arena of polemical debate and missionary activity within Europe and beyond.[8]

The final essay in this collection considers the multiplicity of explanations for the end of witchcraft prosecutions in early modern Europe. Levack's summary is a clear demonstration of the parallels that may be drawn between the complexity of explanations for the origins and conduct of the witch trials and the efforts made in recent scholarship to explain their decline. His analysis explores several potential and plausible approaches, some of which have a local or regional relevance, others which relate to a less tangible shift in intellectual perception and yet others which simply defy assessment or quantification of their impact. What is abundantly clear is that various pressures were exerted upon the early modern image of the witch, ranging from the judicial (including debates over the legitimacy of evidence obtained under torture), the religious (including debates over the sovereignty of God and the scriptural justification for witch-hunting), social and economic factors and the shifting sands of beliefs about witchcraft as medieval scholasticism, which had accommodated the actions of demons, was eroded by neo-platonic models which invited a more naturalistic interpretation.[9] The most plausible 'many reasons why' explanation for the rise and decline of witchcraft and witchcraft trials is symptomatic of the broader problems encountered, as we have seen, in any scholarly approach to the realms of the religious, magical and demonic in late medieval and early modern Europe.

Notes

1.	In the context of the scholarship of the Reformation, the debate over 'disenchantment' owed much to the work of Robert Scribner, especially (1993), 'The reformation, popular magic and the "disenchantment" of the world', *Journal of Interdisciplinary History*, 23(3), 475–94. A good analysis of recent writing on the subject, and its problems, can be found in Walsham, A. (2008), 'The reformation and the disenchantment of the world reassessed', *Historical Journal*, 51(2), 497–528, and in Marshall, P. (2011), 'Disenchantment and re-enchantment in Europe 1250–1920', *Historical Journal*, 54(2), 599–606. For other considerations of Weber's thesis and its impact see Schroeder, R. (1992), *Max Weber and the Sociology of Culture*. London: Sage; Schroeder, R. (1995), 'Disenchantment and its discontents: weberian perspectives on science and technology', *Sociological Review*, 43, 227–50; Spierenburg, P. (1991), *The Broken Spell: A Cultural and Anthropological History of Preindustrial Europe*. London: Macmillan; Weber, M. (1976), *The Protestant Ethic and the Spirit of Capitalism*, 2nd edn. London: George Allen & Unwin; Weber, M. (1991), *General Economic History*. New Brunswick, Canada: Transaction; Whimster, S. and Lash, S. (eds) (1987), *Max Weber, Rationality and Modernity*. London: George Allen & Unwin; Chalcraft, D.G. (1994), 'Bringing the text back in: on ways of reading the iron cage in the two editions of the protestant ethic', in L. J. Ray and M. Reed (eds), *Organising Modernity: New Weberian Perspectives on Work, Organisations and Society*. London: Routledge, pp. 16–45; Brubacker, R. (1984), *The Limits of Rationality: An Essay on the Social and Moral Thought of Max Weber*. London: George Allen & Unwin.

2.	Moore, R.I. (1987), *The Formation of a Persecuting Society: Authority and Deviance in Western Europe, 950–1250*, 2nd edn. Oxford: Oxford University Press; Nirenberg, D. (1996), *Communities of Violence: Persecution of Minorities in the Middle Ages*. Princeton: Princeton University Press; Oldridge, D. (2005), *Strange Histories: The Trial of the Pig, the Walking Dead, and Other Matters of Fact from the Medieval and Renaissance Worlds*. London: Hambledon; Goodich, M. (ed.) (2006), *Voices from the Bench: The Narratives of Lesser Folk in Medieval Trials*. Basingstoke, Hampshire:

Macmillan; Delumeau, J. (1990), *Sin and Fear: The Emergence of a Western Guilt Culture, 13th–18th Centuries*. New York: St Martin's Press; Forster, R. and Ranum, O. (eds) (1978), *Deviants and the Abandoned in French Society*. Baltimore: Johns Hopkins University Press; Geremek, B. (1987), *The Margins of Society in Late Medieval Paris*. Cambridge: Cambridge University Press; Grell, O.P. and Scribner, R.W. (eds) (1996), *Tolerance and Intolerance in the European Reformation*. Cambridge: Cambridge University Press; Kagan, R.L. and Dyer, A. (eds) (2004), *Inquisitorial Inquiries: Brief Lives of Secret Jews and Other Heretics*. Baltimore, MD: Johns Hopkins University Press; Kaplan, B.J. (2007), *Divided by Faith: Religious Conflict and the Practice of Toleration in Early Modern Europe*. Cambridge, MA: Harvard University Press; Laursen, J.C. and Nederman, C.J. (eds) (1998), *Beyond the Persecuting Society: Religious Tolerance before the Enlightenment*. Philadelphia, PA: Pennsylvania University Press; Milner, S.J. (ed.) (2005), *At the Margins: Minority Groups in Premodern Italy*. Minneapolis, MN: University of Minnesota Press; Richards, J. (1991), *Sex, Dissidence and Damnation: Minority Groups in the Middle Ages*. London: Routledge; Swanson, R.N. (1995), *Religion and Devotion in Europe, c. 1215-c. 1515*. Cambridge: Cambridge University Press.

3. Some of these questions are addressed in the articles and introduction to them in Part I.

4. The 'twilight zone' is borrowed from Scribner, R.W. (1984), 'Ritual and popular religion in catholic Germany at the time of the reformation', *Journal of Ecclesiastical History*, 35(1), 47–77.

5. The vocabulary is evident in Thomas, K. (1971), *Religion and the Decline of Magic*. New York: Scribner; and Gentilcore, D. (1992), *From Bishop to Witch*. Manchester: Manchester University Press. For more detailed discussions of late medieval Catholicism in England and Europe see Duffy, E. (1992), *The Stripping of the Altars: Traditional Religion in England, c. 1400-1580*. New Haven, CT: Yale University Press; van Engen, J. (1986), 'The christian middle ages as an historiographical problem', *American Historical Review*, 91, 519–52; Reynolds, S. (1991), 'Social mentalities and the case of medieval scepticism', *Transactions of the Royal Historical Society*, 1, 21–41; Hendrix, S. (2004), *Recultivating the Vineyard. The Reformation Agenda of Christianisation*. Louisville, KY: Westminster John Knox Press; for the earlier period see Murray, A. (1992), 'Missionaries and magic in dark-age Europe', *Past and Present*, 136, 186–205.

6. Scribner, 'The reformation'; Scribner, R.W. (1986), 'Incombustible Luther: The image of the reformer in early modern Germany', *Past and Present*, 110, 38–68; Scribner, R.W. and Johnson, T. (eds) (1996), *Popular Religion in Germany and Central Europe 1400-1800*. Basingstoke, Hampshire: Macmillan; Karant Nunn, S. (1997), *The Reformation of Ritual: An Interpretation of Early Modern Germany*. London: Routledge; Cressy, D. (1989), *Bonfires and Bells: National Memory and the Protestant Calendar in Elizabethan and Stuart England*. London: Weidenfeld and Nicolson; Hutton, R. (1994), *The Rise and Fall of Merry England: The Ritual Year, 1400-1700*. Oxford: Oxford University Press; Walsham, A. (1999), *Providence in Early Modern England*. Oxford: Oxford University Press; Clark, J.C.D. (2007), 'The re-enchantment of the world? Religion and monarchy in eighteenth-century Europe', in Michael Schaich (ed.), *Monarchy and Religion: The Transformation of Royal Culture in Eighteenth-Century Europe*. Oxford: Oxford University Press; Crawford, J. (2005), *Marvellous Protestantism: Monstrous Births in Post-Reformation England*. Baltimore, MD: Johns Hopkins University Press; Bossy, J. (1983), 'The mass as a social institution, 1200-1700', *Past and Present*, 100, 29–61.

7. See also Parish, H. (2001), ' "Impudent and abominable fictions": rewriting saints' lives in the English reformation', *Sixteenth Century Journal*, 32, 45–65; Walsham, A. (2005), 'Miracles in post-reformation England', in Kate Cooper and Jeremy Gregory (eds), *Signs, Wonders and Miracles: Representations of Divine Power in the Life of the Church*. Woodbridge, VA: Boydell, pp. 273–306; Sluhovsky, M. (1995), 'Calvinist miracles and the concept of the miraculous in sixteenth-century huguenot thought', *Renaissance and Reformation*, 19, 5–25.

8. Moore, R.I. (1985), 'Guibert de nogent and his world', in Henry Mayr-Harting and R.I. Moore (eds), *Studies in Medieval History Presented to R. H. C. Davis*. London: Hambledon, pp. 107–18; Reynolds, 'Social mentalities'; Vauchez, A. (1997), *Sainthood in the Later Middle Ages*, trans.

Jean Birrell. Cambridge: Cambridge University Press; Smith, J. (1990), 'Oral and written: saints, miracles and relics in Brittany, c. 850–1250', *Speculum*, 65, 309–43; Marshall, P. (2003), 'Forgery and miracles in the reign of Henry VIII', *Past and Present*, 178, 39–73; Iliffe, R. (1999), 'Lying wonders and juggling tricks: religion, nature and imposture in early modern England', in James E. Force and David S. Katz (eds), *Everything Connects: In Conference with Richard E. Popkin, Essays in His Honour*. Leiden, The Netherlands: Brill.

9.   Roper, L. (2000), ' "Evil imaginings and fantasies": child-witches and the end of the witch craze', *Past and Present*, 167, 107–39; Roper, L. (2006), 'Witchcraft, nostalgia and the rural idyll in 18th-century Germany', in R. Harris and L. Roper (eds), *The Art of Survival. Gender and History in Europe, 1450–2000*. Oxford: Oxford University Press, pp. 139–58; Elmer, P. (1998), ' "Saints or sorcerers": quakerism, demonology and the decline of witchcraft in seventeenth-century England', in J. Barry, M. Hester and G.Roberts (eds), *Witchcraft in Early Modern Europe*. Cambridge: Cambridge University Press, pp. 145–79; Bostridge, I. (1997), *Witchcraft and Its Transformations c. 1650–c. 1750*. Oxford: Oxford University Press; Prior, M.E. (1932), 'Joseph Glanvill, witchcraft, and seventeenth-century science', *Modern Philology*, 30, 167–93; Clark, S. (1991), 'The rational witchfinder: conscience, demonological naturalism and popular superstitions', in S. Pumfrey, P. Rossi and M. Slawinski (eds), *Science, Culture and Popular Belief in Renaissance Europe*. Manchester: Manchester University Press, pp. 222–48; Midelfort, H.C.E. (1988), 'Johann Weyer & the transformation of the insanity defence', in R. Po-Chia Hsia (ed.), *The German People & the Reformation*. London: Cornell University Press; Sneddon, A. (2008), *Witchcraft and Whigs: The Life of Bishop Francis Hutchinson (1660–1739)*. Manchester: Manchester University Press; Davies, O. (1998), 'Newspapers and the popular belief in witchcraft and magic in the modern period', *Journal of British Studies*, 37(2), 139–65; Davies, O. and de Blécourt, W. (eds) (2004), *Beyond the Witch Trials. Witchcraft and Magic in Enlightenment Europe*. Manchester: Manchester University Press.

CHAPTER 12
THE DISENCHANTMENT OF MAGIC: SPELLS, CHARMS, AND SUPERSTITION IN EARLY EUROPEAN WITCHCRAFT LITERATURE
Michael D. Bailey

In 1917, in a lecture in Munich on 'Science as a Vocation,' Max Weber first articulated his notion of 'the disenchantment of the world,' later also incorporated into his seminal *Protestant Ethic and the Spirit of Capitalism*. He presented disenchantment as a hallmark feature of modern Western society, which had come into full vigor with the Protestant Reformation. Initially Weber described this development, in relation to science, as entailing primarily the conviction that 'there are no mysterious incalculable forces' and that 'one need no longer have recourse to magical means in order to master or implore spirits.' Later, and rather more evocatively in relation to religion, he described it as a historical force that had progressively 'repudiated all magical means to salvation as superstition and sin.'[1] Weber's assertions were hardly uncontroversial, and they have been challenged repeatedly in the century since they were first made.[2] Nevertheless, the basic notion of disenchantment remains very influential on many academic disciplines' understanding of the modern world. Magic and cultural perceptions of the magical occupy a critical place particularly in sociological and anthropological conceptions of modernity, and issues of 'magical thought' and 'superstition' in opposition to 'scientific rationalism' frame discussions not only of the modern West but of instances in which Western modernity confronts the traditional beliefs and practices of other world cultures.[3]

Historians of European magic and witchcraft have also engaged, sometimes overtly but often tacitly, with the themes Weber identified and encapsulated as 'disenchantment.' Keith Thomas in particular, in his groundbreaking *Religion and the Decline of Magic*, made only passing reference to Weber directly but took up the essentially Weberian theme of the degree to which religion (of the more modern, reformed variety) displaced magic from European society. Far from eliminating all magic in the world, however, Thomas concluded that by eradicating the 'magical' practices of the medieval church, Protestantism in England actually promoted concern about witches and popular reliance on cunning folk, astrologers, and other types of common magicians.[4] Following this line of argument, historians have since pushed generalized disenchantment back to progressively later points in European history – the Scientific Revolution, the Enlightenment, even nineteenth-century industrialization. Most recently, historians of the modern period have begun to engage directly with, and further problematize, Weber's analysis by arguing that certain magical beliefs and systems of thought not only endured into the nineteenth and twentieth centuries but were in fact essential elements of European modernity.[5]

An underlying issue plaguing any attempt, save perhaps for the modern period, to historically examine key issues entailed in disenchantment – the emergence of putatively purer 'modern' religious sensibilities compatible with scientific rationalism out of earlier, supposedly muddled 'magical' systems – is the fact, now widely recognized, that the categories of 'religion' and 'magic' in their current forms are almost entirely creations of the post-Reformation era.[6] Some historians of early modern Europe, however, now present an at least quasi-Weberian analysis of certain shifts toward more modern mentalities in the area of ritual during that period. They have also returned to locating the critical force behind these shifts in the Reformation. Protestant authorities, they contend, largely abandoned the view that real efficacy or presence of power was inherent in ritual acts and began to assert the notion of ritual as mere symbolic signification or representation. This process was most clearly evident in Protestant sacramental and above all eucharistic theology, but it also played out in many areas of ritualized activity.[7] While there is no denying the significance of the Reformation in terms of ritual and more general religious developments in European history, there is also considerable danger in positing a single period of relatively sudden, dramatic change, especially when the modern analytical categories employed are largely rooted in Reformation-era debates.[8]

In regard to historical conceptions of magic, shifting notions about the inherent qualities of various kinds of ritualized, magical actions need to be disentangled from the immediate context of the Reformation. In the century prior to the eruption of Protestantism, reformist impulses already animated many clerical authorities, feeding increased concern about proper religiosity, lay piety, and putative superstition.[9] A number of these authorities became particularly troubled by the common spells, charms, healing rites, and other simple ritualized acts widely used by laypeople and also by many clerics.[10] Fearing that these rites entailed at least tacit invocation of demons, authorities judged them to be erroneous and therefore superstitious. In this they followed long-standing Christian conceptions of the potentially demonic nature of virtually all magic. New this time, however, was the degree to which established theories were applied to questions of common practice and belief, and the level of concern these practices now generated. The first half of the fifteenth century, in particular, saw a rash of tracts and treatises produced on the question of superstition.[11] Here, however, the focus is on the treatment of common spells and charms in early witchcraft literature.

As important studies by Stuart Clark and Walter Stephens on late medieval and early modern witchcraft treatises have shown, authorities often deployed the idea of witchcraft as a tool for dealing with basic ontological and epistemological problems of their age.[12] They employed this concept at least partially to resolve dilemmas of uncertainty raised by common spells and other ritual acts. By the early fifteenth century, witchcraft connoted far more – for authorities, at least – than just the performance of simple malevolent magic (*maleficium*). Witches were now constructed as surrendering themselves entirely to demons, entering into pacts with them, and worshiping them as members of diabolical sects that gathered secretly to devour babies, desecrate sacraments, partake in sexual orgies, and perform terrible rites.[13] The explicit (and horrific) association of witches with demons removed all doubt about the essential nature of their acts. In establishing witchcraft as clearly diabolical in nature, authorities were particularly concerned to strip any effective agency from the simple ritual acts that witches employed. The words witches uttered or the gestures they performed could not directly cause magical effects; nor did these formulas have inherent power to bind or compel demons to cause those effects.

Rather, witches' access to and control over demonic power was made to rest entirely on an explicit pact with Satan.

In addressing witchcraft and explicating both the nature of witches' power and the rites by which they might appear to work that power, authorities were also obliged to address the nature of many common healing and protective rites, both official ceremonies and formally approved practices as well as more fully popular improvisations often derived from these – those rites of power that Keith Thomas evocatively, although anachronistically, labeled the 'magic of the medieval church,' and which David Gentilcore more accurately described as constituting a complex 'system of the sacred' that permeated premodern European society.[14] As with witchcraft, authorities again denied any real effect to rites themselves. True agency was either covertly demonic (a frightful possibility) or legitimately divine. Even more than demons, however, divinity could never be compelled or coerced by human acts. Thus ritual forms again became meaningless; so long as intent was good and proper faith was maintained, God should respond. Yet not only did this fly in the face of widespread common beliefs that perceived many church rites, as well as spells and charms based on them, to be automatically efficacious, but it also could be thought to undermine a critical point that witchcraft theorists sought to make: that people should eschew questionable rites, even if their intent was good, and employ only the long approved rituals of the church.

Theorists of witchcraft did not resolve these dilemmas in the course of the fifteenth century. Indeed, as the literature on witchcraft grew more developed and thorough, the problems of properly understanding and categorizing common spells and charms became more complex. Not only did authorities frequently seem to maintain the virtually automatic effectiveness of official ceremonies, but even the most severe opponents of witchcraft still argued for the permissibility of various unofficial rites. Issues of the effectiveness, and appropriateness, of spells and charms, church ceremonies, and sacramentals, as well as the sacraments themselves, continued well into the early modern period.[15] Arguably the two greatest monuments of fifteenth-century witchcraft literature were Johannes Nider's *Formicarius* [Anthill], the most extensive and influential of several early tracts and treatises on witchcraft produced in the 1430s, and Heinrich Kramer's *Malleus maleficarum* [Hammer of Witches], the most important late medieval witchcraft treatise, written in 1486.[16] Both men were members of the Dominican order, which was famous for its pastoral and inquisitorial activities and was in each of these roles deeply involved in investigating and shaping common beliefs and practices.[17] Both were also largely conservative in their thought, grounded in the Thomism of the thirteenth century rather than newer intellectual systems such as nominalism that were developing in the fourteenth and fifteenth centuries. Thus they indicate how growing concerns over spells, charms, and potential witchcraft were rooted in long-established interpretations of Christian belief. Moreover, the two men shared a direct connection, as Kramer drew heavily from and expanded upon Nider's earlier accounts.[18]

Although these works were written in the fifteenth century and reflect a particular strain of thought within that century, insights derived from careful attention to this material carry broad implications for how historians and scholars in other disciplines conceive and periodize a major aspect of Western Europe's development toward modernity. Processes identifiable as 'disenchantment' – notably the conceptualization of much magical and religious ritual as merely symbolic rather than directly effective – were evident already in the fifteenth century, and indeed earlier, and thus nothing like Weber's 'disenchantment of the world' or any concomitant lurch toward modernity should be bound exclusively to the impact of the Reformation. Critically, locating some 'disenchantment' prior to the Reformation helps to decouple these processes from modern conceptions of 'magic' and 'religion' that are products of Reformation-era debates. They are instead revealed to be deeply enmeshed with medieval Christian beliefs about the nature of superhuman powers, whether those of demons or of divinity, and the means by which human beings might interact with, supplicate, or attempt to direct such power.[19] Yet the tensions and uncertainty regarding this interaction evident in fifteenth-century witchcraft treatises, and especially in their treatment of spells, charms, and other superstitions, reveal a heightened concern with these issues and indicate much of the manner in which they would continue to provoke and inform debate throughout the Reformation and at least until the Enlightenment.[20] The fifteenth century was therefore an important connecting juncture between 'medieval' and 'early modern' concerns, and the disenchantment it reveals was not a sudden break with or rejection of earlier magical thought, but a development within it that illuminates continuing concern and debate over magical operations into the modern era.

When confronting common spells and charms, or any other potential superstition, clerical authorities in the fifteenth century, as throughout the Middle Ages, were concerned above all to correct errors and provide clarity, for in the theological parlance of this period, superstition entailed improper belief and improperly understood ritual acts.[21] Yet whatever efforts authorities made to define superstition in the abstract, the often ambiguous nature of actual practice eluded their attempts at certain categorization. They were aware of, and deeply concerned about, these ambiguities, which touched on profound tensions within essential issues of Christian belief, namely the ways in which humans could, and could not, interact with supernatural forces, demonic or divine, and the real meaning of the ritual forms in which that interaction was frequently cloaked.[22] The category of witchcraft, as constructed by authorities at this time, allowed them to define a number of malevolent magical practices as definitively demonic (all witchcraft, in this sense, was inherently superstitious, although not all superstition was necessarily witchcraft). The intense diabolism that informed authorities' developing concept of witchcraft entailed the strong denial of any possible direct effectiveness in the spells or other ritualized performances of witches. Convinced that the power of demons lay behind all acts of witchcraft, clerical authorities worked aggressively to promulgate this point and to disabuse the common laity of any notions to the contrary.[23]

Johannes Nider's *Formicarius* includes a story that illustrates the confusion surrounding common spells that so concerned authorities, and their deployment of the concept of diabolical witchcraft to achieve clarity. Although Nider assured his readers of the absolute veracity of all the examples he presented in this work,[24] the tale is too perfect, and may well have been entirely invented. Nevertheless, it encapsulates Nider's vision of the dangers inherent in commonly used spells and charms, and the message of warning he sought to impart. Sometime in the 1430s, in the southern German diocese of Constance, a man suffering from an injury to his foot visited a friend, a laywoman skilled in healing. Nider named her 'Seriosa,' so we will call her Ernestine here. She was not the first source of relief to which this man had turned. Believing that witches had caused his injury, he had tried numerous cures, including some remedies that church authorities deemed illicit, yet nothing could overcome the initial bewitchment. At last he came to his friend for help. She made the sign of the cross over him, whispered certain words, and immediately his foot was healed.[25] Impressed by her power, yet not recognizing how she had actually cured him, he asked what 'incantations' she had used. At this point the acerbic Ernestine began to chide her friend: 'Whether from weak faith or feebleness,' she addressed him severely, 'you don't adhere to the holy and approved rites of the church, and you often use spells and forbidden remedies to heal yourself.' Such spells drew on the power of demons, she warned, and while they might sometimes cure his physical injuries, they always damaged his immortal soul.[26]

This is a story rife with uncertainty. The injured man appears sure that he was bewitched, but we are not told how he knows this. Various means were available in late medieval society for determining when witchcraft was present, and there were a range of popular experts, witch doctors, and cunning folk who could identify witches. These practices, too, were full of uncertainty, and – given the strife that could arise once accusations of witchcraft began to circulate within a community – fraught with danger.[27] While the man was certain of the cause of his suffering, he had no clear idea how to rectify his situation, trying a number of illicit cures, the 'spells and forbidden remedies' of further witchcraft. Only when these failed did he finally turn to his friend Ernestine.[28] Uncertainty persisted, however, as he did not realize, or properly recognize, what she did for him. She cured him by making the sign of the cross and silently saying the Creed and the Lord's Prayer, yet he assumed that she had performed some spell or incantation. She then informed him, in no uncertain terms, of the actual nature of the power she had employed, of the condemned nature of the cures to which he had turned in the past, and of the spiritual harm he had suffered as a result.

In correcting her friend, Ernestine was made to stand in for theorists of witchcraft and other witch-hunting authorities, a fact that carries significant irony, since if she did in fact represent a real person living in the early fifteenth century, she almost certainly would have been a local healer or cunning woman and would have run some risk of being identified as a witch herself.[29] Yet in the text, she was made to deliver with confident certainty a basic message that Nider and other theorists of witchcraft sought to convey regarding the spectrum of spells and charms available in late medieval Europe: that many of those rites were in fact diabolical witchcraft as authorities understood and constructed it. Witches could cure illness, heal, and relieve suffering, but all their acts, regardless of effect, were inherently evil because the operative power behind them was demonic.[30] Authorities were deeply concerned that people who believed themselves to be bewitched in some way not turn to further witchcraft for relief. As Nider stressed in *Formicarius*, 'rather a person should die than agree to such things.'[31]

Witchcraft theorists were obsessed with the notion that the laity tolerated and actively patronized practitioners of common magic, who were, in their perception, witches. By submitting to the devil, worshiping demons, and engaging in diabolical sabbaths, witches damned themselves, and by performing *maleficium* they harmed others; but perhaps their foulest act, in the minds of clerical authorities, was that by deceiving others about the true nature of witchcraft and tempting them into seeking the aid of witches, they corrupted innocent Christian souls. Horrific images of debased carnality and uncontrolled aggression, especially toward infants, proliferated in treatises on witchcraft, as well as in sermons and other forms of propaganda about witches. These served to cast witchcraft emphatically as the inversion of all proper moral order and to warn people against any toleration of suspected demonic activities in their midst.[32] Most laypeople surely understood at least the basic nature of demonic menace as the church depicted it. They did not, however, seem to connect familiar practices with this menace, or they viewed possible involvement with demons far less seriously than did clerics.

Common discourse about interactions with supernatural or occult forces typically reflected care and hesitancy about engaging with such power, but also some casualness, evidenced by claims that most laypeople did not well or fully understand the specific nature of the operations involved or the powers invoked.[33] According to the early-fifteenth-century Franciscan preacher Bernardino of Siena, for example, the entire city of Siena stood in peril because of its citizens' unconcerned acceptance of the many 'witches' known to inhabit the region.[34]

To clarify and justify their concerns, authorities stressed supposedly direct evidence of the diabolism that witchcraft entailed. For example, in his *Buch aller verbotenen Künste* [Book of All Forbidden Arts], the German courtier Johannes Hartlieb claimed to have personally uncovered such diabolism. In 1447, he was ordered by the duke of Bavaria to investigate a woman who supposedly professed the ability to summon storms and hail, one of the major evils attributed to witches in southern German and alpine lands. Under his questioning, she admitted that, to obtain this power, she had denied God, Mary, and all the saints, as well as her baptism and the other sacraments, and that she had given herself 'life and soul' to three devils. Thereafter, she needed only to call these devils, and they would raise hailstorms wherever she desired.[35] Johannes Nider, too, presented an account of a (male) witch who directly confirmed the demonic nature of his powers, also with reference to storm-raising. Captured by authorities, he confessed that he would go with an accomplice to an open field and there implore the 'prince of all demons', the devil, to send a lesser demon. The witch would immolate a black fowl at a crossroads and throw it into the air as an offering, and the demon would then cause hail and lightning to strike at his command.[36]

Like Ernestine, the woman in Hartlieb's account spoke to confirm the message that authorities sought to impart. As for Nider's weather-working witch, he supposedly confessed to a magistrate who had captured him, who then reported this story to Nider. Assuming that Nider did not simply invent the tale or recast it wholesale in his retelling, certainly the judge could have extracted a confession that suited his own purposes as an authority bent on stressing the demonic nature of much common magic.[37] Interestingly, elsewhere in *Formicarius*, Nider related how this same witch supposedly prevented a married couple from having children over the course of several years. In this account, no overt diabolism was present; the man cast the spell simply by burying a lizard under the threshold of the couple's dwelling, although since the accused in this case had already been deemed a witch, Nider was certain that demonic power was somehow in operation.[38] Amid the doubt and confusion that authorities seem to have faced, and which they certainly feared, regarding the nature of many common magical practices, the figure of the witch, forced either in reality or in exemplary accounts to confess the explicitly demonic basis of her (or sometimes his) power, was made to be reassuringly definitive.

The presence of demonic power behind most forms of magic was a long-established fact in Christian thought, deriving from the earliest church fathers.[39] Late medieval witchcraft theorists simply stressed this point in the face of perceived common uncertainty or lack of proper understanding. Yet in their discussions of the power behind magical acts, they also had to define how humans could access and manipulate that power. Here too they addressed, in an even more nuanced way, the function and real effect of the rites involved. And here too they removed from ritual actions, however complex or simple, any direct operative power. Such a conclusion was relatively unproblematic when applied to witchcraft or other magical actions that authorities sought to denigrate and condemn, but matters became more complicated when authorities turned to approved ecclesiastical or other rites that they wished to valorize, or at least not vilify. While they still maintained that rites had no inherent operative or directive force, they were nevertheless deeply concerned that the proper forms of these rites be maintained, for improper forms could entail dangerous superstition.

Even when it was agreed that 'magic' functioned through demonic power, how did a spell draw on that power? Common people either thought little about such issues or found it expedient to claim disinterested ignorance when questioned by authorities. Learned clerics, however, pondered the matter at length, and not just those who sought to condemn magical practices. Medieval necromancers, learned and literate magicians who were mostly clerics, practiced complex forms of ritual magic and readily admitted to invoking and exploiting demonic power.[40] They maintained, however, that they were in no way subservient to demons, but commanded and compelled them by virtue of the powerful rituals they employed. Most clerical authorities argued strongly against this position, claiming that any invocation of demons involved some degree of supplication and implied at least a tacit pact.[41] Witchcraft theorists, focusing on the very simple rites of common magic, stressed explicit pacts that were necessarily prior to any magical activity. In 1437, the same year Nider wrote much of his *Formicarius*, Pope Eugenius IV issued a statement on witchcraft in a directive to papal inquisitors, declaring that witches worshiped demons and entered into formal, often written pacts with them 'so that by a single word, touch, or sign they might perform whatever harmful magic they desire.'[42] Similarly, Nider recounted how witches might raise storms by stirring water with a broom. This action had no direct effect, either to raise the storm or to compel demons to do so. Rather, demons responded to this sign because of binding pacts that had existed between them and witches since time immemorial.[43]

In this way, witchcraft theorists radically disempowered the simple ritual actions involved in the performance of various kinds of common magic that they perceived to be diabolical witchcraft. Not only did these rites have no causative force, they had no necessary directive effect on the agents (demons) that did cause the magical result. They merely signified the witch's desire. Seeking always to argue that witches were utterly subservient to demons, authorities had every reason to denigrate and dismiss the simple rites that supposed witches performed. Matters necessarily became more complex, however, when authorities addressed various rites that they sought to validate and maintain. Aside from explicating the horrific nature of witchcraft itself, most theorists also sought to clarify how people might properly respond to the threat that witches represented. Certainly this was the case with Nider, whose *Formicarius* was mainly a collection of instructive stories, moral exempla intended for use in sermons delivered to the laity.[44] As noted already, he warned that under no circumstances should people have recourse to further witchcraft to remedy bewitchments. Instead, they should turn to the church and such remedies as prayer and penance, the sign of the cross, meditation on the passion of Christ, pious attendance at church rites and ceremonies, or pilgrimage to saints' shrines.[45]

While such approved rites often closely resembled magic spells and charms in their effects and even in their formulas, for medieval authorities the two systems were entirely distinct and dramatically opposed in the most important way possible. Prayers and approved blessings drew on divine power, while magic spells relied on demons.[46] Yet authorities treated both systems similarly in this sense: if the rites of witches played no part in compelling demons to respond, still less could sanctioned rites, although laudable, compel divine power. These rites, too, were merely signs. In some cases, notably the sacraments, God responded because of a covenant (or, in language that could appear shocking when surrounded by demonological arguments in treatises on magic, superstition, or witchcraft, a 'pact') with the church.[47] More often he responded out of mercy, not because of the performance of some specific rite but because of the internal moral state of the person seeking divine help.[48] Nider, for example, related a long account of a secular judge, Peter of Bern, who conducted numerous witch trials in the early 1400s. He was immune to the power of the witches he hunted because he diligently protected himself with the sign of the cross, but more basically because he always 'acted in good faith.' One morning he failed to make the sign of the cross when he arose, and he was almost immediately struck down and injured by witchcraft. Nider explained, however, that Peter was wrathful that day, and may even have cursed in the name of the devil.[49] Thus his vulnerability to witchcraft was due to his spiritual state, not simply his failure to perform a ritual act.

Nider made the unessential nature of even official ritual clear when he discussed exorcism as a means to counteract bewitchment.[50] Given that witchcraft functioned through the power of demons, many bewitchments could be undone by driving off the demons responsible for inflicting them. This was a power that Christ had promised to the apostles and all faithful Christians in the Gospels.[51] Nider made clear that even informal acts of exorcism performed with faith could be as effective as the formal church rite that clerics performed 'ex officiis.'[52] Such basic rejection of the essential importance of specific ritual forms probably contributed to authorities' willingness to countenance many unofficial rites used against witchcraft. Nider, for example, approved of such practices as ringing church bells to protect crops from storms.[53] He also accepted and essentially recommended in *Formicarius* a counterrite revealed by a witch under interrogation. To disperse hailstorms raised by witchcraft, one could recite this formula: 'I adjure you, hail and winds, by the three nails of Christ, which pierced the hands and feet of Christ, and by the four evangelists, Saints Matthew, Mark, Luke, and John, that you should fall dissipated into water.'[54]

Christian thinkers had debated the significance of specific ritual directed toward an omnipotent and omniscient God since the earliest days of the church, and in the early medieval period, ecclesiastical officials had frequently accommodated themselves to unofficial and even pagan rites, so long as these were purged of any overtly demonic elements and were made to reflect Christian faith.[55] Thus the struggles of late medieval witchcraft theorists to come to terms with the nature and function of various rites must be understood as part of a long tradition running through Christian history, as well as the result of specific debates about the nature of common magical operations and the potential threat of superstition developing in the fifteenth century, largely in the context of witchcraft. Seeking to clarify the absolute demonic nature of witchcraft, authorities aggressively stripped all power from the simple rites performed by supposed witches. Against witchcraft they sought to recommend the power of official Christian rites such as prayer, blessings, or the sign of the cross. While they frequently stressed that formulaic rites could not compel divine power,[56] they certainly did not want to devalue these rituals to the extent they had the rites of witches. Authorities also accepted a number of unofficial rites or practices by which the faithful could counteract demonic witchcraft. Again their underlying position was that God responded to pious intent, not specific ritual formulas. Yet they remained deeply concerned about the particular forms these rites took, for while God responded to true faith, an improperly enacted ritual could allow demonic forces to intrude regardless of the intent of the person performing the rite.

The essential element that made any spell, charm, or other formula illegitimate and illicit, all authorities agreed, was the invocation of demonic rather than divine power. Yet such invocation could be tacit or unintended as well as express, making reliable judgments on particular practices difficult to render. This dilemma of discernment is evident in Nider's account of the lay healer Ernestine.[57] In his relation of events, Ernestine delivered a reassuringly confident categorization of what had taken place. The injured man initially sought relief through illicit means that imperiled his soul. Ernestine healed him using the divine power of prayer and the sign of the cross. Yet the man could not tell the difference. In fact, many common spells and charms incorporated the sign of the cross, along with other gestures and phrases drawn from official ecclesiastical rites, and even the explicitly demonic rituals of learned, necromantic magic might include liturgical elements.[58] Ernestine also employed the Creed and the Lord's Prayer, albeit spoken silently so that her friend was unaware of what she had said. A problem for authorities would have been to determine whether she fully understood her own words, and whether she had delivered them correctly in Latin. Even a slight change in a verbal formula, intentional or inadvertent, could corrupt a wholesome prayer into a demonic invocation.[59]

While late medieval witchcraft theorists frequently expounded the seemingly 'disenchanted' view that ritualized actions lacked any real power to coerce or direct supernatural forces, they could not entirely abandon the notion that improper rites, or improperly performed rites, carried dire consequences. At one point in his writings, Nider discussed certain healing spells and charms commonly used by old women. He recognized that these procedures closely resembled approved blessings and exorcisms. Such actions, he concluded, were inherently legitimate and could readily be permitted to trained clerics, but among the uneducated laity the danger of error and demonic infiltration was too great to allow.[60] Here was a straightforward admission that rites seeking to call on divine power for permissible ends could be fatally corrupted if their forms were mangled. Here was also a straightforward response to such complications surrounding conceptions of ritual practice – deploying the coercive power of the church to restrict to itself all such activity. This was a course increasingly taken in the fifteenth and subsequent centuries. Yet the uncertain status of ritual power persisted. As theories of witchcraft became more developed, the confusion would only grow more pronounced.

Malleus Maleficarum was the most extended and influential treatise on witchcraft composed in the fifteenth century. While it repeated many examples and reiterated many conclusions from earlier treatises, it was also the fullest consideration of witchcraft thus far produced.[61] Its chief author, Heinrich Kramer, delved more deeply than many previous authorities into the nature and function of witchcraft, church rites, and the many common spells and charms that seemed to hover between them. The result was by no means greater clarity. Like all late medieval witchcraft theorists, Kramer feared that many common spells might be witchcraft in disguise. He repeated standard prohibitions against including strange words or unknown names in spells or charms, for these could signify compacts with the devil. Those who used such spells might be entirely unaware of their true character, and the results achieved could be wholly beneficial, but the corrupting power of demons remained.[62] Thus Kramer echoed Nider and other earlier authorities by arguing that no one should seek to relieve bewitchment by recourse to other witches.[63] Like Nider, he recommended ecclesiastically sanctioned remedies such as prayer, confession, the sign of the cross, and exorcism, and he was particularly strong in advocating the use of sacramentals such as holy water, consecrated salt, and blessed candles to combat witchcraft.[64] Nevertheless, he also maintained that the means by which faithful Christians might protect themselves from demonic forces extended beyond the 'remedies of the church.'[65] He thus entered into a detailed analysis of the nature and effectiveness of many ambiguous rites, and he offered complicated conclusions.

One of the more involved analyses of magical rites in the *Malleus* focused, like Nider's tale of Ernestine and her injured friend, on a man afflicted by bewitchment in his foot. A merchant from the German town of Speyer was traveling through the region of Swabia. One day, as he walked with two local servants, a woman approached. The servants warned that she was a well-known witch and he should defend himself with the sign of the cross, but he was obstinate and refused, whereupon he felt tremendous pain in his left foot, so that he could barely walk. After three days of suffering, a local healer was called, who examined the merchant, but only after swearing that he would not employ witchcraft to cure him. The healer first determined that the injury was in fact due to witchcraft by pouring molten lead into water and observing the shapes that formed. He proceeded to visit the merchant for three days, touching the foot and saying certain words over it. On the third day, the injury was cured.[66]

Kramer stated flatly that this healing rite did not entail witchcraft. Nevertheless, doubts remained about the particular power or 'virtue' used to identify and remove the bewitchment.[67] The healer maintained that he was able to divine the presence of witchcraft from the behavior of molten lead because of the nature of lead itself and certain astral forces imbued in the metal, but the degree to which astral bodies could impart occult power to earthly items was a point of considerable debate in this period.[68] Many authorities maintained that much astral magic was simply a screen for demonic operations, since it frequently involved the recitation of secret words or ceremonies that might tacitly invoke demons. Kramer himself noted that astral magic was often merely demonic magic in disguise.[69] Nevertheless, all authorities admitted that astral bodies could impart some special properties to mundane materials. Only a few lines before he raised doubts about the nature of the action of the lead, Kramer had stated that if the lead's response was due purely to astral influence, the rite would be 'blameless and very commendable.'[70]

The real cause for concern in the healer's actions was the nature of the healing rite once witchcraft had been identified. No natural power, Kramer argued, could fully remove a bewitchment, and the healer had, in fact, made no pretense of effecting a natural cure, instead speaking certain ritual words over the foot. Were this rite intended to implore divine aid, the healer should have admitted the possibility that it might be ineffective, since God could not be compelled. Yet this man, Kramer noted, was certain that his actions would produce results. Moreover, the fact that he had performed the ritual of speaking over the foot on three consecutive days was ominous. Authorities frequently stressed that divine power did not need to be supplicated in any particular formulaic fashion.[71] That this healer followed such a precise formula caused Kramer to suspect demonic agency. He accepted that the man had probably not formed an express pact with the devil, yet he could not allow that the healing rite might, by any inherent power, have compelled demons to act. That the rite did appear to produce results therefore indicated a tacit pact, and while the healer was no witch, Kramer still judged him guilty of heresy and superstition.[72]

As already noted, the fear of tacit pacts with demons had always been central to Christian authorities' concern about common spells and charms. For witchcraft theorists of the fifteenth century, this concern supported their basic notions about the essential emptiness of ritual acts – that demons always responded because of a pact and not because of any effect of rites themselves – but also stood in some tension to this notion, causing authorities to lavish attention on the specific forms of various rites, as Kramer did above, attempting to discern whether they might tacitly invoke demons. While this tension was by no means fatal, it was problematic, leading many authorities, like Nider, to suggest that only trained clerics be allowed to perform certain rites because of the possibility of dangerous corruptions in their forms. Kramer, too, addressed such issues, but proved fairly tolerant of a number of common rites. At one point, in fact, he repeated Nider's story about Ernestine healing her friend's foot with the power of prayer and then condemning the other remedies the man had tried. While this tale could be taken to indicate that all spells and charms, aside from official prayers, should be rigidly proscribed because of the danger of demonic corruption, Kramer asserted a different interpretation. Ernestine (again made to play the role of a theologian) had judiciously banned only illicit spells and conjurations; legitimate ones existed and should be permitted to the laity to combat witchcraft.[73]

Kramer discussed such spells and other rites at various points in the *Malleus*, sometimes leaving the precise nature of their operation unexplored, but sometimes attempting to explicate it in detail. For example, when women in German lands suspected that a cow had been drained of milk by witchcraft, they would hang a milk pail over a fire and strike it, and the witch responsible for the theft would feel the blows. Likewise, if a cow was injured by witchcraft, it could be brought into a field, usually on a feast day or holy day, with a man's breeches or other 'foul thing' (*im-mundum*) placed over it, and beaten with sticks. It would then go to the door of the person who had bewitched it, identifying the malefactor.[74] Kramer was quite clear that these rites functioned through demonic agency. Always ready to betray his servants, the devil was perfectly happy for witches to be identified in these ways. The rites were not illegitimate, however, because those performing them merely exploited demons; they did not honor or worship demons in any fashion, nor did they form any pact with them, express or tacit.[75] Rather, albeit with diabolical complicity, these rituals seemed to exert some real force of compulsion over demons.

Kramer's impulse to associate some seemingly direct efficacy with certain ritualized acts applied to divine operations as well as demonic ones. For protection from hailstorms, for example, he reiterated the rite discussed by Nider, in which hail was adjured by the wounds of Christ and by the four evangelists to fall as water.[76] He also recounted another ritual. After hail had begun falling, three hailstones should be thrown into a fire while the Lord's Prayer, the Creed, and the opening words of the Gospel of John were recited. The sign of the cross should be made in the four cardinal directions, 'the word was made flesh' repeated three times, and finally 'by the words of this gospel may the tempest be dispersed' said thrice. Kramer maintained that this ritual conjuration was 'entirely proper, nor should it be judged with suspicion.'[77] Of course, the invocation of divine power provided the main operative force of the rite, but he explicitly concluded that casting hail into the fire, while secondary, was not entirely ineffectual, since those performing the rite thereby indicated their desire to destroy the works of the devil. Thus it was more effective to perform this rite while throwing hail into fire than while casting it into water, because fire would destroy the hail more quickly.[78] While one could construct a rationale that hurling hail into fire was still an essentially empty sign indicating to God an intensity of pious wrath against the devil, thus resulting in a more rapid deployment of divine power, Kramer's bald statement that one form of action was more effective than another seems perilously close to asserting that the particular form of this ritual exerted real force.

A final example will serve to highlight Kramer's complicated, often convoluted position regarding ritual invocations of supernatural power. Authorities frequently had difficulty drawing confessions from suspected witches, for the devil would exert his power to keep them silent. As a means of proof, Kramer recommended that judges 'conjure' suspects to weep, for a true witch would be unable to cry, although she might feign it by smearing her face with spittle. Placing his hands on the suspect's head, the judge should recite the following formula: 'I conjure you by the bitter tears shed on the cross by our savior, the Lord Jesus Christ, for the salvation of the world, and by the ardent tears of the most glorious virgin Mary, his mother, spread over his wounds at evening, and by all the tears that all the saints and elect of God have shed in the world, from whose eyes all tears have now been dried, that insofar as you are innocent you shed tears, but by no means if you are guilty.'[79] Shortly thereafter, Kramer noted that inquisitors in German lands had also had success with placing bits of blessed wax in holy water, invoking the trinity, and forcing suspected witches to drink from this mixture three times. The witches would then break their silence and confess.[80]

Kramer would have perceived in these actions divine power operating through the invocation of holy names and the application of sacramental elements. Yet there is cause for confusion. Why was a man who argued against the need for any specific ritual in invoking divine power so careful to present an exact and fairly complex verbal formula? Why was physical contact, the laying on of hands, required? And what, exactly, was being 'conjured' here? A demon restraining a guilty witch from confessing might legitimately be exorcised, but here the accused was conjured to weep only if she was innocent.[81] In the case of the holy water and wax, why did a man who elsewhere condemned a rite specifically because it was employed a certain number of times here prescribe having the suspect drink three times? There would, of course, be responses to such challenges. The laying on of hands was often described in the Bible, particularly in terms of healing and casting out spirits.[82] The triple application of the holy potion could be characterized as complementing the invocation of the trinity. Yet none of these explanations would entirely alleviate the underlying tensions about the efficacy of ritual and the function of ritual forms evident here.

In identifying magical acts with demonic power, and in their attempts to clearly distinguish the rites of demonic magic from legitimate rituals directed toward God and divine power, late medieval witchcraft theorists engaged with long-standing elements of medieval Christian thought. They did so, however, with a mounting intensity that had not been seen for centuries, arguably since late antiquity.[83] This was at least partly because they increasingly confronted the issue of superstition as a practical problem rather than a purely theoretical theological issue, uncovering and attempting to explicate specific instances of potentially confused belief and questionable practice mainly in the area of commonly used spells and charms. This approach reflected the pastoral 'theology of piety' developing especially in German-speaking lands in the fifteenth century.[84] If witchcraft theorists were themselves not always the most profound theological thinkers, many leading theologians in this period were focusing on similar issues, including magic and superstition, and dealing with specific instances of practice rather than grand abstractions.[85] The concerns these men demonstrated, and their focus, derived from major religious and ecclesiastical developments. Particularly in the wake of the Fourth Lateran Council of 1215, the medieval church had sought to define and enforce correct belief among the faithful in Europe far more assiduously than it had previously. Through the institution of structures as diverse, although ultimately closely related, as legal inquisition, sacramental confession, and pastoral preaching, the church in the late Middle Ages became increasingly involved in investigating and controlling common beliefs and practices.[86]

The intensity of authorities' concerns surely also rested on the growing fear of demons and the devil in the later Middle Ages. This general development has never been fully explained, but its manifestation in many areas of late medieval religious culture is apparent, particularly in terms of a growing preoccupation among clerical authorities to discern demonic activity in areas such as spirit possession, mystical experience, and magical activity with less ambiguity than they had previously allowed.[87] Moreover, fifteenth-century authorities concerned with the operation of demonic power, and thus magical practices, were compelled to understand that operation within a much more rigid and precise system of scholastic demonology that had developed since the twelfth and thirteenth centuries. Demonic activity in the world was now conceived as strictly limited by the accepted laws of essentially Aristotelian physics.[88] Probing more deeply and with new rigor into demonic action and its supposed manifestation in any number of potentially superstitious common spells, charms, and other rites, authorities clearly pressed the limits of traditional approaches to understanding the workings of demonic, and concomitantly divine, power in the world.

Attempting to reinforce their construction of witchcraft as utterly and absolutely diabolical, late medieval witchcraft theorists emphasized traditional Christian doctrine that magic operated through demonic agency, not any inherent power in the spell or the human spell-caster.[89] They thus reveal an element of 'disenchantment' buried at the heart of medieval notions of 'magic' itself. Yet they also reveal the dilemma that such disenchantment presented to Christian thinkers, since it impinged on 'religious' as well as 'magical' rites. For all that Protestantism constructed a new theology of religious ritual, still throughout the sixteenth and seventeenth centuries this tension endured. Indeed, while Protestant authorities regarded the medieval church as profoundly superstitious, their basic definition of superstition as deformed or misdirected worship was essentially medieval, and they remained deeply troubled by what R. W. Scribner so aptly termed the 'twilight-zone' of spells, charms, and potential superstitions that lay between entirely legitimate ecclesiastical rite and wholly condemned demonic witchcraft.[90] It would be left to the Enlightenment to shift the terms of debate decidedly, reconfiguring superstition as an irrational rather than an improper act. 'Magical' rites were no longer condemned because they represented a perverse redirecting of 'religious' devotion toward demons rather than toward the deity. Instead they were derided, along with much formally 'religious' ritual, as silly and nonsensical.[91] Thus the elaborate parsing of proper and improper rites and the convoluted considerations of how they might or might not interact with supernatural entities that had plagued centuries past suddenly became unnecessary, at least for those who considered themselves enlightened.

The fifteenth century was, then, neither an end nor a beginning in terms of 'magical thought' or 'disenchantment' in Europe. It was, instead, part of a profoundly gradual transition whereby foundational Christian beliefs about the functioning of religio-magical rites shifted ultimately to the enlightened rejection (never fully realized in the eighteenth or subsequent centuries) of all 'magic' and much traditional 'religion.' Yet within that slow shift, the fifteenth century was an important moment, for in it we can see the strands connecting concern about witchcraft and superstition back to earlier medieval doctrines of magic and demonic power, as well as the newly heightened tensions and energies that would fuel these concerns in the coming early modern age. Studies of late medieval Europe are often dominated by overarching paradigms of autumnal waning or, more actively, prolonged crises leading finally to the Renaissance and Reformation.[92] Conversely, some scholars have stressed the enduring vitality of traditional medieval beliefs and practices into the fifteenth century.[93] Growing concerns about witchcraft, common spells, and superstitions, however, illustrate how new dynamics and tensions emerging in this period (neither so extreme nor so sudden as to warrant the term 'crisis,' perhaps) interacted within long-standing Christian beliefs and helped drive authorities toward new models of thought and understanding, even as they sought to preserve, reassert, or reaffirm traditional ones.

While the arguments, concerns, and conclusions of witchcraft theorists used to be relegated to the fringe of European history, we now know how central demonological thought was to numerous areas of intellectual activity, certainly in the early modern period.[94] Indeed, many scholars are coming to argue that witchcraft, magic, and magical thought remain integral aspects even of Western modernity. Nevertheless, authoritative denial and intellectual dismissal of magic have been salient features of modern Western culture for several centuries. This 'disenchantment,' whether given that label or not, continues to be viewed essentially in terms of emerging skepticism and repudiation of magical beliefs.[95] Even when Weberian arguments are recast in more nuanced and specific terms, such as conceptions of ritual operations, scholars still tend to seek defining moments of change in which old systems were substantially rejected. Yet elements of disenchantment existed already within premodern European conceptions of magical and other ritual operations. The historical processes of disenchantment, therefore, cannot be understood solely in terms of rejection of magical beliefs motivated by forces external to magical thought, whether Protestant theology, scientific rationalism, or Enlightenment philosophy. Magical beliefs were themselves, in the tensions and ambiguities they produced, an important force driving European culture along a trajectory of disenchantment.[96] The fifteenth century – itself not a point of radical rupture, but a critical juncture when many older, medieval systems and structures can be seen to shift noticeably toward more modern forms – reveals how the long history of magic in Europe is an important element of the putatively modern narrative of disenchantment.

Notes

1. Max Weber, 'Science as a Vocation,' in H. H. Gerth and C. Wright Mills, eds. and trans., *From Max Weber: Essays in Sociology* (New York, 1946), 129–156, quotes from 139; Weber, *The Protestant Ethic and the Spirit of Capitalism*, trans. Talcott Parsons (1930; repr., London, 1992), 61. On the dating of the Munich speech, see Wolfgang Schluchter, 'Excursus: The Question of Dating of "Science as a Vocation" and "Politics as a Vocation,"' in Guenther Roth and Wolfgang Schluchter, eds., *Max Weber's Vision of History: Ethics and Methods* (Berkeley, Calif., 1979), 113–116.

2. A succinct critique of the use of 'disenchantment' to frame modernity is found in Owen Chadwick, *The Secularization of the European Mind in the Nineteenth Century* (Cambridge, 1975), 258.

3. Peter Pels, 'Introduction: Magic and Modernity,' in Birgit Meyer and Peter Pels, eds., *Magic and Modernity: Interfaces of Revelation and Concealment* (Stanford, Calif., 2003), 1–38, discussion of

Weber on 26–29. Randall Styers, *Making Magic: Religion, Magic, and Science in the Modern World* (Oxford, 2004), offers a cogent account of how discourses of magic, especially scholarly ones, are employed to fashion modernity. On the centrality of disenchantment, he notes that all 'dominant [modern] theories of magic have as their objective an insistence that the modern subject conform to an emphatic disenchantment' (13). Catherine Bell, *Ritual: Perspectives and Dimensions* (Oxford, 1997), 177–178, notes Weber's 'lingering influence' on most modern typologies of religion, magic, and ritual. Talal Asad, *Formations of the Secular: Christianity, Islam, Modernity* (Stanford, Calif., 2003), states that disenchantment remains 'a salient feature of the modern epoch' (13), even while later calling the interpretive value of the term into some question (48). For an example of the interrelation of magic and modernity outside the West, see Gyan Prakash, 'Between Science and Superstition: Religion and the Modern Subject of the Nation in Colonial India,' in Meyer and Pels, *Magic and Modernity*, 39–59.

4. Keith Thomas, *Religion and the Decline of Magic* (New York, 1971), esp. 25–112.

5. R. W. Scribner, 'The Reformation, Popular Magic, and the "Disenchantment of the World,"' *Journal of Interdisciplinary History* 23, no. 3 (1993): 475–494, reprinted in Scribner, *Religion and Culture in Germany (1400–1800)*, ed. Lyndal Roper (Leiden, 2001), 346–365; Roy Porter, 'Witchcraft and Magic in Enlightenment, Romantic, and Liberal Thought,' in Bengt Ankarloo and Stuart Clark, eds., *Witchcraft and Magic in Europe: The Eighteenth and Nineteenth Centuries* (Philadelphia, Pa., 1999), 191–282, esp. 255–273. Alex Owen, *The Place of Enchantment: British Occultism and the Culture of the Modern* (Chicago, 2004), esp. 10–11 on the centrality of Weberian disenchantment for studies of modern European magic.

6. Styers, *Making Magic*, 25–68; Stanley Jeyaraja Tambiah, *Magic, Science, Religion, and the Scope of Rationality* (Cambridge, 1990), 4–24. Rich discussion of some of the issues and implications inherent in this development can be found in Talal Asad, *Genealogies of Religion: Discipline and Reasons of Power in Christianity and Islam* (Baltimore, Md., 1993), esp. 1–54; also Asad, *Formations of the Secular*, esp. 21–66.

7. Edward Muir, *Ritual in Early Modern Europe* (Cambridge, 1997), 147–223, with discussion of Weber's influence on 185–186.

8. Philippe Buc, *The Dangers of Ritual: Between Early Medieval Texts and Social Scientific Theory* (Princeton, N.J., 2001), 164–247, offers a bracing critique of how modern conceptions of 'ritual' and 'religion' developed in the Reformation and post-Reformation eras.

9. Francis Oakley, *The Western Church in the Later Middle Ages* (Ithaca, N.Y., 1979), 213–259, remains an excellent introduction; also Euan Cameron, *The European Reformation* (Oxford, 1991), esp. 38–48. More recently, see Christopher M. Bellitto, *Renewing Christianity: A History of Church Reform from Day One to Vatican II* (New York, 2001), esp. 102–118; Scott H. Hendrix, *Recultivating the Vineyard: The Reformation Agendas of Christianization* (Louisville, Ky., 2004), esp. 1–35. More focused is Krzysztof Bracha, 'Kritik an den Glaubens- und Verhaltensformen und an der Aberglaubenpraxis im kirchlichen reformatorischen Schrifttum des Spätmittelalters,' in Paweł Kras and Wojciech Polak, eds., *Christianity in East Central Europe: Late Middle Ages* (Lublin, 1999), 271–282; and Bracha, 'Der Einfluß der neuen Frömmigkeit auf die spätmittelatlerliche Kritik am Aberglauben im Reformschrifttum Mitteleuropas,' in Marek Derwich and Martial Staub, eds., *Die 'Neue Frömmigkeit' in Europa im Spätmittelalter* (Göttingen, 2004), 225–248.

10. On this 'common tradition' of magic in the Middle Ages, see Richard Kieckhefer, *Magic in the Middle Ages* (Cambridge, 1989), 56–80; Karen Jolly, 'Medieval Magic: Definitions, Beliefs, Practices,' in Bengt Ankarloo and Stuart Clark, eds., *Witchcraft and Magic in Europe: The Middle Ages* (Philadelphia, 2002), 3–71, 30–53.

11. For an overview focused mainly on influential Latin treatises, see Lynn Thorndike, *A History of Magic and Experimental Science*, 8 vols. (New York, 1923–1958), 4: 274–307; Françoise Bonney, 'Autour de Jean Gerson: Opinions de théologiens sur les superstitions et la sorcellerie au début du XVe siècle,' *Le Moyen Age* 77 (1971): 85–98; Jan R. Veenstra, *Magic and Divination at the Courts of*

Burgundy and France: Text and Context of Laurens Pignon's 'Contre les devineurs' (1411) (Leiden, 1998), 137–153; Werner Tschacher, *Der Formicarius des Johannes Nider von 1437/38: Studien zu den Anfängen der europäischen Hexenverfolgungen im Spätmittelalter* (Aachen, 2000), 269–291. On the numerous German vernacular catechetical texts dealing with superstition from this period, see Karin Baumann, *Aberglaube für Laien: Zur Programmatik und Überlieferung spätmittelalterlicher Superstitionenkritik*, 2 vols. (Würzburg, 1989). For Spain, see Fabián Alejandro Campagne, *Homo Catholicus, Homo Superstitiosus: El discurso antisupersticioso en la España de los siglos XV a XVIII* (Madrid, 2002). On a single major treatise, that of the Heidelberg theologian Nicholas Magni of Jauer, see Adolph Franz, *Der Magister Nikolaus Magni de Jawor: Ein Beitrag zur Literatur- und Gelehrtengeschichte des 14. und 15. Jahrhunderts* (Freiburg im Breisgau, 1898), 151–195. Those who read Polish (I do not) should also consult Krzysztof Bracha, *Teolog, diabeł i zabobony: Świadectwo traktatu Mikołaja Magni z Jawora De superstitionibus (1405 r.)* (Warsaw, 1999).

12. Stuart Clark, *Thinking with Demons: The Idea of Witchcraft in Early Modern Europe* (Oxford, 1997); Walter Stephens, *Demon Lovers: Witchcraft, Sex, and the Crisis of Belief* (Chicago, 2002).

13. Focused studies on this period are Andreas Blauert, *Frühe Hexenverfolgungen: Ketzer-, Zauberei- und Hexenprozesse des 15. Jahrhunderts* (Hamburg, 1989); Martine Ostorero, *'Folâtrer avec les demons': Sabbat et chasse aux sorciers à Vevey (1448)* (Lausanne, 1995); Ostorero, Agostino Paravicini Bagliani, and Kathrin Utz Tremp, eds., *L'imaginaire du sabbat: Edition critique des textes les plus anciens (1430 c.–1440 c.)* (Lausanne, 1999).

14. Thomas, *Religion and the Decline of Magic*, 25–50; David Gentilcore, *From Bishop to Witch: The System of the Sacred in Early Modern Terra d'Otranto* (Manchester, 1992). A strongly Weberian reading of this system is Lutz Kaelber, *Schools of Asceticism: Ideology and Organization in Medieval Religious Communities* (University Park, Pa., 1998), 101–125.

15. See Thomas, *Religion and the Decline of Magic*; Gentilcore, *From Bishop to Witch*; and several essential articles collected in R. W. Scribner, *Popular Culture and Popular Movements in Reformation Germany* (London, 1987), 1–16, 17–47, 257–275, and Scribner, *Religion and Culture*, 275–365.

16. On Nider, see Tschacher, *Der Formicarius*; Michael D. Bailey, *Battling Demons: Witchcraft, Heresy, and Reform in the Late Middle Ages* (University Park, Pa., 2003). On the *Malleus*, see Günter Jerouschek and Wolfgang Behringer, ' "Das unheilvollste Buch der Weltliteratur"? Zur Entstehung- und Wirkungs-geschichte des Malleus Maleficarum und zu den Anfängen der Hexenverfolgung,' in Günter Jerouschek and Wolfgang Behringer, eds., *Der Hexenhammer: Malleus Maleficarum* (Munich, 2000), 9–98; Hans Peter Broedel, *The Malleus Maleficarum and the Construction of Witchcraft: Theology and Popular Belief* (Manchester, 2003). Although traditionally Jakob Sprenger is listed as coauthor with Kramer, there is strong evidence that Kramer was the chief, probably the sole, author. See Peter Segl, 'Heinrich Institoris: Persönlichkeit und literarisches Werk,' in Peter Segl, ed., *Der Hexenhammer: Entstehung und Umfeld des Malleus maleficarum von 1487* (Cologne, 1988), 103–126; Jerouschek and Behringer, 'Das unheilvollste Buch,' 31–37.

17. On the interrelation of these roles, see Christine Caldwell, 'Dominican Inquisitors as "Doctors of Souls": The Spiritual Discipline of Inquisition, 1231–1331,' *Heresis* 40 (2004): 23–40; also Christine Caldwell Ames, 'Does Inquisition Belong to Religious History?' *AHR* 110, no. 1 (February 2005): 11–37, esp. 17–24.

18. Tschacher, *Der Formicarius*, 22; Jerouschek and Behringer, 'Das unheilvollste Buch,' 13; Broedel, *The Malleus Maleficarum*, 21.

19. On antique conceptions of such interaction, see Dale B. Martin, *Inventing Superstition: From the Hippocratics to the Christians* (Cambridge, Mass., 2004).

20. A detailed study of the concept of superstition in the context of Protestant thought is Ernst Saxer, *Aberglaube, Heuchelei und Frömmigkeit: Eine Untersuchung zu Calvins reformatorischer Eigenart* (Zurich, 1970). On superstition into the Enlightenment, see William Monter, *Ritual, Myth, and Magic in Early Modern Europe* (Athens, Ohio, 1983); Martin Pott, *Aufklärung und Aberglaube: Die deutsche Frühaufklä¨-rung im Spiegel ihrer Aberglaubenskritik* (Tübingen, 1992). While Monter

links superstition to the issue of witchcraft, Pott exposes Enlightenment thinkers' reliance on classical descriptions of *superstitio* and especially *deisidaimonia* (esp. chaps. 2–3).

21. Virtually all late medieval authorities followed the definition of *superstitio* given in the thirteenth century by Thomas Aquinas, *Summa theologiae* 2.2.92.1–2, in *Summa theologiae: Latin Text and English Translation*, vol. 40: *Superstition and Irreverence*, ed. and trans. Thomas Franklin O'Meara and Michael John Duffy (New York, 1968), 2–8. On the origins and earlier use of the term, see Dieter Harmening, *Superstitio: Überlieferungs- und theoriegeschichtliche Untersuchungen zur kirchlich-theologischen Aberglaubensliteratur des Mittelalters* (Berlin, 1979). Baumann, *Aberglaube*, 1: 260, indicates late medieval authorities' heavy reliance on earlier scholastic and patristic authors.

22. On medieval conceptions of the supernatural, and the distinct category of the preternatural, see Fabián Alejandro Campagne, 'Witchcraft and the Sense-of-the-Impossible in Early Modern Spain: Some Reflections Based on the Literature of Superstition (ca. 1500–1800),' *Harvard Theological Review* 96, no. 1 (2002): 25–62. Here I intend 'supernatural' in the commonly understood modern sense, not the technical medieval one.

23. The clearest study of the imposition of elite concerns about diabolism onto more common concerns about *maleficium* in the late medieval period remains Richard Kieckhefer, *European Witch Trials: Their Foundations in Popular and Learned Culture, 1300–1500* (Berkeley, Calif., 1976).

24. Johannes Nider, *Formicarius*, ed. G. Colvener (Douai, 1602), prologue (unpaginated).

25. Ibid. 5.4, 356–357.

26. 'Tunc statim infirmus curatum se sentiens, scire voluit in remedium futurorum quid carminationis virgo applicasset. Quae respondit: Vos, mala fide vel debili, diuinis et approbatis exercitiis ecclesiae non inheretis, et carmina ac remedia prohibita crebro vestris infirmitatibus applicatis; idcirco raro in corpore et semper in anima per talia laedimini.' Ibid., 357.

27. Robin Briggs, *Witches and Neighbors: The Social and Cultural Context of European Witchcraft* (New York, 1996), 169–218; Owen Davies, *Cunning-Folk: Popular Magic in English History* (London, 2003), 62–65, 111–112.

28. Gentilcore, *From Bishop to Witch*, 259, describes how recourse to multiple forms of supernatural aid was quite common.

29. On the relationship of cunning folk to accused witches, see Briggs, *Witches and Neighbors*, 122–123; Davies, *Cunning-Folk*, 2–17; Willem de Blécourt, 'Witch Doctors, Soothsayers and Priests: On Cunning Folk in European Historiography and Tradition,' *Social History* 19, no. 3 (1994): 285–303, esp. 288–296.

30. Nider, *Formicarius* 5.3, 352, and 5.6, 371; Nider, *Preceptorium divine legis* 1.11.x (Milan, 1489) (no pagination).

31. 'Immo potius homo mori deberet quam talia consentire.' Nider, *Formicarius* 5.3, 351–352 (misnumbered for 353).

32. On witchcraft and infanticide, see Richard Kieckhefer, 'Avenging the Blood of Children: Anxiety over Child Victims and the Origins of the European Witch Trials,' in Alberto Ferreiro, ed., *The Devil, Heresy and Witchcraft in the Middle Ages: Essays in Honor of Jeffrey B. Russell* (Leiden, 1998), 91–109. On carnality, the fullest consideration is now Stephens, *Demon Lovers* (although I think he overemphasizes the centrality of demonic sex in intellectual constructions of witchcraft). Stuart Clark, in 'Inversion, Misrule and the Meaning of Witchcraft,' *Past and Present* 87 (1980): 98–127, and more fully in *Thinking with Demons*, has demonstrated how essential the notion of inversion was to the concept of witchcraft.

33. Bengt Ankarloo, 'Witch Trials in Northern Europe, 1450–1700,' in Bengt Ankarloo and Stuart Clark, eds., *Witchcraft and Magic in Europe: The Period of the Witch Trials* (Philadelphia, Pa., 2002), 53–95, 58.

34. A translation of the sermon appears in John Shinners, ed., *Medieval Religion, 1000–1500: A Reader* (Orchard Park, N.Y., 1997), 242–245; original Italian in Bernardino da Siena, *Prediche volgari sul Campo di Siena, 1427*, ed. Carlo Delcorno, 2 vols. (Milan, 1989), 2: 1002–1040. Nider knew of and admired Bernardino; *Formicarius* 4.9, 311–312. On Bernardino and witchcraft generally, see Franco Mormando, *The Preacher's Demons: Bernardino of Siena and the Social Underworld of Early Renaissance Italy* (Chicago, 1999), 52–108.

35. Johannes Hartlieb, *Das Buch aller verbotenen Künste, des Aberglaubens und der Zauberei*, ed. and trans. Falk Eckhard Graf (Ahlerstedt, 1989), 46–48.

36. Nider, *Formicarius* 5.4, 358. Although he was the earliest authority to address the frequent association of witchcraft with women, Nider often related examples of male witches. See Michael D. Bailey, 'The Feminization of Magic and the Emerging Idea of the Female Witch in the Late Middle Ages,' *Essays in Medieval Studies* 19 (2002): 120–134; Bailey, *Battling Demons*, 48–52.

37. On ways in which Nider may have reinterpreted earlier reports, see Blauert, *Frühe Hexenverfolgungen*, 57–59.

38. Nider, *Formicarius* 5.3, 350.

39. The most influential patristic treatment of demons was that given by Augustine, chiefly in his *De doctrina christiana*, *De divinatione daemonum*, and *De civitate dei*, esp. books 8–10. Thomas Linsenmann, *Die Magie bei Thomas von Aquin* (Berlin, 2000), devotes several chapters to the Augustinian background of Aquinas's thought; see esp. 73–98.

40. On medieval necromancy, see Kieckhefer, *Magic in the Middle Ages*, 151–175; more fully, Richard Kieckhefer, *Forbidden Rites: A Necromancer's Manual of the Fifteenth Century* (University Park, Pa., 1998).

41. The most influential authority in this regard was the late-fourteenth-century Catalan inquisitor Nicolau Eymeric. See Michael D. Bailey, 'From Sorcery to Witchcraft: Clerical Conceptions of Magic in the Later Middle Ages,' *Speculum* 76, no. 4 (2001): 960–990, 971–976.

42. '[…] et in signum desuper chartam scriptam vel quid aliud tradunt, cum ipsis obligatoria, ut solo verbo, tactu vel signo malefica, quibus velint, illis inferant sive tollant […].' In Joseph Hansen, ed., *Quellen und Untersuchungen zur Geschichte des Hexenwahns und der Hexenverfolgung im Mittelalter* (1901; repr., Hildesheim, 1963), 17.

43. 'De hoc etiam infra dicetur non autem faciunt ista immediate maleficorum opera actione propria et immediate, sed talia fiunt per demones qui uisis maleficiis immediate ex pacto dudum cum maleficis a principio mundi et tempore ueteris idolatrie habito sciunt qualem effectum debent ad intentionem maleficorum procurare. Ut exempla gratia: Scopa quam malefica intingit in aquam ut pluat non causat pluuiam, sed demon talibus visis qui, si deus permiserit, potestatem habet in omnia corporalia, et in aerem, uentos, et nubes, ut statim talia procuraret et causare ualeat. Maga siquidem signum dat per scopam, sed demon illud procurat et agit ut pluat per demonis actionem.' Nider, *Preceptorium* 1.11.v.

44. Bailey, *Battling Demons*, 99–101.

45. Nider, *Formicarius* 5.4, 356, and 5.6, 370; also Nider, *Preceptorium* 1.11.x.

46. The importance of the distinction is stressed by Richard Kieckhefer, 'The Specific Rationality of Medieval Magic,' *AHR* 99, no. 3 (June 1994): 813–836.

47. Nicholas Magni of Jauer, *Tractatus de superstitionibus*, University of Pennsylvania, MS Codex 78, fol. 58r.

48. Nider, *Preceptorium* 1.11.gg; based on Thomas Aquinas, *Summa theologiae* 2.2.96.4, 80–84.

49. Nider, *Formicarius* 5.7, 380–381. For a fuller account of Peter's witch-hunting activities, see Arno Borst, 'The Origins of the Witch-Craze in the Alps,' in Borst, *Medieval Worlds: Barbarians, Heretics, and Artists in the Middle Ages*, trans. Eric Hansen (Chicago, 1992), 101–122.

50. Nider, *Formicarius* 5.6, 370; Nider, *Preceptorium* 1.11.x.

51. Matthew 12:26–28, Luke 8:29 and 9:42.

52. Nider, *Formicarius* 5.6, 372; also Nider, *Preceptorium* 1.11.nn. Heinrich Kramer drew a similar point in *Malleus maleficarum* 2.2.6, *Nachdruck des Erstdruckes von 1487 mit Bulle und Approbatio*, ed. Günter Jerouschek (Hildesheim, 1992), fols. 85v–86r.

53. Nider, *Preceptorium* 1.11.pp; also Kramer, *Malleus maleficarum* 2.2.7, fol. 91r. On the protective power of church bells, see Thomas, *Religion and the Decline of Magic*, 31.

54. 'Adiuro vos, grandines et ventos, per tres Christi diuinos clauos qui Christi manus et pedes per-forarunt, et per quatuor euangelistas sanctos Matthaeum, Marcum, Lucam, et Ioannem, ut in aqua resoluti descendatis.' Nider, *Formicarius* 5.4, 358.

55. Most detailed is Valerie I. J. Flint, *The Rise of Magic in Early Medieval Europe* (Princeton, N.J., 1991), although Flint focuses too much on an oppositional dynamic between Christian and pagan practices that was probably not so strongly perceived by contemporaries. On this, see Karen Louise Jolly, *Popular Religion in Late Saxon England: Elf Charms in Context* (Chapel Hill, N.C., 1996). See also Kieckhefer, 'Specific Rationality,' for criticism of Flint's inattention to the contemporary distinctions that were made regarding the nature of the power – divine or demonic – perceived to underlie different rites.

56. Nider, *Preceptorium* 1.11.gg; also Nicholas Magni of Jauer, *De superstitionibus*, fol. 27r; Heinrich Kramer, *Malleus maleficarum* 2.2.6, fol. 86v. The ultimate source was Aquinas, *Summa theologiae* 2.2.96.4.

57. Discernment of demons and demonic activity in general was a major issue for late medieval authorities; see Nancy Caciola, *Discerning Spirits: Divine and Demonic Possession in the Middle Ages* (Ithaca, N.Y., 2003), 274–319. Caciola focuses more than I do on the nature of church control in these areas, especially its gendered quality, and she draws useful comparisons to witchcraft.

58. On liturgical elements of common spells, best is Eamon Duffy, *The Stripping of the Altars: Traditional Religion in England, 1400–1580* (New Haven, Conn., 1992), 266–287. On liturgical elements of necromancy, see Kieckhefer, *Magic in the Middle Ages*, 70–74, 160–161, 166–168; Kieckhefer, *Forbidden Rites*, 3, 13–17.

59. 'Questio xxvi vtrum licitum sit per carmina scripta uel uerba sacra benedicere infirmos homines uel iumenta […] Respondet Thomas 2.2, ubi supra, quod sic septem conditionibus seruatis. Una est ut uideatur ne uerba aliquid contineant quod pertineat ad inuocationes demonum expressas uel tacitas. Secunda ne contineant ignota nomina […] Tertia ne materia uerborum aliquid falsitatis contineat […] Sexta ut in alligatione prolatione uel scriptura diuinorum uerborum respectus solum habeatur ad sacra uerba et ad intellectum eorum.' Nider, *Preceptorium* 1.11.gg.

60. 'Questio xxvii unde ortum habeant benedictiones et carminationes quas uetule hodie super infirmos et uiri quidam faciunt? Respondetur quod principium horum fuit sanctissimum, sed sicut omnia demonis instinctu deprauantur mediantibus demonibus et malis hominibus […] Sicuti etiam hodie literatos et sacre theologie doctores noui qui infirmos uisitantes similia uerba egrotis applicauerunt non solum demoniacis.' Ibid. 1.11.hh.

61. On the lack of originality in the *Malleus*, see Brian P. Levack, *The Witch-Hunt in Early Modern Europe*, 2nd ed. (London, 1995), 54–55. In contrast, Broedel, *The Malleus Maleficarum*, makes the *Malleus*'s originality a central theme.

62. Kramer, *Malleus maleficarum* 1.2, fol. 10r; 2.1.16, fol. 76r; 2.2.6, fol. 86v.

63. Ibid. 2.2, fols. 76v–77r.

64. Ibid. 2.2.1–3, fols. 79v–83v, and 2.1, fols. 43v–45r. Broedel, *The Malleus Maleficarum*, 152, notes that sacramentals 'provided the most consistently reliable protection against witchcraft' described in the *Malleus*.

65. 'In contrarium est quod sicut deus et natura non abundant in superfluis, ita non deficiunt in necessariis, quare et necessario fidelibus contra huiusmodi insultus demonum sunt data non solum remedia preseruatiua.' Kramer, *Malleus maleficarum* 2.2, fol. 76v. 'Aliis vero duobus modis

vltimis tollere maleficium potest esse vel licitum vel non vanum secundum canonistas et quod tollerari possunt vbi remedia ecclesie prius attemptata, vt sunt exorcismi ecclesie, suffragia sanctorum implorata, ac vera penitentia, nihil effecissent.' Ibid., fol. 77v.

66. Ibid., fols. 78v–79r.

67. 'Sed qua virtute maleficium fugauit et species rerum in plumbo causauit sub dubio relinquitur.' Ibid., fol. 79r.

68. Kieckhefer, *Magic in the Middle Ages*, 131–133.

69. Kramer, *Malleus maleficarum* 1.2, fol. 10r–v. Similarly Nicholas Magni of Jauer, *De superstitionibus*, fols. 52v–53v and 54v; Hartlieb, *Buch aller verbotenen Künste*, 38.

70. 'Et hoc quod saturni influxum super plumbum tanquam ex eius dominio causatum allegauit irreprehensibilis extitit et potius commendandus fuit.' Kramer, *Malleus maleficarum* 2.2, fol. 79r. Similarly Nicholas Magni of Jauer, *De superstitionibus*, fols. 40v, 61r; Hartlieb, *Buch aller verbotenen Künste*, 80.

71. 'Quinto ne spes habeatur in modo scribendi aut ligandi aut in quacumque huiusmodi vanitate que ad diuinam reuerentiam non pertineat, quia alias omnino iudicabitur superstitiosum.' Kramer, *Malleus maleficarum* 2.2.6, fol. 86v; following Nider (*Preceptorium* 1.11.gg) and ultimately Aquinas (*Summa theologiae* 2.2.96.4).

72. 'Potius videtur quod per aliquid pactum adminus tacitum cum demone initum hoc practicauerit,' and later 'Non tam suspectus quam vt manifeste deprehensus adminus licet non super expresseum initum cum demone pactum tamen super tacitum iudicatur et tanquam pro coniuncto habere et penis adminus in secundo modo sententiandi infra contentis, sed puniri debet cum abiuratione solemni.' Kramer, *Malleus maleficarum* 2.2, fol. 79r.

73. 'Gratia hiuis exempli queritur an non alie benedictiones et carminationes seu etiam coniurationes per exorcismos habeant efficaciam cum hic videantur reprobari? Respondetur quod hec virgo non reprobauit nisi illicita carmina cum illicitis coniurantionibus et exorcismis.' Ibid. 2.2.6, fol. 86r.

74. Ibid. 2.2, fol. 79r.

75. Christians were not forbidden all interaction with demons; as noted above, all the faithful were believed to have some power to exorcise demons. The critical distinction for authorities was that the faithful should interact with demons only in such a way as to 'command or compel' them ('imperando seu compellendo'), never to 'solicit' them: Nider, *Preceptorium* 1.11.kk; similarly Nicholas Magni of Jauer, *De superstitionibus*, fol. 48r.

76. Kramer, *Malleus maleficarum* 2.2.7, fol. 91r.

77. 'Lapilli enim tres ex grandine in ignem sub inuocatione sanctissime trinitatis proiiciuntur, oratio dominica cum angelica salutatione bis aut ter adiungitur, euangelium Johannis, In principio erat verbum, cum signo crucis vndique contra tempestatem ante et retro et ex omni parte terre subinfertur. Et tunc cum in fine replicat trinies verbum caro factum est et trinies ex post dixerit per euangelica dicta fugiat tempestas ista. Subito, siquidem tempestas ex maleficio fuit procurata, cessabit. Hec verissima experimenta, nec suspecta iudicantur.' Ibid., fols. 90v–91r. 'Experimenta' was a common term for the rites of ritual magic, and particularly necromantic conjurations (Kieckhefer, *Forbidden Rites*, 23).

78. 'Respondetur utique per alia sacra verba proiiciens autem intendit diabolum molestare dum eius facturam per inuocationem sanctissime trinitatis destruere conatur. Ad ignem potius quam ad aquam proiicit, quia cicius dum resoluuntur.' Kramer, *Malleus maleficarum* 2.2.7, fol. 91r.

79. 'Coniuro te per amorosas lachrymas a nostro saluatore domino Iesu Christo in cruce per salute mundi effusas, ac per ardentissimas lachrymas ipsius gloriosissime virginis Marie matris eius super vulnera ipsius hora vespertina sparsas, et per omnes lachrymas quas hic in mundo omnes sancti et electi dei effuderunt, et a quorum oculis iam omnem lachrymam abstersit, vt inquantum sis innoxia lachrymas effundas, si nocens nullo modo.' Ibid. 3.15, fol. 107r.

80. Ibid., fol. 108r.

81. One could suppose that Kramer feared the presence of a demon exerting its power to prevent an innocent suspect from weeping, and so the conjuration was directed at this entity, but this would still not necessarily cause the freed suspect to commence weeping, as the conjuration explicitly intended.

82. For example, Christ in Mark 5:23 and 6:5 and in Luke 4:40–41, and various apostles in Mark 16:18 and Acts 8:18 and 28:8.

83. On early medieval confrontations between Christian practice and pagan superstitions, see Flint, *Rise of Magic*, but also Jolly, *Popular Religion*. Yitzhak Hen, *Culture and Religion in Merovingian Gaul, A.D. 481–751* (Leiden, 1995), 154–206, argues strongly that little real pagan practice unaccommodated to Christianity persisted after the seventh or eighth century.

84. On 'Frömmigkeitstheologie,' see Berndt Hamm, 'Frömmigkeit als Gegenstand theologiegeschichtlicher Forschung: Methodisch-historische Überlegungen am Beispiel von Spatmittelalter und Reformation,' *Zeitschrift für Theologie und Kirche* 74 (1977): 464–497; Hamm, 'Von der spätmittelalterlichen reformatio zur Reformation: Der Prozeß normativer Zentrierung von Religion und Gesellschaft in Deutschland,' *Archiv für Reformationsgeschichte* 84 (1993): 7–82, esp. 18–24; Hamm, 'Nor-mative Centering in the Fifteenth and Sixteenth Centuries: Observations on Religiosity, Theology, and Iconology,' *Journal of Early Modern History* 3, no. 4 (1999): 307–354, 325–330. Baumann, *Aberglaube*, 1: 201–202, does not use this term but stresses the desire to create a 'theologia practica' and extend scholastic theology to a wider audience evident especially among what she labels the 'Vienna school' of late medieval authors concerned with superstition.

85. Daniel Hobbins, 'The Schoolman as Public Intellectual: Jean Gerson and the Late Medieval Tract,' *AHR* 108, no. 5 (December 2003): 1308–1337, esp. the chart on 1336–1337.

86. For one approach to this broad subject, see Dyan Elliott, *Proving Woman: Female Spirituality and Inquisitional Culture in the Later Middle Ages* (Princeton, N.J., 2004).

87. Baumann, *Aberglaube*, 1: 318–321, notes but does not extensively analyze the particularly demonized nature of late medieval concern over superstition. On general fear of the devil, see Jeffrey Burton Russell, *Lucifer: The Devil in the Middle Ages* (Ithaca, N.Y., 1984), 295–296; Robert Muchembled, *A History of the Devil from the Middle Ages to the Present*, trans. Jean Birrell (Cambridge, 2003), 20–21. On growing concerns with spirit possession and the discernment of spirits, see Barbara Newman, 'Possessed by the Spirit: Devout Women, Demoniacs, and the Apostolic Life in the Thirteenth Century,' *Speculum* 73, no. 3 (1998): 733–770; Caciola, *Discerning Spirits*, 274–319; Elliott, *Proving Woman*, 264– 296.

88. The most probing study of this development has been Stephens, *Demon Lovers*. While he concentrates on conceptions of demonic bodies and demonic sex, the ramifications of this development were far broader.

89. Peter Brown, 'Sorcery, Demons, and the Rise of Christianity: From Late Antiquity into the Middle Ages,' in Brown, *Religion and Society in the Age of Saint Augustine* (London, 1972), 119–146, esp. 131– 138, although as Brown points out, in late antiquity Christian authorities tended to deemphasize human participation in magic, while late medieval witchcraft theorists focused strongly on human agents, if not human agency.

90. R. W. Scribner, 'Ritual and Popular Religion in Catholic Germany at the Time of the Reformation,' *Journal of Ecclesiastical History* 35, no. 1 (1984): 47–77, 71. Saxer, *Aberglaube*, makes clear the degree to which Calvin's notion of superstition, based on ancient and patristic sources, was similar to that of fifteenth- and sixteenth-century Catholic reformers, and even to that of medieval scholastic theologians, although he of course located superstition in the world very differently than they did.

91. Pott, *Aufklärung und Aberglaube*, 100–124; Campagne, *Homo Catholicus*, 100–112.

92. Overview and trenchant criticism of these models in Howard Kaminsky, 'From Lateness to Waning to Crisis: The Burden of the Later Middle Ages,' *Journal of Early Modern History* 4, no. 1 (2000): 85–125.

93. For example, Bernd Moeller's classic 'Frömmigkeit in Deutschland um 1500' (1965), translated as 'Religious Life in Germany on the Eve of the Reformation,' in Gerald Strauss, ed., *Pre-Reformation Germany* (London, 1972), 13–42; more recently Duffy's magisterial *Stripping of the Altars*.

94. Most thoroughly demonstrated in Clark, *Thinking with Demons*.

95. Styers, *Making Magic*, esp. 38–44; Wolfgang Behringer, *Witches and Witch-Hunts: A Global History* (Cambridge, 2004), 165.

96. On belief as a historical force, see Thomas Kselman, 'Introduction,' in Kselman, ed., *Belief in History: Innovative Approaches to European and American Religion* (Notre Dame, Ind., 1991), 1–15.

CHAPTER 13
THE DECLINE AND END OF WITCHCRAFT PROSECUTIONS
Brian P. Levack

Introduction

During the seventeenth and eighteenth centuries, prosecutions and executions for the crime of witchcraft declined in number and eventually came to an end. The decline occurred in all European countries where witch-hunts had taken place, from Scotland to Transylvania and from Portugal to Finland. The same process took place in those colonial possessions of Spain, Portugal, England and France where ecclesiastical or temporal authorities had brought witches to trial. The decline was marked by an increasing reluctance to prosecute witches, the acquittal of many who were tried, the reversal of convictions on appeal, and eventually the repeal of the laws that had authorized the prosecutions. By 1782 the last officially sanctioned witchcraft execution had taken place, and in many jurisdictions witchcraft, at least as it had been defined in the sixteenth and seventeenth centuries, had ceased to be a crime. Individuals continued to name their neighbours as witches, and in some cases they took violent action against them, but they did so illegally and at the risk of being prosecuted themselves.

The purpose of this essay is to explain how and why the great European witch-hunt declined in intensity and eventually came to an end. It will cover the entire period of that decline, from the time when the prosecutions first began to taper off until the conclusion of the last trial. It does not deal with temporary lulls in the process of witch-hunting. Periodic reductions in the number of trials and executions occurred in almost every European jurisdiction during the sixteenth and seventeenth centuries, and they merit close historical investigation, but they do not concern us here. This essay deals only with the later stages of the process, when witch-hunting finally lost its grip on local communities and when a decline in the number of trials led to their complete termination. In some cases that final decline was related, as either cause or effect, to formal declarations that witchcraft was no longer a crime.

In studying the decline of witch-hunting, we need to distinguish between the number of prosecutions and the number of executions. Marked reductions in both of these totals occurred in the late seventeenth and eighteenth centuries but they did not always coincide. In many jurisdictions, most notably in England and Denmark, the last executions long preceded the last trials. We must also distinguish between the end of large witch-panics or chain-reaction hunts and the end of all prosecutions, including occasional, isolated trials. In many German territories, for example, the great panics, which had always involved charges of collective Devil-worship, had all but disappeared by 1670, but individual trials, and even a few small panics, continued for nearly another one hundred years.

The reduction and eventual end of witch-hunting occurred at different times in the various kingdoms and regions of Europe. In some countries, such as the Dutch Republic, the decline in prosecutions became evident before the end of the sixteenth century, while in others, like Poland, it did not begin until the middle of the eighteenth century. The length of time that the entire process took also varied greatly from place to place. In Scotland, for example, the initial reduction in the number of prosecutions was followed by more than 50 years of trials, whereas in Franche-Comté and colonial Massachusetts witch-hunts came to a complete end only a few years after the courts started to discourage prosecutions. Even the legislation declaring that witchcraft was no longer a crime was passed at different stages of the process. In some kingdoms, such as Hungary and Prussia, the formal decriminalization of witchcraft preceded and was largely responsible for the end of witch-hunting, whereas in Great Britain and Denmark it did not occur until long after the trials had stopped.

Historians of witchcraft have traditionally given much more thought to the question why the trials began than why they came to an end. Until the middle of the twentieth century those who bothered to address the latter question at all attributed the decline in one way or another to the emergence of modern rationalism, the rise of science, or an even vaguer dispelling of ignorance and 'superstition' (Lecky, 1910: 1–138). This interpretation arose during the Enlightenment, and it became the backbone of late nineteenth- and early twentieth-century liberal and Whig historiography. Historians writing in this tradition focused mainly on the content of published witchcraft treatises and the theological and philosophical controversies to which those treatises contributed. They assumed that the decline of witchcraft prosecutions had been caused by a decline in the witch-beliefs of the educated classes and therefore made little distinction between the two developments. The end of the trials thus became synonymous with the enlightened rejection of the demonological ideas that had provided the intellectual foundations of the witch-hunt.

In the last thirty years historians of witchcraft have begun to take different approaches to this problem of the decline of witchcraft. While by no means ignoring the published treatises, whose influence remains a subject of scholarly debate, they have begun to focus on the decisions of the judges, inquisitors, jurists and magistrates who staffed the courts where witches were tried. Historians have, for example, studied the ways in which Spanish Inquisitors, the members of the parlement of Paris, jurists on the law faculties at German universities, and the judges who presided at the English county assizes succeeded in reducing the number of executions for witchcraft within their jurisdictions (Mandrou, 1968; Soman, 1978; Henningsen, 1980; Lorenz, 1995; Sharpe, 1996: 213–34). These studies have shown, moreover, that the judges who brought the trials to an end displayed a much deeper belief in the reality of witchcraft than the 'enlightened' authors of contemporary witchcraft treatises. Further questions regarding the validity of the 'enlightenment model' of the decline of witchcraft have come from social, economic and cultural historians who have suggested that changes in the system of poor relief, the altered mood of local communities in the wake of large witch-hunts, the reform of the profession of popular healers, and the success of the state in christianizing and disciplining the rural population may have played a role in reducing the number of witchcraft accusations and prosecutions (Thomas, 1971: ch. 18; Midelfort, 1972: ch. 6; Várkonyi, 1991–2).

Research on the decline and end of witch-hunting has resulted in the formulation of very few general theories that apply to all of Europe (Soman, 1989). Almost all of the modern scholarship on the subject has had a local, regional or national focus, and interpretations emerging from the study of one locale do not always apply to others (Monter, 1976: 37–41; Soman, 1978; Klaits, 1982; Johansen, 1991–2; Lorenz and Bauer, 1995). The vast chronological gulf that separates the decline of witch-hunting in the Netherlands and France from the parallel phenomenon in Hungary and Poland makes it even more difficult to establish working models or unifying themes (Muchembled, 1991–2). What is more, the developments that account for the initial decline of witchcraft prosecutions in many jurisdictions do not always explain why the trials came to a complete end or why witchcraft officially ceased to be a crime.

This essay will take three different approaches to the problem of the decline of witch-hunting throughout Europe. First, it will identify and illustrate by way of example the general reasons why prosecutions declined in number throughout Europe. It will attempt to be comprehensive in this regard, covering legal, intellectual, religious and social explanations, but it will emphasize changes in judicial procedure and the growth of judicial caution in the trial of witches. Second, it will trace the decline of witch-hunting in five national case studies as a way of illustrating the intersection of some of the general causes discussed in the first part of the essay. These case studies will also establish similarities and differences between the patterns of decline in countries which followed different judicial procedures. The third part of the essay will explore the actual decriminalization of witchcraft in the various countries of Europe and two broad shifts in the administration of criminal justice that accompanied the entire process of decline: the trial of individuals for specific crimes once included within the general category of witchcraft and the prosecution of those who took malicious, violent or otherwise illegal action against persons whom they suspected as witches.

General reasons for the decline in prosecutions

Judicial scepticism and procedural caution

The starting point for any investigation of the decline of witch-hunting must be the development of a growing awareness by those persons who controlled the judicial machinery that many witches were being convicted and executed for crimes they had not committed. This realization, which usually arose in response to the excesses of witch-hunting in certain localities, led judges and other persons involved in the hunts to criticize the ways in which the trials were being conducted. These critiques led in turn to the formulation and implementation of stricter procedural rules for the conduct of witchcraft trials, including greater restraint in the administration of torture and the application of more demanding standards of evidence. As a result of these changes in the judicial process, the trials of witches resulted in a larger number of acquittals, the mass panics in which scores of witches perished no longer recurred, and the courts became increasingly reluctant to initiate prosecutions in the first place.

I have used the phrase judicial scepticism to describe the attitude of those judges, inquisitors, magistrates, and writers who responded to the trials in this way. In the context of witchcraft the word scepticism usually denotes the attitudes of those who doubt or deny the existence of witches or the possibility of their crime. Judicial sceptics did not necessarily adopt such a stance. The essence of their intellectual position was a genuine doubt whether those persons who were being prosecuted were actually guilty as charged, and this concern led in turn to a more general uncertainty whether the crime could ever be proved at law. Some judicial sceptics may have also harboured a more fundamental, philosophical doubt whether witchcraft even existed. But judicial scepticism could, and in many cases did, coexist with a firm belief in the reality and possibility of the crime.

Let us look at five examples of the emergence of this type of scepticism and the role it played in the decline of witch-hunting. In all five cases the process began as a reaction to witch-panics that claimed large numbers of victims. The first was a chain-reaction hunt in the cathedral city of Würzburg which lasted from 1627 to 1629 and took the lives of 160 persons. Like many similar hunts in other German localities, especially in the episcopal principalities, this hunt involved the extensive use of torture. That procedure was used not only to secure confessions and convictions of those who had been accused by their neighbours but also to obtain the names of the witches' alleged accomplices. This tactic allowed for a rapid expansion of the number of victims, but it also led to the naming of witches who did not conform to the traditional stereotype of the witch, which was that of an adult female from the lower levels of society. In the early trials at Würzburg the overwhelming majority of the victims fit this description. At the height of the panic, however, the web of accusations had embraced people 'high and low, of every rank and sex', including clerics, electoral councillors and doctors, city officials, court assessors and law students (Burr, 1903: 29). It also included large numbers of children who at one point supplied more than half the victims (Midelfort, 1979: 282–3). This breakdown of the witch stereotype inclined many members of the community to question seriously whether the officials who were conducting the trials had succeeded in identifying the real witches. It also led to the frightening realization by members of the city's elite that they themselves might just as easily be named as witches. As a result of this crisis of confidence in the mechanisms by which witches were identified and prosecuted, the Würzburg trials came grinding to a halt, and witch- hunting in that bishopric entered a long period of decline. The last trial would not take place until 1749, but never again did the city experience the ravages of witch-hunting as it had in 1627–29.

The excesses of witch-hunting at Würzburg also inspired a devastating critique of the legal procedures used in the witchcraft trials. In 1631 Friedrich Spee, a Jesuit priest who held a professorship of moral theology at the University of Paderborn, published an anonymous treatise, entitled *Cautio Criminalis*, which exposed the insurmountable judicial pressures to which the accused were subject during their interrogations and the unreliability of their confessions as evidence of the crime (Spee, 1631). This book, the work of the quintessential judicial sceptic, emerged from Spee's actual experience as a confessor during the trials at Würzburg as well as from his first-hand experience with another chain-reaction hunt at Paderborn in 1631. The *Cautio* did not at first have a profound impact on the conduct of witchcraft trials, but later translations into German (1647 and 1649), Dutch (1657), French (1660) and Polish (1697 and 1710) enabled it to exercise a moderating influence throughout Europe, even in Protestant lands. It gained its greatest fame from the publicity given it by Christian Thomasius, the Protestant jurist at the University of Halle who relied heavily on it in writing his own treatises on torture and witchcraft in the early eighteenth century. Thus the *Cautio* contributed in this indirect way to the final end of the trials almost 100 years after its author had died (van Oorschot, 1995; Behringer, 1987: 366–99).

The second example of the way in which judicial scepticism developed in response to the excesses of witch-hunting comes from Sweden, where a major chain-reaction hunt took place between 1668 and 1676. Prior to this panic witch-hunting in Sweden had been relatively restrained, mainly as a result of the caution and scepticism exhibited by the clergy and the members of the royal Court of Appeal in Stockholm. In the late 1660s, however, confessions by hundreds of children that witches were taking them to the sabbath at a mythical place called Blåkulla triggered a massive hunt which began in the northern province of Dalarna and then spread to the provinces of Hälsingland, Ångermanland, Gästrikland, Norland, Upp-land and ultimately Stockholm. In response to extraordinary pressure from local communities, King Charles XI appointed a series of royal commissions, consisting of local judges, clergymen and farmers as well as appellate judges and law professors, to try these cases. The lawyers on the commission objected to the acceptance of testimony from children and alleged accomplices, and they entertained serious doubts about the authenticity of the children's statements. But those sceptics constituted a minority, and the commissions secured a large number of convictions. The Court of Appeal provided less support for the panic, but it did confirm a number of sentences sent to it from local courts. The panic did not come to an end until the trials moved south to Stockholm. There the Court of Appeal began to interrogate witnesses directly rather than rely on the criminal dossier submitted by the lower courts. Shortly thereafter some of the children who had lodged the accusations began to confess before the royal commission that their stories were fabricated and that the accused were innocent. The trials came to an abrupt end and the government prosecuted some of the main witnesses, including a thirteen year-old boy (Ankarloo, 1990: 294–300).

The great Swedish trials of the 1660s and 1670s did not bring a complete end to witch-hunting in Sweden, but they certainly marked the beginning of its precipitate decline. It appears that Swedish lawyers, and probably also many members of local communities, experienced a crisis of confidence not unlike that which had occurred in places like Würzburg. After 1676 there were only isolated trials in different parts of the country, and the Court of Appeal, taking more care in the evaluation of evidence than it had in the hunt of 1668–76, confirmed only a few sentences. When another panic occurred in the western province of Värmland in the 1720s, complete with child witnesses, stories of flying to Blåkulla, and the illegal use of torture, the court of Appeal reversed all the sentences and, as it had in 1676, prosecuted those who had brought the charges of witchcraft in the first place. The experience of 1668–76 had introduced a level of caution and judicial scepticism that prevented intense witch-hunting from ever occurring again.

A third large hunt that led directly to the expression of judicial scepticism and the decline of witchcraft prosecutions was the operation conducted by the Spanish Inquisition in the Basque country between 1609 and 1611. This hunt, the largest and most famous in Spanish history, had many of the characteristics of the large chain-reaction hunts, although it did not involve the extensive use of torture. The episode began with the apparently uncoerced confessions of some villagers in Zugarramurdi in the kingdom of Navarre that they were attending sabbaths where they worshipped the Devil with large numbers of their neighbors. A panel of inquisitors investigated these confessions, tried those who had confessed or had been accused, executed six of the witches and another five in effigy, and solicited new confessions by promulgating an edict of Faith by which those admitting their crime would be reconciled with the Church. In the course of the hunt inquisitors received the confessions of some 1,300 children, who admitted that they had been taken to the sabbath. In the midst of this investigation, one of the inquisitors, Alonso Salazar de Frias, became sceptical regarding the reality of the witches' confessions, especially those of the children. He conducted a painstaking interrogation of all those who had confessed, ultimately reaching the conclusion that the entire thing was a 'chimera' and that the confessions were the result of fantasy which had arisen from youthful imagination, parental or clerical suggestion, or local rumour (Henningsen, 1980).

Salazar did not deny the possibility of witchcraft, but his recognition that in this case hundreds of persons had made false confessions and that a smaller number had been wrongly convicted and executed led him to propose a strict set of procedural rules for the Inquisition to follow in all future investigations and trials of the crime. These rules, which included the mandatory review of all sentences by the highest tribunal of the Inquisition in Madrid, had a powerful impact on the prosecution of witches in Spain for the remainder of the seventeenth century (Henningsen, 1980: 358–86). Prosecutions for various forms of magic continued, some of which were classified as witchcraft, but the records of the Inquisition after 1614 reveal few trials for attending the witches' sabbath, and capital punishment for witchcraft became a rarity. The new guidelines did not put an end to prosecutions in the local secular courts, especially in the kingdom of Aragon (Gari Lacruz, 1980; Monter, 1990: 274–5), but there is no question that the steps Salazar and the Inquisitors at Madrid took in response to the excesses of the Basque witch-hunt of 1609–11 marked a turning point in the history of Spanish witchcraft, signaling the beginning of a long decline (Henningsen, 1980: 387–9).

The last two witch-hunts illustrating the development of legal scepticism involved the accusation of witches by persons who were allegedly possessed by demons. These accusations, much more than the naming of accomplices under torture, were the main mechanisms by which these hunts spread. The first occurred in the Roman Catholic bishopric of Paderborn in the late 1650s. It began when two young nuns from the small village of Brakel displayed the symptoms of demonic possession. The symptoms spread rapidly among the female teenage population in the village and ultimately infected about 200 persons in Paderborn itself. The entire episode received great encouragement from Bernhard Loeper, a Jesuit professor of theology at the University of Paderborn who performed a number of exorcisms mainly to prove that the Roman Catholic church was the one true church founded by Christ. As in many cases of possession, the demoniacs accused others of harming them by witchcraft, and these accusations led to the execution of approximately twenty witches and the murder of another ten (Decker, 1995).

During this hunt the bishop of the diocese, Dietrich Adolf von der Recke, engaged in a correspondence with the Vatican regarding the treatment of possession and exorcism. The main spokesman for the Vatican, Ferdinand von Fürstenberg, was highly sceptical of the authenticity of the possessions, and he also made a series of recommendations regarding the proper procedure for prosecuting witches. These recommendations, which reflect the traditional caution of the Roman Inquisition regarding both possession and witchcraft, helped to bring the hunt to an end in 1658. When Dietrich Adolf died in 1661 Fürstenberg was appointed to succeed him. With the knowledge of what had happened a few years before, Fürstenberg insisted upon due process in all witchcraft cases originating within his jurisdiction, and he confirmed only one execution during his entire episcopate. By the time he died in 1683 Paderborn had witnessed its last witchcraft trial, although prosecutions in the neighbouring duchy of Westphalia, which had its own judicial apparatus, continued with a vengeance until the end of the century (Decker, 1981–2).

The witchcraft episode at Paderborn in the 1650s can be compared in a number of respects with the much more famous one that occurred at Salem, Massachusetts, in 1692. This hunt began when a group of teenage girls, manifesting the signs of demonic possession, accused three women of afflicting them by means of witchcraft. The hunt spread rapidly, aided greatly by the girls' identification of other individuals whom they claimed were the source of their afflictions. Further accusations came from other people in nearby towns like Andover who, in the midst of the tremendous fear generated by the trials, accused their neighbours of maleficent and diabolical activities. The number of individuals named as witches rose to almost 200, of whom 30 were convicted and 19 were executed. In the midst of the trials, however, the leading men in the colony, especially the clergy, began to doubt whether those who had been accused and executed were in fact guilty as charged. One of the most prominent ministers, Increase Mather, delivered a sermon in which he claimed it would be better for ten suspected witches to be set free than one innocent one condemned. In response to these concerns the colonial government forbade further imprisonments, released those still in gaol, and dissolved the court that had conducted the prosecutions (Boyer and Nissenbaum, 1974: 9–21; Hoffer, 1996).

There were two main sources of the judicial scepticism that emerged during the Salem trials. The first was a breakdown of the stereotype of the witch, similar to that which had occurred at Würzburg and in other German territories. The original set of accusations at Salem had been directed at old, relatively poor or marginalized women within the community, but as the accusations spread, men and women of much higher social standing, including some wealthy Bostonian merchants and Lady Phipps, the wife of the governor of Massachusetts, were implicated (Boyer and Nissenbaum, 1974: 32; Midelfort, 1979: 285–8). The second source was a growing recognition that the special court of oyer et terminer which had been established to try the witches had failed to adhere to prevailing standards of judicial proof. Contemporary critiques of the trials by Increase Mather, Thomas Brattle, Samuel Willard, Robert Calef and John Hale all focused on the insufficiency of the evidence that was used (Willard, 1692; Mather, 1693; Calef, 1700; Hale, 1702; Burr, 1914: 69–90). In particular they denied the reliability of spectral evidence, the testimony of afflicted persons that they could see the spectres of the witches who were allegedly harming them. The jurors who had returned the guilty verdicts in the trials echoed this line of argument in 1693 when they issued a public recantation, claiming that they had been deluded by the powers of darkness and had condemned persons to death on the basis of insufficient evidence (Drake, 1866). This criticism of the trials and the recantation of the jurors not only brought the Salem witch-hunt to a sudden halt, but it also signaled the end of witch-hunting throughout New England. After 1692 only one witch, Mary Disborough of Hartford, was convicted, and she was reprieved on the grounds that the evidence against her was insufficient (Taylor, 1908). The last trial in New England, which resulted in an acquittal, took place in Massachusetts in 1697.

The judicial scepticism that emerged in the wake of these large witchhunts was in large part responsible for the significant changes that occurred in the conduct and supervision of witchcraft trials in virtually every European jurisdiction in the late seventeenth and early eighteenth centuries. These changes were sometimes prescribed in formal documents, such as the procedural guidelines that Spanish and Italian inquisitors received from their superiors or the edicts that royal governments published concerning the trial of witches. At other times judges and inquisitors made the changes themselves, on their own initiative, during the trials. Four changes in particular had a bearing on the number of witchcraft trials and convictions and executions: 1) the tighter control, supervision and regulation of local witchcraft trials by central or superior courts; 2) the restriction and in some cases the prohibition of torture in witchcraft cases; 3) the adherence of trial judges to more demanding standards of proof; and 4) the admission of more lawyers to represent witches at their trials.

The regulation of local justice

The most clear-cut and decisive change that took place in the conduct of witchcraft prosecutions, one that was linked to the other three, was the greater regulation of local justice by either central or superior judicial authorities. In order to appreciate the importance of such control, we must recognize that the most severe witch-hunts in early modern Europe were conducted by local officials who operated with a certain amount of independence from central state control. This is not to say that central governments did not from time to time participate in or even initiate witch-hunts. In a few instances even the rulers of kingdoms and principalities helped to fuel witch-hunts. King James VI of Scotland played an active role in starting the great witch-hunt that took place in his kingdom in 1591, while Christian IV of Denmark apparently had a hand in the hunt at Køge in 1612 (Larner, 1984: 3–33; Johansen, 1990: 345–6). In seventeenth-century Hungary two Transylvanian princes, Gábor Bathlen and Mihály Apafy, brought charges of witchcraft against their aristocratic enemies, leading to a set of high profile trials (Klaniczay, 1991–2: 75). Even in the early eighteenth century, when witch-hunting was declining in most parts of Europe, the senate of the kingdom of Piedmont initiated a series of witchcraft trials in which the primary victim of the crime was none other than the first-born son of King Vittorio Amedeo II (Loriga, 1994).

It is also true that throughout the entire period of the witch-hunts central state authorities granted local judges and magistrates the legal authority they needed in order to hold witch trials. But there is an enormous body of evidence showing that the areas in which witch-hunting was most intense over a long period of time were those jurisdictions in which central state power was relatively weak (Soman, 1989; Levack, 1996). Indeed, this is one of the main reasons why so many witch-panics took place in the relatively small duchies, principalities, and bishoprics within the Holy Roman Empire. There is also evidence that in those states that did have relatively strong central judicial establishments, the most serious witch-hunts occurred in communities which found ways to ignore or circumvent active state supervision of witch trials.

There were two main reasons why central authorities tended to exercise much more restraint than local judges in handling witchcraft cases. The first has to do with the level of involvement in witch-hunting. Judges from central courts, whether they were hearing cases on appeal or serving as itinerant justices, tended to be less likely than village or municipal judges to share the fears regarding witchcraft that gripped all members of the local communities. It is true that occasionally a zealous witch-hunter or inquisitor coming from outside the community would actually instill fears of witchcraft that had not previously arisen, but the more common sources of witch-hunting were the fears and animosities that prevailed within the local community. The second reason is that central judicial authorities had more legal training than local judges and usually were more deeply committed to the maintenance of what we would today call due process. They were therefore less likely than local authorities to tolerate the gross judicial abuses, such as the improper administration of torture, that frequently characterized local witch-hunts. In his discussion of the proper administration of torture, the Saxon jurist Benedikt Carpzov, observed that in small jurisdictions, county districts, and even in the larger towns, where legally ignorant plebeians and mechanics served as judges, innocent men and women were often tortured and forced to confess. Carpzov, who was no friend to witches, concluded that without judicial supervision the guilty would be set free and the innocent punished (Carpzov, 1670).

The differences in judicial outlook between central and local authorities often resulted in deliberate efforts by judges from the central legal establishment to enforce stricter rules of criminal procedure, to demand that all prosecutions be warranted by central authority, to insist that death sentences in witchcraft cases be reviewed on appeal, and to punish those local officials who violated established procedural norms. These efforts were often sustained over a long period of time, and they did not always meet with success. Occasionally the central authorities tolerated violations of their own high procedural standards. Ultimately, however, the state authorities that made such efforts succeeded in bringing about a permanent reduction in the number of prosecutions and executions.

The classic example of the way in which central authorities contained the witch-hunting zeal of local officials comes from the large portion of northern France that was subject to the jurisdiction of the parlement of Paris, one of the nine royal courts that exercised an appellate jurisdiction in the country. In 1587–8 a large witch-panic broke out in the Champagne-Ardennes region, which fell within the jurisdiction of the Parisian tribunal. In this local panic, which claimed hundreds of lives, all semblance of due process appears to have vanished. In an effort to discover the identity of witches, village judges were using the popular method of swimming those who had been named, a vestige of the medieval ordeal by cold water which was now illegal. Local officials were also torturing suspects without restraint and executing them in summary fashion. In response to this crisis the parlement proposed a policy of obligatory judicial review of all witchcraft convictions, an unprecedented imposition of central judicial authority on the French localities. The implementation of this policy, which involved the punishment of local officials for violating procedural norms, was a most delicate process. Nevertheless, the policy of automatic appeals was formally adopted in 1604 and published as an edict in 1624. From the adoption of that policy one can trace the decline of witch-hunting within the parlement's jurisdiction, even if some of the later sentences were upheld on appeal (Soman, 1986, 1978).

A similar pattern to that which obtained in France can be found in Spain, where witchcraft was considered a crime of mixed jurisdiction and could be prosecuted either by the Spanish Inquisition, an ecclesiastical institution that was under the authority of the king, or the secular courts. The Inquisition was a highly centralized, national institution, consisting of nineteen (ultimately 21) regional tribunals which reported to, and were supervised by, a central court, *la Suprema*, in Madrid. One of the functions of this central tribunal, which was headed by the Inquisitor General, was to enforce procedural rules in the trial of the crimes brought before it. The first set of guidelines, which were issued in 1526 in the wake of a witch-hunt in Navarre, were intended to govern the activities of inquisitors who tried witches in the regional tribunals. These guidelines restricted the practice of confiscating a witch's property, required consultation with the Suprema before convicting a witch a second time, and forbade the arrest or conviction of a witch solely on the basis of another witch's confession. These rules, coupled with a tradition of leniency that those rules encouraged, were in large part responsible for keeping executions for witchcraft in Spain at extremely low levels during the sixteenth century. Indeed, on a number of occasions the Inquisition succeeded in acquiring jurisdiction over cases of witchcraft that had originated in the secular courts and reversed the sentences of death that had been pronounced on the victims (Monter, 1990a,b: 268–9).

The Spanish Inquisition's impressive record of tight regulation and judicial leniency in witchcraft cases did not remain unblemished. A major lapse occurred in the great Basque witch-hunt of 1609–11. As we have seen, however, the inquisitor Alonso Salazar de Frias succeeded in returning the Inquisition to its traditional posture of judicial restraint. The new instructions that Salazar drafted and which the Inquisition issued in 1614 stand as a testament to the efforts of central authorities to regulate the conduct of officials in lower courts in order to contain the spread of witch panics. In addition to restating many of the guidelines of 1526, and issuing new instructions regarding the taking and recording of confessions and denunciations, the Inquisition also dissociated itself from the tactics followed by local authorities who had, 'without any legal authority, exposed the subjects to such abuses in order to make them confess and witness against others'. Moreover, as in France, the Inquisition took steps to punish the parties that had been responsible for these miscarriages of justice, turning them over to the High Court of Navarre and promising that in the future the Inquisition itself would proceed against them with the greatest severity (Henningsen, 1980: 375).

The conflict between the Suprema and local authorities continued after the publication of the new instructions. In a number of cases, most notably in northern Vizcaya, the Inquisition found it necessary to intervene in local witch-hunts conducted by secular authorities, reversing sentences and preventing executions. In a few other localities, most notably in Catalonia and Aragon, it chose to intervene belatedly if at all, and consequently hundreds of witches were executed (Monter, 1990a,b: 275). But in the long run la Suprema, which was the most highly centralized judicial institution in Spain, succeeded in enforcing a policy of judicial caution that not only kept executions for witchcraft at a minimum after 1614 but also brought about their ultimate termination.

The Spanish pattern was in many respects mirrored in Italy, where a centralized Roman Inquisition, which had been established in 1542, maintained control over witchcraft prosecutions long after ecclesiastical tribunals in northern European lands had deferred to secular courts in prosecuting witches. The record of the Roman Inquisition regarding witchcraft is even more impressive than that of its Spanish counterpart. Not only did it develop a strong tradition of leniency in sentencing witches, but it also insisted upon adherence to strict procedural rules in the conduct of witchcraft trials (Tedeschi, 1990). As in Spain, the enforcement of these rules was entrusted to the highest tribunal in the Inquisitorial organization, the Congregation of the Holy Office in Rome. Thus once again, as in France and Spain, a centralized institution assumed the role of regulating justice on a lower level.

The quintessential statement of the judicial caution that characterized the Roman Inquisition was the *Instructio pro formandis processibus in causis strigum sortilegiorum et maleficiorum*. Drafted in the early 1620s during the pontificate of Gregory XV, it circulated widely in manuscript until 1655, when Cesare Carena, fiscal of the Roman Inquisition, annotated and published it as an appendix to his *Tractatus de officio sanctissimae Inquisitione*. Reflecting the influence of the Spanish Inquisition's new instructions of 1614, the *Instructio* dealt with all aspects of criminal procedure, establishing strict rules for examining accused witches, calling for restraint in the administration of torture and recommending particular care in the evaluation of witches' confessions. The most revealing part of this document, however, is the preface, which explains why the instructions had been drafted in the first place. The authors referred to the grave errors that were committed daily by ordinaries, vicars and inquisitors in witchcraft trials, including the use of defective forms of process, the administration of excessive torture, conviction on the most slender evidence, and the turning over of suspects to the secular courts. As Carena observed in his commentary, the atrocity of the crime had led inferior judges to disregard all the rules (Lea, 1939: 952–3). The *Instructio* was intended to remedy this problem.

The instructions drafted by the Roman Inquisition in the 1620s may have had an even more pronounced effect on witch-hunting than the rules adopted by the Spanish Inquisition in 1614. We know for example that in 1649 Cardinal Barberini of the Holy Office used the guidelines contained in the manuscript version of the document to prevent the execution of one of the *benandanti* or sleepwalkers who had confessed to infanticide before the Venetian Inquisition (Ginzburg, 1983: 125–9). After the publication of the *Instructio* in 1657 convictions for witchcraft throughout Italy declined dramatically, even in the secular courts, over which the Inquisition established its jurisdictional supremacy (Martin, 1989: 203–4). Nor did the influence of the Roman Holy Office and its procedures end there. The *Instructio* appeared in many different editions in the late seventeenth and eighteenth centuries, and it was also appended to various editions and translations of Friedrich Spee's *Cautio Criminalis*. In 1669 Cardinal Czartoriski of Poland used the instructions in order to restrain witch-hunting in his native country. The *Instructio* also served as the basis of the advice that Ferdinand von Fürstenberg sent to the bishop of Paderborn in 1657 and which Fürstenberg himself enforced as bishop after 1661, the year in which the *Instructio* was translated into German (Decker, 1995: 112). Just as the publication of demonological works had helped to disseminate the learned concept of witchcraft and thus encourage prosecutions, so the printing of cautious or sceptical works like the *Instructio* helped to make the legal community throughout Europe aware of the dangers of the unrestrained prosecution of the crime.

Even in countries which did not have strong central governments, higher judicial authorities who supervised the conduct of local courts demonstrated an ability to moderate the excesses of witch-hunting. This was particularly true in certain parts of Germany. Most German territories lay within the Holy Roman Empire, a political structure not known for the strength of its central judicial institutions. Indeed, one of the main reasons why the overwhelming majority of European witchcraft prosecutions and executions occurred in German territories, especially those that were relatively small, was the inability of imperial judicial authorities to control the operation of criminal justice in the numerous duchies, principalities and other political units within the Empire. In particular the Empire was never able to develop a regular and effective process by which cases could be referred or appealed to the *Reichskammergericht* or imperial supreme court which sat at Speyer, although that tribunal did succeed in reversing a number of sentences during the period of witch-hunting (Merzbacher, 1970: 63–4; Wolf, 1995: 785). There were, however, two other types of superior judicial institutions in Germany that could, and at times did, exercise a restraining influence on witch-hunting, contributing eventually to its decline. The first were the central courts of the various duchies and principalities, especially those in the largest states, where witch-hunting tended to be more moderate than in the mid-sized territories and bishoprics. Judicial councils in places like Stuttgart, Munich, and Berlin all tended to have this negative effect on witch-hunting, especially in the late seventeenth and eighteenth centuries.

The second set of superior judicial institutions in Germany were not courts at all but the law faculties of the German universities. The imperial code promulgated by Charles V in 1532, the *Constitutio criminalis Carolina* required that when local courts confronted difficult cases, they would consult with the jurists in the law faculty of the nearest university. These consultations, which dealt with the successive stages of arrest, torture and judgment in the criminal process, served as one of the few mechanisms that could prevent local German courts from violating due process and conducting large witch-hunts.

During most of the period of witch-hunting, consultation with the law faculties in cases of witchcraft did litde to restrain witch-hunting. Indeed, the consultations often had the opposite effect, as jurists, being familiar with demonological theory and committed to the rigorous prosecution of the crime, probably did more to facilitate than to restrain the prosecution of the accused and to spread learned witch-beliefs throughout Germany (Schormann, 1977: 9–44, 158; Lorenz, 1982). In the late seventeenth century, however, the consultations began to have the opposite effect, as jurists started to advise the use of extreme caution in the prosecution of the crime and to secure acquittals rather than convictions. This change was particularly evident at the University of Tübingen, which began to recommend against torturing witches and in favour of acquitting them in a majority of cases in the 1660s (Schormann, 1977: 20–1). A similar but less dramatic change occurred at the University of Helmstedt in the 1660s, and that change contributed to the striking decline in the percentage of executions for witchcraft in the principality of Braunschweig-Wolfenbüt- tel, which consulted with the Helmstedt jurists on a regular basis. Between 1648 and 1670 the number of acquittals in witchcraft cases in that principality exceeded the number of capital sentences for the first time (Schormann, 1977: 24, 57).

One of the earliest examples of this insistence on judicial caution by members of the university law faculties comes from an opinion of Ernst Cothmann, professor of law at Rostock in the 1620s, the decade in which the Roman *Instructio* was written. The opinion, which recommended and secured the acquittal of an accused witch, is largely taken up with a critique of the various *indicia*, or pieces of circumstantial evidence, upon which the local judge had based his decision to torture the accused. It also reveals the insufficiency of the proofs that the judge had used to convict her. Just like the *Instructio,* this opinion took local officials to task for proceeding recklessly in the prosecution of witchcraft and thus for sending innocent people to the stake (Hauber, 1738: 2. 27–55). A similar decision, drafted by Paul von Fuchs, a jurist at the University of Duisburg, in 1662 concluded that the burgomaster of the town of Rietberg in Westphalia in 1662, who had been accused of witchcraft, should be acquitted and released (Hauber, 1738: 1. 614–35). That decision apparendy put a permanent end to witch-hunting in Rietberg. A third decision, drafted by the law faculty at the University of Halle regarding the procedures used in the trial of Barbara Labarentin in 1694, had an even wider impact, since it led one of the members of that faculty, Christian Thomasius, to develop his ideas regarding witch trials. In 1699 Thomasius recommended that students in his faculty be taught that witchcraft prosecutions should have their own distinctive form of *inquisitionsprozess*, in which special caution was to be observed (Wolf, 1995: 865). Two years later he published his treatise *De Crimine Magiae,* in which he claimed that all witchcraft prosecutions should be abandoned (Thomasius, 1701). Thomasius's scepticism, therefore, just like that of Spee and Salazar, had its origins in his efforts to contain the excesses of local justice.

The restriction and prohibition of torture

When superior judicial authorities took steps to remedy the procedural abuses that occurred in local jurisdictions they were almost always concerned, at least in part, with the improper administration of torture. This should not surprise us. Not only was torture frequently used in the prosecution of witches, especially in those areas of Europe influenced by Roman law, but as a judicial practice it was particularly open to abuse. When torture was revived in the ecclesiastical and secular courts in the thirteenth century, with the clear purpose of obtaining confessions to concealed crimes, jurists recognized that the procedure might easily lead innocent persons to make false confessions in order to stop the pain. In order to prevent this from happening and thus to make the evidence obtained from confessions more reliable, jurists formulated a set of rules requiring that a certain amount of evidence of guilt be produced before torture could be administered. This evidence was usually weighted as a percentage of a full proof, which in the Roman-canonical tradition consisted of either the testimony of two-eye-witnesses or a confession. One eye-witness or circumstantial evidence that was the equivalent of this half-proof was usually required for torture to proceed. In order to prevent prosecution on trumped up-charges there also had to be evidence that a crime had actually been committed – the famous *corpus delicti*. Other rules governed the duration and intensity of the torture, and all confessions obtained under torture had to be repeated outside the torture chamber. Yet another set of rules was intended to restrict or deny the prosecution of a criminaPs alleged accomplices on the basis of confessions obtained under torture.

These rules did not serve as a rationale for the system of torture, but they did attempt to limit its arbitrary potential and made judges more confident that it would serve its intended purpose. The problem arose when those rules were either relaxed or completely ignored in the interests of obtaining convictions from persons who were assumed to be guilty but for whose guilt there was little tangible evidence. Relaxation of this sort was very common in trials for witchcraft, since it was widely regarded as a *crimen exceptum*, an excepted crime, in which the usual standards of proof did not apply. And while relaxation became the rule in courts administered by trained judges, the complete ignorance or suspension of the rules occurred frequently in trials conducted by untrained laymen or clerics in small communities.

In the seventeenth and early eighteenth centuries the administration of torture in all criminal cases, and particularly in witchcraft cases, came under attack, resulting ultimately in the prohibition of torture in all European jurisdictions. The earliest critiques appeared in the first half of the seventeenth century. In addition to Spee, two Jesuits from Ingolstadt, Adam Tanner and Paul Laymann, wrote large works on moral theology that included sections on the use of torture in witchcraft trials (Tanner, 1626–7: 3. 981–22; Laymann, 1629; Kneubühler, 1977: 142–59; Behringer, 1987: 256–8). Both of these books, like Spee's, reflected first-hand experience with the trials themselves. From the Protestant side came works by Johann Meyfarth, a Lutheran professor from Erfurt whose work betrayed a heavy reliance on Spee, and Johannes Grevius, a Dutch Arminian theologian who condemned the use of torture by Christians for any purpose whatsoever (Grevius, 1624; Meyfarth, 1635).

This body of critical work on torture continued to grow in the late seventeenth century. The appearance of new works at that late date attests to the continued use of the procedure, even after its employment in witchcraft prosecutions had become less frequent. Three of these later works achieved fairly widespread circulation. In 1682 the Burgundian judge Augustin Nicolas wrote a closely reasoned assault on the practice, *Si la Torture est un moyen seur á verifier les crimes secrets: dissertation morale et juridique.* The second work, a dissertation by Meint Johan Sassen, of the University of Halle, was published in 1697 and went into several printings, while the third, which also came from the law faculty at Halle, was a dissertation by Christian Thomasius, the jurist who is known mainly for his earlier work, *De Crimine Magiae* (1701). Thomasius's dissertation on torture, which was published in 1705, also provided the basis for his more comprehensive treatise on criminal procedure in witchcraft cases that appeared in print in 1712 (Thomasius, 1705, 1712, 1986). Thomasius drew heavily on the earlier works of Spee, Tanner, and Meyfarth, but he also gave his treatise a distinctly Protestant flavour. A Pietist known for his anti-clericalism, Thomasius argued in the manner of Grevius that torture was an unchristian means of extorting the truth, that it was never mentioned in Scripture, and that the 'tyrannical' papacy had used it to strike down their enemies under the pretext of heresy and witchcraft (Thomasius, 1705).

The main criticism of torture in all these works was not so much that the procedure was inhumane, although Grevius, Nicolas and Thomasius all made that point, but that the evidence obtained by means of its administration was unreliable, since innocent persons would make false admissions in order to stop the pain. This criticism of torture was therefore just one manifestation of a more general change in attitudes towards legal evidence and proof that will be discussed below. The criticism possessed more than mere academic significance. In those jurisdictions where torture was routinely administered in witchcraft cases, it contributed directly to a reduction in the number of convictions and executions and ultimately to a decline in the number of trials as well.

Before looking at the specific elements of this critique, it is important to make three qualifications. First, the arguments against torture, as they were articulated in the seventeenth century, were not new. Many of the criticisms of the procedure had been advanced in the late Middle Ages in the context of heresy trials, while the judicial reformers and witchcraft sceptics of the sixteenth and early seventeenth centuries, especially the Dutch priest Cornelius Loos (1546–95), had applied them to trials for witchcraft. What made seventeenth-century judges and jurists more receptive than their predecessors to the arguments for restraint and caution was a more general change in attitude towards the evaluation of judicial evidence, coupled with the recognition that justice had obviously miscarried in the large chain-reaction hunts of the seventeenth century.

Second, even when the critics began to command an audience, the witch-hunters always managed to restate the traditional defence of the practice. Shortly after the publication of Adam Tanner and Friedrich Spee's passionate attacks on the system of torture, the Saxon judge and jurist Benedikt Carpzov published his famous *Practica Rerum Criminalium* (1635). In this manual on the criminal law, known later as 'the Lutheran *Malleus*' Carpzov presented a systematic defence of the procedure and claimed that in cases of witchcraft proof was so difficult to obtain that the judge need not be restricted by the rules (Carpzov, 1670: 145–207). For every Hermann Löher, the German judicial official who condemned the torture of innocent witches at Rheinbach in the 1630s and whose opposition to the trials forced him to flee to Amsterdam, there was a Nikolaus von Beckman, the German-born jurist and convert to Catholicism who conducted a number of brutal witch trials near Graz and Steiermark in the 1680s and who complained that the Devil appeared as a squirrel during torture in order to help the guilty survive (Löher, 1676; Robbins, 1959: 308–9; Wolf, 1995: 932). In other words, the arguments of the judicial sceptics, just like those of the philosophical sceptics, were always contested.

Third, the actual abolition of torture in most European jurisdictions came after the effective end of witchcraft prosecutions and sometimes even after formal decriminalization. Only in two countries, Scotland and Hungary, did abolition take place before the last witchcraft trial. Most of the prohibitions of torture formed part of a broader reform of criminal procedure that many continental European states undertook in the last quarter of the eighteenth century and first quarter of the nineteenth. The first country in continental Europe to abolish torture was Prussia in 1754, forty years after King Frederick William I had issued an edict against witch-hunting. The last European territory to follow suit was the Swiss canton of Glarus, which took the step in 1851, long after the last legal execution for witchcraft in that territory (and in all of Europe) in 1782. Moreover, the abolition of torture in Europe was in large part inspired by humanitarian concerns that had not been prominent in earlier critiques. The decline of witch-prosecutions therefore had much more to do with the *regulation* and *limitation* of torture than with its formal elimination.

The seventeenth- and early eighteenth-century critics of torture, writing in the context of witchcraft trials, made four specific points. The first was that torture should not be allowed on the basis of mere ill fame (*infamia*) or insufficient circumstantial evidence (*indicia*). The rationale for torturing witches on the basis of such limited or unsubstantiated evidence was the claim that witchcraft was a *crimen exceptum*, an exceptional crime in which the normal rules of evidence do not apply. Beginning in the 1620s, which was a particularly intense period of witch-hunting in Germany, a number of jurists, most notably Ernst Cothmann, presented the unorthodox but not entirely novel argument that witchcraft was not a *crimen exceptum*. If that were the case, trials for witchcraft would have to conform to the more exacting legal requirements spelled out in the *Carolina*. Cothmann also argued that the less demanding evidentiary requirements in hidden crimes should apply only to the initiation of legal proceedings, not to the administration of torture, an argument that was later fully developed by Cesare Carena in the 1650s (Hauber, 1738; Lea, 1939, 2: 601–4). Soon after the appearance of Cothmann's decision, Paul Laymann argued that in cases of witchcraft and heresy the *indicia* must be *stronger* rather than weaker than in other criminal cases, so much so that judges for all intents and purposes had to be persuaded of the guilt of the accused before resorting to torture, the confession being needed simply to establish the technical requirements of full proof (Laymann, 1629).

A second criticism, closely related to the first, was directed against the arbitrary or excessive use of torture, a practice which once again had been justified on the basis of the exceptional nature of the crime. Extreme cruelty was by far the most widespread abuse of the system, and the criticism of such excesses, on both moral and legal grounds, became the most powerful and enduring argument against the entire procedure. It was central to Hermann Löher's *Hochnötige Klage,* which claimed that victims would confess to almost anything when torture was repeated, as well as to the critiques presented by Spee and Tanner. It is important to note that the same criticism of torture was often voiced by those who accepted the practice under certain circumstances, such as the Spanish and Italian inquisitors who drafted the instructions of 1614 and 1623 respectively. The Roman *Instructio,* for example, prohibited the administration of torture by jerking the ropes in the administration of *strappado,* by attaching weights to the feet, and for periods of more than one hour. Repetition was to be forbidden except in the most serious cases, in which the court was required to consult with the Congregation before proceeding. As this last rule suggests, the criticism of excessive torture was also closely bound up with the regulation of local justice, since the most flagrant abuses of the practice had occurred within relatively small or minor jurisdictions.

The third criticism of torture, which may have done more to reduce the number of prosecutions than any other single factor, was directed at the common practice of torturing those who were named by confessing witches as their accomplices. In ordinary crimes such denunciations could not be admitted as evidence, but once again the definition of witchcraft as a *crimen exceptum* allowed the judge to ignore the standard cautionary rules. The use of torture in this way had become routine in areas where belief in the sabbath was strong, and in some German bishoprics, such as Trier, Bamberg and Würzburg, it had resulted in hundreds of executions. The practice raised two legal questions. The first was whether witches whose torture had led to their conviction could be tortured a second time to extract the names of accomplices. The second was whether those persons whom the convicted witch named as accomplices could themselves be tortured without any other supporting evidence. On both legal questions learned opinion was divided, although it is important to note that the most widely read demonologist of the seventeenth century, the Jesuit Martin Del Rio, had defended the practice in unequivocal terms, and had even claimed that the judge's suggestion of names during the administration of torture was legal. The torture of those persons had been deemed necessary in order to confirm the testimony of the witches (Lea, 1939: 649). The first scholar to engage Del Rio on this issue was Adam Tanner. Tanner did not deny the propriety of seeking evidence from accomplices of those who had confessed to exceptional crimes. But he objected that mere denunciation, even by more than one confessing witch, did not justify either torture or condemnation of those who had been of good reputation prior to their denunciation. The danger was that under torture innocent persons would confess to crimes they did not commit, the same danger that Spee identified in his *Cautio Criminalis*.

The final criticism of torture was a rebuttal of the claim that God would intervene in the process in order to protect the innocent. This same argument had served as a defence of the medieval ordeals before their abolition in 1215. Tanner, Grevius, and even the French jurists who drafted the *Grande ordonnance criminelle* of 1670, which identified torture as an archaic practice similar to the old ordeals, had shown the weakness of this defence (Peters, 1985: 85). Tanner was particularly eloquent in destroying this argument, claiming that if God had permitted martyrdoms, wars and massacres, there was no assurance that he would not permit the execution of innocent persons named as witches by allowing them to incriminate themselves under torture (Tanner, 1626–7).

The arguments of Tanner and Grevius against providential intervention in the torture chamber went hand in hand with criticisms of the swimming of witches, a popular and technically illegal practice which stood as a remnant of the practice of the water ordeal and which had been formally abolished as a method of judicial proof in 1215. Most lawyers, including the German jurist Johann Goedelmann and even Jean Bodin, condemned it, denying that it had any probative value. Goedelmann considered it a superstition invented by the Devil and claimed that judges who used it should be prosecuted (Goedelmann, 1592: 1: cap. 5: 21–30). In England the physician John Cotta characterized this 'Vulgar trial of witchcraft' as a barbarous exercise of 'uncivil force and lawless violence.' Nevertheless it did not lack learned or powerful advocates, including King James VI of Scotland, who claimed it could serve as an indication of the divine will (James VI, 1597: 81; Unsworth, 1989: 96–8). Swimming never became an accepted part of the legal process against witches in England or Scotland, but in some European localities it served as one of the *indicia* that justified the use of torture. In France village judges occasionally authorized its use, although they did so without the permission of the superior courts (Soman, 1986: 11–12; 1989: 6). In Hungary, where the old ordeals persisted well into the eighteenth century, municipal courts used the swimming test and compurgation on a regular basis (Kristóf, 1991–2: 99–100). In parts of Westphalia the swimming test apparently served as a final proof of guilt as late as the seventeenth century (Lea, 1939: 892–3). German jurists, however, uniformly condemned the procedure, and by the eighteenth century it had became the exclusive property of the popular community (Brähm, 1709: 47). In many parts of Europe the swimming of witches continued long after decriminalization (Gijswijt-Hofstra in this volume).

As legal writers and judges began to adopt a more cautious approach to the administration of torture, a more fundamental change in legal procedure began to reduce the premium on obtaining confessions under torture. This was the emergence of the possibility of non-capital punishments in all felony convictions, including witchcraft. Such sentences had always been possible in England, where the witchcraft statutes of 1563 and 1604 had provided for non-capital punishment for certain categories of offences, but these options were more difficult to exercise on the Continent, where judicial discretion was greatly limited and where the only officially recognized punishment for a crime like witchcraft was death. Recognition that the only alternative to capital punishment was acquittal provided judges with a powerful incentive to use torture to extort the requisite confession for conviction. The introduction of transportation, imprisonment and corporal punishment (classified as *poena extraordinaria*) as penalties for major crimes in continental jurisdictions changed all this, while the precedent of punishing a person for the 'suspicion' of a capital crime (*Verdachtstrafe*) without full proof gave judges a legal justification for the new sentences (Langbein, 1976; Damaska, 1978). These sentences were meted out in large numbers in Italy, Spain, and Portugal, where both torture and executions for the crimes of magic and witchcraft almost disappeared in the late seventeenth and eighteenth centuries. The new punishments in witchcraft cases also became common in France after the edict of 1682 and in the Austrian Empire after the promulgation of the *Constitutio Theresiana* in 1768. Both of those laws, just like the Prussian edict of 1714, also made it virtually impossible for judges to administer torture in witchcraft cases.

New standards of evidence

As suggested above, the questions raised regarding the administration of torture in witchcraft cases formed part of a more general set of concerns about the admission and evaluation of judicial evidence. During the seventeenth century judges and legal writers throughout Europe showed themselves increasingly reluctant to accept the evidence that was presented to them to justify the conviction and execution of witches. This caution led to the realization that the crime of witchcraft was extremely difficult, if not impossible to prove. This conclusion may have contributed to, or received support from, a more fundamental belief that witchcraft itself was an impossible act, as shall be discussed below. But the legal conclusion, taken by itself, was of incalculable importance in bringing witchcraft trials to an end. It led directly to the increasing number of acquittals that occurred in virtually all jurisdictions, and it also contributed to the ultimate realization that witchcraft as a crime could no longer be effectively prosecuted.

The sceptical attitude towards evidence in witchcraft cases, just like scepticism regarding the possibility of the crime, was not completely absent in earlier periods of witch-hunting. There had always been judges who demanded that proof of witchcraft be absolutely conclusive before proceeding to sentence. Some of the temporary reductions in the prosecution of the crime in various jurisdictions, such as in Spain between 1550 and 1610, Scotland in the period 1597–1628, and Italy after 1520, can be attributed at least in part to the insistence upon rigid standards of proof. Underlying this caution was the fear that if such standards were not enforced, innocent persons would suffer torture and death. But whereas those early recommendations of caution were eventually ignored or contradicted, on the grounds that society needed to be protected, in the late seventeenth century they found more widespread and lasting acceptance. In this way an erratic pattern of witchcraft prosecution, in which courts oscillated between periods of intense prosecution and relative leniency, gave way to an enduring pattern of judicial caution and restraint.

Scepticism regarding the sufficiency of evidence in witchcraft cases took a number of different forms. It can be seen, first and foremost, in a growing reluctance among judges and legal writers to accept confessions, traditionally regarded as the queen of proofs, as sufficient proof of guilt. This scepticism was not restricted to those confessions that were adduced under torture, which, as we have seen, had their own special evidentiary problems. Judges and lawyers seemed just as unwilling to accept at face value those confessions that witches had allegedly made 'freely'. This scepticism arose mainly when the confessions had a high diabolical content, i.e., when the witches had confessed to either a pact with the Devil or attendance at the sabbath. Reginald Scot had argued that confessions of this sort were the least reliable of all evidence, while the other great sixteenth-century sceptic, Johan Wier (Johann Weyer), attributed them to the mental weakness of the women who had made them (Scot, 1930: 14; Weyer, 1991). An even more sophisticated interpretation of free confessions as the product of dreams or illusions, especially juvenile dreams, emerged during the investigation conducted by Alonso Salazar in the great Basque witch-hunt of 1609–11. By the late seventeenth century judges were willing to accept confessions to witchcraft (or any other crime) only if such confessions were in no way extorted, if they contained nothing that was impossible or improbable, and if the person confessing was not either melancholic or suicidal (Mackenzie, 1678: 86–7; Larner, 1981: 177). In 1788 the Danish jurist Laurits N0rregard, in urging the greatest possible caution in witchcraft cases, warned that the last thing an authority should do would be to believe the accused person's own confession (Henningsen, 1988: 108).

A second and even more frequent expression of judicial caution in the interpretation of evidence was based on the possibility that events attributed to supernatural agency may have had natural causes. This was particularly relevant to charges of *maleficium*, in which it was claimed that witches had inflicted harm by supernatural, i.e., diabolical, means. The sceptical response to such allegations, frequently adopted when lawyers defended witches against such charges, was that the act had natural causes, and that in order to convict a person of the crime, the possibility of natural causation had to be ruled out. Thus in Spain, in the wake of the hunts of 1526 and 1609–11, inquisitors were instructed to inquire whether the maleficent deeds that witches confessed to, such as having killed children or destroyed crops, might have had natural causes (Henningsen, 1980: 371). Inquiries of this sort became more and more common in later seventeenth-century trials. In Italy inquisitors from the Congregation of the Holy Office insisted that in cases of infanticide by witchcraft, the physicians who had treated the children should be examined to discover whether they could determine 'if the illness was or *could have been* natural' (Ginzburg, 1983: 126). The burden of proof was on the prosecution; all that was necessary to secure acquittal was evidence that natural causation was *possible*. In a number of trials in Scotland in the late 1620s, advocates for the witches went to great lengths to prove that malefices might not have been the product of supernatural intervention (Larner, 1981: 178). In securing the acquittal of a witch accused of murder by sorcery in 1662, Paul von Fuchs was content to show that the alleged supernatural cause of the disease which killed his victim could not be proved (Hauber, 1738: 617–21).

Even if the court could be satisfied that harm was done by supernatural means, on the grounds that there was no possible natural explanation of a particular act of malefice, cautious lawyers and officials could demand concrete evidence that the witch had actually been responsible for its infliction. Proof of this sort was obviously difficult to obtain, precisely because the very nature of magic was that it could act on substances at a distance, without direct physical contact. The evidence for commission, therefore, could only be circumstantial, such as the pronouncement of a curse on the victim, close physical proximity between the witch and the victim before the misfortune occurred, or even the report of a glance on the victim that could be represented as the evil eye. To sceptical seventeenth-century legal minds this evidence was not terribly persuasive, and it led some lawyers to claim that the only way to establish the guilt of the witch and demonic agency in the infliction of *maleficium* was to prove that she had made a pact with the Devil (Dalton, 1630; Fox, 1968: 64–5). Of course that undertaking had its own evidentiary problems. In the absence of a confession, courts would have to rely on the discovery of the witches' marks, the content of their speeches, or the testimony of accomplices to prove that she had made a pact (Bernard, 1630: 212–21). The difficulty of convicting persons on those grounds alone became evident in colonial Massachusetts, where judges required evidence of the pact for conviction. Because of that requirement, more than 80 per cent of all witchcraft cases brought before the Massachusetts courts before the Salem witch-hunt resulted in acquittals (Godbeer, 1992: 153–78).

The question whether afflictions were caused by diabolical or natural means arose in a particularly telling fashion in those cases of witchcraft which involved demonic possession. During the seventeenth century, which has been referred to as 'the golden age of the demoniac', witchcraft cases of this sort became increasingly frequent, especially in England and France (Lea, 1939: 1041; Monter, 1976: 60). Demoniacs, very often women and children, identified witches as the cause of their possession, claiming that the witches had commanded demons to occupy their bodies and to afflict them with the fits, contortions and other forms of abnormal behaviour that had become associated with possession. The question naturally arose how such symptoms should be interpreted. Those who did not readily accept a demonological explanation of what had occurred had two alternatives. The first was fraud. In some of these cases the demoniacs staged their fits and then falsely accused individuals for their afflictions. The case of the English teenage girl Anne Gunter, who at the urging of her father feigned various signs of possession and then accused three women from her village of afflicting her in 1604, falls into this category. The other explanation was disease, the argument being that the maladies from which demoniacs suffered, which could be counted among the *maleficia* performed by witches, had natural causes. The most common interpretation of this sort in the seventeenth century was hysteria, or what in England was referred to as the suffocation of the mother. One of the first and most influential treatises to advance this was written by Edward

Jorden, a London physician who was invited to observe both Mary Glover in 1602 and Anne Gunter in 1604 (Jorden, 1603).

The role that cases of demonic possession played in bringing about the decline of witch-hunting has not gone unnoticed by historians (Mandrou, 1968; Walker, 1981: 1, 75–84; Karlsen, 1987: 253–4; MacDonald, 1990: li–lvi). The revelation of frauds associated with possession contributed to greater caution in the handling of all witchcraft accusations, while the highly publicized exorcisms of possessed nuns in France led theologians, especially Protestants, to entertain and advance serious doubts about the extent of demonic interference in the world. But the most direct effect was that it made judges uncertain whether the behavior of possessed persons was sufficient to convict the witches whom they named as the source of their bodily afflictions. In 1697 a Scotsman, James Johnstone, shortly after the conclusion of a case of mass possession-cum-witchcraft at Paisley in his native land (Millar, 1809), observed that 'the parliaments of France and other judicatories who are persuaded of the being of witches never try them now because of the experience they have had that it's impossible to distinguish possession from nature in disorder' (HMC, 1894: 132). The French may have had other compelling reasons for not trying witches in 1697, but Johnstone's explanation at the very least reveals how the evidentiary problems associated with possession could lead to a state of judicial paralysis in witchcraft cases.

Demonic possession also highlighted two further evidentiary problems that had arisen in the context of numerous witch trials. The first arose from the possibility that when possession occurred, demons entered the body directly, without any human agency. This possibility, which was fully accepted in contemporary demonological theory, could also lead to greater reluctance to try witches for causing possession. Indeed, the Roman *Instructio* directly criticized those judges who argued that all possession came from sorcery, claiming that the Devil could vex anyone's body directly with God's permission. Mere possession, therefore, did not provide *the corpus delicti*, the legal prerequisite for further investigation of a crime (Lea, 1939: 958). This line of reasoning was analogous to that of the Spanish inquisitors who argued that storms attributed to the maleficence of witches could very well be sent directly by God to punish people for their sins. In other words, direct supernatural agency, by either God or the Devil with God's permission, could serve as an alternative explanation of the witch's *maleficia*.

A further evidentiary problem connected with demonic possession arose in connection with spectral evidence, which was the testimony by possessed persons that they could see the specters or ghosts of the witches who were responsible for their afflictions. Evidence of this sort had been introduced into witchcraft trials at various times in the seventeenth century. In England it found a place in witchcraft trials as late as 1696 or possibly even 1712 (Kittredge, 1929: 363–4). Opinion on the value of such evidence varied, with writers like George Gifford proclaiming its insufficiency while others accepted its worth. The most effective challenge to its judicial use, however, came from those who claimed that the Devil might have used his powers of illusion to misrepresent innocent persons in spectral form, just as he might have misrepresented innocent persons at the sabbath. It was precisely this line of reasoning that caused the clergy in Massachusetts to abandon the trials that they had originally supported in 1692 and to conclude that some of the victims had been falsely accused. Similar reasoning led German jurists in the late seventeenth century to refuse the admission of spectral evidence unless it was confirmed by other proof (Becker, 1700).

A final source of judicial caution in matters of evidence concerned the acceptance of the testimony of witnesses. In the trial of ordinary crimes excommunicants, children, criminals, heretics, and the defendant's relatives, servants and alleged accomplices were not allowed to testify against him. In many Continental jurisdictions, however, these same persons were permitted to testify against witches, on the grounds that witchcraft was a *crimen exceptum* that would otherwise be incapable of legal proof (Bodin, 1580: lib. 4, cap. 2; Carpzov, 1670: 130; Kramer and Sprenger, 1928: 209). In the seventeenth century children in particular played an increasingly prominent role as witnesses in witchcraft trials (Sebald, 1995: 104–5). The policy of allowing them to testify, however, began to encounter opposition as the trials started to take a heavy toll. In 1584 Reginald Scot criticized Continental judicial procedure precisely on these grounds (Scot, 1930: 11). About the same time the parlement of Paris, denying the entreaties of Jean Bodin, refused to allow testimony from children and other witnesses in witchcraft cases. The exclusion of testimony from unqualified witnesses had the demonstrated ability to bring witch-hunts to a swift end. In 1614 the earl of Dunfermline, the Scottish lord chancellor, successfully derailed a prosecution to which he was opposed by excluding all 14 of the prosecution's witnesses against the accused, arguing that witchcraft was not a *crimen exceptum* and that therefore there was no reason to admit them (Wasser and Yeoman, forthcoming). Many of the acquittals in German witchcraft cases in the late seventeenth and early eighteenth centuries can also be attributed to the enforcement of a more demanding policy regarding the admission of testimony during the trial.

Legal representation

Closely connected to the careful and sceptical handling of evidence was the increasing frequency with which witches gained legal assistance as the trials declined in number. Although witches were entitled to defence counsel in all Continental and Scottish trials, few lawyers took their cases during the peak periods of the great witch-hunt. Not only was legal counsel too costly for the typical lower-class witch, but lawyers were reluctant to defend witches on the grounds that they might thereby encourage the Devil's activities and incur suspicion themselves. There was in fact a considerable literature regarding the propriety of a lawyer's serving as a witch's advocate in such trials, and the warnings given to lawyers in this regard were probably effective in discouraging widespread representation (Kramer and Sprenger, 1928: 217–20). These warnings virtually disappeared in the demonological literature of the seventeenth century.

Although we cannot possibly gain any kind of accurate figures regarding the number of witches who had the benefit of counsel, there is a sufficiently large record of legal representation in the seventeenth century to suggest that the number of cases in which lawyers defended the accused was increasing. The large volume of business that was directed to the appellate courts of France by itself accounts for some of this increase, since legal representation at such trials was mandatory. Even in trials in the first instance, however, lawyers started pleading for witches in greater numbers during the seventeenth century. In Scotland lawyers began to defend witches in the court of justiciary in the 1620s, and in some cases they succeeded in securing acquittals (Larner, 1981: 178–91). Most of those acquittals came after 1670, such as that of the witch known as Maevia, whom Sir George Mackenzie successfully defended before the High Court of Justiciary (Mackenzie, 1672: 185–97). To this can be added the acquittals of Margaret Clerke in 1674 and Bessie Gibb in 1680, each of whom had an attorney, who in the latter case was her own husband (Scottish Record Office, 1674: fos. 181–2; 1680: fo. 103). By the 1660s the legal representation of German witches also seems to have become fairly common (Hauber, 1738: 1. 617–21; Wolf, 1995: 867). In Hungary counsel for accused witches appear as early as the 1650s and receive frequent reference in the records of eighteenth-century cases, when the number of trials finally began to decline (Várkonyi, 1991–2: 470).

Legal assistance of this sort benefited witches more than those accused of any other crime precisely because the evidence in witchcraft cases was so vulnerable to challenge by a person skilled in the law. Lawyers in witchcraft cases could easily raise doubts regarding the supernatural causes of alleged *maleficia*, demand evidence of the *corpus delicti*, and impeach the credibility of witnesses who would not have been allowed to testify in the trial of ordinary crimes. They could also point out the insufficiency of the evidence, especially when it was hearsay, and the irrelevancy of the evidence that was presented in the indictment or the libel. They could even go so far as to deny the existence of witchcraft and call for a ban on the trials, as one Hungarian lawyer did in 1671 (Várkonyi, 1991–2: 470). No wonder that in the previous century Martin Luther, in one of his outbursts regarding the crime of witchcraft, complained that lawyers 'want too much evidence and deny open and flagrant proofs of witchcraft' (Monter, 1976: 31). It was doubtless a similar frustration with the tactics of lawyers that led members of the Spanish Inquisition to complain in 1526 that none of the jurists in Castile believed in witchcraft. Nor should it surprise us that the one person acquitted of witchcraft in the central Scottish courts between 1605 and 1622 had been wealthy enough to hire no fewer than three lawyers (Wasser and Yeoman, forthcoming).

As a result of all these procedural changes and the persistent demands for the exercise of legal caution, witchcraft prosecutions in the late seventeenth and early eighteenth centuries looked very different from those undertaken at the height of the great witch-hunt. Trials tended to last longer and to become more deliberative, as sceptical judges, lawyers, and juries engaged in a scrupulous examination of the evidence brought before them. This tendency towards longer, more exacting trials became most apparent in the central or higher courts, where many cases were heard on appeal, but there is also some evidence of a similar trend at the English assizes. In all the European courts where witches were tried, the summary processes that had been common in the late sixteenth and early seventeenth century virtually disappeared. So did the large chain-reaction hunts. Torture continued to be used in some jurisdictions, but its application was closely regulated and monitored by the superior courts, and many of the witches who were subjected to torture managed to withstand it and thus purge all the presumptions against them.

It should come as no surprise that as a result of these changes the number of acquittals in witchcraft cases began to increase, in some cases quite dramatically. Even more striking was the growing reluctance of judges and officials to initiate witchcraft proceedings. One of the main characteristics of the roman-canonical form of criminal procedure, which was adopted in one form or another in most continental European courts by the sixteenth century, was that the officials of the state could initiate criminal prosecutions by themselves, by virtue of their office, on the basis of ill fame. This procedure by inquisition, which had its origins in the prosecution of heretics in the church courts, had greatly facilitated the development of witch-hunting. Most prosecutions for witchcraft in the sixteenth and early seventeenth centuries had begun in this manner, and in many jurisdictions a legal official, known variously as the procurator fiscal or advocate, acquired the function of bringing such charges before the court.

Now, as the number of prosecutions began to drop off, this pattern of official prosecution began to wane. In the duchy of Württem- berg official prosecutions for witchcraft virtually disappeared after 1660. All subsequent trials began when private subjects brought accusations against their neighbours. In Prussia almost all witchcraft trials in the late seventeenth and early eighteenth centuries originated in private suits. This option had always been available under the system of justice that we broadly label as inquisitorial, and the *Carolina* had specifically provided for it (Goedelmann, 1592: 3: cap. 2; Langbein, 1974: 177–8; Unverhau, 1983: 59–142). What makes the seventeenth century distinctive in this regard was the frequency with which individuals began to exercise that option.

The reduction in the number of official witchcraft prosecutions, coupled with the new policy of restraint in the application of torture and the refusal to consider witchcraft an excepted crime, were largely responsible for giving witchcraft trials their new look. In Germany the courts that tried witches began to adhere much more closely to the criminal procedures set down in the *Carolina*, which had made special provisions for the protection of the defendant's rights (Trusen, 1995: 225). This return to the procedures of the *Carolina* did not constitute a rejection of the system of criminal justice that we generally label inquisitorial. In fact the *Carolina* served as the quintessential statement of inquisitorial procedure. Even when private citizens initiated legal actions, those suits were still handled within the framework of officialized justice. Written depositions were still taken by officers of the court for inclusion within a criminal dossier, while judges, as opposed to lay juries, continued to decide the guilt or innocence of the accused. The essence of the inquisitorial system was not the initiation of cases *ex officio* but the judicial investigation and determination of the crime by the judge regardless of the mode of initiation (Schmidt, 1940: 9; Langbein, 1974: 129–31). This inquisitorial system of justice, especially after its abuses and excesses had been eliminated, proved to be far more effective in bringing an end to witch- hunting than the accusatorial system, as a comparison between the end of witch-hunting in France and England will reveal.

Changes in witch-beliefs

The responsibility for the end of witch-hunting lies mainly with the judges, inquisitors and magistrates who controlled the operation of the judicial machinery in the various secular and ecclesiastical courts of Europe in the late seventeenth and eighteenth centuries. These men not only implemented the procedural changes that we have just discussed but gradually became more uncertain whether the witchcraft accusations brought before their courts were either capable of legal proof or had any foundation whatsoever. As a result of this uncertainty they released an increasingly large number of witches, reversed capital sentences on appeal, and eventually stopped hearing cases altogether.

The behaviour of these judges and officials raises the fundamental question whether the judicial scepticism they manifested proceeded from or contributed to a more fundamental philosophical scepticism or disbelief regarding the power of the Devil, the existence of witches, and the theoretical possibility of their crime. Put another way, the question is whether the men who stopped the trials did so because they no longer believed in witchcraft. As we have seen, the decline of witchcraft prosecutions has traditionally been associated with a rational, scientific, and secular world view that denied the reality of witchcraft and the possibility of demonic intervention in the physical world. Prior to the late seventeenth century such 'enlightenment' was rare. Few educated men denied the existence of witches, and even fewer denied the possibility of their crime, especially its magical component. Those who adopted a sceptical position usually doubted the collective aspects of witchcraft, especially the sabbath, and the explicit pact with the devil, rather than the possibility that a person could harm man or beast by means of the devil's power. It is fairly safe to assume that if jurists in the kingdom of Castile did in fact 'hold it as a certainty that there were no witches', as the supreme council of the Spanish Inquisition claimed in 1526, they were referring to the witches' alleged worship of the devil, not their practice of harmful magic. None of the most famous witchcraft sceptics of the sixteenth century denied the possibility of the crime they were discussing. Certainly Wier and Goedelman did not deny it, however bitterly they attacked the activities of witch-hunters. Cornelius Loos and Reginald Scot came much closer to a full denial, but neither made a categorical statement to that effect. Loos, like almost all the others, denied the reality of the sabbath, night flight, and the explicit pact with the Devil, but not magic itself (Lea, 1939: 603–4). Scot insisted in good Calvinist fashion that the age of miracles had passed and that a sovereign God would not permit human beings to exercise supernatural power, but he did not include the 'working of wonders by supernatural means' in his summary of the 'absurd and impossible crimes' attributed to witches.

Samuel Harsnett, the cleric who did so much to discredit exorcism in early seventeenth century England, came close to denying the reality of witchcraft when he referred to witches as part of 'all that lymphatical chimera', but he went no further than his fellow countryman Scot (Harsnett, 1603: 299). Friedrich Spee, in his passionate plea for the lives of the witches who were forced to confessed in the 1620s in Germany, argued that witchcraft was a terrible crime. His belief in the reality of witchcraft may have actually made his book more acceptable in conservative circles (Monter, 1976: 84–5). Tanner and Meyfarth, like Spee, professed their belief in witchcraft. Of course it is always possible that these men made such cautious statements of orthodox belief in order to avoid the charges of atheism, but aside from Loos's formal recantation in order to avoid execution as a heretic, their expressions of belief bear signs of genuine intellectual discrimination rather than self-serving political convenience.

Among the lawyers, Salazar developed his stinging critique of inquisitorial practice within the context of a firm belief in magic as well as the sabbath. None of the judges who were members of the parlement of Paris during the early seventeenth century ever denied the reality of the crime they were adjudicating, and in some cases they confirmed sentences against the accused. Carena, whose insistence on judicial caution matches that of Salazar and the Parisian *parlementaires*, insisted that there was much illusion but also much reality regarding witchcraft (Lea, 1939: 953). Ernst Cothmann, in a pattern that became increasingly evident in the later seventeenth century, denied the reality of the sabbath but did not dispute that of *maleficium* (Hauber, 1738: 2. 217–55). A few years later Paul von Fuchs, defending his client against charges of witchcraft, disagreed with those unidentified sceptics who said there were no witches, since he believed that magicians did exist and that they should be put to death (Hauber, 1738: 1: 627–8). In Scotland, the famous defender of witches and inveterate critic of those who prosecuted them, Sir George Mackenzie, began his exposition on the subject with a response to Wier, 'the great Patron of Witchcraft', claiming that witches should suffer death not just for poisoning and murder but also for 'enchanting and deluding the world' and that even charmers were guilty of at least apostasy and heresy (Mackenzie, 1678: 81–4). In Denmark, where learned witch-beliefs tended to last longer than in other parts of Europe, it was not until the 1850 that a lawyer, T. Algreen-Ussing, declared the crime of witchcraft to be impossible (Henningsen, 1988: 108).

One reason for the rarity of categorical denials of witchcraft, even among the most sceptical and cautious critics of witch-hunting, was that until the late seventeenth century the philosophical systems that prevailed in academic, theological and judicial circles made the existence of witchcraft possible, even likely. Late medieval scholasticism readily accommodated the operation of demons in the world and provided a solid intellectual foundation for the great witchcraft treatises of the period from 1450 to 1650. Neo-Platonism, which served as the main challenge to scholasticism in the fifteenth and sixteenth centuries, was more predisposed to see magic in natural rather than supernatural or demonic terms, and that outlook gave rise to some of the earliest challenges to learned witch- beliefs (Thomas, 1971: 578–9). But neo-Platonism, with its belief in a magical world of various occult forces and its acceptance of the existence of demonic as well as angelic spirits within that 'natural' world, proved to be an insufficient foundation upon which to mount an assault on the entire set of learned witch-beliefs. A neo-Platonist would have found it difficult to argue that witchcraft and magic were impossible crimes.

Only in the seventeenth century did a new philosophy emerge that had the potential to undermine the belief in the reality of witchcraft. The mechanical philosophy, which ranged itself equally against scholasticism and neo-Platonism, viewed the earth as a machine that followed regular, immutable laws of nature. The challenge that this new philosophy presented to the belief in witchcraft became evident in the work of mechanists Rene Descartes, Thomas Hobbes, and Baruch Spinoza, all of whom denied that spirits, if they existed at all (and the materialist Hobbes would not even accept that), could exercise influence on the operation of the material world. Because of the strength of this philosophical challenge to witchcraft, and the ability of this new philosophy to spread among the learned elite in a culture increasingly dominated by print, the decline of witchcraft prosecutions and executions is often attributed to its influence. Only when the members of the ruling and educated classes began to think in this new way, so it is argued, did witchcraft prosecutions enter a permanent and irreversible decline. According to Trevor-Roper, it was the new philosophy of Descartes that 'dealt the final blow to the witch- craze in western Europe' (Trevor-Roper, 1969: 110).

Categorical statements like this require serious qualification. The mechanical philosophy may very well have helped to undermine the *beliefs* that many educated persons had in the reality of witchcraft (Thomas, 1971: 577; Easlea, 1980: 5, 198), although recent scholarship has tended to minimize its role in this regard, especially in England (Bostridge, 1997: 4, 105, 242–3; Clark, 1997: ch. 19). Whether the dissemination of the new philosophy had anything to do with the decline and end of witchcraft *prosecutions* is much more problematic. The problem is largely one of chronology. We have seen that the decline in prosecutions began in some areas as early as 1600 and in most other areas by 1670, with the exception of a few countries on the eastern and northern periphery of Europe. These were the years when the new mechanical philosophy first made its appearance. The spread of this philosophy, however, was a gradual process, and it was not uncontested. A few natural philosophers embraced the new ideas in the 1650s (Easlea, 1980: 135) but it took some time for mechanism to exercise a more pervasive influence within the universities, the legal profession and the bureaucracies of the state. It is unlikely that the judges and officials who applied the early brakes to witch-hunting during the first 70 years of the seventeenth century were even exposed to, let alone influenced by, the new ideas. When the ideas did reach them, moreover, they had often undergone significant modification at the hands of natural philosophers who had tried to reconcile the harsh mechanism of Descartes and Hobbes with their belief in a providential, if not an immanent God.

The critical period in the reception of the new philosophy appears to have been the years between 1690 and 1720, the period of the early Enlightenment. Thus the new philosophy did not appreciably affect the mental outlook of the educated classes until well after prosecutions had begun to decline in number and in some cases until after they had stopped altogether. In Geneva, for example, the first magistrate to profess an adherence to Cartesian ideas, Robert Chouet, wrote a critical commentary on Geneva's prosecution of witches in 1690, almost 40 years after the last witch had been executed in that republic (Monter, 1976: 38). Even in France, where the new philosophy may have taken root somewhat earlier than in Geneva, Cartesianism probably did not have the negative influence on the level of prosecutions that scholars have often attributed to it (Mandrou, 1968; Trevor-Roper, 1969: 110). Certainly the members of the parlement of Paris who played a decisive role in the decline of French witch-hunting, could not have been influenced by Cartesianism or any other aspect of the 'intellectual revolution' until long after they had brought executions for witchcraft to an end within their jurisdiction in the early seventeenth century. If the new philosophy played any role at all in the decline of witch-hunting, it was at the *end* of the process in the late seventeenth and early eighteenth centuries, when the last trials took place and witchcraft was decriminalized, not in the earlier decades of the seventeenth century, when the initial and usually the most dramatic reduction in the number of trials occurred.

Even in this later period, the extent of the influence of the new philosophy on the process of witch-hunting remains in doubt. This can be seen first by looking at the impact of two of the most celebrated critics of witch-hunting around the turn of the eighteenth century, the Dutch Reformed minister and theologian Balthasar Bekker and the Saxon jurist Christian Thomasius. Both wrote in the 1690s and early 1700s, after the decline of prosecutions had begun in all western European countries, but before the last trials had taken place. The works of both men, moreover, commanded an international audience. Their scepticism was much more fundamental than that of any of their predecessors, especially Wier, and they are both considered to be participants in the early Enlightenment (Pott, 1995). Most important, the two men came to the same crucial conclusion that the crime of witchcraft was not only impossible to prove (the position of the judicial sceptics) but impossible to perform.

Of the two men, Bekker's views were the more radical. His attack on witch-beliefs took the form of a massive treatise, *De Betoverde Weereld,* which was published in four parts in the Netherlands in 1691 and 1693 and translated into English, German and French shortly thereafter. It would be hard to identify a more comprehensive assault upon the cumulative concept of witchcraft before the end of the great witch-hunt. In 1701 the sceptical German jurist Felix Brahm hailed the book as the chief assailant of the superstition of witchcraft (Brähm, 1709; Attfield, 1985: 4). Bekker denied the pact with the Devil, the sabbath, metamorphosis, flight, conception by a demon, demonic possession and the reality of harmful magic itself At the basis of this denial lay a powerful critique of contemporary demonology. Whereas Wier could not bring himself to abandon the belief in a powerful, knowledgeable and deceptive Devil, Bekker denied that the Devil even possessed knowledge, much less a capacity to intervene in the operation of the material world.

The basis of Bekker's argument is two-fold: on the one hand, Bekker was clearly a Cartesian, a rationalist who endorsed the mechanical philosophy and who accepted Descartes' rigid distinction between matter and spirit. He gave an early preview of this outlook in his earlier rejection of the traditional interpretation of signs and wonders as indicators of supernatural displeasure and as portents of the future. On the other hand he was also a biblical scholar in the Erasmian tradition, who argued for a proper historically contextualized interpretation of those Scriptural passages that referred to witches and devils. It was in fact Bekker's biblical scholarship, much more than his Cartesianism, that lay at the basis of his radical conception of the Devil. To claim that Bekker 'had not repudiated belief in the Devil' is to miss the point, which is that for Bekker the devil was merely a symbol of evil and was incapable of exercising power over the physical world, even the power of illusion that figured so prominently in the work of Wier (Trevor-Roper, 1969: 102; Pott, 1995: 190–3). Once the devil was reduced to this status, the possibility that a human being could commit the crime of witchcraft vanished. Indeed, Bekker boldly suggested that when accusations of witchcraft are made, the state should prosecute the accusers, not the accused, a course of action that was becoming common at precisely this time.

The impact of Bekker's book on the prosecution of witches is a matter of some controversy. It obviously had little judicial effect in the Netherlands, where witches had not been tried in decades, or in England, where the last execution had also occurred eight years before the first volume of the book appeared in print. The same could be said of France, which was executing its last witches in the 1690s. But it has been claimed that Bekker's book saved the lives of countless victims in other parts of Europe where his book was read, especially in the German lands near the Netherlands. On closer analysis, however, we realize that there were relatively few prosecutions even in those German lands by the time Bekker wrote. The one northwestern German territory where witch panics continued to take a heavy toll into the 1690s was the duchy of Westphalia. Only in 1696 did the courts in that duchy begin to acquit witches in significant numbers (Decker, 1981–2: 386). It would be difficult, however, to show that the judges in places like Olpe and Hallenberg, where the trials in the late 1690s were held, acted under the influence of Bekker's book. However important Bekker's book may be in the history of learned witch-*beliefs*, its effect on witch-*hunting* was apparently limited. It may have provided a foundation for the decision of some judges and magistrates to abandon prosecutions entirely in the eighteenth century, but even that influence cannot be established.

Christian Thomasius, the jurist who became the chancellor of the University of Halle in Brandenburg, appears to have exercised more influence on the later stages of witch-hunting than Bekker, if only because he wrote as a criminalist and because he and the jurists with whom he was associated were actually involved in the adjudication of the witchcraft cases that were still being heard in German courts. As we have seen, Thomasius was the quintessential judicial sceptic who exposed the evidentiary problems associated with the administration of torture in his dissertation on that subject and who published a full-scale critique on the trial of witches. His most famous work, *Dissertatio de crimine magiae*, which was translated into German as *Kurze Lehr-Satze* in 1703, was also largely concerned with questions of judicial proof. It recommended that when cases of witchcraft came before the courts, judges needed to proceed with great caution, investigate the possibility of deception and demand more proof than was required under the existing criminal law. Even if it could be proved that the Devil had been responsible for the injury or illness that had been inflicted (a point on which Thomasius was himself highly dubious), one could not prove that the accused was responsible for the deed by means of the pact. The entire procedure for trying witches was therefore worthless, and all prosecutions should cease.

The important question here is the content of the witch-beliefs that underlay this demand for judicial restraint. It appears on the surface that the position Thomasius took was just as radical as that of Bekker. In *De Crimine* he stated emphatically that the reason why all witchcraft trials should end was that 'witchcraft is only an imaginary crime'. In a full-scale assault on the cumulative concept of witchcraft, he denied the existence of a pact with the Devil, the sabbath and the influence of evil spirits over corporeal bodies. Thomasius, like Bekker, never denied the existence of the Devil, but his concept of demonic power was so limited that it rendered the crime of witchcraft impossible, with the confessions of witches being the product of either delusion or 'inhuman torture'. Thomasius believed that the power of the Devil was exercised only invisibly in the spiritual sphere; it thus had 'only moral influence' (Pott, 1995: 193–8; Trusen, 1995: 224).

Despite the apparent similarity of Thomasius's position to that of Bekker, there are grounds for drawing a distinction between them. Thomasius was not, like Bekker, a mechanist or a Cartesian. Indeed he admitted in *De Crimine Magiae* that he could not go as far as Bekker in separating the material from the spiritual world. Although he praised Bekker for his destruction of scholastic fantasies, he could not accept his dualism. The intellectual basis of Thomasius' view of demonic power was not Cartesianism, as it was with Bekker, but the theological tradition of German Pietism, which emphasized the sovereignty of God and attributed all misfortune direcdy to him.

The other difference between Bekker and Thomasius is that the latter never denied the reality of certain forms of magic. Thomasius fully admitted that sorcerers and witches could injure people by occult means and that those individuals should be put to death. In defending his book against his critics in 1702 he even made the apparent concession that sorcerers could bring on diseases with the Devil's help. He would not, however, make any concessions on his main point, which was the nonexistence of the pact with the Devil. For Thomasius it was the demonic pact, not the inflicting of harm, that constituted 'the crime of magic'. Thomasius justified this definition of magic on the grounds that according to Saxon and Prussian law, the pact with the devil remained the essence of witchcraft. The reason for declaring the crime of magic to be impossible was that human beings could not make an explicit pact with a physical Devil. The scholastic view that witches could also perform *maleficium* by means of an implicit demonic pact did not enter the discussion.

The philosophical position that underlay Thomasius's judicial scepticism did not go much beyond that of Wier, Scot and the other sixteenth- century critics of witch-hunting. The same can be said for the other jurists who wrote about the crime of witchcraft in the early eighteenth century, like Johann Reiche and Jacob Brunnemann, and the judges who tried the last cases. These men had rejected the reality of the sabbath and the pact with the Devil, but they had not yet embraced a philosophy or a theology that would lead them to reject the reality of natural or even demonic magic. This suggests that in Germany and other lands where witchcraft prosecutions continued into the eighteenth century, the judges who brought an end to the trials, no less than those who had been responsible for their initial reduction in number, were not as 'enlightened' as is often claimed.

Religious changes

Thomasius and Bekker were both committed Protestants who relied extensively upon Biblical citation and ecclesiastical history to destroy contemporary witch beliefs (Haustein, 1995: 249, 259). Both men also claimed that the theory of witchcraft was the invention of the papacy. For Bekker its purpose was to confiscate the property of witches and pay the salaries of inquisitors, whereas for Thomasius, an indefatigable opponent of clericalism, it had emerged in the misguided papal briefs that formed canon law. The prominence of religious themes in the works of these two critics of witch-hunting raises the further and much debated question whether changes in religious thought might have contributed in some part to the decline of witchcraft prosecutions.

This is not the place to evaluate the role of the Protestant and Catholic Reformations in the rise of witch-hunting (Levack, 1995: 100–24). Suffice it to say that the demonization of European culture that preceded and accompanied the Reformation, the reliance upon Biblical injunctions against witchcraft (especially Exodus 22:18), the determination of religious reformers to eliminate magic in its various forms, the subjection of the rural masses to a rigorous moral discipline as part of a program of Christianization, and the determination of public, authorities to establish a godly state by taking legal action against moral deviants and blasphemers all contributed significandy to the intensification of witch prosecutions in the sixteenth and early seventeenth centuries. At the same time, however, it is possible to identify elements of Protestant and reformed Catholic culture that contributed in one way or another to the growing reluctance to prosecute witches in the late seventeenth and eighteenth centuries.

Certainly the Protestant biblicism that had been effectively pressed into the service of witch-hunting could just as easily be used by the opponents of the trials to discredit the entire process. In 1584 Reginald Scot revealed the full potential of this approach in his full-scale assault on prevailing witch-beliefs, *The Discoverie of Witchcraft*. This book, arguably the most radical witchcraft treatise to appear in the sixteenth century, was based in large part on the Bible and the works of its Protestant interpreters. In the seventeenth century other critics of witch-hunting, relying on a growing consensus among biblical scholars, took pains to emphasize that the Bible said nothing about witchcraft as that term was understood in the early modern period and to insist that the condemnation of 'witches' in the Bible should have no relevance to the prosecution of the crime. In 1650 the Alsatian jurist Andreas Sandherr argued before a court at Colmar that witch-beliefs had no biblical foundation (Klaits, 1982: 163), while three years later in England the political thinker Sir Robert Filmer, in the wake of the witchcraft trials at Maidstone, Kent, appended a long discourse on the difference between an English and a Hebrew witch to a tract advising members of juries how to deal with charges of witchcraft.

In similar fashion the Protestant emphasis on the sovereignty of God, which underlay the prosecution of those magicians and witches who were believed to have challenged that sovereignty, could just as easily be invoked to deprive the Devil of much of his alleged worldly power. This line of thought finds its clearest expression in the 'providential' theological tradition that flourished at Tubingen in the sixteenth and seventeenth centuries. Contrary to the position taken in the *Malleus maleficarum*, the theologians at Tubingen attributed all misfortune to the work of a providential God, denying that any intermediate demonic forces played a role in the process. This tradition not only contributed to the moderation and ultimately the decline of witch-hunting in the duchy of Württemberg, but it also made inroads in Denmark, where pastors trained in the Tubingen tradition were largely responsible for the decline of witch-hunting that began in that kingdom as early as 1625 (Johansen, 1991–2: 413–20). One finds a similar theme in the works of some of the early German Pietists, including Christian Thomasius, whose strictly spiritual view of demonic power allowed him to bring faith and reason into harmony.

Perhaps the most important religious source of the decline of witch-hunting was the new attitude of tolerance that began to characterize some Protestant and even a few Catholic communities in the second half of the seventeenth century. There is a solid foundation for this religious tolerance in the Protestant tradition, most notably in the *Heidelberg Catechism*, even though intolerance was more characteristic of Protestant practice during the first century of the Reformation. This Protestant tolerance was manifested mainly towards members of other religious denominations, but the same sentiment could be extended to those suspected of witchcraft, since they were widely regarded as either heretics or at least as religious transgressors. It is probably no coincidence, therefore, that witch-hunting first began to decline in the Dutch Republic, a country known for its early religious tolerance. When Bekker pleaded eloquently in 1691 that Protestants should not pass judgment on other Christians, he was reflecting a Dutch tradition that reached back to Erasmus in the early sixteenth century (Stronks, 1991: 154–5). It was also no coincidence that Poland, the Roman Catholic 'state without stakes', not only tolerated religious diversity but also did not prosecute many witches in the sixteenth century, although both religious persecution and witch-hunting did develop belatedly in that kingdom in the late seventeenth century.

Not unrelated to this new spirit of tolerance was the abandonment of the determination by both Protestant and Catholic public authorities in many states to use their secular power to create an ideal Christian community. This determination to establish a godly state, which was widely evident in many small German states as well as in Scotland, Denmark and colonial Massachusetts, often involved the imposition of a strict moral discipline on the population. In response to clerical pressure, the legislatures of these states had passed laws against blasphemy, drunkenness, adultery, and sodomy as well as witchcraft, and on the basis of these laws the courts had prosecuted these sinners with a vengeance. In some cases this effort to impose God's will on the people was inspired by millenarian fervour. In the late seventeenth and eighteenth centuries, however, the various states of Europe abandoned this type of moral crusading, a process indicative of the secularization of both law and politics. The end of prosecutions in many of these states can be linked, at least in general terms, with this change in thinking regarding the functions of the state (Midelfort, 1972: 127; Larner, 1981: 57–9, 193–9; Roeck, 1988; Ankarloo, 1990: 291–2).

In establishing the religious sources for the decline of witch-hunting, it is important to maintain a sense of perspective. Opposition to the trials on religious grounds was more than balanced by the determination of zealous clerics and laymen to keep the trials going. Among the Protestant theologians and pastors who spoke or wrote about witchcraft in the late seventeenth and early eighteenth centuries there was a wide range of sentiment, just as there had been in the late sixteenth century, but more of it was enlisted in support of witch-hunting than against it. Let us not forget that Bekker directed his work against two of the most respected Calvinist theologians in the Netherlands in the seventeenth century, Johannes Coccejus and Gisbertus Voetius; that the leadership of the Reformed Church expelled him from his ministry for his faulty exegesis of the Bible regarding the power of the Devil; and that the large number of Dutch polemicists who attacked his book anchored their position in Calvinist theological orthodoxy. In similar fashion Thomasius encountered strong opposition from the theologians at German universities, including Johann Weidner, of the University of Rostock, who in 1722 attacked both Thomasius and his stalwart supporter Jacob Brunnemann, and who defended the proposition that the Devil can transport witches through the air and breed with them corporeally.

Some of the strongest defenders of witch-hunting during the period of decline, including a number of judges and jurists, grounded their position on a biblical fundamentalism that flourished within the Protestant tradition. In England the learned judge Matthew Hale, who presided over the trial and conviction of three witches at Bury St Edmunds in 1662, explained that his belief in the reality of witchcraft derived from the Bible. Hale's religious views also led him to adopt a mechanical world view that allowed for the operation of a supernatural will, a modification of Descartes' philosophy espoused by the natural philosopher Jean Baptiste van Helmont (Cromartie, 1995: 206–8). A friend and admirer of Hale, the nonconformist Richard Baxter, likewise based his *Certainty of the World of Spirits* (1691) upon his Protestant views, supplemented by uncorroborated experience. The core of the Cotton Mather's treatise on witchcraft, *The Wonders of the Invisible World* (1692) consisted of propositions, corollaries and conjectures revealing an uncompromising biblicism. A biblically based demand for the continued prosecution of witches also emerged in Hungary, where in 1758 the Palatine Lajos Batthyany protested against Empress Maria Theresa's recently announced policy of leniency towards witches on the grounds that the Bible confirmed the existence of witches (Klaniczay, 1990: 171).

The Bible remained a main source of witch-beliefs long after the trials had ended. In 1738 E. J. F. Mantzel, a professor at the University of Halle, defended the prosecution of witches on the ground that they, 'having denied God and made a pact with the Devil, should be punished with death in accordance with divine command' (Mantzel, 1738). In 1760 the Danish jurist C. D. Hedegaard claimed that 'when one believes the Scriptures or the revealed word of God', the reality of sorcery or witchcraft 'cannot generally be denied' (Henningsen, 1988: 107). The eighteenth- century English Methodist preacher John Wesley declared that 'giving up witchcraft is, in effect, giving up the Bible', while his contemporary, the systematic English jurist William Blackstone, stated even more emphatically that 'to deny the possibility, nay, the actual existence of witchcraft and sorcery is at once to contradict the revealed word of God' (Blackstone, 1769: 4: 60; Wesley, 1906: 3: 330). In 1773 the Presbyterian clergy of the Church of Scotland, citing the Bible as their authority, made a common declaration in the reality of witchcraft, just as they had in 1736, the year in which the witchcraft statute of 1563 had been repealed.

Social and economic changes

In this survey of general reasons for the decline of witch-hunting we have focused almost exclusively on the work of those persons who controlled the judicial machinery and the writers who might have influenced them. But what about the members of the lower classes, who were primarily responsible for bringing the initial accusations of *malejicium* against their neighbours and for testifying against them in court? Without their support witch-hunting would not have been successful, at least not over a long period of time. Could these same members of the lower classes have been at least partially responsible for the decline of witch-hunting? Did the number of trials decrease because fewer members of the lower classes were attributing their misfortunes to the magical powers of their neighbours? If that were the case, the lower number of formal accusations might very well be explained by social, economic and demographic change.

There is little doubt that the dramatic changes in the fabric of European social life during the period 1550–1650 contributed to the great European witch-hunt. Over-population, an unprecedented rise in prices, a decline in real wages among the poor, chronic famine and dearth, especially during years of climatic severity, periodic outbreaks of the plague, extraordinarily high levels of infant mortality, migration of the poor from the countryside to the town, pestilence among men and beasts, and the social dislocations that resulted from widespread domestic and international warfare often lay at the root of those personal conflicts that found expression in witchcraft accusations. The question for our purposes is whether there was a sufficient improvement in, or reversal of, these adverse economic and social conditions to bring about a reduction in the number of charges brought before the courts.

It is true that the demographic explosion of the sixteenth and seventeenth centuries came to an end around 1660, and the inflation that had been fueled primarily by that demographic growth also showed signs of levelling off. Real wages registered some improvement, and the effects of warfare on the civilian population were greatly reduced. Whether these improvements made daily village life more secure and personal tensions in small communities less acute is certainly problematic; one could argue that significant changes in the quality of rural life did not take place in most European countries until the nineteenth century. The same might be said of the quality of medical care in those same communities; the country physician did not replace the wise woman in rural areas until long after the witch-trials were over. The most that we can say with any degree of certainty is that communal provision for the poor became more systematic and effective in most European countries after 1660, and that may very well have eliminated some of the social tension between the dependent members of the community and their more well-off neighbours (Thomas, 1971: 581; Labouvie, 1995: 73–6).

In the final analysis it remains impossible to determine to what extent the social and economic improvements and the changes in culture that did take place after 1660 helped to reduce the number of formal accusations made by members of the lower classes. It is difficult enough to identify the social and economic tensions that lay behind the specific quarrels leading to witchcraft accusations, but at least we have some tangible evidence, in the form of depositions taken from witnesses, to work with. But when communities did *not* bring charges of witchcraft against their neighbours, at least not as frequently as they had in the past, they rarely left written evidence regarding the reasons for their inaction. The most that the legal record tells us is the suggestive report from the Scottish justiciary court in 1671 that two witches were set free because 'there was no one to insist', i.e. for lack of a formal accuser (Scott-Moncrieff, 1905: 56). We can only speculate, therefore, whether the decline in formal accusations reflects a real reduction in the number and gravity of personal conflicts at the village level or the more pragmatic calculation that judicial authorities would not be receptive to complaints brought before them.

There are of course other possibilities. One is that popular witch beliefs actually changed, following the same pattern that occurred first among the more highly educated members of society. One possible source of such a transformation would have been the sermons of sceptical and tolerant ministers, such as those delivered by Danish pastors trained in the providential tradition in the middle of the seventeenth century or the more admonitory one given in the next century by Joseph Juxon, the vicar of Twyford, after a local witch-swimming (Johansen, 1991–2: 415–18; Gaskill, 1994: 91). Sermons served as one of the few vehicles for contact and interaction between popular and learned culture during this period. But there is little evidence that popular beliefs actually changed in response to such religious instruction, either before or after decriminalization, and there is much to suggest that they continued in their earlier form. Indeed, the frequency with which local communities took illegal counter-action against suspected witches suggests strongly that popular witch-beliefs persisted for many generations after the trials had stopped. As one scholar has observed, witchcraft 'died hard in the public mind–if it died at all' (Carnochan, 1971: 389). In her contribution to this volume Marijke Gijswijt-Hofstra provides substantial evidence to support this observation.

Another possibility is that people stopped bringing charges against witches because the prosecutions themselves became too costly. We know from isolated examples that the confinement and trial of witches could be terribly expensive, even when the assets of the accused were used to defray the cost of incarceration and transportation. These financial burdens arising from the prosecution of witches fell on the entire community. In order to avoid further expenses a number of accused witches were actually released from gaol, and that result might easily have made villagers more reluctant to support further prosecutions (Monter, 1990a,b: 273; Levack, 1995a,b: 180–1). It is unlikely, however, that the larger patterns of decline can be attributed to such financial considerations. It is more likely that residents of villages and small towns would have abandoned witch-hunting after experiencing the fear that gripped the entire community during the panics. The realization that no one was safe from the cycle of accusations and implications, coupled with the recognition that innocent people were being executed, was just as capable of affecting the members of the lower classes as the members of the local ruling elite.

In any event we still do not have any hard evidence showing that members of the lower classes became reluctant to accuse and prosecute witches. Faced with a dearth of evidence from popular sources, we can only return to the sources we do have, which are statistics showing a reduction in the number of trials and executions, the records of those trials that ended in acquittals, and the statements of those individuals who criticized the process of witch-hunting. These sources suggest that the main reason for the decline in prosecutions was the increasing reluctance of lay and clerical judicial authorities to convict persons of witchcraft, an attitude that was only occasionally and belatedly reinforced by a growing scepticism regarding the possibility of the crime. It remains to be seen, however, how this reluctance to convict actually brought about a reduction of witchcraft prosecutions in different parts of Europe.

Bibliography

Ankarloo, B. (1990) 'Sweden: The mass burnings (1668–76)', in B. Ankarloo and G. Henningsen, eds (1990): 285–317.
——— and Henningsen, G. eds (1990) *Early Modern European Witchcraft: Centres and Peripheries* (Oxford).
Attfield, R. (1985) 'Balthasar Bekker and the decline of the witch-craze: the old demonology and the new philosophy', *Annals of Science*, 42: 383–95.

Barry, J., Hester, M. and Roberts, G. eds (1996) *Witchcraft in Early Modern Europe: Studies in Culture and Belief* (Cambridge).

Baxter, R. (1691) *The Certainty of the World of Spirits* (London).

Becker, A. (1700) *Disputatio Juridica de Jure Spectrorum* (Halle).

Behringer, W. (1987) *Hexenverfolgung in Bayern: Volksmagie, Glaubenseifer und Staatsräson in der Frühen Neuzeit* (München).

—— (1995) 'Der "Bayerische Hexenkrieg". Die Debatte am Ende der Hexenprozesse in Deutschland', in S. Lorenz and D. R. Bauer, eds (1995): 287–313.

Bernard, R. (1630) *A Guide to Grand Jury Men... in Cases of Witchcraft* (London).

Blackstone, W. (1769) *Commentaries on the Laws of England* (Oxford).

Bodin, J. (1580) *De la démonomanie des sorciers* (Paris).

Bostridge, I. (1997) *Witchcraft and its Transformations c.1650-c.1750* (Oxford).

Boyer, P. and Nissenbaum, S. (1974) *Salem Possessed* (Cambridge, Mass.).

Brähm, F. (1709) *Disputatio Inaug. de Fallacibus Indicüs* (Halle).

Burr, G. L., ed. (1903) 'The witch persecutions', *Translations and Reprints from the Original Sources of European History*, 3: no. 1 (Philadelphia).

—— ed. (1914) *Narratives of the Witchcraft Cases* (New York).

Calef, R. (1700) *More Wonders of the Invisible World* (London).

Carnochan, W. B. (1971) 'Witch-hunting and belief in 1751: The case of Thomas Colley and Ruth Osborne', *Journal of Social History*, 4: 389–403.

Carpzov, B. (1670) *Practicae novae imperialis Saxonicae rerum criminalium* (Leipzig).

Clark, S. (1997) *Thinking with Demons: The Idea of Witchcraft in Early Modern Europe* (Oxford).

Cromartie, A. (1995) *Sir Matthew Hale, 1609–76* (Cambridge).

Dalton, M. (1630) *The Country Justice* (London).

Damaska, M. (1978) 'The death of legal torture', *Yale Law Journal*, 86: 860–84.

Daston, L. (1987) 'The domestication of risk: Mathematical probability and insurance 1650–1830', in L. Krüger, L. Daston, and M. Heidelberger, eds *The Probabilistic Revolution* (Ann Arbor): 237–60.

Decker, R. (1981–2) 'Die Hexenverfolgungen im Herzogtum Westfälen', *Westfälische Zeitschrift*, 131/132: 339–86.

—— (1995) 'Die Haltung der römischen Inquisition gegenüber Hexenglauben und Exorzismus am Beispiel der Teufelsaustreibungen in Paderborn 1657', in S. Lorenz and D. R. Bauer, eds (1995): 97–115.

Drake, S., ed. (1866) *The Witchcraft Delusion in New England* (Roxbury).

Easlea, B. (1980) *Witch-hunting, Magic and the New Philosophy: An Introduction to Debates of the Scientific Revolution 1450–1750* (Hassocks).

Favret-Saada, J. (1977) *Les mots, la mort, les sorts* (Paris).

Feather, J. (1985) *The Provincial Book Trade in Eighteenth Century England* (Cambridge).

Fox, S. J. (1968) *Science and Justice: The Massachusetts Witchcraft Trials* (Baltimore).

Gari Lacruz, A. (1980) 'Variedad de Competencias en el delito de brujeria 1600–1650 en Aragon', in *La Inquisición Española: nueva visión, nuevos horizontes* (Madrid): 319–27.

Gaskill, M. (1994) 'Attitudes to crime in Early Modern England with special reference to witchcraft, coining and murder', Ph.D thesis (University of Cambridge).

Ginzburg, C. (1983) *The Night Battles: Witchcraft and Agrarian Cults in the Sixteenth and Seventeenth Centuries*, trans. J. and A. Tedeschi (London).

Godbeer, R. (1992) *The Devil's Dominion: Magic and Religion in Early New England* (Cambridge).

Goedelmann, J. G. (1592) *De Magis, Veneficis et Lamüs* (Frankfurt).

Grevius, J. (1624) *Doma Tribunal Reformiatum* (Hamburg).

Hale, J. (1702) *A Modest Inquiry into the Nature of Witchcraft* (Boston).

Harsnett, S. (1603) *A Declaration of Egregious Popish Impostures* (London), reprinted in F. W. Brownlow, *Shakespeare, Harsnett and the Devils of Denham* (Newark, 1993).

Hauber, E. D., ed. (1738) *Biblioteca sive acta et scripta magica* (Lemgo).

Haustein, J. (1995) 'Bibelauslegung und Bibelkritik: Ansätze zur Uberwin- dung der Hexenverfolgung', in S. Lorenz and D. R. Bauer, eds (1995): 249–67.

—— (1980) *The Witches' Advocate: Basque Witchcraft and the Spanish Inquisition (1609–1614)* (Reno, Nevada).

—— (1988) 'Witch persecution after the era of the witch trials', *ARV. Scandinavian Yearbook of Folklore*, 44: 103–53.

HMC (1894) *The Manuscripts of the Duke of Roxburghe*. Historical Manuscripts Commission Fourteenth Report, Appendix III (London).

Hoffer, P. C. (1996) *The Devil's Disciples: Makers of the Salem Witchcraft Trials* (Baltimore).

James VI (1597) *Daemonologie* (Edinburgh), ed. G. B. Harrison (London, 1924).

Johansen, J. Chr. V. (1990) 'Denmark: The sociology of accusations', in B. Ankarloo and G. Henningsen, eds (1990): 339–65.

—— (1991–2) 'Witchcraft, sin and repentance: the decline of Danish witchcraft trials', *Acta Ethnographica Hungarica*, 37: 413–23.

Jorden, E. (1603) *A Briefe Discourse of a Disease Called Suffocation of the Mother* (London).

Karlsen, C. (1987) *The Devil in the Shape of a Woman: Witchcraft in Colonial New England* (New York).

Kittredge, G. L. (1929) *Witchcraft in Old and New England*, (Cambridge, Mass.).

Klaits, J. (1982) 'Witchcraft trials and absolute monarchy in France', in R. Golden, ed. *Church, State and Society under the Bourbon Kings of France* (Lawrence, Kans.): 148–72.

Klaniczay, G. (1990) *The Uses of Supernatural Power: The Transformation of Popular Religion in Medieval and Early Modern Europe* (Cambridge).

—— (1991–2) 'Witch-hunting in Hungary: Social or cultural tensions?', *Acta Ethnographica Hungarica*, 37: 67–91.

—— (1994) 'Bûchers tardifs en Europe centrale et orientale', in R. Muchembled, ed. *Magie et sorcellerie en Europe du Moyen Age à nos jours* (Paris): 215–31.

—— Kristóf, I. and Pócs, É., eds (1989) *Magyarországi Boszorkányperek* I and II (Budapest).

—— and Pócs, É., eds (1991–2) *Witch Beliefs and Witch Hunting in Central and Eastern Europe*, Special Issue *Acta Ethnographica Hungarica*, 37.

Kneubühler, H.-P. (1977) *Die Überwindung von Hexenwahn und Hexenpro- zess* (Diessenhofen).

Kramer, H. and Sprenger, J. (1928) *The Malleus Maleficarum*, ed. M. Summers (London).

Kristóf, I. (1991–2) ' "Wise women", sinners and the poor: The social background of witch-hunting in a 16th-18th century Calvinist city of Eastern Hungary', *Acta Ethnographica Hungarica*, 37: 93–119.

Kunstmann, H. H. (1970) *Zauberwahn und Hexenprozess in der Reichstadt Nürnberg* (Nuremberg).

Labouvie, E. (1995) 'Absage an den Teufel. Zum Ende dörflicher Hexeninquisition im Saarraum', in S. Lorenz and D. R. Bauer, eds (1995): 55–76.

Langbein, J. H. (1974) *Prosecuting Crime in the Renaissance: England, Germany, France* (Cambridge, Mass.).

—— (1976) *Torture and the Law of Proof* (Chicago).

Larner, C. (1981) *Enemies of God: The Witch Hunt, in Scotland* (Baltimore).

—— (1984) *Witchcraft and Religion* (Oxford).

—— Lee, C. H. and McLachlan, H. V. (1977) *Source-Book of Scottish Witchcraft* (Glasgow).

Laymann, P. (1629) *Processus iuridicus contra sagas et veneficos* (Cologne).

Lea, H. C. (1939) *Materials Towards a History of Witchcraft*, arr. and ed. by A. C. Howland, 3 vols (Philadelphia).

Lecky, W. E. H. (1910) *History of the Rise and Influence of the Spirit of Rationalism in Europe* (London).

Levack, B. P. (1995) *The Witch-Hunt in Early Modern Europe*, 2nd ed. (London).

—— (1996) 'State-building and witch-hunting in early modern Europe', in J. Barry, M. Hester and G. Roberts, eds (1996): 96–115.

Löher, H. (1676) *Hochnötige unterhanige wemütige Klage der frommen Unschültigen* (Amsterdam).

Lorenz, S. (1982) *Aktenversendung und Hexenprozess* (Frankfurt am Main).

—— (1995) 'Die letzten Hexenprozesse in den Spruchakten der Juristfakultäten: Versuch einer Beschreibung', in S. Lorenz and D. R. Bauer, eds (1995): 227–47.

—— and Bauer, D. R., eds (1995) *Das Ende der Hexenverfolgung* (Stuttgart).

Loriga, S. (1994) 'A secret to kill the king: magic and protection in Piedmont in the eighteenth century', in E. Muir and G. Ruggiero, eds *History from Crime. Selections from Quaderni storici* (Baltimore and London): 88–109.

MacDonald, M. (1990) *Witchcraft and Hysteria in Elizabethan London: Edward Jorden and the Mary Glover Case* (London).

Mackenzie, Sir G. (1672) *Pleadings in Some Remarkable Cases* (Edinburgh).

—— (1678) *The Laws and Customs of Scotland in Matters Criminal* (Edinburgh).

Mandrou, R. (1968) *Magistrats et sorciers en France au XVIIe siècle: une analyse de psychologie historique* (Paris).

Mantzel, E. (1738) *Ob wohl noch Hexenprozesse entstehen möchten* (Rostock).

Martin, R. (1989) *Witchcraft and the Inquisition in Venice, 1550–1650* (Oxford).

Mather, I. (1693) *Cases of Conscience Concerning Evil Spirits Personating Men* (Boston).

Merzbacher, F. (1970) *Die Hexenprozesse in Franken* (Munich).

Meyfarth, J. (1635) *Christliche Erinnerung an gewaltige Regenten und gewissen- haffte Pradicanten wie das abscheuliche Laster der Hexerey mit Ernst auszurotten* (Schleusingen).

Micale, M. (1995) *Approaching Hysteria: Disease and its Interpretations* (Princeton).

Michelet, J. (1862) *La sorcière* (Paris).

[Middleton, C.] (1749) *A Free Inquiry into the Miraculous Powers Which are Supposed to Have Subsisted in the Christian Church* (London).

—— (1751) *Vindication of the Free Inquiry* (London).

Midelfort, H. C. E. (1972) *Witch Hunting in Southwestern Germany, 1562–1684* (Stanford).

—— (1979) 'Witch hunting and the domino theory', in J. Obelkevich, ed. *Religion and the People* (Chapel Hill, NC): 277–88.

Millar, J. ed. (1809) *History of the Witches of Renfrewshire* (Paisley).

Monter, E. W. (1976) *Witchcraft in France and Switzerland: The Borderlands during the Reformation* (Ithaca and London).

—— (1990a) 'Scandinavian witchcraft in Anglo-American perspective', in B. Ankarloo and G. Henningsen, eds (1990): 425–34.

—— (1990b) *Frontiers of Heresy: The Spanish Inquisition from the Basque Lands to Sicily* (Cambridge).

—— (1991–2) 'Variations sur le énigme: la fin des bûchers de sorcellerie', *Acta Ethnographica Hungarica*, 37: 373–8.

Oorschot, T. G. M. van (1995) 'Ihrer Zeit voraus: Das Ende der Hexenverfolgung in der *Cautio Criminalis*' in S. Lorenz and D. R. Bauer, eds (1995): 1–17.

Peters, E. (1985) *Torture* (Oxford).

Pott, M. (1995) 'Aufklärung und Hexenglaube: Philosophische Ansätze zur Überwindung der Teufelspakttheorie in der deutschen Frühaufklärung', in S. Lorenz and D. R. Bauer, eds (1995): 183–202.

Robbins, R. H. (1959) *The Encyclopedia of Witchcraft and Demonology* (New York).

Roeck, B. (1988) 'Christlicher Idealstaat und Hexenwahn zum Ende der Europaischen Verfolgungen', *Historisches Jahrbuch*, 108: 379–405.

Schmidt, E. (1940) *Inquisitionsprozess und Rezeption* (Leipzig).

Schormann, G. (1977) *Hexenprozesse in Nordwestdeutschland* (Hildesheim).

Scot, R. (1930) *The Discoverie of Witchcraft*, ed. M. Summers (London).

Scottish Record Office (1674) JC 2/14. Books of Adjournal of the High Court of Justiciary, 1673–8.

—— (1680) JC 2/15. Books of Adjournal of the High Court of Justiciary, 1678–82.

Scott-Moncrieff, W. G., ed. (1905) *Proceedings of the Justiciary Court from 1661 to 1678* (Scottish History Society, 48).

Sebald (1995) *Witch-Children* (Amherst, NY).

Sharpe (1996) *Instruments of Darkness: Witchcraft in England, 1550–1750* (London).

Soman, A. (1978) 'The Parlement of Paris and the Great Witch Hunt (1565–1640), *Sixteenth Century Journal*, 9: 31–44.

—— (1986) 'Witch lynching at Juniville', *Natural History*, 95: 8–15.

—— (1989) 'Decriminalizing witchcraft: Does the French experience furnish a European model?', *Criminal Justice History*, 10: 1–22.

[Spee, F.] (1660) *Advis aux criminalistes sur les abus qui se glissent dans les procès de sorcelleries* (Lyon).

Stronks, G.J. (1991) 'The significance of Balthasar Bekker's *The Enchanted World*' in M. Gijswijt-Hofstra and W. Frijhoff, eds *Witchcraft in the Netherlands*: 149–56.

Tanner, A. (1626–7) *Theologia Scholastica* (Ingolstadt).

Taylor, J. M. (1908) *The Witchcraft Delusion in Colonial Connecticut, 1647–1697* (New York).

Tedeschi, J. (1990) 'Inquisitorial law and the witch', in B. Ankarloo and G. Henningsen, eds (1990): 83–118.

Thomas, K. V. (1971) *Religion and the Decline of Magic: Studies in Popular Beliefs in Sixteenth- and Seventeenth-Century England* (London).

Thomasius, C. (1701) *De Crimine Magiae* (Halle).

—— (1705) *De Tortura ex foris Christianorum proscribenda* (Halle).

—— (1712) *De origine ac progressu processus inquisitorii contra sagas* (Halle).

—— (1986) *Über di Hexenprozesse*, ed. R. Lieberwirth (Weimar).

Trevor-Roper, H. R. (1969) *The European Witchcraze of the Sixteenth- and Seventeenth-Centuries and Other Essays* (New York).

Trusen, W. (1995) 'Rechtliche Grundlagen der hexenprozesse und ihrer Beendigung', in S. Lorenz and D. R. Bauer, eds (1995): 203–26.

Unsworth, C. R. (1989) 'Witchcraft beliefs and criminal procedure in early modern England', in T. G. Watkin, ed. *Legal Record and Historical Reality* (London): 71–98.

Unverhau, D. (1983) 'Akkusationsprozess-Inquisitionsprozess. Indikatoren für die Intensität der Hexenverfolgung in Schleswig-Holstein', in C. Degn, H. Lehmann and D. Unverhau, eds *Hexenprozesse: Deutsche und Skandinavische Beiträge*, Studien zur Volkskunde und Kulturgeschichte Schleswig Holsteins 12 (Neumünster): 59–142.

Várkonyi, A. (1991–2) 'Connections between the cessation of witch trials and the transformation of the social structure related to medicine', *Acta Ethnographica Hungarica*, 37: 426–77.

Walker, D. P. (1981) *Unclean Spirits: Possession and Exorcism in France and England in the Late Sixteenth and Early Seventeenth Centuries* (London).

Wesley, J. (1906) *The Journal of the Rev. John Wesley*, 4 vols (New York).

Weyer, J. (1991) *Witches, Devils, and Doctors in the Renaissance: Johann* Weyer, '*De Praestigüs Daemonum*' ed. G. Mora and B. Kohl, with E. Midelfort and H. Bacon, trans. J. Shea (Binghamton) (orig. 1568).

[Willard, S.] (1692) *Some Miscellany Observations on Our Present Debates respecting Witchcrafts* (Philadelphia).

Wolf, H.-J. (1995) *Geschichte der Hexenprozesse* (Erlensee).

CHAPTER 14
THE CESSATION OF MIRACLES
D. P. Walker

I have not been working long on this Protestant doctrine of the cessation of miracles,[1] but I have done enough to realize how large the subject is and what a lot I still have to learn. I say this not so much to excuse the deficiencies of this paper as to make an appeal for all the relevant information my readers can give me. According to this doctrine miracles, such as were performed by Christ and his disciples and by Moses and the Prophets, ceased either soon after the Apostolic Age, or (it is more usually thought) when Christianity was firmly established, perhaps in the time of Constantine, or at the latest by about A.D. 600. They did not of course cease abruptly, but tailed off gradually. In any case, the evident purpose of the doctrine was to prove that all medieval and especially all contemporary Catholic miracles were either fakes or diabolic wonders, and to account for the lack of Protestant miracles. In the late sixteenth and early seventeenth centuries this doctrine was firmly and widely held by English Protestants. It is with this period and country that I shall be mainly concerned.

It is likely that in England the cessation of miracles became such a prominent and tenaciously held doctrine at this period partly because of the controversies arising out of Puritan attempts in the 1590s to cast out devils and the savage suppression of these attempts by Anglican prelates, as I suggested in my book, *Unclean Spirits*.[2] In these controversies both sides made explicit their basic assumptions about supernatural occurrences, and were thus led to a principle that they both accepted: the cessation of miracles. This principle is clearly and emphatically expressed in the *Dialogicall Discourses of Spirits and Divels* (1601) of John Deacon and John Walker,[3] and in the Puritan John Darrel's replies.[4]

But the doctrine certainly had earlier roots. Luther had sometimes preached the cessation of miracles. In a sermon of 1535 on Matthew 8: 1–14 (the cleansing of the leper and the healing of the centurion's servant),[5] he distinguished two kinds of miracles: first, miracles of the soul that is transformed by faith; and second, miracles of the body, such as these cures. The first kind is by far the greatest, for Christ 'marveled' at the centurion's faith; they are done daily and will continue until the Last Day. The second was always rare, and such miracles were done by God only to establish the new Church, its baptism and teaching. Now that Christianity rests securely on the Scriptures, these miracles of the body have ceased, just as, when the children of Israel had reached the Promised Land, the miracle of the Exodus no longer continued, and to ask now for miraculous signs (*Wunderzeichen*) would be to doubt the truth of the Gospels. But Luther does not here mention modern Catholic miracles, and may be thinking only of the lack of Protestant ones.

The wish to discredit contemporary Catholic miracles and to justify the lack of Protestant ones is conspicuous in Calvin's dedication to the king of France of his *Institutes*,[6] but here and elsewhere in the *Institutes*[7] and in his commentaries on the Gospels,[8] the cessation of miracles appears only as a recommended opinion, and not, as it later became, a dogmatically asserted principle. For example, on the end of Saint Mark's Gospel (16: 15–20), where the resurrected Christ sends forth the Apostles to 'preach the gospel to every creature,' saying.

> And these signs shall follow them that believe: In my name shall they cast out devils: they shall speak with new tongues: They shall take up serpents; and if they drink any deadly thing, it shall not hurt them: they shall lay hands on the sick, and they shall recover.

Calvin comments cautiously:

> Although Christ does not express whether he wishes this to be a temporary gift, or to reside perpetually in his Church, it is however more probable that miracles, which were to make famous the new and still obscure gospel, were promised only for a certain time.[9]

Moreover, in this *Traité des reliques*, where one would certainly expect to find the doctrine, Calvin does not mention it.[10]

The English Protestants were divided on an important point. The Puritans believed that diabolic phenomena, such as possession and witchcraft, were still going on, whereas at least some Anglicans included these in the class of miracles and therefore maintained, cautiously but sometimes explicitly, that present-day demoniacs and witches could do nothing superhuman and were either diseased or deluded or fraudulent.[11] Although I consider this Anglican line extremely important. I am here concerned only with the general thesis, accepted by both Puritans and Anglicans, that the miracles in the Bible are historically true, but that no such miracles have occurred for about a thousand years.

Another reason that this doctrine was so prevalent in the two decades around 1600 was the Catholic use of contemporary miracles for anti-Protestant propaganda; this made it urgent to have a simple compendious, and effective means of exploding all modern miracles. The Catholic exorcisms at Denham in 1585–86, closely connected with the Babington plot against Elizabeth, became widely known through Samuel Harsnett's book. *A Declaration of Egregious Popish Impostures* of 1603.[12] The exposure of the anti-Huguenot demoniac, Marthe Brossier, as fraudulent in 1599 by the French physician Marescot was quickly translated into English.[13] In his anti-Protestant work, the *Disputationes de controversiis*, published in the 1580s and 1590s, the great Jesuit polemicist, Robert Bellarmin, used the continuance of Catholic miracles and the lack of Protestant ones as a God-given mark of the true Church.[14]

But the greatest boost to the Protestant interest in and anxiety about miracles was given by Justus Lipsius's two treatises, published in 1604 and 1605, shortly before his death, about miracles performed at two shines of the Virgin Mary, one in the town of Hall, and one at Montaigu near Sichem, both in the Catholic Netherlands.[15] These two little books had enormous repercussions. They produced an immediate flood of polemical literature on both sides,[16] and in England Lipsius's miracles soon became the stock example of ridiculous but dangerous popish 'lying wonders.' Protestants everywhere were probably genuinely shocked that the great humanist scholar and historian, the apparently irenic promulgator of Christian neo-Stoicism, who had spent thirteen years teaching at the new Protestant university of Leiden, should not only return to the faith of his youth (if indeed he had ever left it), but should also publicly defend the most obviously superstitious and idolatrous practices of that degenerate faith. Moreover, although the two books were not violently polemical in tone, the miracles recounted in them were explicitly presented as divine proofs of the true Church, as evidence of God's approval of the cult of saints and of the Virgin, and of God's support for the Catholic side in the present wars in the Netherlands.[17]

These miracle books of Lipsius remain rather puzzling. On the one hand, I am inclined to accept his statement that he did have a sincere devotion to the Virgin Mary and a serene belief in the miracles worked by these two images of her. From his youth onward he had chosen Mary as his patron saint, and regularly prayed to her when he had to give an important public lecture, usually with good results (*felici ferè successu*).[18] He bequeathed his fur coat to a statue of the Virgin in a church at Louvain (unfortunately it did not fit her),[19] and on his deathbed, when his Jesuit confessor urged him to make a vow to visit the Virgin at Montaigu if he should recover, he replied, 'Reverend Father, I no longer wish for life: but if the blessèd Virgin wishes to devote me to her service and the benefit of the Church, I will not refuse the task' (*non amplius R*[vde] *Pater, mihi vita in voto est; si tamen velit me vovere Diva Virgo ad suum scrvitium et Ecclesiae utilitatem, non recuso laborem*).[20]

On the other hand, there are curious ineptitudes in the two books. For example, in the preface to the first of these – *Diva Virgo Hallensis* (The Virgin of Hall) – although he announces that in recounting these miracles he is exercising his usual profession of historian, he tells us that one of the daughters of the duke of Brabant, who brought the image to Hall in the thirteenth century, gave birth to 364 children at once. Lipsius comments, 'This would seem more like fable than history, were it not that all our Annals agree in asserting it.'[21] Indeed, in both books he is clearly not so much concerned with presenting convincing historical evidence that miracles did occur at these two shrines as with edifying and entertaining the reader. He is afraid that a long catalog of similar cures might become boring: he therefore puts some of them into verse,[22] and tells in elaborate detail any of the miracles that have the attractive fairy-tale quality of the *Golden Legend*.[23] The first miracles are, as Lipsius himself says, 'both serious and funny' (*seria simul & jocosa*). Two of these occurred at the siege of Hall in 1580, when a soldier, Jan Zwyek (Joannes Zwyckius), impiously said that he was going to cut off the nose of that little woman of Hall, 'meaning the mother of God: but she had overheard the boast, and devising a fitting punishment [*talionis poenam machinata*], procured that one of the first bullets fired took off his nose.'[24] The unfortunate Zwyck then became the laughingstock of his comrades, who were always telling him to go to Hall and get back his nose. Another soldier said he would take the image to Brussels and burn it; he had his mouth and chin removed by a cannonball.

It is really not surprising that the Protestant adversaries of Lipsius should jeer at his miracles and constantly recall the wretched Zwyck's nose. Sir Edward Hoby, for example, a distinguished diplomat who had a controversy with an English Jesuit named John Floyd (who appears again in this story), in a pamphlet of 1609, having recalled some of the more entertaining of Lipsius's miracles, including 'how she [the Virgin] made John Swiekius lose the best nose in his face,' concludes:

But the truth is, we have too many of these alreadie, unlesse they were better: and yet I will not say, but that Lipsius is worth reading by the fireside, when men roste crabs, to drive a man out of a melancholic fit. For I thinke sobrietie it selfe could not chuse but change countenance to have him tell these ridiculous jests so seriouslie, as if he did verilie beleeve them to be true. For our parts, wee are not ashamed to confesse, that we have no other miracles, than those which were wrought by Christ, the Prophets, and Apostles.[25]

The doctrine of the cessation of miracles had one glaringly weak spot: its lack of scriptural support. In the New Testament, when Christ confers wonder-working powers on the Apostles and those whom they should convert, as in Mark 16 (already quoted) and in John 14:12 ('He that believeth on me, the works that I do shall he do also; and greater works than these shall he do'), there is nothing whatever to indicate that these powers were limited in time. For Protestants, who had made Scripture the supreme – indeed nearly the sole – religious authority, this lack was a very grave defect. The doctrine therefore needed arguments to prop it up, arguments that could, if possible, be supported by biblical texts. The line of argument was as follows:

First, it is assumed, as has been seen in Luther and Calvin, that God does miracles only to establish a new religion, and that, as it becomes established, the miracles gradually cease. Richard Sheldon, a convert from Catholicism who had been a Jesuit, in his *Survey of the Miracles of the Church of Rome* (1616), gives this assumption a semblance of biblical authority by drawing the parallel, like Luther, with the Exodus: as the pillar of fire and manna ceased when the Jews entered Canaan, so Christians now no longer need the power of miracles given to Peter and Paul to guide the first believers through 'the wilderness of Gentilisme, or of Pharasaicall pride.'[26]

It follows from this assumption that the miracle working faith proclaimed by Christ in Matthew 17:20 ('Verily I say unto you. If ye have faith as a grain of mustard seed, ye shall say unto this mountain. Remove hence to yonder place; and it shall remove; and nothing shall be impossible unto you') – that this faith is distinct from justifying faith and is no longer granted. James Mason, in his *Anatomie of Sorcerie* (1612), having stated that 'it is more than probable that miracles are now ceased' and dated the cessation from the time of Constantine, when Christianity was publicly professed by godly emperors, quotes John Chrysostom on the above text.

> Since nowadays those miracles are not done in the Church, should we therefore say that Christians are bereft of faith? God forbid that we should have such a bad opinion of the people of God. Justifying faith is with us, but what is called the faith of miracles has ceased.[27]

I have not yet been able to find this comment on Matthew 17:20 in Chrysostom's works, either genuine or spurious, but it is also cited by Deacon and Walker and by Sheldon.[28]

This distinction between miraculous and justifying faith can also be supported by a famous text of Saint Paul in 1 Corinthians 13:2: 'And though I have all faith, so that I could remove mountains, and have not charity, I am nothing.' Calvin, in the *Institutes*, eager to deny the Catholic doctrine that faith without charity is unformed, explains that by 'faith' Saint Paul here means merely the power to work miracles, which is a particular gift of God, 'which a wicked man can have and abuse it' (*lequel un meschant homme peut avour et en abuser*).[29] But commenting on Matthew 17 and the similar pronouncement in Matthew 21:21, Calvin dismisses these promises of miraculous powers as hyperbolic figures of speech (*hyperbolica loquendi forma*).[30]

The argument then goes on to show that those Catholic miracles which are not obviously faked or ridiculous, like Zwyck's nose, are the 'lying wonders' of Antichrist, predicted by Saint Paul (2 Thessalonians 2:9) and by Christ in Matthew (24:24): 'For there shall arise false Christs, and false prophets, and shall show great signs and wonders: insomuch that, if it were possible [εἰ δυνατόν] they shall deceive the very elect.' Antichrist is named in the Bible only in the

Epistles of Saint John (1 John 2 and 4: 2 John, verse 7), but other eschatological texts, such as the two just cited, and chapters 11 and 13 of Revelation, were taken to refer to him. From these sources, combined with early medieval prophecies, such as the Pseudo-Methodius *Revelations*, a full and relatively stable picture of Antichrist was built up.[31] He will be a diabolically inspired man who in the Last Days will both persecute Christians and try to mislead them by claiming to be Christ and performing wonders: after a short reign of about three and a half years, he will be destroyed by Christ or his agent. There was also a typology of Antichrist, the types being found both in the Bible and in later secular history. For example, a famous type of Antichrist as deceiver and wonder-worker was Simon Magus (Acts 8 and 18); of Antichrist as persecuting tyrant, Nero.

This tradition was radically transformed early in the Reformation. For Protestants, Antichrist was no longer an evil man in the future, but an existing institution, namely the papacy, and for many, the whole Roman Catholic church.[32] Although earlier heretics, such as Lollards, Hussites, and some Joachimites, had attacked particular popes as types of Antichrist, this firm identification of Antichrist with the Roman church was something new – new interpretation of the biblical texts in question. It raised many historical and eschatological problems. The various solutions of these resulted in great variety and vagueness about the beginning and duration of Antichrist's reign and the placing of the millennium, the binding of Satan for a thousand years, predicted in Revelation 20. John Foxe, for example, in the first edition of *Actes and Monuments* (1563), had a millennium in the past, lasting until A.D. 1000, when Satan was released, according to Revelation (20:3), 'a little season,' and Antichrist's reign began: but in the 1583 edition the millennium was shifted forward to last from the time of Constantine until the fourteenth century. But, although Antichrist's open reign began so late, with the persecution of Wycliffe and Huss, the corruption of the Church was far advanced long before this, by the seventh century at the latest, when, as has been seen, true miracles ceased. This early deprivation of church was generally agreed, in spite of many variations with regard to the exact phraseology of Antichrist's official reign and to the part played by the Turks and Islam as an Antichrist complementary to the papacy.[33]

One point about Antichrist on which nearly all Protestants and all Catholics were in agreement was that his satanic wonders were not supernatural, but only superhuman. This is a particular application of a general and widely held principle about the limitation of diabolic powers; it is, for example, the guiding thread of the Calvinist Johann Wier's careful investigations of demoniacs and witches.[34] The Devil cannot break the laws of nature, but can only move things about with superhuman speed; trouble men's animal spirits, thus producing illusions; and perhaps speed up natural processes. But he cannot create something out of nothing (such as manna), raise up the dead, or make the sun stand still.[35] The limitation was of course by no means clear-cut, since no one could be quite sure what the laws of nature were. But, be that as it may, it was agreed, as the Protestant convert Sheldon says, that all diabolic wonders are done 'by the secret, hidden, quicke and speedy application of naturall causes.'[36] And the Jesuit exegete Cornelius à Lapide comments on 2 Thessalonians 2:9:

Neither Antichrist, nor the Devil, nor angels can do a true miracle, but only God. For a miracle is what is done above all power of nature, and what exceeds and transcends the powers of all natural causes and creatures. Antichrist therefore will not do true miracles but false and lying ones.[37]

This limitation of the Devil's powers is essential if miracles are to be taken as signs of divine approval of the person who performs them or of the church in which they are performed: for otherwise there is no way of distinguishing them from lying wonders. But from the Protestant point of view, it had the disadvantage that not all Catholic miracles could be quickly dismissed as the works of Antichrist, since some of them apparently did transcend the natural order – such as the raising of the dead. Hence one finds some Protestants who hold the view, already implied by Calvin, that God does sometimes allow Satan to perform supernatural miracles, and that the only way of detecting these is by seeing whether the doctrine of the performer is in conformity with Scripture. George Thomson, who published one of the earliest and most savage attacks on Lipsius's miracles, the *Vindex Veritatis* (1606), asserts that God does allow false prophets to do true miracles, in order to test the constancy of the faithful. He can quote, very appositely, Deuteronomy 13:1–4:

> If there arise among you a prophet, or a dreamer of dreams, and giveth thee a sign or a wonder, And the sign or wonder come to pass, whereof he spake unto thee, saying Let us go after other gods, which thou hast not known, and let us serve them: Thou shalt not hearken unto the word of that prophet.

Calvin could also cite Augustine writing against the Donatists, who are not to be believed even if they do perform miracles. He accepts the miracles done by Vespasian and Hadrian, vouched for by Suetonius and Tacitus, as evidence that God allows true miracles to occur among the heathen.[38] The wonders of Antichrist will be supernatural, for, in 2 Thessalonians 2:9 τέρασιν φεύδους (literally 'with wonders of a lie') means not lying false wonders (*prodigiis mendacibus* in the Vulgate), but true miracles used to back up false doctrine.[39] The true Church is founded, not on miracles, but solely on the canonical Scriptures.[40] Most Protestant writers against miracles do not take up this extreme position; for it has the serious defect of making the miracles in the New Testament quite pointless. The safer and more usual line was to state that the Church was founded on the canonical Scriptures and the miracles recounted therein, which are recognizably different from diabolic wonders.

After this brief sketch of the Protestant arguments in favor of the cessation of miracles, I now come to the Catholic answers to these arguments. My main sources are Bellarmin; Justus Lipsius; Robert Chambers – a Catholic priest living in Brussels who, in 1606, published an account and defense of the Virgin's miracles at Montaigu, and dedicated it to James I;[41] John Floyd (or Flood) – the English Jesuit whose *Purgatories Triumph over Hell* (1613) contains a chapter on Lipsius's and other modern miracles,[42] which sparked off Protestant replies such as Sheldon's *Survey of Miracles*; and finally, the French Jesuit Louis Richeome, whose *Trois discours pour la religion catholique: Des miracles, des sainets, et des images*, dedicated to Henry IV, appeared in 1597.[43] Richeome relies heavily on Bellarmin, but he is much fuller and more persuasively eloquent – his eloquence is highly praised by that connoisseur of French religious literature, Henri Bremond.[44]

In answering the argument that miracles have ceased because, now that Christianity is established, they are no longer necessary. Catholics are willing to make some concessions. Richeome admits that 'the miracles that were only necessary at the beginning of the Church have ceased, the necessity having ceased'; but, he goes on, other miracles continue, 'although less frequent, the necessity also being less.' Of the first kind is the gift of tongues, which lasted only a few years. Nevertheless, even this gift still continues in a certain sense, in that members of the Church now speak all manner of tongues, from China to Peru, and yet the Church herself speaks only one language everywhere: Latin. Wherever a Catholic goes, 'he hears God praised in the language of his mother.' But the Protestants, having no missionaries, are confined to the few tongues of Europe, and they have no common liturgical language; they are neither catholic nor united.[45]

Bellarmin also accepts the principle that 'miracles are necessary for persuading [people] to a new faith or [confirming] an extraordinary mission'; but he adds that this is not their only function. As witness given by God (*testimonia Dei*), they also often have the purpose of glorifying saints, proving their sanctity and the truth of their faith.[46] Moreover, like Richeome, Bellarmin claims that Calvin's doctrine *is* a new faith, and that he pretends to an extraordinary mission to reform the Church; on both counts he needs the confirmation of miracles.[47]

In general, the Catholics are in a strong position when maintaining that miracles are still necessary to guide Christians at a time when multiple heresies are rife and atheism is rearing its ugly head. According to Floyd, all ages have their scoffers at Divine Providence, and therefore their miracles, which, by punishing the wicked and rewarding the faithful, vindicate God's dominion, though these are carefully and sparingly distributed so as not to infringe on human free will. Then he asks, 'Now in what age since the comming of Christ hath either piety more needed a spur, or impiety a curb, then in this we live in?' The world is full of wolves in sheeps' clothing – that is, of heretics. 'Why then should we bynd the hands of God, that he may not send downe Miracles upon the world, which doth so need them? That he may not scarre ravenous wolves with thunderbolts from heaven in these days, as well as in former ages?'[48]

Another strong argument in favor of the continuing necessity of miracles was their use in converting the heathen. I have already shown Richeome taunting the Protestants with their lack of foreign missions. Bellarmin recalls the innumerable miracles of Saint Francis Xavier in the Far East, and then draws a series of contrasts between the saint's life and death and Luther's. One enters the Society of Jesus; the other deserts his monastery. One keeps his vow of chastity; the other breaks it and marries. One makes a special vow of obedience to the pope; the other attacks the Vicar of God. One has a 'singular gift of miracles,' and his body is preserved after death, 'against the order of nature,' with an odor of sanctity; the other could 'not even resuscitate a fly' (*ne muscam quidem resusoitare*), and his corpse rotted in freezing weather, 'against the order of nature,' so that it stank through a metal coffin.[49]

The missionary argument was so strong that Protestants had to make some concessions to it. Sheldon, the former Jesuit, after implying that most of the missionaries' miracles are fakes, admits that the Jesuits begin by preaching the apostolic doctrine of faith in Christ and that it is quite possible that God does confirm this with miracles, though of course they later introduce their idolatrous superstitions.[50] Floyd quotes a similar concession in Philip Nicolai's *De regno Christi*, where the missionaries miracles are admitted as credible because the Jesuits begin by preaching 'as Lutherans or Evangelicals.' The English Jesuit comments bitterly:

> I think sobriety will smile at the Protestants felicity in this point who may sit by the fire side, or ly quiet in their warme beds whilest the Jesuits go into barbarous countries to worke Miracles, to prove, forsooth their Ghospell that Fryars may marry Nunnes, and be saved in idle life by sole faith.[51]

With regard to the Protestant doctrine of Antichrist, the Catholics naturally keep to the traditional picture of him and his wonders. These wonders, Floyd and Richeome argue, will not be beneficial to body and soul, as are Catholic miracles, but merely astonishing tricks, such as are described in Revelation 13, 'making the picture of a beast speak, bringing down fire from heaven, faygning himself dead and rising again.'[52] Floyd also argues that if all present-day miracles are to be ascribed to Antichrist – to the powers of the Devil – then the love and fear of God will be greatly diminished. Recalling the vindictive miracles at the siege of Hall, he writes:

> If God when Hereticks blaspheme his *Mother*, and play with her *nose*, strike their tongues out of their heades, and their *best noses* from their faces, Heresy teacheth them to turne their hartes that want tongues, & their faces without noses against heaven, and call the Author of that miracle, Divell.[53]

Justus Lipsius, in the preface to his first miracle book, asks the question, Why are miracles nowadays not usually done in the name of God or Christ, but in that of saints, especially of the Virgin Mary? The answer is. There is no need now to prove the divinity of Christ, which all Christians accept; but the cult of saints and of the Virgin, attacked by so many new heretical sects, does need the support of God's approval expressed in miracles.[54] Lipsius here points to a very important aspect of modern Catholic miracles. They were of a kind that could be and was used, not only as a mark of the true Church, but also to validate practices and doctrines that were rejected by Protestants as idolatrous and superstitious: the Mass, the cult of the Virgin and of the saints as intercessors, and, going with this cult, the reverence of images and the magical power of relics.[55] For Protestants, of course, this use of miracles confirmed the belief that they were the lying wonders of Antichrist – not merely fake wonders, but deceiving and pernicious ones. But the Catholics could show, quite convincingly, that miracles of this type had frequently occurred before the supposed beginning of Antichrist's reign, which, as was shown, was usually dated by Protestants not earlier than A.D. 500.[56]

In this historical debate a crucial authority, respected by both sides, was Augustine, but he was a double-edged weapon. His pronouncements on miracles in some of his earlier writings, especially those against the Donatists (such as the *De unitate Ecclesiae*), could be used to support the Protestant contention that miracles art not a sufficient mark of the true Church,[57] and they were so used by Mason and by Sheldon.[58] In Augustine's *De vera religione*, written about 390. Sheldon and Thomson found almost the whole doctrine of the cessation of miracles:

> Since the Catholike Church hath been diffused over the whole world, neither are those miraculous things permitted to endure unto our times, lest the mind should alwaies seeke visible things, & by the custome of them, mankind should waxe cold, at the new appearance whereof, it was all on fire. (Sheldon's translation)[59]

But they forbore to mention Augustine's *Retractationes*, where he explains that he meant only that certain kinds of miracles – such as the gift of tongues – no longer happened, and that, when he wrote that book, he had already witnessed the healing of a blind man at the tombs of Ambrose and many other newly discovered martyrs at Milan.[60] Deacon and Walker, honestly but indiscreetly, cite both the book and the retraction.[61]

But, on the other hand, there is the long chapter in the last book of the *City of God* (22.8), in which Augustine recounts with great enthusiasm many miracles of his own day, including those wrought around Hippo by the newly arrived relics of Saint Stephen. This was a trump card in the Catholics' hand, and Bellarmin, Richeome, and Floyd all play it.[62] There was little the Protestants could do about it. However, since Augustine begins his chapter by stating the case he is going to refute – 'But how comes it, say they, that you have no such miracles nowadays, as you say were done of yore?' – some of them had the impudence to cite this chapter as evidence of the early cessation of miracles, for example, Sir Edward Hoby and the editor of the eminent Puritan divine William Perkins's *Discourse of the Damned Art of Witchcraft* (1608).[63] Sheldon tries several ways out of the difficulty, none of them very convincing. He suggests that the chapter contains later interpolations, or alternatively, that these are not examples of pre-Antichrist miracles confirming the cult of saints, as Floyd claims, since the congregation may only have honored Saint Stephen, and not prayed for his intercession; or yet again, that even if they did pray to the saint, this does not justify present-day abuses of such prayers – just as the brazen serpent once cured snakebites, but was later rightly destroyed by Hezekiah because it was being worshiped as an idol.[64]

The Protestants, however firmly they held to the belief that modern Catholic miracles were either fraudulent or proofs that the Church of Rome was Antichrist, must have felt some anxiety about their own lack of miracles. By widening the connotation of the term *miracle*, it was possible to claim that they, too, had signs that God was on their side. I have shown Luther arguing that the invisible miracles of conversion and spiritual regeneration are greater than any physical wonders, and that they still continue in the true Church. This ancient doctrine is prominent in Saint Augustine, and it could also be used by Catholics. The same applies to the miracles of nature, which people fail to appreciate as such only through long habit; Richeome has an enormous digression on these.[65] More satisfying and reassuring was the extension of the term *miracle* to cover outstanding instances of Divine Providence. Sheldon, Hoby; and others claim as miraculous signs of God's approval of the English Reformation the preservation of Elizabeth's life in spite of all the popish plots to assassinate her, the Spanish Armada, and the Gunpowder Plot – quite an impressive little list.[66]

Bellarmin and Richeome maintain that both Luther and Calvin had attempted to perform miracles, but had failed ignominiously.[67] These highly suspect stories, which also appear in the Jesuit Thyraeus's monograph on demoniacs of 1596–98,[68] are taken from Catholic biographies of the two reformers. Luther is said to have tried in 1545 to exorcise a demoniac girl in a church at Wittenberg, but the possessing devil terrified him and locked him in the sacristy. The story about Calvin belongs to a class of miracles named by Richeome 'miracles in reverse' (*miracles a reculons*), of which he gives several examples. The earliest of these is from Gregory of Tours, who tells of an Arian heretic who induced a man to feign blindness in order to confirm the truth of his heresy by performing a false miracle of healing; the man was struck with real blindness. Calvin, according to Jerome Bolsec's life of him (1577), persuaded a married couple, recent and impecunious immigrants to Geneva, in return for financial support to pretend that the husband was sick, and finally he was to feign death. Accompanied by many friends, Calvin then walked, as if by chance, near the house, heard the wails of the widow, and entered. Everyone knelt, and Calvin prayed that God would show his power by restoring the corpse to life, thus demonstrating Calvin's divine mission to reform the Church. He took the dead man's hand and commanded him in the name of the Lord to arise. But, by a just judgment of God, the simulated corpse was truly dead.

There was one kind of miracle that few disputed at the time but that raised insoluble problems for English and French Protestants: touching for the King's evil – the power of the French and English kings miraculously to cure scrofula. Here inevitably I rely heavily on Marc Bloch's fine study. *Les rois thaumaturges* (1924). Many Catholics – Richeome and Robert Chambers, for example – refer to saints.[69] But most Protestants ignored these awkward miracles and passed over them in silence.

I shall end this discussion by giving one example of the problems these miracles raised for a Protestant who was unable to evade the difficulty: the king of England, James I. James, in his *Daemonology*, first published in 1597 and reissued in 1603, the year he came to the throne, had proclaimed the now familiar doctrine: Since the establishment of Christ's 'Church by the Apostles, al miracles, visions, prophecies & appearances of Angels or good Spirits, are ceased; which served only for the first sowing of faith, and planting of the Church.'[70] Bloch quotes an anonymous letter, sent by an Italian to Rome in October 1603,[71] which clearly shows the painful conflicts produced by the rite of touching for a monarch who believed firmly both in the divine right of kings (which this ceremony was designed to confirm) and in the cessation of miracles. While his scrofulous subjects were waiting in an antechamber, James, before touching them, had a sermon preached by a Calvinist minister.

> Then he himself said that he found himself perplexed about what he had to do, that, on the one hand, he did not see how he could cure the sick without a miracle, and miracles had now ceased and were no longer wrought; and so he was afraid of committing some superstition; on the other hand, since this was an ancient custom and beneficial to his subjects, he was resolved to try it, but only by way of prayer, in which he begged everyone to join him. He then touched the sick. ... It was noticed that while the king was making his speech he often turned his eyes towards the Scots ministers who were standing nearby, as if expecting their approval of what he was saying, having beforehand conferred with them on the subject.

James did what he could to cleanse the ceremony of popish superstition. He no longer made the sign of the cross when touching the sick person, and the gold coin that was hung around his neck no longer bore the cross or the inscription from Psalm 118:23: 'This is the Lord's doing; it is marvelous in our eyes' (*A Domino factiom est istud, et st mirabile in oculis nostrist*).[72]

Notes

1. So far as I know there is very little modern work on this subject: but see Keith Thomas, *Religion and the Decline of Magic* (London, 1971), pp. 80, 124, 256, 479, 485.

2. D. P. Walker, *Unclean Spirits: Possession and Exorcism in France and England in the Late Sixteenth and Early Seventeenth Centuries* (London, 1981), pp. 66–70, 72–73.

3. John Deacon and John Walker, *Dialogicall Discourses of Spirits and Divels* (London, 1601); idem, *A Summarie Answere to All the Material Points in Any of Master Darel His Bookes* (London, 1601).

4. John Darrel, *A Survey of Certain Dialogical Discourses* (n.p., 1602); idem. *The Repile of John Darrell, to the Answer of John Deacon, and John Walker* (n.p., 1602).

5. Martin Luther, *Werke,* 107 vols. (Weimar, 1910), 41:18–21.

6. John Calvin, *Institution de la religion chrestienne,* 5 vols., ed. J.-D. Benoit (Paris, 1957), 1:33–36.

7. Ibid., 4:473–74, 485–87.

8. John Calvin, *In Novum Testamenum commentarii,* 59 vols. (Brunswick, 1891), 1:400–401 (on Matt. 10: 1–8). 973 (On Matt. 24:23: 'Quum antichristos et mendaces prophetas Dornium miraculis armatos fore pronbuntiet, non est eur tantopere superbiant papistae hoc obtentu. vel ipsorum jactantia territemur. Miraculis superstitiones suas confirmant; nempe quibus praedixit filius Dei, labefactandam esse multorum fidem. Quare tantum apud prudentes momenti habere non debent, ut per se sufficiant ad probandum hoc vel illud doctrinae genus. Si excipiant, hoc modo everti ac in nihilum redigi miracula, quibus tam legis quam evangelii sancita fuit autoritas: respondeo, certam spiritus notam illis insculptam fuisse, quae dubitationem et errandi metum fidelibus eximeret').

9. Ibid., p. 1211: 'Quanquam aulem non exprimit Christus, veline hoc temporale esse donum, an perpetuo in sua ecclesia residere: magis tamen probabile est, non nisi ad tempus promitti miracula, quae novum et adhuc obscurum evangelium illustrent.'

10. John Calvin, *Traité des reliques* (Geneva, 1543), in idem, *Three French Treatises,* ed. F. M. Higman (London, 1970).

11. See Walker, *Unclean Spirits,* pp. 66–70, 72–73.

12. See ibid., pp. 43–49.

13. Ibid., pp. 33–42, 65–66.

14. Robertus Bellarminus, *Disputationum … De controversüs Christianae fidei, adversus huius temporis haereticas,* 3 vols. (Ingolstadt, 1586–93), edition revised by Bellarmin, 4 vols. (Venice, 1596). I shall quote from *Disputationum …* (Ingolsiadt, 1605), 2: 348–62 (*De notis ecclesiae,* cap. 14. nota llma: Gloria miraculorum).

15. Justus Lipsius, *Diva Virgo Hullensis: Benefica eius & Miracula fide alque ordine descripta* (Antwerp; 1604); idem, *Diva Sicheniensis sive Asprecollis; Nova eius beneficia & admiranda* (Antwerp, 1605); *cf. Bibliographie Lipsienne: Oeuvres de Juste Lipse,* 1st ser., 3 vols. (Gent, 1886), 1:535–98: 2:167–87.

16. *cf. Bibliographie Lipsienne,* 1:535–98; 2:167–87: J. L. Saunders, *Justus Lipsius: The Philosophy of Renaissance Stoicism* (New York, 1955), pp. 51–53: Lipsius, *Opera omnia,* 4 vols. (Vesaliae, 1675), pieces at the beginning of vol. 1.

17. Lipsius, *Diva Virgo Hallensis,* pp. 15, 18; idem. *Diva Sichemiensis,* in *Opera omnia,* 3:1295, 1298–99.

18. Lipsius, *Diva Virgo Hallensisis,* p. 1.

19. *La correspondance de Juste Lipse conservée au Musee Plantin-Moretus.* ed. A. Gerlo (Antwerp, 1967), p. 256 (account of Lipsius's death – 23 March 1606 – by Franciscus Van den Broek, Fr. Minor, an eyewitness).

20. Ibid., p. 259.

21. Lipsius, *Diva Virgo Hallensis,* p. 12: 'Rem fabulae, quam historiae propiorem, nisi eam Annales nostri constanti assensu tradidissent.'

22. Lipsius, *Diva Sichemensis,* in *Opera onmia,* 3:1296.

23. E. g. Lipsius, *Diva Virgo Hallensis,* pp. 25–27 (story of the servant about to be crucified for having lost a falcom).

24. Ibid., pp. 23–24: 'See suis manibus Hallensi mulicruclae (Dei parentem intelligebat) nasum abscissurum. … Diva audierat, & quasi talionis poenam machinata, procurat glande plumbeâ, inter primas excussa, scurrae illi ipsi nasum auferri.'

25. Edward Hoby, *A Letter to Mr. T. H. Lute Minister: Now Fugitive* (London, 1609), pp. 100 (the falcon story cited in note 24 above), 101–2.

26. Richard Sheldon, *Survey* (London, 1616), pp. 50–51.

27. James Mason, *Anatomie* (London, 1612), p. 7: 'Cùm hedie ista sc. miracula in ecclesia non fiant, an propterea dicemus Christianos destitui fide? avertat deus, ut de populo dei tam male sentiamus. Adest fides justificans, sed ea quae miraculorum dicitur, jam desijt.'

28. Deacon and Walker, *Dialogicall Discourses*, p. 300: Sheldon, *Survey*, p. 35.

29. Calvin, *Institution*, 3:25.

30. Calvin, *In Novum Testamentum*, 1:728: 'Certum quidem est. hyperbolicam esse loquendi formam, quum fide pronuntiat transferri arbores et montes.'

31. Richard Kenneth Emmerson, *Antichrist* (Manchester, 1981).

32. Ibid., pp. 206–ff.

33. See Katherine Firth, *The Apocalyptic Tradition in England. 1530–1645* (Oxford, 1979).

34. Johann Wier, *Histoires disputes et discours des illusions et impostures des diables*, 2 vols. (1579; reprint, Paris, 1885), 1:56–59.

35. Louis Richeome, *Trois discours pour la religion catholique; Des miracles, des sainets, et des images* (Bordeaux, 1597), pp. 182–85: *Bellarminus, Dispuationum*, p. 349; Mason, *Anatomie*, pp. 16–18; Edward Hoby, *A Curry-Combe for a Coxe-Combe* (London, 1615), p. 221.

36. Sheldon, *Survery*, pp. 39–40.

37. Cornelius à Lapide, *Commemaria in Seripudam Sacrum*, 21 vols. (Paris, 1857–63), 19:157. cap.2, sec. 9: 'Nee Antichristus, nee daemon, nec angeli possunt facere verum miraculum: sed solus Deus. Miraculum enim est quod fit super omnem naturae vim, quodque omnium naturalium causarum et creaturarum vires excedit et transcendit: Antichristus ergo faciet miracula non vera sed falsa et mendacia.'

38. G. Thomson, *Vindex Veritatis: Adversus Iustus Lipsium Libri duo* (London, 1606), pp. 94–96.

39. Ibid., pp. 104–5.

40. Ibid., p. 99.

41. Robert Chambers, *Miracles Lately Wrought by the Intercession of the Glorious Virgin Marie at Montaigu* (Antwerp, 1606). This was answered by Robert Tynley, archdeacon of Ely, in *Two Learned Sermons… In the Seconde, Are Answered Many of the Arguments Publised by Rob. Chambers Priest, concerning Popish Miracles; amd Dedicated (Forsooth) to the Kings Most Excellent Maiestie* (London, 1609).

42. I. R. [Floyd], *Purgatories Triumph* (n. p., 1613), pp. 124–55 (chap. 5, 'The miracles of the B. Virgin at *Hall, and Sichem*, and other Catholike Miracles are proved Authenticall, against the Prophane jestes of the *Letter*, and *Countersnarle*. And that they cannot be Antichrists Wonders'). Both works referred to are by Edward Hoby; for *Letter*, see note 25 above: the *Countersnarle* was published in 1613.

43. See note 35 above.

44. Henri Brémond, *Histoire littéraire du sentiment religieux en France*, II vols. (Paris, 1924), 1:18–67. He does not mention this work of Richeome.

45. Richeome, *Trois discours*, pp. 134–36; *cf.* pp. 123–24, on Protestants' lack of spiritual support.

46. Bellarminus, *Disputationum*, pp. 349–50; *cf.* Richeome, *Trois discours*, pp. 188–91.

47. Bellarminus, *Disputationum*, p. 353; Richeome, *Trois Discours*, pp. 192–94.

48. Floyd, *Purgatories Triumph*, pp. 130–31.

49. Bellarminus, *Disputationum*, pp. 356–57.

50. Sheldon, *Survey*, p. 185.

51. Floyd, *Purgatories Triumph*, p. 152.

52. Ibid., p. 151; Richeome, *Trois discours*, p. 213.

53. Floyd, *Purgatories Triumph*, pp. 148–49.

54. Lipsius, *Diva Virgo Hallensis*, p. 18.

55. Chambers, *Miracles Lately Wrought*, sigs. C3v–C4: *Bellarminus, Disputationum*, p. 357.

56. Floyd, *Purgatories Triumph*, pp. 144–47.

57. Augustine, *De unitate Ecclesiae, liber unus* (= *Ad Catholicos Epistola contra Donatistas*, in Migne, *Patrologiae Cursus, series Latina*, vol. 43, cols. 428–30, cap. 19), mentions also recent miracles at Milan, saying: 'Quaecunque talia in Catholica (sc. ecclesia) fiunt, ideo sunt approabanda, quia in Catholica fiunt; non ideo ipsa manifestatur Catholica, quia haee in ea fiunt'; *cf.* idem, *De utilitate credeni*, cap. 16, and on this *Retractationum libri duo*, l. cap. 14 (Migne. *PL*, vol. 42, col. 90; vol. 32. col. 606).

58. Sheldon, *Survey*, pp. 32–33.

59. Ibid., p. 121; Thomson, *Vindex Veritatis*, p. 79; Augustine, *De vera religione, liber unus*, cap. 25 (Migne, *PL*. vol. 34, col. 142): 'Cum enim Ecclesia Catholica per lotum orbem diffusa atque fundata sit, nec miracula illa in nostra tempora durare permissa sunt, ne animus semper visibiha quaereret, et corum consuetudine frigesecret genas humanum, quorum novifate flagravir.'

60. Augustine, *Rectractationum libri duo*, 1:13:7 (Migne *PL*, vol. 32: cols. 604–5).

61. Deacon and Walker, *Dialogncall Discourses*, p. 333.

62. Bellarminus, *Disputationum*, pp. 359–60; Richeome, *Trois discours*, pp. 269, 288: Floyd, *Purgatories Trumph*, p. 145.

63. Hoby, *Curry-Combe*, p. 217; William Perkins, *A Discourse of the Damned Art of Witchcraft* (Cambridge, 1608), dedication signed by Thomas Pickering.

64. Sheldon, *Survey*, pp. 66–72.

65. Richeome, *Trois discours*, pp. 16–ff.

66. Sheldon, *Survey*, pp. 313–15; Hoby, *Curry-Combe*. p. 219

67. Bellarminus, *Disputationum*, pp. 351–53; Richeome, *Trois discours*, pp. 149–206.

68. Petrus Thyraeus, *Daemoniact, Hoc est: De obsessis a spiritibus daennotiorum hominibus*, 2d ed. (Cologue, 1598), pp. 126–28.

69. Richeome, *Trois discours*, pp. 171–72; Chambers, *Miracles Lately Wrought*, sig. B4.

70. James I, *The Works* (London, 1616), p. 127.

71. Marc Bloch, *Les rois thaumaturges* (Strasbourg, 1924), p. 337: 'Chese trovava perplesson in quel ch'haveva di fare rispetro, che dell'una parte non vedeva come potessero guarire i infermi senza miracolo, et gia li miracoli erano cessati et non si facevano piu: et cosi haveva paura di commettere qualche superstitione; del'faltra parte essendo quella usanza anticha et in beneficio delli suoi sudditi, se risolveva de provarlo, ma solamente per via d'oratine la quale pregeva a futti volessero fare insieme con lui; et con questo toceava alli infermi … Si notava che quand'il Re faceva il suo discorso spesse volte girava Pocchi alli ministri Scozzesi che stavano appresso, com aspettando la loro approbatione a quel che dieeva, havendolo prima conferito con loro.'

72. Ibid., p. 338.

INDEX

Note: Letter 'n' followed by locators refer to notes.

Index

Index

Index

Index

Index

Index